Palgrave Macmillan Studies in Banking and Financial Institutions

Series Editor: **Professor Philip Molyneux**

The Palgrave Macmillan Studies in Banking and Financial Institutions are international in orientation and include studies of banking within particular countries or regions, and studies of particular themes such as Corporate Banking, Risk Management, Mergers and Acquisitions, etc. The books' focus is on research and practice, and they include up-to-date and innovative studies on contemporary topics in banking that will have global impact and influence.

Titles include:

Mario Anolli, Elena Beccalli andTommaso Giordani (*editors*)
RETAIL CREDIT RISK MANAGEMENT

Seth Apati
THE NIGERIAN BANKING SECTOR REFORMS
Power and Politics

Caner Bakir
BANK BEHAVIOUR AND RESILIENCE
The Effect of Structures, Institutions and Agents

Alessandro Carretta and Gianluca Mattarocci (*editors*)
ASSET PRICING, REAL ESTATE AND PUBLIC FINANCE OVER THE CRISIS.

Dimitris N. Chorafas
BASEL III, THE DEVIL AND GLOBAL BANKING

Dimitris N. Chorafas
HOUSEHOLD FINANCE
Adrift in a Sea of Red Ink

Dimitris N. Chorafas
SOVEREIGN DEBT CRISIS
The New Normal and the Newly Poor

Stefano Cosma and Elisabetta Gualandri (*editors*)
THE ITALIAN BANKING SYSTEM
Impact of the Crisis and Future Perspectives

Juan Fernández de Guevara Radoselovics and José Pastor Monsálvez (*editors*)
CRISIS, RISK AND STABILITY IN FINANCIAL MARKETS

Juan Fernández de Guevara Radoselovics and José Pastor Monsálvez (*editors*)
MODERN BANK BEHAVIOUR

Franco Fiordelisi and Ornella Ricci (*editors*)
BANCASSURANCE IN EUROPE
Past, Present and Future

Jill M. Hendrickson
FINANCIAL CRISIS
The United States in the Early Twenty-First Century

Otto Hieronymi and Constantine Stephanou (*editors*)
INTERNATIONAL DEBT
Economic, Financial, Monetary, Political and Regulatory Aspects

Paola Leone and Gianfranco A. Vento (*editors*)
CREDIT GUARANTEE INSTITUTIONS AND SME FINANCE

Philip Molyneux (*editor*)
BANK PERFORMANCE, RISK AND FIRM FINANCING

Philip Molyneux (*editor*)
BANK STRATEGY, GOVERNANCE AND RATINGS

Victor Murinde (*editor*)
BANK REGULATORY REFORMS IN AFRICA

Bernardo Nicoletti
CLOUD COMPUTING IN FINANCIAL SERVICES

Özlem Olgu
EUROPEAN BANKING
Enlargement, Structural Changes and Recent Developments

Fotios Pasiouras
GREEK BANKING
From the Pre-Euro Reforms to the Financial Crisis and Beyond

Daniela Pîrvu
Corporate Income Tax Harmonization in the European Union

Ramkishen S. Rajan
EMERGING ASIA
Essays on Crises, Capital Flows, FDI and Exchange Rate

Allesandro Roselli
Financial Structures and Regulation: A Comparison of Crises in THE UK, USA and Italy

Yasushi Suzuki
JAPAN'S FINANCIAL SLUMP
Collapse of the Monitoring System under Institutional and Transition Failures

Gabriel Tortella and José Luis García Ruiz
SPANISH MONEY AND BANKING
A History

The full list of titles available is on the website:
www.palgrave.com/finance/sbfi.asp

Palgrave Macmillan Studies in Banking and Financial Institutions
Series Standing Order ISBN 978–1–4039–4872–4

You can receive future titles in this series as they are published by placing a standing order. Please contact your bookseller or, in case of difficulty, write to us at the address below with your name and address, the title of the series and the ISBN quoted above.

Customer Services Department, Macmillan Distribution Ltd, Houndmills, Basingstoke, Hampshire RG21 6XS, England

Spanish Money and Banking

A History

Gabriel Tortella

and

José Luis García Ruiz

palgrave
macmillan

First published 2013 by
PALGRAVE MACMILLAN

Palgrave Macmillan in the UK is an imprint of Macmillan Publishers Limited, registered in England, company number 785998, of Houndmills, Basingstoke, Hampshire RG21 6XS.

Palgrave Macmillan in the US is a division of St Martin's Press LLC, 175 Fifth Avenue, New York, NY 10010.

Palgrave Macmillan is the global academic imprint of the above companies and has companies and representatives throughout the world.

Palgrave® and Macmillan® are registered trademarks in the United States, the United Kingdom, Europe and other countries

ISBN: 978–0–230–34765–6

This book is printed on paper suitable for recycling and made from fully managed and sustained forest sources. Logging, pulping and manufacturing processes are expected to conform to the environmental regulations of the country of origin.

A catalogue record for this book is available from the British Library.

A catalog record for this book is available from the Library of Congress.

To the memory of Rondo Cameron

Yo vi en corte de Roma do es la santidad
que todos al dinero facen gran homildad
gran honra le facían, con gran solemnidad
todos a él se humillan, como a la majestad

I saw in the Court of Rome, where sanctity resides,
that everybody pays great respect to money,
they greatly honor it with great solemnity,
all bow to it, as they would to majesty

— Juan Ruiz, Arcipreste de Hita, *14th century*

Madre, yo al oro me humillo,
él es mi amante y mi amado,
pues de puro enamorado
de continuo anda amarillo.
Que pues doblón o sencillo
hace todo cuanto quiero
Poderoso caballero
es Don Dinero

Mother, I bow to gold,
he is my lover and beloved
and he is so much in love
that his color is always yellow.
Since as doubloon or as simple coin
he does whatever I wish,
A powerful lord
is Mister Money

— Francisco de Quevedo, *17th century*

No te me engrías, dinero,
que aunque sin cesar te busco
ya sabes que no te quiero.

Don't be conceited, oh money,
because although I constantly look after you
you know I don't love you.

— Jorge Guillén, *20th century*

Contents

List of Tables

List of Figures

List of Data Appendices

Preface and Acknowledgements

In December 2010, through Professors Philip Molyneux, Santiago Carbó and Gregorio Núñez, Gabriel Tortella was asked whether he knew of somebody who would be willing and able to write a history of Spanish money and banking for Palgrave Macmillan. This was a project which had been entertained by Tortella for many years and had not been undertaken just for lack of time and publisher. So he offered himself as a prospective author. When he was accepted in principle by Palgrave Macmillan, he started thinking about the magnitude of the project and proposed as an associate author José Luis García Ruiz, a seasoned bank historian with whom he had collaborated in several books and articles on banking, monetary, and business history. There was agreement on all sides and the project went forward.

What the reader now has in his/her hands is the outcome of the project. We think this is the first book in English on the topic, and one could say that the same is almost true regarding the Spanish language. We think the subject is interesting and not only for those attracted to Spanish history. All national monetary and banking histories are unique cases, but some are more unique than others, and we believe this to be the case of Spain. But it will be for each reader to judge.

Obviously we have followed a chronological scheme and have tried to write as clearly as possible and to avoid technicalities unless it was really necessary. We were surprised when compiling the bibliography to see how much has been published on the subject, something which made a synthesis all the more desirable. Let us hope this one fulfils its role adequately. Let us add that we have had to translate a considerable number of texts, and not only from Spanish. All translated texts are by us unless specified otherwise.

We want to thank Professor Clara Eugenia Núñez for reading most of the book and making very useful comments. Miguel Ángel Prieto, of Banco Popular, and Rafael Bermejo (recently retired from the board of BBVA), who have lifelong expertise in banking, gave us invaluable advice, read the book, and made very timely remarks. We also want to thank Professor Molyneux for his effective editing. The responsibility for the text, however, is exclusively ours.

1
Introduction

1.1 Distinctive traits

The history of the Spanish banking and monetary system shows some distinctive traits, which make its study interesting. In the first place, it is a long history, and its evolution shows not a steady progression, but an alternation of booms and busts which somehow follow the ups and downs of the Spanish economy and politics. Other distinctive traits are the following:

1.1.1 Wealth of precious metals

Although Spain has traditionally enjoyed an abundance of mineral wealth, precious metals have not been among the most plentiful. Silver and gold were mined since Roman times at least, but the relative abundance of precious metals in medieval Spain was more due to trade with Africa, Eastern Europe, and the Middle East than to the output of local mines. This in fact was the case with the whole of Western Europe in the late Middle Ages: it produced less gold and silver than its expanding economy required, but its favourable trade balance with those areas brought in extra inflows of gold and silver (Vicens Vives, 1959, Chs. 18, 21, 22; Bautier, 1971, pp. 161–9; Vilar, 1972, pp. 61–82; Le Goff, 2010, pp. 139–42).

The discovery of America, as is well known, put into Spanish hands the fabulous wealth of Mexican and Peruvian gold and silver mines. For over a century the inflow of precious metals, especially silver, contributed to remarkable prosperity in Spain and vested enormous power in the hands of Spanish kings. Then the classical example of big power overreach occurred. The finances of the Spanish Crown were in trouble since the mid-sixteenth century (Carande, 1965), and provoked recurring suspensions of payments from the second half of that century on. This ruined Spanish bankers and in the end caused shortage of gold and silver in the country, which had seemed to own unlimited supplies of precious metals. All this brought about the decline of Spain in the seventeenth century, with its concomitant recourse to debasing the currency (the *vellón* episodes) and to repeated military defeats and political retrenchment.

The economy recovered gradually during the eighteenth century, but a monetary problem subsisted. Because silver was abundant in Spain its coins had a high tenor of this metal. In other words, silver was undervalued in the Spanish monetary system; as a consequence, the famous pesos or *reales de a ocho* were internationally appreciated and increasingly exported. This was helped by the fact that Spanish products were overpriced and the country tended to have an external commercial deficit. This also thwarted its industry. This monetary problem plagued Spain until the mid-nineteenth century, when a series of monetary reforms finally aligned Spain's bimetallic (gold–silver) ratio with that of the rest of Europe.

1.1.2 Silver standard

As most European countries, Spain practised a bimetallic standard in the early modern period. Increased economic integration during the nineteenth century, as well as the vagaries of the bimetallic ratio, made most countries, following England, to adopt the gold standard. For a series of reasons we examine in Chapter 5, Spain chose a divergent path and adopted a silver standard. It thus became one of the few Western countries to use a different monetary system from the last decades of the nineteenth century until the Great Depression. The silver standard became in fact a fiduciary standard, as the price of silver fell throughout this period. The Spanish monetary authorities, however, showed restraint in the creation of money. In spite of this moderation, there is no doubt that its monetary system contributed to isolate the Spanish economy. The consequences of the silver-fiduciary standard were complex: while the isolation of the Spanish economy was on the whole bad, the non-subjection to the gold straitjacket and the economic isolation turned out to be very helpful at the height of the Great Depression.

1.1.3 Relatively early 'central' bank

It seems somewhat paradoxical that, in spite of the relative underdevelopment of its banking sector, Spain should have created rather early an official bank: the Bank of Saint Charles (*Banco de San Carlos*), founded in 1782. As most other banks of its nature, the Saint Charles was created to solve a pressing public financial problem. The relative inexperience of its founders and managers, however, and the mounting fiscal problems it was supposed to solve, soon put it in a situation of de facto suspension of payments. After several decades of virtual inaction, it was thoroughly reorganized and, through a series of reforms and readaptations (it was renamed as Spanish Bank of Saint Ferdinand or *Banco Español de San Fernando*), it slowly converged towards adopting the structure and functions of a central bank under the name Bank of Spain (*Banco de España*). This process was not concluded until late in the twentieth century.

1.1.4 Late development of a modern banking sector

The Bank of Saint Charles was the first joint-stock bank in Spanish history. It would take more than 60 years for another joint-stock bank to be established in Spain: the Banco de Isabel II, in 1844. In the following years some other joint-stock banks were created, most of them short-lived. From the mid-1850s, however, the number of joint-stock banks grew by leaps and bounds, to nearly 60. Unfortunately, this was an ephemeral episode, and the number of banks fell to less than 15 in the early 1870s. From then on the number of banks grew very slowly and their size was rather modest, so that the Bank of Spain could be seen figuratively as a giant among pigmies (and only few of them at that). A clear discontinuity took place after the 1898 defeat in the Spanish–American War. In a few years Spanish public finances were put in order and a series of new modern banks were created – some of them with capital repatriated from the former colonies. A similar discontinuity was taking place in the whole economy, which started to diversify and modernize at around these same years: basic industries developed, agriculture started a slow process of modernization, urbanization accelerated, and demographic transition took place. Economic growth and banking growth proceeded in a parallel fashion for most of the twentieth century.

1.1.5 Slow diffusion of banknotes

The diffusion of banknotes was also a very gradual affair. Although their circle of acceptance expanded somewhat during the booms of the early 1840s and 1860s, their diffusion became really widespread only in the last decades of the nineteenth century, so that one can say that it was the peseta and the Bank of Spain's monopoly of issue that made banknotes popular.

1.1.6 'Mixed banking' and 'banking repression'

As in some other countries, these phenomena took place in the twentieth century. The big joint-stock banks that were established in the early decades practiced mixed banking with the active support of the Bank of Spain and the government. They actively promoted industrial firms and public utilities, acted like holding companies and controlled industrial groups, while at the same time dealing in commercial banking, attracting deposits, making short-term loans, and discounting. This went on roughly until the end of the Franco dictatorship. The banking crisis of the late 1970s and early 1980s put an end to this banking schema, which had been accompanied by active banking repression – tight government controls of interest rates, restriction of competition, government intervention in banks' policies such as distribution of dividends, fields of investment, creation of branches, and so on – which the banking sector as a whole had accepted gladly during the dictatorship, as it permitted almost riskless profits. While it is true that banking repression was common in the world after the Great Depression, it was more intense and longer lived under Francoism than in most Western countries. The panorama changed radically in the last quarter of the century, with liberalization and industrial crisis, which were accompanied by mergers, divestment, and internationalization.

1.2 Banking and money in the medieval and early modern periods

The first banking transaction recorded in Spanish history is contained in the opening passages of the *Poema del Cid*, the epic poem written in the twelfth century narrating the exploits of the medieval Castilian hero in the mid- and late-eleventh century. The *Poema* contains many economic references: the Cid's exploits have two aims, to clear his name and to become rich and powerful. The hero had incurred the king's displeasure and had been ordered to leave Castile. His exploits are seen as an enterprise to restore his honour and riches as the best way to regain the king's goodwill, and to return to Castile enjoying the esteem of the people. The first thing the hero needs is money to pay his men and to provide victuals, so he tells one of his lieutenants (Martín Antolínez, whose pay he promises to double) to contact two Jewish bankers (Rachel and Vidas) in the city of Burgos and ask them to lend him 600 marks; the Cid has nothing to offer as collateral, so he contrives a ruse whereby he deposits two boxes full of sand with the bankers telling them they are filled with gold jewellery from the Moorish kings' tribute. Confiding in his word, the bankers lend him the 600 marks (one half in gold, one half in silver) and even pay Martín Antolínez, thirty marks (five per cent of the loaned sum) as the commission he has asked for. So this is how the Cid managed to get the capital necessary to finance his enterprise.

When after a series of conquests, which make the Cid rich and powerful as intended, he sends an emissary back to Castile to offer the king gifts, the bankers ask him for the money the Cid owes them. They claim they would even accept the return of the principal without interest, they are in such need. They are promised much more and they reply: 'May God allow it! Otherwise we will leave Burgos and go to meet him'.

This is the last we hear about the loan and we do not know whether the money was in fact returned and whether some interest was paid. We do not even know whether the bankers opened the boxes and found out the Cid's deceit. However, the story is full of subtle twists. The Cid was banished from Castile by the king because he had been accused of covertly keeping a share of the Moorish tribute the Castilian king sent him to collect in Seville. The accusation was false, and the proof is that he had no money to finance his enterprise. But he lied to the bankers, telling them that what was in the boxes was the part of the tribute he had retained, and he asked them to keep his secret. So he had to lie to the bankers, who believed him, because he had been honest with the king, who did not. It is paradoxical that the bankers trusted him when, by implication, he was telling them that he had deceived the king. So much for the proverbial Jewish mistrust and avarice.

Be it as it may, the poem gives us a lot of information about medieval banking in Spain. It was written around 1150, and refers to events which took place some 70 years before, so we are not dealing with Renaissance banking here, but with a much earlier period. It shows that there were well-known Jewish bankers in medieval Burgos, a commercial city whose wealth derived from the wool trade; bankers charged interest: when they were asked for the loan, Rachel and Vidas answered: 'We must gain something in our dealings', and were ready to renounce to it when they saw the loan in peril. It is interesting also that bankers paid commission to intermediaries who brought business to them. Martín Antolínez asked for the commission as a matter of fact: 'I brought you good profit'. And of course loans on collateral appear to have been common: both lender and borrower seem to take depositing specie as collateral as a normal part of the transaction. Whether the story is literally true or not, it gives us a glimpse on banking in medieval Castile.

We find historical references to bankers later on in the Middle Ages, established in the main commercial centres of the two largest kingdoms, Castile and Aragón, such as Medina del Campo, Burgos, Valladolid, Segovia, Toledo, Madrid, Seville, Barcelona, Valencia, Mallorca, Saragossa, and so on. These earlier bankers were most commonly money changers: words such as *cambio, canvi, campsor* were used to designate them. In northern Castile they were especially active in trade fairs and in the pilgrimage road to Santiago de Compostela, a road which attracted travellers from all over Europe (Ruiz Martín, 1970, pp. 5–12; García de Valdeavellano, 1960, pp. 71, 136). In Aragón, where fairs were less important, those early bankers were involved in financing trade and commerce, largely maritime. Bills of exchange were used in fourteenth-century Barcelona, but banking was the object of state and municipal regulation since at least a century earlier (Usher, 1967, pp. 237–46). This city was also the cradle of one of the earliest municipal banks, the *Taula del Canvi* (1401), whose name, literally meaning 'Table of Change', is another clear indication of the main activity of bankers in medieval Spain. The Taula, however, was mainly devoted to attracting deposits and servicing the city's financial needs. Its role has been decried for unfairly competing with private moneylenders (Vicens Vives, 1959, pp. 212–13; Usher, 1967, Ch. X). In spite of its shortcomings, the Taula was imitated in other Aragonese cities, such as Valencia, Gerona, and Saragossa, and had a remarkably long life.

The expulsion of the Jews from Spain in 1492 was a severe blow to the banking system. As already reflected in the *Poema del Cid*, Jews played a prominent role in the Spanish medieval credit system, as they did in many other European countries (Sánchez Albornoz, 1956, pp. 114, 190–227). The

Jews' absence could not be wholly filled by native Christians. As Carande (1965, p. 263) wrote, 'Spanish merchants, largely due to their own shortcomings, were subject to the competition of foreigners [...] and saw themselves displaced by them in their own country'; another – Christian – minority, the Genoese, stepped into the breach. This was the case especially in Seville, the city whose trade with the Americas (and silver inflow therefrom) turned it into a great commercial centre during the reign of Charles V (1516–56). In the long run, however, the Seville bankers' close links with the chaotic finances of the Spanish Crown drove many of them to bankruptcy or closure, and prevented the Spanish banking system from developing as those in northern Europe did. In early-sixteenth-century Seville, nonetheless, bankers (mostly converted Jews and Genoese) flourished. They financed the large flows of trade which went through its harbour, usually combining the normal financial activity (deposit taking, giro payment, lending to public and private borrowers) with money changing and trading in their own name. They also lent to the Crown, whose political and military enterprises required increasing amounts of financial resources. The most common instrument in these operations was the *asiento*, a contract to supply a specified amount of merchandise (most commonly, specie) at some predetermined location, typically, in Italy or the Low Countries. These deals were extremely profitable, and attracted financiers from all over Europe. The risks involved, however, were high and increasing. The *asientos* were usually payable against the silver shipments arriving from the Americas, and 'any delay in the arrival of the silver fleets caused such tightness in the money market that the solvency of the bankers was severely threatened' (Pyke, 1966, p. 87).

The monetary system – the set of monetary units – which Spain used through the early modern period well into the nineteenth century was created by Ferdinand and Isabella, the Catholic Monarchs, at the close of the Middle Ages. As in many other matters, in those monetary, the Catholic Monarchs marked the transition from the medieval to the early modern era in Spain. They put an end to political and economic confusion and set the basis of the national state. Not everything they did was successful (witness the Inquisition, mercantilism, and the imposition of religious and cultural uniformity), but many of the things they did left a deep imprint – for better or worse.

The Catholic Monarchs found a chaotic monetary situation upon their joint assumption of the crown, 'one of the most deplorable our history registers', according to the author of an official history (Surrá, 1862, p. 31). Their monetary reform of 1497 established a trimetallic system whose main units were: the *excelente*, a gold coin (also called ducat, *escudo*, or *doblón*); the *real de plata*, a silver coin (later known as *real de a ocho*, *peso duro*, *thaler*, or dollar) and the *blanca*, a *vellón* coin. (*Vellón* is a confusing word; it has two meanings: one, tuft of hair or fleece of wool; two, an alloy of copper and silver. The first meaning derives from *vello*, which means body hair. The second from the French *billon*, meaning this alloy.) There was a medieval relic, however, not even the Catholic monarchs could do away with, and this was the *maravedí*. Originally a gold coin used by the Almoravids, who invaded the Peninsula from Africa in the eleventh century, the *maravedí* underwent a series of metamorphoses until finally it became a pure unit of account. The Catholic monarchs used it to establish the equivalences between their three monetary units: the *excelente* was worth 375 mrs, the *real de plata* 34 mrs, and the *blanca* 0.5 mrs. These coins changed names, but they remained the basic monetary units for three and a half centuries. Only the *blanca* disappeared in the long run and was confusingly replaced by the *real de vellón*, a new unit created by Charles II in 1686.

Although the Catholic Monarchs probably hoped that their trimetallic system should be in use throughout all their kingdoms, in fact it worked almost exclusively in Castile; the Aragonese kingdoms maintained a silver system directly derived from the Carolingian division of the *libra* (pound) into 20 *sueldos* (*solidus*, shilling) or 240 *dineros* (*denarius*, penny). These monetary systems converged slowly due mostly to Gresham's Law, which operated at full speed in the seventeenth century. Navarra, although annexed by Ferdinand, originally King of Aragón, adopted the Castilian system early in the sixteenth century. The gold–silver relation established by the Catholic Monarchs was of 10.11 (that is, one unit of gold was equivalent to 10.11 units of silver). No great changes took place in the Spanish monetary system during the sixteenth century, except for the substantial inflow of silver, and, to a lesser extent, gold, from the Americas, especially during the second half, that is, the reign of Philip II (1556–98). This entailed a gradual modification of the official gold–silver ratio, which was about 12.1 by 1600 (Hamilton, 1948, p. 83). Spain exported a large amount of the bullion it imported in order to finance her European wars and her commercial deficit. In spite of this and of the three state bankruptcies under Philip II, however, the monetary system was not greatly affected, chiefly because Philip II made a point of not having recourse to debasement in spite of his fiscal tribulations.

Philip II inherited a troubled financial system: no wonder his first bankruptcy was declared in 1557, a year after he assumed the crown. His financial legacy, however, was even more troubled: his reign not only commenced, but also ended in bankruptcy. He had to suspend payments in 1596, two years before his death. He had also suspended payments in 1575, when he reached a sort of forced agreement with his creditors under the name of *medio general*. Although it is said that 'the prudent King', as Philip II was called, was not as fond of war as his father, he was involved in military struggles for all of his reign. Of course the best known and most ruinous of these was the '80-year war', against the Protestants in the Netherlands, which started in 1566 and lasted well into the next century. Connected to this was the ill-fated *Armada* expedition in 1588. But there were many other wars, internal and external. Constant conflict explains that in spite of a more than tripling (they multiplied by a factor of 3.5) of the Crown's ordinary revenues between 1555 and 1598, its indebtedness kept mounting; expenditure in the same time span increased fourfold.

Philip III's reign (1598–1621) was marked by the legacy of his father but included a dangerous innovation: the recourse to the debasement of coinage (the *vellón* alloy surreptitiously replacing silver) to finance the unmanageable deficit. In spite of the Cortes (Parliament)'s protests, the issuing of copper coins went on; once debasement had taken place, there was no reason to even keep the face value of money near the value of its metallic content: in 1602 copper coins were minted with the same intrinsic characteristics as those of 1599, but with double denomination. By the time the king obtained a substantial tax hike in 1607 in exchange for a promise to stop debasement, the fabulous sum of 22 million ducats worth of copper coinage had been issued (Hamilton, 1948, esp. pp. 56, 70), more than double total budget income in 1598 (Gelabert, 1997, p. 29). This did not prevent a new suspension of payments in 1606.

In spite of his promise, Philip III, alleging that the deficit was insurmountable, asked the Cortes to allow him a new debasement in 1617. His plea was granted and a new copper coin was issued, until the Cortes again obtained a promise to suspend new copper coinage in exchange for a new tax increase in 1619. But issuing new coin was not the king's only means of debasing the currency: another expedient was crying up the money. This was done for the first time in 1603 and frequently repeated under Philip III and Philip IV. The operation was as follows: the public was ordered to take their copper coins to the mints; there the coins were re-stamped at double their face value. The owners were reimbursed with half the coins (same face value as they had turned in), plus a little extra for the nuisance. The other near half was pure profit for the government, minus the cost of re-stamping. Of course the profits would be higher if the crying up was done for higher face values. The operation made the buying of new copper bullion unnecessary; the problem, however, was lack of public enthusiasm: lesser and lesser amounts were taken to re-stamping every time. The situation was memorably described by Hamilton (1947, pp. 9–12, 36–7):

> the large output of copper money by the best machinery then known [...] and crying up the coinage, when the King was too poor to buy copper, shook the foundations of Spanish life [...]. While universally envied because of her monopoly of the American of gold and silver mines, Spain saw her precious metals driven out of circulation in the second quarter of the seventeenth century by a cumbersome and unstable medium of exchange [...]; often the gold and silver that flowed in from the Indies never entered circulation in Spain. The private treasure was sequestered by the Crown for remittance abroad, along with the public treasure;

> and the owners were indemnified in vellon [...]; several years' work with the contemporaneous account-books [...] have given me the impression that vellon constituted at least 92 per cent of the money spent in the 1650s. Apparently, the percentage rose to well above 95 during the next three decades of monetary disturbance and economic decline [...]. Not only were silver coins extremely scarce, but a significant portion of those available was degraded [...] and late in 1650 it was discovered that silver reals of defective fineness, coined in Peru [...], were circulating in Castile [... And t]o aggravate the evil, unbridled inflation was generally followed by sharp deflation, mistakenly conceived as a remedy.
>
> [...P]rogressive debasement and overissue of fractional coins drove the precious metals out of circulation, thereby forcing the mistress of Mexico and Peru onto a cumbersome and unstable copper standard. The brusque alterations of monetary inflation and deflation – obviously far worse than either separately – [...] were at once a result and a fundamental cause of the economic decline.

The paradox of the mistress of Zacatecas and Potosí being reduced to the almost exclusive circulation of copper coins is not difficult to explain. According to our calculations (Tortella, unpublished), Spain retained in minted form only 15 per cent of gross silver imports (gold imports were much less in weight and in value). Silver remittances levelled off and then decreased in the seventeenth century. The increase in the money supply that this inflow of precious metals brought about was offset by price increases, so that, in real terms, the money supply hardly grew at all in the reign of Philip II. The levelling off, and then the fall in the importation of precious metals after 1595 left a gap in the money supply which was filled by *vellón* coinage. Prices also levelled off and even decreased during the first two decades of the seventeenth century, as silver disappeared from circulation and was replaced by copper (Hamilton, 1934, Chs. 2, 8, and 9; Andrés, 2006).

Tax revenues also faltered in the seventeenth century (on seventeenth-century financial problems see Sureda, 1949; Domínguez Ortiz, 1960, 1984; Ruiz Martín, 1990; García Sanz, 1991; Pulido, 1996; Sánchez Belén, 1996; Gelabert, 1997). There were several causes for this. First of all, there was over-taxation, which ruined the Castilian economy and shrunk the tax base (a clear early example of the 'Laffer curve'). This was understood by contemporaries and has been confirmed by modern research. The tax system was regressive and penalized the cities versus the countryside and commoners versus churchmen and nobles. Industry and trade, therefore, were discouraged. The flourishing sixteenth-century Castilian textile industry was taxed and regulated out of competitiveness (García Sanz, 1994, esp. p. 424). There also was the sale of patents of nobility and *hidalguías* (gentry), which reduced the number of taxpayers and thereby increased the tax burden on commoners; it has been estimated that about one million taxpayers 'disappeared' in Castile between 1591 and 1631. A third perverse mechanism was the general insecurity of markets and property rights generated by the periodic state bankruptcies and confiscations, compounded by the increasing uncertainty about the value of money as the seventeenth century progressed. To the self-defeating bias of the tax system must be added the ineptitude and corruption of bureaucrats and tax farmers. It has been calculated that as much as 40 per cent of assessed taxes were lost in collection (the Count-Duke of Olivares, Philip IV's *valido* – right-hand man, approximate equivalent to Prime Minister – believed the proportion to be 70 per cent: Elliott, 1963, p. 307).

The climax of disaster arrived under Philip IV (1621–65). He ascended to the throne in a bad year, because it marked the end of a 14-year truce in the Netherlands. To strengthen his army the new king immediately had recourse to all the means at his command. He lowered interest rate on loans to the state, confiscated private silver remittances, which were forcibly exchanged for public debt, and had new recourse to bankers' *asientos*; but the easiest and cheapest expedient was to issue new copper money. During the 1621–26 period about 14 million ducats worth of debased coin were issued (Hamilton, 1948, pp. 60, 70). From then on the new debasements were made by means of crying up. In spite of all these and many other expedients, the government suspended payments in 1627 and a new *medio general* was proclaimed.

In times of such difficulties the inequities in the distribution of the fiscal burden became glaring. Castile paid a disproportionate share of the Crown's revenues and the opinion became extended in government circles that the imbalance ought to be redressed not so much on ethical grounds as on those of necessity: Castile was exhausted and impoverished: the time had come for other kingdoms (Aragón, Portugal, the Basque provinces) to lend a hand. The champion of this idea was the Count-Duke of Olivares, who, as its basic aim was to strengthen common defence, called the project *Unión de Armas* (Union of Arms) (Elliott, 1986, Ch. VII). But Olivares' project misfired. The attempt to put the *Unión de Armas* into practice provoked widespread rebellion. In 1640 both Catalonia and Portugal revolted and seceded from Castile. It took 12 years to subdue Catalonia; Portugal gained definitive independence.

This marked the zenith of Castile's fiscal efforts and the end of its hegemonic ambitions. The treaties of Münster (1648, peace with the Netherlands) and the Pyrenees (1659, peace with France) sealed Castile's admission of defeat. But earlier, in a desperate effort to fight on all fronts, recourse was made to inflation again. In 1641 copper coins were re-stamped twice. Afraid of the widespread protests against inflation, the government then decided to cry down the money in 1642. This only made things worse, as it implied outright expropriation of the holders of coin. The government promised compensation, but this never arrived. Then silver was cried up again

(Hamilton, 1948, pp. 64–5). All these expedients, and many more (such as the plans to organize a network of *erarios*, or public banks, to drain savings from the wealthy: Ruiz Martín, 1970, pp. 62–96; Schwartz, 1996) were to no avail. After a frantic effort which increased the state's debt and exhausted all possibilities, a new suspension of payments was declared in 1647. After this many established bankers stopped extending credit to the Crown. From that time on the feeling was widespread that the effort had been excessive. After concluding the Peace of Münster the king stated that he had signed it in order to 'alleviate' Castilian taxpayers (Gelabert, 1997, p. 122). But nothing more drastic could be done as long as wars went on. Peace with Portugal was not signed until 1668. The last decades of the seventeenth century saw a clear retrenchment, but intermittent war with France prevented the fiscal rearrangement that was thought to be essential. A series of moderate measures were taken, such as the creation of a *Junta de Alivios* (Council of Alleviations), which tried to limit expenditure and to lower taxes. The state remained in arrears, however.

All this fiscal and monetary chaos was deleterious to the banking system. The expulsion of the Jews left it in shambles in the early sixteenth century; however, the lure of American silver and the great business opportunities in Seville and Madrid attracted foreign bankers, especially Genoese. There were Spaniards left, mostly converted Jews (*conversos*) and, specializing in the grand affairs of state, German bankers, the most prominent among them the Fuggers of Augsburg. But the structural imbalance of the Spanish state in the long run ruined those who dealt with it, or at least exhausted their liquidity. The state borrowed but rarely repaid fully. The best deal was for those who retired while the going was good. Charles V treated his German bankers as well as he could. He repaid them with land and concessions when he was short of money, which was virtually always. He gave the Fuggers the concession of the Almadén mercury mines and later on repaid them with land in Spain and in Germany. Mining was good business, but required investing in it; something similar can be said of landowning. Gradually the Fuggers retired from money lending; they were not ruined, but their assets became illiquid (Kellenbenz, 1978, pp. 19–21). For smaller firms things became more complicated, especially when Philip II repeatedly stopped payments and confiscated specie shipments. The Genoese and some Spaniards united in a *Compañía del Medio General* in order to pressure and scrutinize the government after the suspension of 1596; and again, after Philip III's suspension in 1608, they constituted a *Diputación del Medio General* with a similar purpose: to appropriate public income before it could be disbursed (Ruiz Martín, 1970, p. 45; De Carlos, 2006). The mistrust and retrenchment of German, Genoese and local bankers no doubt contributed to the Crown's decision to debase the currency. From that time on Portuguese bankers appeared on the scene, gradually replacing the Italians, but the continued arrears and repudiations by the Crown drove many of them to termination. Furthermore, quite a few Spanish and Portuguese bankers suffered harassment by the Inquisition. By the late seventeenth century, the delays and bankruptcies on the Spanish treasury, plus religious persecution, drove most bankers, Portuguese, Genoese, and Spanish, out of business (Sanz Ayán, 1988, pp. 136–40, 313–433; Gelabert, 1997, pp. 76–7).

After the economic chaos of the seventeenth century, the eighteenth was one of relative stability. Philip V made several minor innovations. One of them was the introduction of a new gold coin, a new type of *escudo* commonly called *veintén* because it was valued at 20 *reales de vellón*. Another was lowering the bimetallic ratio to discourage silver extraction. Possibly the most important of these reforms was to establish a two-tier monetary system. Under Philip V the old gold and silver coins remained; but new, slightly debased versions were also issued. The distinction thus was made between 'national money', used for international operations, and 'provincial money', intended for day-to-day transactions. The Bourbons also introduced a certain discipline in the issuing of *vellón*, which contributed to price stability and to greater confidence in the monetary system.

Not all was well, however. The system remained seriously impaired by a number of factors. In the first place, while the two-tier system had its advantages, it also contributed to internal confusion. Furthermore, the War of Succession (1701–14) had left a considerable amount of foreign, mostly French, coins in Spain, which also circulated currently and added to the uncertainty. Furthermore, the habit of clipping and sweating the coins was prevalent, so that defective pieces of indeterminate value were mixed with newer ones. To this must be added the circulation of coins from non-Castilian kingdoms (Valencia, Aragón, the Canary Islands) as well as American coins. And to top it all off, *vellón* coins of varying proportions of silver (mostly pure copper) were the main circulating medium for petty transactions.

During most of the eighteenth century banking was carried out by 'merchant capitalists', that is, traders who undertook banking operations on the side. Many of these were the descendants of Italian, mostly Genoese, families established in Spain many years before. One example of these has been studied by Maixé (1994), the Barcelona house of *Bensi and Merizano*. Maixé shows the network of relations of this house with other houses (mostly Italian) in Madrid, in other Spanish ports, in Genoa and in several important European centres. French bankers, perhaps due to a Bourbon being on the throne, became numerous and active. Madrid became the financial centre of the country (Zylberberg, 1983) more to cater to the needs of the court and bureaucracy than to those of agriculture or industry. There were no specialized bankers and these tradesmen's companies were very small, typically individual enterprises or very reduced partnerships. The only large and somewhat more specialized lender appeared in Madrid around the mid-eighteenth century: the guilds or *gremios*. As a bureaucratic metropolis, Madrid had numerous craftsmen and shopkeepers who organized themselves in guilds; some of these guilds had very wealthy members, whose dues and savings could be put to profitable use by lending, and, especially, tax farming. As the business was profitable, the guilds also accepted deposits and became increasingly specialized in banking operations. Soon the five richest guilds (silk tissues, jewellery, haberdashery, spices, and druggists) constituted in 1667 a *Compañía de los Cinco Gremios Mayores de Madrid* (Company of the Five Major Guilds of Madrid), which became the 'most potent capitalist institution in Castile' (Ruiz Martín, 1970, p. 158; Capella and Matilla, 1957), practicing banking, commerce, contracting, industry, and insurance, and operating as banker to the state. The *Cinco Gremios* also operated internationally. The *Cinco Gremios*, however, ended up having the same problems as earlier lenders to the state. The wars of the late eighteenth and early nineteenth centuries brought about increased state expenditure and insolvency. The Peninsular War ruined the *Cinco Gremios*, which after decades of pleading and suing the state, was liquidated in 1846.

2
Money and Banking in the Twilight of Empire

2.1 Fiscal and monetary problems: the *Vales Reales*

The eighteenth century was one of slow recovery for the Spanish economy as a whole, thanks largely to internal peace, to legal and administrative modernization by the Bourbon kings, and especially thanks to the gradual opening of the Spanish Americas to trade with the metropolis, which had been subject to tight restrictions before. In 1778 transatlantic trade with Spanish America was open for the most important ports on both shores of the Atlantic and for a series of Pacific harbours also. The so-called Free Commerce Decree of 1778 was followed by a brief trade boom, but politics put an end to this hopeful development.

During the War of the American Revolution, Spain sided with France in support of the future United States of America against England; for both European countries the war effort turned out to be very costly. For Spain military expenditures shot up while revenues fell due to conflicts at home and abroad. Naval warfare took place not only in the Caribbean and the Gulf of Mexico, but also in the Mediterranean, especially around Minorca and Gibraltar. Spanish American revenues used to be a substantial proportion of total government revenues and Britain's naval blockades were often able to intercept the trade and the remittances, which had just started to soar only a few years before.

The Spanish government soon felt the difficulties of the situation: expenditure about doubled revenue. The King (Charles III) and his government were looking for a way to finance this deficit without burdening their subjects with new taxes. They found a solution under the inspiration of a French banker and businessman long established in Spain, François Cabarrus. In 1780 the government issued a novel type of public debt, the *vales reales* (a literal translation would be 'royal vouchers'), which were supposed to play the role of paper money while also yielding a 4 per cent interest rate. The first issue of the *vales* in October 1780 was successful, and so were the following two in October 1781 and July 1782 (Herr, 1978). As White (1987) has remarked, the *vales* had many points in common with other hybrid monetary-public-debt instruments issued at around this time in other countries, such as the *assignats* in revolutionary France and the Treasury notes emitted by some American colonies. However, in order to increase the acceptability of the *vales*, Cabarrus resuscitated an old idea many times revived but never before put into practice, and proposed to the king the creation of a national bank.

2.2 The Bank of Saint Charles

With the gradual revival of prosperity since the mid-eighteenth century, the schemes and proposals for public banks had been frequent, but it was not until the needs of the Crown became pressing that one of these plans was made into a reality. The Cabarrus project was accepted and the National Bank of Saint Charles was established in June 1782 'under Royal protection'.

There is no doubt that the immediate purpose of creating the Bank was to provide a backing for the *vales*: the Bank's charter made this very clear in its preamble. However, this same document invested the new institution with a strange assortment of missions, one of which was not even closely related to banking: this was the supplying of victuals, clothing, weapons, ordnance, etc., to the army and navy. Possibly Cabarrus thought that this would be a solid and profitable business (the *Cinco Gremios* had been frequent contractors with apparent success), or the king and his government thought this would be a way of centralizing and controlling a crucial military function; but in this they all turned out to be gravely mistaken. Earl J. Hamilton (1970, p. 204) remarked that Alexander Hamilton, the American revolutionary politician and financier, was, at approximately the same time, making a parallel error when he proposed that the First Bank of the United States undertake a similar mission, but this scholar found no evidence of any relation between the two financiers that could explain such unfortunate coincidence.

2.2.1 The Bank's charter

The charter carefully enumerated the three missions or purposes of the Bank. The supplying of the army was number two. Number one was to discount letters, *vales*, and bills (article 2); interestingly enough, the text specified that the Bank would enjoy no monopoly on these matters, while it would be sole supplier of the army; the procurement contracts still in vigour, however, would be respected albeit not renewed (article 3). The third mission of the bank was to make foreign payments and transactions on account of the government (article 4). In a strict literal interpretation this meant transferring funds for the embassies and diplomatic missions but the text itself made clear that this could include any kind of foreign monetary transactions. In fact, exporting silver on account of the government and on its own account turned out to be one of the most lucrative of the Bank's activities (Tedde, 1988, p. 127). The charter's text presents some contradictions and omissions, probably due to last-minute amendments. For example, it says peremptorily that the bank could not 'under any motive or pretext' undertake any other mission than the three previously enumerated, and should not mix itself in any commercial operation, 'so as not to do any harm to private persons'. This must have meant that the Bank should not compete with merchants, and a strict interpretation of the text would have excluded the Bank from many common operations of commercial banking. For instance, nowhere is it said that the Bank could lend to merchants or businessmen unless it was by means of discounting bills and letters. However, an exception clause was added in that the king could authorize or commission operations which could 'favour agriculture or factories', something which might be, and was, construed as permitting ordinary loans to business (article 29).

Indeed, the charter seemed to give wide latitude to the Bank's managers and shareholders when it said that as in designing any 'establishment it [was] difficult to avoid some shortcomings. [...] Shareholders in their General meetings [would] be free to accord what they deem necessary, as long as they should follow the spirit of the present rules and announce it to the public' (article 45). The will of the monarch to interfere as little as possible and to give a wide leeway to shareholders is evident in several other articles as well, including no. 22, according to which if the king or any member of his family owned shares of the Bank, his or their voting rights would be the same as those of any other shareholder. These voting rights were rather egalitarian: any person owning a minimum of 25 shares could vote, but nobody, no matter the number of shares he or she owned, had right to more than one vote.

No mention was made in the charter of the right of the bank to issue banknotes, but the possibility of merchants making payments among themselves by means of credits and charges on their accounts at the Bank (girobank payments), 'as is practiced in Holland', was admitted in article 44. This same article assumed that merchants would pay interest for their deposits in the Bank, with which this institution tacitly renounced attracting substantial resources by means of current account deposits. In spite of the silence of the charter about banknotes, the first shareholders meeting asked for permission to issue them and it was granted. Later on, however, the Bank developed a system called '*vales-dinero*' (money vouchers) whereby the Bank would transfer one *vale* to anyone depositing 300 reales in silver, and would convert back this *vale* into silver on sight. This in fact was equivalent to a current-account silver deposit with a 4 per cent interest, but it was developed after 1794, when the Bank's activity was already quite reduced, and its quantitative import does not seem to have been substantial.

It is obvious that no idea, even remote, of a central bank existed in the minds of the writers of the Bank of Saint Charles' charter. It has even been said by Earl J. Hamilton (1970, p. 229) that, according to its charter, the Saint Charles was really no bank at all. He was right in that it was conceived, first and foremost, as an aid to the state (or the Crown), in supporting the *vales*, in provisioning the army, and in managing its international payments. Secondarily, it was seen as a help to commerce, agriculture, industry, and public works, with the clear proviso that it should not compete unfairly with other bankers and merchants (article 2). It is worth mentioning, in this respect, that, although an instrument of the state, the Bank was organized as a private corporation, the property of its shareholders, with relatively small intervention by the Crown ('The economic government of the Bank must be entirely in the hands of the Shareholders', article 13), and with the intention that the number of these should be as widespread as possible, so that, if feasible, the number of shares should be expanded so that 'no citizen of these kingdoms and of the Indies should be excluded from the benefits that this establishment may produce' (article 12). Perhaps the true merit and originality of the Bank of Saint Charles was more in its organization as a novel type of corporation than as a bank.

The shareholders appointed eight directors, two of them charged with the military supplies. This group of eight directors soon turned out to be a confused and unwieldy body, unable to act or control properly, so that Cabarrus, who was not elected one of them, but was appointed 'honorary director' by the first general meeting, became *de facto* president until his demise in 1790.

2.2.2 Early years of relative prosperity, 1782–90

The Bank's capital was fixed at 300 million reales, a figure judged excessive by many. However, Cabarrus considered that the ambitious and complex missions of the Bank required such volume of capital: in a way, he thought of shareholders as surrogate depositors, whose money would be employed profitably and who would receive good dividends, so that their number would keep expanding. Furthermore, by the time the Bank was founded, the volume of *vales* in circulation was 451.8 million reales (Herr, 1978, p. 124), and nobody knew how many would be submitted for redemption. However, 300 million reales was a very high figure for the Spanish economy, and in spite of the generous example of the king and his family, the subscription took much more time and effort than expected. Convents and pious institutions were pressured to buy shares, and so were villages and cities, which were even encouraged to levy special taxes for that purpose (Tedde, 1988, p. 73). Cabarrus and his associates managed to sell about one-fifth of the bank's equity in France, something which provoked the wrath of the count of Mirabeau, who wrote a booklet pointing out the several contradictions in the plan of the Bank of Saint Charles and trying to dissuade Frenchmen from buying its shares. Mirabeau even compared Cabarrus to John Law, saying that a Frenchman would do in Spain what a Scotsman had done in

France. This *bon mot* was frequently repeated and did considerable harm to Cabarrus' prestige. In the end, however, he managed to sell a good number of shares in France and in Spain, and make a tidy profit of it (Tedde, 1988, pp. 87–110; T. Tortella 1986, *passim*, esp. pp. 389–408).

For the Bank one of the steadier sources of profits was the export of silver. Spain at that time played the role of *entrepôt* between Europe and its American colonies. The colonies produced mostly agricultural products that – except for cocoa beans and a series of durable products such as quinine bark, *cochinilla* (a red dye), and some other dyes – were of very difficult transportation. Their really valuable exports were mining products such as gems, gold, and silver. This last metal, being the most abundant, was Spanish America's main export. The colonies had a few craft industries such as textiles, aimed almost exclusively for internal consumption. They imported large amounts of industrial products, from linen and other textiles to weapons, books, tools, and so on. Spain provided some industrial products, such as clothing, liquors, and books, and some agricultural products such olive oil, but it re-exported to Spanish America large amounts of industrial goods from England, France, Italy, Holland, Germany, and other European countries. Silver settled Spanish America's commercial deficit with Spain, and then Spain's commercial deficit with the rest of Europe. In controlling a large amount of the silver flow from Spain to the rest of Europe, the Bank of Saint Charles had a sure source of profit for no other reason than that silver commanded a lower price in Spain than north of the Pyrenees. The Bank had to fight for its monopoly because many other merchants had been profiting from this same operation; and it also had to urge the government to repress silver contraband exports. In spite of these problems, silver exports were a very substantial source of profit for the Bank, especially during its first years (Table 2.1, Col. 1). Cabarrus and his fellow directors were very keen on obtaining high profits especially at that time because they wanted to distribute high dividends to

Table 2.1 Bank of Saint Charles: profits from silver exports as percentage of total profits, paid-out capital as percentage of total liabilities, and discounts as percentage of total assets, 1784–90

	Silver Profits (% of total)	**Capital (% of liabilities)**	**Discounts (% of assets)**
1784	67.7	50.3	7.1
1785	45.1	85.4	15.6
1786	50.8	76.8	10.9
1787	21.5	79.7	7.3
1788	32.0	80.1	10.2
1789	31.1	79.4	9.1
1790	22.4	65.2	10.1

Source: Calculated from Tedde (1988), Table V.2, p. 118, and Table VII.5, p. 186.

attract additional shareholders, as capital was not totally disbursed when the bank opened for business. They also wanted to reinforce the credit and prestige of the Bank, and in addition to have as much cash in hand as possible to shore up the value of the *vales*. In this they were lucky, because the end of the American War (Treaty of Paris, 1783), restored confidence and the *vales*, which had depreciated somewhat in previous years, regained their par and even traded at a slight premium occasionally for the rest of the decade. They were also helped by the increase in the output of American silver and in the volume of commerce which had followed the liberalization of transatlantic trade in 1778.

In the following years silver exports diminished considerably and so did their profit rate, although it remained considerable. The French Revolution and the international wars that followed it put an end to the relatively placid life of the Bank of Saint Charles in its first eight years. In the short run, however, it permitted higher rates of profit in the exportation of silver: although its volume (at least that exported by the Bank) diminished, the price of silver shot up as a consequence of the insecurity in Europe. All in all, during the 1780s, silver exports yielded an average 2 per cent profit on the Bank's capital.

Examining the Bank's balances as presented by Tedde (1988, pp. 185–6) one is surprised by the absence or small weight of two items which are characteristic of commercial banks and more specifically of official or state banks even in that period: banknote issue and customers' deposits. We have already commented on the Bank's deposit policy: its creators conceived of deposits only as part of the giro payment system, a service the Bank offered to their customers and for which it charged a fee in the form of interest rate. But we have seen that the Bank intended to issue banknotes and that, early on, it applied for, and obtained, a permit for it. The banknotes of the Bank of Saint Charles received the name of *cédulas*, a polysemic word which may mean written instrument, legal document, identity card, license, or IOU, among other concepts. Although the *cédulas* appeared repeatedly on the liability side of the Bank's balances for very small amounts, they circulated in significant quantities only for two short periods: in the summer of 1783 and in the years 1797–1800. It is obvious that, lacking the attraction of the 4 per cent interest offered by the *vales*, the public saw no advantage in holding them; they therefore submitted the *cédulas* for redemption in silver as soon as they fell into their hands. In the summer of 1783 the new notes were put into circulation by the state, which purchased them from the Bank and used them to pay salaries and supplies; but employees and suppliers lost little time before going to the bank to exchange their *cédulas* for silver, so that of the 18.3 million reales that had been put into circulation between late May and early July, nearly 17 million had returned to the Bank's vaults by 31 July. No more attempts were made to put the *cédulas* into circulation at this time (T. Tortella, 1997, pp. 65–71). As a consequence of all of this, capital was usually much more than 50 per cent of the Bank's liabilities (Table 2.1, Col. 2), something which justified, at least to some extent, Earl J. Hamilton's doubts about its real nature as a bank.

Another remark must be made at this point: Hamilton himself (1947, *passim*) and others have considered the *vales* as paper money; however, it is debatable to what extent they played this role rather than that of ordinary bonds or debentures. The *cédulas* episode makes one doubt that the Spanish public at that time was prepared to use paper money. As we shall see later on, paper money (fiduciary) circulation remained very limited in Spain until well into the second half of the nineteenth century. Furthermore, the *vales* were issued in very high denominations, which made them hardly suitable for daily transactions. The first issue of vales had a unitary value of 600 reales, and was followed by two more issues of so-called *medios vales* (half *vales*) of 300 reales each. Now, 300 reales was about the monthly wage of a doorman at the Bank of Saint Charles (T. Tortella, 1997, p. 49) or of a trained mason or carpenter in or around Madrid (calculated from Hamilton, 1947, appendix V) in 1782. It is hard to conceive that currency units of this denomination should have circulated frequently at the time, not even the quarter *vales* of 150 reales when they were issued in 1794. Furthermore, they had to be transmitted by endorsement and renewed annually; their value depended therefore on their expiration date so that, rather than paper money, they were a 'disturbance to circulation', according to Ramón Santillán, the first historian of the Bank (Santillán, 1982 [1865], I, p. 10)

A typical operation of central banks is the discount and negotiation or resale of bills of exchange, and this was listed as the number one mission of the Bank in its statutes. However, although these operations were duly reflected in the Bank of Saint Charles' balance sheets, these show that discounts and negotiation of bills averaged about 10 per cent of total assets during these early years (Table 2.1, Col. 3), a fact which moved Santillán, to say that its capital was much in excess of what was needed for its ordinary banking operations (Santillán, 1982 [1865], I, p. 12).

The Achilles heel of the Bank of Saint Charles however, was its second mission, the provisioning of the army and navy. This was a complex operation, comprising the purchase and transportation to many different and distant places of very diverse commodities such as grain and other victuals, clothing and footwear, weapons, wood, ropes, tools, ordnance, and so on. Furthermore, the type of contract between the Bank and the government required a very detailed accounting of all these operations, to be submitted for approval. All these tasks turned out to overwhelm the Bank: the accounts were late and incomplete, and the prices charged much higher than planned. The Bank was accused of profiteering and the government delayed its payments or rejected the Bank's invoices, so that losses started mounting. In spite of this, the Bank under Cabarrus did not admit the reality of these losses, which were written down on its ledgers as government debt accruing interest. We have seen that the Bank of Saint Charles' founders, and especially Cabarrus, had been optimistic about this supply contract because the *Cinco Gremios* had apparently reaped profits from this activity before. The question then should be, why did the Bank fail where the *Cinco Gremios* had succeeded? There may be several explanations: the one offered by Santillán would have pleased Adam Smith: a simple partnership is more agile and its members work harder, while 'a corporation must by its very nature have a more expensive and generally less dedicated and provident administration'; he even described what nowadays is called by economists the 'agency problem' (Santillán, 1982 [1865], I, p. 10). There may be something to that; as we saw, some of the Bank's directors were accused of overcharging in their purchases. Furthermore, the *Cinco Gremios* had probably gradually built a network of agents and commissioners which the Bank had to assemble anew, possibly even with the enmity of the personnel of the *Cinco Gremios*, which considered the Bank as an intruder (Tedde, 1988, pp. 73–5). The Bank also had the misfortune that prices, especially those of grain, shot up after 1782. Many attributed these rises to the Bank's operations; here the accusations were unfounded. Inflation was general in Spain at that time; the government, however, wanted the contractors to stick to the agreed-upon prices and withheld payment.

But this was not the only egregious error of the Bank's directors. Another was the heavy investment of money and effort they made into the project of a canal to permit navigation from Madrid to Seville, and thereby to the sea. This was an impossible task due to the dryness of the Castilian plateau and to the mountain chains lying across it. The works were started in 1786 and continued for several years; they never produced a real of profit and were abandoned around 1790. The Bank also made other, more rational public work investments, but with very little profit.

Another Cabarrus project which was ruinous for the Bank was the Company of the Philippines, whose object was to develop commerce between Asia, Spanish America, and the Peninsula. The company was established in 1785 and appeared to make some profits initially but it was soon heavily in debt with the Bank, which put an end to its loans in 1789, when the company's debt was 18.4 million reales.

Cabarrus' boundless optimism also moved him to try to obtain a quick profit by having the Bank buy French public debt bonds in 1788 to the tune of 22 million reales. Naturally, this turned out to be an almost total loss.

2.3 War and decline

But it was the provisioning fiasco which in the end brought Cabarrus' downfall. In view of the growing tensions between the Bank and the government relating to this matter, the 1790 shareholders' meeting decided, with the government's full agreement, to suspend the contract. This, plus the recriminations he received for his other failed projects, moved Cabarrus to resign his post in the Bank. In October of that year the *Cinco Gremios* recovered the provisioning contract which they had lost eight years before. But this was not the end of the Bank's troubles in this matter. It had to transfer all the provisions in its power to the *Cinco Gremios*, plus grant them a tide-over loan. Times had changed, however, and the *Cinco Gremios* never repaid their debt. On the contrary, this had grown to 53.4 million reales by 1796, at which time the government took over the provisioning business. But that sum was never paid back and accrued to the accumulating arrears of the state towards the Bank.

The fall of Cabarrus was precipitous, following his resignation from the Bank. After a brief brush with the Inquisition, he was jailed, on 25 June 1790, accused of fraudulent exports of silver on the purported evidence of a letter. He languished in prison for five years without trial. In 1795, Manuel Godoy, then all-powerful *valido,* freed him and returned his bails, properties, titles, and honours (he had been made a count in 1789). A factor contributing to his recovery was no doubt that his daughter Teresa, married to Jean-Lambert Tallien, the hero of the 'Thermidorian restoration' in France, was one of the most powerful – and beautiful – women in France at that time. Although reinstated as a Bank director, Cabarrus did not recover his former influence there until after the Napoleonic invasion, when he became Finance Minister of Joseph Bonaparte.

The Bank was reorganized after the resignation of Cabarrus, and its governing personnel was profoundly renovated. But the turmoil of the French Revolution affected all of Europe and Spain was no exception. The execution of Louis XVI in 1793 was followed by Spain's declaration of war on France, a war which lasted for three years and left the Spanish Treasury in a state of near bankruptcy. To meet the French invasion of Catalonia in 1794 the government issued new *vales reales* in 1794–5 in far larger quantities than before; this caused their depreciation by about 20 per cent in 1797.

Meanwhile, after making peace with France, Spain changed sides and joined her new ally in declaring war on England in 1796. The French not only could not help Spain economically, they demanded support from their southern neighbour, whose government was in dire straits. The *vales* plummeted again. In order to stop the fall, the government looked for sources of income which could serve to back the *vales*. They made wealthy families and groups pay. In the end the Crown started selling Church lands, thus opening the way, as Herr (1978, p. 119) pointed out, for the *desamortización* ('disentailment' is the closest English synonym) of the lands of the Church and the nobility, an essential chapter of social modernization which different European countries carried out almost invariably under revolutionary processes. In Spain, although this was only a modest beginning, the selling of Church lands was started by the old monarchy in 1798. This fiscal squeeze was felt across the Atlantic also, and contributed to alienate churchmen and

Table 2.2 Bank of Saint Charles, balance sheet, 1801

Assets	Million reales	Liabilities	Million reales
Cash	3.1	Capital	240.0
Royal Treasury	193.2	Subsidiary Fund	10.4
Public Works	13.9	Profit and Loss	11.7
Nonperforming Debtors	19.2	Dividends in Arrears	6.8
Bills	0.6	Other	6.9
Madrid Town Hall	6.3		
Company of the Philippines	21.0		
Agents	3.2		
Loans on Shares	12.1		
Other	3.2		
TOTAL	275.8	TOTAL	275.8

Source: Tedde (1988), Table IX.2, p. 266.

landowners, thus fostering colonial revolt (Bazant, 1977, pp. 5–6). Another desperate government measure was to declare the *vales* inconvertible in 1799. Meanwhile, the Bank, endeavouring to shore up the *vales*, decided to make a second attempt at issuing the *cédulas* it kept since 1783, in the hope that they would replace silver and *vales*. The idea seemed to work for a year or two: as the *vales* depreciated, the volume of *cédulas* in circulation went up, reaching a maximum of 29.1 million reales by October 1798. From then on, however, their circulation decreased and they were down to less than 2 million by September 1801 (T. Tortella, 1997, Chs. 14 and 15, esp. Table 7). The mistrust of the public in the government and the Bank as war continued no doubt contributed to their lack of appetite for both *cédulas* and *vales*. The quotation of the *vales* recovered somewhat with the Peace of Amiens (1802). But by that time the Bank, after depleting its last reserves of silver in redeeming the *cédulas* and lending the rest to the government, was in a hopeless state of illiquidity. Its directors thought they would have to suspend payments in 1801. Its balance sheet of 1801 (Table 2.2) is representative of the situation. In fact, its basic structure had not changed for ten years and was not going to vary much thereafter.

The balance sheet shows a bank almost reduced to paralysis. Its capital, though pared down from 300 to 240 million reales in 1794, was 87 per cent of total liabilities. If we added to it the Subsidiary Fund, this would total more than 90 per cent, most of the rest being profits and dividends in arrears. It is hard to imagine where these came from, as most of the Bank's assets were frozen: the mountainous debt of the Treasury had been accumulating for almost two decades, and only a meagre and irregular trickle of interests flowed from it; most of the rest was long-delinquent debts, on the origin of some of which (Public Works, Philippines Company) we have already commented. Most of the nonperforming debt was the French 1788 bonds. The Madrid Town Hall debt was there at least since 1795 and was a little reduced after 1801, but not much. The relations with the private sector were practically nil. The discounts of bills had been steadily going down almost since the 1790 crisis (Tedde, 1988, p. 273). The renewal of the hostilities with England in 1804 of course was no help at all. But worst was to come.

2.4 War and stagnation

In 1808 Spain changed partners again in the protracted warfare which followed the French Revolution. This time, however, the change was due not to a government decision but to a popular upheaval which started with the rebellion of the people of Madrid against the French allies of their sovereigns. The rebellion was seconded almost everywhere and war ensued. Soon the French controlled most of the Peninsula, save the city of Cadiz in Spain and Lisbon in Portugal. In many areas of Spain, however, war had become *guerrilla* ('little war'; that is where and when the word originated). José I (Bonaparte) ruled precariously from his court in Madrid. A government emanating from an almost spontaneous Cortes, assembled in Cadiz, resisted and did little more effective than legislate, including a Constitution proclaimed in 1812. The royal family was in the hands of Napoleon. The Bank of Saint Charles split; its nominal head remained in Madrid; but its most important branch had been founded in 1785 in Cadiz, the harbour which had controlled the commerce with Spanish America for most of the eighteenth century and where the silver remittances arrived. This permitted this 'more national' of the two Banks (Santillán, 1982 [1865], I, p. 98) to be of more help to the loyalists than the Madrid headquarters were to the *afrancesados* ('Frenchified'). But even more decisive in expelling the French, aside from Napoleon's blunder in invading Russia, were a group of Spanish bankers cooperating with the Rothschilds in support of Wellington's army campaign starting out from Lisbon (Ferguson, 1999, pp. 83–8; López-Morell, 2005, pp. 31–5). By the end of 1813, French armies had left Spain and the field was open for the return of the young king from his confinement in southern France.

Ferdinand VII's reign (1814–33) was an unmitigated disaster for Spain. He restored absolutism through and through, blocking any hint of modernization or progress. His finances were archaic (he considered budgets dangerous liberal innovations) and he brutally ruled a bankrupt country for many years. There were several military rebellions against him but only one succeeded, in 1820, from Cadiz, led by Coronel Rafael del Riego. A confused liberal regime ensued, which tried to modernize the country at full speed, with mixed success. The experiment was interrupted by a new French invasion, this one to restore absolutism, in 1823. Meanwhile the Spanish American colonies had been lost and the country could not count on those blessed silver remittances. In the last years of his reign, Ferdinand finally and dimly realized that he had to accept the advice of a few moderate liberals to modernize the country enough to be able to attract some foreign credit. He may have belatedly realized that Spanish America had been lost at least in part due to his financial incompetence. There were no bankers inside Spain capable of making a substantial loan to Ferdinand (the paralytic Bank of Saint Charles was out of the question), but thanks to his moderate ministers he found a Spanish banker in Paris, Alejandro Aguado, who could lend him at exorbitant prices in 1826. Ferdinand was thus able to introduce a few improvements in the last years of his reign. In the economic sphere these were: a Commerce Code, the Madrid Stock Exchange and the reorganization of the Bank of Saint Charles into the Bank of Saint Ferdinand in 1829.

3
Banking in War and Peace

3.1 Some institutional groundwork: the Commerce Code, the Madrid Stock Exchange, and the Bank of Saint Ferdinand

The Spanish Bank of Saint Ferdinand was established by a royal decree on 9 July 1829. It was part of a set of financial innovations introduced in the last years of the reign of Ferdinand VII, which included the Commerce Code of May of the same year and the founding of the Madrid Stock Exchange on 10 September 1831. These three innovations were largely due to the talent of the jurist Pedro Sainz de Andino, who wrote the charter of the Bank and of the exchange, and proposed the writing of the code and, once the royal agreement was obtained, carried out the redaction of the whole book himself. This considerable wave of financial innovation was made possible not only by the remarkable abilities of Sainz de Andino but also by the political and financial evolution of Spain in those years. The final years of Ferdinand's reign witnessed a certain mellowing of the old ferocious autocrat. The causes of this relative redress were economic and dynastic. Incompetent economic management kept his government in permanent insolvency, which contributed to the defeat of the Spanish colonial armies in America and to the consequent loss of the empire. For a better financial performance the king was forced to turn to abler officials and bankers, who happened to be less reactionary than his former ministers and counsellors. In addition, this moderating of his original despotism disappointed several of his formerly staunch supporters, who shifted their allegiance to his brother Charles, his heir apparent – as his first three marriages had produced no live heirs. However, he married María Cristina of Bourbon-Parma, his niece, in 1829, and she gave him two daughters. By then he was quite ill and it was obvious that he would have no male heir. Invoking the French *Salic law*, which excluded females from succession, Charles contested his niece Isabel's title to the throne. In this he was supported by the extreme right, while the liberals stood by Ferdinand's daughter, a fact which pushed him further towards the political centre.

The chronic deficit of the Spanish state during and after the Peninsular War made repayment of its huge debt to the Bank of Saint Charles impossible. The solution to the impasse was for the Bank's shareholders to accept a steep reduction of their claims, from some 310 million reales to 40 million. This was to be the capital of a renewed Bank of Saint Charles, although in the last minute the decision was made to call this novel, reduced version of the old Bank, Spanish Bank of Saint Ferdinand, thus placing it under the invocation of the reigning king's patron saint and avoiding the term 'National', at the time reminiscent of the French Revolution (Tedde, 1999, p. 25). The old Saint Charles's shares were exchanged for those of the new Bank at a rate of 5 to 1. At their current market price, this was advantageous for the shareholders.

The leading organs of the Saint Ferdinand were as follows: (i) a 'Royal Commissary', appointed by the Crown with powers of inspection; (ii) a board (*Junta de Gobierno*) composed of a director, a sub-director, seven ordinary members, and five trustees (*síndicos*). Director and sub-director were appointed by the Crown out of three names for each post submitted by the stockholders; the members and three trustees were appointed by the stockholders and two trustees were appointed by the Crown; (iii) the meeting of stockholders (*Junta General*), which could only be attended by those owning a minimum of 25 shares.

The bank's charter designed it as a bank of issue and discount, and a lender to the government, but not as a deposit bank in the modern sense. It could issue notes in Madrid, and discount bills of exchange wherever its branches or correspondents operated. The charter initially stipulated that depositors should pay interest, although this was corrected in 1833, when deposits became free of charge. The removal of interest was followed by a surge in deposits, but it took more than a decade for them to become a substantial item on the Bank's balance sheet.

This did not seem to pose any serious problem with the Bank in its early years. Excess of funds rather than shortage seems to have been the concern of its managers. In their first meeting (1 February 1833), stockholders learned that about half of the capital had been idle since the Bank was established. The reason is not hard to find. The Bank of Saint Ferdinand was conditioned by the stormy history of its predecessor, and this legacy prevented it from displaying an aggressive operational attitude. For over a decade the overriding aim of the Bank's managers was to dispel the disreputable image of the Bank of Saint Charles by enhancing the Saint Ferdinand's respectability, keeping its assets as liquid as possible, and guaranteeing the convertibility of its banknotes. To these ends the Bank restricted its note issue and was parsimonious with loans and discounts. Unfortunately, after 1833, the breaking of civil war pressured the bank to lend to the government and to accentuate its conservatism towards the private sector.

It was in their first meeting that the Bank's shareholders made deposits free. They also voted to admit government bonds and the Bank's own shares as collateral for loans. They also took a rather curious decision: to discontinue publication of the Bank's balance sheets, with the aim of keeping closed 'the vault where the mystery of credit must be locked [...because...] once this mystery is published, its virtue is destroyed' (Banco Español de San Fernando, 1833, pp. 53–4). This decision remained in vigour until 1852, and is a telling example of the banking ideas in Spain at the time. Santillán, who countermanded this agreement on becoming the Bank's governor, acutely criticized the 'mystery' doctrine three decades later (1982 [1865], I, p. 164). Fortunately for scholars, Pedro Tedde has reworked the Bank's balances from its books and published them in his monumental history (Tedde, 1999).

3.2 Monetary and fiscal effects of the fall of the empire

The repercussions of the loss of the empire in continental America for the Spanish economy must have been considerable, although economic historians debate how much so. For Vicens Vives (1959, p. 549) the independence of the colonies was 'a very serious setback' and a 'brutal event'; for his disciple J. Fontana, the falls in the volume of trade and remittances were decisive factors in the 'bankruptcy' of the Spanish state (1974, p. 75 and *passim*). For Prados de la Escosura, however, the consequences of the loss of the colonies were 'less ample and profound' than suggested by other historians. He estimated the direct loss at 6.7 per cent of national income (1993, pp. 273, 284), which at first blush does not seem shattering. One must take into account, however, that a large part of Spanish income was produced by subsistence agriculture, which naturally was hardly affected by the independence of the Empire, at least in the short run. The impact of independence upon trade and government revenue, however, was much more serious. It also had long run monetary consequences (Tortella and Comín, 2001, pp. 161–70).

Although the monetary system was not legally modified during the early decades of the nineteenth century, colonial emancipation and the war against Napoleon greatly altered it. The French invasion divided the country into two areas, the conquered and the free, whose extensions varied according to the military alternatives. Furthermore, in the unconquered and liberated areas, several political units existed at different times which tried to finance their war effort by issuing money and establishing new mints. In addition, in the French zone, which from 1809 to 1812 comprised most of Spain, French coins circulated freely in substantial amounts, and they tended to displace Spanish money by virtue of Gresham's law, as their silver content was less. Portuguese and English coins also circulated, although in smaller amounts.

These additions to the money supply did not bring about its expansion; they just partially offset decrease due to monetary extraction. Spanish coins were exported or hoarded because of their high silver content and also because of the chronic deficit in the balance of trade (Prados de la Escosura, 1993; Carreras and Tafunell, 2005, Table 8.4). The consequence of monetary contraction was, naturally, deflation. Prices fell precipitously from around 1815 to 1830. Then they steadied from around 1830 until the mid-1850s, although with ups and downs around a horizontal trend. The Carlist civil war, for instance, made them go up; then they went down again from the late 1830s to the mid-1840s. Deflation contributed to the stagnation of the economy in the 1820s (Fontana, 1973, pp. 262, 332–5; Prados de la Escosura, 1988, Table 1.2, p. 45), caused peasant unrest, and was one of the sources of the political instability of the period. The Carlist war was largely a peasant war; it was preceded by another peasant rebellion in the late 1820s (the so-called War of the Aggrieved), and unrest in the countryside was endemic during the 1820s. To this unrest contributed the attempts to shore up public finances by increasing fiscal pressure. The remedy to deflation would not have been too difficult: diminishing the silver content in coins plus lowering the seigniorage price would most probably have stopped the hemorrhage. This was tried by the liberals during the *Trennium*, but that simple solution was abhorrent to Ferdinand and his ministers, probably because of their love of tradition and of a shortsighted fear of losing revenue, so they abolished the liberal measures after the restoration of absolutism in 1823.

Another hard problem was public finance. For centuries Spain had used remittances from the Americas to fill the gap between its expenditures and its revenues. The independence of the colonies put an end to this situation; nevertheless, the governments were slow to adapt to the new conditions. The old, antiquated tax system stayed in place, with minor changes, until 1845. The liberals tried to introduce a tax reform in 1821 but the attempt was short-lived. The governments of Ferdinand were totally opposed to any reform which would make taxes more equitable and flexible because this may put into jeopardy the privileges of the nobility and the clergy. This left Spanish finances in a situation of permanent deficit. Ferdinand tried to solve this problem by borrowing, but Spain was quite indebted already and, having lost the American remittances, bankers were reluctant to lend to it; the few who would, asked for high interest rates and very tangible guarantees. Furthermore, Ferdinand had repudiated the loans contracted by the liberals during the Liberal Triennium (1820–23), and this complicated matters even more. So Ferdinand and his Finance Minister, the moderate Luis López Ballesteros, finally were able to find two bankers in Paris, who would be willing to lend to the depleted Spanish state: the first was Louis Gebhard, a Frenchman, whom Ballesteros described as 'a poor banker', and who, early on, in 1823, signed a contract to float a loan for some 334 million reales at an outrageous interest rate plus commission and expenses (Fontana, 1973, pp. 206–15). Whatever the conditions, however, Gebhard could not carry out his commitment, and remitted very small fractions of the sums agreed upon. He himself looked for the support of other bankers and finally contacted Alejandro Aguado, who agreed to take up about half of Guebhard's commitments and was able to acquit himself faster and more effectively than the Frenchman. He thereby became the court's favourite banker – in fact, the only one – and was made marquis of *las Marismas*. But Aguado, able though he was, could not work miracles. At the end of Ferdinand's reign, the Spanish state was insolvent and penniless. According to Fontana (1973, p. 324), all that was left in the Royal Treasury in December 1833 was 37,000 reales. At that time the yearly expenditure in personnel of the Bank of Saint Ferdinand was 167,000 reales (Tedde, 1999, pp. 31–2).

3.3 How to pay for the war

Ferdinand died on 29 September 1833. He had compared himself to a beer bottle cork, and predicted that when he died there would be a spurt and spillover in Spain. On this he was right. Before year's end his brother Charles was at the head of a rebellion for his pretended rights to the throne: thus started the Carlist civil war, which lasted for the rest of the decade and caused very serious and painful problems to a country already in a parlous state.

The war posed almost insurmountable difficulties to a treasury as broke as the Spanish was. This explains two paradoxes of this period: how could a war against a rebellion which was almost penniless, reduced in numbers, and bottled up in the slopes and valleys of the Pyrenees last so long; and second, how was the Spanish state, in its destitute and disorganized situation, able to win a war at all. The explanation to the first paradox was that the Spanish state was also penniless, indebted, disorganized, and divided; the explanation to the second was that it still retained a few assets which proved decisive in the end. These assets were: the remains of the colonial empire, Cuba, Puerto Rico, the Philippines, and other minor dependencies; some mining sites, especially the mercury lode of Almadén; the vast extensions of barely tilled lands possessed by the Church, the nobility, and several public bodies, such as villages, towns, and the state itself; and the Quadruple Alliance. The Bank of Saint Ferdinand should very possibly be added to this list.

The Quadruple Alliance was signed in 1834 by Britain, France, Spain, and Portugal with the purpose of helping these two last countries to defeat the threats posed by Don Carlos and Dom Miguel, pretenders to the throne in Spain and Portugal respectively, both of whom had resorted to armed rebellion (López-Morell, 2005, p. 70). The treaty tried to compel both pretenders to abandon their respective countries and contained vague compromises for the two northern powers to intervene militarily if necessary. Although the Alliance did not operate smoothly, and both Britain and France avoided armed intervention (only some small voluntary columns were sent in

1836), the treaty could be a source of credit, at least for Spain: rumours of a French intervention in support of the Spanish government made the price of Spanish bonds go up in several occasions and thereby made possible the flotation of new Spanish debt.

Cuba, Puerto Rico, and the Philippines were rich colonies producing appreciated staples such as sugar and tobacco; Spain increased its fiscal pressure there and their remittances were still a valued asset for the Spanish treasury. The mine of Almadén in Ciudad Real, south of Madrid and near Andalusia, belonging to the Spanish state, produced mercury, a vital ingredient in the refining of silver ore. The metal was mostly exported to Mexico and it had been a rich source of profit since the sixteenth century.

As to arable land, there were very large tracts of it in the hands of institutional owners who cultivated them inefficiently or not at all. Although density was low, Spanish population had been increasing and the pressure to redistribute these lands was growing. This redistribution was called *desamortización* (disentailment) because institutional owners were commonly called *manos muertas* (dead hands), and their lands were said to be *amortizadas*, as in most cases they were legally unable to dispose of their property. Some of this distribution had taken place on a small scale since the mid-eighteenth century, and the liberals in the Triennium had tried it in a somewhat larger scale, but the bulk of these lands remained in the dead hands of institutional owners when the Carlist war started. *Desamortización* was anathema to conservatives and one of the main planks in the liberal programme. Among liberals, however, there was discussion about how to carry out disentailment; some wanted land to be given away for free or at a very low price to poor peasants and to soldiers who had fought against the French; others saw the selling of those lands for what the market would carry as a way to redress public finances.

Soon after the war started the effects of the Quadruple Alliance were evident in a bold move by Nathan Rothschild of London. Early in 1834, after the signing of the treaty, he promised to lend the Spanish government a considerable sum. This provoked dissension among the Rothschild brothers (Ferguson, 1999, p. 359), but in the long run it proved an astute move. The contract was finally signed in Paris (7 June 1834), not by Nathan, but by his brother James, the head of the Paris branch, and it provided Spain with 15 million francs. In exchange the Spanish government undertook to submit to the Cortes a bill recognizing the Triennium debt (as we know, Ferdinand VII had refused to recognize this debt, which was largely in foreign hands, and had become a long-standing subject of dispute) as soon as possible and also made James official banker of the Spanish court. It is true that the new Finance Minister (the count of Toreno) dithered about the contract and that repayment was slow, to the desperation of Nathan. However, his son Lionel was sent to Madrid in August and he obtained (by bribing the Queen Regent and Toreno) the Almadén contract which the Rothschilds had been seeking for years. This was a superb coup. The Rothschilds had been already in the Almadén business, as 'sleeping partners', for some years; their interest in Almadén was all the greater as brother Solomon, head of the Vienna branch, exploited the other large mercury lode in Europe, in Idria (Slovenia). Controlling Almadén and Idria, the Rothschild brothers could have the monopoly of European mercury, and this is what Lionel obtained from Toreno. Furthermore, the recognition of the Triennium debt was enacted by a law in November 1834. When Lionel left Spain in the spring of 1835 with all his aims attained, he left behind Daniel Weisweiller, to organize the Rothschild branch in Madrid. Weisweiller had been an employee of the Rothschilds in Frankfurt, but soon became acclimated in Madrid and became one of its leading bankers. He associated to his office a group of Spanish employees, some of whom later became independent and notable financiers. The most notable of these was Estanislao Urquijo, a Basque of humble origins who worked with Weisweiller from 1835 to around 1848, when he was established on his own.

The war divided Spanish society into absolutists (Carlists) and liberals. Ferdinand's widow, Cristina, was no liberal, but allied herself to them so they would defend her and her daughter's rights. The liberals on their part were far from united; they had to achieve a transition to parliamentary politics while fighting a civil war, creating modern institutions anew, managing the desperate financial plight Ferdinand had left, and dealing with the Queen Regent, who mistrusted all politicians but the most conservative. In these circumstances, there were very frequent cabinet changes. Prime ministers succeeded each other at the rate of more than one per year, and ministers, especially Finance Ministers, had an even faster turnover. Toreno became Prime Minister in June 1835 and chose Juan A. Mendizábal to replace him as Finance Minister. Mendizábal was a liberal banker who fled Spain in 1823 and established himself in London, where he made a fortune in banking and commerce (importing Spanish wines was one of his trades). He was still in London when he was appointed minister, but by the time he arrived in Madrid in September he found himself Prime Minister, thanks, it appears, to anti-clerical disorders in Barcelona and other cities, and to the influence of the British ambassador, Charles Villiers. Mendizábal was well connected in London and there was hope that these contacts, plus his financial abilities, would solve the multifarious problems of the liberal establishment.

In truth, Mendizábal, who combined the premiership and the finance portfolio, did not disappoint the hopes that had been pinned on him: he was the only man with a coherent plan about what to do in the dire circumstances in which he took power, and with the energy needed to put it into effect. However, he was not able to surmount the chaotic social conditions and the machinations of the queen and the politicians, so his government lasted barely eight months. In this short time, however, he achieved an economic and social revolution which would mark the

Spanish nineteenth century: the *desamortización* of the properties of the monastic orders. Although his tenure as Prime Minister was short, Mendizábal held the finance portfolio several times afterwards, and his influence over liberal governments lasted for at least a decade. He was a *Progresista,* as the left-wing liberals called themselves, while the more conservative wing called themselves *Moderados.* Through his influence and his stints at the ministry he was able to complete the disentailment of church lands later, adding those of the so-called secular institutions to those of the monastic orders. The Church was compensated in public debt bonds and the lands and other properties were sold in auction; a combination of cash and public debt securities were accepted in payment for the purchased parcels: Mendizábal hoped this would raise the desirability of those securities and permit the floating of further loans. His colleague Nathan Rothschild, however, was sceptical about how fast disentailment would work its financial effects: 'It is like telling me at seven o'clock when I want my dinner [that] there is a calf feeding in a field a mile off' (Ferguson, 1999, p. 365). The Rothschilds in fact were little inclined to take Spanish debt paper; for the remainder of the decade they made plenty of short-term loans to the government on very solid guarantees, such as future revenues from Almadén and promissory notes on Cuba and the Philippines remittances, and little more. All in all, however, the Church land disentailment was a key factor in the financing of the war. According to the calculations of a contemporary economist (C. Labrador, quoted in Tedde, 1999, p. 127) the war cost the Spanish treasury some 4,000 million reales; in the five years after the disentailment law (19 February 1836) the land sales contributed 1,700 million to the treasury (Tortella and Núñez, 2011, p. 92), more than two-fifths of the total cost. In addition, as Mendizábal claimed repeatedly, the buyers of this land became 'a copious family of landowners' supporting the liberal cause. To this must be added, naturally, the increase in agricultural output and taxes that the more intensive cultivation of the newly acquired parcels of land brought about.

Mendizábal also decreed a levy of 100,000 men to be added to the army (which meant almost doubling those already in the field), admitting a considerable payment in lieu of enlistment; this reduced the number of men actually recruited to some 70,000, but contributed to their provisioning. Furthermore, in order to provide the funds immediately needed, Mendizábal carried out a series of very ingenious operations with public debt securities, which permitted to obtain the necessary means while the disentailment machinery was being put in place (Fontana, 1977, pp. 145–6, 167–74; Tedde, 1999, pp. 56–7). Later on, when he was no longer in power, the promissory notes of the buyers of disentailed land were used by the government as securities to obtain credit from the Bank of Saint Ferdinand and from numerous private bankers in Madrid.

The Bank certainly was a solid support to the government in spite of initial and occasional resistance. It was approached for help very soon after Ferdinand's death and not without a certain reluctance on the Bank's part, who alleged that the government was already in arrears, its board finally agreed to advance two-thirds of what the government had asked for (Tedde, 1999, pp. 47–8). This became a pattern: during the war, and for several years thereafter, the government pressured the Bank for money, offering all kinds of securities as guarantee. The Bank resisted, asked for the reimbursement of old debts, demanded solid guarantees and high interest rates, and finally agreed, usually lending only a fraction of the original request. In several occasions the Bank ended up collecting taxes and other exactions for the government, and keeping a share in concept of interest and commission (Tedde, 1999, Part Two, *passim*. What follows is largely drawn from this work). Not only did the Bank wholeheartedly, although with caution, support the government's war effort with its credit, it also acted as the government's agent, fiscal and otherwise, mediated with other financial institutions, bankers and suppliers (*Ibid.*, p. 69), discounting promissory notes from the disentailment sales (pp. 79, 121), and so on. It was characteristic of the Bank's role as government's agent that the Saint Ferdinand's secretary was one of the signatories of the agreement with James de Rothschild of 7 June 1834 (*Ibid.*, p. 49; López-Morell, 2005, p. 70); it is also symbolic of the bank's cooperation in the disentailment operation that it accepted as guarantees church jewels and even bells (Tedde, 1999, pp. 90–1).

The Bank's involvement in the war marked a shift in the structure of its operations, as is shown in Table 3.1 and Figure 3.1, which are calculated from Tedde's reconstructions of the Bank's balance sheets. We have used bills of exchange as a proxy for the Bank's credit to the private sector.

Table 3.1 Bank of Saint Ferdinand: loans to private (bills) and public sectors (as percentage of assets)

	Bills	**Government**
1830	1.1	28.7
1831	13.0	19.1
1832	24.2	11.0
1833	24.1	11.1
1834	36.0	9.8
1835	22.0	18.6
1836	7.1	35.5
1837	3.6	64.3
1838	1.3	63.1
1839	0.5	56.9
1840	10.3	60.8

Source: Calculated from Tedde (1999), Tables II.3, IV.5 and VI.3.

Tedde's balance sheets include an item on the asset side called 'Public Sector' and this is reflected in Column 2 of the table. Very probably, the unbalance between the private and public sectors was even larger, because the other large asset item in the balances is '*Comisionados*', the Bank's agents in the provinces and abroad, and, according to Tedde (1999, p. 128), the largest part of the holdings of these agents were government securities, although we cannot separate private from public assets under this rubric. The figures in Table 3.1, therefore, are only indicative. They show, in any case, that in its early years the Saint Ferdinand was increasing its share of credit to the private sector and restricting its credit to the government; this trend, however, was sharply interrupted after 1834 and, from then on, credit to the government grew by leaps and bounds, while credit to the private sector was neglected until it approached zero in 1839.

According to Tedde, the credit extended by the Bank of Saint Ferdinand to the Spanish Treasury during the war was about 8 per cent of total war cost. And he adds (1999, p. 127):

> Aside from the importance of this contribution – far from negligible – we have been able to show that the financial effort by the Bank in the civil conflict as congregator of private lenders, mediator with foreign bankers or coordinator of diverse credit operations, was even more determinant.

By the summer of 1839 both sides in the war were exhausted and depleted, but the Carlists more so. After long and tortuous negotiations, the generals of the two armies (Baldomero Espartero for the liberals, Rafael Maroto for the Carlists) signed a peace agreement at Vergara in the Basque country on 31 August 1939, accompanied by an accolade (*el abrazo de Vergara*). Its most important clause was that both armies were to merge and the liberal government to prevail. Adding all those new soldiers to the payroll was an

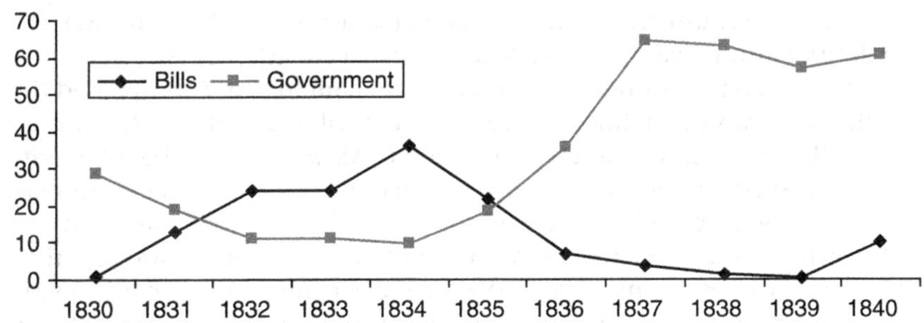

Figure 3.1 Bank of Saint Ferdinand: loans to private (bills) and public sectors (percentage of assets)

Source: Table 3.1.

expensive proposition for the government. Furthermore, the war was not totally finished: in southern Catalonia the Carlist bands continued fighting for almost another year. The liberals had won but Spain had to pay a very high price, largely on credit.

3.4 The peace dividend: the Banks of Isabel II and Barcelona

The end of the Carlist War was a boost to the Spanish economy, although none of the long-term economic problems was solved, especially those of the public debt and the chronic budget deficit. Early in 1840, the war officially over, the government was letting the Bank of Saint Ferdinand know that it still needed 5 million reales for military operations (Tedde, 1999, p. 120). In truth the war went on in Valencia and Catalonia, and the mop-up operations continued until the final defeat of the Carlists in the summer of 1840.

Politically the end of the war also brought about rapid changes. The foremost hero of the war, General Espartero, became the head of the Progressive Party; the Queen Regent, María Cristina, never concealed her *Moderado* sympathies. Santillán (1996, p. 276), a *Moderado* himself, admitted that 'The Moderate Party [...] was really the party of the Queen mother.' There was some confrontation between her and Espartero in Barcelona, just after the defeat of the Carlists. Espartero was immensely popular there. She was forced to appoint him Prime Minister, something she did reluctantly, and thereafter she abdicated, and left the country. He became the sole arbiter of the situation and was soon elected Regent by the Cortes, Isabel being barely ten. Espartero was a good soldier but as a politician he was mediocre or worse. In the next three years he managed to stir up the enmity not only of the *Moderados* but of a large part of his own party as well. In November 1842 the same Barcelona which had acclaimed him two years earlier rose against him. Espartero took this as just a military problem and had that cradle of Progressivism bombarded: more than 400 houses were destroyed and the city was punished with extra taxes (Soldevila, 1959, VII, p. 162). His popularity plummeted. In the summer of 1843 a coalition of Moderates and Progressives, led by another war hero, General Ramón Narváez, deposed the regent. Isabel was proclaimed of age and crowned queen at 13. Her mother was recalled to Spain and a ten-year period of *Moderado* rule (the 'Moderate Decade') ensued, under the benevolent protection of the new queen and her mother. Isabel inherited her mother's partiality for the Moderate Party.

Meanwhile, free from the fears and uncertainties of civil war, Spanish capitalism was beginning to stir. We have clear indications that growing optimism drove investment up. The Mercantile registers of Madrid and Barcelona both show sharp increases in the establishment of new companies and in their combined capital figures (Tedde, 1999, pp. 143–5). Banks and insurance companies were most numerous among the new corporations created under this euphoric climate and the liberal clauses of the Commerce Code. In the industrial sector, the textile cotton industry in Barcelona and other smaller towns recovered and started to employ machinery imported from England. In the Basque country the first corporation devoted to mining the local iron ore was founded in 1841.

Furthermore, there were hopes that Alejandro Mon, a prestigious Minister of Finance, was going to fix the budget problems and take the first steps towards solving the conundrum of the public debt. The quotation of public debt bonds in the Madrid Stock Exchange more than doubled between 1838 and 1846 (Hoyo, 2007, p. 176, weighted index). Mon really had a plan and carried out a considerable part of it. One part of the plan was to rearrange the 'floating debt', that is, the innumerable promissory notes the government had given to suppliers and bankers during the war, many of them with the proviso that they could be used to pay taxes for their nominal value, having been surrendered at large discounts. He converted all these into a new type of bond not acceptable for tax payments and asked the Bank of Saint Ferdinand to handle the management of this new debt. In truth, this was a stopgap solution, because large budget deficits subsisted. The other part of the plan was a profound reform of the fiscal system, the so-called Mon-Santillán Reform, because Santillán was the author of the main blueprint (Tortella and Comín, 2001, pp. 161, 170–2). The reform, enacted in 1845, certainly modernized and made more fair the archaic fiscal order, but its basic flaw was that it could not do away with deficits, largely because its main revenue was a land tax, and landowners were able to prevent government agents from collecting accurate information in a cadastre, there consequently being enormous tax evasion.

Meanwhile, optimism endured and company creation proceeded apace. This renewed activity demanded financial services and several banks were founded. Most of the new financial and insurance companies, however, just as the fond hopes about the public debt, were short-lived. Nevertheless two banks of issue were founded in 1844, which were to leave a deep imprint in Spanish history.

The first of these was the *Banco de Isabel II*, among whose founders was the most colourful of Spanish nineteenth-century businessmen, José Salamanca. He could also be called 'the Spanish robber baron' but his audacity, dash, and vision somehow compensated for his lack of scruples. He had arrived in Madrid from his native Málaga in the 1836 as a deputy to the Cortes, and was helped in his first steps in business by a wealthy relative. His Andalusian charm opened many doors for him and he soon had amassed a fortune in the stock exchange, dealing in Spanish debt, and farming the salt state monopoly. For this he needed political contacts, but he was past master at mixing business and politics.

There were some other notable financiers on the board of the Isabel II, but Salamanca was the guiding spirit. The statutes of the bank allowed it to issue banknotes under a different name. The Saint Ferdinand was not fooled by this ruse and immediately opposed the Isabel II by all available means, including judicial, seeing it as a serious competitor and justly claiming that its charter violated the Saint Ferdinand's official monopoly of issue in Madrid. It was to no avail. Both banks soon opened hostilities: the Saint Ferdinand refused to accept its competitor's money while the Isabel II accumulated large amounts of its rival's notes and presented them for redemption all at once hoping to provoke bankruptcy. It appears that this operation was carried personally by Salamanca, who hauled bags of banknotes on a carriage, but he did not reach his goal: thanks to emergency help from the Rothschilds and from Madrid bankers, the Saint Ferdinand could stop Salamanca's blows (Tedde, 1999, pp. 183–4).

The *Banco de Isabel II* was indeed a competitor for the older bank. It was conceived as a commercial bank, and intended to take advantage of the official institution's limitations; its nominal capital of 100 million reales was more than double the paid-up capital of the Saint Ferdinand. The Isabel II introduced several innovations which jolted the Saint Ferdinand out of its staid habits. It was active in lending to the burgeoning new mercantile, industrial, and railroad companies, accepting their shares as collateral. Among the companies which received generous credit was the railroad from Madrid to Aranjuez (a riverside resort where the royal family had an impressive and frequently used palace), belonging to Salamanca. Given the volatile conditions in Madrid and the commercial nature of the bank, this liberality with loans was dangerous. Even more dangerous was accepting its own shares as collateral, which the Isabel II did, not being authorized to it by its statutes. Another, more orthodox, innovation of the new bank was to open a branch in Cadiz, which put the Isabel II's notes in circulation there, where they were eagerly accepted. The Isabel II also innovated in putting into circulation banknotes of small denominations, and also in making ample use of its issuing licence, thus contributing to popularize fiduciary money. All this shook the Saint Ferdinand from its torpor. It immediately publicized its readiness to intensify its operations with the private sector, and reminded its customers that it charged no fee for deposits, something which until then 'had been generally ignored by the public'. It also made known that current account deposits were free as well, facilitated the concession of loans and discounts and made an effort to speed up its operations. It also imitated its rival in expanding its note issue, so that Madrid's banknote circulation increased from 24 million reales in January 1844 to 110 million in September 1845 (of these 60 million were the Saint Ferdinand's notes, which had thus multiplied its circulation by 2.5 in a year and a half; the rest, of course, were the Isabel II's).

The other new bank of issue was established in Barcelona. In contrast with the *Banco de Isabel II*, it was extremely conservative and enjoyed a long life. According to Castañeda (1991, pp. 339–41) 'it is paradoxical [after the steps towards industrialization which had taken place in the 1830s] that Catalonia should have lacked private banks and financial institutions' before 1844. He attributes this paradox to several causes; but the really important one was the lack of specialization among Catalan merchants and industrialists: until the mid-1840s there were, he says, neither banking houses nor bankers in Catalonia. He cites Vilar (1962, III, p. 419), who wrote that at the end of the eighteenth century, 'all Catalan businessmen practice banking as monsieur Jourdain spoke in prose [that is, unconsciously....] Credit is mobilized without coordination, but spontaneously.' Merchants discounted bills, made loans, kept deposits in current account, and practised insurance among themselves without abandoning their merchandise trade. Castañeda adds (p. 347) that '[a]ll the evidence suggests that, during the first third of the nineteenth century, the supply of financial assets was sufficient, in normal years, for the existing demand in Catalonia. Otherwise, money would have become more expensive and banking would have become a very profitable activity and banking houses would have turned up, which is what happened in the eighteen-forties.' In 1840 the economic revival increased the demand for money. Financial resources turned out to be insufficient in the face of the abrupt increase of commercial activity. Money became more expensive, interest rates went up. This made clear that specialized bankers were needed.

The *Banco de Barcelona* was founded by Manuel Girona, a young (26) scion of a family of merchants who also practised banking and had a company called *Girona Hermanos, Clavé y Compañía*. Girona had obtained the licence for his bank in 1842, but the political upheavals in the city delayed its constitution and opening until 1844 and 1845. The Barcelona had a nominal capital of 20 million reales, but started out with only 5 million paid up. It more than once had recourse to asking shareholders for 'passive dividends', that is, for additional disbursements, which were returned to them later when the emergency had passed. In this way, the bank used the large difference between paid-up and nominal capital as a safety buffer to be used in troubled times. It was a commercial bank of issue and was authorized to open branches in Catalonia and the Balearic Islands. It opened three branches with mediocre success; the ones in Tarragona and Reus were short-lived: they were merged, closed, reopened, and closed definitively in 1854. The Mallorca branch was more active, perhaps because it was farther from Barcelona, as, according to Blasco and Sudrià (2010, p. 48), 'the strong control exercised by the central office [made the branches] highly ineffective'. Another distinctive operation by the *Banco de Barcelona* in its early years was lending on merchandise as collateral, mostly cotton bales; this was natural, as Barcelona was becoming specialized in the cotton textile industry and many of the bank's customers (and board members) were merchants and/or industrialists. These collateral loans, however, turned out to be dangerous in the 1847–8 crisis and they were toned down afterwards.

If most banks founded during this period were short-lived, a few of them had a longer trajectory. This was the case not only of the *Banco de Barcelona*, but also of a sort of merchant bank, the *Sociedad Valenciana de Fomento*, the *Caja de Descuentos Zaragozana* and the *Caja de Ahorros de Madrid*.

The *Sociedad Valenciana de Fomento* (Valencia Development Company) was founded in 1846 by José Campo, a Valencian businessman and politician who was defined in 1871 by a *Crédit Lyonnais* agent in Madrid as 'a smaller-size Salamanca, except that he is less *sympathique*, he has less *esprit*, and his manners are more gross' (Crédit Lyonnais Archives, Paquet CEES 73.247, Dossier 'Banques'). This unflattering description was not totally inexact. As Salamanca, Campo adroitly mixed business and politics, was not too encumbered by legal scruples, promoted railroad companies, was interested in the introduction of innovations, was ennobled with a marquisate, and his fortunes experienced frequent ups and downs. He also had some points in common with Girona in that his father was a merchant who, when he saw that his son had considerable business abilities, created a family company, initially devoted to dealing in fruits and groceries, but which the younger Campo steered towards banking. He then became councillor in the Valencia Town Hall and later on became mayor of the city. Meanwhile he had introduced gas illumination and running water in the city, and had started railroad lines connecting Valencia to the tracks leading to Madrid and Barcelona. To help finance these enterprises in 1846 he founded the Valenciana which, although chiefly a business bank, issued short-term promissory notes which circulated as means of payment; this was quite irregular, as it was not authorized to issue banknotes. All in all, however, it was a remarkable financial innovation in the Spain of the time: although possibly inspired in other French models, it was founded six years before the Crédit Mobilier.

The *Caja de Descuentos Zaragozana* (Saragossa Discount Bank) was founded in that city in 1845. It was a commercial bank created by a former Progressive Finance Minister. Probably the competency of its founder and director, as well as its specialization in short-term credit, are the main explanations for its ability to sail through the 1847–8 crisis.

The *Caja de Ahorros de Madrid* (Madrid Savings Bank) was founded on 25 October 1838. It was the first of its class in Spain, although it had some interesting forerunners in the *Montes de Piedad*, charitable pawnshops whose origins go back to medieval times. These pawnshops were intended to supply small loans at reasonable interest rates, thereby protecting modest borrowers from the extortion of usurers. The first pawnshops of this class were established in England, Spain, and Italy as early as the fourteenth century. The name *Monte di Pietà* originated in Italy, where these institutions developed more steadily in the early modern period. The first regular *Monte de Piedad* using that name was founded in Madrid in 1702 under Franciscan auspices, as was the most frequent case in Italy. The problem of these institutions, however, was the liabilities side of their ledger: they had no capital and no shareholders; they needed an initial endowment to start business, and frequently this was insufficient as a source of funds. It was logical, therefore, that they should cooperate with savings banks whose problem was the opposite: they collected funds but, in so far as they were charitable – not financial – institutions they had no obvious investment outlet for the funds they collected. It seemed logical, therefore, that the *Cajas* should be associated with the *Montes*, as their charitable aims were similar and their economic activities complementary.

This was the case in Madrid, which was the cradle of the first Spanish *Monte* and the first *Caja*. Both institutions were formally independent, but they soon signed an agreement whereby all the funds deposited with the *Caja* would be lent to the *Monte*. The Madrid *Caja* was the first of a series of savings banks that were created under the auspices of a royal order of 1835 which recommended and stimulated the establishment of savings banks in Spain, with a double aim: to promote the thrift spirit among the poorer classes, and to favour the formation of a ready pool of investible funds the state could dip into. Naturally, that royal order was inspired by the return after 1833 of liberal exiles who had witnessed the virtues of savings banks in Paris and London and at the same time by the dire straits of the state's finances. Other *Cajas* were established at around this time in other cities, such as Granada (1839), Sagunto and Valladolid (1841), Seville, Santander, La Coruña and Valencia (1842), Barcelona (1844), Burgos and Cadiz (1845) (Titos, 1989, 1993).

3.5 The first capitalist crisis

It is difficult to pinpoint exactly how the 1847–8 all-European crisis, which originated in London and Paris, was transmitted to Spain, but the fact is that it reached awesome proportions there. One obvious channel was foreign trade: both official and estimated figures show Spanish exports falling after 1846 (Tena, 2005, pp. 600, 603). We do not know, however, whether this fall was due to a dip in demand or to a shortfall in supply, as the 1847 crop was bad and the government clamped a temporary stop on food exports. Be it as it may, the estimated export figures in constant monetary units fell by 37.8 per cent from 1847 to 1848, and the 1847 level was not reached again until 1853. Unfortunately we lack reliable estimates of other balance of payments figures. The estimated budget data we have show falls of receipts in 1847–8 in taxes related to consumption (excises) or to output such as duties on mortgages or on industry, and a long stagnation in the land tax (Comín, 1990, p. 60). Signs of distress abounded in the Spanish economy. Bankruptcies and closedowns multiplied after 1846 and the Madrid Stock Exchange index fell steeply in 1847 and 1848 (Hoyo, 2007, pp. 176–7). Mercantile register data show a precipitous fall (53 per cent) in capital invested in new companies in Catalonia in 1849 (Tafunell, 2005, p. 770). The deposits at the *Caja de Madrid* fell by 1.2 per cent in 1848, but the number of depositors fell by 32 per cent, which means that the poorer classes were the hardest hit (calculated from Titos, 1989, p. 565). Most of the banks founded just a few years before closed their doors and railroad companies halted their work, except for the Barcelona–Mataró line, which was inaugurated in 1848, the first in Spain.

For the *Banco de Isabel II* the consequences of the crisis were fatal. Several of the companies which failed had received credits from the bank which they would never be able to repay. Other companies which did not altogether go out of business simply suspended payments. Such was the case of the Madrid–Aranjuez railroad, lavishly financed by the Isabel II. In addition, the collateral deposited with the bank by these companies could only be liquidated at great loss, as its quotation in the stock exchange was falling rapidly, and the Isabel II had valued the securities used as collateral at their market value when the going was good. This was not only the case of the equity of the Madrid–Aranjuez railroad, but also that of the Isabel II's own shares, which had often been bought only to be used as guarantee with the bank.

The situation of the Bank of Saint Ferdinand was also shaky, but for altogether different reasons. The Bank had increased its cooperation with the government after the war even more than before so that credits to the public sector hovered around 50 per cent of its total assets during these years (probably the proportion was even higher, because other items, such as 'Correspondents', usually included a large share of government debt). The Saint Ferdinand had signed a contract with the state in 1844 whereby the Bank would become the state's cashier or treasurer, that is, would collect a series of taxes and advance the government monthly sums on account of the tax receipts. Meanwhile, the Bank had continued neglecting the private sector, except in 1846, when the competition of the Isabel II spurred it to increase its loans and discounts to that sector. The crisis, however, had very probably expanded the government's deficit (we lack reliable figures: see Comín, 1990, pp. 35–9) and forced it to borrow larger amounts from the Bank (Tedde, 1999, p. 188). The Saint Ferdinand's solvency, therefore, totally depended on the state's capacity and willingness to repay its debts.

Early in 1847 both banks were on the verge of suspending payments. The holders of the banknotes whose circulation had surged so suddenly in the previous years queued in front of both institutions to have them exchanged for gold and silver coins. The banks had trouble to 'satisfy these exigencies' and had recourse to desperate expedients, such as restricting teller's hours and dumping securities at a loss. At this moment, however, there was one of the frequent changes of government and Santillán was appointed Minister of Finance. In his own words (1996, p. 307), that of the banks 'was the conflict I had to attend to most urgently, and I found no more effective remedy than to merge both banks into one'. One of the reasons for this combination was putting an end to the rivalry between the two banks and to the coexistence of two issuing institutions in Madrid, something of more than dubious legality. A decree of 25 February ordered the merger. Santillán's plan was to appoint a commission to evaluate the banks' respective balance sheets and to apportion the capital in the new bank (which would be called New Bank of Saint Ferdinand) to the old shareholders according to this valuation. However, that government lasted only two months, and a new one was formed on 28 March. The leading member of this new government was none other than Salamanca, who, 'indebted for enormous quantities to the *Banco de Isabel II* and to a considerable number of banking houses of the first rank, could find no other means of getting out of this morass than by becoming Finance Minister'. So he pulled all his political strings to convince the queen to provoke a crisis and appoint the new government – with the help of a handsome general she was infatuated with (Santillán, 1996, pp. 311–12). Once in power, Salamanca appointed the commission supposedly to evaluate the assets of both banks, but this body limited itself to 'confusedly admit all the credits and all the liabilities of both' banks at face value, which was 'the shortest way, but at the same time the most fatal for the Bank of Saint Ferdinand' (Santillán, 1982 [1865], I, p. 256). The puzzling question is why did this commission, where shareholders of the Saint Ferdinand were a majority, make a decision which was so obviously against their own interests, and in favour of those of their old rival? The answer is simple: the government menaced them with stopping the payments it owed the Bank, thus 'threatening [it] with bankruptcy', because without the repayment of at least part of what the government owed it, which was the best part of its assets, the Bank would not be able to 'face its obligations, made more pressing by the crisis'; to add to the pressure, the contract making the Bank the government's cashier was suspended, although it was restored in November, after the Salamanca cabinet fell in September (Santillán, 1996, pp. 317–18; 1865, I, p. 273).

A consequence of the merger was the birth of a new bank of issue: the Isabel II's Cadiz branch, which had been operating under the title *Banco Español de Cádiz, Sucursal del Banco de Isabel II* (Spanish Bank of Cadiz. Branch of the Bank of Isabel II) and issuing the banknotes of its parent institution, became independent by dropping its branch character and issuing its own notes. This was possible because a new bank of issue just established under the title *Banco de Cádiz* absorbed the old branch.

If things were not complicated enough for the Saint Ferdinand, in June 1848 its director, Joaquín Fagoaga, absconded with a large amount of money and securities. As Santillán wrote, this caused 'enormous losses to the Bank, not only materially, but also by hurting its credit, which was even worse, as it put it in the most pitiful prostration' (Santillán, 1982 [1865], I, pp. 289–90; Tedde, 1999, pp. 225–6).

At that moment the *Banco de Barcelona* was also experiencing grave difficulties. In February it was discovered that considerable quantities of cotton had disappeared from the warehouses where the bank kept the merchandise deposited by its clients as collateral for loans. It was soon found out that most of the subtractions had been carried out by the clients themselves, the owners of the raw cotton. As was the case with the embezzlement in the Saint Ferdinand, these robberies not only entailed serious direct losses, but they also greatly affected the credit of the bank. Things became worse a few days later, when news of the dethronement of Louis Philippe in Paris caused a panic in Barcelona, where customers of the bank congregated to demand conversion of banknotes into specie. Soon the bank was short of silver so it had to severely diminish its loans and discounts and shorten its teller hours. In March it asked its shareholders for a 'passive dividend', which was punctually paid. Furthermore, several board members brought specie to the bank in exchange for notes, the exact opposite to what the majority of customers were doing. The forthrightness of executives and shareholders was known to the public and quickly restored confidence in the institution, which by early May was returning back to normal. The losses of that year were, nonetheless, considerable: they were due to the reduction of operations, in addition to the selling of assets and merchandise, often at a considerable discount in order to obtain specie readily. From that time on the bank reduced its operations with goods as collateral, manned its own warehouses (instead on renting them as before), restricted its banknote circulation, while expanding its current account deposits, and accumulated large proportions of cash. It became more cautious and conservative than before (Cabana, 1978, pp. 31–3; Blasco and Sudrià, 2010, pp. 158–69).

The *Moderado* governments constituted as a response to the crisis were longer and more solid than their predecessors. They were headed by two strong men, Ramón Narváez, a general, and then, in the early 1850s, Juan Bravo Murillo, a lawyer. Both men belonged to the right wing of the party and had, therefore, strong misgivings about *laissez-faire*. Their governments issued repressive economic laws. In January 1848 a law was issued which in practice forbade corporations, putting an end to the rather liberal regime of the 1829 Commerce Code. The only exceptions to the blanket prohibition were banks of issue, transportation companies (canals, railroads, and thoroughfares), companies enjoying privileged status and 'companies whose purpose was the public welfare'; these companies, though, should be approved by the Cortes, except for the last ones, which only needed a royal decree.

A year later (4 May 1849) a new banking law was approved which further reduced the possibilities of incorporation, for it outright forbade the creation of new banks of issue. Therefore, the only economic activity left specifically open for incorporation was transportation. The 1849 Banking Law clearly intended to grant the Bank of Saint Ferdinand the monopoly of issue in Spain, something it in fact did with the only exceptions of Barcelona and Cadiz. It was largely inspired by the English Peel Act of 1844, perhaps because Britain was one of the few large countries in Europe where there had been no revolution. The Spanish law divided the Saint Ferdinand into an issue department and a banking department, as the Peel Act had done with the Bank of England. The law was not very popular with the Bank's board and in fact it was not really applied. It was in vigour only for two years, during which the Bank did little more than liquidate its assets and reduce its liabilities. The new law also limited the maximum banknote circulation to one half of the disbursed capital, but this only applied to the Saint Ferdinand, as the bylaws of the Barcelona and Cadiz banks were not modified. This clause made life difficult for the Saint Ferdinand and was soon annulled. Other minor reforms of the law lasted longer, such as abolishing the posts of royal commissary and director, and substituting those of governor and two deputy governors. The new posts were to be directly appointed by the Crown, instead of jointly by the Crown and the stockholders as before.

In December of the same year Santillán was appointed governor of the Bank of Saint Ferdinand, a post which, with only a brief interruption, he would fulfil until his death in 1863. From that post he devoted himself to two main tasks during the early years: on the one hand, to straighten as much as possible the tangled accounts of the Bank, getting rid of the overvalued assets inherited from the Isabel II and resisting the constant urgings from the government for new advances; and, on the other hand, to draft a series of bills which were eventually enacted: a banking law of 1851, and another one of 1856. He was quite successful in both tasks; having a military training, he was a strict disciplinarian: he pursued the Bank's debtors persistently, and firmly resisted the government's threats and entreaties for extraordinary advances, to the point that in April 1854 he was dismissed by the government; by August, however, he was reinstated. The result of his efforts was that, after experiencing losses in 1848, the Bank became profitable in the following years and by 1851 its balance sheet was back to normal: the ratios of banknotes/capital and banknotes/specie were within the legal limits (they had not been in the stormy years of crisis), and, most importantly, credit to the private sector amply exceeded that to the state. The Bank's capital was also reduced (Tedde, 1999, pp. 249–51). As to the Bank's legislative activity, it responded to Santillán's ideas: he considered the 1849 law excessively restrictive, so the project he submitted and which was finally enacted on 15 December 1851 admitted the possibility of creating new banks and permitted a higher banknote/capital ratio. This ratio was 0.5 in the old law, and was raised to 1 in the new; even so, it soon became evident that, with the economic recovery which took place in the 1850s, even this ratio was too low. It was expanded in 1856. The 1851 law also abolished the division of the Bank into two departments, issue and banking, which Santillán never liked.

Santillán's stern resistance to accommodating the credit demands from the government produced intense irritation in the circles of power as we have seen. In 1852 it moved the Prime Minister Juan Bravo Murillo to establish a novel public financial institution, the *Caja de Depósitos* (could be translated as National Savings Bank) (Tedde, 1999, pp. 251–3). The *Caja* was a sort of state deposit office: it paid a 5 per cent interest rate to depositors and also was official custodian of judicial deposits, a role the Saint Ferdinand had been playing until then. It turned out to be a complete success in its own terms. Deposits more than tripled in 1853 and they went on increasing, with some fluctuations, until 1864. Although it had been founded as a competitor, the *Caja* soon became complementary to the Saint Ferdinand. The *Caja* invested practically all of its funds in public debt, whose yields were ordinarily one point above its passive interests; so, at least for the time being, it enjoyed a smooth and profitable ride. This in turn relieved the Bank from the burden of state pressure for funds, and enabled it to provide adequate service on the floating debt, and also to devote more funds and attention to the private sector. The danger of this arrangement was that, if confidence in the government was shaken and the prices of the public debt declined for a prolonged period, the *Caja* would be in serious trouble to repay its depositors and this might trigger a crisis. Unhappily, this is what happened after 1864 (Tortella, 1977, pp. 75–9).

3.6 Monetary reform

The complex and archaic monetary system was reformed by a decree of 15 April 1848 which marked a very clear, if partial, improvement. The main novelties were the proclamation of the silver *real* as the official monetary unit (the old units were the *maravedí* and the *real de vellón*), the introduction of the decimal division instead of the cumbersome former system where the *real de vellón* was, usually and approximately, equivalent to 34 *maravedís*, and a new bimetallic ratio, which made silver a little more expensive in terms of gold. This last measure was very opportune for two reasons: (i) Spanish coins traditionally undervalued silver, which caused chronic extraction and deflation; (ii) the discovery of gold mines in California and Australia at around this time caused further raises in the relative price of silver, thus furthering the undervaluation of this metal in Spain. The upward trend in the relative price of silver continued for about 20 years, as the price of gold kept going down. By virtue of Gresham's law, silver tended to disappear from circulation and be replaced by gold. This made the Spanish authorities to panic and suspend gold coinage in 1851, but the suspension was terminated by another decree in 3 February 1854 (Fernández Pulgar and Anes, 1970, pp.147–66).

It must be said that the 1848 decree was preceded by an earlier decree (31 May 1847), dating from the short spell of José Salamanca at the Ministry of Finance, relating with these matters. Salamanca's decree was very similar to the one issued ten and a half months later, so a large share of the credit for the reform must be attributed to that clever double crosser who, while playing tricks to save his patrimony, showed intelligence and foresight in monetary matters (he was most probably inspired by Paradaltas, 1847). Nevertheless, such was the hatred his wiles provoked that most of his work was annulled by the governments which followed: that was why his monetary decree was not given time to be put into practice although less than a year after its annulment, a very similar measure was enacted.

Unfortunately, the 1848 decree was not followed, as it should have been, by a full recoinage, so that monetary confusion persisted. This was augmented by the circulation of Catalan copper coins (commonly called in Spain *calderilla*, small change). The face value of these copper coins was higher than their metallic content, so the trend was for Spain to export silver coins and to import copper, which was immediately taken to be minted. Catalan small change thus circulated widely outside Catalonia, and was used even for large settlements, including payment of salaries, which in fact meant the deterioration of some incomes. It took long for the government to solve this problem by limiting the purchasing power of copper coins and eventually by withdrawing them from circulation.

The 3 February 1854 decree, without changing the essentials of the monetary system, in addition to going back to gold minting, again lowered the silver content of Spanish coins, something which, at least for some time, counteracted the deflationary tendencies derived from the undervaluation of silver. It was evident, however, that the demand for money was growing faster than its supply, especially during the boom years of the Crimean War (1853–6).

4
Banks and Railways: From Boom to Bust

4.1 Progressive economic policies

In the summer of 1854, a protracted *pronunciamiento* by General Leopoldo O'Donnell toppled the *Moderado* government of Luis Sartorius, count of San Luis; new elections produced a Progressive Cortes; the new government was headed by none other than Espartero, who reluctantly gave Leopoldo O'Donnell, a Unionist general, the Ministry of War. The Unionists were centrist liberals, who wanted to end the division between Progressives and Moderates. They were inspired by a young journalist, Antonio Cánovas del Castillo, who was to become the undisputed leader of the centre–right in the last quarter of the nineteenth century. The success of the rebellion was partly due to its promises to put an end to the corruption of the moderate governments, whose railroad concessions to their cronies, especially Salamanca, had scandalized public opinion (on Salamanca's railroad combinations, López-Morell, 2002) and to do away with the circle of right–wing buddies (*camarilla*) who surrounded the queen, particularly her mother and her morganatic husband. Unionists and Progressives had repeatedly denounced that, due to the speculative character of railroad concessions, very little actual construction had taken place during those years. In addition, the Crimean War, while enriching grain producers and exporters, had produced bread price increases which had caused deterioration in the standard of living of the poor and thereby fomented unrest. The rebels had also raised hopes by promising to lower taxes.

In consonance with the Progressive programme, the new Cortes produced a flurry of legislation, which included a new general *desamortización* law, a railroad law, and two laws regulating banks of issue and business banks. These new measures produced almost immediate effects; however, the Progressives' intention to enact a new constitution could not be carried out, because the clashes in the cabinet between Progressives and Unionists gave the queen, who was especially displeased with the *desamortización* law, the opportunity to dismiss Espartero in the summer of 1856; O'Donnell and Narváez repressed the scattered riots and mutinies organized by the Progressives against the dismissal of Espartero, and things went back to normal. There followed a long decade when Narváez and O'Donnell alternated in power, sometimes replaced at the head of the government by friends and confederates. In September 1868, however, a new *pronunciamiento* by Progressive and Unionist generals produced a revolution, much more radical than that of 1854. This time the queen was dethroned amid deep social upheaval. We will examine this 'Glorious Revolution' in the next chapter.

One of the keystones of the Progressive programme was disentailment. Previous disentailement laws had dealt with Church properties. The new *desamortización* law (1 May 1855) was defined as 'general', because it also included properties in secular hands, such as municipalities, lay institutes, and the central state itself. In principle, it would sell all land not in private hands already. Pascual Madoz, the Finance Minister – author of a reputed multi-volume geographical, historical and statistical dictionary of Spain – who submitted the bill, spoke of 'completely doing away with the dead hand, [which is] a deadly hand' (cited in Paredes, 1991, p. 264). The reason for general disentailment was not only ideological: the government was trying to find an alternative source of funds after a series of taxes had been abolished in accordance with the Progressives' programme, and indeed in this it was successful. Land sales, which were less than 1 per cent of total government revenue before 1855, jumped to 6.1 per cent in 1856 and, following a decrease after the ousting of Espartero, they expanded in the 1860s, reaching a yearly average above 10 per cent. There were some problems however: in the first place, the new disentailment provoked strong opposition from the Vatican and open hostility from the queen, who only signed the bill when Espartero told her revolution might occur if she did not sign. Second, it left many poor peasants, who until then had subsisted by encroaching upon public lands, without means of subsistence. And third, subsequent governments reinstated the old taxes and used the additional revenues to finance a series of foreign adventures in Morocco, Cochin-China, Mexico, Perú and Puerto Rico, so that the deficit problem subsisted and expanded.

Another pillar of Progressive policies was the Railroad Law, enacted on 3 June 1855. The Progressives considered the building of a railroad network as the key to economic development both through the surge of investment it should bring about and through the benefits of cheaper and faster transportation. They wanted the network built, and built fast, so the public might see how more efficient than the moderates they were, and also how more honest. The decision was made to leave the construction and management to private initiative but to assign planning, supervision, and stimulus to the state. A basic radial network was drawn up that would determine which lines would be the objects of concessions. The law offered subsidies that would be subject to competitive bidding, and softened the rigours of the 1848 company law for railroad companies. Additional advantages were special guarantees to foreign investors, tariff remission for the importation of foreign railroad equipment, right of way privileges, and land grants. In order to prevent the most scandalous cases, in addition to determining beforehand the priority trunk lines, all concessions had to be approved by the Cortes.

To complete this legislative edifice some measure which would facilitate investment seemed necessary. This was the role of the twin banking laws of 28 January 1856 (the following summarizes Tortella, 1977, pp. 79–97; see also Sánchez-Albornoz, 1975). The initiative for a bank-of-issue law was originally taken by Santillán himself on behalf of the Bank of Saint Ferdinand. He felt that more fiduciary circulation was needed, and had been petitioning several Finance Ministers for a change in the Bank's charter without success. Furthermore, several applications for bank licences were submitted to the Cortes in 1854 and 1855. The Saint Ferdinand also wanted permission to increase its capital and to open branches in the provinces. The demand for banking services had increased with economic recovery and the impulse to trade by the Crimean War. But, in addition to the Saint Ferdinand's lobby, there was another group in the Cortes whose interests were parallel, though not convergent. This was a coalition of provincial businessmen and left-wing politicians who wanted more banks and were somewhat resentful of the Saint Ferdinand's privileges. Rather than increasing the powers of the old Bank, they wanted more independent institutions as they thought competition was healthy and desirable. The debate between these two groups in the Cortes was long: the Saint Ferdinand was frequently berated in the discussion, but in the end it managed to keep a privileged, albeit not monopolistic, position. To start with, its name was changed to *Bank of Spain* (*Banco de España*), something Santillán had also strived for. The result of all this parliamentary jousting, however, was a partial defeat of Santillán and considerable legal confusion. Santillán was defeated in that the principle of plurality of banks of issue became established. The Bank of Spain's monopoly of issue would be confined to Madrid and perhaps a few other cities. Article 4 of the law said that 'in each town only one issuing institution shall be permitted, be it an unofficial bank [*banco privado*] or a branch of the Bank of Spain'. The confusion derived from the fact that the law contained contradictory clauses: one seemed to give precedence to the branches of the Bank of Spain, another seemed to give it to other, nonofficial banks. The end result was that the Bank of Spain established only two branches, in Valencia and in Alicante. In other towns independent banks of issue were established, to a maximum number of 21 in 1864 (including the Bank of Spain but not its two branches). Other features of the Banks-of-Issue Law could be summarized as follows: (i) the volume of banknotes issued by each bank could not exceed the triple of paid-in capital or of specie reserve, whichever was smaller. Except for the Banks of Barcelona and Cadiz, the capital of all banks of issue had to be fully paid in before they started operations; (ii) government supervision was to be exercised through the governor of the Bank of Spain and through the royal commissaries of the other banks; (iii) banknote holders and current account creditors of the banks were legally considered as ordinary depositors, that is, received privileged creditor consideration. This was intended to favour the growth of demand deposits and the circulation of banknotes; (iv) banks had to be incorporated, their shares to have a nominal value of 2,000 reales and be fully paid up, maximum and minimum denominations of banknotes were to be 4,000 and 100 reales, banks were chartered by government decree, they could not make loans against their shares as collateral, their loans to the Treasury were strictly regulated, they were under obligation to publish their balance sheets monthly in the *Gaceta de Madrid* (the official gazette), and the distribution of profits was subjected to some rules intended to provide for a reserve fund; (v) article 14 seemed to exclude investment banking from their purview.

The second banking law dealt with merchant or investment banks (called *sociedades de crédito*, credit companies). In 1855 several French banks had submitted projects for opening branches in Spain. The most important request had come from the brothers Émile and Isaac Pereire, the founders and directors of the *Crédit Mobilier*, at that time reaching the apex of its power and prestige (Cameron, 1961, p. 157). The Spanish government intended to turn the bill granting the Pereires their bank charter into a 'general law' regulating credit companies. But competition among the leading members of French finance, which had been brewing for years (Cameron, 1961, pp. 134–44; Gille, 1967, II, pp. 183ff.; Ferguson, 1998, pp. 56–65, 82–5; López-Morell, 2005, pp. 155–7) spread south of the Pyrenees and, on the same day the Pereire's bill was submitted to the Cortes, a counter manoeuvre prepared by the Rothschilds in Paris came to light in the Spanish parliament. Weisweiller (now associated with Ignatz Bauer) organized a group of distinguished Madrid bankers, headed by the ex-Minister of Finance, Alejandro Mon, who hurriedly created a Mobilier-type corporation called *Sociedad Española Mercantil e Industrial* (SEMI, Spanish Industrial and Mercantile Company) and instantly applied for a charter, unctuously claiming that they had 'no less right than any other [company] to the benevolence and protection of the legislative body and of the government' (see the text of the banking laws in Tortella *et al.* 1970, pp. 322–7).

The Rothschild petition was followed by a third one from France: Alfred Prost and his associates, the brothers Louis and Numa Guilhou, had also applied for a Spanish branch to be called *Compañía General de Crédito en España* (General Credit Company in Spain, usually called *General de Credito*). It was decided in the Cortes that the Credit Companies Law, of general application, would be separated from the law granting the three French banks their concessions. The most hotly debated topic in the Credit Companies Law was that dealing with short-term bonds. Several deputies suspected that these bonds were going to circulate as *de facto* banknotes, and asked why should all the safety clauses be introduced in the Banks-of-Issue Law if credit companies were going to be allowed to issue those short-term bonds which in fact would be ordinary banknotes with another name. In France a clause had been introduced in the Crédit Mobilier's charter whereby the maximum volume of these bonds in circulation, plus current account deposits, could not exceed twice the paid-in capital. This put a clear limit to its capacity to issue these bonds, especially if the Mobilier had a large number of companies among its clients, because these would open current account deposits thereby reducing the possibility to issue those short-term bonds. This limitation had worked in France and a similar clause was incorporated to the Spanish law. It seriously limited the ability of those companies which really were merchant banks to issue surrogate banknotes; however, it turned out that several credit companies in the provinces, where they had little chance of playing the role of investment banks, fiercely competed with banks of issue and became a source of instability.

The definitive version of the law allowed credit companies a wide range of activities, from making loans to the government, and collecting taxes to practising industrial promotion and commercial banking. They could start business with a minimum paid-in capital of 10 per cent of the nominal figure. They could also issue long-term bonds up to ten times the capital if it were fully paid in, and five times the paid-in capital otherwise. Authorization to set up a credit company could be obtained by government decree or by a law issued by the Cortes. As with banks of issue, credit companies were required to publish monthly balance sheets in the *Gaceta de Madrid* and the government had the right to inspect them at any time. Finally, when applying for a charter, the prospective company should make a deposit of 10 per cent of the value of the first planned share issue.

4.2 The effect of the banking laws

Table 4.1 reflects the immediate effects of the 1856 banking laws. The total number of joint-stock banks jumped from 5 to 19 in a matter of two years.

Table 4.1 Joint-stock banks in Spain, 1844–74

	Banks of issue	Credit companies	Other	Total
1844	3	0	0	3
1855	3	0	2	5
1857	10	6	3	19
1860	11	8	3	22
1865	21	35	2	58
1870	16	14	0	30
1874	1	13	8	22

Source: Tortella (1977), pp. 14–15.

The number of banks of issue increased much faster, suggesting that the note-issuing privilege was a powerful lure to bank promotion. Later on, credit companies grew by leaps and bounds, probably attracted by the *de facto* issuing privilege embodied in the possibility of circulating short-term bonds.

The table also reflects the sharp decline after 1865, which probably was steeper than the data show, due to the fact that, although bank foundations were meticulously documented and published in decrees, dissolutions and cessations were less rigorously recorded.

One new bank of issue was founded in 1856 and six in 1957. The *Banco de Málaga* was licensed in the summer of 1856 and opened its doors for business in September. Málaga was not only a busy port, but also the site of an iron mining and smelting industry. The owner of the iron furnaces was Manuel Agustín de Heredia, a relative by marriage of José Salamanca, to whom he lent money in his early years in Madrid. There had been several applications for a bank in Málaga earlier, but the permit was not granted until the 1856 banking laws were enacted. Among the banks of issue established in 1857 (Seville, Saragossa, Valladolid, La Coruña, Santander, and Bilbao), the latter ones were to become, more than a century later, the leading banks in Spain. Santander and Bilbao are busy northern ports. Santander was the main exporter of grain and flour to the Americas, especially to Cuba, and was closely connected with Valladolid, the leading city of the Old Castille wheat-producing region. Bilbao, like Málaga, was an active port but also had excellent iron mines nearby and was becoming an iron-smelting centre.

Other smaller banks of issue were established in the following years most commonly in ports or in commercial inland cities, such as Jerez, Reus, Pamplona or Vitoria. It was quite common that banks of issue and credit companies, especially in secondary places, should compete as creators of bank money, the monetary use of short-term bonds by credit companies being a contentious topic. The rivalry was especially heated in Valencia between the branch of the Bank of Spain and two credit companies. One of these was the Valenciana, which adapted its charter so as to become a company under the 1856 law. Another credit company was established in 1858 by a group of local businessmen who had tried to found a bank of issue, in which they were frustrated by the arrival of the branch of the Bank of Spain. They then decided to open a credit company under the name of *Crédito Valenciano*, and proceeded to issue short-term bonds. Meanwhile, the Valenciana had been issuing promissory notes which circulated as banknotes with a wide acceptance for many years. The Bank of Spain asked the Valencia authorities to retire these notes and bonds, but this was not easy. The public used them widely, and preferred them to Bank of Spain's paper money. The tensions and hostilities lasted for several years, and probably were detrimental to the local economy (Tortella, 1977, pp. 139–44; Ródenas, 1978).

Meanwhile, the big French credit companies had started early to unfold their plans. The word big is right, because their capital figures were out of proportion with those of the rest of Spanish banks. This was notably the case with the *Crédito Mobiliario Español*, whose nominal capital was 456 million reales, which was fully paid up in 1864; at that time the paid-up capital of the Bank of Spain, by far the largest corporation (after the *Mobiliario Español*), was 160.4 million. The *Mobiliario Español* started out with 68.4 million paid up and with an impressive cast of French and Spanish businessmen and aristocrats on its board. The Pereires had grandiose plans for Spain, but their star project was their railroad company, the *Caminos de Hierro del Norte de España* (North of Spain Railroad, Norte for short). They had secured a line going north from Madrid to France, crossing the Pyrenees at Irún-Hendaye, and passing through Segovia, Palencia, Burgos, Vitoria, and San Sebastián. They had soon secured collateral branches to the main northern ports: Santander, and, later, Bilbao, Oviedo, and La Coruña. The Mobiliario also tried to open banks of issue in several provincial capitals, but was received with hostility and withdrew. It also made loans to the government, no doubt knowing that this was a key which opened many ministerial doors. By the end of 1856 the Mobiliario had almost 43 per cent of its assets in Norte, but it had made other investments, such as the Barruelo coal mines, between Burgos and Santander, the Gas Company of Madrid, and an interest in the Córdoba–Seville railroad. The Pereires hoped that Barruelo, and other mines they bought, would provide coal for their locomotives and for their gas company. They were disappointed: coal has never been Spain's forte.

They were clearly disgruntled to see their former boss and current competitor James de Rothschild creating a rival company in Spain, the SEMI. They complained to their shareholders (April 1856) that 'Spain has adopted, perhaps letting herself be driven further than she ought to, all the projects' of new credit companies. The Rothschilds, in any case, were less sanguine about the economic future of Spain than the Pereires, perhaps because they had been working there for about 20 years. The capital of the SEMI, although large by local standards, was relatively modest. It reached a paid-up maximum of 91.2 million reales by 1857, which was reduced to 60.8 million in 1861, no doubt reflecting the disappointment the board transmitted to shareholders in 1860 when its report complained about the lack of legal encouragement to investment in Spain and the scarcity of domestic capital.

The board of directors of the SEMI was, like that of the Mobiliario, studded with prestigious names. Its president was Alejandro Mon, and its vice presidents were Manuel Collado and Juan Sevillano (ennobled with a dukedom), both bankers, deputies and recent Finance Ministers under Espartero – with very short tenures. Furthermore, Collado and four other members of the board were also on the Bank of Spain's board. One of them was Urquijo. Of course Weisweiller and Bauer were on the SEMI's board too.

Aside from a loan to the government (in fact, the three French credit companies participated in a 200 million reales loan, jointly subscribing 80 per cent of it), the SEMI's almost exclusive concern was railroads. Its rail corporation was the *Compañía de los Ferrocarriles de Madrid a Zaragoza y Alicante* (Railroad from Madrid to Saragossa and Alicante, commonly known as MZA), established shortly after the SEMI was constituted. Almost three quarters of the Madrid–Alicante line were already in service when MZA was founded; the Madrid–Aranjuez line had been prolonged to Almansa by Salamanca, who had also secured the rights to the Almansa–Alicante connection on the Mediterranean, and sold line and rights to James de Rothschild and to a group of associates in 1856. He was a vice president in MZA. Meanwhile, the Madrid–Saragossa line, acquired separately, was only starting to be built, with SEMI as its contractor; it was completed by 1863. MZA and SEMI made an effort to expand their network in southern Spain: in this they were successful. They failed, however in their attempt to obtain a connection with France through the Pyrenees, which they had planned as an extension of the Saragossa line and as a direct challenge to the Norte's Irún–Hendaye link. It was much later that, by means of absorptions and buyouts, they were able to secure the linkup with France through Catalonia.

The third large French bank, the *General de Crédito*, was more diversified in its investment outlets and less strong in its railroad undertakings. Its paid-up capital was 40 million reales in 1856, and reached 133.2 in 1859. Its main rail network was the Seville–Jerez–Cadiz line. It was located in what was possibly the most economically active area of Andalusia with its wine, mining and commercial activities, but the network became bottled up when MZA secured de Córdoba–Seville concession. It also took part in a modest Catalan railroad connecting Tarragona to Norte's Barcelona–Saragossa line. The General de Crédito compensated the limitations of its railway lines with a wide range of industrial ventures. It brought about the merger of two insurance companies into one, *La Unión*, which later on merged with *El Fénix*, a creation of the *Crédito Mobiliario Español*. The General de Crédito also undertook other very ambitious ventures. In 1857 it created the *Compañía General de Minas de España* (Spain's General Mining Company), capitalized at 60 million reales, which bought copper mining fields in Huelva, lead mines in Jaén, coal mines in León, and so on. It also operated a number of gasworks in several cities, and opened the *Sociedad General Española de Descuentos*, a network of discount houses similar to Prost's *Compagnie Générale des Caisses d'Escompte* in France (Gille, 1967, pp. 311–14; Tortella, 1977, pp. 111–27; Tedde, 1978, Ch. 1; Ferguson, 1998, pp. 84–5; Comín *et al.*, 1998, I, pp. 66–81; López-Morell, 2005, Ch. 4).

Several Spanish credit companies were created in the wake of the new legislation and following the example of the French companies: the most important ones were the Valenciana and the Catalana. The Valenciana was, of course, the old bank created by José Campo in 1846; only days after the Credit Companies Law was approved the Valenciana petitioned the queen to be allowed to become a credit company, but it took three years for the licence to arrive. Perhaps the Bank of Spain lobbied against it. Be it as it may, the Valenciana stuck to its mixed commercial and investment activities. Its paid-up capital reached a maximum of 21.2 million reales by 1865. The Valenciana had undertaken the water works in Valencia, financed the Valencia–Játiva railway and was building the Játiva–Almansa line which would link Valencia to the Madrid–Alicante railway. It was also negotiating with the Catalana to pool their resources for a Valencia–Tarragona line. In addition, it was involved in real estate development around the city of Valencia and in government and municipal loans. Its 1856 balance sheet shows that the water works and the railroads were the best part of its investments, which were about one half of its assets, commercial credit being about 20 per cent.

The *Sociedad Catalana General de Crédito* was founded in February 1856 by a group of Barcelona merchants and businessmen, with a paid-up capital of 36 million reales. Its first chairman was Antonio Brusi, the director of the *Diario de Barcelona*, Spain's oldest daily, and among its members Ramón Bonaplata, one of the introducers of the steam engine in Spain, and member of a saga of textile and metallurgical entrepreneurs. The Catalana was clearly an investment bank: although it also practised commercial banking (its explicit policy was to be an industrial bank and only devote surplus funds to loans on collateral and discounts), its main concern was the construction of railroads in Catalonia. One of its first loans was to the Barcelona–Saragossa railroad which was thus able to continue its works which were halted by lack of funds. The Catalana also undertook, as we have just seen, the construction of the Tarragona–Valencia line jointly with the Valenciana. Even more important was the building of the Barcelona–France line, which continued the Barcelona–Mataró track. The *Catalana* mediated between two companies, one building along the coast, the other pushing inland: they joined forces and the Catalana became their contractor. Other minor investments of the Catalana were some insurance companies, a mining company, and a small interest in the Suez Canal. It is remarkable that the Catalana did not own one single share of an industrial company (Tortella, 1977, pp. 127–35).

There were other, lesser credit companies in Barcelona and Valencia established under the wing of the new legislation. We already saw the *Crédito Valenciano* embattled with the Valenciana and with the Bank of Spain. The *Crédito Valenciano* went on and in 1859 won the contract to improve the Valencia harbour, an activity which became its most important long-term investment, although its commercial portfolio took a far larger fraction of its assets. Later it opened a branch in Alcoy, a textile city, and it appears to have carried out fairly successful business there. In Barcelona there were four other incorporated banks, among them a *Crédito Mobiliario Barcelonés*, which extended commercial credit in Barcelona, invested in a timber venture in Asturias, and opened a branch in Tarragona.

4.3 Free banking?

There is no doubt that the economic policy of the Progressive party was a shot in the arm to the lethargic Spanish economy. On the one hand, it provoked an injection of foreign investment and entrepreneurial initiative, which obviously had a contagious effect on the rather inert local economic agents. On the other, it solved, at least momentarily, the endemic monetary problem, that is, the chronic deflationary tendency derived from monetary extraction, due to high silver content in Spanish coins and to regular deficits in the balance of payments.

Table 4.2 and Figure 4.1 show the partial monetary effect of the banking laws of 1856. We say 'partial' because the figure only reflects the money created by the banks of issue during the period we are studying. This is only a part of the total supply of money. To this should be added the stock of specie in circulation, which around 1865 was about 1,100 million pesetas in gold and 250 million pesetas in silver. In addition, the short-term bonds and current-account deposits of the credit companies should be added. These, however, did not amount to much: the largest credit companies did not issue short-term bonds, and their deposits were not very large. The companies which issued short-term bonds were Lilliputian compared with the large ones. The great unknown here is the extraction of specie, which we know to have been considerable. Nuño *et al.* (2011) used an estimate for extraction which we do not consider as totally reliable. It is very probable that there was a continual drain of silver at this time, mostly due to a continued commercial deficit, accentuated from the mid-1850s on by the importation of railroad material; this, however, was offset by capital imports, especially from France; at least in the late 1850s a sizable part was channelled through the French credit companies.

All this means that we cannot be sure of how the money supply evolved at this time. All we can say with confidence is that bank money, which was around 10 per cent of the money supply in 1865, had more than doubled in the four years following the banking laws. Then it dipped in 1861, recovered and reached a maximum in 1863. It went down from then on, for reasons that we will examine presently. The dip in 1861 was closely related to the breakout of the American Civil War, which caused alarm and a withdrawal of capital, especially in Cuba, and an increase in the price of cotton, at the time a vital raw material.

Some writers have used the term 'free banking' when referring to this period of Spanish banking history (Pascual and Sudrià, 1993); this expression may be colourful, but it is not strictly appropriate. As Nuño *et al.* (2011) have

Table 4.2 Money created by the banks of issue, 1856–73 (thousands of pesetas; 1 peseta = 4 reales)

	Banknotes	Deposits	Specie reserves	Bank money
1856	56,980	56,459	48,265	65,174
1857	71,564	50,733	45,263	77,034
1858	85,993	63,464	50,621	98,836
1859	112,290	82,458	64,796	129,952
1860	118,208	69,201	52,999	134,410
1861	99,971	53,573	47,634	105,910
1862	99,965	72,398	51,770	120,593
1863	117,828	76,262	55,463	138,627
1864	124,779	38,132	45,044	117,867
1865	114,668	43,448	54,549	103,567
1866	89,769	47,253	64,037	72,985
1867	95,359	80,706	70,122	105,943
1868	102,882	58,259	58,692	102,449
1869	95,970	76,717	79,149	93,538
1870	99,111	119,981	138,846	80,246
1871	122,155	127,528	161,945	87,738
1872	114,794	112,986	127,152	100,628
1873	97,302	78,620	73,769	102,153

Source: Tortella *et al.* (1970), p. 285.

written, banks of issue were strictly regulated and enjoyed local emitting monopolies under the 1856 law; both conditions were very far from what is considered 'free banking'. Credit companies were much freer, even when it came to using semi-monetary instruments, such as short-term bonds; but they were subjected to a series of limitations and regulations that restricted their freedom considerably. While the term 'free banking' is exaggerated, it must be admitted that the years when the 1856 laws were in vigour constituted the period when banking corporations have enjoyed a wider degree of freedom in Spanish history. The disastrous end of the 1856 experiment may be the reason they have been tightly regulated since then.

Table 4.2 and Figure 4.1 also show an interesting fact: deposits and specie reserve were of similar magnitude and fluctuated together; for this reason, fiduciary circulation (banknotes) and total bank money also were closely related. Banks obviously made their specie reserve a function of their deposits. During the crisis, after 1864, these two variables went up while banknotes in circulation went down (Tortella, 1977, Ch. VII).

Spanish authorities tried to offset the endemic problem of specie extraction. The discovery of gold mines in North America, South Africa, and Australia around 1848 had flooded markets with this metal, whose price in silver terms went down. As we saw in Chapter 3, Spanish authorities hesitated about what to do about this. In 1854 they had lowered the silver

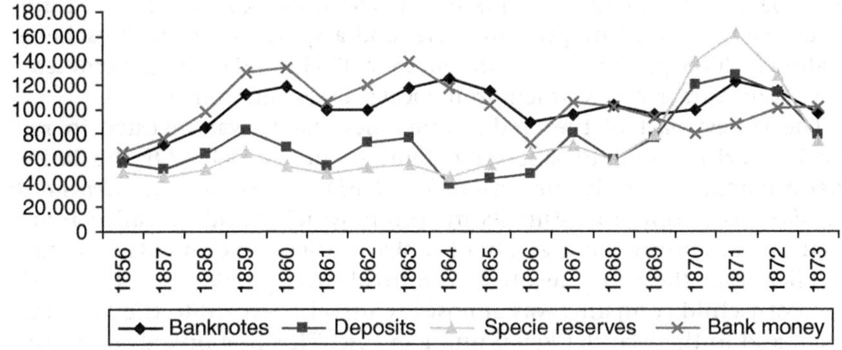

Figure 4.1 Money created by the banks of issue, 1856–73 (thousands of pesetas; 1 peseta = 4 reales)
Source: Table 4.2.

content of coins. In 1861 they ordered the coinage of small gold pieces, so as to facilitate the circulation of this metal, which was replacing silver by virtue of Gresham's law. In 1864 a full-fledged monetary reform tried again to solve the problem of the overvaluation of silver. To start with, a new monetary unit was established, the *escudo*, worth ten reales or one half peso. The escudo was defined in terms of silver at the old bimetallic ratio (15.476). However, the smaller denominations, peseta and real, would be minted in 'rich *vellón*' or low-tenure silver, that is, with a relatively high content of copper. Smaller coins would be issued in bronze and they should replace the old Catalan copper pieces. It was hoped that the rich *vellón* coins, which would be those more in circulation, would not be extracted. The new system may have worked, but it was not given time to be really put into practice; a full recoinage could not be carried out due to the onset of the 1860s crisis, which was especially severe in Spain. Then, a new, more lasting monetary reform took place in 1868 (Sardà, 1948, Ch. VI; Fernández Pulgar and Anes, 1970, pp. 170–7; Tortella and Comín, 2001, p. 174).

4.4 Lost illusions

There was a second wave of bank foundations after 1859, as can be appreciated from Table 4.1. The number of banks of issue more than doubled between 1859 and 1864, while their combined paid-up capital increased from 206 to 307 million reales, or almost 50 per cent in these five years. Obviously, the new banks were smaller than the old. The expansion was even more spectacular for credit companies, whose numbers grew more than fourfold in these five years, and whose combined capital multiplied by 2.6. Here also the new companies were smaller. As with all economic cycles, there was a strong psychological component in this boom. The universal faith in the future of railroads, fostered by price increases and a spurt in the stock exchange (Tafunell, 2005, p. 827; Hoyo, 2007, pp. 35–7, 49–53) and by the government's optimism, attracted investment from local sources and from abroad.

The largest part of the credit companies' assets was invested in railroad securities and, to a lesser extent, in public debt. Of the largest credit companies, only the *Crédito Mobiliario Español* and the *General de Crédito* made some investments in sectors which could be called industrial, such as mining and gas, but the size of these investments was much smaller than the sums devoted to railroads and public debt. The SEMI, the Rothschild company, was almost exclusively devoted to the MZA railroad, and to the Alar del Rey–Santander line. This line linked the Norte's main track with Santander, but it was originally owned by an independent company (called *Ferrocarril de Isabel II*); perhaps the SEMI supported it (it had some 30 per cent of its equity) in the hopes of encroaching upon the Pereires' northern empire. In the long run, however, the Pereires absorbed it (Sánchez-Albornoz, 1969). The SEMI had little faith in Spain's economy, and wisely started divesting itself of its railroad interests and devoting its resources to speculating in public debt – something James de Rothschild and Daniel Weisweiller were past masters at – and to ordinary commercial credit after 1860. The largest Spanish credit company, the Catalana, did something similar, selling its Valencia–Tarragona railroad building rights to the Valenciana in 1859 and disposing very profitably of most of its railroad shares in 1860. As the board communicated to the shareholders in 1862, they had decided to 'limit the circle of our businesses for the time being and [...] only take part in those of short-term realization'. Both banks turned out to have been prescient.

But these were exceptions: most of the new and old credit companies devoted the largest part of their investments to railroad securities; and the banks of issue also contributed, in less direct ways, to the railroad boom. If we examine the *Banco de Barcelona*'s loan portfolio, for instance, we can see that loans on railroad companies' bonds and shares as collateral were 3.5 times larger than loans on industrial securities. Loans on public debt bonds were even larger, 5.2 times those on industrial securities (Tortella, 1977, pp. 192–4). This might seem surprising in Spain's most industrialized city. The *Banco de Bilbao*'s board at the time of its constitution was composed of exactly the same persons as that of the Tudela–Bilbao Railroad Company, founded at around the same time. The *Compañía General Bilbaína de Crédito* was a credit company, a subsidiary of the *Banco de Bilbao*, created in 1862, whose main aim was to manage the bank's interests in the Tudela–Bilbao railway. The founders of the Bilbaína were all members of the Bilbao's board. In Barcelona the relationships between the bank and the Catalana were almost as close. The close links between local banks of issue and some credit companies were then quite common. Such was the case with

Table 4.3 Combined volume of paid-up capital in Spanish corporations, main sectors (millions of reales)

	Manufactures	Credit companies	Railroads
1859	399.2	373.2	1,375.6[a]
1861	389.0	420.4	2,069.6
1864	393.6	970.8	2,619.2
1866	266.0	916.8	2,795.6

[a] Nominal capital.

Source: Tortella (1977), p. 289.

the links between the *Banco de Valladolid* and the *Crédito Castellano* (which became the contractor of the Isabel II railroad) of the same city, and of the *Banco de Sevilla* and the *Crédito Comercial de Sevilla*. These relationships were advantageous to both sides in the short run: they permitted the banks of issue, more tightly regulated, to participate in the juiciest businesses of the time, namely and particularly, railroads. For credit companies the relative solvency of banks of issue made them a convenient source of loans.

All in all, the combined effects of the Progressive 1855–6 laws became a powerful inducement to invest, and overinvest, in railroads. Table 4.3, based on data provided by the *Anuarios Estadísticos* (statistical yearbooks) of the period, shows how the paid-up capital of railroad companies and credit companies grew during these years while industrial companies stagnated.

Unfortunately, the boards of the SEMI and the Catalana were right in their misgivings about the railroads and the Spanish economy as a whole. Spanish railroads turned out to be a bad investment in the end. All the hopes, fast building and heavy investment were sorely disappointed when the main lines were completed. The plan of the Progressives had worked too well: prior to 1855 only 440 km had been built, whereas 4,436 km were built in the 1857–67 period, which meant a 443.6 yearly average: in other words, more was built in a single year of the post-Progressive period than in all the *Moderado* ten-year period. But success brought disappointment, because revenues turned out barely sufficient to cover running costs. After years of extolling the economic virtues of railways, the *Gaceta de los Caminos de Hierro* (the Spanish *Railway Gazette*) was forced to admit the bitter truth in 1864: 'We must confess it: Spanish railways have not fully met the sacrifices of the government nor the hopes of the capitalists'. The same picture was drawn by a modern scholar in 1961: 'When the construction period came to a close and the railways had to pay dividends out of earnings they discovered that their revenues not only did not permit them to distribute benefits but in many cases were insufficient to cover the interest on bonds' (Cameron, 1961, p. 265). This discovery was devastating to the credit companies, which had invested so much in railways and now found that they could not be reimbursed and, in many cases, not even receive interest on the bonds subscribed. Frequently the credit companies in turn were indebted to the banks of issue, so the whole credit system so hastily built up started to fall down like a house of cards.

We may ask, why had Spanish politicians and investors been so wrong? After all, Spain is a dry and mountainous country where transportation problems have been endemic. If railways could and did solve the transportation bottleneck, how come they were not profitable? One single word can answer this question: underdevelopment. The country was not developed enough to pay for that enormous investment effort. There were some farsighted people who had anticipated such result. In *El Economista* one could read the following in 1856: '[W]here there are no products roads, canals and railways are of no use' and '[W]ith the capital that is being devoted to the acquisition of transportation facilities one could acquire other goods, and to build a railway when there is little to be carried on it is to act like a doctor who buys a carriage without having any patients.' There were two additional problems: one, building the track was more expensive in Spain due to the mountainous terrain; two, the distances between large population centres in Spain are very long. The track between Madrid and the coasts must cross many kilometres of almost empty extensions. All this makes for high fixed and variable costs. In the 1860s traffic density was not enough to pay for these long hauls. It has been pointed out that Spanish railroads started to be moderately profitable only in the 1880s (Barquín, 1999). To use a once fashionable expression, Spanish railways were built ahead of demand. In the process of adapting to this circumstance, they brought down the banking system.

4.5 The onset of a long depression

Several additional factors contributed to the banking debacle. The end of the American Civil War in 1865 caused a sharp fall in cotton prices, something which ruined many businesses and banks which had invested heavily in marginal lands that were profitable at the former high prices (a classic on the topic is Landes, 1958). There was also the increasing pessimism in international circles provoked by the tensions between Prussia and Austria, which would precipitate war in 1866. All these caused interest rate increases and capital scarcities in international markets, augmenting the difficulties of the troubled Spanish banks.

Another internal factor should be taken into account. Flushed with optimism with the boom of the early 1860s and the extra revenues provided by the *desamortización*, the O'Donnell governments embarked on a series of foreign adventures in Morocco, and so on (see above), which exhausted the already wobbly Spanish budget, so that at the time when the banks came into dire straits the government turned to them in search of substantial advances. Another considerable public expenditure item during those years was railway subsidies. To compound problems, the London and Amsterdam Stock Exchanges had been closed to Spanish securities since Bravo Murillo's 1851 debt reform, which in fact was a partial repudiation. In 1861 it was the Paris Exchange which was closed to Spanish loans in retaliation for the government's procrastination in carrying out even Bravo Murillo's leonine clauses. In view of all this 'the Spanish government, effectively excluded from foreign financial markets, eked out its meagre resources with revolving short-term advances from French bankers' and pressured the Bank of Spain and other Spanish banks for additional resources (Cameron, 1961, pp. 404–10; Tortella, 1977, pp. 74–6). This put a strain on the Bank of Spain's assets so that it had to restrict banknote circulation in order to keep it within legal limits. Even so, it still had trouble converting notes to specie when required by the public. The notes started circulating at a discount. Then the government adopted a typically devious way to enforce banknote circulation: it directed the mercantile courts not to issue verdicts in cases involving banknote convertibility complaints. All in all, the banks of issue as a whole played a deflationary role, thus aggravating the depression which set in after 1864. Many banks of issue, however, survived the crisis thanks to this defensive attitude, but several went down, most commonly those that had close links to credit companies.

In spite of all government's efforts, the Madrid *Audiencia Territorial*, the highest instance below the Supreme Court, ruled in December 1865 that the Bank of Spain should redeem its notes on sight and in full. Tensions increased between the government and the bank, whose governor resigned in March 1866. The government then unveiled its own plan to solve the crisis: it had been negotiating a loan with a syndicate of London bankers, led by the recently incorporated Overend, Gurney & Co. The English group would be granted a charter for a 'Spanish National Bank', which would absorb and replace the then existing banks of issue, starting with the Bank of Spain itself. The new bank would have a capital of 1,200 million reales, of which 600 immediately subscribed. The bill authorizing the new bank was passed by the Cortes. Manuel Alonso Martínez, the Finance Minister, announced that the government would fulfil all its compromises. British bondholders were elated and petitioned the London Stock Exchange to readmit Spanish bonds. The Bank of Spain, however, was not happy and vowed to resist the Minister's designs tooth and nail. Then the bomb fell: London was also in the throes of a crisis, and Overend, Gurney suspended payments on 10 May. It was, in Landes' words (1958, p. 245), 'rotten from top to bottom', and its incorporation had been just a desperate expedient to bring in capital (on the London situation, Cottrell, 2009).

The last hopes for a painless solution to the Spanish quagmire crashed down with Overend, Gurney: the British loan was now out of the question; so was the projected National Bank, and what little confidence was left in the Spanish public evaporated. A long chain of bank failures ensued. For two years the banking system had been tottering on the verge of bankruptcy until the last attempt at a salvaging operation failed. In Barcelona, the Catalana and the *Crédito Mobiliario Barcelonés* suspended payments on 12 May. The stock exchange was closed and all other banks suspended activities, except for the *Banco de Barcelona,* which in the end was the great beneficiary of the crisis. Panic spread throughout the country. According to our figures in Table 4.1, 28 banks went out of business between 1865 and 1870, but, as we said before, official figures understate reality. Credit companies were the most vulnerable because they had been more reckless and made the stronger commitment to railways, but several banks of issue, especially those that had worked closely with credit companies, also went bankrupt. Such was the case particularly with the banks of Valladolid and Seville. In Valladolid the bank and the credit company, the *Crédito Castellano,* had several board members in common. Those of the Crédito bribed some other members to form a majority and vote to sell the bank's silver and gold reserves to the Crédito for worthless promissory notes. Something similar happened in Seville. In contrast, the *Banco de Bilbao* showed a financial acumen which has obviously lasted long since then and served it well. When the Tudela–Bilbao railroad suspended payments and reached an agreement with its creditors it was the *Bilbaína de Crédito* which took the loss and was dissolved. The Bilbao still managed to recover 10.4 million reales from the railroad company's bankruptcy. The crisis had different outcomes in the different cities, and it would be excessively long to tell the various sad and depressing stories. (For a comprehensive survey, Tortella, 1977, Ch. VII; see also Sánchez-Albornoz, 1963, 1966, 1968). Let us say a few words about Madrid. Of the three French credit companies only the *Crédito Mobiliario Español* survived. The *General de Crédito* suspended payments in 1864 and went into liquidation. The SEMI was quietly dissolved in 1868; facts had confirmed James de Rothschild's lack of trust in the Spanish economy. The *Crédito Mobiliario Español* withstood the crisis and the demise of its senior partner in Paris: the *Crédit Mobilie*r suspended payments and entered into receivership in 1867. Most other Madrid banks also closed during those years (for a recent analysis, Moro et al., 2013).

The crisis also had political dimensions: Alonso Martínez resigned scarcely a month after the 'National Bank' fiasco. Two weeks later there was a military mutiny in Madrid. It was sternly repressed, but the queen dismissed the cabinet and called her trusted Narváez to head a new government. General Narváez ruled with an iron hand, but he died in April 1868. In September of that year, a revolution broke out.

5
The Peseta and the Bank of Spain

5.1 Revolutionary policies

On 18 September 1868 a group of generals led by Francisco Serrano and Juan Prim rebelled against the government and the queen. In two weeks the queen had left the country and the rebels were in power, Serrano as premier, Prim as War Minister (they would become regent and premier respectively after a new constitution was approved). This was not one more *pronunciamiento*; it was considered by its planners, by its followers, and by most historians since then, a revolution; it is commonly called 'the Glorious Revolution', a sort of equivalent to the English revolution almost two centuries before. Unfortunately, the Spanish version was less successful, and after six years (*Sexenio Democrático* or *Revolucionario*) of kaleidoscopic governments, rebellions and wars, the formerly hated Bourbon dynasty was restored in the person of Alfonso XII, Isabel's son.

The revolutionaries were a heterogeneous group, but they covered a wide band in the political spectrum. Serrano was head of the Unionists and Prim of the Progressives. This means centre and centre–left, but they were supported by most parties of the left, such as the Democrats, the Republicans, Anarchists, Socialists, Internationalists, and other members towards the end of the spectrum. One could say that the revolution was supported by all but the right and the far right, that is, the diehard Moderates and the Carlists. Government bankruptcy, increasing fiscal pressure, economic depression, dictatorial methods, and widespread corruption had made the queen and her ministers unpopular in almost every quarter of the country.

The causes of the revolution, therefore, are fairly clear. On the political plane, Isabel's systematic exclusion of the Progressives from power, in addition to the unfair electoral system based on restricted suffrage and boss control, pushed Progressive politicians to seek the support of the military in order to get back in power. In 1868 Prim promised (and his partners went along) to hold elections by universal suffrage, and of course the promise was kept. Elections to constituent Cortes took place in December. The Cortes wrote a new constitution which was proclaimed early in June 1869. It was a monarchical constitution, but it also veered to the left. Male universal suffrage would elect both chambers, and the king's powers were quite limited. Furthermore, as the Bourbons were excluded from the Spanish throne, a new royal dynasty had to be found. Prim, now Prime Minister, had his way and a scion of the Italian reigning family, Amedeo of Savoy (*Amadeo de Saboya* in Spanish) was selected after almost two years. The trouble was that, when he landed in Spain, Amadeo learned that his main supporter, Juan Prim, had been assassinated. From then on things went from bad to worse. There were rebellions and wars of independence in Cuba and Puerto Rico. Amadeo had no supporters: for most monarchists he was almost a usurper and for the growing number of republicans he was just another tyrant. The Carlist party took advantage of the situation and opened hostilities.

Amadeo, whose reign had started in January 1871, abdicated in February 1873. The Carlist War, the financial chaos, his lack of popularity, the constant bickering among the political parties, the arrogance of military officers, the snubs from the Madrid aristocracy, all converged to convince him that he was sitting on a powder keg. On his abdication, the republic was proclaimed and the powder keg exploded. In the Mediterranean regions of Andalusia, Murcia, and Valencia, far left rebellions broke out against a republic the rebels considered too conservative. The government found itself trying to impose federalism and democracy, while waging two civil wars and a colonial war, on a backward country lacking true democratic traditions, without a decent administration, and financially bankrupt, where presidents replaced each other at a rate of one every two and a half months. The military grew restless and at the end of 1873 they dissolved the Cortes and installed a sort of republican dictatorship under Serrano. The liberal coalition that had led the revolution was back in power, but only for a year. In the last days of December 1874 another *pronunciamiento* proclaimed Alfonso de Borbón, a lad of 17, King of Spain. The monarchy thus restored lasted until April 1931.

The main economic causes of the revolution were examined in Chapter 4 – a banking and financial crisis due to the default of the railways and to gaping budget deficits. To this must be added two crop failures in 1866 and 1867, which, according to Sánchez-Albornoz (1968, pp. 45–6), caused hunger, a fall in the birth rate, and a jump in the death rate. This was the fearsome situation faced by the revolutionaries in September 1868.

Within the multifarious revolutionary coalition the only party having a more or less coherent economic programme were the Progressives, and this programme was, by and large, to establish a liberal economy. There was a substantial minority in the party, however, mostly in Catalonia, which, while advocating *laissez-faire* in the domestic sphere, favoured tariff protection, especially for the textile industry. There were other additional factors militating against the full implementation of the Progressive *laissez-faire* programme. One was, of course, the misgivings of the other parties, which were rather partial to Spain's long interventionist tradition, although they had no clear alternative blueprint to that of their Progressive partners. Another problem was the complex economic situation which painfully affected Spain by depriving it of the foreign loans which might have helped to solve its most pressing difficulties. The European crisis of the 1860s, although less profound than in Spain, was prolonged and aggravated with diplomatic entanglements and wars, such as the Austro-Prussian war, the Franco-Prussian tensions about Italy and Spain, the Franco-Prussian war, and the Paris Commune; all this created a climate of tension which discouraged capital exports. Furthermore, the unsettled political situation in Spain, the social unrest, and the Cuban war (which had started as the revolution was unfolding), made day-to-day problems such as finding the money to pay the monthly salaries of public servants (with special attention to those of the armed forces) more pressing than the fulfilment of any long-range programme.

In spite of all of these major impediments, a substantial part of the liberal programme was enacted (often by decree) and it constituted the most coherent and explicit effort to establish economic liberalism in Spanish history. The first piece of revolutionary economic legislation was a decree of monetary reform (19 October 1868) whose chief aim was to align Spain with the Latin Monetary Union. The treaty creating this union had been signed in 1865 by France, Belgium, Switzerland, and Italy. Other countries were subsequently invited to adhere, among them Greece and Spain. Greece joined as a full member; Spain never did, but took some preparatory steps, the main one being this monetary reform. The union's main feature was bimetallism, contrasting with Britain's gold standard. The adoption of gold by Germany in 1875, however, and the spread of this standard afterwards definitively debilitated bimetallism. Nevertheless, in 1868, the year when Greece joined it, the union seemed attractive, especially as ready convertibility of the Spanish currency into those of the countries of the union would make capital movements easier. Bankers and railroad managers were solidly in support of the reform. Carrying it out was a sign of the government's willingness to get into better terms with its international creditors.

The kernel of the reform was a new monetary unit, the *peseta*, equivalent to four *reales*. The peseta was a coin originating in Catalonia, which had been circulating widely since the early eighteenth century. It became the new monetary unit simply because its value was very close to that of the franc at the time; this was no mere coincidence: the franc and the peseta had one single ancestor, the *livre tournois*, which had been introduced in Catalonia in the seventeenth and eighteenth centuries by French troops, and coined in Barcelona under Philip V (Vilar, 1972, pp. 337–9; Sédillot, 1979, p. 72); the reform decree made its silver content exactly 5 grams, the same as that of the franc. The bimetallic ratio was fixed at 15.5, as in the

Latin Union. The preamble of the decree made clear the reasons for reform. It said that subsequent recoinage would 'erase forever the Bourbon lilies' from the Spanish currency and added that it was convenient to tighten 'the bonds of friendship which link us to the other European nations'. Gold coins and fractional currency in copper and bronze would circulate also.

The problems of the public debt and the crisis of the railway companies were the most pressing issues for the provisional revolutionary government. The inability of the former administrations to solve them had swayed many conservative politicians and men of wealth to support the revolution and thus made it possible. Many of these people had purchased railroad securities and now expected the government to bail them out of their predicament. In February 1866 there had been a petition to the queen pleading for increased railway subsidies. The roster of its signatories makes interesting reading: there were bankers such as Ignacio (Ignatz) Bauer, one of Rothschild's agents in Spain; Jaime Girona, brother and partner of the president of the *Banco de Barcelona*; Jorge Loring, of the *Banco de Málaga*, and so on; it also included businessmen and politicians such as José Salamanca, José Campo, Alejandro Mon, Juan Bravo Murillo, and Francisco Serrano. This is a select group of powerful men – although not all of them supported the revolution, two and a half years later were clearly disturbed by the economic situation. Another sign of the hopes aroused by the revolution was that Spanish debt bonds rose in the stock exchanges of Madrid, Paris, and even London, in the days that followed its proclamation.

Laureano Figuerola, the Finance Minister, an accomplished economist, free trader, teacher, and writer, was immersed from the start in trying to solve the puzzle of increasing public debt, dwindling tax receipts, and bankers demanding to be repaid. Figuerola believed in transparency and accountability, so he immediately published figures showing the Treasury's indebtedness: they were awesome. The government had immediate debts amounting to 600 million pesetas and its liquid assets were less than 100 million. The main creditors were, first of all, the *Caja de Depósitos*, which had been purchasing public debt with abandon and whose total credit to the government amounted to 310.8 million. The problem with the Caja was that most depositors had short-term or on-sight accounts; in the end the depositors were forced to accept government bonds as repayment and the Caja was liquidated. Bankers, many of them foreign, made the second category of creditors, for a combined total of 85.9 million (Tortella, 1977, p. 518; Titos, 1979; Gonzalo, 1981, esp. Ch. VIII). Most of the rest was short-term, or *floating*, debt. The prospects of settlement were not good, because the tax system was in bad shape: one of the consequences of the revolution was that people stopped paying taxes, as one of their grievances against the queen and her ministers had been increasing fiscal pressure. One frequent revolutionary cry had been *¡Abajo los consumos!* ('Down with excises'). Figuerola tried to tax alternative sources, although he did not succeed: the new imposts failed. But this was medium term, anyway. He first had to solve the immediate problem of liquidity. With this in mind, he tried to get a loan for 100 million in the markets while at the same time searching the help of the Rothschilds. Although the government offered an interest rate of 10 per cent, the loan only produced about one-fourth of its planned yield, so the bankers became indispensable. They agreed to float a new loan for some 320 million on the condition that a part of their contribution should go to subsidize the railroad companies, with special consideration to MZA. Figuerola had to agree. A joint committee of the government and railroad companies was appointed to distribute the subsidies. Naturally, MZA was clearly favoured (Tortella, 1977, p. 520; López-Morell, 2005, pp. 232–4). As Figuerola proclaimed, 'Cheap capital is a privilege of rich and powerful countries, and if Spain must pay a high price for the funds its needs, the blame lies with those governments which impoverished the country with their continuous blunders'. Let us say in passing that the preambles to revolutionary economic laws and decrees, written by Figuerola and by Manuel Ruiz Zorrilla, Minister of *Fomento* (Economics), form a remarkable compendium of economic liberalism.

While the loan was being negotiated, the government went on bravely with its *laissez-faire* programme: a new decree in October 1868 abolished the old 1848 law restricting the establishment of corporations. One of the chief economic ideas of the revolutionaries was that economic liberty would bring about economic growth, and with it increased budget revenues and fiscal balance, which in turn would bring about foreign credit, which would foster investment and further more economic growth. The preamble of this decree extolled corporations as an 'invention of the American genius' which had permitted 'the thousands and thousands of wonders the powerful England and the great Republic of the United States have performed in the brief span of half a century'. The abolition of the restrictive 1848 law gave new force to the old Commerce Code, considerably more liberal. On 10 December a new decree made banking freer by abolishing the inspectors of credit companies and the royal commissaries of banks of issue, with the exceptions of the Bank of Spain and the *Banco de Barcelona*, whose governors were to be appointed by the government. These exceptions show how revolutionaries had to compromise their principles when questions of finance were involved. As neither the Bank of Spain nor the *Banco de Barcelona* played the role of a central bank, the reason for the government wanting to conserve some control over them was their size and the fact that they operated in Spain's two largest cities; they could hence render considerable services to the government.

Laissez-faire legislation in matters of incorporation was carried to its logical conclusion with the law of 19 October 1869, which established general free incorporation for 'local banks, agrarian banks, banks of issue and discount, credit companies, mortgage loan associations, public works contractor companies, manufacturing companies, docks and storage companies, mining companies, life funds, foundations, and any other type of associations having as their object any commercial or industrial enterprise'. All that was required to establish a company, according to the law, would be the signing of a notarized document with the basic particulars of such company, and its inscription in the Mercantile Register. Regarding banks of issue, the law was extremely liberal, much closer to 'free banking' than their predecessors: the limit to banknote issue, for instance, was to be established by the bank's statutes. Three months later a new law gave general authorization to revise the statutes of banks and credit companies. Nevertheless, some limitations subsisted: the banks enjoying a monopoly of issue in a given town would continue to do so until their charters expired. This in fact excluded the possibility of opening new banks of issue in most important cities, though not in all of them as some banks of issue, those of Seville and Valladolid, for instance, had been forced to close.

No legal limits were set to the issuing of shares, bonds, or any other credit instruments. Furthermore, the law explicitly declared that 'the companies established after the publication of this Law will *not* be subjected to the inspection or the vigilance of the government' (emphasis added); a remarkable statement, even more so in traditionally interventionist Spain. The reason for this frank hands-off policy was spelled out in the preamble to the law, which condemned the futile interventionism of former governments, which sent inspectors and commissars to banks and credit companies, but could not prevent the collapse of the banking system. Excessive control was counterproductive: it not only inhibited the enterprising spirit, but also 'lulled the shareholders into a mortal confidence'.

The keystone to this liberal arch was commercial policy. Figuerola proposed a moderately *laissez-faire* tariff law, which was approved in July 1869. The Figuerola tariff, as it has been known since then, contained a clause (called 'Fifth Base') whereby the duties would be lowered in two steps, each after a six-year period. So, its liberalism was postponed to a later date. Meanwhile, its original duties made it moderately protectionist, which was already an advance by comparison with earlier tariffs. This moderation did not make Figuerola any less unpopular with his fellow Catalans, who considered him a traitor for being a free trader and for living in Madrid. They were wrong: industry did well under the new tariff.

5.2 A brief respite

Some economic improvement took place thanks to the new economic policies, but it was not sufficient to bring about the swift increases in revenue which Figuerola expected. The evidence we have suggests that the liberalizing policies were successful, at least in the short run. According to Carreras *et al.* (2005, p. 1341), Spanish income per capita declined from 1863 to 1869, while it grew steadily from 1869 to 1873 at an average yearly rate of 7.8 per cent, all in real terms. More disaggregated variables, such as cotton imports or iron output also show vigorous growth during the 'revolutionary sexennium' in spite of war and political chaos. This contradicted the dire predictions of the protectionists, who foretold the ruin of industry, and of the economy in general, as a consequence of Figuerola's moderately protectionist tariff. Another strategic sector which was favoured by liberal policies was railroads. Not only did they receive subsidies, but they also benefited from legislation making mergers easier, and also from the increase in traffic brought about by the lowering of tariffs.

The banking sector also reflected the short lease of life provided by the liberal legislation. With somewhat renewed activity, the demand for credit went up. In contrast with the banking debacle of the pre-revolutionary years, there was a modest revival of banking institutions after 1870. The new banking corporations were neither banks of issue nor credit companies, but a less stereotyped set of institutions, along the lines of the 1869 Corporation Law, rather than along those of the more rigid laws of 1856.

The most prominent banks founded after the revolution were mortgage banks. This was logical. After the straitjacket of pre-revolutionary laws had been removed, the forces of the market pointed towards agriculture as the main sector in need of financial services. The increasing weight of agriculture in the Spanish financial markets derived from the *desamortización* programme, which had stimulated a massive transfer of real estate from the dead hands of the Church, the nobility, and the town halls into the more alive hands of middle- and upper-middle class individuals who purchased them, in most cases, to obtain a profit. This created a demand for fixed and variable capital in agriculture, and thereby a demand for financial services to help purchase this capital.

One of the banks founded at this time was the *Banco de Castilla*, established in 1871 as a mortgage bank. With a paid-in capital of 2.5 million pesetas, it had bonds in circulation to the tune of 66.1 million by December 1872, almost 80 per cent of which were sold in England. Among the founders and managers of the Castilla were Jaime Girona, Antonio Vinent, Rafael Cabezas, and Jorge Loring. We already know Girona and Loring. Vinent was a Catalan banker established in Madrid who made 'frequent loans to the Government' and Cabezas was a politician and banker who, according to a *Crédit Lyonnais* agent in Madrid, was not very rich, unlike Girona, Vinent, and Loring, but had 'a lot of administrative intelligence and *savoir faire*'. He knew uncommonly well the corridors of Spanish power and had 'some influence in all Spanish ministries'. He also was 'the official representative of the *Banque de Paris*'. This French bank was just about to merge with the *Banque de Crédit et des Depôts des Pays Bas*, of Antwerp, and become the *Banque de Paris et des Pays Bas*, commonly called Paribas. Paribas was an international conglomerate, not just Franco-Belgian: it also included London bankers, such as Bischoffsheim & Goldschmidt. One of its purposes was to build the 'cross-border alliances necessary to compete with the Rothschilds in future international operations and thus to avoid the fate of the Pereires', who had lost most of their power after the demise of the French Crédit Mobilier (Bussière, 1992, pp. 27–8). The same French agent informed that in reality the *Castilla* had been founded by Adrien Delahante, a member of a saga of French bankers, and was just a branch of the *Banque de Paris* (Crédit Lyonnais Archives, Paquet CEES 73.247, folder 'Banques'; Baumier, 1988, Ch. 1, esp. p. 16; Bussière, 1992, Ch. 1). In fact the Castilla seems to have been a sort of *pied-à-terre* in Paribas' plans of penetration in Spain, which was to be one of its fields of expansion. Paribas, when it was only *Banque de Paris*, had granted a loan to the Spanish government, which was guaranteed with promissory notes of buyers of disentailed lands. The *Banque de Paris* was authorized to issue mortgage bonds (*billetes hipotecarios*), but it preferred to create the *Castilla* and let this bank issue the bonds (Tedde, 1974, p. 258). This explains the high proportion of the *Castilla*'s bonds sold in London. Later on the *Castilla* abandoned its original specialization in agricultural credit and became an investment bank.

Another credit institution founded during these years was the *Banco Popular Español de Barcelona* (no to be confused with another, longer-lived *Banco Popular*, founded in Madrid in 1926), whose main business was to lend to municipal governments with the promissory notes from the sale of municipal lands as collateral. Most of the Popular's loans were employed in public works. It issued bonds, a substantial share of which was bought by Frenchmen.

The few banks created in the early 1870s, therefore, seem to have all specialized in credit related to real estate operations; none more so than the semi-official *Banco Hipotecario*. The idea of creating a public bank devoted to making advances to the government on the guarantee of the promissory notes of the buyers of nationalized land had already been mooted in the 1850s, when the *desamortización* law was being discussed, but nothing came of it then. Later on Salamanca submitted a similar project in 1863, but again to no avail. It is possible that the opposition of the Bank of Spain may have accounted for these failures. If the *Banco Hipotecario* idea finally became real it was most probably due to the financial difficulties of the Spanish government in the post-revolutionary period. Its immediate origin was another loan by Paribas, this one for 100 million pesetas at 12 per cent interest, which was reasonable in the circumstances. In the spring of 1872 the problems of the Spanish government were mounting. With the war in Cuba still raging, and scattered Republican rebellions erupting in several cities, the Carlist war broke out in the Basque Country and Catalonia; the real threat, however, was not military but financial. The Carlist pretender was aware of this, as he wrote to his brother: 'regardless of whether we win or lose actions, as long as we persist, the government, which does not have one cent, will irremediably fall' (Fernández Almagro, 1968, p. 135). The Paribas loan, therefore, was sorely needed. In order to pressure the government Paribas appended a clause to the loan contract whereby the interest rate would be upped to 16 per cent if the Hipotecario were not chartered. In spite of this, the opposition to the project in the Cortes was stiff, and came from the conservative side, which would appear surprising at first blush considering that the new bank was intended to supply credit to landowners. The explanation lies in the fact that the main antagonist was the Bank of Spain, which saw in the project a new version of the 'National Bank' idea of 1866, and in the Hipotecario a dangerous competitor. But the advantages of the new bank were overwhelming: it was not only that a loan at a reasonable rate was vital to the government; the private economy also required a source of credit at a non-usurious price. With the government absorbing large amounts of credit, the private sector was really starved of it and forced to pay rates which not infrequently reached 60 per cent. The Cortes was in no mood to force the government and the farmers to pay outrageous rates of interest to maintain the Bank of Spain's partial monopoly. The Hipotecario bill (whose first articles unilaterally lowered the interest rate paid by public debt bonds) was approved by a wide margin. The cooperation with Paribas intensified: the bank floated another loan in Paris, this one for 250 million; in exchange for this, the Hipotecario became the government's agent in all matters of land credit, disentailment, and public debt, in addition to being authorized to do business with the public and to issue mortgage bonds. In 1875 the right to issue mortgage bonds became a privileged monopoly, just as the Bank of Spain feared. But it was to have its compensation too, and fairly soon.

The Hipotecario was a new *Banco de Castilla* only with an official seal. Among its founders were Loring, Girona, Vinent, Cabezas, and the top brass of Paribas: Delahante, Henri Bamberger, Edmond Jean Joubert, and A. J. Stern. The board again included Loring and Cabezas (who became *de facto* co-presidents), Bamberger and Joubert. Soon afterwards they had the flair to appoint as a new member Antonio Cánovas del Castillo, who in two years was to become Prime Minister and the leading statesman in Spain until his death in 1897. (A summary of the early relations of the *Banco Hipotecario* and the Spanish government is contained in 'Banque Hypothecaire d'Espagne, Extraits des Rapports d'Assemblées de Paribas' in Paribas Archives, Cont. 63, Dossier 11, Folder Banque Hypothecaire d'Espagne; see also Tortella, 1977, pp. 532–41, and Lacomba and Ruiz, 1990, Ch. 1.)

5.3 Free banking no more

In spite of their hopes and blueprints, the revolutionaries were unable to solve the economic problems they had set out to unravel in 1868. This is often seen almost as a personal failure of Figuerola, who was often thought of as the economist of the revolution. It is possible that his failure may explain, at least in part, Spain's longstanding mistrust of economic liberalism. Be it as it may, historical perspective makes us think that the failure should be attributed to the uncommon difficulties of the task at hand and to the hostile political circumstances. Spain was at the time a backward country with a penchant for violence, rebellion, and war, things which, among others, forced increased expenditure on an already bankrupt state. Democracy and liberalism, such as the revolutionaries decreed and practised, could not work in nineteenth-century Spain; rather they fostered mutiny and turmoil. A more authoritarian regime might have succeeded better, as the relative success of the Restoration in the years that followed would suggest. The fact is that, after the Savoy monarchy, the republic, and the republican dictatorship failed, the hated Bourbons returned to the throne and stayed there for 55 years.

The last years of the 'Revolutionary Sexennium' were really desperate. The only two possibilities the government had of dealing with its intractable fiscal problems were to sell its assets and to negotiate one more loan. In 1873 the Río Tinto copper and sulphur mines were sold to an international consortium led by a London banker of Scottish origin, Hugh Matheson, for 92.7 million pesetas (López-Morell, 2005, pp. 309–14). But this was only a temporary solution. War expenditures devoured most available resources and the international crisis of 1873 made international borrowing even more difficult than usual. The moment Serrano came back to power, this time as 'head of the provisional government of the Republic', in January 1874, the *Gaceta de los Caminos de Hierro* (4 January 1874) proclaimed boldly: 'The Spanish state is virtually bankrupt'. The only solution was one more loan. This is what the new Finance Minister, José Echegaray, an engineer who received the Nobel Prize for Literature in 1904, set out to do as soon as he reached office. The possibilities of a foreign loan, however, were dim. The international crisis still lingered; furthermore, the Hipotecario had been organized a year before and its relations with the Spanish government were somewhat strained already over what the bank claimed to be breach of contract ('Banque Hypothecaire d'Espagne', in Paribas Archives, cited earlier, and Lacomba and Ruiz, 1990, pp. 64–8). In addition, the new, unelected Spanish government was not recognized by the leading European states. A substantial domestic loan did not look very probable either, in the depressed state to which the wars had put the country. The Spanish banking system was in shambles: of the approximately 60 incorporated banks of 1864, only 25 remained in March of 1874, most of them in a precarious state (they were those listed in Tedde, 1974, p. 263, in addition to the nine banks of issue that were absorbed by the Bank of Spain). Spanish banks, therefore, were out of the question too – unless, of course, recourse was had to the Bank of Spain. And this is what Echegaray endeavoured to obtain as soon as he took charge of his post. Little over two weeks after the government was constituted, he sent the Bank a proposal to exchange a new and advantageous charter for a loan; this is what had been done in the case of the Hipotecario in 1872, and in those more momentous cases of the Bank of France in 1800 and the Bank of England in 1694. In 1874 there was little the Spanish government could seriously offer but monopolies and privileges. This is how and why Echegaray, who had signed the very liberal law decreeing, among other things, total banking freedom in 1869, ended up four and a half years later, giving the Bank of Spain the monopoly of banknote issue and other privileges.

It was not an easy affair. The Minister was loath to betray his principles to the extent of explicitly giving the Bank the monopoly of issue, and the draft he sent the Bank carefully avoided offering it, although it came quite close. But the Bank wanted it and had the big trump in his hand: the lure of a fat loan. The problem was, the monopoly meant depriving the other banks of issue of the privilege embodied in their charters. They were sounded out and showed themselves rather hostile to the idea. The Bank presented a counterproposal in February in which the provincial banks were offered to become branches of the Bank of Spain and their shares exchanged for those of the Bank at par. This was quite advantageous to most of them. The discussion went on and transcended to the public; economists did not believe Echegaray, the ultra-liberal of 1869, would betray his principles to the extent of granting the monopoly (for the discussion, Bank of Spain Archives, Secretaría, folder 647; Tortella, 1977, pp. 541–6; see also Tedde, 2006; Tortella, 2006). He did grant it, however, with a decree of 19 March, whose preamble made quite clear that that the main reason for the reorganization of the banking system was the government's financial plight. Politics is the art of the possible. The decree's articles openly proclaimed the monopoly of issue conferred upon the Bank of Spain and invited the provincial banks of issue to merge with it by exchanging their shares for those of the Bank at par value. This was a good proposal for shareholders in most cases; for managers, however, the transaction, even if profitable, might not have compensated for the loss of their independence: this may be why several of these banks resisted what they said – not unreasonably – was an arbitrary measure. The debates and disputes were reflected in the pages of the *Gaceta de los Caminos de Hierro*. The decree also provided for an increase in the capital of the Bank of Spain to 100 million pesetas and permitted its fiduciary circulation to reach up to five times that figure. In payment for all these privileges the Bank would lend the government 125 million pesetas.

After months of struggle and resistance, most provincial banks of issue agreed to merge with the Bank of Spain: these were those of Pamplona, Oviedo, Vitoria, Balear, Málaga, San Sebastián, La Coruña, Jerez, and Saragossa. They became branches of the Bank of Spain. The *Banco de Sevilla*, which was not functioning but not officially dissolved, made a feeble attempt to merge with the Bank of Spain but was rejected (Castañeda, 2001, pp. 40–5; see also Anes, 1974, pp. 130–3). Five provincial banks of issue refused to merge, struggled to keep their status, and finally reconverted as commercial and deposit banks; these were the banks of Bilbao, Santander, Barcelona, Tarragona, and Reus. Of these, the first three were the strongest and most solvent among the surviving institutions, and the last three were Catalan.

It may seem surprising that the shareholders of the Bank of Spain were not all convinced that their new status was a good thing, but they showed some resistance in the meeting summoned to approve the changes deriving from the decree of 19 March. Some were afraid the Bank would not be able to take up its new responsibilities, others were motivated by their hostility to the government; in the end, however, the dissenters were outvoted (Castañeda, 2001, pp. 12–19). All in all, Echegaray's government benefited but little by his travails and his betrayal of his principles: nine months after the decree ending the plurality of banks of issue was published, the Bourbon monarchy was restored, and it was its governments that took advantage of the reorganization of the banking system and of the Bank of Spain's largesse.

5.4 The bank and the peseta

In the very last days of 1874, a group of generals under the leadership of Arsenio Martínez Campos proclaimed *Alfonso de Borbón* king of Spain. At the time the future monarch was a cadet at the Royal Military Academy at Sandhurst, in England. Isabel had abdicated her rights in his favour four years before. Antonio Cánovas del Castillo, who headed the Alfonsine party, was appointed Prime Minister. Thus commenced the period in Spanish history known as 'the Restoration', a long span which could be considered ended in 1923, when general Miguel Primo de Rivera assumed dictatorial powers with the acquiescence of the then king, Alfonso XIII, or, alternatively, in 1931, when Alfonso abandoned Spain and the second republic was proclaimed. The secret of the Restoration's relatively long life and stability lies largely in Cánovas' political intelligence: he imposed the rule of bipartisanship and promoted the alternation of both parties in government. He soon found in Práxedes Mateo Sagasta his adequate counterpart at the head of the Liberal Party (Cánovas called his own party Liberal–Conservative), and promulgated a new (1876) constitution tailored to his plans for the new monarchy and regime. When the king died in 1885 his level-headed queen, Maria Cristina of Habsburg-Lorraine, became regent and soon afterwards gave birth to a posthumous son who was crowned in 1902 as Alfonso XIII. Cánovas was assassinated by an anarchist in 1897 and Sagasta died naturally in 1903. The passing away of these two men, plus the economic and social development of the country, thanks in large part to the peace brought about by the Restoration, made this regime more and more obsolete in the twentieth century.

In the economic sphere, the monopoly of issue vested upon the Bank of Spain by the decree of 19 March 1874 was an unintended gift from the republic to the monarchy. Of course the Restoration also inherited a poisoned legacy in the almost unmanageable situation of the public debt and budget deficits; by way of compensation, however, they received an improved military situation: the Carlists were bottled up in the Pyrenees and the anarchist–cantonalist rebels had surrendered in January 1874; the Carlists made peace very soon after the monarchy was restored. The Cuban rebellion still smouldered, but was finally defeated in 1878. Thanks to the end of wars, military expenditures could be reduced. Another positive economic sign was the stock exchange, which rebounded in Madrid, and especially in Barcelona, after 1875.

The monopoly of issue turned the Bank of Spain into a 'new financial power' as the decree said, giving it a measure of strength it had never enjoyed before. Its fiduciary circulation could be expanded up to 500 million pesetas, an enormous figure when one considers that the combined fiduciary circulation of all banks in early 1874 had stood below 60 million. Furthermore, the Bank could still increase its capital by 50 per cent, which would move the limit of circulation to 750 million. The Bank used this possibility to popularize banknotes and the relatively new monetary unit, the peseta, but, most of all, the new purchasing power was applied to acquiring public debt bonds, thus alleviating the financial needs of the government: the correlation between banknotes in circulation and loans to the government was evident (Anes, 1974, pp. 146–57; Anes, 1994; Tortella, 1999, pp. 163–5). Thus started the process which economists called 'direct monetization of the public debt'. The Restoration ministers made an effort to balance the budget, something which was facilitated by the end of the wars, but liquidating the enormous debts that the revolution and the Isabeline governments had left took a long time. During those years the state necessitated a reliable and steady source of credit to tide it over, and he found it in the 'new financial power' of the Bank of Spain. In the long term, vesting the privilege of banknote issue upon the Bank of Spain was a good move; it caused, however, a considerable amount of immediate problems and difficulties (Tortella, 2006).

As was mentioned earlier, there were misgivings even among the shareholders of the Bank. There was some opportunistic political opposition to the March decree from monarchists who did not want the Bank to prop up the republic; other misgivings were more legitimate: some were afraid the Bank might have trouble doubling its capital in the difficult circumstances of 1873; others fretted that absorbing so many banks at a time and creating a branch network would necessitate an excessive effort and involve high risks; still others thought the decree might be illegal. All these fears turned out to be unfounded, but there was justification in doubting the lawfulness of at least some points of the 19 March decree, such as the one depriving the provincial banks of issue of their privilege while their statutes were still in vigour. In fact several provincial banks protested this measure and one of them, the *Banco de Bilbao*, put up a stiff resistance which lasted almost four years during which time the Bilbao's banknotes remained in circulation in the city. The government was obliged to confirm the decree by law in 1876 so as to override the Echagaray law of 1869, which said that the provincial banks of issue could not be deprived of their privileges as long as their concessions were in vigour. At this point we may ask whether the high-handedness of the March decree was necessary, and our conclusion is that it was not. Only five banks did not merge with the Bank of Spain; of these only three were located in large commercial cities (Barcelona, Bilbao, and Santander) and the concessions of these banks had only a few years left to run. Considering that the Bank of Spain took ten full years to establish a truly national fiduciary circulation (meaning that its banknotes were convertible in any branch), waiting until the privileges of the three provincial banks ran out would not have made so much difference, and would have avoided a great deal of tension and hostility especially in Barcelona and Bilbao (Castañeda, 2001, pp. 11–20; Anes, 1974, pp. 125–57).

Table 5.1 shows the growth of the money supply (Col. 5): it nearly doubled in the last 25 years of the nineteenth century, growing at an average yearly rate of 2.4 per cent. This was nothing extraordinary at the time (or now), but it was certainly faster than it had grown in previous decades and probably faster than it had ever grown in Spain for a long period. After all, these were decades of economic growth, not at an accelerated pace, but steadily. Per capita income grew between 1875 and 1900 at an average yearly rate, in constant pesetas, of 0.84 per cent, not very impressive by twentieth-century standards, but quite acceptable for the nineteenth century, and, again, probably unprecedented, although the former 25-year period was also of substantial, although less regular, growth (Carreras *et al.*, 2005, pp. 1335–6). It was logical that in a time of growth the demand for money should have grown too and the Bank of Spain stepped into the breach by multiplying its banknote issue. Money demand and supply, however,

Table 5.1 Components of the money supply (cols 1–4, percentages; col. 5, millions of current pesetas)

	Silver	Gold	Banknotes	Deposits	Money supply
1875	27.6	56.6	6.8	9.0	1,766
1881	28.5	34.9	17.6	19.0	1,960
1885	33.2	28.8	21.8	16.1	2,118
1890	31.8	14.3	31.6	22.3	2,287
1895	28.6	4.7	44.5	22.2	2,139
1900	25.4	0.0	46.6	28.1	3,220

Source: Tortella (1974) (These figures differ slightly from the ones in the Appendix.).

moved in a rather parallel way, and the result was a remarkable stability of prices (Maluquer de Motes, 2007). The demand for money from the public and from the government was expanding fast and the Bank found itself several times in need to curtail its banknote emissions for fear of overstepping its rigid limits. According to the March 1874 decree, the maximum was 750 million pesetas (five times its capital). As banknotes outstanding were fast approaching the cap figure in 1888, the Bank was forced to curtail banknote circulation and make a growing number of payments in silver, something which caused problems, among them carrying inconveniencies if the sums involved were large. The government felt compelled to pass a new law in 1891 doubling the maximum volume of circulation, and renovating the privilege of issue for another 30 years. In exchange for this, the Bank extended a 150 million pesetas loan to the government. The public debt problem at the time was not as acute as in the past. In 1881 Finance Minister Juan Francisco Camacho carried out a reform which introduced novelties that made Spanish bonds more attractive: first, payments became punctual; second, foreign debt was paid in gold. From the Camacho reform on, the volume of Spanish debt in circulation went down substantially, external debt decreased relative to the total, and quotations became higher and steadier (Comín, 1994a).

The cap to banknote issue had to be raised again to 2,500 million by a decree of 1898, during the Spanish–American War over Cuba and the Philippines. The government had tried to finance the war by having recourse to the Bank's credit; as a consequence the banknote issue got out of hand and inflation appeared. But immediately after the end of the war, in 1899, another decree lowered the cap back to 2,000 million. The 1898 decree is interesting also because it made the maximum banknote issue independent from capital and linked to a series of reserve assets, not only specie but also public debt bonds and some private securities. In addition, this required reserve was made progressively more stringent as the volume of banknotes in circulation approached the cap.

Another remarkable feature presented in Table 5.1 is the disappearance of gold from circulation (Col. 2): it went from being more than half the circulating medium in 1875 to vanishing from the money supply. We will consider the causes of this phenomenon later. Silver, by contrast, remained a fairly stable element within the circulating medium, its share oscillating between one-third and one-fourth within the money supply. Possibly the most relevant feature in the table is the substitution of bank money for metal in the Spanish money supply: bank money (banknotes plus deposits) went from less than 16 per cent in 1875 to almost 75 per cent of the total mass of money in circulation in 1900. This was part and parcel of the process of economic growth, but we can be certain that, without the monopoly of issue and the network of branches created by the Bank of Spain, the modernization of the means of payment would have been much slower.

The fact is that during this period the Bank of Spain grew disproportionately within the Spanish banking system. Its branch network went from 2 in 1874 before the March decree to 17 at the end of the same year; by 1900 it had 58 branches distributed rather evenly over the peninsula and the Balearic and Canary islands. As we will see, 'private' (non-official) banks did not start building up their branch networks until well into the twentieth century.

This was the period when the Bank of Spain was not only the centre of the financial sector, it really was a giant among pygmies. Since the early twentieth century 'private banks' grew in numbers and size and the share of the Bank of Spain shrank in quantitative terms. But by the end of the nineteenth century, thanks to its branch network and its monopoly of issue, it was the only truly 'national bank', as it liked to call itself. In terms of paid-in capital, the Bank had 150 million pesetas, 40 per cent of total paid-in capital of joint-stock banks. In terms of deposits the disproportion was even starker: the Bank held 75 per cent of the total, not including savings banks (total combined capital of other banks calculated from Tedde, 1974, pp. 329–30; current account deposits in Tortella, 1974, p. 492).

Throughout this period the Bank remained 'official' but privately owned. It was official in that the government appointed its governor, it enjoyed a privileged status and was the banker of the state, not only in terms of making loans and absorbing great quantities of public debt, but also in having a role of counsellor in financial matters, although the ministry carried the initiative in monetary and financial policy. In fact, as we will see, there was little real monetary policy; it was fiscal matters that determined the economic policies of the Spanish government.

Neither was the Bank of Spain a central bank in the modern sense: in matters of policy it was subordinated to the ministry; its relations with other banks were more competitive than cooperative, something which often drew bitter complaints, especially in Barcelona and Bilbao. It did not act as lender of last resort. It was not properly a bankers' bank, as it dealt directly with the public and competed with other banks in several areas. In general it was more concerned with its profits and its rapport with the government than with acting as the executor of a monetary policy having a bearing and a repercussion on the economy of the country as a whole, or on financial international relations. In spite of all this, by virtue of its sheer size, its policies, even if not intended to, had a bearing and repercussions upon the Spanish economy.

5.5 Picking up the pieces of the banking system

The dire state the Spanish banking system was left in after ten years of crisis is reflected in a table in Tedde's work (1974, p. 263), listing the banking corporations existing in Spain at the end of 1874. Their number was 16, including the Bank of Spain, the Hipotecario, and the five banks of issue that did not merge with the Bank of Spain. This leaves 9 non-issuing banks, the old 'credit companies' of which there were 40 in 1864; 2 of these 9 were the recently established *Banco de Castilla* and *Banco Popular*, so that of the original 40 credit companies, less than one-fifth remained. The largest of these was, of course, the *Crédito Mobiliario Español*; there was also the Catalana, a distant second. All in all, of these 16 surviving banks, 4 were in Madrid (including the Bank of Spain and the Hipotecario), 4 in Barcelona, and then there was one each in the following cities: Bilbao, Santander, Tarragona, Reus, Zaragoza, Pamplona, La Coruña, and Palma de Mallorca. There was not a single one in Andalusia or Valencia, two large and economically active regions, where the only joint-stock banks at that moment were the branches of the Bank of Spain. To this should be added 39 banking partnerships (commonly called 'banking houses' or 'merchant capitalists'), according to Canosa (1945, p. 39), who gathered his figures from tax rolls. There had been 82 of these partnerships in 1866, according to the same source. Some of these houses, such as Weisweiller and Bauer, and Urquijo, were considerable. Most of them were small and short-lived (García López, 1985).

By century's end the Spanish banking system comprised some 30 corporate institutions (Calculated from Tedde, 1974, pp. 329–30). At that time, the number of unincorporated banking houses, according to Canosa, was around 25. Two things can be deduced from this: one, that, while joint-stock banks increased in numbers, the number of banking houses diminished, a modernizing trend; another, that, even after a quarter century of recovery, and of moderate though steady economic growth, the number of banks in Spain was still way below the number in the 1860s. The banking–railroad episode which we examined in Chapter 4 had been a unique bubble in nineteenth century history. But although it was unique in its size, it was not the only one. There was a comparable episode in the early 1880s, commonly known as the *febre d'or* ('gold fever' in Catalan), a speculating frenzy occurring mostly in Barcelona, probably linked to Camacho's successful public debt conversion and in general to the optimism deriving from the stability brought about by the Restoration.

This, however, was not an episode exclusive of Spain. The crisis of the early 1880s and the ensuing depression was an international phenomenon which affected France with special force (see, for instance, Lewis, 1978, esp. Ch. 2). In fact, there were several parallels between the Spanish and the French economies at the time: after suffering war and disorder in the early 1870s, both countries put their political and economic houses in order and enjoyed a boom in the second half of the decade. There were some differences though: in France the boom was linked to railway construction (the Freycinet plan to expand and improve the network); in Spain, by contrast, after the frenzy of the late 1850s and early 1860s, railroad construction proceeded at a slow pace. In France the fear of inflation put an end to the railway subsidies and expenditures linked to the Freycinet plan, while at the same time a new and ambitious bank, the *Union Générale,* failed dramatically in 1882 (Cameron, 1961, pp. 198–9; Bouvier, 1960).

In Spain the optimism was fuelled by political stability, monetary expansion, moderate interest rates, and the success of Camacho's debt reform. This was exacerbated by a wave of stock exchange speculation in Barcelona, where banks and insurance companies were founded in unbelievable numbers. In a city where there were just four banks a few years before, 14 banks were established in 1881–2; in the rest of Catalonia, where there had been none previously, 11 banks were founded in the same span of time; almost all of them failed in the ensuing years. Other regions of Spain, especially Madrid, also suffered from the crisis, although the previous euphoria had been less marked than in Catalonia. In Madrid the swings were less pronounced, but a few new banks disappeared almost instantly after being established. The ensuing depression, in France and Spain, no doubt aborted two plans, in 1882 and 1884, mooted by Paribas and the *Crédit Lyonnais,* to inject new money into the old *Crédito Mobiliario Español* and to reform it with the help of other banks, among them a new Spanish institution, the *Banco Hispano Colonial* (Sánchez-Albornoz, 1977, p. 171; Tedde, 1974, pp. 292, 301; Paribas Archives, Fonds Cabet, Espagne, File 14); a similar plan, however was carried out 18 years later.

The *Crédito Mobiliario Español* certainly lost its spark after the demise of its French parent, the Spanish crisis and, finally, the death of Isaac Pereire in 1880. It became just a manager of its holdings with an almost total lack of initiative. In addition to the Norte railway network, its most important holding was an insurance company, *La Unión y el Fénix Español,* which was number one in its field for almost a century.

The *Banco Hispano Colonial* was perhaps the outstanding bank created during this period. Its founder was Antonio López y López, a self-made man who started his meteoric business career in Cuba, then established himself in Barcelona, and was ennobled as marquis of Comillas (his native town near Santander). One of Comillas' lines of business was maritime navigation, so his rapport with Cuba endured. He had a lasting business entente with Manuel Girona and other members of the business elite in Barcelona and Havana. This is why he was asked by the Spanish government in 1876 to coordinate a big loan (100 million pesetas) to enable the army to defeat the rebels in Cuba; Comillas obliged, and founded the Hispano Colonial as an instrument to carry out the negotiations and management of the complex operations of this loan, which was assured with the revenues of Cuba's customs. Such was the power of Comillas that the contract the bank signed with the government vested the Hispano Colonial with the management of Cuba's custom duties.

The war ended in 1878 and many people expected the bank to fold up; instead, it obtained a new contract with the government and became a sort of agent for managing colonial finances; somebody in the government said that it should play in the colonial sphere the same role the Bank of Spain played in the metropolis. It also kept its control over Cuba's customs. In addition, the *Hispano Colonial* became a business bank, investing in and promoting businesses, especially those related to the interests of the Comillas–Girona group. It often worked in tandem with the *Banco de Castilla* and with the *Crédito Mercantil*, a credit company founded by the Girona family in the 1860s to act as a business bank complementary to the *Banco de Barcelona*. The Hispano Colonial became very active in the last years of the century, after the Cuban war started again in 1895. When this war ended with the loss of Cuba, Puerto Rico, and the Philippines, the Hispano Colonial reverted to its investment bank posture, but it never recovered the strength and vitality it exhibited in its early years (Cabana, 1972, Ch. I; Rodrigo, 2000, Ch. 2; Tedde, 1974, *passim*). The truth is that the Hispano Colonial, the *Banco de Castilla*, and the Hipotecario, the most powerful and successful banks created in the last quarter of the nineteenth century, owed much of their success to their special relationships with the Spanish state, as was also the case with the Bank of Spain.

The Hipotecario derived substantial profits from the monopoly of mortgage credit and of issuing special mortgage bonds. It soon discovered that loans to agriculture were less profitable and easy to manage than urban mortgage loans and also that ordinary shorter-term loans, and especially credit to the government, were more profitable than mortgage loans. In consequence, its much touted role of financing agriculture became rather marginal after all (Lacomba and Ruiz, 1990, esp. Chs. III and IV).

Nothing much need be said about the old banks of issue reconverted as commercial banks. The Barcelona went on with its cautious policies while competing with the local branch of the Bank of Spain. According to Tedde (1974, pp. 307–8), it still hoped to recover its banknote-issuing privilege. Its founder and president, the very influential Manuel Girona, rarely a daring visionary, was getting on years; after he died in 1905, however, the *Banco de Barcelona* quickly ran into problems. In fact, after the 1880s crisis the whole Catalan banking system went into a slow decline which lasted for over a century, provoking much soul-searching among Catalan politicians and scholars. This is the period when, by contrast, the Basque banks developed steadily until they became, together with those of Madrid, the strongest group in Spain. The contrast between the two northern banks, Bilbao and Santander, was telling. The *Banco de Santander* stagnated during this period, carried down by the decline of the city as an exporter of flour and grain to the colonies, while the *Banco de Bilbao* greatly benefited from this city's development as an iron and steel centre. The Bilbao intensified its relation with the nascent Biscayan industries and became a well-managed, thriving business, so much so that a competitor appeared in 1890: the *Banco del Comercio*; the Bilbao, however, soon absorbed it; ten years later, nevertheless, another, stronger competitor was established: the *Banco de Vizcaya*. The rivalry between the Bilbao and Vizcaya banks lasted for over 80 years (on *Banco de Santander*, see Gutiérrez Sebares and Hoyo, 2007–8, I, Ch. 2; Martín Aceña, 2007, Chs. 1–2; on *Banco de Bilbao* and *Banco de Vizcaya*, see González *et al.*, 2007, Ch. 1).

Two banking houses stood out in the final years of the century, one in slow decline, the Rothschild branch, the other in impressive ascent, Urquijo. About Weisweiller and Bauer a French banker had written the following in 1871: 'they sometimes do business with the government but they have a reputation of being excessively Jewish, that is to say, that they charge too much for their loans; there are, nevertheless Spanish bankers who, Christian though they are, deserve even more this reputation. [... But the fact is that] whenever the government can do without Weisweiller & Bauer they do so gladly' (Crédit Lyonnais Archives, Paquet CEES 73.247, Folder 'Banques'). This may be the reason the Rothschild branch changed tack and devoted more money and interest to industrial and mining enterprises and less and less to government finance in the last decades of the nineteenth century. In addition to their old participation in the Almadén mercury business, they now patronized two prosperous mining concerns: Rio Tinto and Peñarroya. In the Rio Tinto company they acquired a controlling interest in the late 1880s, just before this company had its most profitable period; very possibly the Rothschilds had a hand, not only a share, in this prosperity. Peñarroya was a large lead deposit the bankers acquired in 1881 and developed successfully. Together with the MZA railroad, these two mining enterprises were the core of the Rothschild estate in Spain. Daniel Weisweiller was almost retired by this time and Ignacio Bauer was not very young either. They both passed away in the 1890s and their successors were not as able as they had been; the Rothschild house slowly faded from the Spanish scene in the early twentieth century (López-Morell, 2005, Chs. 7–8).

Estanislao de Urquijo had been an employee and apprentice of Weisweiller who established himself on his own in the 1840s. He soon became very successful dealing in the stock exchange and lending to the government. According to the *Crédit Lyonnais*' agent in Madrid, Urquijo was 'a very intelligent businessman. He is at the head of the Spanish Bankers group, who almost every time they meet heed his advice as the law. This is the reason why he is called here the *Cabestro de Toros*, that is to say, the leader of the herd' (see Crédit Lyonnais Archives, *Ibid.*). His support of King Amadeo brought him the marquisate of Urquijo. While he continued doing business with the government under the Restoration, he also imitated his old boss Weisweiller and became increasingly interested in industry. He died in 1889 and was succeeded as the head of the house by his nephew Juan Manuel de Urquijo (who also inherited the title). Under Juan Manuel the bank became decidedly industrial, with investments in the leading companies in the fields of tobacco, iron and steel, mining and metallurgy, paper, shipbuilding, electricity, and so on (Díaz Hernández, 1998, esp. Chapter III; Puig and Torres, 2008, pp. 17–32). These bankers, the Rothschilds and the Urquijos, were obviously adapting themselves to the changing Spanish economy and society: on the one hand, we have seen that the Restoration governments were able to redress somewhat the threatening public debt problem of previous decades; they were therefore better able to deal with bankers, to bargain more successfully, and to pay lower interest rates. Lending to the government was no longer the heady and fabulously profitable business it had been before. Furthermore, the Bank of Spain, the Hipotecario, and the Hispano Colonial held a place of choice in dealings with the state. Private banks and banking houses were pushed to second rank. On the other hand, the country was developing economically, cities were growing, industry and public works were expanding: textiles, food processing, mining, metallurgy, chemicals, electricity, transportation, urban infrastructure and utilities, were all sectors with increasing potential. It was natural that the more alert bankers, such as the Rothschilds and the Urquijos, should pay increasing attention to these promising new sectors.

Savings banks developed quite fast, at least in terms of numbers, during this period. There were 9 of them in 1874 and 43 in 1900. By that date the combined deposits of the savings banks amounted to 131 million pesetas, about 25 per cent of total combined bank deposits excluding the Bank of Spain, and 10 per cent including it. This turned them into a strong potential source of financial funds in a growing economy. Although they were still considered as charitable institutions, their financial role was far from negligible. Many of them, as we saw in Chapter 3, worked in tandem with the *Montes de Piedad*, following the example of the Madrid *Caja*, whose deposits were one-third of all savings banks deposits (Tortella, 1974, I, p. 499 and II, pp. 544–7). The *Caja de Madrid* soon found itself in a quandary: it collected more money than the *Monte* could absorb, so it had to find other remunerative outlets for its deposits; it started buying public debt bonds, but later diversified and acquired private securities, such as railroad bonds and Bank of Spain shares. Thus the *Cajas* were impelled, somewhat reluctantly, to assume an increasing role in the financial market, a role that would expand in the twentieth century (Titos, 1989, 1991).

While the total volume of deposits in savings banks expanded, the average deposit remained constant around 700 pesetas, which indicated that the number of modest savers grew remarkably during this period, one more sign of economic improvement. Women flocked to savings banks: they were 36 per cent of all customers; but this figure is an understatement. If we add deposits in the name of children, they combined to make 57 per cent of all savings banks customers. Domestic servants (84 per cent of them women) were another substantial group of depositors. Women (servants and non-servants, plus those having some other profession) probably were more than half of depositors, as women servants plus non-servants already were 48 per cent.

Stock exchanges also developed during this period. The Madrid Stock Exchange, the oldest and largest official market (it had replaced an older *bolsín*, or unofficial exchange) had been devoted almost exclusively to trading public debt bonds, but in the last decades of the nineteenth century it started to quote private securities such as Bank of Spain shares, railroad bonds, securities of insurance companies, other banks, and utilities. Meanwhile the unofficial Barcelona stock exchange had started functioning in 1851, and it was more specialized in private companies' securities (Fontana, 1961). New *bolsines* were established in Bilbao and Valencia. The one in Bilbao became the second official *bolsa* in Spain in 1890.

Spanish stock exchanges remained, nevertheless, thin and unstable. The country still being in its early stages of development, its savings were but a small fraction of total income, as the frequent recourse to the Paris and London stock exchanges by Spanish governments and corporations indicates. On the other hand, recent studies show that joint-stock companies, the only listed in the stock exchanges, remained a minority of all Spanish companies (Hoyo, 2007, esp. pp. 27–40).

5.6 Monetary doubts and the silver standard

The first reaction of the Spanish government facing the uncertainties brought about by the Franco–Prussian war was to imitate other European countries and prepare for the gold standard by suspending silver coinage in 1870. This was followed by a turnaround in 1873, when gold minting was suspended and silver seigniorage was lowered. The reason for this about face was that the price of silver was falling, largely due to Germany's impending adoption of the gold standard and to increasing silver output in the United States (Nevada) and Mexico; this made minting gold relatively more expensive and a virtually bankrupt state, as the Spanish was, could not afford such an expensive monetary system. The dilemma between wanting to be on the gold standard like other European countries and the fear of the excessive economic and political costs of such standard tore Spanish governments from that moment on, until the Great Depression put an end to gold being a regular domestic means of payment anywhere.

By 1873 the price of silver was 2 per cent under the parity established in 1868. At that point, adopting the gold standard would have reduced the Spanish money supply by about 20 per cent (Tortella, 1974, pp. 136, 206–7). Such a contraction would have had terrible consequences in such a fragile economy as Spain, still reeling from the crisis of the 1860s, with two civil wars and a colonial war looming and the state prey to all sorts of political uncertainties. However, if the bimetallic standard were maintained, gold would gradually disappear from circulation by virtue of Gresham's law ('cheap money drives out expensive money'), as silver had been driven out in the former decades when it was gold's price that was falling.

The price of gold kept going up for the remainder of the nineteenth century. By 1876 it was 14 per cent above the 1868 parity. The possibility of establishing the gold standard, as Germany had just done, was getting dimmer. But the Spanish government, flushed with the recent monarchist victory and encouraged by the inflow of foreign capital attracted by the peaceful state of the country, made a new attempt at establishing the gold standard in 1876 and proposed to start minting new gold coinage. It never got around to actually doing it. The price of gold kept going up (in 1879 it was 20 per cent above the official parity); the government decided to stop and wait; but the trend was inexorable: gold was becoming more expensive by the month. Furthermore, the 1882–83 crisis hurt Spanish exports of agricultural products and caused a dip in the influx of capital. Juan Francisco Camacho meanwhile was carrying out his reform of public finances and, in order to make Spanish foreign debt more attractive, made it payable in gold and charged the Bank of Spain with fulfilling this task. The Bank saw its gold reserve go down swiftly; in view of this, apparently with the government's agreement, the Bank's top officials quietly instructed its tellers in Madrid and at its provincial branches to stop redeeming banknotes in gold (Jiménez, 1905, p. 240; Sardà, 1987 [1948], p. 172). The measure caused protests, but the Bank and the government insisted it was legal, although the matter was more than debatable. Thus, in this surreptitious manner, Spain abandoned bimetallism and adopted the silver standard in 1883. According to Teresa Tortella (2010, pp. 38–9), the Bank avoided publicity for fear of provoking a panic.

More than a decision, the adoption of the silver standard was a non-decision. It was, as Sardà wrote, 'more than a deliberate ideal of Spanish governments, a concession to reality'. Nobody acknowledged responsibility for it and Spanish governments kept proclaiming periodically their intention to establish the gold standard, but never daring to make the decision. One of the main obstacles was the Bank of Spain itself, which, afraid of losing its gold reserve if convertibility were restored, always advised against it.

In a few years gold had disappeared from circulation. A part of it returned to the Bank of Spain's vaults, where it was now secure from the public's demands. A part was used to pay foreign bondholders, not all of them really foreign, however, as Spanish citizens, attracted by the gold settlements, illegally bought external debt bonds through intermediaries. The rest was hoarded or exported.

In late-nineteenth-century conditions, the silver standard was really a fiduciary standard, that is, a monetary system where the intrinsic content of the circulating medium was way below its face value. The typical example of a fiduciary standard is banknotes, ornate pieces of paper whose intrinsic value is a very small fraction of their purchasing power. Such was also the case of silver coins in late-nineteenth-century Spain, when, for instance, in 1886, the intrinsic value of a silver peseta coin was 75 cents, and by century's end was less than 50 cents. In these conditions for the Spanish government minting silver was extremely profitable and if it did not mint more it was because its officials were afraid the exchange rate of the peseta would go down for it.

The silver standard had advantages and disadvantages. On the negative side, it isolated Spain economically and thereby almost assuredly discouraged larger influxes of foreign capital. Foreign investors should, to a certain extent, have been wary of the uncertainties inherent to a non-convertible monetary unit. The value of the peseta fluctuated in international markets with respect to the currencies of gold-standard countries, which were the main capital exporters. However, save in the years of the Cuban war (1895–8), Spanish governments showed restraint in the creation of money, the Spanish price level remained fairly steady, and so did the quotation of the peseta. It only went down in the years of the war, and a drastic stabilization plan in 1899 soon restored its value.

On the positive side, the gold standard would have implied either an enormous effort or a brutal deflation, or most probably both. For a poor country in the process of catching up gold as a circulating medium was a non-affordable luxury. A moment when Spain could have adopted the gold standard would have been in the wake of the First World War, when it had accumulated such quantities of gold that the Bank of Spain held one of the largest reserves in the world. But again, the government hesitated and this was a good thing in the end, because, when the depression came, during the crisis of the spring of 1931, the Bank of Spain was able to increase its banknote circulation considerably, thus guaranteeing the solvency of the banking system, quickly restoring confidence, and avoiding a painful bank crisis such as the ones which took place in Austria, Germany, or Italy (Tortella, 1999, pp. 174–7).

In fact, as the best Spanish economists pointed out at the time, Spain did not have a true monetary policy. The decisions made in this realm were in reality little more than responses to budgetary problems. The chronic fiscal deficit (with the exception of the surpluses obtained by the stabilization plan just referred to) caused deficits in the balance of payments, which in turn caused gold losses. Monetary policy was guided almost exclusively by the desire to minimize these losses and to cushion the Spanish economy from them. The irrelevance of this monetary policy has been confirmed by means of an econometric exercise by García Ruiz (1996, pp. 132–4), where it is shown that causal dependence was strong from income to money, and weak in the opposite direction for the 1856–1913 period.

Nor was Spain's case as unique as it seems. Other countries in similar stages of development, in Europe and America, struggled to maintain the gold standard and finally dropped it. Such was the case of Portugal, the second country in the world to adopt the gold standard (in 1854), which abandoned it in 1891; or of Italy, which adopted bimetallism in 1861, abandoned convertibility in 1866, resumed it in 1883 (really in silver only, like Spain), and again abandoned it altogether in 1894. Mexico, a great producer and exporter of silver, adopted the gold standard in 1905 only to abandon it forever in 1910. In other Latin-American countries, such as Brazil, Chile, and Colombia, the gold standard was adopted and quickly dropped (Martín Aceña and Reis, 2000). To repeat: the gold standard was a luxury developing countries could hardly afford. Spain was no exception.

6
A Renewed Banking System

6.1 Stabilization and regeneration

The loss of the colonies in America (Cuba, Puerto Rico) and Asia (Philippines) in 1898, at the hands of the United States, was a blow to the Spanish collective consciousness. But there was reaction to the 'Disaster of 1898' and Spain soon evolved from complaining about the *males de la patria* (woes of the fatherland) to facing problems boldly (Velarde, 1999; Maluquer de Motes, 1999). The liberal–conservative minister Raimundo Fernández Villaverde drew up a successful stabilization plan in 1899–1900 based upon a tax reform which balanced the budget for almost a decade (a record in modern Spanish history) and even provided a project of income tax (Comín, 2002). Villaverde's plan also permitted a substantial reduction in the volume of public debt. Some thought, however, that the reform had to go further and put an end to the 'soft nationalization' that had characterized nineteenth-century Spain (De Riquer, 1994). According to this school of thought (the *regeneracionistas*), it was necessary to espouse a newly minted Spanish nationalism, recognizing regional differences but at the same time pursuing the integration of the Spanish market and giving the state a greater role in economic modernization.

Antonio Maura was the politician who best understood the need for a proper 'Regenerationist' reaction. Maura broke away from the Liberal Party in 1901, proposing a 'revolution from above', that is, from the state down. Shortly thereafter, in November 1903, Maura was named head of the Conservative Party, which he sought to transform completely. Maura's programme eventually materialized in the creation of a doctrine combining the protectionist Cánovas Tariff (1891) with new elements of nationalism and interventionism. This doctrine, popularly called *Maurismo*, would remain influential, in successive versions, for much of the twentieth century (Perpiñá, 1972; Fusi and Palafox, 1997).

As set out in Appendices 2 and 3, under the economic Regenerationist programme, Spanish GDP per capita grew between 1899 and 1913 at around

1–2 per cent per year (estimates differ) and the investment rate (Gross Fixed Capital Formation/GDP) went from 5.79 per cent in 1875–98 to 8.91 per cent in 1899 to 1913. One could see a takeoff *à la Rostow* of the Spanish economy during these years. Catalan and Basque nationalists however made themselves felt after the 'Disaster'; regional nationalism was fuelled by fear for the loss of colonial markets. After 1917, liberal and conservative Prime Ministers included Catalanists in their governments. The most notable of these Catalanists was Francesc Cambó, a lawyer and financier who led the conservative *Lliga*, dominated Catalan politics until the civil war, and made remarkable contributions to economic policies in the 1920s. Nationalist and working-class agitation took place in the early 1920s, in the midst of the business bonanza that started with the First World War, which was produced by an export boom favoured by the country's neutrality. The bonanza was not free from serious problems: it was short-lived, inflationary, and caused social and economic polarization. After the war distortions became apparent, many improvised industries collapsed, and depression set in. Inflation and war profiteering provoked serious social tensions (Sudrià, 1990).

Social conflict intensified in 1919, the year of the strike in the large electricity company *La Canadiense* (part of the Pearson international group), an episode which led to an escalation of violence in Barcelona which culminated in the assassination of the provincial governor in 1920. Amid a very tense social climate, the president of the Council of Ministers, Eduardo Dato, was also assassinated in Madrid in March 1921. In the two and a half years that elapsed between the murder of Dato and the coup by Primo de Rivera, social tension came to a head, even though economic growth was considerable between 1919 and 1923 (yearly per capita GDP growth was about 3 per cent). On 13 September 1923 Alfonso XIII acquiesced when the Captain General of Catalonia, Miguel Primo de Rivera, published a manifesto announcing that the army had decided to intervene and suspend the 1876 Constitution, taking public disorder as a pretext. Parliament was dissolved. The political system of the Restoration was over, although economic *Maurismo* (albeit not Maura himself) would be the leading inspiration during the ensuing six years of dictatorship.

The development of economic nationalism between the colonial crisis and the rise to power of Primo de Rivera has been the origin of a debate about the relationship between political and corporate power in the first third of the twentieth century. For Juan Velarde and his disciples, it seems clear that the state was captured by rising corporate power, where the role of banks was outstanding (Velarde, 1953; Muñoz, 1969; Roldán and García Delgado, 1973; García Delgado, 1985). In what might be called 'the theory of capture', authors have joined from positions as antagonistic as Marxism (Tuñón, 1975) and liberal economics (Fraile, 1991). However, Cabrera and Del Rey (2002, p. 405) have argued that 'the nationalist discourse was not invented by businessmen, no matter how much they liked it and ended up adopting it in their claims and demands.' According to these authors, political power acted with considerable independence from businessmen and bankers, in the years before the coup of 1923 and during the dictatorship of Primo de Rivera, which lasted until January 1930.

6.2 The new banks

The 1885 Commerce Code provided the legal basis for the Spanish banking system until 1921, when a banking law (the Cambó Act) was approved. The 1885 Commerce Code maintained the old distinction between 'credit companies' and 'banks of issue and discount'. Commercial credit transactions should not exceed a maximum of 90 days (although extensible through renewals), but credit companies were authorized to purchase and deal in public debt bonds and securities of private companies. Thus, legislation discouraged long-term lending (financing needed for industrial activities) by commercial banks but permitted merchant banks to play the role assigned by Alexander Gerschenkron (1962) and Rondo Cameron (1967) in the backward countries, that is, the promotion of companies by participating in their capital, something which would contribute to fostering economic growth.

Fernández Villaverde's stabilization plan (in addition to the $20 million compensation for the loss of Spain overseas colonies paid by the US government according to the Treaty of Paris) improved the quotation of the peseta, which in turn attracted investment from abroad. The colonial war also had accelerated repatriation of capital. Between 1892 and 1902, remittances from the Americas to Spain amounted to some 1,000 million pesetas (Sardà, 1987 [1948], pp. 193–6). Much of this money would be applied to creating new financial institutions in the early years of the new century, especially credit societies comparable only to those of the 1856–64 period or the 1880s (the *febre d'or*), but this time with much more lasting effects. Up to 50 banks were created between 1899 and 1914 (Table 6.1).

The Basque Country and Madrid were the areas where most of the new banks were established: in the Basque Country, a new type of relationship between banks and industrial firms was developing into what became known as 'mixed banking', a model pioneered by Germany and also followed by Italy; Madrid was on its way to becoming a national financial centre, in a process similar to what happened in other European countries. Among the new Basque institutions we must highlight the *Banco de Vizcaya* (1901) and the *Crédito de la Unión Minera* (1901), specializing in electrification and mining, respectively. In Madrid, the outstanding new institutions were the *Banco Hispano Americano* (1900) and the *Banco Español de Crédito* (Banesto). Banesto was established in 1902 on the basis of the old *Crédito Mobiliario Español* with new capital and reorganization from Paribas (García Ruiz, 2007c, 2007d). The underdevelopment

Table 6.1 Joint-stock banks created in Spain in 1899–1914

	Head office	Duration	Cause of disappearance
Banco Agrícola de San Isidro	Madrid	1899–1900	Dissolution
Banco Asturiano de Industria y Comercio	Oviedo	1899–1970	Absorption by Banco de Bilbao
Banco de Gijon	Gijon	1899–1977	Absorption by Banco Hispano Americano
Banco Guipuzcoano	San Sebastian	1899–2011	Absorption by Banco Sabadell
Banco Castellano	Valladolid	1900–70	Absorption by Banco de Bilbao
Banco de Andalucía	Seville	1900–8	Dissolution
Banco de Burgos	Burgos	1900–28	Absorption by Banco Español de Crédito
Banco de Cartagena	Cartagena	1900–23	It became Banco Internacional de Industria y Comercio
Banco de Valencia	Valencia	1900–2012	Absorption by CaixaBank
Banco de Vigo	Vigo	1900–25	Dissolution
Banco de Vitoria	Vitoria	1900–2004	Absorption by Banco Español de Crédito
Banco Hispano Americano	Madrid	1900–92	It became Banco Central Hispano
Banco Mercantil	Santander	1900–46	Absorption by Banco de Santander
Crédito Industrial Gijonés	Gijon	1900–8	Dissolution
Crédito Industrial y Comercial	Santander	1900–1	Dissolution
Banco de Vizcaya	Bilbao	1901–88	It became Banco Bilbao Vizcaya
Banco Naviero	Bilbao	1901–1	Dissolution
Banco Vascongado	Bilbao	1901–2	Dissolution
Crédito de la Unión Minera	Bilbao	1901–25	Dissolution
Crédito Popular Madrileño	Madrid	1901–8	Dissolution
Fomento Agrícola de Menorca	Ciudadela	1901–11	Dissolution
Sociedad Aurora	Bilbao	1901–1	Dissolution
Banca Marsáns	Barcelona	1902–42	Absorption by Banco Hispano Colonial
Banco Español de Crédito	Madrid	1902–2012	Absorption by Banco Santander
Crédito Barcelonés	Barcelona	1902–8	Dissolution
Banco de Alayor	Alayor	1903–11	Dissolution
Banco Popular de León XIII	Madrid	1904–47	It became Banco Popular de Crédito y Descuento

continued

Table 6.1 Continued

	Head office	Duration	Cause of disappearance
Crédito Mercantil de Menorca	Mahon	1905–54	Absorption by Banco Español de Crédito
Banco Aragonés de Seguros y Crédito	Saragossa	1906–69	Absorption by Banco Mercantil e Industrial
Banco Comercial Español	Valencia	1906–27	Absorption by Banco Español de Crédito
Banco del Comercio	Mahon	1906–11	Dissolution
Banco de Ferrerías	Ferrerias	1908–65	It became Banco Comercial de Menorca
Banco Ibérico	Madrid	1908–08	Dissolution
Banco de Aragón	Zaragoza	1909–71	Absorption by Banco Central
Banco de San Sebastian	San Sebastian	1909–75	Absorption by Banco Hispano Americano
Banca Arnús Garí	Barcelona	1910–42	Absorption by Banco Español de Crédito
Banca Arnús	Barcelona	1910–48	Absorption by Banco Central
Banco de Albacete	Albacete	1910–21	Absorption by Banco Central
Banco Zaragozano	Zaragoza	1910–2004	Absorption by Barclays Bank
Crédito y Fomento de Ahorros	Barcelona	1910–26	It became Crédito y Fomento
La Vasconia	Pamplona	1910–66	It became Banco de la Vasconia
Sindicato de Banqueros	Barcelona	1910–99	Absorption by Bancaja
Banco de Menorca	Mahon	1911–51	Absorption by Banco Central
Banco de Tolosa	Tolosa	1911–69	Absorption by Banco Central
Banco Herrero	Oviedo	1911–2002	Absorption by Banco Sabadell
Banco Riojano	Logrono	1911–25	Dissolution
Banco Agrario de Baleares	Palma	1912–53	Absorption by Banco de Santander
Banco Popular de Manacor	Manacor	1913–27	Dissolution
Banco Comercial de Ciudadela	Ciudadela	1914–47	Absorption by Banco de Crédito Balear
Banco Cooperativo del Comercio y de la Industria	Madrid	1914–31	Dissolution

Source: García Ruiz (2007a), Appendix I, updated with information from the *Asociación Española de Banca* (Spanish Banking Association).

of Catalan banking was now becoming more noticeable; scholars have attributed it to factors on the demand side (predominance of small and medium enterprises with a high level of self-financing) and on the supply side (poor management of financial institutions, with an inclination towards stock-market speculation) (Sudrià, 1994 [1982], 2007). Other relevant banks included in the table were the *Banco Guipuzcoano* and the *Banco de Vitoria* in the Basque country, the *Banco de Valencia* and the *Banco Zaragozano* in two important provincial capitals, and the *Banco Herrero* in Asturias, which had a significant role in the financing of mining, metallurgical, and chemical industries. In Barcelona three merchant banks were founded, the *Banca Marsans*, the *Banca Arnús*, and the *Banca Arnús-Garí*, often involved in stock-exchange operations; the Arnús and Arnús-Garí houses were the product of a family split, as their names suggest (Cabana, 1972, Ch. IV). In the Balearic Islands there was a remarkable wave of bank creation in this period, probably due, among other reasons, to the close connections of the islands with Cuba (Méndez Vidal and Hernández Andreu, 2013, pp. 176, 183).

The expansion which took place between 1899 and 1914, however, was not without risks. Out of the 50 banks created, 13 were liquidated within the period while the Goldsmith ratio (Financial Assets/GDP) fell from 37–9 per cent to 32–5 per cent (Appendix 9). Some critical commentators asked for state intervention to solve what they considered to be the problem of insufficient credit in Spain (Canals, 1916). This initiative would seem unnecessary when during the business boom of the First World War the number of banks increased from 52 in 1915 to 91 in 1920 (Muñoz, 1969, p. 46). Among the institutions that emerged in these years were the *Banco Urquijo* (1918), the *Banco Central* (1919) and the *Banco de Cataluña* (1920). The Banco Urquijo was the old Urquijo banking house gone public. Foreign banks also increased their presence, and their number of branches rose from 20 in 1916 to 43 in 1920 (García Ruiz, 2001). The nationalist–statist ideology, however, scored a point when the Law for the Protection of National Industry was approved in 1917; it was largely the consequence of an outcry against foreign banks and the excessive conservatism of Spanish ones, especially the Bank of Spain. Those critics demanded longer-term credit for businesses and their claims found a powerful echo in the Cortes. Salvador Canals and Cambó, both Catalan deputies, managed to insert a clause in the 1917 law which recommended the creation of a state bank to supply long-term credit to industry. Three years later the *Banco de Crédito Industrial* (Bank for Industrial Credit) was created by a consortium of banks with the support and supervision of the state. Spain was not the only country where a bank of this nature was established at this time: in France and Belgium similar institutions had been founded in 1919 (Tortella and Jiménez, 1986, pp. 22–35).

6.3 Monetizing the public debt

During the 1873–96 period, the world economy was affected by a deflationary trend, whose causes and consequences were examined at the International Monetary Conferences of 1878, 1881, 1889 and 1892. Economists who attended these meetings linked deflation to the gold standard, as the yellow metal shortages constituted a severe restriction to the liquidity of the financial system, and some of them recommended a return to traditional bimetallism. The exploitation of the mines of the Transvaal (South Africa) since the early 1890s put on the market large quantities of gold and the doubts over the monometallic standard ended. In Spain, Vicente Ortí Brull, inspector of branches at the Bank of Spain and a member of the Conservative Party, published an interesting book on this topic where he gathered differing opinions of economists (Ortí, 1893), but he was wrong in predicting that the world would return to bimetallism (it should be kept in mind, however, that France did not abandon this standard *de iure* until 1926).

In the final years of the nineteenth century, the only supporters of the gold standard in Spain appeared to be the old liberals of 1868, such as the sexagenarian Gabriel Rodríguez, founder of *El Economista*, who in a speech in 1892 criticized the monetization of public debt and the abandonment of gold and the exclusive use of silver for the simple reason, according to him, that governments made good profits by minting cheap silver, while gold remained in the 'prisons of the vaults of the Bank [of Spain]' (Rodríguez, 1892, p. 30). Rodríguez wanted to make the Spanish economy respectable through a return to the gold standard discipline, although this might require the withdrawal of no less than two-thirds of the banknotes in circulation (Rodríguez, 1892, pp. 37–9). Of course, he found unacceptable that the Bank should convert notes into gold for its distinguished clients and into silver for the rest, but this is what, under the counter, probably occurred until the Civil War (T. Tortella, 2010, pp. 38–9).

The Catalan business class and politicians were ranged squarely against the gold standard because they thought that it was part of a free-market economic order that they mistrusted. For Federico Rahola, general secretary of the employers' association (*Fomento del Trabajo Nacional*), monetary systems only reflected the interests of the countries involved (Rahola, 1892, p. VI). Having no gold or silver mines, Spain should be pragmatic and put the protection of producers above all. The journalist José G. Ceballos Teresí, founder of the journal *El Financiero*, collected opinions on the currency issue, showing that the Catalan stance began to be shared by leading Conservative Party economists linked (Ceballos Teresí, 1931).

The most influential champion of the gold standard was a leading politician, Raimundo Fernandez Villaverde, the Conservative Party leader, whose stabilization plan had put Spain's finances in order. On 16 January 1890, Fernández Villaverde made a public speech at the Royal Academy of Moral and Political Sciences which caused great impact (Fernández Villaverde, 1890). He agreed with the French–Italian economist and banker Henri Cernuschi on the impossibility of the *'monométallisme bossu'* (hunchback monometallism), that is, the coinage of gold while keeping a large amount of depreciated silver in circulation (a silver 'hump'). Fernández Villaverde stated that Spanish bimetallism had become in practice silver monometallism, where the face value of coins exceeded by about 30 per cent their intrinsic value. He found this situation dangerously inflationary. The only way out of this impasse was the demonetization of silver, which was no longer a means of international payment, and the gradual introduction of the gold standard. In this he differed from Cernuschi, who was an ardent bimetallist.

According to Martín Aceña (1993, pp. 143, 159–60), in 1910–14 the exchange rate of the peseta was close to its theoretical parity and it would have been very easy to adhere to the gold standard. He notes that the main drawback of being out of the international monetary system was that Spain lost the opportunity to be one of the major recipients of foreign investment, which would have allowed more vigorous growth. As we saw before, however, the gold standard in Spain may have posed serious deflationary problems; perhaps, apart from fulfilling foreign debt commitments, 'financing imports of food and raw materials was the best use for [the gold reserves]', according to Tortella (1974, p. 481; 1981, p. 160).

One of the main clauses of Fernández Villaverde's stabilization plan had been a cap on the permitted banknote circulation of the Bank of Spain, from 2,500 to 2,000 million pesetas. A strict quantitativist, Villaverde wanted to put limits to the growth of the money supply, in order to achieve price stability and a stable quotation of the peseta. He knew that government deficits were the main cause of banknote expansion and so his fiscal reform made possible ten years of budget surpluses, something which finally brought about a reduction in the volume of public debt in circulation. Furthermore, a law of 13 May 1902 (he was no longer in power, but his principles had been widely accepted) put serious obstacles to loans by the Bank of Spain to the Treasury. This posed no problem while the budget was in surplus; but from 1909 on deficits returned, caused by the increases in military expenditure due to troubles in the Spanish Morocco Protectorate. The solution to this conundrum was what was called the 'indirect monetization of the public debt'. In the years immediately before the First World War, Spanish banks were large enough to be able to purchase substantial amounts of public debt bonds. In order to make these bonds attractive to them, the government pressured the Bank of Spain to accept them as collateral, at low interest rates and with a favourable tax treatment. For the banks this made purchasing public bonds very convenient: they guaranteed an acceptable rate of interest and were quite liquid, as they could be pawned at the Bank of Spain at any moment for interest rates that were ordinarily below the bonds' yield.

These agreements were confirmed and reinforced a few years later, in 1918. A year earlier, the *Comité Central de la Banca Española* (Central Committee of the Spanish Banks), which coordinated regional bankers' associations, was established. On 1 July 1918, the *Comité Central* signed a deal with the Bank of Spain whereby the Bank would grant national banks (that is, excluding foreign institutions) a bonus of 1 per cent on the rediscount of bills of exchange (article 1) and would automatically grant credits on collateral of public funds for 80 per cent of their value (article 2) (the text of the pact is reproduced in Ministerio de Hacienda, 1921). The pact confirmed former agreements and encouraged banks to invest large sums of money in public funds, that is, it meant 'indirect debt monetization'. These agreements had several important effects. In the first place, they permitted non-inflationary financing of budget deficits, as banks ordinarily kept public debt bonds in their vaults and only pledged them when they felt short of liquidity. Before the agreements, the relation between budget deficits and banknote issuing by the Bank of Spain was quite close; after the new loan policy was in place, there was a large gap between both variables (Tortella, 1999, pp. 163–5). Secondly, these agreements created the main economic bond between the Bank of Spain and private banks; rediscounting became a secondary kind of recourse for commercial banks. Third, for the banks, purchasing public debt bonds was a convenient complement to acquiring and dealing with industrial securities, more subject to the vagaries of the market; by combining public and private securities in their portfolio, the banks were insured against sudden jumps in liquidity preference. Fourth, these arrangements permitted the new big banks to take an active part in the industrial expansion which took place during the early decades of the twentieth century. A final consideration: the Bank of Spain was able to sustain the activities of the 'mixed banks' in support of industrial development because it was not encumbered by the rules of the gold standard. All the actors involved in this play tacitly knew that in a crunch the government would raise the top to banknote issue; this is what happened in the spring of 1931 (Ortiz-Villajos, 2001, pp. 157–8; Martínez Méndez, 2005; Tortella, 2006, pp. 128–34).

6.4 Towards a true central bank

Renewing the issuing privilege of the Bank of Spain always posed problems, because there were sections that were critical of its high profits and conservative policies. There was rather heated public discussion when the Bank's privilege was renewed in 1891. When Ángel Urzáiz, Minister of Finance in a Liberal cabinet, tried in 1902 to undertake a comprehensive reform of the Bank of Spain to bring it closer to the Bank of England, with a separate Issue Department, and to move rapidly towards integration in the international gold standard system, many dissenting voices were heard. These reforms were not popular among the most significant industrial producers and there was a press campaign from Catalonia against Urzáiz (*Revista de Economía y Hacienda*, 1902). The Urzáiz project failed, and so did others by Juan Navarro Reverter (1906), Augusto González Besada (1908), Tirso Rodrigáñez (1912) and Santiago Alba (1916) (Adrados, 1918). Everything presaged the outbreak of a major controversy in 1921, the date of expiry of the privilege of issue of the Bank of Spain. Books and pamphlets were released with all kind of opinions, but critics agreed that a privileged institution such as the Bank of Spain should allow greater state participation in profits (Paret, 1921). The most radical critic, who signed with initials probably to avoid unpleasantness, suggested that the Bank of Spain should be completely nationalized, something which only took place more than 40 years later (A. V. del R., 1918).

The Bank of Spain was publicly defended by the count of Torreánaz, a director of the institution, who was opposed to a bank controlled by the state, which would only be a 'factory of paper money' (Conde de Torreánaz, 1915, p. 30). In a similar vein, Emilio Miñana and Juan Antonio Galvarriato (1918, p. 55) defended the survival of a 'privileged private bank of issue, unique in the whole country, sufficiently independent from political influence and enjoying the privilege for long enough to not fear changes that could endanger its solvency and credit'.

An official commission to study the extension of the privilege of the Bank of Spain was created by a royal decree of 5 September 1918. All the reports coincided in one respect: they all criticized the scant support the Bank of Spain gave to the private sector (Ministerio de Hacienda, 1921, Chapter IV). Let us remind that the Law for the Protection of National Industry had just been approved. In its conclusions, the commission, which completed its work by 11 March 1919, requested the following: (i) there should be representatives of agriculture, trade and non-privileged domestic banks on the board of the Bank of Spain; (ii) the required bimetallic reserve backing banknote circulation should be lowered to 45.33 per cent; (iii) the maximum banknote issue should be increased to 6,000 million; (iv) the 1918 agreement between the *Comité Central de la Banca Española* and the Bank of Spain should be ratified. The commissioners, therefore, sought a compromise solution, stimulating the Bank of Spain to lend to the private sector and to expand the money supply. Table 6.2 shows the evolution of the legal limits to banknote circulation and of the required bimetallic reserve or coverage backing banknote circulation.

When the time came to renew the privilege in 1921, the Minister of Finance was Francesc Cambó, who wanted to carry out a comprehensive reorganization of the entire banking system. The Banking Law of 1921 (commonly called the Cambó Act) was passed with difficulty on 29 December, thanks to an intervention by the Prime Minister, the charismatic Antonio Maura, who had to work hard to achieve the necessary consensus (Gómez Ochoa, 1991). The problem was that Cambó had sought to strengthen the state's

Table 6.2 Basic legislation on the issue of banknotes by the Bank of Spain, 1874–1920

	Maximum authorized (million pesetas)	**Bimetallic coverage**
Decree of 19 March 1874	500	25 per cent
Law of 14 July 1891	1,500	33.33 per cent
Law of 17 May 1898	2,500	50 per cent
Royal decree of 2 August 1899	2,000	60 per cent[a]
Royal decree of 5 August 1914	2,500	68 per cent
Royal decree of 10 March 1917	3,000	73.33 per cent
Royal decree of 6 August 1918	3,500	77.14 per cent
Royal decree of 2 January 1919	4,000	80 per cent
Royal decree of 27 December 1919	4,500	82.22 per cent
Royal decree of 7 October 1920	5,000	66 per cent

[a] As amended by a law of 13 May 1902.
Source: Ministerio de Hacienda (1921).

control over the Bank of Spain and the private banks by imposing the presence of government representatives in all credit institutions. In the end, the Cambó Act settled for a 'smooth evolution' towards making the Bank of Spain into a 'bank of banks', and setting limits to its privileged relationship with the state. Ultimately, monetary and exchange rate policies would be the competence of government (Pons, 2012, pp. 77–80).

Regarding private banks, the law entrusted them to a new regulatory body, the *Consejo Superior Bancario* (CSB, High Council for Banking), dominated in fact by the big banks, which meant, according to Olariaga, letting the banks 'to be ruled by themselves as they pleased' (Olariaga, 1921, p. 3). The CSB should compile the statistics of the sector, establish accounting systems, and set the working rules for the banks inscribed in a new Register of Banks and Bankers. The registered banks would enjoy bonuses in their operations with the Bank of Spain and in the payment of taxes, and could be integrated into the clearing houses that were to be created. Foreign banks were excluded from these benefits because they could not be registered (if they wanted to compensate documents they should do it through a registered bank).

Modern banking theory attributes four main functions to a central bank: (i) to issue legal money; (ii) to be the banker of the state; (iii) to conduct monetary policy; (iv) to be a bank of banks and lender of last resort. There is a debate among historians about the performance of these functions by the Bank of Spain at the stage we are considering. For Rafael Anes (1995, p. 120), the Bank of Spain during the Restoration was an 'efficient bank for the government and a good interpreter of monetary policy'. By contrast, Martín Aceña (1995) thinks that the development of the functions of the

Bank of Spain as a central bank was harmed by the absence of the rules of the gold standard, the low degree of competition and openness of the Spanish economy, the excessive closeness between the Bank and the Ministry of Finance, and the lack of expertise of the monetary authorities.

According to Walter Bagehot (1873), a modern central bank should assume the role of bank of banks to the point of acting as 'lender of last resort'. The Bank of Spain did this for the first time in January 1914 when it saved the *Banco Hispano Americano* from an undeserved bankruptcy (García Ruiz, 1999). Despite its spectacular initial success, and the soundness of its policies, the Hispano, founded in 1900, was forced to suspend payments on 11 December 1913. How could this happen? The answer is simple: the Hispano was a victim of the Mexican Revolution. The bank's strong ties with Latin America (its founder and many of its board members had made their fortune overseas), in particular in Mexico, were well known so many inferred that the share of Mexican securities in the Hispano's portfolio should be very high, which was not true. The teller windows of the Madrid bank were closed between 11 December 1913 and 9 January 1914 because the Bank of Spain took all that time to approve a loan to save the Hispano, a very reliable entity that soon afterwards would lead the ranking of Spanish banks. The loan was for 12 million pesetas – the Hispano had asked for 60 million – and a personal guarantee was required from every member of the Hispano's board. The Bank of Spain behaved as a very reluctant lender of last resort.

Its response to the crisis caused by the end of the economic boom associated with the First World War was even worse. The Bank did nothing to avoid the bankruptcy of the venerable *Banco de Barcelona* in 1920, after a failed currency speculation (Cabana, 1978). Then in 1923–24 when half a dozen banks closed doors and others went through great hardship – due to the postwar recession – the Bank of Spain, according to Martín Aceña (1995) first tried to ignore the situation; then under pressure from the government it argued that other banks' problems were not its responsibility. In the case of the Central, which, five years after starting business had its first crisis induced by the bankruptcy of its largest shareholder, the *Crédito de la Unión Minera*, the Bank of Spain only acted as a lender of last resort because it was so ordered by the head of the government, the dictator Primo de Rivera, in person (Tortella, 2007). In another field, but in the same vein, the Bank of Spain did not accept joining the clearing houses created according to the Cambó banking law until 1930, seven years after they were established, and it declined over and over again to establish a money market of the 'open market' type (García Ruiz, 1993). As we shall see, it was not until the crisis of 1931, that the Bank of Spain began to be a real 'bank of banks' and lender of last resort.

7
From Dictatorship to Republic: Spain and the Great Depression

7.1 The growth of a state banking sector

A decree of 15 September 1923 appointed General Miguel Primo de Rivera 'president of the military directorate in charge of the government of the state', whose decisions had to be countersigned by the king. That same day, civil governors were replaced by military governors in all provinces. The new government suspended the 1876 Constitution giving as its motives its intention to restore social order, which was disturbed by struggle in the streets, and to correct the unfavourable course of the colonial war in Morocco. By and large, these goals were achieved. Social conflict was largely resolved thanks to the accommodating attitude of socialist leaders towards the new regime (unlike the anarchists, who were harshly repressed). The socialist union, the *Unión General de Trabajadores* (UGT) agreed in 1926 to enter the *Comités Paritarios* (Joint Parity – i.e., employers–workmen – Committees) that, under the chairmanship of the Minister of Labour, Eduardo Aunós, laid the foundations of collective bargaining in Spain; the general secretary of the UGT, Francisco Largo Caballero, was appointed councillor of the state, while his party, the *Partido Socialista Obrero Español,* was not persecuted. Regarding the pacification of Morocco, in September 1925 a successful Franco–Spanish major pincer offensive on Alhucemas Bay and south of the Rif mountains was launched, which defeated the rebels. In the last days of that year, Primo de Rivera replaced the military directorate with a civilian one, where José Calvo Sotelo was appointed Minister of Finance.

Spanish output under the dictatorship expanded due in part to a public works programme undertaken by the government and to the favourable international atmosphere of recovery from the ravages of the First World War (Velarde, 1973). However, the growth model implemented by the Minister of Finance was marked by three heterodox notes: protectionism, nationalism, and interventionism. Foreign observers perceived this and, for example, the 1929 report on Spain by the British Department of Overseas Trade expressed concern about: (i) the existing proposals to limit imports of machinery and equipment for public works; (ii) the diffusion of nationalist theories seeking to exclude the participation of foreign capital in railways, refining and distribution of petroleum, mining and water engineering; (iii) the interventionist attempts and movements leading to the nationalization of banks and insurance companies. According to the report, the current prosperity in Spain was 'ephemeral' and induced by a public deficit that had hitherto been funded at low interest rates, but which was beginning to worry bankers (Department of Overseas Trade, 1930).

Calvo Sotelo's model was not completely new. It had been around at least since the years of *Maurismo*, as we saw in the previous chapter. Calvo Sotelo had been a follower of Maura in his youth (Bullón de Mendoza, 2004, Ch. 2). As Minister of Finance of the dictatorship he put the model into practice with all its consequences. His main concern was to obtain the resources needed to launch a vast programme of public works (water works, renewal of rail infrastructure and equipment, electrification, and new road construction) by means of a 1926 special budget. A tax reform aimed at increasing revenue through a new tax on income, failed, and the fight against tax fraud obtained very meagre results (for these attempts to increase and spread the tax burden, Calvo Sotelo was labelled a 'bolshevik' by large landowners, and the dictator himself asked him to desist). A substantial share of the floating debt was consolidated, but public funds remained under automatic pledge by the Bank of Spain–private banks agreement of 1918. In compensation for the failure of his tax reform, and as an alternative source of funds, Calvo Sotelo created the *Compañía Arrendataria del Monopolio de Petróleos, S. A.* (CAMPSA, Company for the Leasing of the Oil Monopoly), which was entrusted with the distribution, refining and production of petrol (Tortella *et al.*, 2003). The oil monopoly imitated somewhat similar institutions being established in France and Italy, and, at the same time, it satisfied Calvo Sotelo's staunchly nationalistic and xenophobic ideology. The big banks supported the idea enthusiastically and became the main shareholders of the Arrendataria. In contrast, these same bankers were very suspicious of the group of public banks that were being promoted by the dictatorship, even though in some cases private banks became shareholders of the public ones.

The nationalist economic creed of the dictatorship was clear and often proclaimed. However, it was sometimes applied with flexibility. This was the case, for instance, with commercial policy. Traditional Spanish protectionism had been invoked, renewed, and refined by the 1922 Cambó Tariff – the other contribution by the Catalan politician to the Spanish economic panoply. This tariff, adopted in reaction to the end of the export cycle after the First World War, had established especially high duties for industrial goods. Under the dictatorship, these duties were softened by the application of second column preferential rates. In the 1920s, nationalism did not prevent foreign technology transfers or the installation in Spain of iconic multinationals, such as the International Telephone and Telegraph which helped to create the *Compañía Telefónica Nacional de España* (Telefónica, recently rebaptized Movistar), a company that would exploit the telephone monopoly established in 1924 (Calvo, 2010). The dictatorship was partial to monopolies. The regime's interventionism was also reflected in its penchant for regulation: it created, for example, the *Consejo de Economía Nacional* (National Economy Council) in 1924, or the *Comité Regulador de la Producción Nacional* (Regulatory Committee of the National Production) in 1926. The *Consejo* was a general advisory and regulatory body; the *Comité Regulador* was empowered to authorize the establishment, expansion, and relocation of industrial enterprises. Due to the limitations of budgetary resources, the dictatorship preferred regulation to direct financial help. In the banking field, the dictatorship eased the tax measures against foreign banks that had been taken in 1920–2 to curb their rapid expansion, but it applied unreservedly the discriminatory measures contemplated in the 1921 Banking Law (García Ruiz, 2001).

To financially support the government's economic plans, Calvo Sotelo gave a big boost to public banks. By that time, there were two of these in addition to the Bank of Spain: the Hipotecario, which was prodded by Calvo Sotelo to focus its loans towards small property, whose governor was to be appointed by the government and a growing share of whose profits would accrue to the state (Lacomba and Ruiz, 1990, pp. 293–301); and the *Banco de Crédito Industrial* which was thoroughly reformed and streamlined by Calvo Sotelo (Tortella and Jimenez, 1986, pp. 42–56). The dictatorship's public works programme was a boost to the Hipotecario. There were also two small public credit institutions which were not actually banks, but rather branches of the administration: the *Caja Central de Crédito Marítimo y Pesquero* (Central Fund for Credit to the Maritime Industry and Fisheries, 1919), which was not really operative until after the Civil War (Sánchez Blanco, 1992), and the *Servicio Nacional de Crédito Agrícola* (National Service for Agricultural Credit, 1925) which in its first five years of activity only granted 120 million pesetas in credits to about 29,000 farmers (Gámez, 1997); the *Servicio Nacional* would be reorganized and renamed *Banco de Crédito Agrícola* (Agricultural Credit Bank) in 1962.

Before becoming Minister of Finance, Calvo Sotelo was director of local administration, and from that position he enacted the Municipal Statute (1924), the Provincial Statute (1925) and launched the *Banco de Crédito Local* (Bank of Credit for the Local Administration, 1925). Three months after the approval of the Municipal Statute, a Catalan financier, Eduard Recasens, founder and director of the *Banco de Cataluña* (1920) had sent a letter to the dictator where he proposed the creation of a 'Municipal Bank of Spain', a private institution supervised by the state, whose main purpose would be to lend to local and municipal bodies and would be financed through bond issues. Calvo Sotelo presided over the commission to study the proposal (Bullón de Mendoza, 2004, pp. 143–4). A royal order of 6 February 1925 granted the management of the newly created *Crédito Local* to the *Banco de Cataluña* (Solé, 1976; Cabana, 2003; González Ruiz and Matés, 2008).

The only public bank founded while Calvo Sotelo was minister was the *Banco Exterior de España* (Spanish Bank for Foreign Trade), established by royal decree on 12 August 1928. The Exterior would be managed by a consortium called *Crédito Nacional Peninsular y Americano* (Peninsular and American National Credit), where the *Banco de Cataluña* and the *Banco Central*, the two financial institutions that enthusiastically backed Calvo Sotelo's policies, were shareholders. Calvo Sotelo was also chairman of the *Central* for a few months in 1930 (Bécker, 1988; Tedde, 1993; Tortella, 2007, p. 219). The share capital of the Exterior was set at 150 million pesetas and its object was defined very broadly and put at the service of an ambitious 'neomercantilist program' (Tedde, 1993, p. 41), which included the state monopoly of export credit insurance through a company called *Crédito y Caución*. The Exterior took its first steps in the summer of 1929, a few months before the outbreak of the Great Depression, which caused a serious crisis in world trade, thus crippling the bank's activity. When the crises of the Cataluña and the Central took place during the Republican years, the Exterior was in serious danger (the Civil War, as we will see, served to rescue the Central and the Exterior).

A decree law of 9 April 1926 established that the registration and inspection of savings banks, which until then was ascribed to the Ministry of the Interior, would from then on depend of the Ministry of Labour; and a new rule was added, requiring, for the first time, a mandatory investment ratio: 50 per cent of deposits of savings banks should be invested in government securities (Titos, 1999, pp. 146–7). Previously, these banks had been submitted to very light regulation, which in fact, was limited to the seven articles of a very short law of 29 June 1880, which had recommended the collaboration of savings banks and *Montes de Piedad*, the creation of 'school savings accounts' in learning centres to encourage the virtue of saving, and had classified savings banks as 'charities', thus granting them tax benefits. In the 1920s, with savings banks' share in total bank deposits approaching 20 per cent (Appendix 10), politicians took advantage for the first time of their ambiguous legal status to impose mandatory investment ratios on them. The subsequent legal provisions – a royal decree of 21 November 1929 and the Statute of the General Popular Savings Banks of 14 March 1933 – merely confirmed this new trend of government control.

7.2 The gold question

During the First World War (1914–18), the belligerent countries were unable to maintain the currency convertibility required by the gold standard because monetary expansion undertaken to finance the war effort was inconsistent with the required ratios of specie reserve. With the cessation of hostilities, the reorientation of military industry to civilian purposes led to a short recession (the 'crisis of the armistice'), which was also accompanied by inflation. All these events were discussed at international conferences held in Brussels (1920) and Genoa (1922), where a return to the gold standard was seen as necessary to restore the economic balance. However, there were many difficulties. On the one hand, many economies had been strongly affected by the war and required a considerable reconstruction effort; on the other, gold production was insufficient to meet liquidity needs. Furthermore, price levels in many countries were much above those of the prewar era.

The solution was found in an agreement at the Genoa Conference, which allowed central banks to maintain reserves either in gold or in hard currencies issued by rich countries that would become 'centers of gold'. The idea was to establish what was called the 'gold exchange standard', with the primary goal of saving on precious metal, but inevitably distinguishing between 'key currencies' and 'peripheral currencies', the former belonging to those countries which maintained the convertibility of their banknotes into gold exclusively. This scheme gave a privileged and hegemonic position to the issuers of 'key currencies'. The United Kingdom and United States supported decisively the new standard and obtained the status of 'key currencies' for the pound sterling and the US dollar, respectively.

The Primo de Rivera dictatorship did not adopt the 'gold exchange standard', although the Bank of Spain had accumulated substantial reserves of the yellow metal, thanks to the export boom Spain enjoyed during the First World War. Improvements in internal and external peacekeeping strengthened the peseta by 1926, but the persistence of budget and balance of payments deficits and the reticence of foreign investors towards the nationalist policies of Calvo Sotelo soon caused the peseta to weaken (Figure 7.1). In particular, the creation of the *Compañía Arrendataria del Monopolio de*

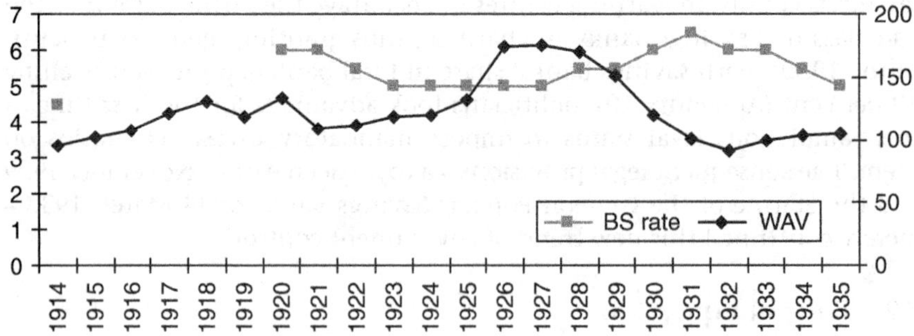

Figure 7.1 Weighted average value (WAV) of the peseta and discount rate of the Bank of Spain (BS rate), 1914–35 (the WAV is recorded on the right-hand side scale and the discount rate on the left-hand side scale)
Source: Martínez Méndez (1990).

Petróleos provoked the hostility of the big oil companies, which did their best to discredit the Spanish currency, dumping on the market the pesetas they received as indemnity for the expropriation of their assets.

The decline of the peseta in international markets worried the government, especially Calvo Sotelo. When the peseta's exchange rate went up he had boasted that this was proof of the dictatorship's success, so its fall now made him and his government look bad. On 25 June 1928 Calvo Sotelo established a *Comité Interventor de Cambios* (Committee for the Intervention of the Exchange Rate) to try to stop the downslide, something which provoked a long and heated debate in the press. The debate was marked by the intervention of Cambó, who was supported by the prestigious economist Antonio Flores de Lemus and by the French economist Charles Rist. Calvo Sotelo, following the example of Mussolini, was determined to defend a strong peseta, something which proved impossible, even with intervention in the exchange rate. He also wanted to restore full gold convertibility. In order to prepare the way, Calvo Sotelo summoned a committee, presided by Flores de Lemus, to study the problems involved in the adoption of the gold standard. He also asked Rist for a separate report. To Calvo Sotelo's discomfiture, the two economists believed that Spain should tackle budget deficits and stabilize the peseta before establishing a commitment to convertibility. In the end, the weakness of the peseta contributed to the fall of Calvo Sotelo and the dictatorship in January 1930 (Hernández Andreu, 1980; see the report of the Commission on the gold standard in Consejo Superior Bancario, 1929).

The dictatorship (*dictadura* in Spanish) was followed by the *dictablanda* (wordplay: in Spanish *dura* means *hard* and *blanda*, *soft*). The *Dictablanda* was devised as a transitional regime to prepare the country for return to democracy and it lasted until April 1931, when, in view of the outcome of municipal elections, the Second Republic was proclaimed. During the *Dictablanda* period two notorious 'errors' were made: 'Berenguer's error' (expression coined by the philosopher José Ortega y Gasset) and 'Argüelles' error' (named after the Minister of Finance Manuel Argüelles). The former expression referred to the inability of General Dámaso Berenguer, the head of the transitional regime, to restore constitutional order, and the latter expression referred to the excessive fiscal orthodoxy of a minister who sought to put an end to the public deficit with a sharp cut in public spending at a time when the Great Depression was spreading across the world (García Delgado, 1979). Manuel Argüelles was a monarchist banker with very orthodox views who wanted to return to balanced budgets, as Flores de Lemus and Rist had recommended; but this deflationary policy in the middle of the Great Depression brought stagnation, popular discontent and, in the end, the departure of Alfonso XIII into exile.

By the time the king left Spain and the Republic was proclaimed (14 April 1931) the international economic (and political) situation was deteriorating rapidly. In Britain the May and the Macmillan reports unveiled serious problems at the Treasury and the balance of payments in the spring and summer of 1931. Distrust in the pound ensued and caused massive capital withdrawals, which could not be stopped with interest rates rises. On 21 September 1931 the United Kingdom abandoned the gold standard, with the result of depreciation during the following seven months of about 40 per cent in the value of sterling against the dollar. Germany had abandoned de facto convertibility, and introduced exchange controls and deflationary policies to prevent the fall of the Deutsche mark. Chancellor Heinrich Brüning thought that with these measures he would be able to restrain capital flight, but he only caused a rise in the unemployment rate up to 30 per cent and desperation of the population who sought salvation in the Nazi programme of Adolf Hitler.

The influence of the pound was now reduced to the 'sterling area'. On 20 April 1933, as part of President Roosevelt's New Deal programme, the United States also abandoned the gold standard. The US dollar's exchange rate dropped; it depreciated about 60 per cent. Many countries in the Americas linked their currency to the US dollar forming a 'dollar area'. Lack of cohesion in the actions of the 'gold centers' was shown again in the failure of the World Economic Conference of London in June–July 1933.

After the flotation downwards of the pound and the dollar, France cherished the idea of imposing the hegemony of the franc through a 'gold bloc' (*bloc d'or*), which was established on 8 July 1933, five days after the failure of the London World Economic Conference. The adherents to the bloc were France, Belgium, Switzerland, Italy, the Netherlands and Poland, with Spain, Turkey, Latvia, Lithuania and Danzig as mere supporters. It can be argued, as it was then, that France was Spain's main trade partner and that this justified this country's support of the gold bloc, but certainly this alignment brought about a significant appreciation of the peseta. This probably was another error, but it must be remembered that the weakness of the peseta had contributed mightily to the discredit of the dictatorship. Since 1933 not only the weighted average nominal value of the peseta rose, but, because Spanish prices held up, the average in real terms increased in a greater proportion, so that the loss of competitiveness was very acute. Spain's situation was similar to that of the gold bloc countries, which saw economic difficulties aggravated by monetary orthodoxy. On 1 October 1936, the French franc abandoned gold convertibility; six days before France had promoted the signing of an agreement with Britain and the United States to try to keep exchange rate stability (Eichengreen, 1995, pp. 378–80). By that time, however, the Civil War raged in Spain.

7.3 The advantages of a lax monetary standard

The spring and summer of 1931 had dramatic overtones in most European countries. In Spain the drama was double, because, to the fearsome consequences of the economic crisis, those of a political crisis were added. The hesitating *Dictablanda*, after a year of dithering, had decided to call municipal elections as a first trial before elections to the Cortes. The poll took place on 12 April 1931 and the victory of the republicans in all the big cities was known by the 14th. As it was widely recognized that elections in small towns and rural districts were often subject to bossism and rigging, the results were considered as a clear victory of the left; spontaneous demonstrations took place in many cities and the king left the country to avoid a bloodbath. The Republic was proclaimed, and new, constituent parliamentary elections were immediately announced.

The economic effects of political transition were serious: 'The proclamation of the Republic had in itself caused a grave financial crisis in Spain. Wealthy Spaniards had immediately begun to transfer their capital to foreign banks, and the international financial community reacted skeptically to the new regime' (Jackson, 1967, p. 78). The dimensions of the capital flight were quite large. According to Martín Aceña (1984, pp. 615–17)

> All in all, between 30 March and 30 September demand and savings deposits decreased by about 1,300 million pesetas, which was equivalent to a sudden reduction of 20 per cent. The magnitude of the crisis can be better understood if we take into consideration that [the Spanish] percentage of reduction was greater than that experienced by American banks during the same period.

However, as has been often remarked, this was not followed by a series of bank failures, as happened in other countries, even though some institutions, such as the *Banco Central*, were in serious trouble. Only the middle-sized *Banco de Cataluña* was let to sink, and this for political reasons: it had been too friendly with the dictatorship (Cabana, 1965, 2003; Tortella and Palafox, 1983, pp. 52–6). This resilience of the Spanish banking system was due to two factors: first, the Bank of Spain, at the behest of the government, followed a Bagehotian policy of lending freely at high interest rates; and, second, the mechanism of automatic credits with public debt as collateral gave banks considerable leeway. The Bank of Spain abandoned its former reluctance to be lender of last resort, and, for example, early in July took the unprecedented step of rediscounting the Central's entire portfolio, with the pledge of all the bank's assets as guarantee. The government, meanwhile, had issued two decrees in May raising the fiduciary circulation ceiling, first to 5,200 million, then 6,000 million. Fiduciary circulation, which was at 4,815 million in April, reached a maximum of 5,469 in August. This was an unequivocal sign that both the Bank of Spain and the government had decided to follow a liberal lending policy. It obviously contributed to restore confidence (Tortella, 1999, pp. 174–6; Banco de España, 1934).

While monetary policy saved the day in 1931, other aspects of economic policy, including later monetary policies, were less fortunate. The overriding preoccupation of the successive republican governments was to prevent the fall of the exchange rate of the peseta; in the circumstances of the 1930s this was a serious error; let us not forget, however, that in this the Spanish government was not alone. Most countries were reluctant to abandon the gold standard, which implied fixed exchange rates; France, often Spain's model, was the outstanding example. Keynes' *General Theory* was not published until 1936, much too late for Spanish politicians to have grasped the message of countercyclical fiscal policies, neo-mercantilist commercial and exchange-rate measures, and the easy-money gospel.

The Republican Constitution of 1931 was orthodox in fiscal matters. This, however, did not prevent deficits in the budgetary liquidations of 1931–35: these deficits amounted to 0.2 per cent of GDP in 1931; 0.7 in 1932; 1.1 per cent in 1933; 1.6 per cent in 1934; and 0.9 per cent in 1935 (Calculated from data in Carreras and Tafunell, 2005). As is well known, in the three republican elections the vote swung widely, from the moderate left in 1932–33, to the moderate right in 1933–35, to the left in 1936. Fiscal policies swung also. The left veered towards higher expenditure, especially in education and public works, while the right made efforts to balance the budget. Conservative fiscal policy resulted in an increase in unemployment, which was an important element in the victory of the Popular Front in 1936. With the left in power in 1931–33, public investment returned to 1929 levels, offsetting to some extent the decline in private investment caused by the crisis. With the right, private investment recovered, but, due to falling public investment, in 1935 the overall investment level stood at 67 per cent of that reached in 1929 (Carreras, 1985).

Keeping in mind this performance of investment, the interest rate policy carried out by the republican governments after 1931 seems to have been inappropriate (a long series of nominal interest rates in Appendix 8). As shown in Table 7.1 and Figure 7.2, Spain enjoyed low real interest rates in 1930 and 1931, but not in subsequent years, when it refused to follow the policy of 'cheap money' that helped the British authorities to deal with the crisis. In 1931, the discount rate of the Bank of Spain rose from 6 to 6.5 percent when it finally decided to act as lender of last resort and to prevent the capital flight that accompanied the establishment of the Republic. From then on it would take four years to get a meagre 1.5 points of reduction in the discount rate of the Bank of Spain, while drastic 'cheap money' policies were implemented almost everywhere else. A law of 26 November 1931, sponsored by Indalecio Prieto, the socialist Finance Minister, had ordered that three members appointed by the government to represent the interests of the national economy should be added to the board of the Bank of Spain. The obsession with the peseta exchange rate, however, prevented these members to demand a lowering of the discount rate.

Table 7.1 Discount rates of central banks, in real terms, of a large sample of European countries, 1930–35 (percentages)

	1930	1931	1932	1933	1934	1935
Austria	14.75	14.73	4.44	8.73	2.34	4.25
Czechoslovakia	15.44	13.78	13.79	6.27	0.72	-0.55
France	15.71	17.05	14.66	7.11	7.49	5.08
Germany	13.93	17.84	18.79	6.85	–1.88	0.72
Italy	15.93	19.21	11.97	13.43	4.61	-5.73
Netherlands	15.21	17.25	15.98	5.94	2.50	3.17
Spain	5.73	5.24	8.39	10.04	3.80	4.46
Sweden	16.72	13.28	5.65	5.73	–4.07	–3.67
Switzerland	13.89	14.38	14.82	6.41	3.53	2.50
United Kingdom	15.42	16.43	5.60	2.00	–2.00	2.00

Source: García Ruiz (1993) p. 609.

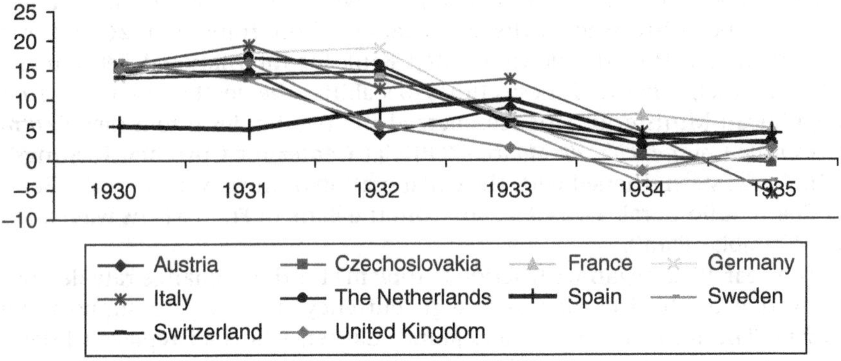

Figure 7.2 Discount rates of the central banks, in real terms, of a large sample of European countries, 1930–35 (percentages)
Source: Table 7.1.

Economía Española, official organ of the *Unión Económica* (Economic Union, the main employers' organization during the Second Republic), repeatedly complained about the high interest rates and the credit rationing practised by banks. Its director, Mariano Marfil, pointed out in December 1933 that 'the demand of trade and industry, for several years, has been the reduction of the discount rate, because few countries in the world have interest rates as high as ours' (*Economía Española*, 19, 1934). In 1936, an influential economist of the time, Josep A. Vandellós, lamented that many employers had been in great difficulties due to the lack of affordable credit (Vandellós, 1936). The main stumbling block for this was the Bank of Spain, whose Research Department was initially opposed to following the path of cheap money taken by the United Kingdom (Banco de España, 1932) and only began to recognize the negative impact of high rates on economic recovery in May 1935 (Banco de España, 1935). Evidence on the scarcity of loanable funds, however, is contradictory: while business circles moaned about lack of funds, banks complained about the trouble they had to find 'adequate and profitable employment' for their resources due to 'the patent inactivity of industry, commerce, and business in general'. Whether the blame should fall on supply or on demand, therefore, is a moot question (Tortella and Palafox, 1983, p. 51).

What is clear, nevertheless, is that Spanish governments carried out an active policy of sustaining the peseta exchange rate. The Committee for the Intervention of the Rates of Exchange (1928) of the dictatorship gave way during the *Dictablanda* to not one, but two regulatory bodies: the *Centro Regulador de Operaciones de Cambio* (Center for the Regulation of Exchange Operations) and the *Centro Oficial de Contratación de Moneda* (Official Center for Currency Dealings). Pierre Quesnay, who was a disciple of Charles Rist, had been involved in the stabilization of the franc in 1926 and was general manager of the newly created Bank for International Settlements (BIS) in Basel, supported these efforts to stabilize the peseta. Prieto, the first Republican Minister of Finance, merged the two bodies into a new *Centro Oficial de Contratación de Moneda* (Official Center for Currency Dealings), which was strengthened with the collaboration of the governor of the Bank of Spain, Julio Carabias, and a loan from the Bank of France (this was called the 'Carabias Plan').

The year 1932 began with serious problems for the exchange rate defense body due to the lack of the foreign currency necessary to support the peseta. The minister of finance, Jaume Carner, who had replaced Prieto, was forced to let the peseta float, as had been done sometimes in the past when resources were also scarce. Carner's forecast was that the peseta would collapse, but the opposite happened: the peseta stopped falling against the French franc and the US dollar (its exchange rate had gone up against sterling since September 1931). This unexpected stabilization was explained as the result of recent intervention efforts and of the favourable evolution of the balance of payments (Sardà, 1936; Vandellós, 1936).

This *de facto* stabilization of the peseta against the French franc lasted until the outbreak of the Civil War. Capital inflows in 1934 and 1935 contributed to maintain this situation. The conclusion of all this is that the exchange rate policy of the Second Republic since the spring of 1932 prevented the adoption of more robust countercyclical policies. In the months of the Popular Front there was some hope of change in this mistaken course – the Research Department of the Bank of Spain, always cautious, even said in

April 1936 that 'it would be necessary to make a radical devaluation' (Banco de España, 1931–36) – yet nothing was done about it. One could say that while the freedom from the 'golden fetters' saved the day in 1931, Spain showed a longing for these fetters in defending its exchange rate and so blindly following the policies of the gold bloc from 1932 on.

According to Joan Sardà, mistakes in monetary policy were 'one of the contributing factors to the social unrest of the time and perhaps of the civil war of 1936' (Sardà, 1987 [1970], p. 424). Angel Viñas has said that the Republic was unable to escape from the myth cultivated by the dictatorship of a strong peseta, being unaware of the negative consequences that derived from such policy during the Depression (Viñas *et al.*, 1979, I, p. 120). Martín Aceña recognizes that excessive appreciation of the peseta was 'probably the biggest mistake of the republican authorities', but he does not share the view that it entailed a highly restrictive monetary policy (Martín Aceña, 1984, pp. 295–306). His data show that, after the severe crisis of the spring–summer of 1931, the money supply recovered (on the evolution of the money supply, see Appendix 7). But it did so at a slow pace that was insufficient to pull the economy out of stagnation. If we include in the estimation of the money supply the deposits of foreign banks operating in Spain, which is more correct than leaving them out, the 1931 fall in the amount of money in circulation is shown to have been deeper and its recovery much slower from 1932 to 1934 (Table 7.2). It is quite obvious that Spanish monetary policy in those years converged with the French, which has been repeatedly criticized for its procyclical character since the classical work by Paul Einzig (1935). It is true that France broke with monetary discipline in the night from 25 to 26 September 1936, and that this was experienced by many as the liberation from an economic burden, as had happened previously in other gold bloc countries. But by then it was too late for Spain.

Sardà's thesis about the influence of monetary policy on the outbreak of the Civil War is somewhat exaggerated, as it seems clear that there were other more important factors, such as social violence, political polarization (in 1933, the son of General Primo de Rivera created *Falange Española* as

Table 7.2 Rate of growth of money supply (M3), including and not including foreign bank deposits, 1923–34 (percentages)

	1923	1924	1925	1926	1927	1928	1929	1930	1931	1932	1933	1934
Without foreign banks	4.1	−1.2	0.9	−0.9	6.3	6.7	7.1	6.5	−2.5	0.9	2.2	3.1
With foreign banks	2.9	−1.3	0.6	−0.4	7.0	5.4	9.4	5.7	−3.6	0.1	1.6	1.8

Source: García Ruiz (2006), p. 640.

a political party inspired by Italian fascism), numerous conspiracies, the controversy over the autonomy of Catalonia, the Basque Country and Galicia, or the polemical land reform. Moreover, unlike other countries such as the United States or Germany, where the banking crisis was a key factor in the Great Depression, the Spanish banking system as a whole avoided failure: the worst it experienced was a contraction in profits. The more affected institutions were those banks that had been linked to the dictatorship of Primo de Rivera (Cataluña, Central, Exterior), where political factors played a crucial role. Central and Exterior survived the hostility of left-wing republican leaders and were saved from bankruptcy by the Civil War (Tortella, 2001, 2004).

8
Banking under Franco

8.1 The economic consequences of war

The programme of the Popular Front, winner in the elections of February 1936, was not revolutionary in banking matters, because the liberal republicans in the coalition never accepted the state control of banks proposed by the working-class parties. In any case, the programme had little time to be applied as the Civil War broke out only months later, on 18 July. At that time, there were 2,013 banking offices in Spain (including head offices) of which 25 belonged to foreign banks. Only 35 per cent of the offices and 25 per cent of the employees were located in Franco's 'national zone' from the beginning, because the coup was more successful in rural than in urban areas. The bankers were not in the plot (with the exception of Juan March, a controversial banker from Mallorca), but the 'nationalists' soon managed to gain their trust: in October 1936, the Republican government turned the CSB into an appendage of the Ministry of Finance, while in the 'national' zone the operations of a *Comité Nacional de la Banca Privada* (National Committee of the Private Banks, since 1938 called *Comité Central de la Banca Española*, the denomination of the prewar bankers' association), were subject to close supervision, although the bankers were given 'an acceptable margin for their initiative' (Sánchez Asiaín, 2012, pp. 455–8).

The Civil War led to the breakup of the monetary union achieved in 1868. From 12 November 1936 all banknotes that were not stamped by them were declared invalid by the nationalists and, since the spring of 1937, only 'nationalist' banknotes circulated in that zone. Soon, the 'nationalist' peseta strengthened its exchange rate relative to the 'republican' peseta, because the republican side was plunged into monetary and productive chaos. Whereas the business of banking in the republican zone was geared towards financing current expenditure (salaries), the banks in the national zone could, since August 1937, invest in the so-called National Services (organizations in charge of the requisition of some crops, such as wheat, cotton and almonds, in order to distribute food products through rationing schemes), although they had to accept low interest rates and zero charges (Sánchez Asiaín, 2012, pp. 476–88). These patterns of investment banking help to explain the inflation differential between the two sides: from the beginning of the war to its end prices in the 'national' zone multiplied by 1.4, while in the republican zone they multiplied by more than 15 (Martín Aceña, 1994).

The war ended on 1 April 1939 and the process of restoration of the monetary union of the country began with the *Ley de Desbloqueo* (Monetary Unfreezing Act) of 7 December 1939, which was completed with a second *Desbloqueo* law of 13 March 1942 that unified the two Banks of Spain that had appeared, one in each zone (the 'nationalist' Bank had been created in Burgos, the capital of the Franco side; the 'republican' Bank was the old Madrid headquarters) into one single unit: the new Bank of Spain. The Franco dictatorship faced the problem of the coexistence of republican pesetas – 'red pesetas', as they were called – with 'national pesetas' in the same markets. In the case of the banknotes issued by the republicans since the outbreak of hostilities, the solution was simple and radical: their character of legal tender was denied and so their holders were the victims of a punitive forfeiture. For bank accounts, the so-called Larraz Plan was implemented. It was due to the Minister of Finance José Larraz. This plan established a scale of depreciation depending on the date of the operation. In spite of some inevitable arbitrary aspects, the Larraz Plan has been generally considered as fair enough, or at least, as a lesser evil; its fiercer opponents were the hardliners of the new regime who wanted not peace but victory after the war and clamoured for the confiscation of republican bank deposits (Sardà, 1987 [1970]; Martín Aceña, 1994; Larraz, 2006, Ch. 6).

The Civil War victors tried to magnify the number of victims and the destruction that occurred during the war, in their search for a culprit for the poor performance of the Spanish economy during the first 15 years of the Franco regime. Gabriel Jackson revised the death toll downwards, so that there were, in his opinion, no more than 125,000 killed in the battlefield, while 10,000 people fell in air raids, 50,000 died of disease and malnutrition, 20,000 for reprisals in the republican zone and a maximum of 200,000 for executions in the nationalist zone between 1936 and 1944 (Jackson, 1976, p. 14). The latest available data up the republican repression to 50,000 victims, while the Franquist repression (war and postwar) would drop to 150,000 (Juliá, 1999, p. 410), or even to 130,000, according to more recent research (Espinosa, 2010, p. 78). Be it as it may, there was huge loss of human capital for the Spanish economy, to which must be added the fall due to non-fatal victims and exiles (approximately 220,000 people in a permanent way, according to Barona, 2011, p. 161; for an estimate of the loss of human capital, Núñez, 2003, pp. 40–53).

As for the destruction caused to agriculture, a report by the *Servicio de Recuperación Agrícola* (Office for Agricultural Recovery) informed just after the war about a loss of 1,350 million pesetas, which can not be considered catastrophic because these were crops which could easily recuperate and such was the case of livestock (Barciela, 1987). In June 1940, the director general of devastated regions provided data on damage to urban property, based on the 46,000 files on case studies that had been conducted for the purpose, stating: 'The amount of damage according to all the files under examination is about 1 per cent of the total value of the Spanish urban wealth; an amount, you see, not too alarming' (Moreno, 1940, p. 13). A new public bank, the *Instituto de Crédito para la Reconstrucción Nacional* (Institute of Credit for the National Reconstruction) granted 35 million pesetas in 20-year loans and 3 per cent of interest to address this problem. This bank was reorganized in 1962 and renamed *Banco de Crédito a la Construcción* (Bank of Credit for Construction).

The losses of industrial equipment were very moderate, due to the fact that factories were usually in the outskirts of towns where battles and bombardments were less intense, to the inaccuracy of aerial bombardment, and to the attitude of the authorities on both sides, opposed to the burning and looting of factories (Catalan, 1995, pp. 41–59). Companies were able to adapt to the situation with remarkable agility and, after initial collapse, industrial profits (in constant pesetas) in 1939 were on a par with those of 1935 (Tafunell, 1998). The biggest losses were concentrated in infrastructure and transport equipment. The war severely affected railway transportation (30 per cent of locomotives, 60 per cent of passenger cars and 40 per cent of freight wagons were destroyed), shipping (with a loss of capacity of 22 per cent), the state car fleet and the communications network. In this Spain was not different from countries involved in the Second World War (Catalan, 1995, pp. 44–5).

The so-called New State of Franco exacerbated the protectionist and nationalist orientation of the previous regimes. It proclaimed autarky as its ultimate aim and its policies were imbued with heavy doses of authoritarian interventionism. The ultimate expression of this policy was the creation of the *Instituto Nacional de Industria* (INI, National Institute for the Industry) in 1941 (San Román, 1999). Although there is still some confusion about macroeconomic figures, as one would expect in this dark period of Spanish history, the overall economic result of this autarkic phase of Francoism (1939–59) is clear: it was a complete failure. Estimates of the yearly index of industrial production and the Europe-wide comparative studies confirm that it was a long and black parenthesis in the history of Spanish industrialization, with discrimination against consumer goods in favour of capital goods, something that aggravated the suffering of the population (Morellá, 1992) without visibly improving productivity. The long postwar stagnation did not tally at all with what happened contemporaneously in Europe, where reconstruction was rapid, particularly after 1948, when the Marshall Plan was put into effect; Spain, due to the dictatorial nature of its political regime, was left out of the Marshall Plan.

8.2 Suffocating under Fascism: the banking law of 1946

Postwar banking legislation and policy followed the same interventionist trend as the rest of government policy. A series of legal measures tried to bring about the normalization of postwar banking. Among these there were some decrees severely restricting the possibilities of founding new banks and limiting the freedom of action of those in existence (on the number of banks, see Appendix 6). For instance, a decree of 17 May 1940 expressly prohibited the opening or relocation of new banks, branches and agencies. It was the consecration of the *status quo* principle in banking, which, however, would soon be relaxed in its practical application for large institutions. The deputy governor of the Bank of Spain, Luis Sáez de Ibarra, in 1954 justified the exceptions simply by saying that they had made possible 'the economic growth, driven by the fruitful peace that the country has been enjoying' (Sáez de Ibarra, 1954, p. 24). The new legal framework was completed by establishing 'banking secrecy' in the tax reform of 16 December 1940, which permitted the non-collaboration of the banks in the detection of fiscal fraud, and establishing a limit to the distribution of dividends (decree of 31 December 1941). The limitation of banking dividends had two purposes: one, to avoid an image of rich shareholders in an impoverished country; and two, to prevent bank shares to crowd out public debt bonds in financial markets. The banks responded to this by means of frequent share splits.

The Cambó Banking Act of 1921 had a deadline of 25 years. A new law was needed, and it was approved on the very final day of the deadline. The Banking Law of 31 December 1946 (often called the Benjumea Law, because the Finance Minister at the time was the Andalusian engineer Joaquín Benjumea) had posed problems and debates, because the opinions of the Franco government and of the ruling elite were divided on the topic of banking. The Falangists demanded nationalization, as their programme announced. The monarchists and conservatives, instead, took a less extreme view. A cautious liberal economist, Luis Olariaga, a university professor and distinguished Bank of Spain economist and board member, wrote that strong state intervention in the Spanish banking sector was not justified because banks had sailed through the Great Depression virtually unscathed (on Olariaga, see Cepeda, 2003). Even totalitarian governments, such as those of Germany or Italy, although putting the reins of monetary policy in the hands of the state, did not nationalize banks, nor did they rule over day-to-day operations of their central or commercial banks (Olariaga, 1989, pp. 122, 226; see also his *Informe sobre la necesidad y condiciones de una reforma bancaria en España* or *Report on the Necessity and Conditions of a Bank Reform in Spain*, dated 1942, in folder 18549 of the Spanish Ministry of Finance Archives).

In the end, the liberal–conservatives won the day. Neither the Bank of Spain nor the private banks were nationalized; the state, however, kept considerable authority and regulatory power in its hands. The main traits of the law were as follows: (i) the control over the Bank of Spain by the Ministry of Finance was reinforced; (ii) the Bank of Spain was directed to abstain from dealing directly with the public in commercial operations, one more step towards making it a bank of banks; (iii) the separation between the internal and external aspects of monetary policy was accentuated, and the latter was entrusted to the *Instituto Español de Moneda Extranjera* (IEME, Spanish Institute of Foreign Currency), created on 25 August 1939 as a branch of the Ministry of Commerce (Martínez Ruiz, 2000); (iv) there was almost total renunciation to monetary instruments as a means of economic policy: interest rates were kept low and unchanging; (v) the oligopolistic structure of the banking sector was respected; (vi) practically all aspects of the structure and operations of banks, including interest rates, were tightly regulated (Sardà, 1987 [1970]).

In general, the Benjumea Act was in line with the past: the preamble said that 'no fundamental innovation' was intended. The law did not even nationalize the Bank of Spain, as many expected, placing it among the 8 central banks in the world, out of a total of 57, that remained totally private in the late 1940s (Kriz, 1948). Public banks maintained their prewar status and the self-regulatory body of private banks, the CSB, was restored.

When the bill was discussed in Parliament, Franco had distanced himself from the totalitarian regimes defeated in the Second World War. Meanwhile, however, 'financial repression', that is, steady government intervention in the financial systems, had spread throughout the world (Sayers, 1962), so that private banks still had much to fear. The bill, which was not very interventionist, received six amendments in the parliamentary debate, two of which were inspired by radical Falangist principles. The Falangists criticized the restoration of the CSB, 'a classist body similar to an employers' association', and the similarity of the bill to the Cambó Act, something which was, according to the amendment, equivalent to 'prejudging the goodness of the [liberal] system of that time'. Three other amendments went against the only items in the project that the banks considered harmful because they empowered the Minister of Finance to establish compulsory reserves by private banks in the Bank of Spain for up to 20 per cent of deposits. The amendments warned against the 'serious alarm' that this could cause to the public and the futility of such reserves against inflation as long as the automatic granting of credits against the pledging of public funds would be kept; this in practice meant the indirect monetization of the public debt, something the government was interested in. The last of the six amendments opposed the 'humiliation' that would be inflicted upon the saving banks by subjecting them to some extent to the CSB (Spanish Ministry of Finance Archives, folder 59252).

The Benjumea Act incorporated the four non-Falangist amendments, something which caused great anger in the *Movimiento Nacional*, the official party which had been created on the basis of *Falange Española*. According to the

Falangists, not to have nationalized the Bank of Spain and the public banks, and not to have established mandatory coefficients to regulate liquidity or investment by private banks, as had been imposed upon savings banks since 1926, was unacceptable. They also said that the Benjumea Act was in open contradiction with the 'social orientation' of the New State for assuring high profits to banks whose number was limited by law (Paris Eguilaz, 1947). By contrast, liberal writers were pleased with the law, in particular with the removal of the Bank of Spain from commercial banking operations, which opened new horizons for private banking (Olariaga, 1946). Naturally, the bankers were also satisfied, and stated that institutions had been reinforced without resorting to harsh, detailed, and completely unnecessary regulations (Ridruejo, 1954). But on one thing all factions agreed: foreign banks should be subjected to the principle of international reciprocity and to the requirement of guarantees in the form of deposits with the Bank of Spain. To put an end to what a union boss called 'a picture of colonial atmosphere' (Sanz, 1948, p. 166), all applauded the 'voluntary nationalization' process under a law of 11 July 1941. 'Voluntary nationalization' meant the free transfer of the activity from a foreign bank to a national bank with government support. In practice it would entail the withdrawal of the foreign bank from the Spanish market. This move for nationalization failed because some foreign banks (Bank of London and South America, *Crédit Lyonnais, Société Générale de Banque, Banca Nazionale del Lavoro*) were aware that if they abandoned the Spanish market at that moment it would be very difficult to come back. In any case, the impact of the Great Depression and the wars had made their market share almost negligible (García Ruiz, 2001).

In spite of what may appear as some measure of harmony, there was no mutual current of sympathy between the dictatorship of General Franco and the banks. A totalitarian regime was hardly compatible with bankers who were inspired by liberalism (García Ruiz and Tortella, 2003; Tortella and García Ruiz, 2004). What happened in 1946 should be understood as a tacit agreement between the political and the economic powers to respect each other as long as the first received the necessary cooperation from the second. The banks did cooperate. The law of 26 December 1958 on 'official institutions for medium and long term credit', which authorized the Minister of Finance to set mandatory investment coefficients in public funds, was a norm that only recognized *de iure* a *de facto* situation. Shortly after the enactment of the Benjumea Act, in a circular letter of 6 November 1947, Luis Sáez de Ibarra, former head of the *Dirección General de Banca y Bolsa* (DGBB, General Directorate of Banks and the Stock Exchange) (1941–46), deputy governor of the Bank of Spain (1947–56) and, as such, president of the CSB, invited banks to follow 'faithfully the Spanish banking tradition regarding the possession of a strong provision of public funds'. Sáez recommended that national and regional banks should invest 45 per cent of their deposits in public funds and local banks up to 50 per cent. This circular

Table 8.1 Weight of public debt in Spanish bank portfolios, 1920–59

	Public debt in portfolio/ Total public debt (%)	Pledged amount/ Total public debt (%)		Public debt in portfolio/ Total public debt (%)	Pledged amount/ Total public debt (%)
1920	7.7[a]	4.5	1945	Na	3.7
1925	7.7[a]	9.1	1950	31.1	17.3
1930	11.9	6.5	1955	37.9	14.4
1934	14.4	5.6	1959	43.8	23.3[b]
1941	26.0	4.9			

[a] 1922; [b] 1958.
Source: Ministerio de Hacienda (1961), pp. 5–8.

letter ended with a warning, or rather, a veiled threat: the Bank of Spain would monitor compliance to these 'suggestions' and take it into account when the time came to aid financial institutions in case of need (Spanish Ministry of Finance Archives, folder 19954).

The Sáez de Ibarra's 'recommendation' would be repeated in 1950, with the explicit threat of a reduction of the rediscount limits in the Bank of Spain to those institutions that failed to reach the 45 per cent objective in the coming months, because this policy was practised 'in all modern states that are undergoing a stage where big public spending or large economic investments are convenient or needed' (Spanish Ministry of Finance Archives, folder 19961). Thus, it is not surprising that, in the late 1950s, the share of public funds in bank portfolios began to be overwhelming. With large masses of public debt in their portfolios, banks did not hesitate to use their right to pledge, automatically and without restriction, those bonds in the Bank of Spain, thereby aggravating the problem of inflation (Table 8.1). In view of this, the law of 26 December 1958, inspired in more liberal and market-minded principles than prevailed in the 1940s, eliminated the more than 40-years-old agreement on automatic pledging as a liquidity facility, replacing it with wider use of the rediscount lines, a more orthodox mechanism that put an end to the indirect monetization of the budget deficit.

8.3 Gradual recovery and runaway inflation: the role of the bank oligopoly

The end of the civil war and the beginnings of official autarky coincided with the outbreak of hostilities of Second World War, which might suggest that autarky was imposed on Franco by international circumstances. But the thesis that economic isolation was consistent with the principles of the New State has been proved long time ago (Viñas *et al.*, 1979). Autarky brought the end of the process of moderate but sustained growth, which had been recorded in Spain during the early decades of the twentieth century; it also brought about, in consequence, the widening of the distance between Spain and the more developed European countries (Carreras, 1990). However, we should distinguish the 1950s from the 1940s, as the average annual growth rates of industrial production accelerated progressively during those years at the following rates: 0.8 per cent in 1940–45; 3.6 per cent in 1945–50; 7.7 per cent in 1950–55; and 8.2 per cent in 1955–58 (Morellá, 1992). The support that the United States gave to the Franco regime in 1950–53, to take advantage of the geostrategic possibilities of Spain in the Cold War, helps us to understand these figures: the sixth Franco government, formed in July 1951, prompted the shift to a model with higher doses of economic rationality, initiating what has been called the 'hinge decade', an intermediate step between the autarkic 1940s and the relative openness of the 1960s (García Delgado, 1987).

For the Spanish economy as a whole, this 'hinge decade' recorded average yearly growth in per capita GDP at market (constant) prices of about 5 per cent, much higher than the rates recorded in the 1940s, which were below 2 per cent (Tortella and Garcia Ruiz, 2012, p. 49). The acceleration of growth in the 1950s was not accompanied by higher inflation, just the opposite: the average inflation rate fell from 12.2 per cent in the 1940s to 5.5 per cent in the 1950s (Appendix 5). In any case, the growth of prices was a constant concern during the early Francoism and research has insisted on the contribution of the banking oligopoly to aggravating this problem. According to this literature, it was in the interest of the largest banks to eliminate competition, not only ensuring a highly rewarding financial margin thereby, but also causing undesirable social effects such as charging higher prices for credit and thus boosting inflation (Muñoz, 1969; Pérez, 1997).

According to this view, the banking oligopoly had two key strategies: (i) cross-shareholdings and cross-directorships among banks and between banks and the largest Spanish companies; (ii) cartelization (market sharing, price agreements). These strategies are almost a necessary consequence of the practice of mixed banking. On the topic of the first of these strategies several problems arise, however. The presence of cross-directorships is often misleading because, as Rafael Termes, a distinguished banker in the 1970s and 1980s, wrote, the Board of Directors knows what happened in the past, the Executive Committee knows what is happening now, but only the very top management (chairman, CEO, general managers) know what is most important: what shall happen in the future (Termes, 1991, II, p. 1684). Business history shows again and again how dangerous it is to draw conclusions from quantitative studies that are not sufficiently critical of their sources. Furthermore, to pillory the banks for promoting and holding shares of industrial firms is to ignore the economic theory that supports the role of mixed or universal banking in accelerating growth in underdeveloped economies without solid entrepreneurial traditions (Gerschenkron, 1962;

Cameron, 1967; Tortella and Núñez, 2011, pp. 491–3). Moreover, when in 1963 the Bank of Spain began to request information from banks on credit to their subsidiaries, it turned out that the volume of this credit was not very high: it was around 4 per cent of total credit in national banks; 3.5 per cent in regional banks; and 3 per cent in local banks (Spanish Ministry of Finance Archives, folder 29578). Spanish banks were never as universal as German banks, which are the model for this type of banking (Martín Aceña and Pons, 1994).

About cartelization, the available studies show that the cartel agreements were not strictly respected, so it can be said that during the Franco dictatorship there was more competition among banks, especially in the market for deposits, than has been thought (Garcia Ruiz, 2002). State intervention in interest rates stems from a law of 27 August 1938 (although there were some precedents in earlier legislation), which put this and all the other aspects of credit policy under the command of the Ministry of Finance. On 25 November 1938, a government order fixed maximum rates for bank and savings bank deposits, while the commission rates adopted on 15 January 1936 were kept untouched. The commission charges were the only element of the cost of banking operations that had previously received (since 1927) systematic regulation by the state. The order of 1938 was privately qualified as 'ominous' by Pablo Garnica Echevarría, chairman of Banesto and of the *Comité Central de la Banca Española* (García Ruiz, 2002, p. 367).

After the war, the three largest Madrid banks (Hispano, Banesto, Central) joined the three largest banks from the Basque Country (Bilbao, Vizcaya, Guipuzcoano) and three banks from the East Coast (*Internacional de Industria y Comercio*, Valencia, Castellón) to sign an agreement on passive (maximum) and active (minimum) interest rates and charges that would take effect on 1 January 1941. The Ministry of Finance was informed of the agreement, and considered it acceptable, except for proposing the creation of a private court to punish the violations of the rules. The *Comité Central de la Banca Española* was successfully involved in making the *arreglo* (arrangement, agreement) known and, on 19 February 1941, it was signed by 32 banks (out of 114 registered) in its own headquarters. In case of non-compliance the culprit would not receive a penalty, but only a warning (private or public, depending on the seriousness of the matter). On 22 March 1941, the final version of the *Arreglo moderador de la competencia bancaria* (Arrangement to Moderate Banking Competition) was passed, although without the seal of approval of the DGBB. Therefore, the *Arreglo* would simply be a private pact among the signatories.

On 3 September 1941, Luis Sáez de Ibarra was appointed director general of the DGBB. During his tenure in the Ministry of Finance (1941–6), not wanting to offend his predecessor, he did nothing to officially endorse the *arreglos*, but as deputy governor of the Bank of Spain (1947–56) he looked eagerly for a new agreement that should be more comprehensive and more punitive to the violators. On 19 November 1949 such an agreement was signed under the name of *Acuerdo interbancario sobre intereses de cuentas pasivas* (Interbank Agreement on Passive Interest Rates). Sáez himself put his signature on the document, which was publicized in specialized magazines such as *España Económica y Financiera*. The deputy governor would monitor compliance, while at the same time he was pressuring for the purchase of public funds by private banks, as we have seen. The vast majority of banks adhered to the agreement. They also adhered, in 30 June 1952, to another agreement called *Ordenación reguladora de condiciones bancarias* (Regulatory Arrangement of Banking Conditions), comprising passive and active interest rates which was again an initiative by Sáez de Ibarra who at the time was vice president of the CSB. This initiative was later sponsored by the DGBB, which would form part of the body in charge of punishing the breaches to the *Ordenación*. It is obvious that Sáez de Ibarra was a central figure in the relationship between the banks and the authorities during the early Francoism.

Nevertheless, interbank agreements so painstakingly achieved were a failure in practice. This was acknowledged by the *Anteproyecto de reglamentación bancaria* (Draft on Banking Regulation) submitted in January 1960 by the bankers Ignacio Villalonga (Central) and Luis Usera (Hispano): 'The intense competition in banking has resulted in part in the granting of special interest rates to checking accounts, savings accounts and time deposits [....] All those covenants [the *arreglos*] were instruments of noble purposes, but they were broken frequently' (García Ruiz, 2002, pp. 375–6). Villalonga and Usera admitted that some accounts had received up to ten times the maximum agreed interest rates. From the *Anteproyecto* came out the *Convenio de Condiciones Bancarias* (Bank Terms Convention), which was adopted in February 1960 under the 'pressing requirements' of the DGBB. The *Convenio* had 27 rules, of which the following are noteworthy: the first, which states that the document should be of a 'strictly reserved character' and would be put under the custody of the CSB; the third, which set maximum interest rates for deposits of all types and fixed maturities for time deposits; the fourth, which established minimum interest rates and charges for discounts and loans; the fifth, which created private courts for conflicts in applying banking regulation; the nineteenth, which proposed secret polling with the aid of white and black balls to determine the guilt of those accused of breach of faith; the twenty-second, which set as penalties fines, investments in public funds, reduction of the rediscount limits, cuts in dividends to be distributed, and the application of some other punition; and the twenty-seventh, which abolished the private courts that were supposed to control the application of the *Ordenación* of 1952 (García Ruiz, 2002, p. 376).

In sum, it is difficult to attribute to the banking oligopoly a relevant role in causing the inflationary pressures of the 1940s and 1950s, as the oligopolistic agreements, attributable largely to the government's initiative, failed to be consistently applied. The causes of inflation were rather the general application of the autarkic model (1940s) or the semi-autarkic one (1950s), which dominated economic policy until the 1959 Stabilisation Plan.

8.4 Sharp reversal: the stabilization plan of 1959

After a new banking law was adopted in April 1962, Luis Olariaga wrote that banks could not be accused of provoking inflation, because if they had created an excessive volume of means of payment it was due 'solely to the need to serve the economic policy of the government agencies' (*Estabilización monetaria y progreso de la economía española*, August 1962, a text preserved in the Spanish Ministry of Finance Archives, folder 17527). Olariaga was right. The 'financial repression' of the early Francoism had all the components to produce inflation: banking *status quo* (or *numerus clausus*), control of interest rates, investment channelled by the government, reliance on public banking, compulsory purchase of public debt and external capital controls (Shaw, 1973; McKinnon, 1973; Reinhart and Sbrancia, 2011). Therefore, the responsibility for inflation mostly fell on economic policy.

Mandatory bank investments were channelled by the state towards the acquisition of public funds, but there had also been forced loans. A law of 17 July 1946 ordered Spanish banks, banking houses and savings banks to put at the disposal of the *Servicio Nacional de Crédito Agrícola*, for improvements on farms, up to 1,000 million pesetas, for which they would be rewarded with a meagre interest rate of 2 per cent, when individual farmers would pay 3.5 per cent and farmer associations, 2.5 per cent (the requested figure rose to 2,500 million in 1954 and 4,000 million in 1956). To this credit line an annual contract with the *Servicio Nacional del Trigo* (SNT, National Wheat Agency, created by a decree of 23 August 1937, which was supposed to prevent fluctuations in price and supply, but whose effect was scarcity and black market) was added, which also yielded low interest rates (and no commissions for the first ten years). A law of 22 December 1949 added another forced loan for 100 million pesetas, this one bound for the *Caja Central del Crédito Marítimo y Pesquero*, a lifeless institution for lack of resources since its founding in 1919; in 1952, the Ministry of Labour (traditionally dominated by the Falangists) wanted to add another forced loan of 500 million to facilitate the transition from steam to diesel in the propulsion of ships, but failed in the face of firm opposition by bankers (Spanish Ministry of Finance Archives, folder 19959). More successful was the *Instituto de Crédito para la Reconstrucción Nacional*, which a little earlier, by a law of 15 July 1952, got 700 million from bankers for poor tenants who wanted to purchase the houses where they lived. To these figures, 150 million would be added for the *Caja Central de Crédito Marítimo y Pesquero* by a decree law of 11 September 1953 (expandable to 250 under certain circumstances).

Table 8.2 Share of financial institutions in combined bank deposits in four Western European countries, 1960

	Spain		Germany		France		Italy	
	Number	Share (%)	Number	Share (%)	Number	Share (%)	Number	Share (%)
Central bank	1	1.7	1	0.2	1	1.2	1	0.5
Commercial banks	108	73.2	337	32.6	384	45.1	156	51.0
Savings banks	84	23.5	867	41.5	584	31.9	89	19.4
Postal savings Banks	1	1.7	15	4.2	1	12.5	1	19.2
Others	0	0.0	2.555	21.6	3.793	9.3	223	9.9

Source: Ministerio de Hacienda (1961). Figures differ slightly from those in the Appendix.

Under pressure from bankers, an order of 11 November 1949 allowed that the securities that served as instruments for agricultural credit could be discounted at the Bank of Spain, a measure which opened the door for turning these loans into a factor as inflationary as the automatic pledging of public funds. But again the main price demanded by banks to the state for their support was their hegemony in the financial system (Table 8.2). The Ministry of Finance, dominated by people trained in economics, was always willing to concede that hegemony, while the Ministry of Labour, the fortress of Falangist thought, made every effort to erode the power of private banks in favour of savings banks or to obtain (unsuccessfully) that mutual credit institutions should grant 'labour credits' to 'give workers a chance to avoid usury' (Spanish Ministry of Finance Archives, folder 19959). When in 1960 the *Ordenanza Postal* (Postal Regulation) vested the post offices with banking functions, banks demanded that those functions be reduced to the 'minimum necessary', under the threat of filing an appeal in court (Spanish Ministry of Finance Archives, folder 19965).

Finally, on 21 July 1959, a momentous decree law was issued; commonly known as the *Stabilization and Liberalization Plan,* it sought an 'economic rearrangement' based on the following: (i) budget and price stabilization through higher taxes and credit restrictions in order to reduce the public deficit; (ii) progressive liberalization of imports and control of monopolistic practices in the domestic market; (iii) a favourable attitude towards foreign investment, which had been subjected to severe restrictions up to then; (iv) convertibility of the peseta within the Bretton Woods framework after sharp devaluation and currency market regulation. The authorities expected that these measures would produce the 'internal and external stability of [the Spanish] economy, the equilibrium of the balance of payments, the strengthening of trust in our currency and, in sum, the normalization of our economic life'. The text was submitted to Parliament by the Minister of Commerce Alberto Ullastres, and was immediately supported by leading economists as Joan Sardà, Manuel Varela or Enrique Fuentes Quintana, who knew how to interpret the recommendations of the first OEEC (from 1960 onwards, OECD) report on Spain (March 1959) and contributed to the writing of the plan (commonly known as 'Plan Sardà'). The greatest resistance to the plan came from the Falangist factions and even from Franco himself (Fuentes Quintana, 1984 and 2003, and interviews collected in Perdices and Baumert, 2010).

The Stabilization and Liberalization Plan was a sudden turnaround in the unorthodox path of development of semi-autarkic Spain. In 1959–60 the rate of increase in per capita GDP at constant market prices was negative, but it was obvious that the plan followed the correct approach, to reach its aim, i.e., that in the following years Spain could enjoy what later on was called the 'Spanish economic miracle'. As indicated before, the Sardà Plan's measures to combat inflation were tax increases to reduce the public deficit and the setting up of a ceiling on bank loans, but the truth is that there was a wage freeze as well, which undoubtedly contributed to the stabilization effort. It is also true that the Money/GDP ratio rose, but this was due to the sharp fall in the denominator. The banks met the goals fixed by the government for credit contraction. They supported the Stabilization Plan without hesitation, though adding a request: 'the cessation of public appeals to the services of the banking sector [that is, of credit for official purposes]' (*Oficina de Coordinación y Programación Económica*, 1959, p. 116).

8.5 A small relaxing of the grip: the banking law of 1962

After stabilizing prices in 1959–60, policymakers discussed how to liberalize an economy hitherto subject to so many interventionist measures. In the end, they opted for gradualism, liberalizing first the real sector (the 1960 tariff) and then the monetary and financial sector (from 1962 onwards), that is, in an order that may be deemed appropriate (McKinnon, 1991; García Ruiz, 1992; Lukauskas, 1997). Both types of liberalization were discussed and agreed upon with the groups with interests at stake. Thus, before approving a new banking law, the Minister of Finance Mariano Navarro Rubio carried out consultations with financial institutions, business representatives and some advisory organizations such as the *Consejo de Economía Nacional*. The result of the consultations was collected in a memo that is one of the most interesting reports ever presented on the Spanish financial system (Ministerio de Hacienda, 1961).

Navarro Rubio's proposal comprised the following steps: (i) to restructure the monetary authority in order to improve its performance; (ii) to stimulate bank specialization so as to boost medium- and long-term bank lending, while at the same time trying to put limits to the expansion of the economic power of the banks over non-financial companies. Private banks, through a consensus report emanated from the CSB, accepted both points and added to them the need to reform the *status quo*, allowing more banks in the market (with a minimum capital of 20 million pesetas) and more branches (2,000). The CSB report was accompanied by three separate opinions: one from the *Banco de Bilbao*, which called for the complete abolition of the *status quo*; a second from Banesto, which argued that the figure of 2,000 for new branches was excessive; and a third, from Joaquín Sánchez Torres, the owner of *Sucesores de Clemente Sánchez*, a Caceres' banking house, who judged excessive the minimum capital figure for new entrants and claimed for more help to aid in the expansion of small banks across the country, including Madrid and other important places (Ministerio de Hacienda, 1961, pp. 42–4 and 51–2).

The new banking law (the Navarro Rubio Act) was approved on 14 April 1962; several decree laws would later develop what was only a 'framework law' (*ley de bases*). In it the ministry's intentions were fully reflected. The Bank of Spain and the public banks were nationalized, though *Banco Exterior de España* was not, for reasons never explained. Banks were compelled to specialize by having to choose between becoming 'commercial banks' (retail banking) or 'industrial banks' (wholesale banking). As for the *status quo*, the law had opted for a middle way: there was no more *numerus clausus* but the approval of banks for registration became dependent upon the approval of the CSB, while the opening of branches was subjected to some 'expansion plans' determined by some objective criteria to be approved by the government each year. As a result of the cumbersomeness of this procedure, it would take ten years to reach the figure of 2,000 new bank offices, even though improved client service through easy accessibility of bank offices was the main way to compete, as price competition remained strictly forbidden.

In addition to the Navarro Rubio Act, other far-reaching measures were taken to improve operational conditions, such as the introduction of the *Central de Información de Riesgos* (CIR, Risk Information Center) by a decree of 7 July 1962 and an order of 13 February 1963. The CIR operated within the Bank of Spain and permitted the central bank to accumulate quantitative information on loan risks above a minimum (in principle, 5 million pesetas), and this information was later on made available to private banks. The CIR was an institution of the type established for the first time in Nazi Germany (1934), which however had been adopted later on by democratic countries such as France (1946) and Italy (1962). The French model, very centralized, was adopted in Spain, against the opinion of some private banks who were opposed to sharing the information that had been gathered individually (Prado, 1983).

CIR information completed that from the *Registro de Aceptaciones Impagadas* (RAI, Registry of Unpaid Acceptances), which contained details on unpaid commercial bills. The RAI started functioning in 1922 within the *Asociación de la Banca Española del Centro de España* (Association of the Spanish Banks of Central Spain). Its creators were so convinced of its importance that even foreign banks were invited to participate (*Memoria de la Asociación de la Banca*

Española del Centro de España, 1921, Appendix, Document 17). The Civil War paralyzed the functioning of the RAI, but it was revived in 1941 under the auspices of the *Comité Central de la Banca Española*, though only in Madrid. In 1950, the CSB promoted the extension of the RAI throughout Spain (CSB, Circular Letter 319), and in February 1976 began the computerization of the service (CSB, Circular Letter LXXVI/77). The combination RAI–CIR greatly reduced the transaction costs of Spanish banking.

The Navarro Rubio Law of 1962 was a sharp break with the past. How was it received? In a previous paragraph we have shown the discomfort the Benjumea Act provoked in the Falangist sector of Francoism. Sixteen years later, the banks had proved to be one of the more solid mainstays of Spanish economic development; so the Falangist economist Higinio Paris Eguilaz, so belligerent against private banks in 1946, had to admit that without the intermediation of those banks Spanish savings 'would not have been properly invested for lack of people with the capacity to assume the risks involved in establishing [the] type of industries [that trigger economic development]', adding that 'the dilemma in Spain has not been choosing between independent firms on the one hand and corporations collaborating with banks on the other; the truth is that at a certain stage of industrial development, without the intermediation of the banks the expansion would have been very slow' (Paris Eguilaz, 1959, pp. 74–5).

The *Escuela de Organización Industrial* (School for Industrial Organization), a Taylorist educational institution founded in 1955 by the Ministry of Industry, and its factotum, Fermín de la Sierra, held a consistently critical position towards banks, in line with the 1941 law that created the *Instituto Nacional de Industria*. In this law the erection of the Instituto and the creation of public industrial enterprises by this holding was justified alleging that Spanish banks diverted savings towards short-term operations and neglected industry 'to the detriment of the country's interests'. In 1951, De la Sierra published a pioneering study on the concentration of banking institutions, which portrayed them as an oligopoly: the five big banks (Banesto, Central, Hispano, Vizcaya, Bilbao) accumulated in their hands offices (72 per cent in Madrid; 68 per cent in Barcelona; 64 per cent in Bilbao), capital (45 per cent), deposits (65 per cent of demand deposits) and industrial participations (50 per cent), and they expanded their sphere of influence by means of cross-directorships with other banks and large companies in key sectors (coal, steel, electricity, cement, chemicals). Soon after, Juan Velarde, a Falangist economist of great erudition, associated this oligopolistic power of the banks to the economic decline of Spain in the long term (Velarde, 1953).

The adoption of the Navarro Rubio Act did not satisfy those who denounced an excess of banking power. In 1963, the *Escuela de Organización Industrial* released a survey on the attitudes of Spanish businessmen towards banks, where unfavourable opinions (43 per cent) were very close to the favourable ones (45 per cent) and a majority of respondents thought that the banking sector was too backward (De Miguel and Linz, 1963).

The attempted merger of Central and Hispano in 1965 set off alarms among critics. The Ministry of Finance supported the operation, but Franco himself objected to the emergence of a 'monster bank' and even went on to say: 'I prefer bank nationalization to these monopolies' (Franco Salgado-Araujo, 1976, pp. 458–9). The projected merger was aborted and this gave hopes to those who supported greater state intervention in banks. Velarde was happy to report that 39 of the 91 components of the Privy Council of the Count of Barcelona, Don Juan de Borbón, pretender to the throne of Spain as successor of his father Alfonso XIII, were leaders of large banks (Velarde, 1966). In this light, banking power appeared as Franco's enemy because everyone remembered that in a manifesto issued in Lausanne on 19 March 1945, at a time when many hoped that Franco would fall after the defeat of the Axis powers, the Count of Barcelona had noted that the Franco regime was inspired in the 'totalitarian systems of the Axis powers' and therefore was 'contrary to the character and the tradition' of the Spanish people. There were bankers also in the circle of Don Juan's son, Prince Juan Carlos, as he had been housed in Las Jarillas, a rural property of the Urquijo family, when he stepped on Spanish soil for the first time in November 1948 (he had been born ten years earlier in Rome). Some years later, some bankers would support him in the so-called Operation Prince, which promoted his appointment as Franco's successor, something which took place in 1969. The promoters of the 'Operation Prince', led by men of Opus Dei (a Catholic organization which since the mid-1950s was able to place its members in senior posts of the Franco Administration, including the cabinet, which always contained several of them since 1957), expected Don Juan Carlos to lead a peaceful transition to democracy after Franco's death; their hopes were eventually fulfilled.

8.6 The new financial order quickly disintegrates

In 1967 there was a curious confluence: Falangists and communists – or better, crypto-communists, as the *Partido Comunista de España* (Communist Party of Spain) was outlawed – joined forces to openly request the submission of banks to the control of the state. In the book *Los monopolios en España* (1967) a friendly conversation between Velarde and the then communist Professor Ramón Tamames was reproduced, where the reader can appreciate the coincidence of their views. Fairly different opinions were voiced elsewhere. Ignacio Villalonga, chairman of the *Banco Central*, wrote a justly famous article in 1961 in which he praised and justified the role of banks in Spanish economic development along lines that were quite similar to Alexander Gerschenkron's (1962) or Rondo Cameron's (1967) arguments on related topics, although these authors wrote from a more general and scholarly perspective. According to Villalonga, financial institutions, acting as mixed or universal banks, had stepped into the breach of weak private industrial initiative, acting not only as bankers, but also as entrepreneurs, thus avoiding a greater presence of state or foreign capital (Villalonga, 1961). There was also a debate in the media on this same topic between Tamames and Prados Arrarte, the head of the Banco Central's research department (see a summary in Moya, 1975).

Disciples of Velarde (José Luis García Delgado, Santiago Roldan, Juan Muñoz) joined the fray in the following years in their crusade to denounce the power of banks in Spain (García Delgado and López Muñoz, 1968; Muñoz, 1969). According to their data, in 1966–7 the six largest banks exerted their influence over about 1,000 companies through the presence of their top officials on the companies' boards of directors. This was evidence that the large Spanish banks, supposedly commercial, maintained their character of promoters of companies against the precepts of the Navarro Rubio Act. Furthermore, five groups had developed (those of Banesto, Hispano-Urquijo, Central, Bilbao-Vizcaya, and Popular-Atlántico), which jointly controlled 68.9 per cent of paid-up capital of all private banks in the country, 78.9 per cent of total deposits and 80.9 per cent of all branches. This was, according to these authors, unquestionable proof of the high degree of oligopoly in the Spanish banking sector.

While the facts adduced by the bank's critics are undeniable, it must be admitted that the 1960s were a time when these financial institutions were submitted to a high degree of 'financial repression': a law ordering them to specialize, tight control of interest rates and of the opening of branches, directives telling them to channel substantial fractions of their investment towards the objectives of the three four-year Development Plans the government had issued and were in operation between 1964 and 1975, and so on. Prados Arrarte complained in 1959 that part of the banks' loans went to cover 'unpaid expenses of the public sector' (Prados Arrarte, 1959, pp. 16–17) and, far from this situation being redressed, the 1960s saw a 'boom of intervention in financing' (Poveda, 1980, p. 91). To appease the banks, they were allowed to rediscount the securities issued by the borrowers in the Bank of Spain. In other words, the top banks constituted an oligopoly of sorts, but they clearly were under the heel of the authorities.

On 23 July 1969, the '*Matesa* scandal' exploded like a bombshell and forced policy makers to review the entire network of state-controlled financing. The scandal uncovered for all to see the flimsiness and vulnerability of all this financial scaffolding. *Matesa* (*Maquinaria Textil del Norte, S. A.*, Northern Textile Machinery, Inc.), a private company of Catalan origin, had received very large and numerous loans from the *Banco de Crédito Industrial* to finance the exportation of the state-of-the-art looms Matesa's factories produced. This was by virtue of a law which subsidized exports of machinery and other industrial goods with preferential official credit. The

Banco de Crédito Industrial had asked for, and obtained, the responsibility to administer and finance that programme. This was a foolish decision, for it was not organized to deal with foreign commerce operations, a field the Banco Exterior should have been better prepared for. In our case, the only problem was that a good proportion of Matesa's exports were bought by the company's own branches in foreign countries. This was discovered by Ministry of Commerce officials, and given wide publicity. Matesa and *Crédito Industrial* were run by people linked to Opus Dei, and this fact was used by Falangists to attack their two political *bêtes noires*, Opus Dei and bankers, who joined in the defence of economic liberalism and advocacy of the integration of Spain in democratic Europe after the dictator's death. The Falangists hoped to be able to use the scandal to prevent the appointment of Don Juan Carlos as Franco's successor and king, but they failed. Juan Carlos was appointed in due time, and Opus Dei remained strong in the next cabinet reshuffle. It became obvious to everybody, however, that excessive government meddling with the banking system was counterproductive and that further liberalization was necessary (Tortella and Jiménez, 1986, ch. VI).

The reforms came about slowly but surely. A new Law on Organization and Management of Official Credit, of 19 June 1971, created the *Instituto de Crédito Oficial* (ICO, Official Credit Institute), as an agency that sought to improve and streamline its predecessors (*Comité de Crédito a Medio y Largo Plazo*, 1958; *Instituto de Crédito a Medio y Largo Plazo*, 1962) in the control of state banks. The law also simplified the mandatory investment coefficients and eliminated the possibility of rediscount or pledging in the Bank of Spain, as an anti-inflationary measure. The law also showed itself less favourable to bank specialization and slightly less unfavourable to the participation of foreign banks than previous legislation. Foreign banks were now authorized to participate in operations in Spain as long as management control remained in Spanish hands. Shortly afterwards, the oil crises of 1973 and 1979 would cause severe problems to industrial banks and lead them to merge with the universal banks they came from, while foreign banks would be allowed to settle in Spain in normal conditions, through branches or subsidiaries, although there were limitations on the number of branches until 1993 (Álvarez and Iglesias-Sarriá, 1992; Álvarez, 1998).

Recent research has found that the Navarro Rubio Act failed to impose discipline on interest rates, just as other previous attempts had failed in this field (García Ruiz, 2002). The interbank arrangement of 1960, which we discussed earlier failed in practice, in spite of the 'juries' that were in charge of informing the DGBB on the violations, which were supposed to be severely punished (fines, forced investments in public funds, reduction in the rediscount limits, cuts in distributed dividends, higher charges on interbank transactions) but were not. Navarro Rubio issued ministerial orders that appeared in October 1964 in the *Boletín Oficial del Estado* (BOE, the official gazette), trying to fix interest rates and fees for all types of financial institutions, and entrusted the inspection on this subject to the Bank of Spain in the case of commercial banks and to the *Instituto de Crédito de las Cajas de Ahorros* (Credit Institute of Savings Banks) in the case of savings banks. Interbank lending would be the only operation free from state interference.

While the power to fix most bank interest rates remained with the Ministry of Finance, a novelty had been introduced in 1966: the rates fixed by the ministry would no longer be floors, but ceilings, because now the aim was not to eliminate competition, as before, but to establish caps to lower the price of credit and thus, through the reduction of financial costs to companies, to dampen inflation. It should also be noted that credits with a term of two or more years were unregulated.

After 1969, banks were required to publish their preferential rates in the legislative gazette. From that date until 1985 it is possible to follow the evolution of these rates in *Cifras y relaciones significativas de los balances de la banca privada*, a publication of the CSB. Judging by the diversity of rates declared, it can be said that very soon national banks tended to follow their own policies, not coordinated with the rest, although regional, local or industrial banks were even more independent. In addition, since the late 1960s, some banks, taking advantage of the freedom with which industrial banks operated – most of them were the subsidiaries of commercial banks – started to practice 'financial engineering' or launched imaginative products like the then famous 'accounts with insurance' package the *Banco de Vizcaya* and the *Banco de Santander* launched in 1968, banks that were beginning to challenge the big banks of Madrid, increasingly asleep on their laurels.

The interest rate regime was barely altered by the financial liberalization reforms of August 1974; apart from their updating, as had been previously done in 1966, 1967, 1970, 1971, and 1973, the reforms only added the liberalization of passive operations for a term of 24 months or more. Meanwhile, an order of 29 February 1972 had started the liberalization of commissions: in interbank operations they were declared free, and for the other operations, although commissions were still regulated, banks were given a considerably wider leeway. All this meant the return by 1972 to a certain price competition.

After 1960 there were no more interbank *arreglos*, but, at the suggestion of Ignacio Villalonga, the presidents of the big banks started to meet monthly to coordinate their actions aside from the rest (Tortella, 2000b, p. 360). Villalonga was a follower of the Austrian School of Economics, but in practice he could not forget that he was the chairman of the Banco Central, an institution with a large portfolio of industrial holdings, which required a style of management oriented towards avoiding ruinous competition. In 1970, just appointed chairman of Banesto, José María Aguirre

Gonzalo began to organize weekly meetings, lunch included, in which the first in the ranking – at the time Banesto, Central since 1977 – would act as host. These meetings were known as the 'Club of the Big Seven' (the hosts just mentioned plus Hispano, Bilbao, Vizcaya, Santander, and Popular) and had an open character, as the monetary authorities were also invited to the luncheons. Large financial institutions and policymakers shared a common goal: to curb the *extratipos* (passive interest rates above the legal limits) or 'special conditions' (for example, allowing early withdrawal of the interest or the principal on time deposits), whereby mainly medium and small banks attracted deposits. The club was able to agree to distribute a circular letter among the banks asking them to stop unfair competition and sue competitors who violated the rules (the full text of the letter was published in *Doblón*, July 1975). Its success was as limited as that of the 1941–60 *arreglos*.

8.7 The onset of bank reform in the last years of dictatorship

The financial repression that followed the Second World War delayed the modernization of the financial sector in most countries. Until the 1960s no modernization was noticeable; at that point in time modernization could be characterized by globalization, computerization and liberalization. For Charles P. Kindleberger (1984), the starting point of the modernization process was the sudden appearance of a 'Euromarket' for currencies in the late 1950s, when European banks, particularly in London and Switzerland, began negotiating in dollars. There were three causes of the appearance of the eurodollar market: (i) the preference for the US dollar by Sir George Bolton, the chairman of the very British Bank of London and South America; (ii) Regulation Q of the Federal Reserve, which since 1933 limited the interest rates of the deposits offered by US banks in the domestic market, but not abroad; (iii) the discovery of the possibilities of working simultaneously in different time zones to maintain constant activity. We can consider also the fact that the Gosbank (the most important bank of the USSR) sought to keep its dollars in non-US banks to avoid seizures in the context of the Cold War.

Between 1960 and 1970, in the OECD countries, the number of foreign banks increased from 175 to 527, reaching up to 1,165 in 1980 (Bröker, 1989, pp. 153–4); if we include subsidiaries, the figures rise to 564 in 1970 and 1,664 in 1980 (Tschoegl, 1987, p. 68). This development was carried out by US institutions: the 8 American banks with foreign offices in 1960 jumped to 151 (899 offices) in 1986 (Huertas, 1990, p. 253). The largest number of institutions were concentrated in London: in 1974, according to *The Banker*, there were 264 foreign banks in the city, compared to only 114 in the Wall Street district of New York. This was due to the fact that in London there was much less regulation than in New York, but things just started to change in 1974, when the United States began to relax the application of Regulation

Q and the Interest Equalization Tax was abolished (since 1963 this tax fell upon the purchase of foreign securities). Ten years later, in 1984, the number of foreign banks in New York (307) was closer to that of London (403). To the presence of subsidiaries or branches of foreign banks we should add another form of internationalization: the formation of 'financial clubs' in the wake of the *Société Européenne de Développement Industriel*, founded in Paris in September 1957, with the participation of Paribas and Deutsche Bank, six months after the Treaty of Rome that gave birth to the European Economic Community (EEC). The European-wide market which the EEC promoted led to the creation of those clubs, but, as many other business alliances, they were short-lived.

The computerization of banking, from accounting to commercial service (terminals, Automatic Teller Machines or ATMs), was a process that began in the 1960s also. At first, computer systems had a centralized structure, with a powerful central computer located in a data centre, but since the late 1970s regional and local computers increased their importance, favouring decentralization of decisions. At the same time, speed and security in the transmission of data improved, while new optical fibre lines reduced costs enormously. The process was very rapid, and in 1973 it was possible to found the Society for Worldwide Interbank Financial Telecommunication (SWIFT), with 239 banks from 15 countries, to exchange international payment orders in an automated way.

The consequences of computerization went beyond the increase in capacity and speed of data transmission, because it induced substantial changes in the traditional activity of banks, their structures and even the organization of their staffs (Bátiz-Lazo *et al.*, 2011). Telematics boosted financial disintermediation, as new agents (insurance companies, real estate companies, department stores and so on) could perform banking functions by exploiting the new database management. The competitive answer from the banks was to generalize personal guarantee credit, which French banks (*crédits en blanc*) and English banks (the Midland Bank pioneered in this field since 1958) had begun to offer to their best clients in the 1930s and 1950s, respectively (Banque, 1932, 12, p. 214; Holmes and Green, 1986). In addition, new technologies favoured the emergence of scale economies, so that the big banks improved their chances against smaller-sized institutions. In the end, staff reorganization was inexcusable, increasing the number of people in commercial tasks at the expenses of those in administrative tasks (Fundesco, 1988).

Financial liberalization also progressed in the 1960s, but it did so very slowly. Germany released a mildly liberal banking law in July 1961, but controls remained on interest rates and restrictions on access of foreign banks; in fact, until 1984 there was no real liberalization of the German financial system (Giannola, 1990). France advanced on the path of liberalization in 1966, but leading French banks continued to be in the hands of the state. Furthermore the price of money was subjected to severe financial repression (Bröker, 1989). In the late 1960s, all countries regulated interest rates in one way or another; still in the mid-1980s only banks from Germany, Italy and the Netherlands enjoyed complete freedom in this field. In some countries such as Austria, Belgium and Switzerland interbank agreements were legalized, and in many others the authorities maintained discretional controls on this subject. Banking reforms in the 1970s were primarily concerned with putting an end to specialization and advancing towards universal banking (Denmark, 1974; Belgium, 1975; Germany, 1976; Holland, 1978, Great Britain, 1979), of course without neglecting safety and stability in their institutions.

The modernization process, however, was carried out without major convulsions in Europe. In the 1960s, there were significant banking concentration processes throughout the ECC, which lasted into the next decade, but rather than by financial crises, they were determined by scale and scope economies (those obtained from the use of a common structure to expand the range of products) (Bröker, 1989, pp. 211–12). As a precaution, Germany introduced deposit insurance in 1966, although this did not become operational until 1977, after the crisis of the Herstatt Bank in 1974. Deposit insurance was introduced in 1973 in Britain (and was reformed in 1979) and in 1979 in France. Italy resisted this formula until the crisis of the *Banco Ambrosiano* in 1982.

Spain was not aloof from any of the major changes (internationalization, computerization and deregulation) that took place in banking since the 1960s, but at first the pace of its progress was among the most conservative. For Lukauskas (1997) and Pérez (1997) there is no doubt that this was because the regulator had been 'captured' by those powerful banks that had been identified by Fermín de la Sierra and Juan Velarde; by contrast, Pons (2002) believes that political power was autonomous and acted judiciously, seeking above all to boost the development of the national economy (for a nuanced position on this issue, see Pueyo, 2006).

In 1977, there were 4 branches of foreign banks (0.7 per cent of deposits) operating in Spain, 48 international banks had a representative office and 20 Spanish banks had minority foreign shareholders; in turn, the Spanish financial system kept 65 branches and 160 representative offices operating abroad (*Economía,* 1 June 1978). It was evident that the Spanish market ought to be opened to international competition to a much greater extent. The first step was taken by a decree of 23 June 1978, which for the first time since the Civil War allowed the authorization of branches of foreign banks.

Change accelerated in the 1970s, the computerization of Spanish banks brought about not only expansion and improvement of their services, but also personnel cost savings and less labour disputes. According to the available censuses, the staff of Spanish banks had grown apace in the 1940s and 1950s, but it would grow still more in the 1960s, when it doubled; the growth

Table 8.3 Evolution of the number of bank offices and bank employees in Spain, 1919–90

	Total bank offices	**Total bank offices five big banks**	**Total bank employees (in thousands)**
1920	351 (1919)	160 (1921)	
1930	2,013 (1936)	856 (1931)	18.3 (1933)
1940	2,013 (1936)	959 (1941)	33.6 (mid-1940s)
1950	2,368	1,427	47.2
1960	2,805	1,673	69.0 (1963)
1970	4,402	2,473	131.8
1980	13,348	6,891	180.3
1990	16,989	7,631	158.2

Sources: Total bank offices: Appendix 12, adding 96 head offices and 25 offices of the foreign banks in 1936 (*Mundo*, 23 June 1940). Total bank offices of the big five banks: 1921, 1931, and 1941, Ridruejo (1954); for the rest, *Anuarios estadísticos de la banca privada*. Total bank employees: 1933, *Memoria* of the *Asociación de la Banca Española del Centro de España*, documents 35, 36, and 37; the 1940s, in Sanz (1948), p. 165; 1950, in *Revista Sindical de Estadística*, 1951, 3; 1963, in *Revista Sindical de Estadística*, 1965, third quarter; the rest in *Anuarios estadísticos de la banca privada*.

would continue in the 1970s, reaching a total workforce of over 180,000 employees in 1980 (Table 8.3). According to the *Estadística de Salarios* (*Wage Statistics*), from the *Instituto Nacional de Estadística* (National Institute of Statistics), average earnings per hour worked in the financial institutions sector had increased from 30.04 pesetas in 1963 to 86.08 pesetas in 1970 and 518.80 pesetas in 1980; that is, salaries in 1980 were 17.3 times those of 1963 in nominal terms and 2.7 times in real terms (we have discounted the high inflation of the period with the cost of living index of the *Instituto Nacional de Estadística*). It does not seem that this significant growth in labour costs might have dissuaded banks from recruiting more employees; this is explained by the need to meet a network of offices that had skyrocketed from 2,697 in 1960 to 13,223 in 1980. The rapid growth of the financial sector, whose contribution to GDP in 1980 stood at 5.2 per cent – in Germany, for instance, it was 3.5 per cent (OECD, 1989) – explains the above figures. However, this rapid growth also caused high structural costs, which were becoming a burden. As we will see in the next chapter, the response of the banks to this problem was to enhance computerization, which had been left behind up to then.

The first solid liberalization step was taken on 9 August 1974, when the Council of Ministers approved two decrees and five orders signed by the Minister of Finance Antonio Barrera de Irimo that were published in the official gazette (BOE) of the next day. The Barrera Reform differed from the Navarro Rubio Act in that it tried to promote competition in Spanish banking. On the one hand, the reform decreased market segmentation between commercial banks and industrial banks (one of the decrees said that 'specialization [...] should increasingly obey more to the will and vocational orientation of financial institutions and less to a legal imperative') and between banks and savings banks (for example, it allowed the latter access to the clearing houses of Madrid, Barcelona, Bilbao and Saragossa, established by the former). On the other hand, the reform established more objective criteria for approving the expansion of branch networks (from then on it would depend on the amount of capital and reserves), and the creation of new banks; it also liberalized the whole range of interest rates in operation with a maturity of more than 24 months. One of the August decrees allowed specialized banks with up to 15 per cent of foreign capital (this was the origin of Aresbank, in 1975, and Saudesbank, in 1979, Arab institutions among whose specialties was the recycling of petrodollars); this decree was followed by another, of 31 October 1974, that admitted foreign capital to assist Spanish banks in serious problems.

When the Barrera Reform was passed, about a third of the deposits were already entrusted to savings banks. The figures in Appendix 13 show that, among savings banks, *La Caixa,* founded in 1904, exerted a clear lead, followed at a distance by *Caja Madrid* (1838), *Caja de Barcelona* (1926) and *Caja de Zaragoza* (1876) (on *La Caixa,* see Nadal and Sudrià, 1983; on *Caja Madrid,* López Yepes and Titos, 1995; on *Caja de Zaragoza,* Forniés, *et al.,* 1976). Soon afterwards came a royal decree, of 27 August 1977, whose article 20 permitted savings banks 'to perform the same operations as banks perform, with no other limitations than those applicable to the latter'. As a compensation to banks, a law of 25 March 1981 abolished the privilege savings banks had enjoyed in the mortgage market at the expense of commercial banks since 1942. From that moment on, the level field in competition between commercial banks and savings banks sought by the Barrera Reform was completely guaranteed.

9
Transition to Democracy, Oil Crisis, and Further Bank Reforms

9.1 Political and economic reform: its implications for the banking system

Franco's dictatorship ended with his death on 20 November 1975. From that moment on the transition towards democracy proceeded not without serious hindrances, but carried over by popular enthusiasm and faith in the benefits of a democratic system. It took a complex process of dismounting a dictatorial order which Franco himself said that he would leave 'well tied and knotted' when he died. Untying the knots took one year and a half. Alexander's method with the Gordian knot was carefully avoided. Every step was achieved through consensus. Spaniards, politicians and constituents alike, had developed a strong and lasting distaste for swords. The first democratic elections in 41 years finally took place in June 1977. Constituent Cortes were elected by universal suffrage and they promulgated a constitution in December 1978. As political reform advanced, economic reform proceeded in a parallel way. Fiscal and financial reforms were carried out, to which we will refer presently. Meanwhile, to consolidate these political and economic reforms, and with almost unanimous popular support, Spain began a process of integration into the European Economic Community (since the Maastricht Treaty of 1992, European Union, EU) that culminated with its admission as a full member on 1 January 1986.

The 1976–85 period included the oil crises that ended the 'Golden Age' in the Western world. The economic and political postwar order, where economic growth had been complemented with the growth of the Welfare State, was put under stress and many in the political elite, persuaded by the thought of Professor Milton Friedman of the University of Chicago, thought that the only way out was to boost the economy by going deeper into the processes of internationalization, liberalization, and technological innovation. As we have seen in the previous chapter, these measures and processes had been applied in the sphere of European banks since the 1960s and were not completely unknown in Spain.

Within the EEC, internationalization was conditioned by Directive 77/780/EEC, which laid the foundation for the creation of a Single European Market where banks should be able to operate throughout the whole area of the EEC on the basis of a single authorization, subject to compliance with a set of uniform rules. The Directive 89/646/EEC followed, allowing the EU basic legal framework to be implemented at the national level from 1 January 1993 (Strivensr, 1992; Canals, 1994; Ontiveros, 1997). Meanwhile, Britain and Switzerland had completely abolished exchange controls (1979–80), Japan had allowed its banks to deal in foreign currencies (1980), Germany had authorized the purchase of bonds by non-residents (1981), the United Kingdom had eased the access of foreigners to their stock markets (1982–86), and the United States had abolished taxes on the interests of foreign investments in bonds (1984) (Jones, 1990). The result of these and other similar measures was greater market integration, but also a fall in margins and growing instability. Furthermore, the outbreak in 1982 of a debt crisis in the Third World had diverted international financial flows from underdeveloped countries – traditional destination for foreign investment – towards Western countries, contributing to their 'financialization' (excessive weight of the financial system).

Technological innovation during this period was marked by the extraordinary spread of ATMs: around 1990 there were over 100 ATMs per million population in many European countries, including Spain (the first Spanish ATM was installed in 1973 in Toledo by the *Banco Popular*, on a trial basis). This innovation had originated in the English-speaking world in the 1960s, but 20 years later numerous European companies were competing in the field of telecommunications. Not all new products were successful, however: for example, the home banking terminal, launched in 1980 by the First Interstate Bank, Los Angeles, did not reach the intended diffusion. In addition, more ease and speed in financial transactions was bringing increasing difficulties in controlling risk, so Arthur Andersen advised to design very refined systems for this purpose (Arthur Andersen, 1986).

But the biggest fear of banks was that improved telecommunications would open the door to 'disintermediation', that is, to an understanding between lenders and borrowers around traditional intermediaries (Ballarín, 1985). The response of banks was to develop strategies of *Allfinanz* (Global Finance), that is, the creation of groups that would combine commercial banking, investment banking, participation in other financial institutions (for example, insurance companies) or service firms, all offered by a large bank. These strategies were successful in the United Kingdom and Germany, but much less so in France or Italy. This happened because in the former countries the regulatory framework was soon relaxed, while in the latter doing away with regulation took a long time, a retardation which is attributed to the greater weight of public banks in these countries, where many large banks were nationalized after the Second World War. The liberalization of the 1960s and 1970s, aimed at creating more competition in the market, was leading to deregulation, that is, to less state intervention and surveillance. To this end, banking laws were enacted in Germany (1984), which reinforced the tradition of universal banking, and in Britain (1986, 1987), where the reform raised the possibility of 'securitized' loans, that is to say, loans transformed into securities, something which blurred the boundaries not only between commercial banks and investment banks, but also between banks and stock exchanges (The Institute of Bankers, 1986; Giannola, 1990).

All countries of Western Europe advanced along the path of deregulation, although at different paces. Spain, which started from high levels of financial repression, advanced at breakneck speed, as we saw in the previous chapter; in the end this led to a major financial crisis. According to Carmen Reinhart and Kenneth Rogoff (2011, p. 159), the Spanish financial crisis that began in 1977 was the first of the five big crises experienced by the developed world after the Second World War (the others would be the Norwegian of 1987, the Finnish of 1991, the Swedish of 1991, and the Japanese of 1992). Somehow, the Spanish crisis, discussed in detail in the next section, reflected the celebrated phrase 'Goodbye Financial Repression, Hello Financial Crash' of the Cuban–American economist Carlos F. Díaz-Alejandro (1985) (on the opening of the Spanish financial sector, see Lukauskas, 1997; Pérez, 1997).

The United States had taken steps towards deregulation since 1974, but the venerable Glass-Steagall Act of 1933, with its radical separation between commercial banks and investment banks, withstood its critics for a long time (Benston, 1990; White, 1992). Regardless of their specialization, US institutions responded well to the prototype of the bank of the future, which for many was a 'financial high-tech & large scale production' institution (Arthur Andersen, 1986), able to develop automatic banking and home banking as alternatives to attention in the office, to offer 24-hour services and to manage a huge amount of magnetic cards (see Canals, 1994; few, like Gardener, 1992, believed any other type of banking could succeed). The Glass-Steagall Act was considered by many as a burden on Wall Street, but it was not removed until the approval of the Financial Services Modernization Act (or Gramm-Leach-Bliley Act) of 1999, which was an openly deregulatory law which in the end allowed too many excesses (Levine, 2010). This deregulation came to Europe when there were already voices claiming for 're-regulation', not in the area of 'economic regulation' (prices, profits, number of agents), but rather in that of 'safety-and-soundness regulation' (basic requirements of solvency and asset quality to be met by institutions to prevent abuses and excesses) (Dermine, 1990, can be considered a pioneering work in this direction; White, 1992, clearly distinguishes between the two types of regulation).

9.2 Fighting the banking crisis

The immediate response of the big Spanish banks to the liberalization package of 1974 was the circular letter of 1975 from the Club of the Big Seven that tried to do away with the *extratipos* (passive interest rates above the legal maximum) and all 'special conditions' (conditions of dubious legal status to make the products more attractive) for some bank deposits (see p. 134). This proposal for a gentlemen's agreement was not respected and, in the summer of that year, the chairman of Banesto and great promoter of the club, José María Aguirre Gonzalo, complained to the press about the breakdown of 'bank solidarity' (*Doblón*, July 1975). But all talk about *extratipos* became obsolete after the ministerial orders of July 1977, which went further in the liberalization of interest rates, starting with operations exceeding the one-year term. In spite of this, there is evidence that, in June 1980, some bankers searched for a new interbank agreement to introduce a cap on passive interest rates; Aguirre Gonzalo's comment to this attempt was that everything that might be agreed upon in this matter was doomed to failure (García Ruiz, 2002, p. 380). From January 1981 onwards, only deposits of up to six months term and special accounts (for stock market investment or to collect emigrants' savings) remained regulated; but this was not for very long; finally, an order of 3 March 1987 abolished the maximum passive rates and removed the caps on charges in the active operations, while the transparency of information to clients was reinforced and a Claims Service of the Bank of Spain was created.

The orders of July 1977 were part of the reformist policies implemented by the centrist government of Adolfo Suárez, who had won the 15 June 1977 general election. The vice president in charge of economic policies was the celebrated Spanish economist Enrique Fuentes Quintana, who some years later remembered as 'bitter' a meeting in late 1977 with representatives of the largest national banks, who considered any liberalization 'dangerous' and 'inappropriate' (Fuentes Quintana, 1991, pp. LXIII y LXIV). Nevertheless, two bankers, José A. Sánchez Asiaín, chairman of the *Banco de Bilbao*, and Rafael Termes, managing director of the *Banco Popular*, seemed willing to discuss the issue, and it was a relief to the government that Termes was elected president of the bankers' association, the *Asociación Española de Banca* (AEB) in November. Fuentes Quintana was in a negotiating mood, which led to the signing of the so-called Moncloa Pacts (wide political agreements to tackle the crisis) in October 1977, but his Smithian vision was not well understood and he resigned in February 1978. Soon afterwards, Fuentes Quintana criticized Spanish bankers' 'propensity to the *siesta*', that is to say, their resistance to modifying a type of banking whereby they had reaped oligopolistic rents, not from perfect oligopoly, but oligopolistic anyway (*Economía y Diálogo*, 1, 1979, special issue on banking and democracy).

The criticisms by the bankers to the Smithian convictions of Fuentes Quintana were shared by some experts, such as Professor Antonio Torrero, who always thought that freedom in banking should have its limits (Torrero, 1982, p. 153). The Bank of Spain, under governor José María López de Letona, supported institutional solutions to the problems of the sector, such as the *Fondo de Garantía de Depósitos* (FGD, Deposit Insurance Fund) created by a royal decree of 11 November 1977, to confront the coming crisis in the *Banco de Navarra* and a long list of other subsequent failures. The FGD was inspired, as other such institutions elsewhere in Europe, by the Federal Deposit Insurance Corporation, created in the United States in 1933. The FGD was established with contributions from the banks, at a rate of 1.2 per 1,000 deposits. Mistrusting each other, the bankers supported the governor's proposal of introducing external financial audits and even the establishment of a 'Center for Interbank Market Risk', where the indebtedness of financial institutions in the interbank market should be registered (the measure was included in the final summary of the *V Jornadas de Mercado Monetario*, organized by Intermoney in 1978). All in all, however, the Rooseveltian approach prevailed and soon there were different FGDs for banks, for savings banks, and for credit cooperatives.

The *Banco de Navarra* fell victim to the practice of granting high *extratipos* to depositors, who, however, after the intervention of the bank, in January 1978, saw their money back, even above the limit of 500,000 pesetas established in the deposit insurance agreement. This crisis was followed by those of many other banks which succumbed to external (oil crises) and internal (the necessary restructuring and liberalizing of the economy, for many reasons, among them the wish to join the EEC) economic problems and also political problems, as the transition from dictatorship to democracy was not free of hindrances and tensions. To this must be added many cases of incompetence and lack of scruples, especially among the new bankers who had joined after 1962. On the one hand, political transition brought about a period of withdrawal of deposits and capital flight; on the other hand, high oil prices and international crisis hit industry and tourism severely, causing, among other things, a sharp rise in unemployment and a wave of bankruptcies and closures (Betrán *et al.*, 2010). Between 1977 and 1985, more than one half of the banks and about one-third of the resources and bank employees were affected by one of the fiercest financial crises in Spanish history. (The three largest economic crises in modern Spanish history have been the banking and railroad crisis of the 1860s, the oil and political crises of the 1970s and 1980s, and the bursting of the building and financial bubble starting in 2007.) The coincidence of the liberalization programme with a downward turn in the economic cycle ravaged many banks, and the need to neutralize the social effects of the crisis on the political transition to democracy brought the total cost of recovery to very high figures (nearly 1.5 trillion pesetas of 1985), with a huge contribution of the public sector

(75 per cent) (Cuervo, 1988, p. 212; his figures have been often questioned, but there is no alternative estimate). As an orientation, GNP was 28.2 trillion in 1985. The sharing of the burden of loss was controverted because although the crisis of the real economy had been a factor in the financial crisis, bad management by banks had been another in many cases. Rafael Termes, the former president of the bankers' association, believed that banks with severe management problems should not have been rescued (De Juan, 1983; Termes, 1995).

Perhaps the most striking cases of banking collapse are the following three. First was the Urquijo, whose rescue weighed heavily upon the Hispano. Both institutions were bound by a covenant ('The *Las Jarillas* Pact') signed in 1944. The Urquijo, incorporated in 1918, was the first industrial bank in Spain and as such it underwent periodic liquidity crunches. The *Las Jarillas* Pact, engineered by Juan Lladó, who would soon thereafter become the Urquijo's chairman until 1978, was intended to solve this problem by linking both banks. The much larger Hispano would share the profits of industrial dividends in good years and help the Urquijo when the crunch came (the CEO of the Hispano at the time of the pact, Andrés Moreno, had worked in the Midland Bank and admired the English model of banking, clearly oriented towards commercial banking) (García Ruiz, 2007c; on the history of the Urquijo, Puig and Torres, 2008). The crisis of the Urquijo, overburdened by its industrial portfolio in the early 1980s, led to a new pact: the Hispano bought the Urquijo in 1983. But the industrial portfolio of the Urquijo weighed so heavily on the Hispano that the Bank of Spain had to intervene, appointing Claudio Boada, a reputed manager, as chairman of the Hispano and organizing a special rescue operation. In the end the Urquijo was sold to *Banca March* in 1988 (Puig and Torres, 2008, pp. 206–60).

The second case is *Banca Catalana*, an institution promoted and directed for many years by Jordi Pujol, who in 1980 was elected president of the Generalitat de Catalunya, a position where he remained for 23 years. In 1982, *Banca Catalana* was intervened by the Bank of Spain for its insolvency, due to the mistakes committed by their managers while trying to do 'Catalan banking', that is, banking in favour of what they considered to be 'Catalan interests' (Cabana, 1988, p. 131; Cabana, a historian and Pujol's brother-in-law, was senior manager and vice president of the bank). *Banca Catalana* was sold to the *Banco de Vizcaya* in 1984. Pujol was not prosecuted, but he was interrogated by a judge for the failure of the bank.

Someone who was prosecuted and even imprisoned was the main character of the third episode that deserves to be highlighted – José María Ruiz Mateos, an Andalusian entrepreneur who owned a holding group, *Rumasa*, which controlled several banks, some of them of considerable importance, such as the *Banco Atlántico*, and several industrial companies. Rumasa became insolvent and, in 1983, the socialist government of Felipe González intervened to expropriate it and sell its parts separately. This intervention was followed by a long process with criminal and political aspects (Argüelles, 1992).

Although other financial crises took place simultaneously in Europe, there is no doubt that the Spanish crisis was the most serious, a fact which can be explained, to some extent, because Spain had been left out of the wave of mergers and acquisitions that took place in the continent since the 1960s (remember that the Franco government in 1965 thwarted the merger of the *Banco Central* and the *Banco Hispano Americano*, which served as a warning to other institutions). With the Navarro Rubio Act, a considerable number of small and medium banks entered the financial market, the *Banco de Navarra* one of them, led by people not sufficiently trained and experienced, and determined to get rich quickly (Tortella, 1996). Afterwards, during the expansion which followed the liberalization process started in the early 1970s, many small new banks were unable to take advantage of the scale economies that Fanjul and Maravall (1985) found in Spanish banking during that period (see also Maravall, *et al.*, 2009).

The crisis was inevitable and it affected the new institutions (of small and medium size) more than the traditional (large). Several traditional banks in the end benefited from the crisis as they were able to acquire at acceptable prices some failed banks after these were restructured and restored by the FGD after 1980 (previously, *Corporación Bancaria*, a private company created *ad hoc* by the Bank of Spain in March 1978, had run the intervened financial institutions). Some analysts criticized what they said was an unjustified favour to big banks, but the truth is that they collaborated in the recovery, sometimes with very negative consequences (for example, the case of the Hispano and the Urquijo). But most writers agreed that there was a historical need for Spain to acquire some efficient Chandlerian 'modern enterprise' (large, diversified, led by professional managers), as a way to meet the challenges of the European Common Market and, at the same time, to take advantage of the economies of scale we just referred to (García Ruiz and Tortella, 2007).

Today, the Spanish banking system has two flagship international institutions: Santander and BBVA. Their existence proves that the pessimistic predictions of two reports written around this time did not come true. The first of these was produced at the time of Spain's accession to the EEC (Arthur Andersen, 1986) and the other when the EU was being born (Dixon, 1991). The first report stated that Spanish banks would not be able to compete because of their excessive operating costs (a network too heavy and not competitive, high staff costs), the deficient training of their managers, and excessive regulation. The second report said that foreign banks would enjoy excellent opportunities to expand in Spain, due to the lack of competitiveness of its local banks in the Single European Market.

Faced with such pessimistic forecasts, Jack Revell, a socialist economist who founded the Institute of European Finance at the Welsh Bangor

University, found, in a 1984 report, that Spanish banks enjoyed adequate capitalization, and, in another report of 1987, that there was a future for these banks if the best managed institutions (Popular, Santander, Vizcaya) controlled the decadent Madrid big banks (Banesto, Central, Hispano). Revell was right in general, but erred in the combinations he proposed for the forthcoming merger wave (Vizcaya–Central, Santander–Banesto, Popular–Hispano or Popular–Hispano–Bilbao – he considered this last one to have an intermediate level of efficiency), because what actually happened was that the Basque banks combined to give birth to BBVA and Santander absorbed the Madrid banks, except the Popular, which chose to pursue an independent path (on the 'struggle for independence' of *Banco Popular*, see Tortella, *et al.*, 2011).

Shortly before the crisis, about one half of the Spanish population had no bank account and public opinion tended to think all the banks were the same thing, as there was no real competition (Asociación Española de Banca, 1979). The crisis of 1977–85 was expensive, but thanks to it, remarkable progress towards the necessary renewal was possible. In the mid-1980s, the Spanish banking system began to be comparable to those of other major Western Europe countries (Tables 9.1 and 9.2). Spain had a number of domestic banks in proportion to its population about the EEC average, but the penetration of foreign banks was low (although comparable to that in Denmark, Italy, or Portugal). Moreover, the degree of 'bancarization', measured by the Goldsmith ratio (Financial Assets/GDP), denoted maturity in the financial system (the contribution of the Spanish financial sector to GDP formation, 6–7 per cent, was superior to those of many other neighbouring countries). Positive aspects were also the adequate capitalization and the high intermediation margins, although this was related to the high market power achieved in an institutional framework that discouraged competition (Martínez Méndez, 1991).

Table 9.1 Dimension of banking in Western Europe in late 1980s

	Banks per million inhabitants (1986)	**Offices per million inhabitants (1986)**	**Assets of financial institutions/ GDP (%) (1986)**	**Share of foreign banks/ Total assets (%) (1987)**	**Investment abroad/ Total world investment of banks (1988)**	**Average position of big five in the world ranking (1988)**
France	6.9	179.0	175	16	8.8	5
G. Britain	10.1	251.3	220	60	5.8	13
Germany	5.0	104.4	107	4	8.0	9
Italy	2.8	102.7	105	3	4.5	19
Spain	3.5	426.9	138	11	0.9	35

Sources: The first and second columns come from Canals (1991); the rest in Dermine (1990), where Caminal, *et al.* (1990) is included.

The most worrying feature for analysts was the disproportionately high number of financial institution offices (including banks, savings banks and other intermediaries) in Spain. The number per million population (around 850) was the highest in the developed world, followed at a distance by those of some small countries as specialized in finance as Luxembourg or Switzerland. As was stressed by the Research Department of the *Banco Hispano Americano*, this had been a consequence of the disorderly expansion that followed liberalization: two-thirds of the bank branches had been opened after 1974 (Banco Hispano Americano, 1986, p. 18). Fortunately, this finding contrasted with the number of bank employees, which was around the EU average (3 per cent of total employment), although the implementation of generous internal promotions to ease social tension – bank officers rose from 26.57 per cent of staff in 1978 to 45.99 per cent in 1990, according the *Anuario Estadístico de la Banca Privada* – had led to a significant increase in labour costs. It seems surprising that the excess of offices coexisted with low population density, as the marginal benefit of opening a new office is lower when the density is low. What had happened in Spain was that efficient competition via prices had been replaced by inefficient competition via offices (Neven, 1990; Fuentelsaz and Salas, 1994). Among other drawbacks, an oversized branch structure induced higher liquidity ratios because banks had to keep their cash holdings scattered in space (Villalonga, 1956, p. 25, had warned about this problem years before).

Another element that differentiated the Spanish financial system from that of the EEC was the small size of the largest Spanish institutions. In the world rankings published by *The Banker*, they were always classified

Table 9.2 Structure of banking in Western Europe in late 1980s

	Equity/ ATAs (%) (1986)	**Degree of external openness[a] (1987)**	**ATMs/ Million of inhabitants[b]**	**Result before taxes/ ATA (%) (1986)**	**Market share of the big five (%) (1988)**	**Government debt/Total assets (%)[c] (1987)**
France	2.5	34	130	0.38	50	5.8
G. Britain	5.4	65	120	1.18	36	1.6
Germany	4.6	11	35	0.79	44	16.6
Italy	5.0[d]	13	30	0.50[d]	55	35.4
Spain	5.6	8	70	0.81	46	37.4

[a] The degree of openness is the ratio of combined external assets and liabilities to total assets of banks.
[b] Quoted in Dermine (1990), p. 166, using as source *The Economist*, 1988, but without expressing the year of the estimate.
[c] Including mandatory cash reserves and funding of the state Central Administration.
[d] Figure of 1985.

Sources: The first and fourth columns come from Canals (1991), the rest in Dermine (1990), where Caminal *et al.* (1990) is included. ATA = Average Total Assets.

far behind those of the leading EU countries. The problem was not low concentration, as was sometimes said, as the market share of the top five institutions was similar to that of France, Germany, or Italy, and higher than that of Britain. Rather, the small size seemed to be the result of the absence of vigorous competition, something that historically had tended to stunt the development of the large Spanish banks, despite the positive trend in their income statements. The deputy governor of the Bank of Spain, Mariano Rubio, did not hesitate to denounce that if the banking business had flourished since the end of the Civil War it was 'because legislation and action by the authorities had tended to limit competition and to set official interest rates of almost all operations at a level that ensured very satisfactory margins' (Rubio, 1983, pp. 357–8).

The low level of internationalization also helps explain the small size of Spanish banks. The chairman of the *Banco Central*, Alfonso Escámez, said in 1982: 'It is curious that we have grown faster in six or seven years abroad [...] than in sixty years here [...]. It seems clear that it was not a bad idea to go out' (*Dinero*, December 1982); the chairman was right in general terms, although the figures he offered to back his statement did not take into account the impact of inflation and changes in the peseta–dollar exchange rate. In the late 1980s, Spanish international financial activity was less than 1 per cent of the world total, and the degree of openness of the country's institutions (Foreign Assets and Liabilities/Total Assets) was less than 10 per cent. Traditionally confined to the domestic market, Spanish banks had inevitably reflected the relative backwardness of the country. The only advantage of this isolation had been that at the beginning of the Latin American debt crisis the country risk accumulated by Spanish banks represented only 6,199 million dollars, that is, 1.97 per cent of the world debt, and only 29 per cent of that amount was loans to the private sector (Termes, 1991).

Finally, it should be noted that the banking crisis of 1977–85 put an end to a bank–industry relationship that had never been as strong and consistent as in Germany, had been weakened in the previous years due to the problems of Spanish industry and to the existence of more profitable alternatives, and that in some cases had caused true over-indebtedness in companies which, as they faced huge excess capacity, had no other solution than selling out to foreign capital (Torrero, 1991; Zoido, 1998; Valdaliso, 2004; García Ruiz, 2009).

9.3 Financing the welfare state

The welfare state was born to solve a market failure: the majority of individuals are unable to privately secure essential aspects of their daily lives, such as having a decent pension when old age prevents them from continuing work or having adequate insurance protection from accidents and diseases

(Comín, 2010). In 1883, two years after the implementation by Otto von Bismarck of social security in Germany, a *Comisión de Reformas Sociales* (Commission for Social Reforms) was established in Spain that, in time, led to the birth of employer's liability insurance (1900) and to the *Instituto Nacional de Previsión* (National Institute for Providence). The impulse came, as in Germany, from the conservative elites who understood that through the implementation of a scheme of social insurance they would be able to hold back the advance of revolutionary movements. In 1900, a Conservative Party leader, Eduardo Dato, sponsored a law on the responsibility of employers in the accidents of their workers, which stimulated employers' interest in private liability insurance schemes. In 1908, another Conservative Party leader, Antonio Maura, created the *Instituto Nacional de Previsión* to complement private retirement insurance plans.

During the interwar period, a liberal leader, the count of Romanones, introduced the first mandatory worker retirement insurance, to be managed by the *Instituto Nacional de Previsión*. During the Second Republic, in 1931–33, the socialist Minister of Labour, Francisco Largo Caballero, transformed the employers' liability insurance from voluntary to mandatory, with a model of conditioned private management that has survived to this day. The First Francoism provided mandatory health insurance (1942). Finally, the Basic Law on Social Security of 1963 introduced in Spain a 'pay as you go' system of social security starting 1 January 1967. Two Franquist laws, the Law of Financing and Improvement (1972) and the General Law of Social Security (1974), established that the system would be financed by contributions from employers and employees, to which should be added a public provision that would be included as an annex to the general budget of the state from 1975. There would be contributory and non-contributory benefits.

The governments of the transition to democracy period attached great importance to social security, creating, first, the Ministry of Health and Social Security (1977) and, then, the Ministry of Labour and Social Security (1981), a reform which made sense because the coverage of unemployment (in a country with high structural unemployment) and pensions (in a country with an aging population) carried more weight than health insurance. Moreover, the 1978 Constitution defined Spain as a state with 'Autonomous Communities' (a sort of asymmetric federalism) and soon competences on health were transferred to the regions, while the central government kept the management of unemployment insurance (and subsidies) and pensions. At all levels of the state, social expenditure as a percentage of GDP increased until the mid-1990s. When this variable was close to its peak of 23 per cent, the socialist government of Felipe González thought that it was necessary to introduce a reform that would ensure basic benefits to all Spanish citizens, benefits which could be supplemented privately by those who wanted and could afford this additional expenditure, without excessively burdening the social security system.

If social spending grew, so did spending on education, which, as was the case with health, was progressively transferred to the Autonomous Communities. By 1990, combined public spending at all levels of the state exceeded 40 per cent of GDP for the first time, twice the level reached in the times of late Francoism. Funding for this increased spending required active fiscal policies, which had to be coordinated with the active monetary policies that had started to be implemented in the last years of the Franco dictatorship.

August 1973 may be marked as the beginning of modern active monetary policy in Spain, which, after the liquidation of the *Instituto Español de Moneda Extranjera*, would also include external policies, centred upon the exchange rate (Pérez and Rojo, 1977). The paradigm of Milton Friedman's new monetarism was very much in vogue and the instrumental variable chosen by the Bank of Spain was the monetary base. This was a very noticeable novelty over the traditional use of the discount or rediscount rate of the Bank of Spain as the benchmark variable in Spanish monetary policy. The Research Department of the central bank, led by Luis Ángel Rojo, discarded interest rates as an instrumental variable for two reasons: (i) it was convenient to stimulate the growth of interbank markets and to adopt the interest rates formed in them as benchmarks; (ii) management of the monetary base would grant some operational autonomy to the Bank of Spain, as management of interest rates would have required frequent consultation with the Ministry of Finance. Let us remind the reader that, as interest rates on interbank loans were excluded from the regulation of 1964, they were fixed through very particular interbank exchanges that were settled by means of checks drawn against current accounts at the Bank of Spain; these checks in Madrid were carried by motorists who used to have a stop at the *Café Comercial*, where they sometimes would exchange checks thus forming a sort of spontaneous clearinghouse (Pérez, 2012, p. 60).

The control of the monetary base was achieved through loans from the Bank of Spain to the banking system. Every day, the Bank of Spain would distribute a certain amount of credit according to each bank's equity resources and at an interest rate set by the Bank itself, but then these monies could be redistributed by the banks among themselves at rates freely fixed by them. This system would soon be replaced by an auction system. The maximum maturity of these loans was ten days, so the banks could meet their reserve requirements which were established every ten days. The negotiation was carried out by telephone. In 1976, the Telephone Money Market, directly inspired by the US FedWire, was created. From the beginning, interbank market flows were followed with interest by the Bank of Spain inspectors, who would consider it alarming if an institution increased sharply its demand for funds (this was how the problems of the Rumasa holding were first detected).

In April 1982, the *Certificados de Regulación Monetaria* (Certificates of Money Regulation), a kind of bonds to control the liquidity of the monetary system, were created. They would be distributed among banks through periodic auctions. But the *Certificados* were not as successful as expected and in the fall of 1983 there was worry that the Bank of Spain might incur losses. The problem was that the credit of the Bank of Spain to the Treasury was not remunerated and the Bank's liabilities had been put into circulation at relatively high interest rates. To tackle the problem, governor Mariano Rubio and deputy governor Luis Ángel Rojo designed a reform requiring banks to increase their cash ratio so the demand for *Certificados* would increase; the reform also included improving public debt markets and putting a limit to the amount of public debt bonds the Bank of Spain could purchase in primary markets; this, of course, shifted the burden of financing the mounting public debt onto the private sector, and should serve as a certain discouragement for the government to become excessively indebted; and, finally, the reform also included further liberalization of the credit system, in prices (interest rates) and in quantities (diminishing investment ratios) (Pérez, 2012).

That reform created a modern public debt market in 1987, but as an emergency measure a mandatory investment ratio in *pagarés del Tesoro* (Treasury notes) was established in 1984. These Treasury notes would be placed among clients through the banking networks. In order to facilitate their placement, a law of 29 May 1985 exempted these assets from tax withholding, while for other securities the rate of tax withholding was fixed at 18 per cent. The Treasury notes would be fiscally 'opaque' and therefore very attractive for 'black money', that is, for income that had not been declared to the tax authorities. The socialist Minister of Finance Miguel Boyer supported these measures while his secretary of state José V. Sevilla opposed them, so he was replaced by José Borrell. Boyer and Borrell later explained that in this way black money remained in Spain and contributed to public needs at a low cost (the yield of the notes was very low). In 1992, the enacting of a new income tax law put an end to this exceptional situation. The black money invested in the old notes would not be inspected anyway if it was placed in new notes with tax withholding, low remuneration and six years' maturity without advance repayment (Ayuso and Escrivá, 1997).

10
The Challenge of the European Market

10.1 Bank mergers and concentration

In 1992, the banker Alfredo Sáenz announced that Spanish banks, in a few years, would come to a true 'crossroads' that would make it difficult for them to obtain capital (Sáenz, 1992). The expected increase in competition, internally (by disintermediation) and externally (from the Single European Market of 1993), would cause a reduction in profitability and an increase in risk. These factors would depress the supply of capital to the banks, precisely at a time when it would be increasingly necessary to them in order to meet the requirements of the re-regulation that was in progress since 1988, when the Basel Committee, created by the BIS in 1974 in response to the Herstatt Bank crisis, had reached an agreement known as Basel I (1988), which involved the establishment of minimum capital levels for banks (the 'Cooke ratio'), starting from 1993. This agreement was internationally accepted and applied, so it was to be in vigour in Spain too.

One way to solve the problem of shortage of capital was to rationalise banking structures through mergers and acquisitions. By 1980, the heads of the seven major banks were divided on this issue. Those against mergers were Banesto (José María Aguirre Gonzalo believed in specialization), Popular (Luis Valls Taberner advocated independence because of the specificity of his bank, very specialized in business retail banking), Vizcaya (Ángel Galíndez argued that efficiency had nothing to do with size – in this he concurred with Valls), and Santander (Emilio Botin II liked small banks, as they were operational and agile). By contrast, in favour of mergers were Bilbao (José Ángel Sánchez Asiaín considered it vital to find an optimum size), Hispano (Luis Usera believed that the Spanish market could be adequately served by two or three big banks), and Central (Alfonso Escámez saw mergers as the only way to survive in the future). Naturally, the banks' opinions were those of their chairmen (*Dinero*, August 1980). Apart from the effects of the crisis, the lack of a common view helps to explain why, shortly before Spain joined the EEC, the large Spanish banks had not made any progress in

Table 10.1 International rankings of the big Spanish banks, 1970–91

		Position in world ranking[a]	Position in European ranking[a]	World indicator[b]	European indicator[b]
1970	Hispano	71	29	5.25	3.03
	Banesto	81	36	6.00	3.47
	Central	107	48	8.73	5.05
	Bilbao	109	50	9.12	5.28
	Vizcaya	140	60	11.88	6.87
1975	Central	78	38	4.68	3.59
	Banesto	84	42	5.44	4.17
	Hispano	93	46	6.35	4.88
	Bilbao	95	48	6.66	5.11
	Vizcaya	110	55	8.35	6.41
1980	Banesto	78	39	4.56	4.24
	Central	88	46	5.31	4.94
	Bilbao	103	51	6.78	6.30
	Hispano	112	58	7.22	6.71
	Vizcaya	116	59	7.48	6.95
1985	Central	100	46	6.34	4.82
	Banesto	101	47	6.37	4.85
	Hispano	122	54	7.64	5.82
	Bilbao	130	57	8.39	6.39
	Exterior	133	59	8.62	6.56
1991	BCH[c]	31	16	4.19	2.60
	BBV[d]	37	18	4.35	2.69
	Banesto	59	28	5.67	3.51
	Santander	69	34	6.67	4.13
	Caja Madrid	96	48	13.11	8.12

[a] The ranking of 1970, the first of *The Banker*, was ordered by total assets; those of 1975, 1980, and 1985, by total assets less off-balance sheet risks; and that of 1991, by the tier I capital (capital plus reserves), as defined by the BIS.
[b] The world/European indicator has been obtained dividing the average of the total assets of the five major world/European banks by the total assets of each Spanish bank. In 1975, 1980, and 1985 the off-balance sheet risks were subtracted.
[c] BCH was born from the merger of Central and Hispano.
[d] BBV was born from the merger of Bilbao and Vizcaya.
Source: *The Banker*.

concentration and their international ranking was lower than that ten years earlier (Table 10.1).

In view of the above considerations, in addition to the fear of takeovers of some large Spanish banks by foreign entities, around 1987, the government and the Bank of Spain were calling for mergers among Spain's largest institutions (for a not very recent but concise survey of Spanish bank mergers see Tortella, 2001). Sánchez Asiaín was in agreement, and, on 30 September 1987, he took the first step by proposing an understanding to Pedro de Toledo, just appointed chairman of the Vizcaya, almost next door. Not finding the expected response, two months later, Sánchez Asiaín tried to take over one of the big Madrid banks. He fixed his eyes first on the Hispano, under Bank of Spain ward since 1985. He probably did not like what he saw, or was rebuffed, so he then turned to Banesto, offering the shareholders of this bank a takeover bid, which was at first friendly and then became hostile (González *et al.*, 2007, Ch. VI). The operation failed due to the intervention of two major shareholders (Juan Abelló and Mario Conde) who had just taken control of the institution. Shortly afterwards, on 17 May 1988 a document of intent for a merger 'pure and simple' between Banesto and Central was signed, after the possibility of a merger with Hispano or Popular was ruled out (Banco Español Central de Crédito, 1988).

According to this document of intent, the chairmen of Central and Banesto, Mario Conde and Alfonso Escámez, respectively, would stay in their posts until the end of the merger process. Meanwhile, Escámez would assume the presidency of the *Banco Español Central de Crédito* (BECC) and Conde that of its executive committee and the post of CEO. After the transition, Conde would become executive chairman of the BECC and Escámez would be relegated to the presidency of a new advisory board. It had been decided that the merger should be slow so as to favour the natural convergence of both companies (as explained to *Dinero*, 3 June 1988). The approach seemed flawless and was supported by the rating agency Moody's, but on 28 February 1989 Conde sent a letter to Escámez where he expressed his desire to withdraw from the transaction. Escámez did not conceal his bewilderment, and even sadness, caused by the failed attempt to merge with Banesto (*La Gaceta de los Negocios*, 29 March 1989). The main reason for Conde's turnaround had been the opposition of the economic and monetary authorities to the merger.

To understand what had happened we must go back to November 1977, when the merger between the *Banco Central* and the *Banco Ibérico*, a smaller bank, was announced. This operation allowed Central to become the leader of Spanish banks in assets, displacing Banesto (for the following see García Ruiz, 2012). Banesto's reaction was to acquire *Banco Coca* a month later, with the sole guarantee of Ignacio Coca's wealth. Coca, the bank's president and almost sole owner, was a banker from Salamanca who had been very successful in a financially backward region such as Old Castille (Coronas Vida, 2012). Banesto bought Coca blindly (without due diligence) in a foolish attempt to regain leadership of the banking systema as soon as possible. The operation was a disaster, as the Coca's business network had serious undeclared problems. Ignacio Coca committed suicide in June 1986, leaving debts to the tune of 45,000 million pesetas, which could hardly be covered with the 15,000 million pesetas of his net wealth. To the 'Coca error', the Banesto of Aguirre Gonzalo (non-executive chairman) and Pablo Garnica Mansi (CEO) added the 'Bandri-Cadesbank error' in September 1978, which was the acquisition of two banks with those brand names controlled by Jaime Castell. In the spring of 1980, the *Banco Catalán de Desarrollo* (Cadesbank) had to be restructured by the FGD, while the redressing of the *Banco de Madrid* (Bandri) became the sole responsibility of Banesto (it took five long years). There was a third mistake: the 'BGN error'. At the time José María López de Letona was restructuring Bandri (1984–85), an inspection of the Bank of Spain disclosed that the *Banco Garriga Nogués* (BGN), a Catalan subsidiary of Banesto since 1952, and which had been managed since 1977 by Javier de la Rosa, had serious problems: half of its investments were dubious and five clients connected with De la Rosa concentrated 55.4 per cent of the credits granted.

On 17 February 1986, the governor of the Bank of Spain sent the chairman of Banesto, Pablo Garnica, a report that would have serious consequences. The supervisor said that Banesto had to mark down 95,000 million pesetas as additional losses on its balance sheet, of which 44,000 belonged to BGN, 12,800 to *Banco Coca* and 8,000 to Bandri. A month later, José María López de Letona was appointed CEO of Banesto with the aim of carrying out a complete restructuring of the bank. Letona was a distant relative of the governor of the Bank of Spain and there were directors of Banesto who viewed his entrance in Banesto, a conservative institution, as intervention by the socialists in power (Prime Minister Felipe González was socialist and the governor of the Bank of Spain, Mariano Rubio, was an uncommitted sympathizer). On 25 June 1986, two grandchildren of the founders of Banesto, Ricardo Gómez-Acebo and César de la Mora, were appointed to the executive committee against López de Letona's wishes.

In June 1987 it was agreed that López de Letona would become the bank's chairman starting 12 December, but the plans went awry in August when Juan Abelló and Mario Conde bought more than 2 million shares of Banesto. Abelló and Conde were members of the executive committee when the *Banco de Bilbao* launched its takeover bid; they led the opposition of traditional 'Banesto families' to an operation that they alleged was politically motivated. On 30 November 1987, Conde became chairman of Banesto. Soon afterwards, the syndics of the stockmarkets of Madrid, Barcelona and Valencia rejected the validity of the takeover bid and the *Banco de Bilbao* gave up on the operation. Conde became a hero in the eyes of many Banesto shareholders.

In October 1988, Conde was forced to accept the appointment of three independent directors imposed by the government to monitor the course of events; in addition, there was an exchange of directors with the *Banco Central*. At the end of the year, Conde acknowledged that Banesto had lost market share and that its default ratio was high, but he relied on the bank's patrimonial assets to generate ancillary profits in order to attend to the provisions required by the Bank of Spain, which amounted to 80,000 million pesetas. In early 1989, the distrust towards Conde by the three independent directors and by the Central's directors was evident. In February 1989, when the project of creating the BECC was abandoned, Abelló, Conde's associate for many years, broke away from him and left Banesto. Shortly afterwards, in the spring–summer of 1989, three of the five historical families of shareholders also left the bank (Banesto had been controlled by these families almost from its foundation in 1902), with a harsh disavowal of the accounting manipulations by Conde's men to simulate profits in 1988 and of the failed quest to absorb the Central. Conde's reaction was to appoint a team of faithful collaborators to replace his critics; he then would involve Banesto in dubious operations with the help of his cronies in the following years. So dubious were these operations, and so disastrous their results, that Banesto was intervened by the Bank of Spain in December 1993, auctioned a few months later, and acquired by the *Banco de Santander.*

In the *Banco Central,* the main consequence of the failure of the BECC project was the withdrawal of *Cartera Central,* a holding company which controlled the participation of the Kuwait Investment Office (KIO), from the equity in the bank. KIO had been purchasing Central's shares since October 1986; some Spanish partners had joined in late 1987 and they combined to create *Cartera Central* in 1988. *Cartera Central* had opposed the merger with Banesto; however, they soon afterwards abandoned their attempt to take over or take an active part in the Banco Central to discourage Escámez's resistance to enter into risky operations and, of course, to sell out the bank to foreign capital (largely Kuwaiti in this case). Escámez was a banker of the old school, whose motto was 'we strive to create enterprises' (Escámez, 1987, p. 15). What had attracted him to Banesto had been the possibility of increasing the commitment of Spanish banks to industry. By a stroke of luck, the position of *Cartera Central* against the merger had helped to save him from falling into the clutches of Conde, the only leading Spanish banker (with Ruiz Mateos) to have been sent to jail in Spain since the time of Cabarrus.

But, as we noted at the beginning of this chapter, Escámez was convinced of the need for his bank to be very large to face the strategic challenge of competition within the EEC. This explains why, on 14 May 1991, he signed a new document of intent towards a merger with an old acquaintance: the Hispano. At that time the Santander of Emilio Botín III, who had succeeded his father in 1986, had broken away from the traditional conservatism of his institution and seemed ready to pounce on the decaying Madrid banks (Tortella, 2001). The Santander had started its career towards the top from being a rather obscure provincial establishment in 1946, when it absorbed the *Banco Mercantil* under the guidance of its chairman, Emilio Botín II, and with the support of Ignacio Villalonga of the *Banco Central.* It had been a complex manoeuvre, because the Mercantil was bigger than the Santander, and Banesto had also been planning to absorb the Mercantil. The Santander had been one of the founders of the Central in 1919, but in the 1940s the Central was very much the senior. The good personal relations between Villalonga and Botín made both banks partners in many significant businesses, especially hydroelectrical works and bank absorptions. By the 1970s the Santander was among the *Big Seven*, and in the 1990s it became the top Spanish bank after purchasing Banesto in 1994 (Tortella, 2001; Martín Aceña, 2007, Ch. 5). It was fear of being taken over by the Santander that pushed Central and Hispano into each other's arms and to give birth to the *Banco Central Hispano Americano* (BCH) in the summer of 1991, thus in fact culminating an old merger project going back to 1965 (Banco Central Hispano Americano, 1991).

The share exchange ratio would be: five shares of the Central for six of the Hispano, according to the specific weights determined by Price Waterhouse. The government expressed its support by the granting of 93,000 million pesetas in tax exemptions, which was the maximum possible legal dispensation, over 269,000 million pesetas of capital gains resulting from the merger. When the transaction was made public, Minister of Finance Carlos Solchaga was jubilant: 'please, conceal my joy', he admonished the journalists in the corridors of the Cortes. In October 1992, Escámez left the presidency of the BCH and let the managers of the Hispano, very close to the centres of political power since it had been intervened in 1985, to take control of the bank. After his recent experiences, for Escámez (1992, p. 24) the main question was not whether the merger united homogeneous or complementary institutions, but whether it was possible or not to exploit economies of scale and economies of scope (Gual and Vives, 1991, noticed that in banking scope economies are more frequent than scale economies).

The new but old BCH coexisted for a few years with another megabank, the *Banco Bilbao Vizcaya* (BBV), born in June 1988 from the merger of the two largest banks in the Basque country. This operation and the attempt to create the BECC convinced Emilio Botín III, chairman of the Santander, that Spanish banking had entered a phase of total restructuring and this conviction had encouraged him to launch a 'supercuenta' in September 1989 to increase deposits at a fast rate albeit paying up to 11 per cent on call accounts. After the Banesto's intervention, Botín III paid a huge sum of money to gain control of this bank in 1994; then, at the beginning of 1999, he absorbed the BCH, which allowed the birth of the BSCH, the base of the current Banco Santander (Martín Aceña, 2007; Guillén and Tschoegl, 2008). After so much resistance to Santander by Escámez and Amusátegui in 1991, the latter one meekly surrendered the BCH to Botín only eight years later. The BBV's response to the growth of Botín's bank was to merge in that same year (1999) with a recently formed conglomerate of all the public banks, named *Argentaria*. Thus was formed the BBVA, whose chairman, from January 2000, would be Francisco González, the man who had presided over Argentaria between 1996 and 1999 (when the conservative José María Aznar was president of the Spanish government). The Galician González was reluctantly admitted by the Basque bourgeoisie (González *et al.*, 2007), but had to be accepted, among other reasons, because there was a latent conflict in the BBV between the managements of the two original banks, the Bilbao and the Vizcaya, since the merger. Created in 1991 by a former high official on the Vizcaya, Francisco Luzón, Argentaria included the six public banks of 1962, as well as the Exterior and the *Caja Postal*, an institution born in 1909 whose branches were the public post offices; in 1972, the *Caja* had been reorganized as '*Caja de ahorros del Estado*' ('state savings bank'). The only surviving public bank was the ICO, established in 1971 and still operating today.

10.2 A new role for the Bank of Spain

The biggest challenge the Bank of Spain had to face in the late twentieth century was the intervention of Banesto in 1993 (García Ruiz, 2012). This was the answer to a series of bad, sometimes criminal, decisions that had been taken in Banesto for four and a half years, between July 1989 and December 1993. The starting point was the reorganization of 27 July 1989, when chairman Mario Conde appointed a man very close to him as general manager, while credits to the tune of 2,000 million pesetas were granted to firms related to his personal interests. Soon afterwards, Conde had the idea to create the *Corporación Industrial* (Industrial Corporation), a holding company to gather all of Banesto's equity participations, something which was made possible by the tax credits granted in April 1990 by the socialist government. The corporation would include prestigious companies such as *Acerinox, Agromán, Asturiana de Zinc, Carburos Metálicos, Petromed, Sansón, Sniace, Tudor* or *La Unión y El Fénix Español*. These were leading firms in the fields of iron and steel, mining, metallurgy, building and contracting, chemicals, petrol, electricity, and insurance The Serratosa family, owner of a good fraction of *Valenciana de Cementos* (a cement company) was opposed to joining Industrial Corporation, fearing that the Valenciana, linked to Banesto for years, might be badly managed by Conde (as a result, *Valenciana de Cementos* would end up being the gateway of *Cemex* – the giant Mexican cement company – into Spain).

Seconded by a docile board of directors, Conde started practising 'financial engineering' in total opposition to the traditional Banesto culture, which was based on the employment of the bank's own resources and on supporting the real economy. Conde outsourced a significant portion of management and created an internationally extended network of subsidiaries that served to channel investments with dubious purposes. The *Annual Report* of 1991 notes that, since its foundation, Industrial Corporation had invested about 138,000 million pesetas, while more than 95,000 had been divested. Such unusual behaviour was justified, according to the report, by the pressures by the Bank of Spain for Banesto to reduce risk concentration in subsidiaries (1990) and to increase equity (1991). But the fact is that, in late 1991, things were not going well and Conde had to resort to new 'creative accounting': for instance, the accounts of the healthy Portuguese bank *Totta e Açores*, partly owned by Banesto, were included in the balance sheet of this bank in order to make it look better, but causing a conflict with the directors of Totta, who justifiedly considered the operation improper.

By mid-1992, Conde was worried about his inability to relaunch Banesto. Reports from the rating agency Moody's were very unfavourable. Conde then went to J. P. Morgan, looking for support. In the Banesto board of directors meeting of 27 November 1992, two senior executives of the US investment bank said that, if Conde's path was followed, Banesto would again lead Spanish banking. In that same meeting, Enrique Lasarte, a close friend of Conde, became the new CEO, replacing Juan Belloso, who had resigned, and Arturo Romaní, another friend of Conde, was promoted to vice chairman. The support of J. P. Morgan took shape in February 1993, when the entry of Corsair Partnership in Banesto's capital was announced. This was a limited partnership of the state of Delaware, whose sole general partner was Corsair, Inc. (100 per cent of J. P. Morgan), but where there were a total of 46 investors (incidentally, 'Corsair' was the name of John Pierpont Morgan's yacht, which was sold to the US government and used in the war against Spain in 1898).

The sale of the *Banco de Madrid* to a subsidiary of Deutsche Bank allowed Banesto's balance sheet for the first quarter of 1993 to show a profit before tax of 17,400 million pesetas. Soon afterwards, in May, J. P. Morgan presented a plan to recapitalize Banesto, involving a capital increase of 130,000 million pesetas and an issue of subordinated debt. Corsair participated in the part of the capital increase allocated among directors, managers, employees and institutional investors. But J. P. Morgan never directly invested in Banesto and refused to underwrite the issue of subordinated debt. In the *Memorandum of International Information*, which encouraged prospective investors to subscribe new shares, the liquidation value of Industrial Corporation was estimated at over 211,000 million pesetas by 11 June 1993. Conde seemed willing to continue to cover the losses of Banesto's banking business with capital gains on the sale of an industrial portfolio that embodied a huge contribution to the economic development of Spain.

The Executive Committee of the Bank of Spain, at its meeting of 28 December 1993, found that Conde had gone too far in juggling accounts and hiding losses and ordered the intervention of Banesto. The situation detected by the central bank was such that, to 30 June, the requirements of provisions to balance the accounts of Banesto amounted to more than 503,000 million pesetas (Price Waterhouse upped that figure to 605,000 million for the end of the year). There were problems with asset quality and contingencies not covered, a chronic shortage of equity, risk concentration (the risk in the Banesto Group companies exceeded 64.3 per cent of equity), with the estimates of the proft and loss accounts of recent years, and with cash management. The Bank of Spain considered the situation 'exceptionally serious' and determined to apply the Law of Discipline and Intervention of Credit Institutions of 1988 to protect the interests of shareholders and depositors and to ensure proper functioning of the financial system. A manager from the *Banco de Vizcaya*, Alfredo Sáenz, was appointed new chairman and the board was replaced in its entirety. The intervention was followed by a lawsuit that ended with heavy prison sentences for Conde (over 20 years) and his collaborators.

The governor of the Bank of Spain who intervened Banesto was professor Luis Ángel Rojo, a man linked to the central bank since 1971, where he had been head of the Research Department (1971–88), deputy governor (1988–92) and governor since the summer of 1992 (he was in this post for eight years). The Banesto intervention led to its restructuring with funds from the FGD and then its selling at auction, where it was acquired in April 1994 by the *Banco de Santander* (the loss suffered by the FGD was of about 193,000 million pesetas – almost 1,160 million euros – according to Aríztegui, 2012, p. 172). Rojo's decisions regarding Banesto were almost unanimously applauded and a law of 1 June 1994 consecrated the autonomy of the Spanish central bank, which was one of the Maastricht Treaty requirements to access the Economic and Monetary Union (EMU, or Eurozone, as it was commonly named later; Appendix 4 shows the convergence of Spain with the EMU countries). Hereafter, the governor and the deputy governor of the Bank of Spain would be elected for six non-renewable years. The sole restrictions to the Bank's operations would be that its main target should be price stability and the prohibition to grant overdrafts or any sort of monetary financing to the public sector, something which was in line with the future Eurosystem, that is, the system of central banks of the Eurozone, to which the Bank of Spain would belong from 1 January 1999.

In the Eurosystem, the Bank of Spain, as all other national central banks, had to cede monetary policy competence to the European Central Bank (ECB), but it kept supervisory functions. Rojo understood that the elimination of the currency-exchange risk opened the doors to financial expansion in Europe to a degree as had never been known before and he was very concerned about it. Upon taking the office of deputy governor, Rojo had written that financial innovation was not always an unqualified social good, that it could adversely affect the average quality of loan and credit portfolios and that, through off-balance sheet operations, it could raise substantial problems of risk information; to Rojo, financial stability was a value that should be protected even at the cost of some inefficiency (Rojo, 1988). Soon afterwards came times of euphoria as the Bank of Spain led by Mariano Rubio and Luis Ángel Rojo did not hesitate to curtail credit growth by means of quantitative restrictions – credit had been growing at around 20 per cent annually – established between mid-1989 and late 1990. Rojo was convinced that crises are always forged in previous years of great prosperity, something which has been validated by recent research (Jiménez and

Saurina, 2006). The experience with the Banesto of Mario Conde (1988–93) only reaffirmed Rojo's convictions.

Rojo's last major contribution to the stability of the Spanish financial system was a circular letter of 1999 (9/1999) instructing banks to constitute countercyclical provisions that would become known as 'dynamic provisions' (Poveda, 2000; Saurina, 2009; Poveda, 2012). These were a new type of provisions that institutions should accumulate during their boom years of low default ratios for use when the inevitable crisis would manifest itself. Each financial year, a gross provision should be calculated, applying different coefficients to credit exposures according to their potential insolvency; from gross provision credit deterioration should be subtracted to obtain the desired level of net provision. Dynamic provisions would be redesigned by a new Bank of Spain circular of 2004 adapted to the Basel II standards. Nevertheless, dynamic provisions were not accepted as capital, because the BIS believed that the role of capital should be to cover unexpected losses. This has always been problematic for dynamic provisions. It has also been noted that, from a certain standpoint, these provisions could be a 'perverse incentive' to lend in an irresponsible way, because the banker could think that they would cushion him/her against the consequences of defaults (Terceiro, 2012, p. 188). But the overall assessment of dynamic provisions has been positive, and the International Accounting Standards Board (IASB) has designed a loan accounting system inspired by their philosophy. The Basel III agreement (2010) allowed national regulators to require 2.5 per cent more of capital in periods of high credit growth as a countercyclical capital buffer.

10.3 Expansion abroad

After the Civil War, the fierce nationalism of the Franco dictatorship hampered the arrival of foreign capital, something which contributed to delay the postwar recovery of the Spanish economy. Since 1959, Spain's regulatory environment became more flexible and Spain again received capital fluently, first from the United States and then from European countries, which took longer to normalize relations with Franco's government. In a somewhat unexpected way, the capital inflow showed a declining trend during the 1990s, in contrast with an increasingly vigorous outflow. So, at the end of the twentieth century, the net capital balance was negative: Spain had become a net exporter of capital (Durán Herrera, 2005, p. 85). The vectors of this investment outflow were a group of newly minted multinationals, where the two largest banks, Santander and BBVA, were leaders.

Financial repression in this area dated back to the Law of Monetary Crimes, of 24 November 1938, which characterized as such the acquisition of goods and rights abroad without the pertinent administrative authorization.

Measures of this type remained in place even after the Stabilization Plan and liberalizing measures of 1959, as the Franco regime considered that, given its level of development, the country could not afford capital outflows. It was not until a decree of 1 March 1973, followed by another of 14 April 1978, that the restrictions over direct investment began to be relaxed. In 1979, thanks to a royal decree of 14 September and an order of 15 October, the required administrative authorization gave way to a simple verification of the authenticity, consistency, and conformity with the legal framework of the investments. After Spain joined the EEC in 1986, the legal foreign investment regime was adapted progressively to the freedom of capital movements prevailing in the organisation; there was a period of adaptation, which ended in 1992.

Between 1959 and 1973, Spanish direct investment abroad amounted to 274.18 million dollars; the main exporting sectors were banking (28.3 per cent), trade (25.4 per cent), and manufacturing (22.3 per cent). The geographical destination of these investments were Latin America and Europe (mostly, France and Portugal), Africa (especially, the Maghreb) and the United States (Moreno Moré, 1975). These patterns continued in 1974–78, which, for Durán Herrera (2005, p. 91), shows that 'cultural proximity is an important explanatory factor' of foreign investment. In the 1970s investment abroad momentarily became more industrial, with a strong preference for Latin America. But in the 1980s, marked by the liberalization of 1979, industrial investments declined in favour of financial ones: up to 62.25 per cent of the investments in the period 1986–90 were related to that sector (Durán Herrera, 2005, p. 93). Available data for 1993–2003 show the following distribution by sector: primary, 14.2 per cent; secondary, 24.7 per cent; tertiary, 61.1 per cent, with an outstanding participation of banking and insurance, transport and communications (Durán Herrera, 2005, p. 98). Therefore, it can be said that banking has had a considerable weight within the foreign investment of the Spanish economy.

The importance of the Latin American area has been paramount for Spanish investment since the mid-1970s. According to Giráldez Pidal (2002, p. 44), in the period 1975–83, this area accounted for an average of 34.1 per cent of direct investments; its share fell to 23.1 per cent in 1984–95, but it recovered in 1996–99 and reached 58.7 per cent, nearly double the share of its immediate follower, Europe. At that time, after a severe Latin American debt crisis, Spain made a risky bet in which it was not followed by the major Western countries (Giráldez Pidal, 2002, p. 46). A characteristic feature of Spanish investment compared to that of other developed countries was the small presence of the manufacturing sector, which is not surprising given Spain's weakness in R & D. But other 'intangible assets', related to management skills, are more important than R & D in finance, construction and utilities, and in these lines of business the Spanish multinationals bloomed (Guillén, 2005, pp. 13–16).

Around 1986, the year when Spain joined the EEC, a wave of investment in Spain was unleashed that was not immediately matched by Spanish outward investment. In the early 1990s, however, Spanish businessmen reacted and embarked on a process of very rapid creation of multinationals, which raised the stock of foreign investment from 1 to 35 per cent of GDP between 1980 and 2004 (Guillén, 2005, p. 11). Somehow, Spanish businessmen understood that only by growing bigger through investing in Latin America would they be able to withstand the onslaught of the large European companies in the EMU. Thus, Spain joined the select club of countries with multinationals, following a pattern that was consistent with the classic 'Investment Development Path' (Dunning, 2001); but this was done by burning stages, and therefore at the cost of high indebtedness.

The investment of banks abroad attracted much attention of economic theorists in the 1980s, who attributed it to several factors: according to some authors, there were push factors in the countries of origin, such as the high cost of capital, that is, high Tobin Q ratios, or, in other words, high market value of capital compared with its book value (Aliber, 1984); other authors attributed it to domestic over-regulation (Sengupta, 1988), while others focused upon the convenience of risk diversification by geographical dispersion (Grubel, 1985) or the need to serve corporate clients in their international expansion (Channon, 1988). Scholars in this field suggest that the process of multinationalization of Spanish banking institutions was due to a combination of all these factors, but in the cases of real success (Santander and BBVA) what weighed above all else were their links to large non-financial Spanish multinationals (Telefónica, Iberia, Endesa, Iberdrola, Repsol) that had entered Latin American markets before them (Berges, *et al.*, 2012).

The banks usually have two options for channelling their investments abroad: subsidiaries and branches (Cerutti, *et al.*, 2007). Spanish investment began with subsidiaries in Latin America and the English-speaking world (United Kingdom, United States) and continued with branches in Continental Europe, after the creation of the Eurozone, something that favoured choosing EU countries when investing abroad. The European directives of 15 December 1989 and 14 June 2006 made branches more convenient than subsidiaries in the EU, as neither a specific authorization nor a minimum capital are required for the former and supervision from the home country is allowed. However, in Latin America subsidiaries show advantages over branches, because, as crises are more frequent in emerging countries and subsidiaries have their own legal and economic autonomy, they permit better insulation of problems so that their short-term difficulties affect the parent institution less.

The internationalization of the *Banco de Santander* started in 1988 when Emilio Botin III signed an alliance with the Royal Bank of Scotland to improve the capacity of the Spanish bank to face competition from foreign competitors once Spain joined the EEC (Guillén and Tschoegl, 2008). Botín thought that another way to deal with the new competition should be to gain market share, which was achieved by launching the *supercuenta* by surprise, and by acquiring historical Madrid banks (Banesto, 1994; BCH, 1999). These transactions were made at high cost, but allowed Santander to have enough muscle to tackle international expansion. The next international steps were taken with the acquisition of *Banca Serfín* (Mexico, 1999) and *Banespa* (Brazil, 2001), while the BCH's experience in Latin America was taken advantage of in Chile and Argentina to form *Santander Chile* and *Santander Río* (the basis for this one was the historical *Banco Español del Río de la Plata*) and there were movements in the United States starting from Puerto Rico. The Santander's interest in the European market resulted in the purchase of the British Abbey National Bank in 2004. The successful internationalisation of Santander, led by Botín III and his qualified managers (such as Alfredo Sáenz, CEO since 2002, or Francisco Luzón, responsible for the expansion in Latin America since 1996), has turned Santander into the undisputed leader of the Spanish market and a bank able to gain leadership in the Eurozone.

The BBVA case is quite similar to that of *Santander*: first, the megabank was created; then came the expansion across Latin America (Arroyo, Larrinaga y Matés, 2012). As noted, the BBVA is the result of the 1988 merger of *Banco de Bilbao* with the *Banco de Vizcaya* to give birth to the BBV, which became BBVA after merging in 1999 with Argentaria. During its short existence, the BBV took control of many Latin American institutions: *Continental*, in Peru, 1995; *Probursa*, in Mexico, 1995; *Ganadero*, in Colombia, 1996; *Francés*, in Argentina, 1996; *Banca Cremi y Oriente*, in Mexico, 1996; *Provincial*, in Venezuela, 1997; *BHIF*, in Chile, 1998; *Excel Económico*, in Brazil, 1998; *Poncebank*, in Puerto Rico, 1998. But, the first great operation, the acquisition of the control share package of the Mexican Bancomer in 2000–01, was only possible for a megabank such as BBVA. Since 2003, investments were resumed, with the purchase of the total capital of *Bancomer* and of *Hipotecaria Nacional* (2004) and new interventions in Colombia (*Granahorrar*, 2005) and Chile (*Forum*, 2007). Unlike Santander, BBVA has shown no interest in the Eurozone (apart from Spain and Portugal) and has shifted its internationalization process towards the United States (with the help of Bancomer) and Asia (through an alliance with the Chinese Citic Group).

In the early twenty-first century, the expectations created by the introduction of the single currency produced a proliferation of branches of foreign banks in the Eurozone. Spanish banks participated in this process, including savings banks, which had been absent from the expansion in Latin America. Lacking this experience, the foreign branches of savings banks were not successful and their managers decided, since 2003, to concentrate their efforts on the booming Spanish property sector with the results that are well known. By contrast, Santander and BBVA persisted in their multinational strategy, which would allow them to balance risks and to compensate and offset the weaknesses and problems of the Spanish market in the years of crisis with the profits made in overseas markets.

10.4 Europhoria

From 1 July 1990, there was freedom of capital movement among the countries of the EEC, with some exceptions, such as Spain, where, due to its recent incorporation to the organization, that freedom was delayed until February 1992, coinciding with the signing of the Maastricht Treaty that gave birth to the EU. Soon after came the first crisis: in the summer of 1992, the Bundesbank, chaired by Helmut Schlesinger, raised interest rates to restrain domestic spending and so curb the inflation linked to German reunification (the currency of West Germany was equated to that of the German Democratic Republic for purely political reasons: it was a bad economic blunder). The European Monetary System (EMS) that linked the exchange rates of the EEC currencies since 1979 was put to the test. Germany was asked to rectify but its answer was that a realignment of parities was needed. While this debate was taking place, four currencies (Italian lira, Portuguese escudo, Spanish peseta and British pound sterling) suffered attacks by speculators who were convinced that it would be impossible to maintain the exchange rate regime (George Soros earned 1 billion dollars by betting against the pound). The result was that, in mid-September, the pound and the lira left the exchange rate mechanism of the EMS and the peseta was devalued by 5 per cent against the mark. In November, the peseta was devalued again (6 per cent against the mark), dragging down the Portuguese escudo. It was then realized that the introduction of the peseta in the EMS in 1989 by Minister of Finance Carlos Solchaga had been a mistake. The benchmark rate of 1989 had been fixed too high because the market rate at that time, in a moment of strong inflow of foreign capital attracted by the recent accession of Spain to the EEC, despite the fact that the Spanish economy was still suffering from severe structural weaknesses and imbalances, was well above a long-term equilibrium point.

The EMS crisis of 1992 did not impede the advance towards the EMU designed in Maastricht, and on 1 January 1993 the European Stability Mechanism (ESM) was born, as foreseen in the Single European Act of 1986 and in the Maastricht Treaty of 1992. Currency tensions returned in May 1993, when the peseta and the escudo had to be devalued again (the peseta was devalued by 8 per cent against the mark). When the French franc was threatened, in August 1993, it was decided to widen the fluctuation bands of national currencies around the average value to 15 per cent, which in practice meant that the EMS was no longer operating. Markets had triumphed over political wilfulness. Tensions continued in the following years and, for example, the peseta was once more devalued by 7 per cent against the mark in 1995. It was not until May 1998, that the path to monetary union was resumed, a path which this time led quickly and successfully to the implementation of the euro as the sole currency of the Eurozone on 1 January 1999 (although actual euro notes and coins would not circulate until 1 January 2002). The exchange rate for the peseta was established at 166.386 pesetas per euro, which enshrined the low value of the peseta after the four devaluations decreed by Felipe González in 1992, 1993, and 1995. After these devaluations wages were allowed to grow faster than inflation, against the advice of the Bank of Spain. On retirement, governor Rojo confessed that this had been his greatest failure. Unlike Franco Modigliani, who succeeded in convincing the Italian authorities to remove the 'scala mobile', that is, the indexation of wages, in Spain, Rojo's proposals to put an end to this threat to stability and competitiveness were never heeded (the first warning in Rojo, 1981).

The Spanish crisis of 1992–93, which pushed the unemployment rate above 20 per cent, has been explained by the loss of competitiveness caused by the heavily unbalanced policies of the late 1980s, when the whole stabilisation effort rested upon monetary policy (Malo de Molina, 2005). Competitiveness losses implied a sharp deterioration in the balance of payments, which was met with successive devaluations. The autonomy of the Bank of Spain, enshrined in 1994 within the framework of the implementation of the Maastricht Treaty, helped to establish medium-term goals for inflation, which were accepted first by the socialist minister Pedro Solbes (July 1993–May 1996) and then by the conservative minister Rodrigo Rato (May 1996–April 2004); price stability facilitated the incorporation of Spain to the Eurozone in 1999. This happened at a time when a climate of euphoria pervaded among economic regulators and agents, who neglected to discuss in depth the pros and cons of that event. The consequences of such oversight were bitterly lamented ten years later.

'Europhoria' explains why the Eurozone started out with little fiscal and political integration. Instead, the European authorities relied on a Stability and Growth Pact, proposed by Germany and signed in 1997 by all EU member states. The pact was based on the Maastricht Treaty and declared that countries should keep their budget deficits below 3 per cent of GDP and their public debt below 60 per cent of GDP. In Maastricht these criteria had been set as necessary to access the Eurozone, with the addition of another three: (i) inflation not above 1.5 percentage points over the average of the three least inflationary countries; (ii) long-term interest rates not above 2 percentage points on the average of the three least inflationary countries; (iii) not having practised currency devaluations in the previous two years. The pact put in the hands of the European Commission and the Ecofin (the Council of the Ministers of Finance of the EU) the monitoring of the steady compliance to the main conditions of stability in order to ensure the viability of the EMU. Today, it is thought that the EU should have gone further in the monitoring of public finances (fiscal union) and financial institutions (banking union) to avoid the serious crisis that has engulfed the euro since 2010 (on the banking union, see Commission of the European Communities, 2007; European Central Bank, 2009).

The main consequence of 'europhoria' for Spain, between 1999 and 2007, was a change in its external financial position, measured by the difference between its external assets and liabilities. According to the *Cuentas Financieras de la Economía Española* (in the BIEST Database) this position deteriorated due to the continuous advancement of financial liabilities along with a decline in assets since 2003. The explanation of the gap lies in the internationalization of Spanish financial institutions, which accelerated in the final years of the twentieth century, as exchange risk decreased, being nil since 1999 within the Eurozone (the exchange risk is a factor that financial institutions take very much more into account in their international operations than other companies, as their only commodity is money). But, by 2003, the acquisition of financial assets abroad slowed down, because a part of the financial system, the savings banks, considered that the best place to invest was the domestic market.

The degree of financial openness, measured as the sum of foreign assets and liabilities in relation to the whole range of assets and liabilities, increased from 15.1 per cent in 1998 to 19.5 per cent in 2008 (Malo de Molina, 2012, p. 204). Behind these figures was the ability of financial institutions to mobilize resources from abroad to fulfil the requirements of the Spanish domestic economies and firms that wanted to keep high levels of spending over revenue generation. Borrowing by households and businesses was boosted by the low interest rates set by the ECB's monetary policy, when demand conditions in Spain would have required higher rates. Low interest rates were widely applied in Spain thanks to the generalized introduction of variable interest rates in loan agreements, especially mortgages.

In late 1998, the balance of net financial transactions with the rest of the world was near zero for Spain, that is to say, the country did not need outside funding. But the very strong growth in credit demand of the next years could not be met by domestic bank deposits alone. The process of banking integration in Europe prompted Spanish banks to borrow abroad to close the gap. The result was that in 2007 external financing needs already exceeded 9 per cent of GDP (Malo de Molina, 2012, p. 205).

10.5 Financial markets v. financial institutions

In 1952, the economist Joan Robinson summed up in the phrase 'where enterprise leads, finance follows' the idea that in the Keynesian paradigm the real economy is much more important than the financial economy (Robinson, 1952). Twenty years later, a critic of Keynesian economics, Robert Lucas, proposed the 'neutrality of money' in the process of economic development (Lucas, 1972), which was the topic of his acceptance speech for the Nobel

Prize in 1995. There is no unanimity on this point, however: from different perspectives, many economists have opined that finance is a causal factor in economic development. Among these economists we can include critics of financial repression (Shaw, 1973; McKinnon, 1973), but also economists such as Bagehot (1873), Schumpeter (1934), Gerschenkron (1962), Cameron (1967) and Goldsmith (1969). More recently, Ross Levine has proven in many studies that financial intermediation is a factor of economic growth (Levine and Zervos, 1998; Demirgüc-Kunt and Levine, 2001). Easterly, *et al.* (2000) agree, but warn that too much financing can also cause problems (as it happens with 'financialization').

A related question is: what type of financing is more convenient, that coming from stock markets or that coming from banks? Each company has a 'capital structure' (resources) that is determined by a combination of equity and debt, to which sometimes is added some hybrid form which has elements of both. In 1958, Franco Modigliani and Merton Miller published in the *American Economic Review* an influential article where they claimed that the configuration of a company's resources does not affect its value, a conclusion which could be construed as to justify unlimited external borrowing, although the norm would be a balance between funding sources. It was the well-known 'Modigliani–Miller Theorem', which undoubtedly helped their authors to win the Nobel Prize. However, Modigliani and Miller pointed out that their 'principle of irrelevance of capital structure' was valid only in a perfect market, which automatically converted the theorem into an ahistorical one (in history, markets have never been perfect).

In 1984, Stewart C. Myers opposed the so-called Pecking Order Model to the simplicity of Modigliani and Miller. The model is so named because its origin was in the observation of the pecking of birds. In their activity, birds as other animals, respect hierarchies: those that eat first are those higher up in the social ladder. Myers warned that the financing of businesses begins by issuing shares, continues with borrowing from banks and the cycle may end with the issuance of new shares. This last phase occurs when there is no alternative, because straight borrowing is often less expensive than issuing shares. In 1997, Jonathan B. Baskin and Paul J. Miranti issued a global history of corporate finance that had great impact and served to support the Pecking Order Model vs. the Modigliani–Miller Theorem. One could generalize, and state that countries need financing from banks in the early stages of economic development, but that afterwards, in more advanced stages, it is better to rely on markets. Raghuram Rajan and Luigi Zingales (2003) explain well the recent convergence of the continental European model (based on financial institutions) with the Anglo-American model (based on financial markets). This evolution is welcome for these authors because they find that financial markets are more efficient than financial institutions (Rajan and Zingales, 1998).

In Spain, until the mid-1980s, there were four official stock markets located in Madrid, Barcelona, Bilbao, and Valencia, to which a special market for government debt was added in 1987. A royal decree of 3 April 1987 ordered the creation of a system of electronic accounting for public debt and the organization of a *Central de Anotaciones de Deuda Pública* (Public Debt Registry), managed by the Bank of Spain (Aríztegui, 2012). This market, and its secondary market, did not operate in the official stock markets, but more informally, through 'Treasury desks', thus avoiding the rigidity and the expenses of the traditional dealers. It was a model inspired in the market for the US Treasury debt. Thus, the standard stock markets would be limited to the negotiation of bonds and shares issued by private companies in a spot market, because there was no organized market for derivatives (futures and options). The post-negotiation in the stock exchanges was in charge of auxiliary services that depended on the syndics.

The application of the Securities Market Act in 1988 (28 July) brought about a major change in the structure and functioning of the securities markets in Spain (García Hermoso and Zubiría, 1990). A *Comisión Nacional del Mercado de Valores* (CNMV, National Commission for the Securities Market), created on the model of the Rooseveltian Securities Exchange Commission (SEC), began to operate in 1989. Since then, the CNMV has been operating autonomously, but respecting the laws of the EU; for example, since 2004 the CNMV has ensured that the consolidated financial statements of listed companies were prepared in accordance with the International Financial Reporting Standards, elaborated by IASB and accepted by the EU legislation (Moreno, 2006).

In March 1989, forward operations were authorized; in June 1990, the *Fondtesoros* (investment funds in Treasury securities) were born; and in December 1991, official derivatives markets were regulated. All these regulated products had public debt as an included asset, a fact which allowed the Treasury to count with a regular and orderly base of financing since the early 1990s. After a tax reform in 1992, the controversial *pagarés del Tesoro* disappeared and the Treasury would issue *letras* (bills), *bonos* (bonds) and *obligaciones* (debentures), depending on whether the term was short, medium or long, respectively. These securities would be traded on the platform *Sistema Electrónico de Negociación de Activos Financieros*. In 2001, this platform formed a holding with two non-official markets: *Asociación de Intermediarios de Activos Financieros*, a bond market, and *Mercado Español de Futuros Financieros*, a derivatives market. In the following year, the merger of the holding and the four official stock exchanges gave birth to *Bolsas y Mercados Españoles* (BME). A subsidiary of BME, *Iberclear*, would be responsible for registration, clearing and settlement of transactions from the different markets and platforms. BME also incorporated Latibex, a market for Latin American securities denominated in euros (CNMV and Banco de España, 2007).

Banks and savings banks were admitted as members of the stock exchanges in 1993, competing with the securities agencies that had replaced the old *agentes de cambio y bolsa* (official dealers). Very soon, the investment services firms, controlled by the banks, would lead the stock market trading. Non-residents accessed the new markets especially through the branches of foreign investment banks, benefiting from an appropriate tax treatment consisting of reimbursement of the withholding taxes. The presence of banks in the stock markets would be completed with the Bank of Spain's entry in the capital of BME (Restoy and Rodríguez, 2010; Restoy and Sánchez de la Peña, 2012).

In 1998, the government of José María Aznar granted favourable treatment to the *Sociedades de Inversión de Capital Variable* (SICAVs), investment funds, usually very exclusive, which are the favourite formula for wealthy families to manage their financial assets (Restoy and Sánchez de la Peña, 2012, pp. 280–1). Aznar allowed the SICAVs to negotiate outside the regular or continuous market (where securities are continuously priced and traded in an auction format). In 2005, the socialist government of José Luis Rodríguez Zapatero improved the status of SICAVs by abolishing the requirement of official listing to continue receiving a favourable tax treatment. Consequently, the vast majority of these societies abandoned the regular stock markets and went to the *Mercado Alternativo Bursátil*, a special stock market for small and medium enterprises that grew out of BME. As shown in Table 10.2, a unique feature of the distribution of the household financial assets in Spain is the weight of unlisted shares.

The approval of the Securities Market Act increased the propensity of Spanish families to accumulate part of their financial wealth in stocks, thus initiating a process of convergence with the structure of the family portfolios of financial assets in other European countries. However, the convergence

Table 10.2 Distribution of household financial assets in Western Europe, 2010 (percentages)

	Cash and deposits	Investment funds and listed shares	Bonds	Pension and insurance funds	Others
France[a]	32.0	26.1	1.7	40.2	0.0
Germany	37.9	16.6	8.2	33.0	4.4
Italy	30.2	28.8	19.2	18.6	3.2
Spain	48.7	12.9	2.9	14.3	21.2[b]
United Kingdom	27.8	11.8	1.2	52.8	6.3

[a] 2009.
[b] Mainly, unlisted shares.
Source: Inverco (2011).

soon reached its limits and bank deposits have remained the most common form of financial asset in Spanish families' portfolios. Investment funds and pension funds failed to win the confidence of the public and corporate bond issues never lost their residual character. The derivatives of bonds must include public debt, and in this line of business the introduction of the euro moved the investors towards the German bond, which is the benchmark of the public debt in euros. Better luck had the derivatives of stocks, even though the negotiated volume fell far short of those in the leading countries.

A distinguishing feature of the Spanish financial system has been the role played by the banking system in the years of the housing boom as issuers of a huge volume of asset-backed securities, a volume which was only surpassed in Europe by the United Kingdom (Restoy and Sánchez de la Peña, 2012, p. 279). The explanation of this phenomenon is that although the strong growth in demand for credit could not be met by bank deposits alone, the banks used their experience in the stock markets to fill the gap by means of securities issues and asset securitization. The phenomenon would continue even after the outbreak of the crisis as Spanish banks needed more equity to offset the increase of delinquencies and to fulfil the subsequent provisions.

The existence of a common currency in the Eurozone increased the need for convergence in the functioning of the national financial systems. The *Lamfalussy Report* (2001) addressed this question by proposing harmonization measures, as in the Markets in Financial Instruments Directive (MiFID, 2004), which sought the maximum harmonization of investment services in the 30 countries of the European Economic Area (the 27 EU countries plus Iceland, Norway and Liechtenstein) (Gil, 2008). Under the umbrella of MiFID, true systems of multilateral negotiations were created, which specialized in derivatives, easy to operate and with the promise of high returns because they were highly speculative. At the beginning of the current crisis, the *Larosière Report* (2009) considered that it was necessary to erect a supervisory architecture for the financial system at the community level, so that the technical committees of banking, stock markets and insurance should become true 'European authorities', starting with the European Banking Authority, as the crisis was hitting very hard at this sector of the financial system.

10.6 More changes in the banking system

The banking business changed a great deal at the turn of the century (on the evolution of the composition of assets and liabilities in banking, see Appendix 11). Traditional banking, based on the intermediation between depositors and borrowers, has now changed and banks have become providers of services to investors (mutual funds, pension funds) and companies (securitization, insurance, and so on) and have also become investors of their own resources. The universal banks of today not only practise traditional retail banking, but they also practise very sophisticated investment banking, asset management (assets external to the balance sheet), investment of own equity (a concept that has expanded), and insurance (bancassurance).

In the 1980s, banks were alarmed by the spread of 'disintermediation', that is to say, the preference of clients for operating directly in the financial markets, which were becoming more accessible through the internet, bypassing the traditional financial intermediaries. This question was raised in the United States, where, in effect, disintermediation was reaching significant levels, but these fears were premature in Europe. The reaction of US banks was to submerge themselves into the stock markets so as to become a part of them. This is how the model of 'originate and distribute' arose. The model implied the securitization of loans: the bank originated the operation, but then divided it into securities that were placed on the market. The model assumed that the bank renounced to charging interest rates and was satisfied with the commissions collected, just as a simple stock market dealer (Vives, 2012, p. 388).

Branches were no longer offices designed for cash transactions and the classic intermediation, but became places endowed with a high level of investment in information and communication technologies, which were operated by a few highly skilled employees endowed with high levels of human capital. In Spain, the transformation was less innovative than in the Anglo-Saxon world; for example the model of 'originate and distribute' had little acceptance. Clients were conservative as well and internet banking spread slowly, because customers greatly appreciated having a branch close to home and personal relations with their bankers. In fact, if savings banks gained market share at the expense of commercial banks in Spain, it was in part due to the greater extent of their branch network, although their huge involvement in real estate loans and ideological reasons were also relevant.

The institutional framework in which financial institutions operated at the end of the century was shaped by the liberalization enacted in the 1980s. After some early interventionist moves (reserve requirements and mandatory investment in public debt were increased in 1984), the socialist government of Felipe Gonzalez accepted full liberalization of rates and fees in 1987. Two years later, in 1989, the same government approved a timetable for the full liberalization of investment, which would mean the end of the mandatory investment ratios in 1992 (they went from 10.625 in 1987 to 0 per cent in 1992). An order of 21 February 1990 reduced the minimum cash reserve ratio (liquid assets/deposits) from 17 to 5 per cent, thus releasing extra resources for investment (to avoid momentary problems due to lack of investment outlets, *Certificados de Regulación Monetaria* at 6 per cent were offered); the ratio would be lowered further in subsequent years and ended up at 2 per cent. Regarding the opening of offices, commercial banks could do it with complete freedom after 1985 and savings banks after 1988. This was the last step necessary to complete the process initiated in 1985 towards a full operational equality of savings banks and commercial banks. To prevent abuses of the new freedoms, the Discipline and Intervention of Credit Institutions Act of 29 July 1988 would act as a Damocles' sword, especially after its application in the 'Banesto affair'.

In the case of foreign banks, two royal decrees of 1988 and 1995 set rules for their harmonization with national banks in the mid-1990s. Interestingly, this welcoming attitude was not followed by a major presence of foreign banks in the Spanish market. On the contrary, foreign banks realized that it was very difficult and potentially expensive to compete with the services offered by the dense network of branches of the national banks, not only a very expensive structure but also much appreciated by the Spanish clients. Before and after being allowed to freely open branches in 1993, foreign banks preferred to limit structural costs and obtain resources in wholesale markets (mainly, the Spanish interbank market), although the cost of this funding was higher than funding through deposits. In the process, Spanish banks learned from their foreign competitors (for example, on the use of the wholesale markets or on the convenience of variable interest rate loans), and not vice versa, but in the end Spanish banks retained their hegemony in their national market.

Spanish bank liberalization was consistent with what was happening throughout the Western world. In this liberal atmosphere the BIS felt obliged to establish internationally accepted solvency requirements. Since the early 1990s, the regulatory agreements known as Basel I (1988), II (2004) and III (2010) were successfully put in force. They contained increasing demands for capital ratios, and preferred shares (perpetual equity, without political rights but with a high remuneration, although conditioned to the existence of profits) and subordinated debt (debt with high remuneration but usually perpetual and of very difficult reimbursement in case of liquidation of the company) were relegated and traditional equity grouped under the names of 'core tier I' (capital) and 'tier I' (capital and reserves) were given preference. In the light of recent experience, the BIS is setting capital requirements that take into account the increased risk incurred when banks have minority stakes (the decisions are not controlled by them) or are dealing in the insurance business. In addition, the BIS is trying to implement uniform liquidity and leverage ratios, something that should be useful for central banks around the world. All this means higher costs for the banks – equity is more expensive than deposits – and less available money for investment, with a change in the makeup of investment, which presumably will rely increasingly on credit and less on longer-term commitments.

The Spanish ratio of credit to the private sector to GDP was 63.1 per cent in 1975 and 169 per cent in 2008; in late 2009, banks had granted nearly

30 million euros in loans and more than 78 million in credit and debit cards, while the volume of accounts indicated a high level of 'bancarization': 27.3 million of current account deposits; more than 54 million of savings accounts; and 19 million of time deposits (Saurina, 2012, pp. 313–14). Of this 'bancarization' commercial banks and savings banks had partaken equally, because, as we saw earlier, both types of institutions had been put on an equal footing after the long banking transition which had started even before the political transition.

A unique feature of the Spanish banking system is its dense branch network. While in the EU the trend since 1997 has been to reduce the number of branches, in Spain this number has continued growing, so that ten years later (by 2007) Spain had the highest branch and ATM density per head of population, although the size of offices has become smaller (Vives, 2012, p. 396). Low population density and the traditional specialization in retail banking help to explain the large number of offices, while the low penetration of the broadband in telecommunications and the poor financial education explain the preference for operating with ATMs rather than on the internet.

If one were to define the Spanish financial system before the Great Recession, as the current crisis is often called, one could say that it was characterized by: (i) strong credit growth, with specialization in real estate; (ii) centrality of financial institutions, that is, banks, even though financial markets had developed in recent years; (iii) coexistence of retail funding (deposits) with wholesale funding (recourse to capital markets); (iv) increasing concentration; (v) high density of the branch network, which attracts retail customers but pushes up costs; (vi) higher 'market power' – as measured by margins, which normally are higher when the level of competition is lower – than in other neighbouring countries; (vii) high profitability, helped by increasing charges and commissions; (viii) solvency at the level of the EU-15; (ix) low default rates; (x) increasing internationalization (Vives, 2012, p. 392; see also Maudos and Fernández de Guevara, 2008). Saurina (2012, p. 343) is more optimistic about the level of competition in the banking system, but he states that 'this increasing competition has not been linear.' A result of the competition had been the loss of market share by commercial banks to the saving banks, so that at the end of the period the commercial banks only were leaders in deposits in one province (Madrid) and leaders in credits in four (one of them, Madrid) (Saurina, 2012, p. 322) (on regional bank financial flows, with historical perspective, see García Ruiz, 2003; 2007b). This feature, of course, is no longer true.

11
The Bursting of the Bubble: Savings Banks, a Death Foretold

11.1 Crisis and denial

There is agreement in calling the crisis that began in 2007 in the United States and in several European countries the 'Great Recession'. The origin of the crisis in the United States lay in the subprime mortgages that had been granted to insolvent or semi-solvent clients by institutions that practised a policy of 'originate and distribute', i.e., of granting credits and then transferring the risk to others through the securitization of these credits. In previous years, in the midst of continuing increases in the price of real estate, rating agencies had assessed positively this way of distributing of risk, regardless of the high probability of default in the medium term of the mortgage contracts that were at the core of these securities.

In the first quarter of 2007, the US housing bubble burst and assets based on subprime mortgages started receiving the name of 'toxic assets' ('troubled' assets was the more pious expression). Financial institutions that had these assets in their balance sheets or off-balance – in the so-called Structured Investment Vehicles – saw their solvency seriously threatened. The shock spread across financial markets and institutions free from toxic assets were affected as well by their difficulties to refinance.

Spanish banks were comparatively little affected by the first wave of crisis, as their direct or indirect exposure to toxic assets was very low. Spanish banks had maintained a retail orientation and were subject to rigorous supervision that had prevented, for example, investment in mortgage-backed securities through Structured Investment Vehicles. The institutions had covered the gap between credit growth and deposit volume by resorting to wholesale market facilities, but these were long-term liabilities and there were few refinancing problems in the short term. The first wave of crisis in Spain did not engulf banks, but building contractors and real estate agents; in this sector, the first failures took place in the spring of 2007 (Tortella and Núñez, 2009, pp. 136–44).

In September 2008, US authorities did not prevent the bankruptcy of the investment bank Lehman Brothers, which had accumulated an extraordinary amount of toxic assets because its chairman and CEO, Richard S. Fuld, had ignored the mortgage crisis of the previous year and had continued to invest in mortgage-backed securities. Panic spread through the financial world, assets were depreciated and bank credit stopped flowing. The financial crisis had become the Great Recession, and this time Spanish financial institutions could not avoid being drawn into it.

The government of José Luis Rodríguez Zapatero watched in horror how a fiscal surplus of around 2 per cent of GDP in 2007 turned into a deficit of more than 11 per cent in 2009; the immediate consequence of the swelling deficit was that public debt increased by leaps and bounds. Rodríguez Zapatero's first reaction had been the same as Fuld's, that is, the denial of a crisis that threatened the entire economic and social development achieved since the mid-1990s and, most important for him, threatened his re-election in 2008. When the Spanish president grudgingly admitted that things were serious he had been re-elected already, but by then it was too late and his policies were desultory. He resorted to increased public spending without a clear comprehensive plan; the consequences of his policies were growing deficits, mounting public debt, and galloping unemployment.

But the problems of the Spanish economy were structural rather than cyclical, as the economic development of recent years had been achieved with a model where construction (residential and non-residential) had carried a disproportionate weight. The construction boom had been fuelled by a series of factors. First and foremost, the low interest rates prevailing since the mid-1990s made buying houses on credit a very attractive investment for households of almost all levels of income. Public housing was also favoured by these same low interest rates, which permitted regional governments to borrow in order to build showy headquarters, sports arenas, congress palaces, underground parking lots, roads and all sorts of fancy buildings which brought in tax income and very possibly under the counter commissions. A strong current of immigration in turn fed the demand for housing and supplied the largely unskilled labour which the building industry demanded. In addition, low population density and sunny landscapes induced Spanish and foreign city dwellers to build second residences preferably but not exclusively near the sea. To all this, the bubble effect was added. Houses are universally considered to be one of the safest forms of investment; real estate prices had been going up for years; so ordinary citizens, realtors and bankers thought one could not go wrong by buying land and building houses. Spanish banks had not invested in securities related to subprime mortgages in the United States, but they had accumulated an extraordinary amount of loans granted to real estate promotors, building contractors and public works contractors in Spain. In this scenario it was rational to expect a sharp deterioration in real estate assets and a sudden stop in public investment in infrastructures at some point in time, so that the central engine of the Spanish economy would cease to function. The trouble was no one could know when this would happen and in the meantime business proceeded as usual, so that when the crunch came few people, including bankers, were prepared for it. The castles built in Spain soon became dusty financial ruins.

The crisis of the *Caja Castilla-La Mancha*, a savings bank, was the first warning of what was coming. The institution, largely in the hands of the socialist regional government, had committed huge sums to real estate transactions and public investments of dubious or null profitability. Rumours about its problems had circulated for over a year, but at the end of 2008 deposit withdrawals were creating an immediate liquidity problem. There were some attempts for a merger, or rather, absorption, by some other *Cajas*, but to no avail. Finally, in March 2009, the Bank of Spain took the decision to intervene and replace the directors with three administrators. The section of the FGD for savings banks allocated 30 per cent of its resources (1,300 million euros) to buy preferred shares that had been issued by *Caja Castilla-La Mancha* in order to make it possible for investors to get their money (Poveda, 2012, p. 261n). The operation was unorthodox because the FGD's mission was to insure deposits, not preferred shares, but these had been placed among small savers as a special type of deposit. In fact, these 'preferred shares', which were issued by other banks also and were to create many problems, really were equity, and it was interesting for banks to issue them because, together with subordinated debt, they helped to meet the equity ratios of the BIS (savings banks, due to their special legal status, had no capacity to raise capital like ordinary joint-stock banks; more about this later).

The government found it necessary to require savings banks to increase their contributions to the FGD from 0.4 to 1 per thousand of deposits (compared with 0.6 per thousand of banks and 0.8 per thousand of cooperatives), which led to protests. To address future problems of equity, a royal decree law in that same year (2009) established the *Fondo de Reestructuración Ordenada Bancaria* (FROB, Fund for Orderly Bank Restructuring). The legal regime of the FROB would be very similar to the FGD, with a governing body where the Bank of Spain would have the last word and the FGD would have a minority presence. Both public bodies charged with shoring up equity (FROB) or deposits (FGD) were entitled to public intervention and management in the affected banks, something which does not happen in similar institutions in other countries. The funding would come, in the case of the FGD, from the regular quotas of the financial institutions, as we know, and, in that of the FROB, from a variety of sources, among them, the public budget.

Since July 2006, the governor of the Bank of Spain was Miguel Ángel Fernández Ordóñez, a man whose previous post had been Secretary of State of Finance (junior minister) in Rodríguez Zapatero's government. The feeling between Fernández Ordóñez and Rodríguez Zapatero was, of course, very good, and this helps to explain his leniency in the crisis of *Caja Castilla-La Mancha* and his passivity at other junctures. As has been justifiedly pointed out, there were serious failings in the supervision by the Bank of Spain, which prevented it from avoiding or at least mitigating the very serious financial crisis that began with this episode and is still not overcome at the time of this writing. However, many analysts, bankers and authorities have found that the standards of the IASB have much to do with the crisis in that they require the valuation of bank assets to be guided by market prices in the very short term. This approach fosters speculative processes so that the IASB has had to limit the application of its 'fair value' concept to instruments on stocks with embedded derivatives and bonds that involve high risk (Manso and Rodriguez, 2008). For loans, the IASB is now considering the use of an assessment system which is quite similar to the 'dynamic provisions' created by Bank of Spain's governor Luis Ángel Rojo.

11.2 Great Recession and europanic

It seems clear that at the heart of the long Great Recession is the financial crisis that began in 2007. The first wave of the crisis in 2007–9 swept 13 countries (Austria, Belgium, Denmark, Germany, Iceland, Ireland, Latvia, Luxembourg, Mongolia, Netherlands, Ukraine, United Kingdom, and United States), with some impact on another 11 (France, Greece, Hungary, Italy, Kazakhstan, Portugal, Russia, Slovenia, Spain, Sweden, and Switzerland). Unfortunately, in several countries where the initial shock was somewhat muted, such as Portugal, Spain, Italy, and Greece, the aftershock was extremely severe, due largely to structural weaknesses. This crisis had a series of features which made it unique, at least since the Great Depression. These features were as follows: (i) it affected hardest the advanced countries, with comprehensive and integrated financial systems, and having large and multinational institutions; (ii) the intervention of the authorities was swift, not vacillating, in the recapitalization of the affected institutions, something which is explained by the existence of strong institutions and by developments in economic theory and history (Eichengreen, 2012); (iii) the intervention was varied and imaginative, and acted both on supply and on demand through fiscal stimulus packages; (iv) the cost was very high in terms of production losses and public debt increase (Laeven and Valencia, 2010; Claessens, *et al.*, 2010). We could add that, in spite of the swiftness of intervention, this crisis is being exceptionally protracted and that it has exhibited the unusual complication that it arrived eight years after the establishment of the euro as the common European currency and just five years after it started circulating effectively. The crisis has made evident the omissions we mentioned earlier and attributed to excessive 'europhoria'. Lack of common banking and fiscal discipline in the EU permitted an orgy of indebtedness on the part of some governments and some financial systems, which weakened trust in European monetary cohesion to such an extreme that at some points in time many doubted that the euro as we know it could survive.

The efforts to address the crisis were coordinated internationally. Since 2009, the G8 (Canada, United States, France, Italy, Japan, the United Kingdom, and Russia) and the G8 +5 (the above plus Brazil, China, India, Mexico, and South Africa) were displaced by the G-20 (the former as well as Saudi Arabia, Argentina, Australia, South Korea, Indonesia, Turkey, and the EU) as a forum for discussion of the world economy (Spain is not a member country, but a permanent guest). At the summit of the G-20 in April 2009 the Financial Stability Board was established as an institution with the mission of helping in the recovery of the financial system and addressing the problems of rapidly growing public debt in many countries. In the Eurozone, the orthodoxy of the ECB forced most states to have recourse to public debt, which was under active trading on primary, secondary and derivatives markets, to finance their deficits. Public debt had the treatment of a financial asset like any other and was subjected to all kinds of speculative mechanisms, as a result of the liberalization and deregulation process that had been implemented before and which had given rise to awkward situations: 90 per cent of derivative products were traded in 'over the counter' (informal) markets. Among these products stood out the 'credit default swaps', which were used to hedge both the risk of corporate bonds and of sovereign debt. At times, the markets went into panic and 'short selling' (betting on falling stock prices) had to be stopped and 'circuit breakers', that is, instruments to contain the massive sales of a financial asset, especially public debt, introduced.

Rating agencies had failed to see the coming crisis, but once it broke they treated debtors with extreme rigour in their listings. In 2009, there was an outcry in Europe against rating agencies and there was even thought about creating European agencies when it was perceived that the main ones were US companies. But the truth is that the agencies were not wrong in all cases. The crisis that began in 2007 came a little late to Greece, but when it did it was discovered that no less than 80 per cent of the Greek bank assets were dubious. Greek deposit insurance coverage rose from 20,000 to 100,000 euros and the Greek central bank had considerable trouble guaranteeing bank liquidity. The cost of the intervention was equivalent to 3.6 per cent of GDP (1.9 per cent in injections of liquidity and 1.7 per cent in recapitalization) (estimates of Laeven and Valencia, 2010).

Addressing the Greek crisis was the responsibility of the PASOK government, which in October 2009 replaced the conservative New Democracy government, after elections that gave a majority to the socialists. The Prime Minister George Papandreou recognized the problems and also made known to the world that New Democracy had forged the public accounts, with the help of

Goldman Sachs, in order to be admitted to the Eurozone in January 2001. In an attempt to enable the government to bail out failed banks, the 2009 budget deficit rose to 12.7 per cent of GDP, and European authorities demanded that Greece reduce this ratio to 2.8 per cent in 2012, which was wildly unrealistic. To advance along this path, Papandreou did not hesitate to complete the freezing of salaries of public employees, which his predecessor had begun. The answer was a general strike. Anticipating difficulties, in March 2010, the Ministers of Finance of the Eurozone agreed to help in the stabilization of Greece. The ECB, led by Jean-Claude Trichet, announced it would accept Greek public funds as collateral even if they were not of the highest quality. Interest rates in Greece, thanks to the euro, had managed to converge with those of the more developed European countries, but they now began to take off again and posed a serious threat to the future of the Greek economy (Figure 11.1). On 11 April 2010, European leaders agreed to a rescue plan for Greece via bilateral three-year loans for 30,000 million euros at an interest rate of 5 per cent, which stood nearly three points below the market rate. The ECB supported the rescue. In spite of all this, the rating agencies did not appreciate Greece's and Europe's effort and downgraded Greek debt to 'junk' level. In response, the ECB said it would accept Greek bonds regardless of their credit rating.

The weekend of 8 and 9 May 2010 were days that Rodríguez Zapatero may never forget. The leaders of the Eurozone, with German chancellor Angela

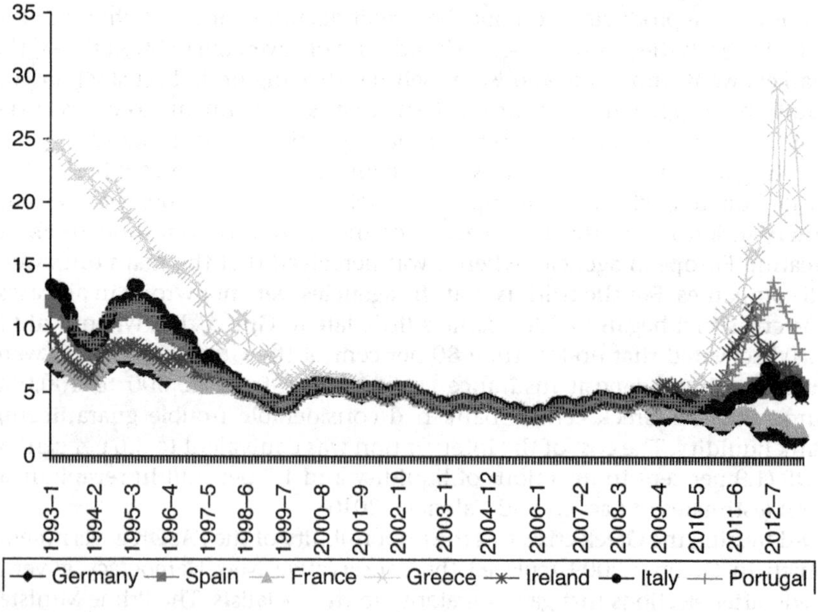

Figure 11.1 Evolution of long-term interest rate in a sample of Eurozone countries, 1993–2012

Source: ECB Statistical Data Warehouse.

Merkel at the helm, decided to protect the euro by increasing the bailout to Greece up to 100,000 million euros. Countries like Spain, which had a high public deficit (the surplus of 1.9 per cent of GDP in 2007 had been transformed into a deficit of 4.2 per cent of GDP in 2008 and 11.2 per cent of GDP in 2009), would have to take drastic measures to avoid following the Greek path. The costly social policies that had characterized Rodríguez Zapatero's government since 2004, and that the socialist leader was committed to maintain despite the crisis, were in danger. Not having foreseen the crisis was structural, and that it required adjustments and reforms of great depth, the measures taken by Rodríguez Zapatero on Monday 10 May and onwards came too late, and were announced in such a reluctant mood that they did not inspire much confidence. This explains why rating agencies such as Fitch (18 May) and Moody's (30 September) withdrew the highest credit rating for Spain. Standard & Poor's had done it earlier, in January 2009.

In a pioneering analysis, Irving Fisher had postulated the relationship between financial crises and the cyclical nature of real economic activity. Economic expansion causes a rise in bank deposits, which soon results in more credits, which in turn stimulates the production of goods. The process becomes unstoppable and eventually allows the financing of unwarranted projects. Finally, defaults arrive and, due to oversupply, prices plunge, triggering a spiral of 'debt-deflation' with devastating consequences for banks, firms and households (Fisher, 1933). The great American economist could have been thinking about Spain, in the period 1994–2007 for the upturn and in the period that began in 2007 for the downturn. In this case, moreover, at the core of the productive system was an industry with a strong tendency to generate cycles: housing.

Between 1994 and 2008, the annual rate of change in the value of the housing stock in Spain grew at a steady rate above 3 per cent. Production and prices grew simultaneously. The strong immigration into Spain in those years helps to explain this apparent paradox (according to the Census of Population, Spain went from 40.8 to 46.0 million between 2001 and 2010, recording the highest ten-year period of population growth in its history), but, certainly, there was also a speculative component in the rate of economic growth. Uriel and Albert (2012) identify four phases in this process: (i) acceleration, between 1994 and 1998, when the Spanish economy found in construction a way out of the crisis of 1992–3; (ii) formation of a speculative bubble, between 1999 and 2006, when prices of land per square metre rose by an annual average of 13.6 per cent, while the average value of stocks rose at 16.2 per cent; (iii) slowdown in 2007 (rates of 6.5 per cent in prices and 9.5 per cent in value of stocks) and 2008 (rates of 1.1 per cent in prices and 3.8 per cent in value of stocks); (iv) bubble burst: in 2009 there were strong negative rates in prices (9.2 per cent) and value of stocks (7.7 per cent), and the unemployment rate leapt from 11.3 to 18 per cent. Rodríguez Zapatero's attempt to stem the decline with an increase in public spending produced a public deficit of 11.2 per cent of GDP. He had rightly insisted that the crisis of the subprime mortgages originated in the United States did not affect Spain, but he had been unable to realize that Spain had a crisis of its own coming.

The European aid approved in May 2010 was channelled through two instruments: the European Financial Stability Facility (EFSF), only for Eurozone countries, and the European Financial Stabilization Mechanism (EFSM), for all of the EU. Both the EFSF and the EFSM would be financed by issuing debt, with the guarantee of the Eurozone countries and the EU budget, respectively. The EFSF was assigned to rescue Greece, and then would do the same with Ireland (November 2010) and Portugal (May 2011); its lending capacity (440,000 million euros) was much higher than that of the EFSM (60,000 million euros). In September 2012, the two instruments joined in the European Stability Mechanism (ESM), whose capacity is the sum of its predecessors, that is, 500,000 million euros. In July 2012, Spain agreed with the EU to receive up to 100,000 million euros to rescue its banks, which had been heavily involved in financing the housing boom and therefore hard hit by the collapse of the sector. By that time Mariano Rajoy's Popular Party had won the elections in November 2011 and he had become President. The Spanish government had to sign a *Memorandum of Understanding*, accepting the implementation of reforms to make easier the reimbursement of the aid. In September, the ECB said it would buy all the necessary public debt of Eurozone countries facing difficulties, in a clear warning to speculators.

The measures taken in the summer of 2012 were effective in controlling the 'europanic' unleashed two years earlier; in addition, the interest rates charged by the EFSF in its bailouts had been reduced, which was a relief for the increasing debt burden. On 12 December Spain received from the ESM an amount of 39,500 million euros to recapitalize its banks; the conditions were good, although there remained the problem of counting the aid as public debt. In any case, the conditions were so attractive that many voices were heard requesting Rajoy's government to ask for another bailout, that of Spain in its entirety, because it was difficult to believe that the conditions imposed would go beyond the Fiscal Compact that had replaced the Stability and Growth Pact in March 2012, with the signature of all EU members except Britain and the Czech Republic. It is said, however, that Rajoy was afraid that the rescue would come accompanied by a political intervention involving the formation of a technocratic government, as had happened in other countries that had been rescued, or in Italy, when in November 2011 the technocrat Mario Monti replaced the controversial Silvio Berlusconi as Prime Minister largely due to EU pressures. The big bailout has not yet been requested (August 2013).

11.3 The vanishing savings banks

In Spain, it was soon found that the most vulnerable part of the financial system were savings banks. At the end of the Franco regime, the main problem with these institutions was the peculiarity of their management bodies, which had imposed a system of cooptation that gave wings to nepotism and inefficiency. The fact that the savings banks, faithful to their original nature of charitable bodies, had no owners, let alone shareholders, posed the problem of how their governing bodies should be appointed. As noted by a former chairman of *Caja Madrid*, Professor Jaime Terceiro, their ownership was neither public nor private, it simply did not exist, and it was unwise to have half of the financial system in these conditions (Terceiro, 2012). The legislation that addressed this problem in the democratic period (royal decree of 1977, and an 'organic' Law About the Governing Bodies of Savings Banks of 1985) allowed the appointment of representatives of regional and local governments to their board of directors, together with representatives of depositors, of labour unions and of various other groups. Curiously enough, according to this law, nobody could own a *Caja*, not even a commercial bank; but *Cajas* could own commercial banks (Maixé, 2012, p. 168). This ultimately meant that the remedy to indeterminacy of ownership was worse than the disease. Regional governments in fact obtained powers of control and supervision over the *Cajas*, which still were owned by nobody. This was a grave imprudence. Regional and local governments at once became administrators of the *Cajas* and their most prominent clients, eager to put their vast resources at the service of policies not always guided by economic rationality. And the *Cajas* hungrily swallowed the bait of the real estate bubble. There were not many able economists on their bloated boards.

A wave of mergers among savings banks had taken place in a parallel way to the one affecting commercial banks in the 1980s and 1990s. But curiously enough, most of these mergers took place within the same region ('Autonomous Communities', in post-Franco democratic Spain), so that the regional governments did not lose their grip on the institutions. After the crisis of *Caja Castilla-La Mancha* in 2009, Rodríguez Zapatero's government encouraged a process of further concentration of the savings banks, in the hope that the larger size of the resulting institutions would dilute the concentration of risks associated with real estate. The savings banks were reluctant to consider outright mergers, in which they were supported by the regional governments, who feared that mergers with savings banks of other communities would deprive them of the financial power they had hitherto enjoyed. These governments promised to be more careful in the future, but they did not want to give up financial resources they considered theirs. This is the origin of the Institutional Protection Schemes (IPSs), an atypical figure in banking regulation in the EU without precedent in Spain. The IPSs involved the pooling of assets and deposits while maintaining the autonomy of management of the institutions involved, something which was bound to lead to many problems. The Bank of Spain authorized the IPSs, but under certain conditions to ensure stability, such as penalizing institutions that broke away from the scheme, and requiring a previous report by the Bank of Spain on the feasibility of the resulting situation (Bank of Spain, 2011).

A royal decree of 9 July 2010 attempted to carry out a fundamental reform of the savings banks, which would affect their equity, their governance and even their institutional nature. The main novelty was that savings banks were allowed develop their businesses through a subsidiary commercial bank to which their financial business could be transferred. The virtue of this measure would be that the subsidiary bank could have access to high-quality equity, i.e., regular shareholders. If the new institutions had trouble placing their shares, the FROB would come in to help, as this fund had been established in order to tackle equity problems in the savings banks. The first intervention of the FROB was to help *Cajasur*, a savings bank from Cordoba, run by the Catholic Church, which had serious problems with defaults in its mortgage loans. It was soon discovered that Cajasur was not alone, because many savings banks had become almost exclusively specialized in real estate and building operations. In fact, they had been specialized in these fields for a long time, even before they were placed on an equal footing with commercial banks. It was these that were relative newcomers to the mortgage business, but they turned out to be more cautious. The savings banks had invested in these operations not only the deposits of their clients but also the resources they obtained through securitization, that is, the issuing of mortgage bonds in wholesale markets. Enough was never enough in the 'brick business'. Furthermore, savings banks had high costs for this same reason (bond issues were more expensive than deposits) and because they had to recruit extra personnel to serve their numerous and eager customers, who flocked to them attracted by their relaxed criteria and easy conditions.

According to Vives (2012, pp. 393–5, 436), between 1997 and 2007, commercial and savings bank deposits combined had grown at an average annual rate of 14 per cent, while loans had done so at 17.5 per cent. Lending to the (non-bank) private sector reached 169.1 per cent of GDP in 2007. What had been the purposes of these loans? In 2007, Spanish bank loans related to real estate operations accounted for 100 per cent of GDP. Of all the credit granted by savings banks, 29 per cent was concentrated in buildings, while this proportion was 25 per cent in commercial banks. In Europe, this type of credit amounted to 12 per cent of the banks' combined balance sheet, while in Spain it was 21 per cent, which gives an idea of the disproportion of the construction sector in Spain (Figure 11.2). How had the gap between loans and deposits been financed? The answer is that it was done by resorting to the interbank market and, if this was not enough, by resorting to other wholesale markets by means of issuing bonds paying high interest rates. However, customer deposits accounted for 48.7 per cent of the balance sheet of the Spanish banking sector, while they only reached 30 per cent in the Eurozone; that is, the recourse to wholesale markets had been higher

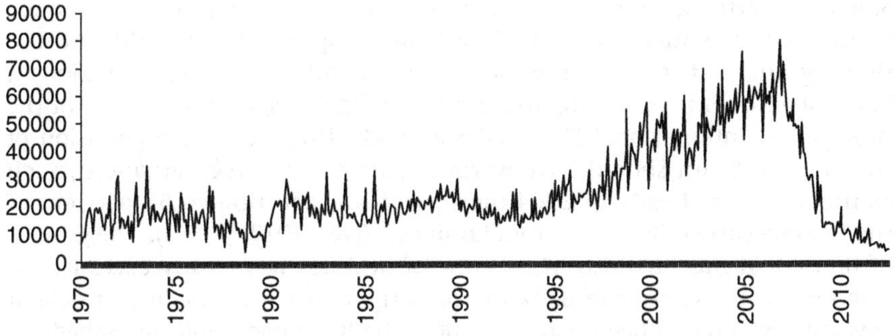

Figure 11.2 Evolution of house starts in Spain, 1970–2012 (monthly data)
Source: BIEST Database (Bank of Spain).

in other countries. Moreover, the Spanish bonds were not securitizations of 'originate and distribute' type; they showed on balance sheets. When in 2009 the issuers of securitized loans were required by the European authorities to retain a 5 per cent interest to cover the risk of loss – as had been required by the US Dodd-Frank Act of 2010 – they were not thinking of the Spanish institutions.

In contrast with the weakness of savings banks, Spanish commercial banks showed undeniable strength due to their previous efforts of diversification and internationalization, and to the prudential rules issued by the Bank of Spain. Spanish commercial banks were also stronger than their counterparts in other countries for they had not abused of structured (off-balance sheet) products. As we have seen, Santander and BBVA were the result of an early process of liberalization and crisis that had created a culture of minimizing costs and fostering profitability, which their executives had used to build a competitive advantage on which to develop their internationalization (more successful in Santander than in BBVA, whose presence in emerging countries may be excessive). This internationalization allowed them to diversify and to obtain resources at a lower cost. Their biggest fear at that time was of a scenario similar to that of 1993, when the rise in defaults was induced by rising interest rates. Most of the more recent operations have been formalized at a variable rate, so now there is no such risk in interest rates but some credit risk remains in the possibility of default due to the falling disposable incomes of customers.

Not all banks behaved as prudently as the Santander and the BBVA, and some scholars attributed responsibilities for this to the supervision of the Bank of Spain. Savings banks and credit cooperatives were largely supervised by the Autonomous Communities, and we know how dangerous this was. However, the Bank of Spain was supposed to supervise the supervisors. (Cooperatives today have a small share in the financial system, but, as shown in Martínez

Soto and Martínez Rodríguez, 2010, they had a promising start in rural areas in the early twentieth century). The Bank of Spain protested this attribution arguing that in the matter of prudential and accounting regulations it had lost autonomy by having to accept EU guidelines, as was the case of the pro-cyclical International Financial Standards. However, the supervision of the Bank of Spain should have warned against some risky situations, such as the fact that already in 2004 mortgage loans contributed 55 per cent of the income earned by banks from families (Vives, 2012, p. 393). The growth of household indebtedness in this line of business was clearly excessive. In response to the crisis, the Bank of Spain tightened the schedule of default coverage, which had been issued in 2004 (the Bank had published schedules since 1978 Prado, 2002). The combination of higher coverage requirements and the difficulty banks found at this time to attract new resources (wholesale markets were drying up), made those institutions peer into the abyss. In order to lower costs, the branch network was urgently downsized.

During Rodríguez Zapatero's mandate,the government tried to make believe that the problems of savings banks were manageable; the stress tests of the European regulators, which threw non-catastrophic results, were adduced as proof. The conservative government of Mariano Rajoy, however, recognized that the European tests had been unable to get to the root of the problem. The July 2010 reform was sadly insufficient to reach the truth of a system of savings banks with serious solvency problems. If Spain persisted in hiding losses, it could travel the road of an unending crisis, a process that had already been seen in Japan after the outbreak of the financial crisis of the 1990s (Caballero, *et al.*, 2008).

One of the worst scandals relating to Spanish savings banks was that of *Caja Madrid*, the second largest in the country, after Barcelona's *La Caixa*. In September 1996, the right of centre Popular Party, the winner of the recent election, and the communist union *Comisiones Obreras* had signed a pact to remove Professor Terceiro from the presidency of *Caja Madrid* and appoint in his place Miguel Blesa, a man close to the new President of Spain José María Aznar. From that moment on, *Caja Madrid* was placed at the service of the politicians of the Community of Madrid and to what was thought to be the engine of the Spanish economic development of the 1994–2008 period: the construction industry.

In June 2010, *Caja Madrid* was merged with the big savings bank of Valencia, *Bancaja*, by means of an IPS, just a few days before the deadline set by the Bank of Spain for banks to request aid from the FROB. One of the outcomes of this merger was *Bankia*, a commercial bank, which went public in July 2011, capturing more than 3,000 million euros that were used to achieve a core tier 1 of 9.9 per cent. Everything seemed to be going smoothly for the institution now led by Rodrigo Rato, a man who had an outstanding political and technical profile: he had been vice president in the Aznar government, in charge of the economy, and later became managing director of the IMF after the socialists came to power. In the ranking of banks, only Santander, BBVA, and *La Caixa* would be ahead of Bankia at the time.

The scandal, however, erupted on 7 May 2012, when Rato, after being pressured by the government of his own party, the Popular Party (back in power after the elections of November 2011 under the leadership of Mariano Rajoy), agreed to be replaced by José Ignacio Goirigolzarri, former CEO of BBVA. It turned out that in the first year of its life, 2011, Bankia had not had more than 300 million euros of profit, as Rato had claimed, but had suffered heavy losses, as the auditing firm Deloitte discovered (these losses amounted to around 3,000 million euros). The merger of *Caja Madrid* and Bancaja had been a disaster, because both institutions were in trouble, especially Bancaja. It transpired that the merger had been a desperate attempt to hide the real situation of both banks. In July 2012, before a parliamentary investigative committee, Rato blamed the Bank of Spain, because, according to him, the merger was carried out under pressure from the central bank; the Bank governor, Miguel Ángel Fernández Ordóñez, protested that the operation had been carried out under the free initiative of both institutions (the truth is that the supervisory powers of the Bank of Spain over the savings banks had been curtailed by the Savings Banks Law of 1985; the last word, however, still belonged to the central bank). It is easy to imagine that there was a political component in the operation, as the Autonomous Communities of Madrid and Valencia had both been long ruled by the Popular Party. Since July, many leaders of this party have had to testify at the *Audiencia Nacional* (a high court) in the 'Bankia case', because a judge had admitted a complaint filed by a minority political party, *Unión, Progreso y Democracia*, which is very belligerent against corruption. This crisis forced Rajoy's government to request from the EU the 100,000 million euros bailout we referred to before.

On 26 November 2012, *Caja Madrid* became a mere foundation, and its example was followed in the next five months by all the savings banks that had lost control of their financial activity. This threat has been hanging over 11 savings banks that since July 2010 had become special foundations with the possibility of controlling a banking company, but without the certainty of being able to. Of the 45 savings banks which existed in 2009, only two of small size had chosen not to change their status, those of Ontinyent (Valencia) and Pollença (Mallorca). At the end of the year, along with Bankia, the FROB controlled the bank incorporating the Galician savings banks (*NCG Banco*) and *Catalunya Banc*, the bank of the *Caixa de Catalunya* (once the second Catalan savings bank). NCG Banco was dominated by Popular Party politicians and Catalunya Banc by socialist politicians. These institutions are to be auctioned in 2013, but not without being previously restructured with the assistance received from the ESM (in contrast with the poor performance of the Galician savings banks, Basque savings banks have done better; in neither of these regions has the building frenzy been as pervasive as in others; see Maixé, 2003; Valdaliso, 2007). The old *Caixa de Catalunya* used to be second only to *La Caixa* (*CaixaBank* today), in that community. *La Caixa*, the former *Caja de Pensiones de Barcelona*, established in 1904, after a process of growth and mergers, and thanks to the competent management by its CEOs (Josep Vilarasau, Isidre Fainé) has been able to remain quite independent from political power, and today is the third bank in Spain, after Santander and BBVA (Appendix 13). We should add that only one commercial bank fell into the hands of the FROB: the venerable *Banco de Valencia*, which had been under the control of a savings bank, Bancaja (Pons and Cuevas, 2007). Both failed miserably. The *Banco* will end its once glorious days, after due restructuring, by being absorbed by CaixaBank. But this was an exception. The soundness of Spanish traditional joint-stock banks has been remarked in the Liikanen report (2012). Also very appreciative of the soundness and resourcefulness of the Spanish commercial banks is the book by Kase and Jacopin (2008), most likely written before the onset of the crisis and which sidelines savings banks. These authors think that the rapid liberalization of banking, in addition to the happy coincidence of a group of very talented CEOs at the top of Spain's leading banks – which in turn is explained by high-quality business schools – powerfully contributed to the ascent of a few Spanish banks to the top world rankings in the last decades of the twentieth century.

Some of the ESM money has been devoted to creating a 'bad bank', an institution which will purchase the toxic assets of the Spanish banking system at low prices; that is to say, it will acquire the huge mass of real estate assets that banks (mainly savings banks) had been gathering through judicial processes for delinquencies. In the last days of 2012, things improved for the Spanish financial sector, due to the coincidence of the arrival of the first tranche of the ESM aid (39,500 million euros, out of a total available sum of 60,000 million until June 2013 and an additional 40,000 million until December 2013). The successful creation of the 'bad bank' (really called *Sociedad de Gestión de Activos Procedentes de la Reestructuración Bancaria* or SAREB – Society for the Management of Assets from Bank Reconstruction) as well as a historic agreement by Ecofin to turn the ECB into a supervisor of those banks whose size could represent a systemic risk are steps which could be considered as favouring a reduction of the high costs of financing of the Spanish economy, which in this way should be able to devote more resources to the expansionary policies needed to cope with an unemployment rate that is over 25 per cent and the cause of serious social problems.

12
Conclusions

To conclude we may ask ourselves whether Spanish banking and monetary history does have 'useful economics' (paraphrasing McCloskey, 1976). We believe it does, and here are some of the topics on which we think this history throws light.

Let us start with the relation between financial and monetary development, on the one hand, and *general economic development*, on the other, a topic which has lately received renewed attention (see, for instance, Sylla, 1998, 2002; Reis, 2005; Beck *et al.*, 2000; Demirgüç-Kunt and Levine, 2001) and is of paramount importance for the study of this branch of economic history. Few authors will deny that there is a relation between the two (or three) variables; but the most frequent belief has been that the financial variable has more often been determined by the 'real' variable, or that, as per Joan Robinson's dictum, the economy leads and finance follows. Sylla (1998) pointed out that this position had been boldly challenged by Rondo Cameron and his collaborators in *Banking in the Early Stages of Industrialization* (1967), where it was stated, based upon abundant historical evidence, that 'the banking system can play a positive, "growth inducing" role as well as responding passively to the demand of financial services' (p. 291). If we accept this statement we find that, according to their effectiveness in promoting development, banking (or financial, not synonymous, but closely related) systems may in fact play three different types of roles in the process of growth: (i) an indifferent passive role; (ii) a facilitating passive role; (iii) an active role. In the second and third cases, financial innovation takes place; in the second case as a response to the demands of the 'real' sector; in the third case financial innovation is spontaneous, takes place, at least partly, ahead of demand, and moulds the directions and ways the 'real economy' will follow. A typical example of the third case was repeatedly studied by Cameron, that is, the instance when bankers became 'real' entrepreneurs themselves. Some Spanish examples of bankers–entrepreneurs would be those of José Salamanca, who combined financial innovation with pioneering railway construction, in the nineteenth century, and Ignacio Villalonga, Emilio Botín II or José Luis Ussía, who combined banking with promoting hydroelectricity enterprises in the twentieth century. Typical examples of bankers who innovated and responded in an agile manner to the demands arising out of economic growth were Manuel Girona of the *Banco de Barcelona*, the founders of the *Banco de Santander* and the *Banco de Bilbao*, and the first two Urquijos in the nineteenth century; and the founders of *Banco Español de Crédito*, *Banco Hispano Americano* and *Banco Central* in the twentieth.

As we pointed out in Chapter 1, the history of Spanish banks shows a clear correspondence with the ups and downs of the 'real' economy, in the early modern era as well as in the modern one. As to what determined what in the early modern ages, we will have a few things to say later. But regarding the modern period there are reasons which make us think that, at some junctures at least, it was banks that pushed the real sector forward. One such moment was the years of the bank–railway bubble, that is, the 1850s and 1860s: in spite of the grave crisis that it engendered, the sudden growth of the banking sector at that time gave the Spanish economy a jump start, which we think was at the origin of the process of gradual growth characteristic of the second half of that century. Another moment when banking growth preceded a long span of economic development was the early years of the twentieth century. For the Spanish economy the defeat in the Spanish–American war and the subsequent loss of the overseas colonies was a blessing in disguise, because the Fernández Villaverde Stabilization Plan and the return of colonial entrepreneurs brought about a sudden repatriation of human and financial capital, which gave another jump start at the economy: three decades of diversification and industrialization followed, at considerably faster growth rates than in the last decades of the nineteenth century. The chronological sequence of these two episodes strongly suggests a banks-to-real-economy direction of causation.

A closely related issue is *the role of the state*. It is related closely for at least two reasons: first, because the development of public finance is a strong determinant of that of private finance. As Alexander Hamilton wrote, 'Public and private Credit are closely allied if not inseparable' (cited in Sylla, 1999, p. 249). The state is the first historical demander of credit and therefore the earliest large customer of banks; the way in which the state behaves as a customer, therefore, largely determines the institutional makeup of the banking sector: how the state demands credit (in the market, directly from some bankers, by coercion, that is, forced loans, and so on), and how it fulfils its obligations (paying punctually, in arrears, or not at all), are also determinant of how the banking sector will be able to organize itself and how it will be able to serve the needs of the private sector of the economy (Comín, 1994b). The other reason the state is one of the main factors in the makeup of the banking sector is that it has legislative and policy powers, i.e., that it dictates the rules whereby the banking sector will be organized and operate. Legislation as well as banking and monetary policies, are vital components of banking history. Let us say at the outset that bad policies and irresponsible behaviour by the state have been serious obstacles, probably the most serious, to bank and financial development in Spain. During the early modern period, irresponsible *fiscal policies* in the sixteenth century brought about three state bankruptcies which ruined Spanish and German bankers. In the seventeenth century there were more state bankruptcies, which combined with extraordinarily inept monetary policies to give an almost fatal *coup de grâce* to the Spanish banking system and to the economy in general.

After about 100 years of sensible albeit not brilliant economic and financial policies, the petrification of the Spanish fiscal system combined with Spain's intervention in the War of the American Revolution, alongside France, for helping America's independence, caused a fiscal crisis in the early 1780s. Although this crisis did not have the revolutionary consequences a parallel crisis had in France, it called for radical financial innovation. The Bank of Saint Charles, like several other official banks of this period, was created as a solution to the state's liquidity problems. It fell a victim to those same problems, however, and was unable to solve them. In fact, fiscal insolvency again became a chronic problem, as it had been in the early modern period, and turned out to be one of the great obstacles to the healthy development of private finance throughout the nineteenth century.

The state, always in arrears and rarely able to properly finance its priorities, systematically crowded out the private sector not only from the open capital market, but also from the asset side of the banks' balance sheets. This has been pointed out repeatedly by many authors (Tortella, 2000a, p. 157, Ch. 7; Reis, 2005, p. 124; Comín, 1996, pp. 179–91 is of two minds about this), and has been considered as an obstacle to the country's economic development. Sylla's 1999 article points out how Alexander Hamilton's policies brought order to a rather messy fiscal and financial situation in the United States after the revolutionary war, and how this set the American banking system on a straight and narrow path (although it strayed several times later on); in another piece (2002) Sylla compares Hamilton to Japan's prince Masayoshi Matsukata, who in 1882 introduced a fiscal and banking reform, which also straightened out Japanese public and private finances for a long time. He draws some parallels between the two characters, among them that both 'came to finance from a military background'. It is a curious coincidence that Ramón Santillán, the author of the fiscal reform that thoroughly modernized the public finances of Spain in 1845 and became the governor of the Bank of Spain – who redressed this bank, thoroughly reformed Spain's system of issuing banks and took the preliminary steps towards making the Bank of Spain a central bank – also had a military background: he had fought in the war against Napoleon, where he was wounded; he abandoned the military career when he was persecuted by absolutist officers under Ferdinand VII, and found refuge and employment in the

Ministry of Finance. Santillán, unfortunately, could not complete his work in that department. Two other ministers did this: Juan Francisco Camacho in 1882 and Raimundo Fernández Villaverde in 1899. Camacho's reform did not solve the problem of the chronic deficit, but put the public debt on a sounder footing and from then on a traditionally intractable problem became manageable; it can be no coincidence that a period of economic growth accompanied this relative improvement. Villaverde was the one who achieved the feat of producing nine consecutive years of budget surplus. Although deficits returned after 1909, from then on until the 1980s Spanish public debt has been well managed and taken up a diminishing share of GNP. Again, it can be no coincidence that Villaverde's stabilization was followed by 30 years of healthy economic growth. So Spanish banking history seems to confirm Cameron's and Sylla's prediction that sound banking and sound public finances can be 'growth inducing' to the real economy.

Another related question is *state regulation*. Evidence tends to indicate that excessive banking regulation may be stifling. It seems to us, however, that here some Aristotelian middle ground is desirable. Total de-regulation, or absolute *laissez-faire*, in banking can be deleterious too, and for a very simple reason: financial markets, unlike most other markets, are not self-regulating. In most real goods markets the law of diminishing returns operates, so that supply curves (identical with marginal product curves) are upward-sloping and meet downward-sloping demand curves at some given point, which determines price and quantity exchanged. This is elementary theory. But in most financial markets the law of diminishing returns does not operate. An issuing bank, for instance, if unrestrained, will issue notes in unlimited amounts, because it makes a profit on each note issued. Maybe very high rates of inflation would diminish the marginal profitability of banknote issuing. But inflation is precisely what we want to avoid, and to avoid running inflation some type of limit to banknote issuing must be established: some specie reserve ratio, some other ratio related to other assets, or simpler quantitative limits. The same principles apply to other, more complex financial assets: as long as there is a profit to be made they will be issued in unlimited amounts unless some legal limits or controls are imposed. The recent 2007–10 financial crisis has demonstrated clearly that financial markets do not 'regulate themselves'. Some measure of state control is required to avoid explosive growth of financial assets.

All this does not mean that tight regulation and numerous controls are desirable, and history also gives some support to this. 'Financial repression' (a general policy of tight regulation of banks in financial markets, which prevailed especially during the Great Depression and lasted until the 1970s, as we have seen) did provide a measure of stability to financial markets, but it put a break on economic growth. This was clear in the Spanish case, where financial repression started already in the 1920s, under Primo de Rivera's dictatorship, which introduced mandatory investment ratios for the private banking sector and also created several state banks for agricultural credit, local governments, the fishing industry, and external trade. The 1921 Banking Law already gave the Finance Ministry a say in setting the Bank of Spain's interest rates; total control by the ministry was established in 1931, and this situation persisted until the 1970s. One can say, therefore that strong financial repression was present in Spain from the 1930s to the 1960s, when the 1962 law softened it a little. The grip of repression was gradually loosened after 1969 and was totally dismantled by the late 1980s. Now the negative record of financial repression in the twentieth century is less clear than that of interference and financial disorder in the nineteenth (on this ambiguity see the 'Conclusions' in Pons, 2002). After all, there was strong economic growth in Spain in the 1960s (and in the 1950s, although with serious imbalances) while financial repression was still fairly strong. And several voices in Spain have claimed that the serious crisis of the late 1970s and early 1980s was precipitated or aggravated by excessive liberalization. According to Lukauskas (1997), however, most of these voices belonged to the enemies of reform. In the Western world, in the 1950s and 1960s growth was spectacular while financial repression, although less stringent than in Spain, was still present. In favour of de-regulation one could say that financial repression had reached its limits by the early 1970s, both in Spain and in the rest of the West, and that de-regulation gave a new chance of growth, which took place in the last decades of the twentieth century.

Going back in time, it has also been pointed out that the strong need for funds by the Spanish state not only impelled it to pressure the Bank of Spain and the private sector for new advances, but also to create public institutions to provide it with additional loans: thus the *Caja de Depósitos* and the *Banco Hipotecario*, and the series of institutions created in the twentieth century to supplement the private financial markets and institutions: *Banco de Crédito Industrial, Banco Exterior,* and so on. Even the *cajas*, the supposedly charitable savings banks, were put at the state's service already under Primo de Rivera, under Franco and even – and with the worst consequences – under the democratic governments of the late twentieth and early twenty-first centuries. This has been a type of government interference that has produced unequivocally negative consequences. The Matesa fiasco in 1969 probably convinced political circles that the public banking sector was inefficient, expensive and possibly corrupt, and so it was privatized in the 1990s and sold to *Banco Bilbao Vizcaya* in 1999.

At the risk of being repetitive, let us reiterate that the contours of Spanish banking history broadly follow those of the whole economy. Strength in the sixteenth century, decline in the seventeenth, slow and incomplete recovery in the eighteenth, and very slow growth, with a series of bumps in the nineteenth. Vigorous growth occurred in the twentieth. Something similar would apply to the Bank of Spain, founded in 1782 under the name Bank of Saint Charles. There is some controversy about dates. Let us remember that the Bank of Saint Charles was, on the whole, a dismal failure and had to be thoroughly reformed and even re-baptized Bank of Saint Ferdinand in 1829. Nevertheless, several authors (Capie, 1999, p. 131; Plessis, 2003, pp. 30–1) place the foundation date of the Bank of Spain in 1856. Now, the readers of the first chapters of the present book know that this is not accurate. The Bank of Spain celebrated its second centennial in 1982; it can be argued that as the Bank of Saint Charles failed (although its doors were never closed), the Bank of Saint Ferdinand was born so there was continuity; be it as it may, the truth is that from 1829 on this institution has been working uninterruptedly until today. True, it evolved and underwent many subsequent changes and reforms, as could not have been otherwise, and as happened to all banks that are several centuries old; among these reforms, its name was changed to Bank of Spain in 1856, but the institution was exactly the same before and after this change of name. In other words, there are many junctures at which the Bank of Saint Ferdinand-Bank of Spain, was reformed, such as 1833, 1848, 1851, 1856, 1874, 1891, 1921, 1931, 1946, 1962, and 1994, for example. Of all these years, 1856 is the least significant, except for the fact that it was the time when the institution was given its definitive name.

One interesting matter relating to the Bank of Spain's evolution is when and how it became a real *central bank*. This topic has been subject to some discussion (see, for instance Tedde and Marichal, 1994) but one must agree with Capie (1999) that, as many other official state banks in continental Europe, the Bank of Spain did not assume this role until the twentieth century. According to Capie the Bank of England started discharging this function much earlier, in the 1870s and in typically anonymous manner, that is, just through open market operations rather than by means of direct help to individual banks (according to Lescure, 2003, pp. 146–8, the *Banque de France* was playing a similar role from 1882 on). The first time the Bank of Spain publicly assumed this role can easily be dated: in 1913, when it rescued the *Banco Hispano Americano*. The Bank did it reluctantly and it obviously did not show any intention to make a public commitment to assume this role again in the future. Probably, however, it was around this time or a few years later when, through its practice of discounting 'automatically' public debt bonds, and with the signing of the 1918 agreement with the private banks, the Bank took a big stride towards assuming this role. The next step came with the Cambó Law of 1921, which made an explicit effort to turn the Bank of Spain into a 'bankers' bank, and to put it on a different, non-competitive plane with respect to the rest of the banking system. Nevertheless, when in 1925 the *Banco Central* asked for support in a panic, the Bank of Spain resisted, and it was only because the ruling dictator himself intervened that the Bank finally acceded to the request. The definitive episode, however, took place in the spring of 1931: at that time, the Bank of Spain, with full government support, showed its willingness to lend freely to banks (with the exception of the *Banco de Cataluña*) and the looming crisis was averted. But one could state that it was when it assumed the compromise to lend 'automatically' with public debt bonds as collateral, with the mechanism of 'indirect monetization of the public debt', that the Bank of Spain really assumed the role of lender of last resort, and this took place in the years of the First World War.

Another interesting feature of the way in which the Bank of Spain assumed its role of lender of last resort was that it gave remarkable solidity to the *mixed or universal character of the Spanish big banks*. By combining public debt bonds and private company securities in their portfolios these banks could promote industry with relatively little risk, as they were assured of the possibility of getting central bank support with public debt bonds as collateral at virtually any time. Now, this was made possible thanks to two features of the financial system: (i) the Bank of Spain was not subjected to the rules of the gold standard; (ii) the role of the Bank in this arrangement was supported by the state, something which increased the confidence, the credit which this arrangement merited on the part of the banking system. To reiterate, this credit was tested in the spring of 1931, when the Bank of Spain lent freely on public bonds as collateral and the interest rate charged on this operation was not raised. The Bank also made clear that it had the full support of the government who, furthermore, raised the ceiling to banknote circulation twice during the month of May. After this dramatic episode Spanish banks sailed through the Great Depression without showing any liquidity strain, in spite of the fall of the prices of securities in the stock exchange.

During most of the twentieth century Spanish big banks practised *mixed or universal banking*. Several authors have wondered whether this was a good thing or bad, whether a more specialized banking system might not have been more efficient and more equitable. We know this sort of debate has been posed relative to other mixed banking systems such as those of Germany, Italy, or Japan, and that there is no agreement among scholars. The same applies in Spain, where some authors have decried the power of the 'banking oligopoly' and denounced the excessive hegemony of the big mixed banks. While many of their arguments are justified, the critics have seldom asked what realistic alternatives were there. Some authors have pointed out that other countries also had mixed banking systems and that such structure has been theoretically justified for the 'early stages of industrialization' by such reputed authors as Gerschenkron or Cameron. A relatively recent and balanced summing up was published by M. A. Pons (2001), who pointed out that the narrowness of the Spanish financial market did not permit large banks to specialize, and that mixed banking was more profitable for them than specialization. Furthermore, she seems to accept the idea that without the support of banks many firms and industries would not have been able to develop. While admitting that mixed banking had its drawbacks, which she largely attributes to the political framework, she thinks, with some reservations, that economic development at this early stage would not have been possible without a mixed banking system.

The reliance on a central bank not subject to the gold standard discipline gave the Spanish banking system a notable resilience or stability. Aside from individual cases, there were no serious *general banking crises* in Spain since that of the 1860s until that of the 1970s and 1980s, precisely when the mixed banking system was disappearing. One could say that this crisis was, among other things, the throes of the mixed banking system. Furthermore, by that time the 'indirect monetization of the public debt' had been abolished, and with it the 'automatic' Bank of Spain credits on public debt collateral. The third large banking crisis in Spanish history is the very recent one, and this has been largely a problem of savings banks, not of the whole system.

We should close on a reference to the Spanish *monetary system*, which has a long *sui generis* tradition. It was *sui generis* in the early modern period by having one of the strongest currencies in history, the prestigious *real de plata* or *de a ocho*. This caused very serious problems, among them what we could call the 'Spanish Dutch silver disease'. If in the twentieth century the Dutch economy lost competitiveness due to a petrol glut, in the sixteenth century Spain was hampered by a silver glut (something similar happened to Mexico in the nineteenth century). In the seventeenth century Spain went from overabundance to scarcity of silver through decades of spendthrift fiscal policies, and its currency became even more *sui generis* due to the bizarre inflationary *vellón* episodes. There was relative monetary normality in the eighteenth century, until the loss of the American colonies caused the fountain of silver go dry and created new problems. Again from the late nineteenth century to the Great Depression, Spanish money became *sui generis* by remaining nominally bi-metallic but really adopting a silver standard when most Western countries had adopted a gold standard. There is no doubt that the *sui generis* character of Spanish money in the early modern era, although universally envied, was a scourge in disguise. About the pros and cons of the silver standard in the gold era, the debate is still going on.

Chronology

1081: the Cid receives a loan from two Burgos Jewish bankers
1401: the municipal bank *Taula del Canvi* in Barcelona opens its doors
1492: Columbus discovers America; expulsion of the Jews from Spain
1497: the Catholic Monarchs create a new trimetallic monetary system (gold, silver, *vellón*) with the *maravedí* as unit of account and the silver real as the main coin
1503: the *Casa de Contratación* (House of Contracts) is created to control and monopolize commerce with the Americas
1516–1700: Spain is the centre of the Hispanic Monarchy of the Habsburgs. It experienced six defaults in 1557–1647 and manipulations of *vellón* coins in the seventeeth century. However, the *real de a ocho* (pure silver) was a true international currency
1500–1650: the 'Price Revolution', caused by the arrival of huge amounts of silver from America
1667: the *Cinco Gremios* company is constituted in Madrid
1701–14: War of Spanish Succession. The reign of the Bourbon dynasty begins in Spain
1778: 'Free Commerce' Decree (between Spain and colonies in America)
1780: first issue of *vales reales*, a sort of paper money invented by François Cabarrus
1782: foundation of the *Banco Nacional de San Carlos* by Charles III
1790: crisis of the *Banco de San Carlos*. Cabarrus is imprisoned for five years
1808–13: the Peninsular War
1813–33: Ferdinand VII keeps the *Ancien Régime* in Spain, with the exception of the liberal *Trennium* (1820–23)
1829: foundation of the *Banco Español de San Fernando* as successor of the *Banco de San Carlos*. Promulgation of the first Commerce Code
1831: foundation of the Madrid Stock Exchange
1833–43: 'Liberal Revolution' that brought about the gradual demise of the institutions of the *Ancien Régime*. First Carlist war. The *desamortización* begins. The Rothschilds begin their operations in Spain
1838: foundation of the first savings bank: *Caja de Madrid*
1843–68: reign of Isabella II, the daughter of Ferdinand VII
1844: foundation of the the *Banco de Isabel II* (by José Salamanca) and *Banco de Barcelona* (by Manuel Girona)
1845: foundation of the *Caja de Descuentos Zaragozana*
1846: foundation of the *Sociedad Valenciana de Fomento* and two banks of issue in Cadiz that merged in 1847

1847–48: first capitalist crisis in Spain. Under the guidelines of Salamanca, as Minister of Finance, the *Banco de Isabel II* merges with the *Banco Español de San Fernando*

1848: monetary reform with the *real* as basic unit and decimal denominations

1849: refoundation of the *Banco Español de San Fernando*, under a banking law inspired by the Peel Act. Ramón Santillán, governor of the *Nuevo Banco de San Fernando*

1851–52: Bravo Murillo's financial reform. Creation of the *Caja de Depósitos*

1856: liberal banking laws dealing with banks of issue and credit companies. The *Banco de San Fernando* is given its definitive name: *Banco de España*

1857–68: rapid growth of banking sector, followed by collapse and crisis

1864: monetary reform with the *escudo* as basic unit

1868–74: *Democratic Sexennium* after the Glorious Revolution of 1868. The heyday of liberalism in Spain. Proclamation of the First Republic (1873–1874)

1868: monetary reform with the *peseta* as basic unit; a halfway step towards the Latin Monetary Union

1872: foundation of the *Banco Hipotecario* in an operation led by Paribas

1874: 19 March: the Bank of Spain receives the monopoly of banknote issue. 29 December: restoration of the Bourbons in Spain (Alfonso XII, 1874–85; Alfonso XIII, 1902–31)

1876: end of the Carlist wars; foundation of the *Banco Hispano Colonial* by Antonio López, marquis of Comillas

1880: first law on savings banks that promotes their merger with *Montes de Piedad*

1885: promulgation of the second Commerce Code

1898: colonial 'Disaster'. Loss of Cuba, Puerto Rico, and the Philippines: Treaty of Paris

1899–1900: Fernández Villaverde's stabilization plan and financial reform.

1898–1914: foundation of fifty banks, among them *Banco Hispano Americano* (1900), *Banco de Vizcaya* (1901) and *Banco Español de Crédito (Banesto)* (1902)

1903: Antonio Maura, head of the Conservative Party with a Regenerationist programme (protectionism, nationalism, interventionism), which was prevalent in the Spanish economic policies until the Sardà Plan (1959), when its dismantling began

1904: foundation of *La Caixa*

1914: the Bank of Spain intervenes as lender of last resort for first time to rescue a sole bank: the Hispano

1914–19: business boom favoured by the neutrality observed during the First World War; foundation of *Banco Urquijo* (1918) and *Banco Central* (1919)

1918: agreement for the automatic pledging of public debt in the hands of the banks between the *Comité Central de la Banca Española* (bankers' association just founded) and the Bank of Spain
1919–23: social violence and military problems in Morocco
1919: foundation of the *Caja Central de Crédito Marítimo y Pesquero*
1920: failure of the *Banco de Barcelona* and foundation of the *Banco de Cataluña* and the public institution *Banco de Crédito Industrial*
1921: Banking (Cambó) Act, a decisive step towards the specialization of the Bank of Spain as central bank and the regulation of the rest of the private banks through a *Consejo Superior Bancario* dominated by the big banks
1923–30: Primo de Rivera dictatorship
1925: foundation of the public banks *Servicio Nacional de Crédito Agrícola* (*Banco de Crédito Agrícola* since 1962) and *Banco de Crédito Local*
1926: mandatory investment ratio in public funds for savings banks. Foundation of the *Banco Popular*
1928–32: intervention in support of the rate of exchange of the peseta
1928: foundation of the public institution *Banco Exterior de España*
1929: report of the *Comisión del Patrón Oro* (Antonio Flores de Lemus), published by the *Consejo Superior Bancario*
1930–31: *Dictablanda* (soft dictatorship)
1931–36: Second Republic
1931: the Bank of Spain intervenes as lender of last resort for the first time to rescue the whole financial system, excluding the *Banco de Cataluña*, that goes bankrupt
1933: the peseta is aligned with the French gold bloc. The *Estatuto de las Cajas Generales de Ahorro Popular*, the basic legal framework of the savings banks to 1977, is passed
1936–39: Civil War. A breakup of the monetary union takes place
1938: interest rates are fixed by the Franco government
1939–75: Franco's dictatorship, where three periods can be established: autarky (1939–51); a 'hinge decade', as transition from autarky to market economy (1951–59); and a 'development', commonly called *desarrollismo*, period (1959–75)
1939–42: monetary reunificaton (Larraz Plan)
1939: foundation of the *Instituto Español de Moneda Extranjera*, in charge of external monetary policy
1940: foundation of the public bank *Instituto de Crédito para la Reconstrucción Nacional* (*Banco de Crédito a la Construcción* since 1962)
1941–60: setup of interest rates by interbank agreements to elude competition
1942: the *Instituto Nacional de Industria*, the main engine for state-promoted industrialization
1946: the Benjumea Act is passed, increasing the control of state over the Bank of Spain, but leaving intact the rest of the banking system

1957: Treaty of Rome that established the European Economic Community. Spain applied for membership in 1962, but due to the dictatorial character of the Franco regime only a preferential commercial agreement was accorded in 1970

1958: Law on Official Institutions for Medium and Long Term Credit that put an end to the automatic pledging of the public debt in the Bank of Spain and a mandatory investment ratio in public funds for the private banks is proposed (it was required in 1965)

1959: Stabilization (Sardà) Plan (a basic programme for the stabilization and subsequent liberalisation of the Spanish economy), which constitutes a true divide in Spanish economic policy in the twentieth century

1962: the Navarro Rubio Act (third Banking Law), which nationalized the Bank of Spain and the public banks (except the *Banco Exterior de España*), segregated 'commercial banks' from 'industrial banks' (investment banks) and began the explicit regulation of quantities (investment ratios), prices (rates of interest) and business conditions. A *Central de Información de Riesgos* is set up within the Bank of Spain

1963: liquidity ratios are implemented for commercial and industrial banks and cash reserve and guarantee ratios for the industrial banks. Limits to industrial securities in the portfolio of the commercial banks are set up.

1964–74: interest rates are established by the government to prevent competition (only interbank rates remained free)

1965: Franco opposes the creation of a megabank by the merger of Hispano and Central

1969: outbreak of the 'Matesa scandal', which brings into question public banks and export-promotion policies and, ultimately, economic interventionism

1970–80: the Big Seven Club, trying to preserve the role of big banks in a period of political, economic and financial transition

1970: compulsory cash reserve ratio for commercial banks

1971: Law of Official Credit, which sets up the *Instituto de Crédito Oficial*. The liquidity ratios are abolished and a guarantee ratio is established for the commercial banks. The mandatory investment ratio in public funds is also abolished and mandatory investment ratios with different purposes are implemented for commercial and industrial banks

1972: the bank charges are liberalized

1973–83: the Bank of Spain effectively takes charge of monetary policy, which includes the external side after the dissolution of the *Instituto Español de Moneda Extranjera*

1973: the first ATM is installed by the *Banco Popular*

1974: Barrera de Irimo Reform, aimed at introducing more competition in banking

1977–2013: democratic Spain, with centre (1977–82, Adolfo Suárez and Leopoldo Calvo-Sotelo), socialist (1982–96, Felipe González; 2004–11,

José Luis Rodríguez Zapatero), and popular governments (1996–2004, José María Aznar; since 19 December 2011, Mariano Rajoy)

1977: interest rates for one- or more-year terms are liberalized. The *Asociación Española de Banca* (a private organisation replacing the semi-public CSB) is established. A decisive push is given to the operational convergence between savings banks and banks

1977–85: banking crisis. The *Fondo de Garantía de Depósitos* is created by the governor López de Letona

1978–93: new foreign banks are admitted in the Spanish markets under certain conditions

1981–87: gradual liberalization of interest rates

1984–92: a reform of public finance, under the guidance of Mariano Rubio (governor of the Bank of Spain) and Luis Ángel Rojo (deputy governor). Mandatory investment ratios are abolished and the cash reserve ratio is lowered to a minimum, while the government uses new, somewhat unorthodox formulas (issue of *pagarés del Tesoro* to channel 'black money')

1985–8: freedom to open branches for banks and savings banks. The control and the supervision of the savings banks are assigned to the Autonomous Communities

1986: Spain becomes full member of the European Economic Community

1987–99: bank merger wave: Santander absorbs BCH, in turn the result of a merger between Central and Hispano, and adds Banesto to its group and creation of BBVA; merger of Bilbao, Vizcaya and Argentaria, which grouped all the public banks, except *ICO*.

1987–2002: reform of the stock exchanges for public and private securities is followed by a spectacular boom and leads to the creation of *Bolsas y Mercados Españoles*

1988: the Securities Market Act modernizes the functioning of Spanish stock markets

1989: Santander launches the *supercuenta* (a call bank account with high yield)

1992–95: crisis of the European Monetary System and four devaluations of the peseta

1992: The Maastricht Treaty proposes the creation of an Economic and Monetary Union as a step towards a European Union to replace the European Economic Community

1993: Banesto is intervened by the Bank of Spain

1994–2008: a period of economic growth largely owing to the construction industry

1994: Law on Autonomy of the Bank of Spain

1995: BBV (later BBVA) starts its expansion through Latin America

1999: start of the European Monetary Union (the Eurozone). *Banco Santander* expands in Latin America. The Bank of Spain establishes the prudential 'dynamic provisions'

2004: Santander buys Abbey National Bank

2009: burst of the construction bubble. Crisis in *Caja Castilla-La Mancha*. Creation of the *Fondo de Reestructuración Ordenada Bancaria*

2010: European rescue of Greece and Ireland. Reform of the Spanish savings banks begins

2011: European rescue of Portugal. The Spanish government adopts measures to reduce the public deficit

2012: after the outbreak of Bankia's crisis, a European rescue of the Spanish banking system is required

Appendix 1 Synthesis of the Spanish economy, 1814–74 (annual rate of change in percentages, except in the case of the investment rate, which is GFCF/GDP)

	GDP[a] per capita Prados de la Escosura	GDP[a] per capita Maluquer de Motes	Investment rate	Prices	Wages	M3 G. R.	M3 C.	B. S. rate of interest
1814–50	0.31–0.44			–1.6	–0.1			
1851	0.9	1.0	6.0	–0.7	0.0			
1852	4.3	3.8	6.8	–2.1	0.0			
1853	–0.2	–0.2	5.8	6.8	–3.6			
1854	0.6	0.4	5.0	6.8	1.9			
1855	3.2	2.6	4.1	0.5	–3.1			
1856	–3.2	–3.7	5.4	6.6	0.0			6
1857	–1.3	0.0	6.9	2.5	5.1	5.7		5.3
1858	1.6	2.9	9.8	–10.4	0.0	4.4		5
1859	4.5	3.1	9.6	0.7	–3.6	9.6		5
1860	3.2	3.2	10.8	7.6	5.6	6.9		5
1861	1.1	0.5	9.7	0.1	0.0	7.2	7.2	7
1862	0.2	0.5	10.1	–0.5	2.9	8.3	8.2	5.5
1863	1.9	2.0	9.4	6.9	–5.1	5.7	4.1	6.5
1864	–0.4	–0.3	8.3	–1.0	0.0	7.3	9.1	8.5
1865	–3.3	–2.8	7.5	–3.7	0.0	4.2	4.2	9
1866	4.7	3.9	6.9	–0.5	0.0	1.9	1.9	7.5
1867	–0.7	–3.0	6.8	–1.0	0.0	7.0	7.1	5
1868	–11.1	–9.2	4.6	7.6	0.0	2.5	2.4	5
1869	2.7	2.2	4.8	–4.0	0.0	3.7	3.7	5
1870	2.3	3.4	5.3	2.3	0.0	5.4	4.3	5
1871	7.4	8.0	5.7	0.2	0.0	5.2	0.3	5
1872	13.2	14.9	5.6	3.0	–2.5	5.8	0.5	5
1873	8.5	5.1	4.8	7.8	–7.4	6.4	0.0	6
1874	–7.1	–6.5	5.4	–1.2	16.1	–14.3	–0.1	6

[a]GDP is at constant prices.

Sources: GDP per capita and Investment Rate in Prados de la Escosura (2003), except for 1814–50 (actually, 1810s–50s), which is Álvarez Nogal and Prados de la Escosura (2011). GDP per capita Maluquer de Motes in Maluquer de Motes (2009). Prices: 1814–29, Nogués (2005); 1830–74, Maluquer de Motes (2007). Wages in Reher and Ballesteros (1993). M3: G. R. García Ruiz (1996); C. Castañeda (2007); B. S. Rate of Interest (discount rate of the Bank of Spain), García Ruiz (1996) (in Castañeda, 2007, rates are 6 per cent in 1863, 8 per cent in 1864 and 6.5 per cent in 1866).

Appendix 2 Annual average rates of change in GDP per capita at constant prices and investment rate (GFCF/GDP, in percentage) in the Spanish Economy, 1875–2011

Years	Historical stages	GDP pc Prados de la Escosura	GDP pc Maluquer de Motes	Investment rate
1875–98	Restoration	0.94	1.32	5.79
1899–13	Regenerationism	1.06	1.86	8.91
1914–18	World War I	–0.57	–0.92	9.76
1919–23	Postwar recovery	2.78	3.05	10.59
1924–29	Primo de Rivera dictatorship	3.16	3.55	14.00
1930–35	'Dictablanda' and II Republic	–0.97	–1.24	12.15
1936–38	Civil War	–11.16	–10.48	10.72
1939–50	Autarky	1.92	1.76	14.31
1951–58	'Hinge decade'	4.85	5.18	20.40
1959–60	Sardà Plan	–0.26	–1.07	18.75
1961–74	'Developmentalism'	6.90	6.64	24.57
1975–85	Oil crises	1.68	0.70	22.81
1986–91	Joining the EEC	4.67	3.82	23.79
1992–93	EMS crisis	0.01	–0.45	22.23
1994–2007	Construction boom	2.71	2.71	26.49
2008–11	Great Recession	–1.23	–1.23	24.86

Sources: GDP Prados de la Escosura, Prados de la Escosura (2003), except for 1994–2011, which is BIEST Database (Bank of Spain). GDP Maluquer de Motes, Maluquer de Motes (2009), except for 1994–2011, which is is BIEST Database (Bank of Spain). Investment Rate, Prados de la Escosura (2003), except for 1994–2011, which is BIEST Database (Bank of Spain).

Appendix 3 Annual average rates of change in prices (consumer prices), Salaries (nominal salaries), and M3/GDP in Spain, 1875–2011 (percentages)

	Historical stages	Prices	Wages	M3/GDP
1875–98	Restoration	0.15	–0.44	1.81
1899–1913	Regenerationism	0.24	1.88	–1.29
1914–18	First World War	9.52	2.27	5.11
1919–23	Postwar recovery	1.97	12.24	2.81
1924–29	Primo de Rivera dictatorship	0.50	1.02	–1.59
1930–35	'Dictablanda' and II Republic	0.12	7.11	2.29
1936–38	Civil War	[a]	0.86	[a]
1939–50	Autarky	11.96[b]	7.38	1.28[c]
1951–58	'Hinge decade'	5.54	16.45	3.31
1959–60	Sardà Plan	4.24	0.03	8.05
1961–74	'Developmentalism'	8.01	13.04	2.57
1975–85	Oil crises	15.04	21.22	0.61
1986–91	Joining the EEC	6.28	8.48	0.53
1992–93	EMS crisis	5.14	7.20	1.43
1994–2007	Construction boom	3.24	4.09	1.30
2008–11	Great Recession	1.90	2.88	1.50

[a] There are not realiable statistics; [b] 1941–50; [c] 1942–50.

Sources: Prices: 1875–1936, Maluquer de Motes (2007); 1939–60, Index of the Cost of Life from the *Instituto Nacional de Estadística*; 1961–2011, Consumer Prices Index from the *Instituto Nacional de Estadística*. Wages, 1875–1991, Reher and Ballesteros (1993), series continued to 2000 with the *Encuesta de Salarios* from the *Instituto Nacional de Estadística* and for 2001–11 with the *Encuesta de Coste Laboral* from the *Instituto Nacional de Estadística*. M3 (wide money supply): 1875–1996, Martín Aceña and Pons (2005); 1997–2011, BIEST Database (Bank of Spain). GDP: 1875–1993, Maluquer de Motes (2009); 1994–2011, BIEST Database (Bank of Spain).

Appendix 4 Convergence indicators of Spain with the countries of the EMU (European Monetary Union), 1960–2011 (GDP pc is GDP per capita in PPP constant euros of 2005)

	GDP pc	On EMU = 100	Unemployment rate (%)	On EMU = 100		GDP pc	On EMU = 100	Unemployment rate (%)	On EMU = 100
1960	5,003	66.50	2.8	104	1986	13,496	62.73	21.3	200
1961	5,621	70.82	2.7	112	1987	14,210	64.57	20.6	193
1962	6,132	73.77	1.9	89	1988	14,901	65.21	19.9	194
1963	6,649	77.01	2.5	121	1989	15,590	65.93	17.3	182
1964	7,012	77.08	3.5	163	1990	16,155	82.16	16.3	187
1965	7,400	78.10	3.3	140	1991	16,528	82.26	15.9	185
1966	7,894	80.28	2.8	114	1992	16,643	82.12	17.7	193
1967	8,164	80.66	3.8	122	1993	16,436	82.04	22.2	206
1968	8,648	81.19	3.8	120	1994	16,797	82.08	24.2	203
1969	9,393	82.47	3.2	115	1995	17,607	84.02	22.7	197
1970	9,816	65.37	6.5	131	1996	17,981	84.69	22.2	189
1971	10,165	65.74	7.3	144	1997	18,627	85.70	20.7	176
1972	10,895	67.68	6.8	130	1998	19,391	86.96	18.7	165
1973	11,637	68.51	6.5	126	1999	20,207	88.28	15.5	148
1974	12,173	69.86	7.0	139	2000	21,050	89.81	13.8	148
1975	12,109	70.34	8.4	142	2001	21,578	90.69	10.4	127
1976	12,367	68.64	8.8	138	2002	21,845	91.48	11.2	132
1977	12,568	68.01	9.2	134	2003	22,149	92.66	11.3	126
1978	12,578	66.33	11.0	154	2004	22,503	92.70	11.1	119
1979	12,472	63.65	12.7	169	2005	22,930	93.45	9.2	102
1980	12,554	63.05	15.4	195	2006	23,502	93.25	8.5	101
1981	12,437	62.54	18.1	205	2007	23,883	92.56	8.3	111
1982	12,525	62.83	19.9	206	2008	23,715	92.07	11.3	151
1983	12,686	62.90	18.2	196	2009	22,661	92.28	18.0	189
1984	12,860	62.40	20.6	201	2010	22,574	90.47	20.1	201
1985	13,111	62.31	21.7	206	2011	22,708	89.95	21.7	215

Source: BIEST Database (Bank of Spain).

Appendix 5 Evolution of total public debt in Spain, 1860–2011 (percentage GDP) (with a comparison with big countries of Western Europe for 1995–2011)

	1860	**1882**	**1901**	**1923**
Spain	63	182	132	60
	1935	*1955*	*1971*	*1985*
Spain	72	40	23	37
	1995	*2000*	*2007*	*2011*
France	56	57	64	86
Germany	56	60	65	81
Italy	121	109	103	121
Spain	63	59	36	69
United Kingdom	51	41	44	85

Sources: For 1860–1985, Comín and Díaz Fuentes (2005), p. 877; for 1995–2011, Eurostat Database.

Appendix 6 Evolution of the number of private (non-public) banks in Spain, 1829–2010

	Banks		**Banks**
1829	1	1930	211
1846	7	1935	210
1855	5	1950	142
1864	57	1960	109
1874	22	1966	126
1880	18	1970	111
1890	40	1973	109
1900	36	1980	125
1905	50	1983	133
1910	60	1990	154
1914	61	2000	139
1923	150	2010	153

Sources: 1829–74, Tortella (1977), Table I.1, pp. 14–15; 1880 and 1890 in Tedde and Tortella (1974), pp. 221–3; 1900–14, Tortella and Núñez (2011), p. 485; 1923–35, Martín Aceña (2012), p. 110; 1950–2010, *Anuarios* from the CSB and the *Asociación Española de Banca*.

Appendix 7 Monetary base and broad money supply in Spain, 1874–1998 (million pesetas)

	Gold	Silver	Monetary base	Money supply		Gold	Silver/ Copper	Monetary base	Money supply
1874	1,131	465	1,722	1,769	1934		523	7,651	15,045
1875	1,058	516	1,731	1,808	1935		512	8,082	15,617
1876	1,003	563	1,802	1,902	1941		45[a]	15,194	35,599
1877	967	596	1,778	1,888	1942		45	17,952	38,348
1878	915	640	1,837	1,951	1943		45	19,240	41,081
1879	793	657	1,764	1,868	1944		45	20,804	46,936
1880	753	657	1,808	1,977	1945		45	21,828	52,677
1881	685	559	1,909	2,065	1946		82	26,189	64,855
1882	774	632	1,941	2,076	1947		164	29,310	75,052
1883	736	685	1,959	2,112	1948		183	30,793	80,395
1884	670	675	1,981	2,128	1949		215	33,072	88,740
1885	619	713	2,093	2,247	1950		251	35,935	101,897
1886	541	665	2,080	2,245	1951		308	41,694	119,658
1887	534	568	2,103	2,253	1952		335	44,107	137,075
1888	480	579	2,185	2,354	1953		373	46,878	152,015
1889	384	669	2,222	2,443	1954		428	53,168	176,774
1890	333	741	2,283	2,462	1955		485	56,566	205,704
1891	263	733	2,334	2,498	1956		620	65,940	241,081
1892	186	726	2,227	2,406	1957		669	79,448	276,123
1893	152	702	2,189	2,363	1958		807	86,586	316,412
1894	117	633	1,987	2,190	1959		2,014	94,005	337,650
1895	106	639	2,143	2,346	1960		3,181	104,362	391,375
1896	67	676	2,259	2,419	1961		3,834	118,553	457,230
1897		691	2,384	2,626	1962		4,363	133,514	551,101
1898		981	3,271	3,538	1963		5,207	156,358	636,216
1899		912	3,299	3,500	1964		5,923	183,461	768,651
1900		789	3,195	3,371	1965		6,605	201,506	912,984
1901		769	3,154	3,444	1966		7,498	229,710	1,042,239

1902	706	3,042	3,272	1967	9,736	257,661	1,202,527
1903	722	3,083	3,401	1968	11,161	282,316	1,428,753
1904	702	3,045	3,377	1969	12,212	309,218	1,696,862
1905	629	2,884	3,259	1970	12,942	358,402	1,952,660
1906	595	2,796	3,239	1971	13,344	434,028	2,432,932
1907	558	2,777	3,242	1972	14,374	513,236	2,986,715
1908	389	2,705	3,188	1973	15,720	586,532	3,706,808
1909	430	2,800	3,340	1974	17,089	714,802	4,411,852
1910	432	2,818	3,427	1975	18,815	824,784	5,229,108
1911	446	2,871	3,533	1976	19,196	930,220	6,353,218
1912	463	3,007	3,692	1977	22,759	1,132,433	7,575,633
1913	484	3,105	3,827	1978	28,445	1,387,476	9,090,995
1914	491	3,378	3,896	1979	36,568	1,591,365	11,004,200
1915	447	3,518	4,323	1980	43,088	1,804,786	12,834,800
1916	459	3,835	4,892	1981	51,993	2,041,000	14,942,100
1917	491	4,592	5,965	1982	67,761	2,432,400	17,212,700
1918	559	5,472	7,646	1983	98,689	2,915,800	19,796,200
1919	570	6,000	8,706	1984	116,446	5,105,600	22,543,400
1920	626	6,702	9,921	1985	131,200	5,636,400	25,252,800
1921	575	6,520	9,843	1986	141,000	6,205,100	28,242,600
1922	544	6,536	10,922	1987	163,900	6,675,900	31,724,000
1923	551	6,667	11,371	1988	214,000	7,560,300	35,777,600
1924	549	6,997	11,236	1989	249,800	9,335,200	40,896,600
1925	548	7,169	11,338	1990	265,300	6,325,700	46,686,000
1926	525	6,812	11,233	1991	280,800	7,717,000	51,778,000
1927	515	6,974	11,942	1992	296,800	7,753,000	54,238,000
1928	502	7,211	12,740	1993	306,000	7,791,000	59,261,000
1929	496	7,335	13,648	1994	333,000	8,594,000	63,676,000
1930	501	7,543	14,528	1995	360,000	8,930,000	70,439,000
1931	685	8,333	14,161	1996	371,000	9,252,000	71,584,249
1932	599	7,975	14,286	1997	354,000	9,862,000	74,116,810
1933	556	7,923	14,593	1998	379,000	n.a.	80,918,869

[a] Since 1941, it is copper because after the Civil War the silver was demonetized.

Source: Martín Aceña and Pons (2005).

Appendix 8 A series of long-term interest rates in Spain, 1850–2011

	Rates		Rates		Rates
1850	9.2	1904	5.2	1958	5.0
1851	8.3	1905	5.1	1959	6.3
1852	6.9	1906	4.9	1960	6.4
1853	6.9	1907	4.9	1961	5.8
1854	8.5	1908	4.8	1962	5.2
1855	9.1	1909	4.6	1963	5.3
1856	7.3	1910	4.7	1964	5.7
1857	7.6	1911	4.7	1965	6.0
1858	7.4	1912	4.7	1966	6.8
1859	7.1	1913	4.9	1967	7.2
1860	6.3	1914	5.2	1968	7.4
1861	6.1	1915	5.6	1969	7.8
1862	5.9	1916	5.4	1970	9.1
1863	5.7	1917	5.4	1971	9.4
1864	6.0	1918	5.1	1972	8.7
1865	7.1	1919	5.2	1973	8.8
1866	8.5	1920	5.5	1974	10.7
1867	8.9	1921	5.9	1975	11.0
1868	8.9	1922	5.7	1976	10.3
1869	11.5	1923	5.6	1977	10.2
1870	11.9	1924	5.7	1978	11.4
1871	10.8	1925	5.7	1979	14.2
1872	11.1	1926	5.8	1980	15.2
1873	13.4	1927	5.7	1981	15.4
1874	17.3	1928	5.3	1982	15.7
1875	13.7	1929	5.4	1983	16.5
1876	11.4	1930	5.6	1984	16.4
1877	8.6	1931	6.3	1985	13.4
1878	7.3	1932	6.2	1986	11.4

1879	6.6	1933	6.0	1987	12.8
1880	5.3	1934	5.7	1988	11.7
1881	3.9	1935	5.2	1989	13.6
1882	4.4	1936	5.3	1990	14.6
1883	6.4	1937	5.2	1991	12.5
1884	6.6	1938	5.0	1992	12.6
1885	6.7	1939	4.9	1993	10.1
1886	6.6	1940	4.8	1994	9.3
1887	6.1	1941	4.6	1995	10.9
1888	5.7	1942	4.5	1996	7.7
1889	5.3	1943	4.5	1997	5.3
1890	5.2	1944	4.5	1998	4.1
1891	5.3	1945	4.5	1999	3.7
1892	5.9	1946	4.5	2000	5.1
1893	5.8	1947	5.5	2001	4.3
1894	5.7	1948	5.5	2002	3.9
1895	5.7	1949	5.5	2003	2.8
1896	6.3	1950	5.5	2004	2.8
1897	6.2	1951	5.5	2005	2.5
1898	7.2	1952	5.5	2006	3.5
1899	6.3	1953	5.5	2007	4.1
1900	5.6	1954	5.5	2008	3.9
1901	5.6	1955	5.0	2009	2.2
1902	5.5	1956	5.0	2010	2.6
1903	5.2	1957	5.0	2011	4.0

Sources: 1850–1998, Carreras and Tafunell (2010), completing for 1937–59 with the interest rate of the lines of credit of the Bank of Spain provided by Martín Aceña and Pons (2005), interpolating in 1937–41 and correcting the figure given for 1954 (from 6.5 to 5.5); 1999–2011, BIEST Database (Bank of Spain).

Appendix 9 Financial assets/GDP in Western Europe, 1900–2010 (percentages)

	1900	1913	1929	1938	1948	1963	1986	2010
France	96	104	90	130	63	104	175	177
Germany	114	158	89	99	107	124	107	197
Great Britain[a]	93–106	103–15	131–55	158–80	177–84	139–62	220	301
Italy[a]	61–69	82–97	95–104	108–37	63–67	114–74	105	231
Spain[a]	37–39	32–35	62–74	79–81	83–90	105–43	138	166

[a] Estimates are offered in a range when they differ.
Sources: 1900–63, Martín Aceña and Pons (2005); 1986 and 2010, Inverco (2011).

Appendix 10 Distribution of the deposits of the financial institutions in Spain, 1900–2000 (percentages and total in million of current pesetas) (there is no information for 1936–41)

	Bank of Spain	Private banks	Savings banks	Rural credit coop.	Postal savings bank	TOTAL	% GDP Prados de la Escosura	% GDP Maluquer de Motes
1900	57.3	31.5	11.2			1,186	11.56	7.93
1901	54.0	34.4	11.6			1,200	11.13	7.31
1902	51.7	34.4	13.9			1,088	10.44	6.80
1903	50.9	34.9	14.1			1,182	10.60	7.23
1904	48.7	36.5	14.8			1,186	10.09	7.32
1905	46.1	38.1	15.8			1,174	10.35	7.30
1906	42.2	41.5	16.3			1,212	10.48	7.25
1907	40.4	42.4	17.2			1,214	10.09	7.08
1908	37.5	44.6	17.9			1,240	10.38	6.98
1909	37.2	44.9	17.9			1,322	10.83	7.55
1910	33.3	48.2	18.5			1,368	11.71	8.21
1911	31.6	48.9	19.5			1,413	11.20	7.67
1912	31.4	48.0	20.6			1,457	11.35	8.12
1913	31.9	46.5	21.6			1,521	11.03	7.87
1914	38.7	39.9	21.3			1,572	11.45	8.36
1915	36.6	44.0	19.4			1,906	12.61	9.54
1916	34.8	46.0	19.2			2,151	12.33	9.51
1917	33.7	49.9	16.4			2,792	14.71	10.91
1918	30.0	56.6	13.3			3,859	16.76	12.80
1919	24.3	61.9	13.8			4,369	17.60	12.72
1920	22.9	63.7	13.3			5,058	17.21	12.53
1921	20.2	64.9	14.9			5,095	18.82	13.27
1922	17.1	69.2	13.7			6,284	22.87	16.22
1923	16.2	69.1	14.7			6,497	23.61	16.57
1924	15.6	67.2	17.2			6,200	20.57	14.89

continued

Appendix 10 Continued

	Bank of Spain	Private banks	Savings banks	Rural credit coop.	Postal savings bank	TOTAL	% GDP Prados de la Escosura	% GDP Maluquer de Motes
1925	20.3	61.4	18.3			6,395	19.99	14.34
1926	16.0	64.9	19.1			6,372	20.41	15.13
1927	14.9	67.2	17.9			7,248	21.65	15.70
1928	12.0	69.1	18.9			8,008	24.49	17.66
1929	11.1	70.0	18.9			8,869	25.19	16.92
1930	9.2	71.5	19.4			9,442	26.80	19.33
1931	13.1	64.4	22.6			8,683	25.11	17.67
1932	10.7	65.7	23.6			9,043	26.14	17.96
1933	9.9	66.0	24.1			9,423	28.54	19.66
1934	8.9	67.0	24.2			9,930	27.30	19.12
1935	11.8	64.5	23.7			11,257	29.94	21.24
1942	17.8	67.7	14.5			23,763	34.28	20.40
1943	14.5	69.8	15.7			26,290	35.23	21.91
1944	14.1	70.1	15.7			31,146	36.14	24.10
1945	9.5	73.7	16.8			35,129	41.08	27.62
1946	8.9	75.0	16.1			43,759	40.45	24.86
1947	7.7	75.5	16.8			50,254	39.98	23.93
1948	5.6	76.1	18.3			55,177	40.66	24.90
1949	5.3	75.8	18.9			62,508	42.97	26.88
1950	5.3	75.4	19.2			72,644	40.47	27.31
1951	3.7	76.5	19.7			85,810	37.56	26.59
1952	4.5	74.2	19.9		1.4	103,070	41.03	30.28
1953	3.5	74.7	20.4		1.4	118,325	43.58	34.02
1954	2.6	75.2	20.8		1.4	136,988	43.61	36.56
1955	4.0	74.1	20.4		1.4	164,767	48.56	41.14
1956	6.5	72.3	19.7		1.4	200,673	47.80	44.17
1957	5.5	72.2	20.8		1.5	225,718	46.08	42.41
1958	6.6	71.1	20.8		1.5	263,975	45.37	40.98

1959	6.6	70.3	21.5		1.6	283,811	46.55	42.61
1960	6.0	70.2	22.3		1.6	333,061	52.57	48.71
1961	4.5	71.1	22.8		1.6	392,906	53.90	50.21
1962	4.1	70.9	23.3		1.7	476,223	55.97	52.54
1963	2.6	70.9	24.5		1.9	549,890	54.20	51.43
1964	2.2	71.0	24.8		2.0	670,914	57.96	55.50
1965	[a]	71.6	26.3		2.1	780,782	57.44	55.68
1966		70.1	27.7		2.2	886,980	56.58	54.53
1967		69.1	28.6		2.2	1,031,097	58.77	55.98
1968		68.4	29.4		2.2	1,238,178	63.47	59.54
1969		68.0	29.9		2.1	1,487,860	67.13	62.48
1970		65.5	32.5	[b]	2.0	1,852,001	75.19	66.47
1971		64.0	33.2	0.8	2.1	2,215,451	79.12	70.46
1972		64.6	32.4	1.0	2.0	2,765,780	84.13	74.95
1973		65.3	31.6	1.2	1.8	3,454,299	86.40	77.64
1974		65.3	31.6	1.4	1.8	4,142,052	83.64	76.02
1975		64.2	32.4	1.5	1.8	4,939,766	84.16	77.22
1976		63.1	33.4	1.7	1.8	5,912,036	83.44	76.80
1977		62.5	33.9	1.9	1.8	7,015,644	77.83	71.83
1978		62.0	34.2	2.0	1.8	8,425,022	76.00	70.47
1979		61.9	34.1	2.2	1.8	10,053,627	77.48	71.89
1980		62.5	33.3	2.4	1.8	11,810,224	77.65	72.89
1981		61.8	33.8	2.6	1.8	13,807,466	81.01	75.95
1982		60.5	35.1	2.6	1.8	16,139,964	81.83	77.20
1983		59.3	35.8	3.1	1.9	17,900,021	79.44	75.19
1984		58.7	37.0	2.7	1.6	19,950,331	78.18	74.26
1985		53.3	41.0	3.6	2.1	21,408,649	75.91	73.13

continued

Appendix 10 Continued

	Bank of Spain	Private banks	Savings banks	Rural credit coop.	Postal savings bank	TOTAL	% GDP Prados de la Escosura	% GDP Maluquer de Motes
1986		55.5	38.9	3.4	2.2	23,332,159	72.18	68.27
1987		55.4	38.2	4.3	2.2	26,569,994	73.16	69.53
1988		52.7	40.9	4.2	2.2	29,935,740	73.84	70.36
1989		50.3	43.6	4.0	2.1	34,045,092	74.51	71.41
1990		50.5	43.4	4.0	2.0	38,476,742	75.28	72.46
1991		50.3	43.1	4.2	2.3	42,898,777	76.27	73.67
1992		48.5	44.8	4.2	2.4	47,979,309	78.89	76.50
1993		47.2	45.9	4.5	2.3	52,386,911	83.13	80.74
1994		46.9	48.3	4.8	[c]	55,436,800	82.34	80.33
1995		48.3	46.7	5.0		62,218,000	85.42	83.62
1996		46.3	48.5	5.2		65,378,338	84.64	82.92
1997		45.9	48.8	5.3		68,363,090	83.31	81.53
1998		44.0	50.1	5.9		70,184,111	80.17	78.19
1999		43.1	50.8	6.2		75,247,903	80.31	77.98
2000		43.0	50.8	6.2		84,798,125	84.06	80.86

[a] Bank of Spain was no longer a deposit bank after the Navarro Rubio Law (1962); [b] Rural credit. Cooperatives were insignificant before 1971; [c] The Postal Savings Bank merged with BBV to form BBVA.

Sources: Deposits, Titos (2003); GDP Prados de la Escosura, Prados de la Escosura (2003); GDP Maluquer de Motes, Maluquer de Motes (2009). Maluquer de Motes's GDP estimate is much higher than Prados de la Escosura's for the first half of the twentieth century.

Appendix 11 Main assets and liabilities of Spanish private banks, 1923–2000 (percentages of total balance)

	Bills discounted	Loans	Public securities	Private securities	Equity	Deposits
1923	22.67	35.82	27.00	14.51	27.56	72.44
1930	21.58	28.86	30.09	19.47	24.17	75.83
1941	12.14	29.43	46.10	12.33	14.40	85.60
1950	32.19	27.64	31.28	8.89	9.48	90.52
1960	40.40	27.82	23.73	8.05	7.11	92.89
1970	51.93	24.28	18.79	5.00	8.52	91.48
1980	43.92	40.76	10.65	4.67	8.17	91.83
1990	18.03	64.68	6.99	10.30	9.65	90.35
2000	77.35		4.53	18.11	10.74	89.26

Sources: 1923, 1930 and 1941, Álvarez Llano and Andreu (1982); for the rest, Consejo Superior Bancario (1975–91) and Asociación Española de Banca (1992–93) (1994–). For 1915, Martín Aceña (2012, p. 106) gives a distribution similar to that of 1923, using the *Anuario Financiero y de Sociedades Anónimas de España* as source.

Appendix 12 Offices and employees of the Spanish private banks by autonomous communities, 1919–2000

Offices, 1919–1936[a]

	Head offices 1919	Branches and agencies 1919	Head offices 1926	Branches and Agencies 1926	Branches and Agencies 1936
Andalusia	0	30	0	103	237
Aragon	4	14	4	44	99
Asturias	4	14	6	41	86
Balearic Islands	12	21	13	25	42
Basque Country	11	50	10	202	182
Canarias	0	1	0	3	14
Cantabria	2	5	3	30	35
Castile and Leon	2	9	3	95	190
Castile-La Mancha	2	6	2	45	132
Catalonia	22	47	28	108	255
Extremadura	0	1	0	24	70
Galicia	3	5	3	30	102
La Rioja	1	4	0	24	42
Madrid	12	16	15	21	45
Murcia	0	10	0	21	37
Navarre	3	24	2	59	87
Valencia	3	13	3	56	237
TOTAL	81	270	92	931	1,892

Offices and Employees, 1950–70

	HO 1950	BRA/AG 1950	EMPLOYEES 1950	HO 1960	BRA/AG 1960	EMP 1963a	HO 1970	BRA/AG 1970	EMP 1967
Andalusia	13	292	4,395	7	382	8,140	8	619	9,420
Aragon	6	118	890	5	137	2,661	2	192	3,081
Asturias	7	84	131	7	95	1,675	6	138	1,779
Balearic Islands	13	43	534	6	46	1,075	5	97	1,388
Valencia	4	258	2,376	3	297	6,750	4	450	7,598
Canarias	1	36	1,046	1	68	1,581	1	119	1,771
Cantabria	1	35	408	1	36	1,183	1	53	1,285
Castile and Leon	12	200	10,106	8	205	3,274	8	329	3,598
Castile-La Mancha	2	129	1,346	1	141	2,692	2	209	2,314
Catalonia	34	311	9,499	25	405	12,032	20	662	16,268
Extremadura	3	74	741	2	98	1,518	2	146	1,641
Galicia	15	110	1,635	10	136	2,971	8	333	4,034
La Rioja	4	39	398	2	33	463	1	40	562
Madrid	14	134	10,265	19	259	15,305	32	391	18,593
Murcia	1	43	451	1	60	1,463	1	109	1,498
Navarre	2	72	642	2	74	731	3	102	839
Basque Country	10	206	1,507	9	201	5,187	7	285	5,071
Other[b]	0	42	876	0	23	253	0	17	230
TOTAL	142	2,226	47,246	109	2,696	68,954	111	4,291	80,970

continued

Offices and Employees, 1980–2000

	HO 1980	BRA/AG 1980	EMP 1980	HO 1990	BRA/AG 1990	EMP 2000	HO 1990	BRA/AG 2000	EMP 2000
Andalusia	5	1,474	16,898	6	2,071	15,509	2	1,888	11,705
Aragon	1	432	5,063	1	543	4,170	1	476	3,030
Asturias	4	392	4,384	2	527	3,921	3	562	2,891
Balearic Islands	3	365	3,150	3	541	2,811	2	535	2,925
Valencia	5	1,399	15,663	5	1,818	13,702	2	1,664	10,244
Canarias	1	338	4,791	1	513	4,543	0	512	3,706
Cantabria	1	197	1,912	1	298	2,092	1	264	1,396
Castile and Leon	3	1,017	8,226	2	1,205	7,135	1	1,137	5,738
Castile-La Mancha	3	529	4,053	1	601	3,303	0	548	2,704
Catalonia	22	2,667	38,628	20	3,089	29,401	12	2,478	19,815
Extremadura	2	386	2,785	2	432	2,310	2	470	2,030
Galicia	7	1,113	9,936	6	1,410	8,836	6	1,372	7,253
La Rioja	1	116	1,009	0	153	947	0	143	742
Madrid	59	1,629	46,404	97	2,250	43,699	97	2,480	37,407
Murcia	1	248	2,816	1	340	2,698	1	353	1,962
Navarre	1	232	1,902	1	292	1,715	1	265	1,234
Basque Country	6	671	11,290	5	731	8,610	8	798	6,472
Otherb	0	18	1,364	0	21	2,758	0	82	1,607
TOTAL	125	13,223	180,274	154	16,835	158,160	139	16,027	122,861

[a]Without foreign banks; bColonial possessions in North Africa and offices abroad.

Source: García Ruiz (2007b), which is based on Álvarez Llano and Andreu (1982) until the Civil War.

Appendix 13 The largest financial institutions in Spain, 1920–75 (share of total deposits of the subsector) and 2012 (share of total assets) (percentages)

	Banks[a]					Savings banks[b]					All[c]
	1922	1934	1947	1975		1928	1940	1955	1975		2012
Banesto	7.0	17.2	21.2	14.2	Barcelona	12.1	9.5	10.1	5.4	Santander	19.0
Bilbao	12.0	12.1	9.6	9.8	Bilbao	10.5	6.0	3.7	2.8	BBVA	15.0
Central	7.0	9.4	14.9	13.2	Guipúzcoa	7.1	5.6	4.0	2.8	CaixaBank	12.0
Hispano	21.6	23.2	28.5	12.8	La Caixa	17.7	25.7	28.1	14.8	Bankia	12.0
Popular			2.0	4.3	Madrid	5.3	3.6	3.2	6.8	Sabadell	6.0
Santander			2.5	6.0	Valencia	5.7	4.9	4.0	4.5	Popular	6.0
Urquijo	7.4	5.8	2.7	1.7	Vizcaína	4.5	4.0	3.8	2.6	Libercaja	4.2
Vizcaya	7.0	8.9	8.4	6.9	Zaragoza	2.9	4.6	6.0	5.4	Unicaja	2.7

[a]Bank groups. Popular was established in 1926 and its share was very small in 1934. Santander was established in 1857, but its share was very small in 1922 and in 1934; [b]In the ranking of the savings banks we have included those that have remained a long time among the biggest; thus, Leon (3.67) was excluded in 1928 and Diputación of Barcelona (3.81) in 1975; [c]Santander absorbed the old Madrid banks (Hispano, Banesto, Central) and BBVA was the result of a merger between Bilbao and Vizcaya. Bankia gathered the savings banks of Madrid and Valencia. Libercaja should be the new name of Caja de Zaragoza (1876), but the project is still pending. The Basque savings banks have merged and rank ninth with a share of 2.6 per cent, followed by Catalunya Banc, with 2.5 per cent, created upon the old savings bank of the *Diputación de Barcelona* (1926) (local government) or *Caixa de Catalunya*. *La Caixa* (now CaixaBank) was founded in 1904 and in 1990 absorbed *Caja de Barcelona*, founded in 1844. Sabadell has its origins in an old Catalan local bank established in 1881 and absorbed Banco Urquijo. Unicaja is a savings bank founded in Ronda (Málaga) in 1909, which has become the biggest financial institution in Andalusia (Molina, ed., 2009).

Sources: For 1920s–1975, banks in Pueyo (2003) and savings banks in Comín (2012); for 2012, Oliver Wyman (2012).

Bibliography

A. V. del R. (1918) *El Banco de España y la reforma del privilegio de emisión* (Madrid: Establecimiento Tipográfico de Juan Pérez Torres).

Adrados, S. (1918) *El Estado y el Banco de España* (Madrid: Hijos de T. Minuesa de los Ríos Impresores).

Aliber, R. Z. (1984) 'International Banking: A Survey', *Journal of Money, Credit and Banking*, 4, 661–95.

Álvarez, P. (1998) *Evolución de la banca extranjera en el periodo 1992–1996* (Madrid: Banco de España, Documento de Trabajo 9802).

Álvarez, P. e Iglesias-Sarriá, C. (1992) *La banca extranjera en España en el periodo 1978–1990* (Madrid: Banco de España, Estudio Económico 47).

Álvarez Llano, R. and Andreu, J. M. (1982) 'Una historia de la banca privada en España', *Situación*, 3 (special issue).

Álvarez Nogal, C. and Prados de la Escosura, L. (2011) *The Rise and Fall of Spain, 1270–1850* (Getafe: Carlos III University of Madrid, Working Paper 11–02).

Andrés, J. I. (2006) 'Finanzas y fiscalidad en Castilla en el siglo XVII: una nota sobre la inflación del vellón' in C. Sánz Ayán and B. J. García García (eds) *Banca, crédito y capital: la Monarquía Hispánica y los antiguos Países Bajos, 1505–1700* (Madrid: Fundación Carlos de Amberes).

Anes, R. (1974) 'El Banco de España (1874–1914): un banco nacional' in G. Tortella (ed.) *La banca española en la Restauración*, vol. I (Madrid: Banco de España).

Anes, R. (1994) 'El Banco de España, la deuda pública y la política monetaria entre 1874 y 1918' in P. Tedde and C. Marichal (eds) *La formación de los bancos centrales en España y América Latina (siglos XIX y XX)*, vol. I (Madrid: Banco de España).

Anes, R. (1995) 'El Banco de España, la deuda pública y la política monetaria entre 1874 y 1918' in P. Tedde and C. Marichal (eds), *La formación de los bancos centrales en España y América Latina (siglos XIX y XX)* (Madrid: Banco de España).

Argüelles, J. (1992) *Vinculación banca-industria bajo una estructura holding: análisis del Grupo Rumasa*, Ph. D. thesis (Madrid: Complutense University).

Aríztegui, J. (2012) 'Luis Ángel Rojo y la regulación financiera de finales del siglo XX' in C. Sebastián (ed.) (2012) *Luis Ángel Rojo. Recuerdo y homenaje* (Madrid: Fundación Ramón Areces).

Arroyo, J. V., Larrinaga, C., and Matés, J. M. (2012) 'La implantación del BBVA en América Latina', *Revista de la Historia de la Economía y de la Empresa*, 6, 281–302.

Arthur Andersen (1986) *The Decade of Change. Banking in Europe: The Next Ten Years* (London: Lafferty Publications).

Asociación de la Banca Española del Centro de España (1919–1934) *Memorias (1918–1933)* (Madrid: ABECE).

Asociación Española de Banca (1979) *Estudio sobre la banca española y las posibles opciones de cambio deseadas por la sociedad* (Madrid: AEB).

Asociación Española de Banca (1992–93) *Anuario estadístico de la banca privada en España* (Madrid: AEB).

Asociación Española de Banca (1994–) *Anuario estadístico de la banca en España* (Madrid: AEB).

Ayuso, J. and Escrivá, J. L. (1997) 'La evolución de la estrategia de control monetario' in *La política monetaria y la inflación en España* (Madrid: Alianza).

Bagehot, W. (1873) *Lombard Street. A Description of the Money Market* (London: H. S. King).

Ballarín, E. (1985) *Estrategias competitivas para la banca* (Barcelona: Ariel).

Banco Central Hispano Americano (1991) *Informe de la fusión* (Madrid: Banco Central and Banco Hispano Americano).

Banco de España (1931–36) *Problemas de la peseta: informes varios* (Madrid: Banco de España, Servicio de Estudios).

Banco de España (1932) *Informe elevado al Excmo. Sr. Ministro de Hacienda evacuando la consulta dirigida al Banco de España acerca de la conveniencia y oportunidad de alteración del tipo oficial de descuento* (Madrid: Banco de España, Servicio de Estudios).

Banco de España (1934) Ritmo de la crisis económica española en relación con la mundial (Madrid: Banco de España)

Banco de España (1935) *La economía inglesa después de la caída de la libra* (Madrid: Banco de España, Servicio de Estudios).

Banco de España (1994) *Informe de la inspección realizada a Banco Español de Crédito, S. A., sobre estados financieros a 30 de junio de 1993* (Madrid: Banco de España).

Banco de España (2011) *Evolución y reforma de las cajas de ahorros* (Madrid: Banco de España).

Banco de España, BIEST Database.

Banco Español Central de Crédito (1988), *Libro de la fusión* (Madrid: Banco Español de Crédito and Banco Central).

Banco Español de San Fernando (1833) *Primera Junta General del Banco Español de San Fernando de los años de 1830, 1831 y 1832* (Madrid).

Banco Hispano Americano (1986) *España y Portugal, nuevos miembros de la Comunidad Económica Europea* (Madrid: Banco Hispano Americano, Servicio de Estudios).

Banque (1932) *La banque et ses services*, 12 vols (Paris: Banque).

Barciela, C. (1987) 'Crecimiento y cambio en la agricultura española desde la Guerra Civil' in J. Nadal, C. Sudrià, and A. Carreras (eds), *La economía española en el siglo XX. Una perspectiva histórica* (Barcelona: Ariel).

Barciela, C., ed. (2003) *Autarquía y mercado negro. El fracaso económico del primer franquismo, 1939–1959* (Barcelona: Crítica).

Barona, J. L. (ed.) (2011) *El exilio científico republicano* (Valencia: Universidad de Valencia).

Barquín, R. (1999) 'El ahorro social: una perspectiva dinámica' in M. Muñoz, J. Sanz, and J. Vidal (eds) *Siglo y medio del ferrocarril en España, 1848–1998: economía, industria y sociedad* (Madrid: Fundación de los Ferrocarriles Españoles).

Barthe, A. (1905) *Estudio crítico de la crisis monetaria* (Madrid: Establecimiento Tipográfico de Jaime Ratés).

Baskin, J. B. and Miranti, P. J. (1997) *A History of Corporate Finance* (Cambridge: Cambridge University Press).

Bátiz-Lazo, B., Maixé, J. C., and Thomes, P. (eds) (2011) *Technological Innovation in Retail Finance. International Historical Perspectives* (London: Routledge).

Baumier, J. (1988) *La galaxie Paribas* (Paris: Plon).

Bautier, R.-H. (1971) *The Economic Development of Medieval Europe* (New York: Harcourt, Brace and Jovanovich).

Bazant, J. (1977) *A Concise History of Mexico, from Hidalgo to Cárdenas, 1805–1940* (Cambridge: Cambridge University Press).

Beck, T., Levine, R., and Loayza, N. (2000) 'Finance and the Sources of Growth', *Journal of Financial Economics*, 1–2, 261–300.

Bécker, F. (1988) *El Banco Exterior de España y su tiempo, 1929–1939*, Ph. D. thesis (Madrid: Universidad Autónoma de Madrid).

Belda, F. (1928) *El patrón oro fantasma* (Madrid: Graficas Reunidas).

Benston, G. J. (1990) *The Separation of Commercial and Investment Banking. The Glass-Steagall Act Revisited and Reconsidered* (London: Macmillan).

Berges, A., Ontiveros, E., and Valero, F. J. (2012) 'The Internationalization of the Spanish Financial System' in J. L. Malo de Molina and P. Martín Aceña (eds) *The Spanish Financial System. Growth and Development since 1900* (Basingstoke and New York: Palgrave Macmillan).

Betrán, C., Cubel, A., Pons, M. A., and Sanchís, T. (2010) *La España democrática, 1975–2009. Economía* (Madrid: Síntesis).

Blasco, Y. and Sudrià, C. (2010) *El Banco de Barcelona, 1844–1874* (Madrid: LID).

Bouvier, J. (1960) *Le krach de l'Union generale, 1878–1885* (Paris: Presses Universitaires de France).

Bröker, G. (1989) *La concurrence dans le secteur bancaire* (Paris: OCDE).

Bullón de Mendoza, A. (2004) *José Calvo Sotelo* (Barcelona: Ariel).

Bussière, E. (1992) *Paribas, 1872–1992: Europe and the World* (Antwerp: Fonds Mercator).

Caballero, R., Hoshi, T., and Kashyap, A. (2008) 'Zombie Lending and Depressed Restructuring in Japan', *American Economic Review*, 98, 5, 1943–77.

Cabana, F. (1965) *La banca a Catalunya* (Barcelona: Edicions 62).

Cabana, F. (1972) *Bancs y banquers a Catalunya. Capítols per a una història* (Barcelona: Edicions 62).

Cabana, F. (1978) *Història del Banc de Barcelona, 1844–1920* (Barcelona: Edicions 62).

Cabana, F. (1988) *Banca Catalana. Diari personal* (Barcelona: Tibidabo).

Cabana, F. (2003) *Eduard i Francesc Recasens: dos empresaris de Reus* (Reus: Cambra de Comerç, Indústria i Navegació).

Cabrera, M. and Del Rey, F. (2002) *El poder de los empresarios. Política y economía en la España contemporánea, 1875–2000* (Madrid: Taurus).

Calvo, A. (2010) *Historia de Telefónica, 1924–1975. Primeras décadas: tecnología, economía y política* (Barcelona: Ariel and Fundación Telefónica).

Cameron, R. (1961) *France and the Economic Development of Europe, 1800–1914. Conquests of Peace and Seeds of War* (Princeton: Princeton University Press).

Cameron, R. (1967) *Banking in the Early Stages of Industrialization: A Study in Comparative Economic History* (Oxford: Oxford University Press).

Caminal, R., Gual, J., and Vives, X. (1990) 'Competition in Spanish Banking' in J. Dermine (ed.) *European Banking in the 1990s* (Oxford: Basil Blackwell).

Canals, J. (1991) 'La rentabilidad de la banca en Europa', *Información Comercial Española*, 699, 99–120.

Canals, J. (1994) *Competitive Strategies in European Banking* (Oxford: Clarendon Press).

Canals, S. (1916) *El problema del crédito en España. Proyecto de un Banco Nacional* (Madrid: Imprenta de 'Alrededor del Mundo').

Canosa, R. (1945) *Un siglo de banca privada, 1845–1945. Apuntes para la historia de las finanzas españolas* (Madrid: Nuevas Gráficas).

Capella, M. and Matilla, A. (1957) *Los Cinco Gremios Mayores de Madrid: estudio crítico-histórico* (Madrid: Imprenta Sáez).

Capie, F. (1999) 'Banking in Europe in the nineteenth century: the role of the central bank' in R. Sylla, R. Tilly and G. Tortella (eds) *The State, the Financial System and Economic Modernization* (Cambridge: Cambridge University Press).

Carande, R. (1965) *Carlos V y sus banqueros*, 2nd ed., 3 vols (Madrid: Sociedad de Estudios y Publicaciones).

Carreras, A. (1985) 'Gasto nacional bruto y formación de capital en España, 1849–1958: primer ensayo de estimación' in P. Martín Aceña and L. Prados de la Escosura (eds) *La nueva historia económica en España* (Madrid: Tecnos).

Carreras, A. (1990) *Industrialización española: estudios de historia cuantitativa* (Madrid: Espasa-Calpe).

Carreras, A. and Tafunell, X. (2010) *Historia económica de la España contemporánea, 1789–2009* (Barcelona: Crítica).

Carreras, A. and Tafunell, X. (eds) (2005) *Estadísticas históricas de España, siglos XIX y XX*, 3 vols (Bilbao: Fundación BBVA).

Carreras, A., Prados de la Escosura, L. y Rosés, J. R. (2005) 'Renta y riqueza' in A. Carreras and X. Tafunell (eds) *Estadísticas históricas de España, siglos XIX y XX*, vol. III (Bilbao: Fundación BBVA).

Castañeda, J. E. (2007) *¿Puede haber deflaciones asociadas a aumentos de la productividad? Análisis de los precios y de la producción en España entre 1868 y 1914* (Madrid: Banco de España, Estudio de Historia Económica 51).

Castañeda, Ll. (1991) 'Sector financer i mercat de capitals al primer terç del segle XIX' in J. Nadal, J. Maluquer de Motes, C. Sudrià, and F. Cabana (eds) *Història Econòmica de la Catalunya Contemporània*, vol. III (Barcelona: Enciclopedia Catalana).

Castañeda, Ll. (2001) *El Banco de España, 1874–1900: la red de sucursales y los nuevos servicios financieros* (Madrid: Banco de España, Estudios de Historia Económica 41).

Catalan, J. (1995) *La economía española y la Segunda Guerra Mundial* (Barcelona: Ariel).

Ceballos Teresí, J. G. (1931) *La realidad económica y financiera de España en los 30 años del presente siglo*, I (Madrid: El Financiero).

Cepeda, I. (2003) *El pensamiento monetario de Luis Olariaga* (Madrid: Instituto de Estudios Fiscales).

Cerutti, E., Dell'Ariccia, G., and Martínez, M. (2007) 'How Banks Go Abroad: Branches or Subsidiaries?' *Journal of Banking and Finance*, 31, 1669–92.

Channon, D. F. (1988) *Global Banking Strategy* (New York: John Wiley & Sons).

Claessens, S., Dell'Ariccia, G., Igan, D., and Laeven, L. (2010) 'Cross-Country Experiences and Policy Implications from the Global Financial Crisis', *Economic Policy*, 62, 267–93.

Comín, F. (1990) *Las cuentas de la Hacienda preliberal en España, 1800–1855* (Madrid: Banco de España, Estudios de Historia Económica 19).

Comín, F. (1994a) 'El papel del presupuesto en el crecimiento económico español: una visión a largo plazo', *Revista de Historia Económica*, 2, 283–314.

Comín, F. (1994b) 'La deuda pública y la formación del sistema bancario en España durante los siglos XIX y XX' in P. Tedde and C. Marichal, eds., *La formación de los bancos centrales en España y América Latina (Siglos XIX y XX), Vol. I: España y México* (Madrid: Banco de España).

Comín, F. (1996) *Historia de la Hacienda pública* (Barcelona: Crítica).

Comín, F. (2002) 'El Plan de Estabilización de Raimundo Fernández Villaverde', *Cuadernos de Información Económica*, 168, 189–96.

Comín, F. (2010) 'Las fases históricas de la Seguridad Social en España, 1900–2000', *Revista de la Historia de la Economía y de la Empresa*, 4, 65–89

Comín, F. (2012) 'The Savings Banks: 1900–1975' in J. L. Malo de Molina and P. Martín Aceña (eds) *The Spanish Financial System. Growth and Development since 1900* (Basingstoke and New York: Palgrave Macmillan).

Comín, F. and Díaz Fuentes, D. (2005) 'Sector público administrativo y estado del bienestar', en A. Carreras and X. Tafunell (eds), *Estadísticas históricas de España, siglos XIX y XX* (Bilbao: Fundación BBVA).

Comín, F., Martín Aceña, P., Muñoz, M., and Vidal, J. (1998) *150 años de historia de los ferrocarriles españoles,* 2 vols (Madrid: Anaya and Fundación de los Ferrocarriles Españoles).

Comisión Nacional del Mercado de Valores and Banco de España (2007) *Los sistemas de compensación, liquidación y registro de valores en Europa. Situación actual, proyectos en curso y recomendaciones* (Madrid: CNMV and Banco de España).

Commission of the European Communities (2007) *European Financial Integration Report.*

Conde de Torreánaz (1915) *Bancos nacionales de emisión y la actuación del Banco de España en la crisis económica de 1914* (Madrid: Imprenta de Jaime Ratés Martín).

Consejo Superior Bancario (1929) *Dictamen de la Comisión nombrada por Real Orden de 9 de enero de 1929 para el estudio de la implantación del patrón de oro* (Madrid: Imprenta de Samarán y Cía.).

Consejo Superior Bancario (1968–85) *Cifras y relaciones significativas de los balances de la banca privada* (Madrid: CSB).

Consejo Superior Bancario (1975–91) *Anuario estadístico de la banca privada* (Madrid: CSB).

Consejo Superior Bancario (1976–82) *Recopilación de circulares (1947–81),* 3 vols (Madrid: CSB).

Coronas Vida, L. J. (2012) *Los bancos y las cajas de ahorros en la historia de Castilla y León. Historia financiera de una región atrasada* (Saarbrücken: EAE).

Cos-Gayón, F. (1891) *Discursos pronunciados en el Congreso y en el Senado con motivo de la discusión del proyecto de ley relativo al aumento de circulación fiduciaria y prórroga del privilegio al Banco de España* (Madrid: Establecimiento Tipográfico Sucesores de Rivadeneyra).

Cottrell, Ph. L. (2009) 'London's First "Big Bang"? Institutional Change in the City, 1855–83' in Y. Cassis and Ph. L. Cottrell (eds) *The World of Private Banking* (Aldershot: Ashgate).

Cuervo, A. (1988) *La crisis bancaria en España, 1977–1985* (Barcelona: Ariel).

De Carlos, C. J. (2006) 'Felipe II y sus banqueros', Sanz Ayán y García García, eds. pp, 329–44.

De Juan, A. (1983) 'La supervisión de las entidades de crédito y ahorro en España' in *Crisis bancarias, soluciones comparadas* (Madrid: AEB).

De la Sierra, F. (1951) 'La situación monopolística de la banca privada española', *Revista de Economía Política,* 1–2, 1–51.

De Miguel, A. and Linz, J. J. (1963) 'Los empresarios españoles y la banca', *Moneda y Crédito,* 84, 3–112.

De Riquer, B. (1994) 'La débil nacionalización española del siglo XIX', *Historia Social,* 20, 97–114.

Demirgüc-Kunt, A. and Levine, R. (eds) (2001) *Financial Structure and Economic Growth. A Cross-Country Comparison of Banks, Markets, and Development* (Cambridge: MIT Press).

Department of Overseas Trade (1930) *Economic Conditions in Spain* (London: His Majesty's Stationery Office).

Dermine, J. (ed.) (1990) *European Banking in the 1990s* (Oxford: Blackwell).

Díaz-Alejandro, C. (1985) 'Goodbye Financial Repression, Hello Financial Crash', *Journal of Development Economics,* 1–2, 1–24.

Díaz Hernández, O. (1998) *El apogeo de una saga poderosa y los inicios del Banco Urquijo, 1870–1931* (Pamplona: EUNSA).

Dinero, Journal.

Dixon, R. (1991) *Banking in Europe. The Single Market* (Londres: Routledge).

Doblón, Journal

Domínguez Ortiz, A. (1960) *Política y Hacienda de Felipe IV* (Madrid: Editorial de Derecho Financiero).

Domínguez Ortiz, A. (1984) *Política fiscal y cambio en la España del siglo XVII* (Madrid: Instituto de Estudios Fiscales).

Dunning, J. (2001) 'The Eclectic (OLI) Paradigm of International Production: Past, Present and Future', *International Journal of the Economics of Business*, 2, 173–190.

Durán Herrera, J. J. (2005) 'La inversión directa española en el exterior y la multinacionalización de la empresa española, 1960–2003' in J. J. Durán (ed.), *La empresa multinacional española. Estrategias y ventajas comparativas* (Madrid: Minerva).

Easterly, W., Islam, R., and Stiglitz, J. (2000) 'Shaken and Stirred: Explaining Growth Volatility', *Annual World Bank Conference on Development Economics.*

Economía, Journal

Economía Española, Journal

Economía y Diálogo, Journal

Eichengreen, B. (1995) *Golden Fetters. The gold standard and the Great Depression, 1919–1939* (Oxford: Oxford University Press).

Eichengreen, B. (2012) 'Economic History and Economic Policy', *The Journal of Economic History*, 2, 289–307.

Einzig, P. (1935) *World Finance, 1914–1935* (Nueva York: Macmillan).

El Economista, Journal (19th century) and daily (21st century)

El País, Daily.

Elliott, J. H. (1963) *Imperial Spain, 1469–1716* (London: Edward Arnold).

Elliott, J. H. (1986) *The Count-Duke of Olivares. The Statesman in an Age of Decline* (New Haven: Yale University Press).

Escámez, A. (1987) *La banca española ante la nueva frontera* (Barcelona: Jornadas de la Cámara Oficial de Comercio, Industria y Navegación de Barcelona, 2 December 1987).

Escámez, A. (1992) *Modelos de fusiones bancarias* (Valencia: Universidad de Valencia, closing session of the Master on Deposit Institutions, 22 June 1992).

España Económica y Financiera, Journal.

Espinosa, F. (ed.) (2010) *Violencia roja y azul. España, 1936–1950* (Barcelona: Crítica).

European Central Bank (2009) *Financial Integration in Europe* (Frankfurt: ECB).

European Central Bank (ECB) Statistical Data Warehouse

Eurostat Database

Fanjul, O. and Maravall, F. (1985) *La eficiencia del sistema bancario español* (Madrid: Alianza).

Feiertag, O and Margairaz, M. (eds) (2003) *Politiques et pratiques des banques d'émission en Europe (XVIIème-XXème siècles). Le bicentenaire de la Banque de France dans la perspective de l'identité monétaire européenne* (Paris: Albin Michel).

Ferguson, N. (1999) *The House of Rothschild: Money's Prophets, 1798–1848* (New York: Penguin Books).

Ferguson, N. (1998) *The World's Banker: The History of the House of Rothschild* (New York: Penguin Books).

Fernández Almagro, M. (1968) *Historia política de la España contemporánea* (Madrid: Alianza).

Fernández Pulgar, C. and Anes, R. (1970) 'La creación de la peseta en la evolución del sistema monetario de 1847 a 1868' in G. Tortella *et al.*, *Ensayos sobre la economía española a mediados del siglo XIX* (Madrid: Banco de España).
Fernández Villaverde, R. (1890) *La cuestión monetaria* (Madrid: Tipografía de Manuel Ginés Hernández).
Fisher, I. (1933) 'The Debt-Deflation Theory of Great Depression', *Econometrica*, 1, 337–57.
Fontana, J. (1961) 'La Vieja Bolsa de Barcelona, 1851–1914' in *La Bolsa de Barcelona de 1851 a 1930: líneas generales de evolución* (Barcelona: Instituto Municipal de Historia).
Fontana, J. (1973) *Hacienda y Estado en la crisis final del Antiguo Régimen español, 1823–1830* (Madrid: Instituto de Estudios Fiscales).
Fontana, J. (1974) *La quiebra de la monarquía absoluta, 1814–1820*, 2nd ed. (Barcelona: Ariel).
Fontana, J. (1977) *La revolución liberal. Política y Hacienda, 1833–1845* (Madrid: Instituto de Estudios Fiscales).
Forniés, J. F., Torres, M. M., and Rubio, A. (1976) *Historia de la Caja de Ahorros y Monte de Piedad de Zaragoza, Aragón y Rioja, 1876–1976* (Saragossa: La Caja).
Fraile, P. (1991) *Industrialización y grupos de presión. La economía política de la protección en España, 1900–1950* (Madrid: Alianza).
Franco Salgado-Araujo, F. (1976), *Mis conversaciones privadas con Franco* (Barcelona: Edicions 62).
Fuentelsaz, L. and Salas, V. (1994) *Spatial Competition in Retail Banking: Theory and Empirical Evidence from Spain and other European Countries* (Bilbao: Fundación BBVA).
Fuentes Quintana, E. (1984) 'El Plan de Estabilización Económica de 1959: veinticinco años después', *Información Comercial Española*, 612–613, 25–40.
Fuentes Quintana, E. (1991) 'Prólogo', en R. Termes, *Desde la banca*, vol. I (Madrid: Rialp).
Fuentes Quintana, E. (2003) 'Joan Sardà y el Plan de Estabilización y Liberalización de la economía española', *Papeles y memorias de la Real Academia de Ciencias Morales y Políticas*, 11, 156–185.
Fundesco (1988) *Las nuevas tecnologías de la información y el futuro del sistema financiero español* (Madrid: Fundesco).
Fusi, J. P. and Palafox, J. (1997) *España, 1808–1996. El desafío de la modernidad* (Madrid: Espasa-Calpe).
Gaceta de los Caminos de Hierro, Journal (19th century)
Gámez, A. (1997) 'La financiación de la agricultura en España: el Servicio Nacional de Crédito Agrario, 1925–1936', *Agricultura y Sociedad*, 82, 219–50.
García de Valdeavellano, L. (1960) *Sobre los Burgos y los burgueses de la España medieval* (Madrid: Real Academia de la Historia).
García Sanz, A. (1991) 'Repercusiones de la fiscalidad sobre la economía castellana en los siglos XVI y XVII', *Hacienda Pública Española*, 1, 15–24.
García Delgado, J. L. (1979) 'La política económica española de 1930: el 'error Argüelles'', *Papeles de Economía Española*, 1, 43–7.
García Delgado, J. L. (1985) 'Nacionalismo económico e intervención estatal, 1900–1930' in N. Sánchez-Albornoz (ed.) *La modernización económica de España, 1830–1930* (Madrid: Alianza).
García Delgado, J. L. (1987) 'La industrialización y el desarrollo económico de España durante el franquismo' in J. Nadal, A. Carreras, and C. Sudrià (eds) *La economía española en el siglo XX. Una perspectiva histórica* (Barcelona: Ariel).

García Delgado, J. L. and López Muñoz, A. (1968) 'Análisis de la banca privada española', *Cuadernos para el Diálogo*, April (special issue), 5–50 (Arturo López Muñoz was the pseudonim of Santiago Roldán López and Juan Muñoz).

García Hermoso, J. M. and Zubiría, S. (1990) 'Reforma y transformación del mercado de valores', *Papeles de Economía Española*, 44, 134–50.

García López, J. R. (1985) 'Banqueros y comerciantes banqueros, clave oculta del funcionamiento del sistema bancario español del siglo XIX', *Moneda y Crédito*, 175, 59–85.

García Ruiz, J. L. (1992) 'Sector financiero y apertura económica: una perspectiva comparada entre España y Argentina', *Ciclos*, 3, 95–112.

García Ruiz, J. L. (1993) 'Banca y crisis económica en España, 1930–1935: un nuevo enfoque', *Revista de Historia Económica*, 2, 595–620.

García Ruiz, J. L. (1996) 'Moneda y finanzas en España, 1845–1921' in J. Hernández Andreu (ed.), *Historia monetaria y financiera de España* (Madrid: Síntesis).

García Ruiz, J. L. (1999) 'La nueva banca mixta en el Madrid de comienzos de siglo' in P. Tedde (ed.) *Economía y colonias en la España del 98* (Madrid: Síntesis and Fundación Duques de Soria).

García Ruiz, J. L. (2001) 'La banca extranjera en España tras la Restauración' en C. Sudrià and D. Tirado (eds) *Peseta y protección. Comercio exterior, moneda y crecimiento económico en la España de la Restauración* (Barcelona: Universidad de Barcelona).

García Ruiz, J. L. (2002) 'Los arreglos interbancarios durante el franquismo', *Revista de Historia Económica*, 2, 365–84.

García Ruiz, J. L. (2003) 'Los flujos financieros regionales en la España del siglo XX: una perspectiva desde la historia bancaria', *Revista de Estudios Regionales*, 67, 15–54.

García Ruiz, J. L. (2006) 'Política y Hacienda en el periodo de entreguerras' in A. González Enciso and J. M. Matés (eds), *Historia económica de España* (Barcelona: Ariel).

García Ruiz, J. L. (2007a) 'Nacionalizando el capital bancario: Banesto y Paribas, 1902–1927', *Investigaciones de Historia Económica*, 9, 79–108.

García Ruiz, J. L. (2007b) 'Nuevos datos sobre flujos regionales de la banca española en el siglo XX', *Revista de Historia Industrial*, 35, 115–40.

García Ruiz, J. L. (2007c) 'Noventa años de gran banca comercial: el Banco Hispano Americano, 1900–1991', *Revista de la Historia de la Economía y de la Empresa*, 1, 117–39.

García Ruiz, J. L. (2007d) 'Banesto, 1902–1993: auge y decadencia de un gran banco mixto', *Revista de la Historia de la Economía y de la Empresa*, 1, 141–63.

García Ruiz, J. L. (2009) 'La banca española y la promoción de sociedades anónimas durante el siglo XX', *Revista de la Historia de la Economía y de la Empresa*, 3, 153–74.

García Ruiz, J. L. (2012) 'La intervención de Banesto en 1993: una perspectiva histórica', *Revista de la Historia de la Economía y de la Empresa*, 6, 307–35.

García Ruiz, J. L. and Tortella, G. (2003) 'Banca y política durante el Primer Franquismo' in G. Sánchez Recio and J. Tascón (eds), *Los empresarios de Franco. Política y economía en España, 1936–1957* (Barcelona: Crítica).

García Ruiz, J. L. and Tortella, G. (2007) 'How Strategy Determines Structure: The Organizational History of the Banco Hispano Americano and the Banco Central, 1900–1992', *Entreprises et Histoire*, 48, 29–42.

García Sanz, A. (1994) 'Competitivos en lanas, pero no en paños: lana para la exportación y lana para los telares nacionales en la España del Antiguo Régimen', *Revista de Historia Económica*, 2, 397–434.

Gardener, E. P. M. (1992) 'Banking Strategies and 1992' in A. W. Millineux (ed.) *European Banking* (Oxford: Blackwell).

Gelabert, J. E. (1997) *La bolsa del Rey* (Barcelona: Crítica).
Gerschenkron, A. (1962) *Economic Backwardness in Historical Perspective* (Cambridge, USA: Harvard University Press).
Giannola, A. (ed.) (1990) *Grandi Banche in Europa: problemi e prospettive* (Naples: Guida).
Gil, G. (2008) 'Perspectivas de los mercados de valores: supervisión y regulación' in *Libro conmemorativo del XX aniversario de la CNMV* (Madrid: CNMV).
Gille, B. (1965–1967) *Histoire de la Maison Rothschild*, 2 vols (Geneva: Droz).
Giráldez Pidal, E. (2002) *La internacionalización de las empresas españolas en América Latina* (Madrid: CES).
Goldsmith, R. W. (1969) *Financial Structure and Development* (New Haven: Yale University Press).
Gómez Ochoa, F. (1991) 'Por una nueva interpretación de la crisis final de la Restauración: el Gobierno Maura de agosto de 1921 y la reforma económica de Cambó', *Investigaciones históricas: época moderna y contemporánea*, 11, 251–72.
González, M. J. (dir.), Anes, R., and Mendoza, I. (2007), *BBVA, 1857–2007. 150 años, 150 bancos* (Bilbao: BBVA).
González Hernández, M. J. (1997) *El universo conservador de Antonio Maura. Biografía y proyecto de Estado* (Madrid: Biblioteca Nueva).
González Ruiz, L. and Matés, J. M. (eds) (2008) *La modernización económica de los ayuntamientos: servicios públicos, finanzas y gobiernos municipales* (Jaén: Universidad de Jaén).
Gonzalo, L. (1981) *El Tesoro Público y la Caja General de Depósitos, 1852–1868* (Madrid: Instituto de Estudios Fiscales).
Grossman, R. S. (2010), *Unsettled Account. The Evolution of Banking in the Industrialized World since 1800* (Princeton: Princeton University Press).
Grubel, H. G. (1985) *Multinational Banking* (Singapur: Institute of Southeast Asian Studies).
Gual, J. and Vives, X. (1991) *Ensayos sobre el sector bancario español* (Madrid: Fedea).
Guillén, M. F. (2005) *The Rise of Spanish Multinationals. European Business in the Global Economy* (Cambridge: Cambridge University Press).
Guillén, M. F. and Tschoegl, A. (2008) *Building a Global Bank. The Transformation of Banco Santander* (Princeton: Princeton University Press).
Gutiérrez Sebares, J. A. and Hoyo, A. (2007–08) *Testigo de una época. El Banco de Santander en la economía de Cantabria, 1857–1945*, 2 vols (Comillas: Amalienborg).
Hamilton, E. J. (1934) *American Treasure and the Price Revolution in Spain, 1501–1650* (Cambridge, MA: Harvard University Press).
Hamilton, E. J. (1947) *War and Prices in Spain, 1651–1800* (Cambridge, MA: Harvard University Press).
Hamilton, E. J. (1948) *El florecimiento del capitalismo y otros ensayos de historia económica* (Madrid: Revista de Occidente).
Hamilton, E. J. (1970) 'El Banco Nacional de San Carlos, 1782–1829' in *El Banco de España. Una historia económica* (Madrid: Banco de España).
Hellmann, T. F., Murdock, K. C., and Stiglitz, J. E. (2000) 'Liberalization, Moral Hazard in Banking and Prudential Regulation: Are Capital Requirements Enough?', *American Economic Review*, 1, 147–65.
Hernández Andreu, J. (1980) *Depresión económica en España, 1925–1934* (Madrid: Instituto de Estudios Fiscales).
Herr, R. (1978) 'El experimento de los vales reales, 1780–1808' in A. Otazu (ed.) *Dinero y crédito, siglos XVI al XIX* (Madrid: Moneda y Crédito).

Holmes, A. R. and Green, E. (1986) *Midland. 150 Years of Banking Business* (London: BT Batsford).

Hoyo, A. (2007) *Economía y mercado de valores en la España contemporánea. La evolución de la Bolsa antes del 'big bang' español, 1831–1988* (Santander: Universidad de Cantabria).

Huertas, T. F. (1990) 'US Multinational Banking: History and Prospects' in G. Jones (ed.) *Banks as Multinationals* (London: Routledge).

Instituto Nacional de Estadística, *Índice del Coste de la Vida* (Index of the Cost of Life) (1939–1960), *Índice de Precios al Consumo* (Consumer Prices Index) (1961-), *Encuesta de Salarios* (1989–2000) and *Encuesta de Coste Laboral* (2000-).

Intermoney (1978) *V Jornadas del mercado monetario* (Madrid: Intermoney).

Inverco (2011), *Memoria* (Madrid: Inverco).

Jackson, G. (1967) *The Spanish Republic and the Civil War 1931–1939, Princeton,* NJ: Princeton University Press.

Jackson, G. (1976) *La República española y la Guerra Civil, 1931–1939* (Barcelona: Crítica) (this second Spanish edition improves the estimates on casualties of the first English edition).

Jiménez, G. and Saurina, J. (2000) 'Credit Risk, Credit Cycles, and Prudential Regulation' *International Journal of Central Banking,* 2, 65–98.

Jiménez, J. M. (1905) *Estudio crítico de la crisis monetaria* (Madrid: Jaime Ratés).

Jones, G. (ed.) (1990) *Banks as Multinationals* (London: Routledge).

Julià, S. (ed.) (1999) *Víctimas de la Guerra Civil* (Madrid: Temas de Hoy).

Kase, K. and Jacopin, T. (2008) *CEOs as Leaders and Strategy Designers. Explaining the Success of Spanish Banks* (Basingstoke, Hampshire: Palgrave Macmillan)

Kellenbenz, H. (1978) 'Los Fugger en España en la época de Felipe II' in A. Otazu (ed.) *Dinero y crédito, siglos XVI al XIX* (Madrid: Moneda y Crédito).

Kindleberger, Ch. P. (1984) *A Financial History of Western Europe* (London: Allen and Unwin).

Kindleberger, Ch. P. (1986) *The World in Depression, 1929–1939,* 2nd ed. (Berkeley: University of California Press).

Kriz, M. A. (1948) 'Central Banks and the State Today', *American Economic Review,* 4, 565–80.

La Actualidad Económica, Journal.

La Gaceta de los Negocios, Journal.

Lacomba, J. A. and Ruiz, G. (1990) *Una historia del Banco Hipotecario de España, 1872–1986* (Madrid: Alianza and Banco Hipotecario de España).

Laeven, L. and Valencia, F. (2010) *Resolution of Banking Crises: The Good, the Bad, and the Ugly* (Washington: *IMF Working Paper* 10/146).

Lamfalussy Group (2001) *Final Report of the Committee of Wise Men on the Regulation of European Securities Markets* (Brussels).

Landes, D. (1958) *Bankers and Pashas. International Finance and Economic Imperialism in Egypt* (Cambridge, MA: Harvard University Press).

Larosière Group (2009) *High-Level Group on Financial Supervision in the EU Report* (Brussels).

Larraz, J. (2006) *Memorias* (Madrid: Real Academia de Ciencias Morales y Políticas).

Le Goff, J. (2010) *Le Moyen Age et l'argent. Essai d'anthropologie historique* (Paris: Perrin).

League of Nations (1926) *Memorandum on Currency and Central Banks, 1913–1925* (Geneva: League of Nations).

Lescure, M. (2003) 'La formation d'un système de crédit en France et le rôle de la banque d'émission: approche comparée' in O. Feiertag and M. Margairaz (eds),

Politiques et pratiques des banques d'émission en Europe (XVIIème-XXème siècles). Le bicentenaire de la Banque de France dans la perspective de l'identité monétaire européenne (Paris: Albin Michel).

Levine, R. (2010) 'An Autopsy of the US Financial System: Accident, Suicide, or Negligent Homicide', *Journal of Financial Economic Policy*, 2, 196–213.

Levine, R. and Zervos, S. (1998) 'Stock Markets, Banks and Economic Growth', *American Economic Review*, 88, 537–58.

Lewis, W. A. (1978) *Growth and Fluctuations, 1870–1913* (London: G. Allen and Unwin).

Liikanen, E. (ed.) (2012) *High-level Expert Group on Reforming the Structure of the EU Banking Sector* (Brussels).

López Yepes, J. and Titos, M. (1995) *Historia de la Caja de Ahorros y Monte de Piedad de Madrid, 1702–1970* (Madrid: CAMP).

López-Morell, M. A. (2002) 'Salamanca y la construcción del ferrocarril de Aranjuez' in M. J. Matilla, F. Polo, and M. Benegas (eds) *Ferrocarril y Madrid: historia de un progreso* (Madrid: Fundación de los Ferrocarriles Españoles).

López-Morell, M. A. (2005) *La Casa Rothschild en España, 1812–1941* (Madrid: Marcial Pons).

Lucas, R. E. (1972) 'Expectations and the Neutrality of Money', *Journal of Economic Theory*, 4, 103–24.

Lukauskas, A. (1997) *Regulating Finance: The Political Economy of Spanish Financial Policy from Franco to Democracy* (Ann Arbor: The University of Michigan Press).

Maixé, J. C. (1994) *Comercio y banca en la Cataluña del siglo XVIII: la Compañía Bensi & Merizano de Barcelona, 1724–1750* (La Coruña: Universidad de La Coruña).

Maixé, J. C. (2003) *El ahorro de los gallegos. Orígenes e historia de Caixa Galicia* (La Coruña: Fundación Caixa Galicia).

Maixé, J. C. (2012) 'Diversity in Banking Systems: France, Italy and Spain, Nineteenth and Twentieth Centuries', in J. Consiglio, J. C. Martínez Oliva, and G. Tortella, *Banking and Finance in the Mediterranean. A Historical Perspective* (Surrey, UK: Ashgate).

Malo de Molina, J. L. (2005) *Una larga fase de expansión de la economía española* (Madrid: Banco de España, Documentos Ocasionales 0505).

Malo de Molina, J. L. (2012) 'The Macroeconomic Basis of the Recent Development of the Spanish Financial System' in J. L. Malo de Molina and P. Martín Aceña (eds) *The Spanish Financial System. Growth and Development since 1900* (Basingstoke and New York: Palgrave Macmillan).

Malo de Molina, J. L. and Martín Aceña, P. (eds) *The Spanish Financial System. Growth and Development since 1900* (Basingstoke and New York: Palgrave Macmillan).

Maluquer de Motes, J. (1999) *España en la crisis de 1898. De la Gran Depresión a la modernización económica del siglo XX* (Barcelona: Península).

Maluquer de Motes, J. (2007) *'La paradisíaca estabilidad de la anteguerra.' Elaboración de un índice de precios de consumo de España, 1830–1936* (Barcelona, UAB Working Paper 2007–07).

Maluquer de Motes, J. (2009) 'Viajar a través del Cosmos: la medida de la creación de riqueza y la serie histórica del Producto Interior Bruto de España, 1850–2008', *Revista de Economía Aplicada*, 51, 25–54.

Manso, E. and Rodríguez, V. (2008) 'La crisis financiera y el valor razonable: debate en torno a su impacto y evaluación de las medidas adoptadas', *Boletín de la CNMV*, 4th quarter.

Maravall, F., Glavan, S., and AFI (2009) *Eficiencia y concentración del sistema bancario español* (Madrid: FUNCAS).

Martín Aceña, P. (1981) 'España y el patrón oro, 1880–1913', *Hacienda Pública Española*, 69, 267–90.

Martín Aceña, P. (1984) *La política monetaria en España, 1919–1935* (Madrid: Instituto de Estudios Fiscales).

Martín Aceña, P. (1985a), 'Desarrollo y modernización del sistema financiero, 1844–1935' in N. Sánchez-Albornoz (ed.) *La modernización económica de España* (Madrid: Alianza).

Martín Aceña, P. (1985b), *La cantidad de dinero en España, 1900–1935* (Madrid: Banco de España).

Martín Aceña, P. (1993) 'Spain during the Classical gold standard years, 1880–1914' in M. D. Bordo and F. Capie (eds) *Monetary Regimes in Transition* (Cambridge: Cambridge University Press).

Martín Aceña, P. (1994) 'Los problemas monetarios al término de la Guerra Civil', *Hacienda Pública Española*, 2, 63–88.

Martín Aceña, P. (1995) 'El Banco de España y las funciones de un banco central, 1914–1936' in P. Tedde and C. Marichal (eds), *La formación de los bancos centrales en España y América Latina, siglos XIX y XX*, 2 vols. (Madrid: Banco de España).

Martín Aceña, P. (2007) *1857–2007. Banco Santander. 150 años de historia* (Madrid: Turner).

Martín Aceña, P. (2012) 'The Spanish Banking System from 1900 to 1975' in J. L. Malo de Molina and P. Martín Aceña (eds) *The Spanish Financial System. Growth and Development since 1900* (Basingstoke and New York: Palgrave Macmillan).

Martín Aceña, P. and Pons, M. A. (1994) 'Spanish Banking after the Civil War, 1940–1962', *Financial History Review*, 2, 121–138.

Martín Aceña, P. and Pons, M. A. (2005) 'Sistema monetario y financiero' in A. Carreras and X. Tafunell (eds), *Estadísticas históricas de España, siglos XIX y XX* (Bilbao: Fundación BBVA).

Martín Aceña, P. and Reis, J. (eds) (2000) *Monetary Standards in the Periphery: Paper, Silver and Gold* (Basingstoke: Macmillan).

Martínez Méndez, P. (1990) *Nuevos datos sobre la evolución de la peseta entre 1900 y 1936. Información complementaria* (Madrid: Banco de España, Documento de Trabajo 9011).

Martínez Méndez, P. (1991) *Los beneficios de la banca, 1970–1989* (Madrid: Banco de España).

Martínez Méndez, P. (2005) *El Banco de España como 'banco de bancos', 1900–1936* (Santiago de Compostela and La Coruña: VIII Congreso de la Asociación Española de Historia Económica, 13–16 September 2005).

Martínez Ruiz, E. (2000) *El control de cambios en la España franquista: el Instituto Español de Moneda Extranjera, 1939–1973*, Ph. D. thesis (Alcalá de Henares: Universidad de Alcalá).

Martínez Soto, A. P. and Martínez Rodríguez, S. (2010) *Rural Credit Cooperatives in Spain (1890–1935): A Good Start was not Enough* (Madrid: Asociación Española de Historia Económica, Documento de Trabajo 1001).

Maudos, J. and Fernández de Guevara, J. (2008) *El sector bancario español en el contexto internacional. Evolución reciente y retos futuros* (Bilbao: Fundación BBVA).

McCloskey, D. N. (1976) 'Does the Past Have Useful Economics?,' *Journal of Economic Literature*, 2, 434–61.

McKinnon, R. I. (1973) *Money and Capital in Economic Development* (Washington: Brookings Institution)

McKinnon, R. I. (1991) *The Order of Economic Liberalization. Financial Control in the Transition to a Market Economy* (Baltimore: John Hopkins University Press).

Méndez Vidal, A. and Hernández Andreu, J. (2013) 'Entrepreneurship and Development: The Minorcan Model (Eighteenth-Twentieh Centuries)' in G. Tortella and G. Quiroga (eds) *Entrepreneurship and Growth. An International Historical Perspective* (Basingstoke: Palgrave Macmillan).

Ministerio de Hacienda (1921) *Ordenación bancaria de España* (Madrid: Ministerio de Hacienda).

Ministerio de Hacienda (1961) *Memorándum sobre el sistema bancario y crediticio* (Madrid: Ministerio de Hacienda).

Miñana, E. and Galvarriato, J. A. (1918) *Los bancos de emisión de la guerra, en la guerra y después de la guerra. El patrón oro en España. La prórroga del privilegio al Banco de España* (Madrid: Imprenta y Encuadernación de Julián Espinosa).

Modigliani, F. and Miller, M. (1958) 'The Cost of Capital. Corporation Finance and the Theory of Investment', *American Economic Review*, 3, 261–97.

Molina, D. (ed.) (2009) *Unicaja, 125 años* (Málaga: Fundación Unicaja).

Morellá, E. (1992) 'El producto industrial de posguerra: una revisión (Índices sectoriales, 1940–1958)', *Revista de Historia Económica*, 1, 125–143.

Moreno, B. (2006) *La Bolsa de Madrid. Historia de un mercado de valores europeo* (Santander: Universidad de Cantabria).

Moreno, J. (1940) *Datos sobre la reconstrucción de España* (Madrid: Dirección General de Regiones Devastadas y Reparaciones).

Moreno Moré, J. L. (1975) 'Quince años de inversiones españolas en el exterior', *Información Comercial Española*, 499, 91–107.

Moro, A., Nuño, G., Tedde P. (July 2013) *A Twin Crisis with Multiple Banks of Issue. Spain in the 1860s* (Frankfurt: European Central Bank Working Paper)

Moya, C. (1975) *El poder económico en España, 1939–1970: un análisis sociológico* (Madrid: Túcar).

Mundo, Journal

Muñoz, J. (1969) *El poder de la banca en España* (Algorta: Zero).

Myers, S. C. (1984) 'The Capital Structure Puzzle', *Journal of Finance*, 3, 575–92.

Nadal, J. and Sudrià, C. (1983) *Historia de la Caja de Pensiones. La Caixa dentro del sistema financiero catalán* (Barcelona: Edicions 62).

Neven, D. J. (1990) 'Structural Adjustment in Retail Banking' in J. Dermine (ed.) *European Banking in the 1990s* (Oxford: Blackwell).

Nogués, P. (2005) 'Análisis de la deflación española de la primera mitad del siglo XIX: una comparación internacional', *Revista de Historia Económica*, 2, 371–405.

Núñez, C. E. (2003) 'El capital humano en el primer franquismo', in Barciela, ed., 27–53.

Nuño, G., Tedde, P., and Moro, A. (2011) *Money Dynamics with Multiple Banks of Issue: Evidence from Spain, 1856–1874* (Madrid: Banco de España, Documento de Trabajo 1119).

Oficina de Coordinación y Programación Económica (1959) *Contestaciones al cuestionario económico del Gobierno* (Madrid: OCPE).

Olariaga, L. (1921) '¿Se va a efectuar realmente una ordenación bancaria?', *El Sol*, 6 December.

Olariaga, L. (1946) *La ordenación bancaria en España* (Madrid: Sucesores de Rivadeneyra).

Olariaga, L. (1987 [1936]) 'El Banco y la regulación monetaria' in *La política monetaria en España*, reprinted in Comisión del Patrón Oro and Luis Olariaga, *El patrón oro, la peseta y la economía española (1900–1936)* (Barcelona: Orbis).

Olariaga, L. (1989) *Escritos varios: advertencias, incitaciones y reformas* (Madrid: Fundación FIES).

Oliver Wyman (2012) *Asset Quality Review and Bottom-Up Stress Test Exercise* (Madrid: Oliver Wyman).

Ontiveros, E. (1997) *Sin orden ni concierto. Medio siglo de relaciones monetarias internacionales* (Madrid: Escuela de Finanzas Aplicadas).

Ortí, V. (1893) *La cuestión monetaria* (Madrid: Imprenta y Litografía de los Huérfanos).

Ortiz-Villajos, J. M. (2001) 'La banca en el periodo de entreguerras: comparación internacional', *Estudis d'Història Econòmica*, 17–18, 141–75.

Paradaltas, F. (1847) *Tratado de monedas, sistema monetario y proyectos para su reforma* (Barcelona: Imprenta de Tomás Gaspar).

Paredes, J. (1991) *Pascual Madoz, 1805–1870. Libertad y progreso en la monarquía isabelina*, 2nd ed. (Pamplona: EUNSA).

Paret, L. V. (1921) *El Estado y el Banco de España* (Madrid: Librería General de Victoriano Suárez).

Paris Eguilaz, H. (1947) 'El problema de la reforma bancaria en España: consideraciones sobre la Ley de Ordenación Bancaria de 31 de diciembre de 1946', *Anales de Economía*, 26, 169–232.

Paris Eguilaz, H. (1959), *La banca privada y la economía española* (Madrid: Diana).

Pascual, P. and Sudrià, C. (1993) *Bancos y moneda en Cataluña, 1844–1859: del monopolio bancario al 'free banking'* (San Sebastián: V Congreso de la Asociación de Historia Económica).

Perdices, L. and Baumert. T. (eds) (2010), *La hora de los economistas* (Madrid: Ecobook).

Pérez, J. (2012) 'Banca central, mercados y estabilidad financiera: algunas experiencias del Banco de España, 1977–1990' in C. Sebastián (ed.) (2012) *Luis Ángel Rojo. Recuerdo y homenaje* (Madrid: Fundación Ramón Areces).

Pérez, J. and Rojo, L. A. (1977) *La política monetaria en España: objetivos e instrumentos* (Madrid: Banco de España).

Pérez, S. (1997) *Banking on Privilege. The Politics of Spanish Financial Reform* (Ithaca: Cornell University Press).

Pérez Requeijo, R. (1893) *El Banco de España y los problemas de actualidad* (Madrid: Imprenta de Enrique Rubiños).

Perpiñá, R. (1972) *De economía hispana. Infraestructura. Historia* (Barcelona: Ariel).

Plessis, A. (2003) 'La création de la Banque de France et la génèse des banques nacionales d'émission en Europe au XIXe siècle' in O. Feiertag and M. Margairaz (eds) *Politiques et pratiques des banques d'émission en Europe (XVIIème-XXème siècles). Le bicentenaire de la Banque de France dans la perspective de l'identité monétaire européenne* (Paris: Albin Michel).

Poema de Mío Cid (1973) edited by Ángeles Cardona de Gibert, Joaquín Rafel, and Luis Guarner (Zaragoza: Ediciones Aubí).

Pons, M. A. (2001) 'Banca e industria en España, 1939–1985: la influencia de la banca universal en el crecimiento económico', *Revista de Historia Industrial*, 19–20, 249–74.

Pons, M. A. (2002), *Regulating Spanish Banking, 1939–1975* (Aldershot: Ashgate).

Pons, M. A. (2012) 'The Main Reforms of the Spanish Financial System' in J. L. Malo de Molina and P. Martín Aceña (eds) *The Spanish Financial System. Growth and Development since 1900* (Basingstoke and New York: Palgrave Macmillan).

Pons, M. A. and Cuevas, J. (2007) 'El papel de la banca regional en España: la evolución del Banco de Valencia', *Revista de la Historia de la Economía y de la Empresa*, 1, 165–91.

Poveda, R. (1980) 'Política monetaria y financiera' in L. Gámir (ed.), *La política económica en España* (Madrid: Alianza).

Poveda, R. (2000) 'La reforma del sistema de provisiones de insolvencia', *Boletín Económico*, 1, 79–91.

Poveda, R. (2012) 'Banking Supervision and Regulation over the Past 40 Years' in J. L. Malo de Molina and P. Martín Aceña (eds) *The Spanish Financial System. Growth and Development since 1900* (Basingstoke and New York: Palgrave Macmillan).

Prado, R. (1983) *La Central de Información de Riesgos* (Madrid: Fundación FIES, Documento 3).

Prado, R. (2002) 'La provisión para insolvencias de las entidades de crédito. Presente, futuro y pasado', *Notas de estabilidad financiera*, 1 (Madrid: Banco de España).

Prados de la Escosura, L. (1988) *De imperio a nación. Crecimiento y atraso económico en España, 1780–1930* (Madrid: Alianza).

Prados de la Escosura, L. (1993) 'La pérdida del imperio y sus consencuencias económicas en España' in L. Prados de la Escosura and S. Amaral (eds) *La independencia americana: consecuencias económicas* (Madrid: Alianza).

Prados de la Escosura, L. (2003) *El progreso económico de España, 1850–2000* (Bilbao: Fundación BBVA).

Prados Arrarte, J. (1958) *El sistema bancario español* (Madrid: Aguilar).

Prados Arrarte, J. (1959) 'La regulación del crédito en España', *Banca y seguros*, 3, 3–22.

Pueyo, J. (2003) 'Oligopolio y competencia en la banca española del siglo XX: concentración económica y movilidad intra-industrial, 1922–1995', *Revista de Historia Económica*, 1, 147–95.

Pueyo, J. (2006) *El comportamiento de la gran banca en España, 1921–1974* (Madrid: Banco de España, Estudios de Historia Económica 48).

Puig, N. and Torres, E. (2008) *Banco Urquijo. Un banco con historia, 1918–2008* (Madrid: Banco Sabadell and Turner).

Pulido, I. (1996) *La Real Hacienda de Felipe II* (Huelva: Artes Gráficas Andaluzas).

Pyke, R. (1966) *Enterprise and Adventure. The Genoese in Seville and the Opening of the New World* (Ithaca: Cornell University Press).

Rahola, F. (1892), 'Prólogo' in E. Viver *Iniciación al estudio de la cuestión monetaria* (Barcelona: Tipolitografía de Luis Tasso).

Rajan, R. and Zingales, L. (1998) 'Financial Dependence and Growth', *American Economic Review*, 88, 559–86.

Rajan, R. and Zingales, L. (2003) *Banks and Markets: The Changing Character of European Finance* (Cambridge, USA: NBER Working Paper 9595).

Reinhart, C. M. and Rogoff, K. S. (2011) *This Time is Different. Eight Centuries of Financial Folly*, 13th ed. (Princeton: Princeton University Press).

Reinhart, C. M. and Sbrancia, M. B. (2011) *The Liquidation of Government Debt* (Cambridge, USA: NBER Working Paper 16893).

Reis, J. (2005) 'Los sistemas financieros de la periferia: una comparación entre Escandinavia y el Sur de Europa durante el siglo XIX' *Papeles de Economía Española*, 105–106, 109–31.

Restoy, F. and Rodríguez, V. (2010) 'Transparency in Securities Markets', *Moneda y Crédito*, 230, 249–69.

Restoy, F. and Sánchez de la Peña, R (2012) 'Spanish Securities Markets: Recent Developments and Key Challenges' in J. L. Malo de Molina and P. Martín Aceña

(eds) *The Spanish Financial System. Growth and Development since 1900* (Basingstoke and New York: Palgrave Macmillan).
Revell, J. (1984) *Changes in Spanish Banking* (Bilbao: Banco de Vizcaya).
Revell, J. (1987) *Mergers and the Role of Large Banks* (Bangor: Institute of European Finance).
Revista de Economía y Hacienda (1902) *La reforma del Banco de España* (Madrid: Imprenta de Ambrosio Pérez y Cía.).
Revista Sindical de Estadística, Journal.
Ridruejo, E. (1954) 'El sistema bancario español' in *Los bancos en la postguerra: ¿vuelta a la normalidad?* (Madrid: Consejo Superior Bancario).
Robinson, J. (1952) 'The Generalization of the General Theory' in *The Rate of Interest and Other Essays* (Londres: Macmillan).
Ródenas, C. (1978) *Banca i industrialització. El cas valencià, 1840–1880* (Valencia: Banc de Promoció de Negocis).
Rodrigo, M. (2000) *Los Marqueses de Comillas, 1817–1925. Antonio y Claudio López* (Madrid: LID).
Rodríguez, G. (1892) *El crédito, los cambios y el presupuesto* (Madrid: Tipografía de Tomás Minuesa de los Ríos).
Rojo, L. A. (1981) 'Desempleo y factores reales', *Papeles de Economía Española*, 8, 124–38.
Rojo, L. A. (1988) 'Innovaciones financieras y política monetaria', *Papeles de Economía Española*, 36, 2–24.
Roldán, S. and García Delgado, J. L. (with J. Muñoz) (1973) *La formación de la sociedad capitalista en España, 1914–1920*, 2 vols (Madrid: Confederación Española de Cajas de Ahorros).
Rostow, W. W. (1960) *The Stages of Economic Growth. A Non-Communist Manifesto* (Cambrige: Cambridge University Press).
Rubio, M. (1983) 'La política de supervisión bancaria' in *Crisis bancarias, soluciones comparadas* (Madrid: AEB).
Ruiz Martín, F. (1970) 'La banca en España hasta 1782' in *El Banco de España. Una historia económica* (Madrid: Banco de España).
Ruiz Martín, F. (1990) *Pequeño capitalismo, gran capitalismo. Simón Ruiz y sus negocios en Florencia* (Barcelona: Crítica).
Sáenz, A. (1992) 'Desafíos bancarios en el fin de siglo', *Boletín de Estudios Económicos*, 145, 223–47.
Sáez de Ibarra, L. (1954) 'La regulación de la Banca española', *Moneda y Crédito*, 51, 15–33.
Salas, V. and Saurina, J. (2003) 'Deregulation, Market Power and Risk Behavior in Spanish Banks', *European Economic Review*, 47, 1061–75.
San Román, E. (1999) *Ejército e industria: el nacimiento del Instituto Nacional de Industria* (Barcelona: Crítica).
Sánchez Asiaín, J. A. (2012) *La financiación de la Guerra Civil española. Una aproximación histórica* (Barcelona: Crítica).
Sánchez Blanco, J. (1992) *Historia del Crédito Social Pesquero* (Madrid: MAPA).
Sánchez Albornoz, C. (1956) *España, un enigma histórico* (Buenos Aires: Sudamericana).
Sánchez-Albornoz, N. (1963) *Las crisis de subsistencias de España en el siglo XIX* (Rosario: Instituto de Investigaciones Históricas).
Sánchez-Albornoz, N. (1966) 'De los orígenes del capital financiero: la Sociedad General de Crédito Mobiliario Español, 1856–1902', *Moneda y Crédito*, 97, 29–68.

Sánchez-Albornoz, N. (1968) 'Los bancos y las sociedades de crédito en provincias, 1856–1868', *Moneda y Crédito*, 104, 39–68.
Sánchez-Albornoz, N. (1969) 'El ferrocarril de Alar del Rey a Santander, 1845–1874', *Moneda y Crédito*, 108, 119–28.
Sánchez-Albornoz, N. (1975) *Jalones en la modernización de España* (Barcelona: Ariel).
Sánchez-Albornoz, N. (1977) *España hace un siglo: una economía dual*, 2nd ed. (Madrid: Alianza).
Sánchez Belén, J. A. (1996) *La política fiscal en Castilla durante el reinado de Carlos II* (Madrid: Siglo XXI).
Santillán, R. (1982 [1865]) *Memoria histórica sobre los bancos Nacional de San Carlos, Español de San Fernando, Isabel II, Nuevo de San Fernando, y de España*, 2 vols (Madrid: Banco de España).
Santillán, R. (1996) *Memorias, 1808–1856* (Madrid: Tecnos y Banco de España).
Sanz, A. B. (1948) *El problema social en la banca* (Madrid: Monografías de Industria y Comercio).
Sanz Ayán, C. (1988) *Los banqueros de Carlos II* (Salamanca: Universidad de Valladolid).
Sardà, J. (1936) *La intervención monetaria y el comercio de divisas en España* (Barcelona: Bosch).
Sardà, J. (1948) *La política monetaria y las fluctuaciones de la economía española en el siglo XIX* (Madrid: Instituto de Economía Sancho de Moncada).
Sardà, J. (1987 [1948]) 'La política monetaria y las fluctuaciones de la economía española en el siglo XIX', reprinted in *Escritos, 1948–1980* (Madrid: Banco de España).
Sardà, J. (1987 [1970]) 'El Banco de España, 1931–1962', reprinted in *Escritos, 1948–1980* (Madrid: Banco de España).
Saurina, J. (2009) *Dynamic Provisioning. The Experience of Spain* (Washington: The World Bank Group).
Saurina, J. (2012) 'Integration, Competition and Stability of the Financial System' in J. L. Malo de Molina and P. Martín Aceña (eds) *The Spanish Financial System. Growth and Development since 1900* (Basingstoke and New York: Palgrave Macmillan).
Sayers, R. S. (ed.) (1962) *Banking in Western Europe* (Oxford: Clarendon Press).
Schumpeter, J. A. (1934) *The Theory of Economic Development. An Inquiry into Profits, Capital, Credit, Interest, and the Business Cycle* (Cambridge, USA: Harvard University Press).
Schwartz, P. (1996) 'Juntar erarios y Montes de Piedad: un arbitrio barroco ante las Cortes de Castilla', *Revista de Historia Económica*, 1, 53–90.
Sédillot, R. (1979) *Histoire du franc* (Paris: Sirey).
Sengupta, J. (1988) 'Internationalization of Banking and the Relationship Between Foreign and Domestic Banks in the Developing Countries', *International Journal of Development Banking*, 1, 25–50.
Serrano Sanz, J. M. (2004) *El oro en la Restauración* (Madrid: Real Academia de Ciencias Morales y Políticas).
Shaw, E. S. (1973) *Financial Deepening in Economic Development* (Oxford: Oxford University Press).
Soldevila, F. (1952–1959) *Historia de España*, 8 vols (Barcelona: Ariel).
Solé, G. (ed.) *Historia del Banco de Crédito Local de España, 1925–1975* (Madrid: BCLE).
Strivensr, D. J. (1992) 'A Guide to EC Regulation: Banking', *International Financial Law Review*, June, 7–12.

Sudrià, C. (1990) 'Los beneficios de España durante la Gran Guerra. Una aproximación a la balanza de pagos española, 1914–1920', *Revista de Historia Económica*, 2, 363–96.
Sudrià, C. (1994 [1982]) 'Desarrollo industrial y subdesarrollo bancario en Cataluña, 1844–1950' in J. Hernández Andreu and J. L. García Ruiz (eds), *Lecturas de historia empresarial* (Madrid: Civitas).
Sudrià, C. (2007) 'La banca catalana en los años de entreguerras y el debate sobre la decadencia: una revisión', *Revista de la Historia de la Economía y de la Empresa*, 1, 269–87.
Sureda, J. (1949) *La Hacienda castellana y los economistas del siglo XVII* (Madrid: Instituto de Economía Sancho de Moncada).
Surrá, J. (1862) *Breve reseña histórico-crítica de la moneda española y reducción de sus valores a los del sistema métrico vigente* (Madrid: Imprenta Nacional).
Sylla, R. (1998) 'Finance and Economic Growth: Three Decades Post-Cameron' in C. E. Núñez (ed.) *Finance and the Making of Modern Capitalism* (Madrid: IEHA).
Sylla, R. (1999) 'Shaping the US Financial System, 1690–1913: The Dominant Role of Public Finance', in R. Sylla, R. Tilly, and G. Tortella (eds) *The State, the Financial System and Economic Modernization* (Cambridge: Cambridge University Press).
Sylla, R. (2002) 'Financial Systems and Economic Modernization', *Journal of Economic History*, 2, 279–92.
Sylla, R., Tilly, R., and Tortella, G. (eds) (1999) *The State, the Financial System and Economic Modernization* (Cambridge: Cambridge University Press).
Tafunell, X. (1998) 'Los beneficios empresariales en España, 1880–1981. Estimación de un índice anual del excedente de la gran empresa', *Revista de Historia Económica*, 3, 707–46.
Tafunell, X. (2005) 'Empresa y bolsa' in A. Carreras and X. Tafunell (eds) *Estadísticas históricas de España, siglos XIX y XX*, vol. II (Bilbao: Fundación BBVA).
Tamames, R. (1967) *Los monopolios en España* (Madrid: ZYX).
Tedde, P. (1974) 'La banca privada española durante la Restauración, 1874–1914' in G. Tortella (ed.), *La banca española en la Restauración*, I (Madrid: Banco de España).
Tedde, P. (1978) 'Las compañías ferroviarias en España, 1855–1935' in M. Artola (ed.) *Los ferrocarriles en España, 1844–1943*, II (Madrid: Banco de España).
Tedde, P. (1988) *El Banco de San Carlos, 1782–1829* (Madrid: Alianza y Banco de España)
Tedde, P. (1993) *El Banco Exterior de España, 1928–1992. Una aproximación histórica*, unpublished manuscript.
Tedde, P. (1999) *El Banco de San Fernando, 1829–1856* (Madrid: Alianza y Banco de España).
Tedde, P. (2006) 'José Echegaray, economista' in F. Comín, P. Martín Aceña and R. Vallejo (eds) *La Hacienda por sus ministros: la etapa liberal de 1845 a 1899* (Zaragoza: Prensas Universitarias de Zaragoza).
Tedde, P. and Marichal, C. (eds) (1994) *La formación de los bancos centrales en España y América Latina (siglos XIX y XX)*, 2 vols (Madrid: Banco de España).
Tedde, P. and Tortella, G. (1974) 'Censos y balances normalizados de los bancos privados españoles, 1874–1914' in G. Tortella (ed.) *La banca española en la Restauración*, vol. II (Madrid: Banco de España).
Tena, A. (2005) 'Sector exterior' in A. Carreras and X. Tafunell (eds) *Estadísticas históricas de España, siglos XIX y XX*, vol. II (Bilbao: Fundación BBVA).
Terceiro, J. (2012) 'Recuerdos de Luis Ángel Rojo' in C. Sebastián (ed.) *Luis Ángel Rojo. Recuerdo y homenaje* (Madrid: Fundación Ramón Areces).

Termes, R. (1991) *Desde la banca*, 2 vols (Madrid: Rialp).
Termes, R. (1995) 'Los últimos doce años del sistema bancario español' in *Historia de una década. Sistema financiero y economía española, 1984–1994* (Madrid: AB Asesores).
The Banker, Journal.
The Institute of Bankers (1986) *Bank Strategies for the 1990s* (London: The Institute of Bankers).
Titos, M. (1979) 'La Caja General de Depósitos, 1852–1874', *Moneda y Crédito*, 151, 79–104.
Titos, M. (1989) 'La Caja de Madrid en el siglo XIX: ¿actividad asistencial o financiera?', *Revista de Historia Económica*, 3, 557–87.
Titos, M. (1991) 'La respuesta histórica de la Cajas de Ahorros a las demandas de la sociedad española', in *Papeles de Economía Española*, 46, 12–38.
Titos, M. (1993) 'Fondation et développement des caisses d'épargne en Espagne au XIXe siècle' in *L'histoire des caisses d'épargne européennes*, vol. II (Paris: Les Editions de l'Epargne).
Titos, M. (1999) 'Las cajas de ahorros, 1853–1962' in P. Martín Aceña and M. Titos (eds) *El sistema financiero en España. Una síntesis histórica* (Granada: Universidad de Granada).
Titos, M. (2003) *El sistema financiero en Andalucía. Tres siglos de historia, 1740–2000* (Sevilla: Instituto de Estadística de Andalucía).
Torrero, A. (1982) *Tendencias del sistema financiero español* (Madrid: H. Blume).
Torrero, A. (ed.) (1991) *Relaciones banca-industria: la experiencia española* (Madrid: Espasa-Calpe).
Tortella, G. (1970) 'El Banco de España entre 1829–1929. La formación de un banco central' in *El Banco de España. Una historia económica* (Madrid: Banco de España).
Tortella, G. (1974) 'Las magnitudes monetarias y sus determinantes' in G. Tortella (ed.) *La banca española en la Restauración*, vol. I (Madrid: Banco de España).
Tortella, G. (1977) *Banking, Railroads, and Industry in Spain, 1829–1874* (New York: Arno Press).
Tortella, G. (1981) 'La economía española, 1830–1900' in M. Tuñón (ed.) *Historia de España*, vol. VIII (Barcelona: Labor).
Tortella, G. (1996) 'La transición bancaria' in S. Juliá, J. Pradera, and J. Prieto, (eds) *Memoria de la Transición* (Madrid: Taurus).
Tortella, G. (1999) 'The Role of Banks and Government in Spanish Economic Development, 1850–1935' in R. Sylla, R. Tilly, and G. Tortella (eds) *The State, the Financial System and Economic Modernization* (Cambridge: Cambridge University Press).
Tortella, G. (2000a) *The Development of Modern Spain. An Economic History of the Nineteenth and Twentieth Centuries* (Cambridge, MA: Harvard University Press).
Tortella, G. (2000b) 'Ignacio Villalonga Villalba, 1895–1973' in E. Torres (ed.), *Los 100 empresarios españoles del siglo XX* (Madrid: LID).
Tortella, G. (2001) 'Bank Mergers and Consolidation in Spanish History' in M. Pohl, T. Tortella, and H. van der Wee (eds) *A Century of Banking Consolidation in Europe* (Aldershot: Asghate).
Tortella, G. (2004) 'Guerra en la guerra: el Banco Central en años difíciles, 1930– 1942' in J. Pérez, C. Sebastián, and P. Tedde (eds) *Estudios en homenaje a Luis Ángel Rojo*, vol. II (Madrid: Editorial Complutense).
Tortella, G. (2006) 'El Banco de España: una nueva potencia financiera, 1874–1914' in *150 años de historia del Banco de España, 1856–2006* (Madrid: Banco de España).

Tortella, G. (2007) 'El triunfo del centralismo: breve historia del Banco Central, 1919– 1991', *Revista de la Historia de la Economía y de la Empresa*, 1, 213–51.

Tortella, G. (unpublished) *El circulante metálico en España: primeras aplicaciones de una estimación para el cálculo de la renta nacional*.

Tortella, G. and Comín, F. (2001) 'Fiscal and Monetary Institutions in Spain, 1600– 1900' in M. D. Bordo and R. Cortés Conde (eds) *Transferring Wealth and Power from the Old to the New World. Monetary and Fiscal Institutions in the 17th through the 19th Centuries* (Cambridge: Cambridge University Press).

Tortella, G. and García Ruiz, J. L. (2004) 'Spanish Banking after the Civil War: A Halting Reconstruction under Fascism' in E. Green, J. Lampe and F. Stiblar (eds), *Crisis and Renewal in Twentieth Century Banking* (Aldershot: Ashgate).

Tortella, G. and García Ruiz, J. L. (2012) 'A Century of the Spanish Economy' in J. L. Malo de Molina and P. Martín Aceña (eds) *The Spanish Financial System. Growth and Development since 1900* (Basingstoke and New York: Palgrave Macmillan).

Tortella, G. and Jiménez, J. C. (1986) *Una historia del Banco de Crédito Industrial* (Madrid: Alianza/BCI).

Tortella, G. and Núñez, C. E. (2009) *Para comprender la crisis* (Madrid: Gadir).

Tortella, G. and Núñez, C. E. (2011) *El desarrollo de la España contemporánea. Historia económica de los siglos XIX y XX*, 3a. ed. (Madrid: Alianza).

Tortella, G. and Palafox, J. (1983) 'Banca e industria en España, 1918–1936', *Investigaciones Económicas*, 20, 33–66.

Tortella, G., Ballestero, A., and Díaz Fernández, J.L. (2003) *Del monopolio al libre mercado. La historia de la industria petrolera española* (Madrid: LID).

Tortella, G., Nadal, J., Anes, G., Anes, R., and Fernández Pulgar, C. (1970) *Ensayos sobre la economía española a mediados del siglo XIX* (Madrid: Banco de España)

Tortella, G., Ortiz-Villajos, J. M., and García Ruiz, J. L. (2011) *Historia del Banco Popular. La lucha por la independencia* (Madrid: Marcial Pons).

Tortella, G. *et al.* (1970) 'Apéndice Estadístico' in G. Tortella *et al. Ensayos sobre la economía española a mediados del siglo XIX* (Madrid: Banco de España).

Tortella, T. (1986) *Índice de los primitivos accionistas del Banco Nacional de San Carlos* (Madrid: Banco de España).

Tortella, T. (1997) *Los primeros billetes españoles: las 'cédulas' del Banco de San Carlos, 1782–1829* (Madrid: Banco de España).

Tortella, T. (2010) *El Banco de España desde dentro. Una historia a través de sus documentos* (Madrid: Banco de España).

Tschoegl, A. E. (1987) 'International Retail Banking as a Strategy: An Assessment', *Journal of International Business Studies*, 2, 67–88.

Tuñón, M. (1975) *Historia y realidad del poder. El poder y las 'elites' en el primer tercio de la España del siglo XX* (Madrid: Edicusa).

Uriel, E. and Albert, C. (2012) *El stock de capital en viviendas (1990–2010) y en otras construcciones (1990–2009) en España, y su distribución territorial* (Bilbao: Fundación BBVA).

Usher, A. P. (1967) *The Early History of Deposit Banking in Mediterranean Europe* (New York: Russell and Russell).

Valdaliso, J. M. (2004) 'Grupos empresariales y relaciones banca-industria en España durante el franquismo: una aproximación microeconómica', *Información Comercial Española*, 812, 163–78.

Valdaliso, J. M. (2007) *BBK (1907–2007). Cien años de compromiso con el desarrollo económico y el bienestar de Bizcaia* (Bilbao: BBK).

Vandellós, J. A. (1936) *El porvenir del cambio de la peseta* (Barcelona: Instituto de Investigaciones Económicas).
Velarde, J. (1953) 'Sobre la decadencia económica de España', *De Economía*, 25–26, 495–549.
Velarde, J. (1966) 'Conexiones entre nobleza de sangre y capitalismo en España', *Mundo Social*, 135, 9–11.
Velarde, J. (1973) *Política económica de la Dictadura*, 2nd. ed. (Barcelona: Guadiana).
Velarde, J. (1999) 'El 98: las nuevas ideas económicas y sus consecuencias' en P. Tedde (ed.) *Economía y colonias en la España del 98* (Madrid: Síntesis and Fundación Duques de Soria).
Vicens Vives, J. (1959) *Manual de historia económica de España* (Barcelona: Teide).
Vilar, P. (1962) *La Catalogne dans l'Espagne moderne. Recherches sur les fondaments économiques des structures nacionales*, 3 vols (Paris: SEVPEN).
Vilar, P. (1972) *Oro y moneda en la historia*, 2nd ed. (Barcelona: Ariel).
Villalonga, I. (1956) *La banca mixta en España* (Stockholm: Institut International d'Etudes Bancaires).
Villalonga, I. (1961) 'La banca española en lo que va de siglo', *Arbor*, 189–190, 93–111.
Viñas, A., Viñuela, J., Eguidazu, F., Fernández Pulgar, C., and Florensa, S. (1979) *Política comercial exterior en España, 1931–1975*, 3 vols (Madrid: Banco Exterior de España).
Viver, E. (1892) *Iniciación al estudio de la cuestión monetaria* (Barcelona: Tipolitografía de Luis Tasso).
Vives, X. (2012) 'The Spanish Financial Industry at the Start of 21st Century: Current Situation and Future Challenges' in J. L. Malo de Molina and P. Martín Aceña (eds) *The Spanish Financial System. Growth and Development since 1900* (Basingstoke: Palgrave Macmillan)
White, E. N. (1987) '¿Fueron inflacionarias las finanzas estatales en el siglo XVIII?', *Revista de Historia Económica*, 3, 509–26.
White, L. J. (1992) 'Why Deregulation Failed in Banking', *Journal of Retail Banking*, 1, 25–33.
Zoido, M. E. (1998), 'Un estudio de las participaciones accionariales de los bancos en las empresas españolas', *Investigaciones Económicas*, 3, 427–67.
Zylberberg, M. (1983) 'Un centre financier "périphérique": Madrid dans la seconde moitié du XVIIIe siècle', *Revue Historique*, 546, 265–309.

Archives Consulted

Bank of Spain, Madrid (Historical Archive and Research Department Library)
Crédit Lyonnais, Paris
Ministerio de Hacienda, Madrid (Spanish Ministry of Finance Archive)
Paribas, Paris

Index

Printed and bound by CPI Group (UK) Ltd, Croydon, CR0 4YY

Alcohol Treatment: A Study of Therapists and Clients

DR J. KEENE

Avebury

Aldershot · Brookfield USA · Hong Kong · Singapore · Sydney

Published by
Avebury
Ashgate Publishing Limited
Gower House
Croft Road
Aldershot
Hants GU11 3HR
England

Ashgate Publishing Company
Old Post Road
Brookfield
Vermont 05036
USA

British Library Cataloguing in Publication Data

Keene, J.
Alcohol Treatment: A Study of Therapists and Clients
I. Title
362.29286
ISBN 1 85628 506 5

Printed and Bound in Great Britain by
Athenaeum Press Ltd, Newcastle upon Tyne.

Contents

Tables

Foreword

The critical issue that this book raises for alcohol experts is this: rather than address the question of whether there is truth in the theory that 'alcoholism is a disease', it might be more fruitful to ask the question of whether it is clinically useful that some patients believe the theory to be true.

It is not often that a new book confronts conventional wisdom, and leads the reader to a new understanding of a moribund field. This work is a landmark study and a fascinating contribution to our understanding of the treatment of alcohol problems. It opens up the 'black box' of treatment , and sheds light on how treatment works from the inside - how it is delivered and why people benefit from it. Its sociological perspective challenges, grappling with the question of what makes treatment effective. It will be essential reading for all those working on the field of alcohol treatment, in the treatment of substance abuse problems, and more broadly for all those who deliver psychological and social treatments.

The alcohol treatment field has been bedeviled by rival theories, and a paucity of substantial evidence for treatment effectiveness. A prolific industry has developed around the question of what 'alcoholism' really is, and how best it may be treated. protagonists have stuck to their theories, in a conflict that smacks of rivalry between competing sects, each holding that their dogma reveals the 'truth' about alcoholism. Clients have been told that the path to abstinence involves commitment to a particular belief system (accompanied by the vociferous rejection of other theories).

This book is ground breaking because Jan Keene has chosen to examine what alcohol therapists actually do, rather than what they say they do. She has also taken a close look at how clients respond to treatment - particularly how they make sense of their drinking problem and its treatment.

Reading the book one is struck by the fact that so few people have tried to examine what is actually going on in treatment. The field has been approached through particular theoretical spectacles; or alternatively by behaviourists who hope that the mystery of treatment will be revealed through the use of more sophisticated measures of patients' attitudes and behaviour. It is perhaps the case that some alcohol treatments work better for some people rather than others, and this in turn has prompted researchers to try to 'match' clients to treatments. What most of them have ignored - and is explored in this book - is that part of the success of treatments may be their ideological or conceptual appeal.

Thus the question is not whether it is true or not that alcoholism is a disease, or whether it is a learned behaviour (that can be unlearned); and the issue is not whether treatment should aim at total abstinence or controlled drinking. Rather, the question might be the acceptability and significance of such 'theories' to the client. AA may work for those who believe its tenets. Belief in the theory, and its appropriateness, may be crucial.

This book goes a long way to develop this argument, backed with data from a study of a treatment centre using the Minnesota Method. The particular black box of treatment that she has opened is one of the most well known, and widest used treatments in the world. Alcoholics Anonymous, and its development in the Minnesota Model claims high levels of success, and attracts prominent celebrity endorsement. Yet few evaluative studies of this treatment model are available for scrutiny.

This book analyses why some people succeed and others fail in treatment, and how clients' views compare with the theories and explanations of the therapists. A key idea is that a crucial variable is the match between client and therapist beliefs.

This book does not say which theory is 'best' - but tries to show how 'theories' work to help people understand and change their behaviour. The implication is that no one theory may make claim to the truth, and that no single treatment modality may have sole rights to the treatment of alcohol problems. Defenders of each position might expand the reach and effectiveness of alcohol treatment if they were to tolerate each other's positions, and strive to obtain the best treatment for the individual, rather than expecting that their treatment model has the answer for everyone with an alcohol problem. Further, if beliefs about alcoholism influence the success of treatment, 'matching' must involve the matching of beliefs. The question turns out to be a pragmatic one: is a theory clinically useful to a patient? In the case of AA, the question is not whether alcoholism is a disease, but whether people may be helped if they believe that it is a disease.

The research logic of this perspective is that behaviourist examinations of treatment - though essential - miss a fundamental point. Controlled outcome studies give little attention to treatment processes or to client interpretations - both of which are significant within AA type treatments. It is not only the measurable patient and therapy characteristics that should be examined, but also the belief systems held by clients and therapists. Hence the desirability of approaches with a qualitative emphasis, and which draw their inspiration from anthropology, phenomenology and discourse analysis. The treatment researcher of the future may just as likely be an ethnographer or sociologist, as a psychologist or psychiatrist.

Professor Gerry V. Stimson
Centre for Research on Drugs and Health Behaviour

Introduction

New approaches to working with alcohol users have developed in the past decade: alongside these, a new professional group of specialist and generic workers has evolved. This group now needs new knowledge from current research and experience, but without losing the wisdom and resources of older beliefs and practices. There are many different interpretations of alcohol dependency, from the social to the medical, each serving different purposes from political to professional. This book is concerned only with the therapeutic usefulness of theories and focuses on two of the most well known treatment models.

Much of the literature in Britain and Australia has reached a consensus focusing on the behavioural treatment of alcohol problems; whereas in the USA (particularly in the northern states) there is a consensus in favour of a completely different model of spiritual disease. As cross cultural influences between the USA and Britain are strong, it is hardly surprising that many professionals are confused about what exactly an alcohol problem is and what should be done about it.

Although academics are aware that there is controversy in the treatment field between the AA abstinence model and those who advocate 'controlled drinking', this is often not clear to generic professionals, nor to clients themselves. In both Britain and the USA the media often reinforce the notion that alcoholism is a disease and lay people commonly share this belief. In contrast, specialist journals and generic professional training, particularly in Britain, can give the message that alcohol problems are behavioural problems and as such can be controlled with cognitive behavioural methods.

The use of the Minnesota Model and AA is widespread in treatment services in both Britain and America yet few genuine evaluative studies of Alcoholics Anonymous or the Minnesota Method are available (Anderson, 1981; Laundergan, 1982; Kurtz, ND and Cook, 1988a and b). Adherents of these models tend to concentrate on teaching the basic philosophy rather than collating and analyzing data. This has resulted in (mainly anonymous) pamphlets describing the philosophy and method, as adherents feel strongly that descriptive personal accounts, within the framework of the recovery process, are sufficient knowledge.

Critics of the model, while developing effective research to evaluate their own methods, have done little better than AA advocates in producing research data to support their views of AA itself. Attempts by 'outsiders' to explain and understand the disease model and Minnesota Method have often been made in a cursory manner, and more significantly are made within the context of behavioural psychology (Heather and Robinson, 1981,1986; and Fingarette, 1988), a theoretical framework which is itself limited (Gorman, 1989).

This book is not written in an attempt to prove which theory and therapy is best, but instead is an attempt to clarify the relative merits of each. It is clear from the literature and research in this field that some theories demonstrably work for some people and not for others (Edwards, 1988; Glass, 1986; Gottheil, 1981; Miller and Hester, 1986) but the question of which theories work best for which people has not been adequately examined. Although the idea of matching clients to different treatments is not new, research concerned with matched studies is extremely sparse (Orford et al.,1979; Marlatt, 1988; Glaser, 1980. Edwards et al., 1988. Lindstrom, 1992).

Work in the area of psychotherapy also sheds light on the therapeutic content of alcohol treatment programmes, particularly that concerned with the content and the function of myth and ideology in self help groups (Antze, 1979) and in psychotherapy generally (Frank, 1959, 1974, 1981). These authors provide thorough examinations of the function of belief and ideology in the therapeutic change process though they do not consider the possibilities of client/therapist interaction in terms of complementary or contradictory sets of beliefs.

The book

This book is divided into two parts. The first part attempts to clarify the present state of affairs in the field of alcohol treatment. It explains how two apparently contradictory and irreconcilable theories of alcohol treatment can exist side by side. The second part of the book focuses on the set of beliefs which has been least researched, those of Minnesota and Alcoholics Anonymous. A study is made of a Minnesota/AA treatment centre using the research methods of both theories; science and descriptive interpretation (Positivism and Phenomenology).

The conclusions reached lead the author to suggest that neither model of alcohol problems should have sole ownership of territorial rights in the alcohol field. The AA and Minnesota models have been developed through subjective interpretation and examination of a (recovery) process but they suffer from a lack of 'scientific' outcome data. Whereas the behavioural model has been developed from a scientific base but remains entrenched within scientific clinical trials which allow no study of either process or subjective interpretation. Each has therefore approached its subject matter by using different methods to acquire different kinds of knowledge; the behaviourists by analyzing alcohol problems in behavioural terms and AA by analyzing these same problems in terms of 'spiritual disease'.

Both models did however develop from the same historical base of medicine and both adhere doggedly to the notion of professional assessment or diagnosis implicit within the medical approach.

It is suggested that it may be this clinical tool that prevents the appropriate matching of clients to one or other model. Diagnosis entails each camp measuring only what fits their own theory and excluding all other interpretations as irrelevant. So an AA therapist will look for symptoms of spiritual disease and behavioural psychologists will look for maladaptive behaviours.

It is commonly believed among service providers that a range of different alcohol services are needed. In order to develop such a range it is first necessary to overcome not only the limits of research, but also those of clinical diagnosis in practice. If we are to utilise more than one clinically useful theory it will be necessary to step outside the theoretical and methodological constraints of each model and devise a means of matching clients to models without using any one diagnostic tool.

In order to match models and individual clients it is essential to clarify the characteristics and significant variables in both. The first step is to understand and classify each model and the second to explore the relevance of individual differences. At present we have some understanding of each model but work on the significance of individual differences has been hindered by methodological and conceptual constraints.

The study described here provides data on treatment process and subjective interpretation to illustrate each of these issues. Firstly the results indicate that the AA model may be useful as a clinical tool even though the theory itself is not scientifically testable. Secondly that individual differences may be significant in determining treatment outcome. Thirdly that the individual differences isolated in this study cannot conceivably be significant within a medical paradigm and are not measurable through diagnosis. It is possible therefore that if individual beliefs about alcohol problems influence treatment process and outcome, matching should occur not only before any one theoretical interpretation but also before any form of diagnosis.

The practical consequences of two sets of professional and lay beliefs resulting from the 'professionalisation' and effective 'de-professionalisation' of alcohol problems raise many difficult issues and lead to the interesting question: what happens when the client believes something different to the therapist ? If the beliefs of clients are significant in treatment outcome, it should be remembered that most clients have not had access to the behavioural or medical models, which remain firmly within the confines of professional training courses and academic journals. They are instead are surrounded by the folklore of AA which has been appropriated by non-professional self-help groups, the media, and more significantly, by lay people themselves. There may of course be far wider acceptance of the beliefs of AA in the USA, but even in Britain there is a curious disparity between the beliefs of the general public and those of the 'professionals'.

The study

The study focuses on the AA and Minnesota Model and illustrates the utility of this model for some clients but not others. AA and the Minnesota Method were chosen, as this model is less well researched in Britain, and because the knowledge base of the therapy is grounded in the qualitative data of subjective experience and treatment process. The theory of Minnesota and AA also emphasises the importance of clients' own beliefs in terms of their treatment prognosis. This type of information was therefore readily available for the qualitative study.

An attempt is made in the study described here to examine the Minnesota Method in terms of the interactions between individuals and the processes involved in therapy, rather than solely in terms of studies of outcome.

The Centre examined in the study was based on both the Minnesota Method and AA, attendance at AA self-help groups being considered a necessary and integral part of the Centre programme. It is one of the few such Centres in Britain which was neither residential nor privately funded, receiving funding from the local Health Authority and central government. Clients attended for individual psychotherapy and group therapy for one or two days a week and stayed for three months to a year.

The empirical case study of the Centre was eclectic, involving both quantitative methods derived from positivist methodology and qualitative methods from phenomenology. However as the study proceeded it became clear that the qualitative data were most useful for analyzing the main research questions. This then gave rise to more general questions about these two methodological perspectives, the study becoming a platform for a much wider consideration of general theoretical issues in this field.

The research question was formulated from the premise that if phenomenological assumptions about subjective interpretation are relevant, the role of a client's beliefs will be important in the treatment process. The study explores the possibility that people showing similar behaviour, but attaching different meanings to it, will respond differently to various types of treatment. In other words, the way people experience treatment for addiction might depend on the availability of theories and methods of helping which are not inconsistent with their own conception of the problem.

The conclusions of this study emphasize the need for a range of responses and stress the importance of assessment in matching clients to different approaches. The research data themselves contribute to these aims by offering an in depth description of one model (the AA disease model) from a possible range, and by proposing an original variable (client/therapist beliefs) of relevance to assessment and allocation.

Part One: an overview of two different theories of alcohol problems

Chapter One examines the early historical development of theory and practice in the field of'addictions', with particular reference to the late 19th and early 20th centuries when alcohol problems mysteriously became the province of both medical science and Alcoholics Anonymous. This examination of historical literature illustrates how contemporary controversies have developed from those of the turn of the Century, demonstrating how alcohol initially became part of the professional territory of doctors and medical science and then became appropriated by Alcoholics Anonymous.

Chapter Two examines present day controversies in the alcohol field and provides a review of academic literature, professional reports and policy documents, in order to examine contemporary approaches in all three areas. It focuses on behavioural models, as much of the recent published research is in this field. The practical utility of 'controlled drinking' theories and methods is evaluated in the light of research findings. This information then allows a comparison with the AA approach below and the 'abstinence' debate is examined.

Chapter Three provides a straightforward description of Alcoholics Anonymous and the Minnesota Method in order to clarify the particular beliefs and theoretical assumptions underlying this treatment. Although research is scarce, descriptions of AA and Minnesota literature together with a review of the relevant academic literature give an understanding of the development of the model. This account also provides the necessary context for the study of AA in Part Two; clarifying the philosophy and theory on which the work of the Centre was based and drawing on AA material used at the Centre by both staff and clients.

Part Two: a study of client theories of alcohol problems

Chapter Four gives an outline of a research project examining the clinical significance of therapist theory and client beliefs within the AA and Minnesota models. The research design is clarified and the relevance of methodological issues discussed, giving an introduction to the questions and methods employed in the study. New ways of researching and understanding the therapeutic process in the treatment of alcohol problems are explored, with particular emphasis on the interaction of client and treatment variables, particularly therapist belief systems.

Chapter Five gives a full descriptive account of the development and day to day work of the alcohol treatment centre studied. This includes both quantitative data relevant to the effectiveness of the programme and qualitative data gathered through non participant observation of all aspects of the Centre's operation. This is supplemented by staff descriptions of themselves, their jobs and their theoretical beliefs.

Chapter Six gives the results of the study of treatment process and interpretation. This focuses on an in depth study of a group of forty clients. Ethnographic data illustrate the progress of clients through the treatment process with the corresponding responses of therapists at each stage. The main data are those relevant to subjective interpretations of events (both client and staff accounts) and those which give an understanding of the actual process of treatment. Sources of data include: staff records, case notes, minutes from meetings, and regular interviews with staff and clients themselves. These data are placed alongside statistical material recording attendance, outcome and Severity of Dependence Questionnaire scores (SADQ) together with monitoring of post-treatment attendance at meetings of Alcoholics Anonymous.

Chapter Seven examines AA and Minnesota treatment in the context of general psychotherapy and considers the therapeutic usefulness of the programme itself, rather than the validity of the underlying theory. This includes a literature survey focused on psychotherapy as a whole and an examination of the therapeutic components involved in 'working the programme' at the Centre. Finally the importance of belief systems in the therapeutic process is discussed.

Chapter Eight reviews the conclusions reached in the book and discusses possible implications for policy and practice in the field. The therapeutic utility of more than one theory and the means of administering a range of treatments are discussed. If it is accepted that more than one theory is clinically useful, it becomes necessary to assess the significance of individual differences and the practicality of matching different individuals to different treatments. It is also essential to ensure that present theories and methods are fully documented and understood in order to provide an accessible and understandable range of treatment options. Finally the practical and administrative difficulties of providing an unbiased eclectic structure for the assessment and allocation of clients are considered.

This book then sets out to clarify the differences between two approaches and highlights the difficulties in communication between professionals, and between professional and clients themselves. It does not recommend either theoretical approach, but rather the development of an academic and clinical environment that allows both to co-exist and an administrative system that matches clients to appropriate treatment models. As such it is hoped that it will be of use to the specialists in the field and to those generic professionals within health care and social work who come into contact with alcohol users. However the theoretical nature of the work also extends the academic debate, to include methodologies and data new to the field, in an attempt to understand the relevance of both treatment process and subjective interpretation to treatment outcome.

Part One

AN OVERVIEW OF TWO DIFFERENT THEORIES OF ALCOHOL PROBLEMS

1 Historical development of theory and practice in the field of 'addictions'

(a) Introduction

This chapter provides a picture of the early historical development of theories of addiction, though focusing mainly on alcohol. The questions raised in the book concern the influence of both therapist theory and client ideas on treatment. It is therefore important to clarify the contemporary beliefs, not only of professionals, but also of those clients who do not read the academic or practitioner journals. Social history is utilised here to provide a means of clarifying how professionals developed theories and practice and also to give some understanding of the beliefs of lay people in contemporary society.

Controversies within the field of addictions affect policy development, research and clinical practice. Research can be constructed around the established methodologies of particular academic disciplines and therapy developed from the cherished beliefs of different types of therapist. It is also possible that what happens to alcohol users in 'treatment' can depend on the theories that they themselves hold. The following chapter sheds some light on why alcohol problems initially came within the respective territories of medical science, psychotherapy and AA.

It is suggested that ideas about addiction developed early in the 19th Century were assimilated into the general culture and understanding of society as a whole, informing the beliefs and attitudes of both lay people and generic professionals. These generally held beliefs are difficult to isolate and identify, but there is little doubt that the public and clients themselves do not necessarily hold with the views expressed in contemporary research literature and specialist journals in Britain.

The chapter is specifically concerned with the conflicts and difficulties

* Addiction is placed in quotation marks, to indicate the controversial status in much of the literature. The term is used throughout the book to incorporate all notions of alcohol dependency.

inherent in integrating the 'disease' model of AA with the developing behavioural and public health models of the late 20th Century. It is necessary to understand the conflicts within the field itself in order to gain a clearer view of the conflicts and ambivalence of individual clients entering treatment.

Professional views client views and Alcoholics Anonymous

In the field of addiction many professions and academic disciplines have attempted to use their own particular theories or paradigms to interpret and explain the phenomenon of addiction. These may take for granted particular methodologies and basic premises or beliefs which are not clearly stated in research publications or clinical protocols.

These issues are discussed in more detail in Chapter Four. However it is important to stress here that this book is concerned with the therapeutic usefulness of theories rather than their scientific credibility. There are various theories and therapies in the field, some of the theories are scientifically tested and useful for prediction, some are only useful for interpretation and others are of less academic credibility altogether but act as useful therapeutic tools.

It is difficult to apply the concept of paradigm change (Kuhn, 1962) to the field of addictions as there is no one paradigm of addiction (Gorman, 1989). However although paradigm change in the social sciences is similar to that in the natural sciences, in the social sciences different disciplines can use mutually contradictory paradigms to interpret the same data. Several paradigms can co-exist, and each can be useful to some extent. This state of affairs is particularly significant in the field of addiction. Professionals from psychiatry, psychology, sociology and other persuasions provide different theoretical understandings of the process of addiction and its treatment. This situation is further complicated by the views and beliefs of lay people generally, clients themselves and self-help organisations, particularly AA.

It is therefore necessary to refer to both social science and medical literature, together with that of AA and Minnesota. In this way a picture can be formed to illustrate how particular models developed at the turn of the century operate in Britain today and why individual therapists and clients themselves believe what they do.

While these different perspectives may complicate the problem, it is of course this wide range of different 'scientific' and 'social' realities in the field of addiction that makes it such fertile ground for this particular investigation into the significance of subjective interpretations and therapeutic process.

(b) Historical context of theories of alcohol misuse and 'addiction'

The following section is concerned with the period of history in which addiction became the province of medical science and the ideas underlying Alcoholics Anonymous were developed. This is not to imply that some kind of linear development of theory has led the field to progress to a more coherent and consistent approach in the late 20th Century. Rather that contemporary controversies can be better understood by analyzing their predecessors, particularly those at the turn of the Century.

The difficulties encountered in the field today are not new, contemporary notions of health promotion and health gain were apparent in the early public health movements of the late 19th Century, parallel to new ideas concerning pathological forms of drug and alcohol use. Theory, practice and policy development in the field of addiction have interacted in complicated ways over the past hundred years. A range of interpretive and explanatory models have been developed, starting perhaps with notions of weakness of will or moral laxity and moving to public health and temperance approaches developed in the 19th Century. The medical disease model of addiction arose as doctors prescribing injectable morphine realised that their patients were physically addicted (the invention of the needle and syringe towards the end of the 19th Century, facilitated the early development of theories of physical addiction).

As doctors claimed legitimate ownership and understanding of the problem of addiction, the research instruments became those of medical science and Positivism. However, as today, the medical profession did not go unchallenged; competing public health and temperance lobbies were joined by the newly developing pharmaceutical profession in claiming expertise and influence in the business of controlling addictive substances. In addition to these fledgling professions, the strong religious and intellectual climate of the time linked physical addiction to moral and spiritual deterioration (the material soul), and so allowed for the development of the moral/spiritual disease model of Alcoholics Anonymous.

This gives a rough picture of Britain at the turn of the Century. Things were different in America and communication was slow. Theory and practice in America diverged from those in Britain at this time, perhaps foreshadowing the opposing paradigms in operation on both sides of the Atlantic today. At the turn of the Century the Americans focused on Prohibition rather than Teetotalism, that is, on the trade rather than the individual.

The strength of the Prohibitionists, or Abolitionists, in America perhaps reflects the political power of lay pressure groups, rather than professions. Whereas the power of the medical profession increased in Britain, resulting in scientific research and theories of pathology; in America prohibition was followed by the development of lay self-help groups.

The dominant treatment model in Northern America today is based on the 'disease' model of AA and reflects the beliefs of the general public. In Britain the dominant models have been developed through medical or behavioural science and remain within the remit of professionals (be they behavioural or medical). They do not necessarily reflect the beliefs of lay people whose own ideas may have more in common with those of the self help groups of AA or possibly to those portrayed in the American media.

The following description is not concerned with the consistency and validity of theory, but with the social influences which have influenced the development of particular theories and practice. Theories may evolve from basic moral or religious philosophies or develop from particular professional perspectives; they can be seen as reasons, rationalisations or justifications of certain policies. Theory can be changed by different professional interests and developing ideologies, which tend to fit the interests of the particular professional group involved. Conversely, existing theory can of course, influence policy and practice. It is difficult to determine whether a theory has been thought out objectively before a particular action or practice, or whether it is simply an explanation or ideology, which fits the interests of the group advancing it, and it is perhaps naive to try. It seems more practical to accept the relationship is interactive, that both need to be taken into account in any understanding of the history of theory development.

(c) History of alcohol use and response

This section will focus on responses to alcohol misuse at the turn of the century in both Britain and America, in order to place AA and the various contemporary models within their historical context. An examination of prominent ideas at this time clarifies how and why the 'disease' model of addiction developed and identifies the predecessors of our contemporary controversies. Although AA was first created and developed in America, the development of spiritual and medical notions of alcoholism first developed in Britain and were later incorporated by Alcoholics Anonymous within the American context. This review therefore covers first the early history and development of British beliefs and then considers the parallel development of American ideas at the turn of the Century.

Beliefs about morality and religion influenced ideas about the nature of man and therefore also ideas about drinking, long before medical or behavioural notions arose. It was only towards the end of the 19th Century that moral and religious interpretations of excessive drinking and drug use were supplemented by a medical model of 'addiction' as the pathological condition of an addict. Ideas of interaction between social conditions and individual use of drugs and alcohol were also prevalent the 19th Century, accompanied by a preventive or public health approach which did not concern itself with theories of the individual psyche or behaviour.

In the 20th Century this pattern of responses was repeated in Britain with notions of individual responsibility being translated into models of individual pathology, which themselves became less prominent, gradually changing in the latter half of this Century into a more social or interactive interpretation. As in the 19th Century, this latter perspective has come hand in hand with a preventive approach which is not particularly concerned with underlying causes, aetiology or generalised explanations of the problem. The public health approach and cognitive/behavioural psychology have been far less influential in America, where the 'disease' model of alcoholism remains the dominant approach in both lay and professional circles.

It has been decided to focus on a particular historical period in order to examine the development of medical science and the disease model of addiction. This is simply because this book is concerned largely with a critique of medical research methodology and clinical diagnosis and a study of Alcoholics Anonymous. As a consequence it has been necessary to exclude much of the later 20th Century developments from this historical review. This is not to undermine the significance of both cognitive/behavioural psychology and psychotherapy, both are examined in greater detail in later chapters.

The most significant addition to the range of 20th Century models of addiction was brought by the newly formed psychological profession. Cognitive/behavioural psychologists applied social learning theory to the phenomenon of addiction, re-defining this as 'addictive behaviour' and utilising behavioural and cognitive methods in its treatment. Although the notion of addiction as a 'bad habit' or maladaptive behaviour was not new, the cognitive/ behavioural approach offered testable hypotheses and new treatment techniques.

The importance of cognitive behavioural interpretations cannot be overestimated today, and as such is discussed fully in Chapter Two. However, these theories initially arose from the research base of medical science and much of psychology is still fixed within this Positivist base. Clinical psychology too, has roots within the medical profession, retaining notions of diagnosis and assessment within a medical framework. Research methodology and clinical diagnosis were both handed down from 19th Century medicine and the significance of this medical inheritance becomes apparent in the following and final chapters. Much of psychology did however break away from the scientific and clinical constraints of medicine. Cognitive/behavioural therapies formed only part of a vast range of psychotherapies developed within the auspices of psychiatry and psychology. These therapies were based on various different models of psychology, many having little theoretical structure and most not testable within a scientific framework. They did not therefore lend themselves to integrative theories of addiction in the way that cognitive behavioural approaches had done.

However the developing psychotherapies were useful to practitioners in many ways. Firstly, 'psycho-dynamic' therapists were able to take advantage of the break from scientific procedures in order to focus on subjective interpretation and the therapeutic process itself, rather than on treatment outcome. Although the aims of therapy and its achievements were often not at all clear, it could be demonstrated that the common components of therapy and particular therapist characteristics were helpful to particular clients. The process of therapy and many therapeutic techniques were found to be useful in helping those with drinking problems, despite the lack of a comprehensive rationale. As psychotherapy in some form plays a large role in many alcohol treatment programmes it is therefore interesting to consider why it has been appropriated. As with Cognitive behavioural psychology, this field has no place within the historical development of addiction at the turn of the Century, but is discussed in some detail in a later chapter (Seven).

This picture is clearly over-simplified, describing the involvement of different disciplines, rather than the development of academic thought or a newly developing paradigm. It is also difficult to clarify exactly what the 'social consensus' might be at any one time, as different professionals hold different views, as do lay people. However the existence and consequent revival of four main interpretive models can be identified: firstly the positivist medical model of individual pathology; secondly the combined spiritual and disease model of AA; thirdly the public health model and the preventive approach; and finally the social learning or behavioural approach. In addition to these theoretical models, the use of psychotherapeutic techniques has been adopted by many irrespective of theoretical base.

Although a sequential progression can be seen in the development of these different approaches, residual beliefs remain from all four within the professions themselves, but more importantly in the minds of the general public. This Chapter describes the historical development of early moral, medical and public health models, in order to give fuller understanding of base from which both AA and the later behavioural model developed.

The past five hundred years

The history of the attempts made to control the use and abuse of alcohol is far longer than the past five hundred years. However, efforts to do something about the use of alcohol had first been formalised and recorded only about five hundred years ago, with the introduction of the first Licensing Laws to control its use.

It is worth giving a brief account of the history of political responses to alcohol use as contemporary beliefs and attitudes can be seen to reflect those of campaigners in the past. This is particularly relevant for lay people and professionals unfamiliar with the academic or practitioner journals, whose views may reflect a wide spectrum of experience, folk-lore and literature. This could include moral, spiritual and other beliefs, rather than the specialist theories derived from particular academic disciplines and research methods.

The first recorded government legislation in Britain in response to alcohol consumption was in 1495, in the reign of Henry VII. This first alcohol specific Act empowered Justices of the Peace to suppress ale houses. This was followed by the first record of drunkenness as a civil offence, in 1552. Several statutes were passed during the time of the Tudors for the prevention or punishment of drunkenness. This continued during the early years of the Stuarts, although governments were aware that these constraints did little good. Williams and Brake (1980) note that 'A statute in 1609 confirmed that despite previous legislation excessiveness and drunkenness increased.'

Early records suggest that in the 16th and 17th centuries the most popular drink had been beer. This changed after 1689 when the government prevented imports and spirits became more common as the distillery trade increased in Britain. At this time there was no duty on spirits and very little tax levied on the selling of beer. By the early 18th Century gin drinking had become widespread and the number of public houses had increased. Some indication of the increase in spirit drinking is given by Williams and Brake, 'In 1684 about 527,000 gallons were distilled, but in 1727 the figure had risen to 3,601,000.' (p.3).

Free licensers and temperance groups: the development of two camps

This state of affairs described in the previous paragraph was criticized at the time and there was much antagonism to the advocates of 'Free Licensing'. The 'Free Licensers' did not think it was possible to achieve changes and were therefore resigned to free licensing, although they did believe that this could not work without popular education. As might be expected, drunkenness was often seen by this group as simply a symptom of underlying social injustice, rather than a personal failing. They were not therefore concerned with drinking itself but only with the inequity and corruption of the licensing system.

Their opponents were people more concerned with drunkenness and drink itself, seeing these as causes rather than consequences of social evils. These people joined the newly formed Temperance groups and it is here that early notions of the nature of the drinking phenomenon are recorded. Temperance groups objected strongly to Free Trade on the grounds that 'Eating of bread and meat moderated hunger, whereas alcohol drinking could actually stimulate thirst.' (see Harrison, 1971 p.345). Harrison quotes Bruce, a contemporary of that time, as stating that 'Excess of supply was not self corrective as it was in other trades.' (p.349).

Whilst there was not yet any fully formed notion of addiction, many felt that alcohol and other drugs were by their nature dangerous, without being able to explain why. 'To defend the free trade in intoxicants was as absurd as to require druggists to leave poison bottles unlabelled.' (ibid. p.349) (NB. The regulation of opium distribution and the labelling of opiates as poison did not occur until the Poisons and Pharmacy Act of 1868.)

It is interesting that Harrison himself, one of the eminent social historians of this period, suggests that 'The free licenser was dominated by a wholly inappropriate model of the drink trade and indeed of human nature. His ideal customer was a self-directed rational citizen who never made unpremeditated entries into a drinking place.' (p.348). Here he incidentally provides an apt illustration of the gap between 'lay' beliefs and those of contemporary 'professionals' in the field, by unwittingly taking a personal position which is opposed to that of both the British academic journals and the public health campaigners of today.

However in the 18th and 19th centuries the government concurred with this stance and moved from free trade to regulation, and free licensing was never revived. Harrison suggests that 'While free licensing may not have endangered sobriety as seriously as Temperance reformers believed, it certainly did not relieve intemperance to the degree that free licensers anticipated.' (p.351), something that could also be said of Health Education and the relaxation of attitudes to drug and alcohol use today.

As a result of the 1736 Gin Act the consumption of spirits was reduced from twenty million to four million gallons by the late 18th Century (Williams and Brake, 1980). The notion that if total abstinence from spirits could be encouraged then the problem would in effect be solved, was not unusual at this time. Though little is remembered about the advocates of this stance today, there is no doubt that it was these people who introduced the idea of total abstinence to the general public, although initially the cause started as applying to spirits only.

Several committees were established at that time to examine the problem of drink and the resulting reports tended to favour legislative interference,'in the public interest, for the correction of evil in society.' The early reign of Queen Victoria saw an increase in the amount of legislation, The Beer House Act of 1853 being the first attempt to limit opening hours.

Those who had initially championed the cause of abstinence from spirits had lost influence by then, only to have their cause picked up and championed by the newly formed Temperance groups. These groups extended the initial notion of abstinence from spirits to incorporate all alcoholic beverages and also concerning themselves not only with the 'reclaiming of drunkards' but also what would today be called preventive and educational work. One of the first of the Temperance groups was the British and Foreign Temperance Society, teetotallers, who regarded abstinence from spirits as illogical without abstinence from beer. Harrison quotes a remark from the *National Temperance Advocate* of June 1843 to the effect that,'We shall have National Education carried on by the people themselves.' (p.351). Rousing rhetoric, and though the objectives may be different, the methods and the ultimate aims were the same as the cry of Health Promoters today. That is that lay people themselves should be responsible, for both prevention and treatment without professional intervention.

Local and national Temperance groups began to become active in the early 19th Century and it appeared as if the problem was coming under control. Williams and Brake note that at that time the revenue from taxation on alcohol was diminishing as the Temperance movement gained momentum. (op.cit., p.6.) However although the Teetotallers had managed to introduce the Temperance movement to Britain, in taking such an extremist stance, they found that they had lost much of the support of the general population. Moderates, politicians and especially members of the drink trade itself could not ally themselves with a cause that alienated a large proportion of the population and threatened to undermine the drink trade entirely. By the mid 19th Century the Temperance movement had come to be seen as 'an amiable fanaticism' (Harrison op.cit. p.353).

A compromise was reached by The Church of England Temperance Society, which helped regain the popularity of the movement in the 1870's by adopting a 'dual basis' of both moderation and teetotal pledges. This moderation gave the movement 'a width of concern and also the financial strength to make its policies feasible.' (ibid., p.353). Having achieved the vocal support of public opinion and the financial support of prominent citizens, the movement was able to enter the political arena.

Politicians as a whole were apprehensive about the 'teetotal vote' as the majority of the general population were not considered to be in favour. Although the Temperance movement remained influential in the early 20th Century, perhaps the most significant group being the United Kingdom

Alliance, by the end of the 19th Century, most Temperance groups were no longer fighting for abstinence nationwide, but were instead involved in lobbying for only limited and specific reforms. (ibid. pp.10-11).

Although there are similarities between the beliefs and controversies of the 19th Century and those of contemporary society, particularly in terms of the present approach of Health Education and the emphasis on the social side of problematic alcohol use, general attitudes to its use and abuse before the 20th Century made little reference to notions of addiction, disease or behavioural problems. The use of alcohol was either seen in moral or religious terms, or alternatively as a social problem or a symptom of social problems.

The disciplines of Psychiatry and Psychology were in their infancy, and it was not until inebriety began to arouse the interests of medical men at the end of the 19th Century and doctors first began to explain morphine use in terms of 'addiction' at the same time, that notions of disease and diagnosis came into play.

Before this time medical and psychological theories remained unconnected with alcohol use and consequently scientific methodologies were not used to research the phenomenon and neither were clinical treatment tools invoked to diagnose and treat it.

The main controversy between Temperance reformers and more general social reformers in the early 19th Century, concerned only drunkenness and remained on the level of social analysis, whether or not this drunkenness was the cause or effect of other social evils. For example Charles Dickens writing at this time argued forcibly that social problems were the cause of drunkenness and opposed 'that monstrous doctrine which sets down the consequences of drunkenness, fifty thousand miseries which are as all reflective persons know, the wretched causes of it.'.

It was only in the late 19th and early 20th centuries that a medical model was developed. This approach was concurrent with the beliefs of the Teetotallers and opposed by social reformers. The forum for the development of the new medical response to inebriety was the 'Society for Promoting Legislation for the Control and Cure of Habitual Drunkards' established in 1876, and the influential 'Society for the Study of the Cure of Inebriety' (S.S.I.) which was formed in 1884 and composed entirely of medical men. This latter organisation was formed by a group of influential medical professionals with the remit 'to investigate the various causes of inebriety, and to educate the professional and public mind to a recognition of intemperance.' (Quoted from the *Proceedings* of the S.S.I. No. 1 July 1884, Parssinen, 1983 p.86).

The S.S.I. viewed intemperance and inebriety as incorporating both drug and alcohol use, and much of the theory incorporates both. The founder of the S.S.I., Dr Norman Kerr, was considered to be to be the 'most important

British spokesman on the question of addiction in the late 19th Century' (Parssinen, p.87). The basic theory proposed by Kerr and the S.S.I. is was a radical departure from previous notions. It was first proposed in the *Proceedings* (1884); 'Inebriety is for the most part the issue of certain physical conditions... the natural product of a depraved, debilitated, or defective nervous organisation,...as unmistakably a disease as is gout, or epilepsy, or insanity.' (ibid., p.87)

Although Kerr and his colleagues were concerned with drug use, they felt that alcoholism was the 'most significant form of inebriety in Britain' and much of the initial theory underlying medical attitudes to drug use was based on Kerr's theories of alcoholism. Kerr pursued the humane implications of the medical model by attempting to obtain public funding for 'retreats for the treatment of inebriates', on the basis that 'If inebriety, like gout or epilepsy, is the result of a physical defect over which the sick person has no control, that is, if inebriety is not a wilful act, then the inebriate should be not be jailed, but hospitalised.' (ibid., p.88.) Without drawing too much attention to contemporary parallels, these proposals were largely unsuccessful. However, partly as a consequence of the work of Kerr and his colleagues, two Acts were passed in the latter half of the 19th Century; The 'Habitual Drunkards Act' of 1879 and the 'Inebriates Act' of 1898, but as Parssinen notes, although 'the Acts did licence a few retreats, they were private and received only nominal public support.' Dr Kerr and the S.S.I. also tried to build a case for compulsory confinement of inebriates: once again they failed. However these attempts by the medical profession to influence social policy produced many 'scientific' publications, which had a significant influence on attitudes to alcoholism at that time. The existence of a growing amount of medical and academic literature at that time is perhaps under-represented in some of the work of politically orientated social historians.

Despite the existence of the S.S.I. and academic literature of the time, it should however be noted that 'After forty years of Temperance agitation, prominent observers were still lamenting the lack of precise information on central aspects of the drink problem.' (Harrison op.cit., p.337) The same can clearly be said of politicians, bureaucrats and professionals today. Although to some extent the moral dimensions of the problem, which were so prominent at the turn of the century, are not significant to professionals and public service providers today, there is no doubt that the general public feels, in agreement with Alcoholics Anonymous that the moral factor is not irrelevant. Although the late 19th Century heralded a new medical literature, the religious or spiritual and moral aspects of drinking remained prominent in the Temperance movement which provided the historical context for the development of AA in the early 20th Century.

The Temperance Movement and particularly the United Kingdom Alliance believed that not only was God on their side, but that the prohibitionist struggle was literally 'Part, and Oh, how large a part, of the great war between Heaven and hell... God is for us and for our work.' (see Civil Rights and Social Duties; *United Kingdom Alliance* 1870. 71, p.89. quoted in Harrison p.372). Harrison states that 'Devout Christians saw the world as deeply corrupted by sin and cynicism; it could be purified only through dramatic reclamation of the individual, or through catastrophic divine intervention. Likewise Teetotallers and Prohibitionists saw social reform entirely in terms of sudden "conversion", whether of the individual or of society as a whole.' (p.380).

These beliefs and priorities may seem out of place to statutory professionals but they formed an integral part of general belief systems prevalent immediately prior to the appearance of Alcoholics Anonymous in both Britain and America as the Temperance movement was at its most influential in Britain in the late 19th and very early 20th centuries. Elements of this basic conviction can be seen during the historical development and contemporary practice of Alcoholics Anonymous. It is, however, important to note that this organisation is concerned with Teetotalism and individual change, not with prohibition or with the Temperance cause of general education and prevention of drunkenness amongst society as a whole.

After the First World War, Temperance societies became less popular and their ideology less compatible with everyday life. Drunkenness itself began to decline, but more importantly perhaps the notion of a drink problem as a moral issue for lay or religious rather than professional intervention began to give way to the view it was medical subject for scientific research and clinical treatment.

America and the development of AA

The above description gives an account of British history, providing information about the foundations on which both contemporary British and American approaches are built. However an understanding of the American context is essential, as historically the development of these ideas and the extent of professional involvement differed in the two countries. In America, emphasis was placed on social rather than medical control and the professional's role was far less prominent. This resulted in less emphasis on scientific research or professional treatment and more prominent lay pressure groups and self-help groups.

Alcoholics Anonymous began in America in the 1930's and although many of its ideas and methods can be articulated in the context of the understandings of alcohol addiction and teetotalism and Temperance in 19th Century Britain, the history of Prohibition in America gives a more comprehensive picture of the specific American influences immediately prior to its inception.

The situation in America parallelled that in Britain. British prohibitionists and American Abolitionists were moving in a rapidly changing environment overlooked by a traditional church perhaps gradually losing its influence and a government gradually increasing its control. However, the medical profession was effectively excluded from the field and instead the Prohibitionist movement in America gained real political power as an independent pressure group. Whereas the movement in Britain had never really achieved this, even though it had become a party issue for a short time, it became sidelined as politically unviable and transformed instead into a professional issue.

The main thrust of the American Prohibition movement was also very different to that of Britain, the focus of change being the trade rather than the individual drinker. This specialisation of approach led to problems later when Prohibition had been achieved and needed to be maintained, but in the initial stages this attitude led to a removal of responsibility from the individual to the 'liquor traffic'(see Kerr, 1985). The American Prohibition movement had been active since the 1850's, though it was not until 1895 that the Anti-Saloon League was formed. This group was important because it achieved political power in America in a way that Temperance societies in Britain had not. The League was united in the belief that to achieve what the Temperance groups were attempting in Britain it would be necessary to destroy the industries that supplied drink.

The campaign in America did however have two dimensions. The Anti-Saloon League was in operation alongside the well established Prohibition movement which had been active throughout the latter half of the 19th Century. The Prohibitionists attempted to reform individuals in the same way as in Britain, by educating them about the harms of drink. At that time in America small pressure groups fighting for specific issues and lobbying government for change had more influence than similar groups in Britain. Boulding (1953) in his book *The Organizational_Revolution*, documents the rise of these groups in American politics. Kerr explains the rise of the Anti-Saloon League within this context of 'expanding and specialising associational activity' (p.5). He states that the League 'specialised by focusing continuing attention on a single issue, (prohibition) and by refusing direct involvement with other issues' (p.6). It is interesting that this stance is reflected in the Alcoholics Anonymous movement, although meticulously avoiding political involvement, it has maintained its identity over the years, partly by refusing to become involved with any issues other than helping individual 'alcoholics'.

The first serious petition for Prohibition was raised by Hobson in 1914. This was popular but it was not until 1919 that a majority of states agreed to the proposal and Prohibition was placed within the American constitution. There is no doubt, as Kerr points out, that the previous sixty years of Temperance campaigning had helped to shape particular ideologies and values. But 'The speed with which America placed Prohibition in the Constitution was largely due to the unremitting political pressure of the Anti-Saloon League' (p.186). American mobilisation for the 1914-18 War was also a contributing factor, as the values espoused by the Temperance groups were those needed for victory at war as well as against drink. However in the post-war years the Anti-Saloon League was unable to agree a strategy for maintaining Prohibition, and the controversy began to revive again. The Anti-Saloon League had focused specifically on the liquor trade and practically ignored the question of personal drinking (Teetotalism had not been the issue). This may have been part of the reason for the popularity of their cause, but after the War there was a good deal of confusion about the aims of the League. As a consequence its power and influence began to diminish. Kerr suggests that this failure to agree on a 'strategy for the post-war years meant that when another national crisis, The Great Depression, occurred the Anti-Saloon League was in no position to stop the repeal of the Amendment.' (p.274).

Although Prohibition is often described as a failure, it is interesting that it did in fact succeed in reducing the levels of alcohol consumption (and alcohol related problems); not only during the period of Prohibition itself, despite the expansion of organised crime and the illicit industry produced, but also after the Amendment was repealed. Kerr points out that the consumption of alcohol was reduced by one third to one half during the period of Prohibition. (p.276).

America and Britain differ less in the overall aims and beliefs of their campaigns but more in the practical and political mechanisms used to achieve results. It is possible that the American prohibition movement did succeed because of the single-minded fight for one limited cause, but this may also have been its downfall.

The Quakers and the 'material soul': addiction to other drugs

Historical material of the development of the Temperance Movement and the Abolitionists is taken from policy documents and leaflets of the time; the development of medical involvement is well documented in professional and academic journals. This is often taken to constitute a comprehensive overview. However this review leaves out less easily accessible information about the influence of religious and moral beliefs on policy and practice. If this historical review were restricted only to the academic and professional literature of the time, the conclusions would be limited. It would become apparent that social and medical interpretations of addiction developed during late 19th Century. But not that this development took place alongside spiritual and moral interpretations and more importantly that notions of pathology were intertwined with spiritual and moral beliefs.

To give a complete picture it is necessary to explain in more detail the underlying base of spiritual and moral beliefs about addiction that prevailed at the time. As the spiritual base provides the foundation for much of the AA philosophy, it is important to provide a clear understanding of this in terms of its historical context. Unfortunately it is difficult to find recorded evidence for these beliefs in either policy documents or professional journals connected with alcohol. However evidence of the religious base to attitudes about addiction in general is available in the literature relating to Opium addiction of the same period. This is perhaps because the of the prominence of the Quakers amongst the early social reformers fighting an early 'war against drugs'. The following analysis of early attitudes to opiate use is included here to clarify the emergence of ideas interconnecting spirituality, morality and pathology in drug addiction as a whole.

The development of theories of drug and alcohol misuse developed alongside each other to some extent in Britain. Attempts to understand alcohol use in terms of 'addiction' or 'inebriety' arose at the same time as theories of opiate addiction. Parssinen (1983) notes that, 'The attempt to define drug addiction as a disease...was derived from and secondary to the more important attempt to define alcoholism as a disease.' (pp.102-3.) This was not the case in America, but the theories underlying the initial development of AA in America were firmly based within the notions of drug and alcohol use established in the late 19th Century in Britain.

Firstly, as G. Harding points out in the introduction to his book, *Opiate Addiction, Morality and Medicine* (1988), 'The history of responses to addiction did not begin with the first addicts.' (p.1). It is difficult to discover a great deal about opium use in Britain before the various professions and the government became concerned. However Berridge and Edwards in their book *Opium and the People* (1981), give a detailed account of the extent of 'working class opium eating' in the 19th Century. They conclude that in the early part of the 19th Century opium use was common amongst the working class, stating that the equivalent of 600mg per head was consumed each year in 1827 and that this increased to three and a half times as much in 1859. This opium was used for many minor ailments as well as more serious illnesses and was sold widely by chemists, many different types of shop-keeper and also by travelling salesmen.

Harding (op.cit.) states that opium eating was 'regarded at worst as a minor vice or a bad habit' continuing, 'the use of opium imported into Britain continued along with an essentially relaxed attitude to its consumption for much of the early 19th Century.' In the second half of the

19th Century various people began to take an interest in opium use generally. Harding records two sources from the mid-19th Century to illustrate the generally held attitude before the changes in the second half of the Century. The first reflects the views on inebriety of the social reformers, 'working class consumption was attributed to poor housing conditions and fever epidemics.' (quoted by Harding from parliamentary paper, *Report to the Commissioners for Inquiring into the State of Large Towns and Populous Districts: XVIII,* 1844.) The second reflects a more medical approach but still views drug use as a response to problems, 'Consumption by the middle classes was held to result from their experience of pressure from severe mental distress.' (quoted by Harding from 'Medicus, Teetotalism and Opium Taking', *Lancet*, 1851, p.694).

The rising influence of the medical profession in the field of drug misuse was paralleled by the influence of the Quaker religion, as many Quakers became involved in the earliest attempts to control opium use. In this way the beliefs of lay people came to influence ideas and attitudes in the same way as the Temperance movement had done.

The issue of opium use was initially raised in Britain because of a concern with the activities of the East India Company and the Indo-Chinese Opium trade, rather than with interest in the widespread use of opium in Britain. This concern was focused by a small number of groups opposed to this trade. The largest and most influential of these groups was the 'Society for the Suppression of the Opium Trade' (S.S.O.T.), an organization founded by the Quakers in 1874. The involvement of the Quakers is of particular significance, as the ideas they expounded were based on their religious beliefs, not merely about the nature of addiction, but also of the nature of man and morality.

These Quaker beliefs not only formed the basis of initial opposition to opium in Britain, but also established the foundation for the early self help groups established to deal with problems of alcoholism in both Britain and America. (The Oxford Group and Alcoholics Anonymous.)

The early theories of addiction derived to some extent from the campaign against the opium trade. The S.S.O.T. succeeded initially in 'raising the issue of non-medical use of opium to the level of a national concern.' (Harding, op.cit.) The many opponents in this debate were the S.S.O.T. and what Parssinen calls the 'opium apologists', the equivalent of the 'Free Licensers'.

The focus of the debate only moved to Britain itself when the first medical practitioners took an interest. As with alcohol, doctors began to extend their professional influence to opiates at this time, though not as a response to general opium use in the population as a whole, but in response to their own mistaken prescribing practice. That is, doctors were initially concerned with the results of the prescription of injectable morphine. Doctors began prescribing injectable morphine for treatment purposes after the invention of the needle and syringe in the late 19th Century. As a result of patients receiving large quantities for prolonged periods of time, the phenomena of tolerance, withdrawal and craving became clearer and consequently a focus of medical attention. This interest was very relevant to the development of theory and practice in the field as the medical profession brought the scientific methodology of clinical research to bear on the study of the phenomenon; firstly because medical research focused on a small group of what came to be known as 'therapeutic addicts' and secondly because scientific research came to be seen as the proper methodology with which to study this group. In addition the simple fact that drug and alcohol use became the remit of the medical profession instilled the implicit assumption that the phenomenon must be of a pathological nature and that clinical diagnosis and treatment were the appropriate tools with which to tackle it.

The medical profession's claim to this territory did not however remain uncontested. Along with the Quakers came public health committees and the newly developing profession of pharmacists, all eager to extend their own professional expertise to include the field of drug abuse. The opposing claims of public health or health promotion and pharmaceutical professions remain today.

However initial ideas about opiate misuse were formulated by the Quakers within the S.S.O.T. and these beliefs remained dominant for many years, informing both lay and professional opinion. The remnants of these beliefs are evident today. Harding summarises the theory and underlying beliefs of the S.S.O.T. as follows; essentially they believed opium use to have 'the property of impairing the habitual user, not just physically, but also morally. In other words this technical language described the manifest symptoms of opium dependence as those of a 'vice' but analyzed its aetiology in terms of a pathologically impaired moral faculty.'

Similarities between this understanding of addiction and that of AA and the staff at the Centre in the study can be seen in the later chapters of this book, when it will become clear that the underlying beliefs of the treatment service have developed from the earliest attempts to construct theory.

Harding explains that these beliefs made sense to the S.S.O.T. because its founders 'subscribed to the Quaker doctrine which was founded on the principle that an individual's "soul" should be regarded...as a physical entity, like a person's body. They could speak of a "material Soul".' (p.34) He continues, 'Those who became dependent on opium were deemed to have suffered a breakdown of the "normal" self-restraining function of the individual which resulted in the irresponsible denial of one's own morality', so opium users became 'willing victims' (p.34). 'The metaphor of a "material Soul" was clearly central to the existence of what might be termed the "moral pathological" model of addiction.' (p.37). Harding concludes that the Quaker notion of a 'pathologically debilitated will' and 'pathologically impaired moral faculty' began to be taken seriously in the late 19th Century as a causal explanation for opiate use by non-Quakers.

The notion of the 'moral faculty' having a physical location was not simply a Quaker innovation in the 19th Century, but there is no doubt that the Quakers established the connection between drug use and the deteriorating moral sense within the culture of the time. The process by which certain beliefs are assimilated into general social 'paradigms' or become cultural norms is difficult to assess, but the remnants of these beliefs are still an integral part of many individuals' attitudes today, perhaps being kept alive by AA itself. This is of significance when considering the implications of these beliefs for those giving and receiving treatment. The beliefs of the Quakers and S.S.O.T. corresponded closely to those held by the early religious groups attempting to deal with alcoholism (eg. The Oxford Group) and with those held by the founders of Alcoholics Anonymous in America. They also correspond closely to the beliefs held by many laymen and professionals who have contact with the 'Anonymous Fellowship' in Britain today, and are still well integrated into the contemporary American approach to alcohol policy and treatment.

It can be seen that the early involvement of the medical profession and public religious groups jointly influenced the development of ideas about alcohol misuse. These ideas became the foundation of two separate approaches to alcohol problems in the 20th century. While the medical profession laid the foundations for 'professional' involvement based on scientific research, diagnosis and treatment, Alcoholics Anonymous developed self help groups based on a mixture of subjective experience and Temperance ideas (drink as the primary cause of the problems), together with Quaker beliefs about the 'material soul' (alcoholism as a'spiritual disease') and personal moral responsibility for 'recovery'.

This then was the historical context from which Alcoholics Anonymous emerged in the 1930's. It will be seen from Chapter Three that the creators of AA adapted the old Temperance and Teetotal beliefs of the late 19th Century, but they did not incorporate notions of Prohibition or social change. They limited their work to recovering themselves and helping other individuals to recover and to this end they incorporated notions of addiction, inebriety and disease developed in the early 20th Century to interpret alcoholism and morphine addiction. Chapter Three describes the initial formation and growth of Alcoholics Anonymous and the theory and method of this approach, examines the ways in which Alcoholics Anonymous have developed and adapted these basic beliefs and the underlying philosophies, and also how the AA programme fits with that of contemporary approaches to drink.

Fundamental disagreements

It is significant that although theories of alcohol misuse and treatment have existed since the late 19th century, the major controversies within the alcohol and drugs fields still exist today as they did a hundred years ago. Although extra players have been introduced in the shape of scientific researchers and the newly established psychiatrists and psychologists, and the religious element has reduced. The controversies between social reformers, Temperance workers and clinicians in the 19th Century are not dissimilar to those of Public Health and Health Education campaigners, AA advocates and clinicians today. It is particularly interesting to note that many of the most recent arguments concerning the development of constraints on drinking hours and legalisation of drugs have much in common with the Free Licensers and Opium Apologists.

However more pertinent to the subject matter of the book are the controversies within the treatment field itself. Should research be the remit of positivist science? Should practice be the remit of professionals (and if so which)? Should the aim of treatment be abstinence or controlled drinking? Perhaps less overt are the disagreements based on differing beliefs about moral responsibility and free will, best illustrated in varying social controls and policing policy.

It is hoped that the historical context gives a greater understanding of the beliefs and methods which underlie the contemporary models examined in this book. Neither the AA or Cognitive Behavioural model follow the medical model slavishly, but both have adopted assessment procedures based on the medical notion of diagnosis. The disease and diagnosis model inform the spiritual disease model of AA and the research methodology and clinical methods of medicine are influential in the methods and research of behavioural science and behavioural medicine.

In summary, it is important to stress that alcohol (and drug) problems have been understood and dealt with, without recourse to doctors, diagnosis or medical science until the end of the 19th Century. With the rise of the medical profession it followed that concepts central to medical practice such as scientific research and clinical diagnosis were unquestioningly accepted as both necessary and appropriate. It is proposed in this book that this may be counter-productive.

2 Contemporary behavioural models and controversies

Alcohol treatment within the statutory professions in Britain is based largely on psychological and medical models. The study in this book examines one of the few statutory services based on the disease model in Britain. In Britain (as opposed to the USA) there is a basic agreement among statutory professionals that addiction is not a spiritual disease, as a consequence the disease model of AA is usually limited to voluntary and residential services.

Although this book presents a study of the AA/Minnesota model, it should be emphasized that the book does not advocate this or any other model, simply highlighting the benefits of a greater understanding of all those available. The study has focused on AA and the Minnesota Method, as there has been little study of these by outsiders. Robinson has discussed AA self help groups in detail and Cook (1988; a,b) has reviewed the literature. Frank (1974, 1981) and Antze (1979) have taken a more independent view of the therapeutic processes of AA. Kurtz (ND) and Denzin (1987; a,b,c.) have attempted overviews, those these texts can seem biased in favour of the underlying assumptions of AA itself.

There has also been much criticism of AA amongst those who have not been through the programme, such as Heather and Robertson (1981, 1986). It is seldom suggested that researchers examine the reasons why AA can be effective, rather than examining the reasons why it is not. AA is seldom represented in British journals or edited collections and only mentioned in passing in literature reviews. Yet AA and Minnesota underpin much American treatment and AA has established self help networks in most countries (Alcoholics Anonymous 1981). It therefore seems strange that this model has been subject to so little study. As Bratt (1953) stated, 'Writing about alcoholism and leaving out what the Americans have to say on the matter would be like writing about Communism and ignoring the lessons from Russia.' (Quoted in Lindstrom, 1992, p.10) AA advocates are themselves equally dogmatic in their criticism and dismissal of alternative approaches, particularly behavioural psychology, as Marlatt (1986) and Fingarette (1988) found out to their cost in the USA.

This section will provide a critique of different models within the context of policy and practice in Britain, outlining the basic positions within different professions and examining theoretical controversies in the literature. In this way AA will be placed in its contemporary context, as the previous chapter placed it within its historical context. Contemporary controversies bear a strong resemblance to those at the turn of the Century. Opinion is divided between those who believe that drinking is a matter of personal choice and habitual behaviour and those who see the problem in terms of loss of self-control and personal pathology. These two directly opposing approaches reflect those of the cognitive/ behavioural approach, most popular in Britain and the AA/ Minnesota approach popular in the USA. This chapter will therefore focus particularly on these two approaches.

Although it will become apparent that there is little common ground between AA and thc cognitivc/bchavioural approach, differences between doctors, psychiatrists and psychologists are less clearly defined. The main issue still remains the relative importance of physical and behavioural factors, but some agreement has been reached by amalgamating biological, psychological and social models. The medical model is perhaps closest to the disease model of AA, but it will become clear in the following chapter that the two approaches have a very different knowledge base.

The chapter is not only concerned with theoretical distinctions, but with the deeper underlying differences between disciplines and professions. In order to examine the usefulness and limitations of different kinds of knowledge about addiction, it is necessary to understand the research status of the methodologies underlying each discipline.

The research methodologies of medicine and psychology are based on positivist premises very different to those underlying AA. However early psychiatric research was closer to the experiential knowledge underlying AA. Published research was often based on descriptive accounts of individual cases, providing qualitative rather than quantitative data and allowing the development of psychodynamic theories of therapeutic process. The influence of case study methods and diagnosis in psychiatric clinical practice remains, but its influence on research is less significant today. Contemporary psychiatric research has more in common with the straightforward experimental methods used to study observable behaviour and physiology. As a consequence perhaps, the attitudes of psychiatrists broadly resemble those of doctors and behavioural psychologists.

There has been a movement in the past twenty years among alcohol specialists to combine biological, psychological and social components of the phenomenon. This has not been a movement to combine the different methodologies of each discipline, but simply to integrate several subject areas for study within one methodology. In Chapter Four it is argued that medical/ behavioural frameworks for defining problems and positivist frameworks for measuring treatment may be inadequate in the field of alcohol. This position is not new (see Cronbach cited in Lindstrom, 1992, p.34). However studies exploring alternative conceptions of treatment have been largely located within the field of psychotherapy rather than that of alcohol. Many therapists have suggested that there is a need for new ways of interpreting therapeutic treatment. Psychotherapeutic research would suggest that treatment should be seen as an interactive process, it being influenced by therapist and client variables rather than those of the theory and method. Frank (1974), Magaro et al. (1978).

It is therefore necessary to examine in which professional territories addiction is located. This chapter examines the extent of the influence of these disciplines, focusing on the similarities and differences between professions and the increasing development of the cognitive/behavioural approach in Britain and Australia.

Policy development in the alcohol field in Britain is strongly influenced by the clinical professions. This is reflected in the continuing debate about the optimum balance of specialist treatment as opposed to generalist primary level services and the more general dispute regarding allocation of resources to preventive, early intervention, or treatment services. These disputes are centred around the aim of intervention (abstinence or controlled drinking) and the positions taken influenced by the particular theory of addiction espoused. The degree of emphasis placed on early intervention methods depends on beliefs about the usefulness of the behavioural approach of controlled drinking for various kinds of alcohol problem. In research, as in treatment, many of the basic underlying beliefs of a particular discipline are taken for granted, thus the initial definition of addiction will be determined by the basic paradigm of each profession and fuelled by the research methodology of each. For example a psychologist might analyze addiction in behavioural terms, as a behavioural disorder, and consequently use empirical methods based on observation of behaviour in order to research the phenomenon.

Positivist research in effect presupposes that the phenomenon can be defined and isolated, all peripheral variables controlled and experimental comparisons made. There is also a further presupposition that data inaccessible to this approach (concerning individual differences, subjective interpretations and the treatment process itself) are superfluous. This would of course be entirely valid if there was general consensus about what addiction is and how to 'treat' it.

However it is doubtful whether the following models can be reconciled: Can drinking problems be seen as cognitive/ behavioural habits? as a biopsychosocial continuum along which everybody can travel under certain circumstances ? and as peculiar to a certain proportion of disease prone individuals ?

It should be noted here that the meaning of 'disease' varies depending on the speaker. The word is not often used by the medical profession to refer to physiological addiction, but can be used by others to refer to AA or the medical model.

Before examining each model of addiction separately it is useful to look at the integral approach. A general overview of different aspects of 'addiction', has resulted in a 'biopsychosocial' model, (Orford, 1985, Galizio and Maisto, 1985). Unfortunately this generalized approach is limited in its clinical usefulness and difficult to test within the framework of a behavioural science, as has been pointed out by Schwartz (1982): perhaps because the increase in subject matter has not being matched with an increase in appropriate methodologies.

However the most comprehensive of the integrated approaches has been developed internationally and is now utilized for both clinical and screening purposes. This is the model of a 'continuum of dependence' originated by Griffith Edwards. Edwards identified alcohol dependence as 'an abnormal degree of psychological dependence, accompanied by evidence of physiological dependence, (that is) a psycho-physiological disorder.' (Edwards et.al., 1977 and 1986a). This model was later developed into the 'Alcohol Dependence Syndrome' by Edwards and colleagues for the World Health Organisation (Edwards et.al., 1977), later being itself integrated into a practically useful tool for screening purposes (AUDIT).

It is significant that the World Health Organisation did not support either the disease or cognitive behavioural approach, simply stating that the syndrome defined a 'cluster' of physiological, behavioural and social phenomena. That is: narrowing of drinking repertoire, salience of drink-seeking behaviour, tolerance, withdrawals and craving, relief drinking and the rapid re-instatement of the syndrome after abstinence. (Edwards et.al., 1976 and 1977.)

Thus the syndrome includes characteristics identified by Alcoholics Anonymous, particularly the salience of drinking and re-instatement of the syndrome (which the WHO refers to as 'remission'), together with behavioural characteristics, such as narrowing of the drinking repertoire. The syndrome therefore can be seen as incorporating aspects of both AA and behavioural models, however the terminology is largely medical, and as such is seen by those outside medicine as too closely related to the disease model. The syndrome has been criticized by both AA advocates and cognitive behavioural psychologists. The former stating that addiction is a disease and not a medical problem (LeFevre ND) and the latter stating that it is based on a medical model and therefore an ineffectual attempt to support the disease model in the face of the evidence of behavioural research. (Heather and Robinson, 1981.)

It can be seen therefore that, despite attempts by Edwards and the World

Health Organisation to overcome controversy and develop an overarching theory and method for screening purposes and diagnosis, both the behavioural psychologists and Alcoholics Anonymous remain intact and autonomous; each offering a comprehensive theory and method of their own.

The Alcoholics Anonymous model will be discussed in greater detail in the following chapter, as although published research examining AA and Minnesota exists it is scarce and not often dealt with in British journals. This chapter deals with the contemporary literature in professional and academic journals, much of which is concerned with the psychological model.

Cognitive and behavioural change methods derive from Social Learning theory and cognitive psychology: they can be very effective for certain conditions ranging from depression to phobias and more significantly for obsessive/compulsive behaviours. (Bandura, 1977, Beck, 1989, Ellis, 1987, Brown, 1984.) These methods have also been demonstrated to be effective in helping people control their drinking and in reducing drink related harm. Though it should be stressed that while observable behaviour can measured scientifically, cognitions cannot. (Heather and Robinson, 1981, 1986, Babor et al., 1986, Chick et al., 1985, Hodgson, 1976, Hester, 1989). As Lindstrom (1992) states 'There is ample evidence demonstrating that brief interventions may be modestly but reliably effective in helping the less serious type of problem drinker.' There is much controversy then, not concerning whether cognitive behavioural methods are useful for alcohol related problems as a whole, but regarding how far the methods are useful when dealing with the biopsychosocial phenomenon of 'addiction'.

If 'early intervention' methods are seen in a preventive light this itself raises methodological issues. It should be asked whether an epidemiological study might not be more appropriate to assess early intervention methods rather than studies of treatment outcome. If these methods are to some extent preventive then epidemiological population measures of incidence and prevalence would be necessary. Although research indicates that non-serious drinkers can be helped to control their drinking at an 'early stage', (Edwards, 1986a) the research cannot distinguish between those who will progress to a 'later' stage and those whose drinking would not become harmful at all. Edwards himself is increasingly unsure of the comprehensiveness and validity of outcome data (1988) and the wisdom of excluding many aspects of addiction in favour of those highlighted by the now popular cognitive behavioural model (1989).

However, despite the growing influence of the cognitive/ behavioural model, the notion of sequential stages of alcoholism which seems integral to behavioural notions of early intervention, is not derived from Social Learning theory itself. It is here, as might be expected that psychologists would question the integrated approach. Hodgson in an article entitled 'The Alcohol Dependence Syndrome a Step in the Wrong Direction' (1980) criticizes the notion of a syndrome as too medical (although he does concede that the concept of a dependence state is valid) and yet if there is no sequential syndrome then the rationale for early intervention is less apparent.

Despite criticisms of the narrow and self limiting nature of the behavioural approach, there is no doubt that much of the most useful recent research in the alcohol field has been carried out by cognitive/behavioural psychologists. This work is listed in a thorough review of early intervention strategies, provided by Babor, Ritson, and Hodgson (1986). This review suggests that 'modest, but reliable effects on drinking behaviour and related problems can follow from brief interventions, especially with the less serious type of problem drinker.' The types of intervention evaluated include information, advice, self help manuals and groups, and periodic monitoring of progress by a health worker. The authors conclude that 'low intensity, brief interventions have much to recommend them as the first approach to the problem drinker in the primary care setting.' This work is corroborated by Chick et al. (1985), who conclude that nurses can effect significant change in patients drinking behaviour, if intervention is made before the problem has become too severe. There are criticisms of the type of controlled experimental/quasi-experimental method used in many of these studies, both in terms of the need for epidemiological data and the bias introduced by a behavioural analysis of problems. But as Babor et al., (op.cit.) point out, the data collected have proved extremely useful, the research indicates that both light and heavy drinking can be brought under individual control and drinking levels maintained or cut down.

The research and discussion concerning the possibility of severely alcohol dependent, or addicted, clients returning to controlled drinking, using the behavioural techniques of early intervention is less optimistic (Lindstrom, 1992). Though there is much controversy over this issue, there is little research to indicate that controlled drinking is a viable option for most severe alcoholics. The discussion in this area centres around the measures used to assess severe dependence or addiction and how to identify those individuals who come into this category.

Edwards concludes that this type of difficulty is compounded by confusion between 'dependence' and 'disability'. He states that because these terms are confused, the problem of definition becomes much worse.

In previous work, Edwards and Orford (1977) had found little difference between treatment approaches and this work is often cited as the best example of an outcome study illustrating no difference between the two options of 'treatment' and 'advice'. This illustrated, as they pointed out, 'A reservation which should properly attach to any too absolute interpretation of a clinical trial is that conclusions based on the averaging process and simple comparisons of group means may fail to bring out important patient type - treatment interactions.' The authors defined different patient types in terms of disability and dependence.

Orford et al. (1979) carried out a two year follow up of this study which confirmed the authors' initial hypothesis, finding that the long term results were different for different categories of client. Those clients considered more seriously dependent achieved better results in the treatment group and others (suffering only disability) did better in the group receiving only advice. There was an interaction between the types of client and the goals they achieved, with the seriously addicted clients achieving better results through abstention and the others tending to achieve good results through controlled drinking.

Edwards believed that if the dependence syndrome were severe, then the chances of returning to controlled drinking were low. If the syndrome were mild, then controlled drinking would be possible. He felt it essential, but problematic, to group subjects in terms of degrees of dependence rather than in terms of disability. Edwards concluded; 'For people who are disabilitated simple strategies of social adjustment or psychotherapy (coping mechanisms) might be useful in reversing the "dependence syndrome". There is an important contrast here with the benefits of such general strategies for severe dependence, where similar approaches may be expected to lead to remission.' (ibid., p.149). That is, what is good for someone not heavily addicted may be a disaster for someone who **is** heavily addicted, and vice versa. (See also Edwards 1988 and 1989).

The significant point raised in their discussion of this study were the difficulties in assigning subjects to groups in terms of whether the drinking caused the disability, or the disability caused the drinking. Edwards is attempting to overcome differences between different theorists and develop 'a shared model of understanding' by defining two types of alcohol problem. It can be seen that the major difference between the two models discussed in this book is the controversy of 'causal direction' or 'primary cause' reflected in Edwards dichotomy between disability and dependency.

Both AA and the cognitive behavioural model aspire to comprehensive coverage of all alcohol problems. Each explaining either disability in terms of dependence (AA), or dependence in terms of disability (cognitive/behavioural). (NB. The results of my study also suggest that the AA approach can be as useful for those who have disabilities as for those who are physically addicted, though the diagnostic procedures used by staff working with the Minnesota Model involve identifying dependency in terms of the symptoms of disability.)

This is not a simple case of confusion about definition. The disease model adherents view the addiction as the **primary** disease which **causes** the disabilities, and would not therefore be able (within their conceptual framework) to separate or distinguish between the two.

The problem of deciding whether dependency has caused certain disabilities or whether certain disabilities had led to and aggravated dependency is not peculiar to Edwards. It seems very difficult, if not impossible, to discover simple objective criteria for assessing this, for professionals and clients alike. This difficulty seems inherent in the phenomenon itself. There is no doubt that there is a correlation between severe dependency and disability, but which causal direction is attributed depends on the initial theoretical structure and beliefs of the observer. An observer believing in the disease model would be more likely to define disabilities as a sign of dependence, whereas a psychiatrist or a psychologist may be more inclined to define dependence as a sign of underlying disabilities.

This situation explains to some extent the confusion of both professionals and clients themselves. The two opposing interpretations tend to divide professionals into two camps, and though they may accept that behavioural techniques do not work at the extreme end of the severity of dependence scale, there is little else on which they will be likely to agree. This seems to be because the underlying beliefs of each camp determine at least to some extent how they **interpret** evidence. Edwards' suggestion that the problem can be solved simply by an accurate assessment with clear distinctions between dependencies and disabilities seems intellectually mistaken.

Although empirical data can be used to test and disprove particular assumptions, the difficulty remains that an abstract, tautologous theory does not produce testable hypotheses and such is the theory underlying the Centre's approach. A review of outcome research on controlled drinking, where behavioural hypotheses can be tested in an objective fashion, demonstrates that these techniques are effective in changing drinking behaviour. This does not however prove that other therapeutic techniques are ineffective or less effective. Demonstrating that a phenomenon can be analyzed in behavioural terms does not undermine the validity of other therapeutic methods.

This problem is often overcome by conceiving of different models of alcohol treatment as a continuum. Sanchez-Craig (1986), states that 'Controlled drinking programmes, which include the option of aiming for abstinence should be offered to problem drinkers.' There is usually little discussion of the theoretical implications of such a pragmatic solution.

These are however the conclusions reached by the main professional protagonists in the field of addiction in Britain today. For example, psychologists, whose approach is summarized in a report from the British Psychological Association *Psychological Aspects of Alcohol* (1987); and secondly psychiatrists, whose approach is explained in several reports by the

Special Committee of the Royal College of Psychiatrists, but perhaps best summarized in *Alcohol, Our Favourite Drug* (1986). Both reports focus on the usefulness of cognitive behavioural techniques with less seriously addicted drinkers, citing the work of behavioural researchers to demonstrate that brief early interventions work very well. Neither report criticizes the limitations of this research.

The Royal College of Psychiatrists in the 1986 Report argues the necessity for the development of a range of services to provide an 'optimum pattern of services'. It recommends a balance of specialist and generalist primary level services, stating that, 'The creation of a cadre of specialists of sufficient size to respond directly to most alcohol-related problems is clearly uneconomic and undesirable.....The trend has therefore been towards ensuring that the care-givers who make first contact have the skills and knowledge to enable them to respond effectively to problem drinkers and their families. In some cases this intervention will be sufficient but others will require specialist support or consultation. Such a strategy implies a local support network of adequately trained specialists.'(p.163) The Royal College also suggests the appointment of a specialist consultant psychiatrist in drugs and alcohol problems. The report is essentially recommending a service which would function on two levels. Firstly, providing a service for the population which either experience minor problems or are seen to be developing serious alcohol problems and secondly dealing with those individuals who have developed serious physical and psychological addictions.

In effect, psychiatrists are perhaps shifting the focus of intervention from psychiatric treatment by defining the problem as less serious and therefore more appropriate for psychological methods. Unfortunately the Royal College do not attempt to define differences between minor problems, major problems and addiction, nor do they offer any theoretical base for their recommendations. The Report does not explain why a consultant psychiatrist should be employed, nor does it clarify what the psychiatrist or the 'adequately trained specialists' would actually do. That is, with which methods and which theories of addiction they would work. It is implicitly assumed that this is generally agreed and understood.

Despite their limitations these recommendations are often reflected in local policy documents. For example the Health Education Advisory Committee for Wales, in its final Report before being disbanded in 1987 *Dealing with Alcohol Problems in Wales*, draws similar conclusions to those of the Royal College of Psychiatrists. This Committee bases these conclusions on the same papers cited by the Royal College (Babor et al., 1985 and Chick et al., 1985), and consequently makes similar recommendations based on the results of the early intervention studies. 'The core concept ... should be that excessive alcohol consumption can be influenced at an early stage by primary care workers.' HEAC, 1987 (26.5).

The cognitive/behavioural approach

It is interesting then that an 'early intervention' policy in Britain appears to be developing as a response to these and other recent research documents. In effect, the reports of The Royal College of Psychiatrists' and the Welsh H.E.A.C. provide suggestions for development of services based on the cognitive behavioural psychological approach, but do little to clarify issues concerning theory and method on which their recommendations are based.

The psychological approach is expounded in more detail by a group of specialist psychologists in a report prepared by the Parliamentary Group of the Standing Committee on Communications, *Psychological Aspects of Alcohol*. Based on the work of six leading psychologists in the field, it was published by the British Psychological Society in January 1987. The basic premise underlying this approach is clearly stated and not unexpected, 'It is a great mistake to regard excessive drinking as a purely medical problem.' The authors then proceed to clarify their position regarding the medical model of addiction, something the Royal College of Psychiatrists had not done. 'Problem drinking obviously has many medical aspects but, in the attempt to change harmful drinking behaviour, the disease theory of alcoholism has been found to be unhelpful and a hindrance to progress in the field.' (p.3) Unfortunately the evidence for this basic premise is not included, leaving the reader in the tautologous position of defining addiction in terms of behaviour and consequently concluding that non behavioural models are largely irrelevant. Interpreted in this way, the implications for alcohol treatment can be seen as very different to those of the disease model and the subject area clearly becomes the remit of behavioural or cognitive/ behavioural psychologists.

The advantage of placing the phenomenon of drinking disorders within the context of Social Learning Theory and cognitive/ behavioural methods is however that they are empirically testable. Thus if the maladaptive behaviour is not changed after 'treatment' in a controlled setting, then the chosen method can be shown to be of no use in dealing with the phenomenon in question. A great deal of research has now been completed in this area which sheds some light, not only on the effectiveness of behavioural techniques in dealing with behavioural disorders, but also on the usefulness of defining alcohol problems and dependency in behavioural terms.

The Psychologists' report defines the psychological approach to addiction as a 'common set of principles (used) to relate the abnormal, harmful use of alcohol to its normal harm-free use.' The authors of the report state that 'drinking problems and alcohol dependence are seen as lying on a continuum, rather than being divided into unhelpful either/or categories.' The issues raised in the report are dealt with in more detail in a special edition of the *British Journal of Addiction* (vol. 82, no.4. 1987). There seems little doubt from the accumulated evidence that psychology has a good deal to offer in the field of addiction.

However, the critics of this approach would suggest that while psychological Social Learning theories and methods of treatment are useful in dealing with psychological dependencies, they have not yet been shown to be effective in serious cases of combined physiological and psychological dependency.

Social Learning theory is a general theory offering an explanation of behaviour formation and maintenance. It assumes that behaviour can be either positively or negatively reinforced and that the sooner the reinforcement occurs the more effective it will be. (Therefore short term positive reinforcement could be seen to outweigh long term negative reinforcement.) The development of behavioural habits can also be influenced by 'modelling' and other social factors such as the need to conform. (Bandura, 1977; Bergin and Garfield, 1971; Bolles, 1979; Catania and Harnad, 1988.)

Most contemporary behavioural psychologists also include a cognitive element in both their theory and practice. The way a person defines or interprets their experience is considered to have a strong influence on their behaviour. (Beck, 1976; Ellis, 1962, 1987; Kelly, 1955; Orford, 1977.) The rationale for developing these cognitive behavioural methods for use with alcohol problems is summarised in the report by the Parliamentary Group (op.cit.). Cognitive processes are now considered influential in both loss of control and relapse (Goldman, Brown and Christiansen, 1987). Cognitive findings are also reviewed by Marlatt (1978) who illustrates the influence of expectation and social cues in loss of control and relapse.

The influence of cognitive psychology is also demonstrated in the work of Orford, Heather, Stockwell, Hodgson and Robertson. Their work on the psychological interpretation of alcohol problems and dependency has to a greater or lesser extent adapted psychology to the particular problems of alcohol. These theories, while developed from rather generalized theories of behaviour, have integrated this with a cognitive approach to encompass the phenomenon of addiction as a subject in its own right. Perhaps the most clinically useful of these approaches is Marlatt's theory of Relapse Prevention. One of the most comprehensive is that of Orford, *Excessive Appetites - A Psychological View of Addictions* (1985). He develops a theory of the addictive process, taking into account biological influences and ideas of restraint, (the counter balancing of incentive and disincentive) and considering the social issue of moral conflict between deviant excess and conforming moderation. He develops this theory within the context of the Social Learning paradigm, but provides a comprehensive and coherent alternative model to that of the 'Addictive Disease', rather than simply interpreting addiction in behavioural terms and advocating general behavioural techniques.

However, cognitive psychology has drawn criticism from within the medical field in a way that behavioural psychology did not. This is simply because cognitive psychology does not allow for observation and measurement. The emphasis on subjective interpretation places this specialism within the phenomenological methodologies rather than with the positivist behavioural sciences. (Despite the attempts of George Kelly to quantify and measure personality in terms of cognitive constructs.)

So while the behavioural approach can be criticized because of the limitations of its theoretical base, cognitive psychology can be criticized for its lack of scientific testing. If behavioural psychologists argue for the scientific status of behavioural psychology, they cannot logically incorporate cognitive psychology within their theory and practice. Yet both Learning Theory and Social Learning Theory do not encompass issues of physiology, nor take account of cognitive processes.

An example of these limitations can be seen when interactions between physiological and cognitive variables appear to influence 'loss of control' and relapse. From the medical perspective, one of the problems inherent in the notion of simply utilizing behavioural techniques is that alcohol has both short and long term physiological effects.

It can, for example be demonstrated that physiological factors influence the significance of psychological expectancy factors. Research with subjects who are physically dependent demonstrates that they respond to the alcoholic content in drinks, whereas the response of less dependent subjects is determined mainly by their beliefs and expectancies about drinking. The effect of an initial drink on a severely dependent subject's craving to drink further is not merely the result of cues, beliefs and rationalization; it occurs without the drinker being aware that he has consumed alcohol. It has been demonstrated that there is a statistically significant increase in craving three hours after a 'primary dose'. (Hodgson and Stockwell op.cit.) The authors state that it is possible to explain this using the behavioural model, but only if it is possible to find out what pattern of reinforcement history differentiates the severely dependent from the less dependent drinker. Hodgson and Stockwell continue, 'Such a learning experience involves a set of discriminative stimuli and also a powerful reinforcer so that, after hundreds of repetitions, the severely dependent alcoholic will tend to experience a compulsion to drink when exposed to the cognitive and physiological cues associated with stopping drinking.' (ibid.) They suggest that this altered physiological state is a component of craving but only for seriously dependent alcoholics for whom it has become a discriminative stimulus. (ibid.). For less serious alcoholics this physiological state is seen only as a component of craving when the alcoholic believes he has consumed alcohol.

A positivist framework allows demonstration of these data, but the results are of course open to different interpretations. So, for the psychologists, physiological factors are interpreted as playing a more significant role amongst heavy drinkers, but have less importance among lighter drinkers. However for AA members, the data would illustrate something different. Here the interpretation would be that physiological factors are significant for those people who are alcoholics but not others.

Marlatt et al., (1973) came to different conclusions when they carried out a similar experiment in order to test whether people addicted to alcohol lose control of their drinking (A premise integral to the disease theory and opposed to the cognitive behavioural approach). They found no difference between 'alcoholics' and social drinkers in alcohol consumption based on the actual primer of drink (physiological stimuli), but found increases based on expectation.

There is therefore conflicting evidence regarding the interaction of physiological or behavioural factors and subjective expectations and cognitions. It is impossible to research these interactions 'scientifically' because subjective interpretation is not observable. Much research is based on apparently positivist methodology, examining observed behavioural and physiological changes, however, this work often invokes both cognitive processes and the notion of craving which cannot be measured in the same way. Craving is not as yet defined in physiological or behavioural terms, instead often involving vague cognitive and emotional concepts far removed from any scientific approach. Research into the concept of craving has been severely restricted due to methodological problems (Tiffany and Drobes, 1991 and Tiffany et al., 1994), but the concept remains a dominant one in the field due to its clinical usefulness.

It is clear that it is necessary to include concepts not accessible to scientific measurement in understanding and working with alcohol problems. Although it may be possible to deal with less serious cases of psychological dependency within a behavioural framework (ie. using methods derived from Social Learning theory), it seems likely that more serious cases involve understanding of both physiological and cognitive variables.

An academic review of the significance of behavioural theories of addiction is available in an article by D.M.Gorman, and a series of responses to his paper. (*British Journal of Addiction,* vol. 84, 1989). Gorman states in his paper that Heather and Robertson claim 'problem drinking' as a new model representing a shift from a 'pre-scientific' to a scientific paradigm within alcohol studies. They see the old disease model as tautologous and not facilitating the testing of hypotheses. Gorman himself suggests that the 'problem drinking' model of the psychologists incorporates a set of assumptions parallel to those of the disease model and so does not represent the type of change in paradigm that they suggest; 'The definition assumes that learning is the cause of all drinking behaviour, and as such, there will never be a case of problem drinking (nor of non-problem drinking) which is not learned behaviour. Like its disease model counterpart, such a model is tautological.... (therefore) the concept defined by Heather and Robertson does not allow a true test of such a hypothesis....as it is fatally flawed by its built-in assumptions about aetiological processes.' He concludes that Heather and Robertson are merely taking one aetiological explanation for granted and dismissing all consideration of any others. (p. 845).

Gorman quotes from a paper by G. Edwards (1985), in which Edwards distinguishes between two interpretations of this 'paradigm change': first Kuhn's notion of paradigm shift and second the perceived conflict between professions for dominance in a field of knowledge. Gorman concludes that 'Heather and Robertson's proposed new problem drinking approach is best understood in terms of the latter.' (p.845). This criticism is interesting as it resembles the situation in the late 19th Century when the medical profession first defined addiction as a medical problem and therefore part of their professional remit. In this instance, Gorman is accusing the behavioural psychologists of a similar misdemeanour motivated by professional power seeking.

Sociological interpretations of professional power are not of course limited to professional infighting. The success of the behavioural sciences in the research field could simply be the tremendous emphasis on measurable variables, due to the dominance of positivist paradigms. Alternatively, in political terms the data derived from the behavioural sciences could allow a conception of individual responsibility at one with contemporary political ideology. Social interpretations provide rationales for the existence of certain theories, so they can be used for the AA model as well as the behavioural model. It has been suggested that the disease model of addiction, revitalized by the Alcoholics Anonymous movement, was accepted for humane and practical reasons rather than its theoretical credibility. 'The promulgation of the disease concepts of alcoholism has been brought about essentially as a means of getting a better deal for the alcoholic rather than as a logical consequence of scholarly work and scientific discoveries.' (Room, 1972). These analyses of social determinants of theory development clarify how opposing models of addiction can co-exist but do not assist in the academic debate.

Instead, clarification and understanding of the limitations of different methodologies are more useful. As Gorman himself points out, academic difficulties arise when the distinction between classification (description) and aetiology (explanation) are blurred and confused. He concludes that the 'field of alcohol studies' has not yet reached the stage where a 'sophisticated understanding of causes has been reached' and he therefore considers it dangerous for the psychologists to make assumptions about aetiological processes when constructing descriptive models. This argument reflects the idea that the field of alcohol studies has not reached the scientific stage of its development and should not therefore function as if it were a science. The implications are that attempting scientific research methods may be less appropriate than descriptive methods based on phenomenological methodologies.

Heather replies to these criticisms by firstly agreeing with Gorman 'that the basic proposition that problem drinking results from learning processes is, in itself, difficult to test'. He insists, however that the learning paradigm is more useful because 'it relates the study of problem drinking to a much wider body of knowledge.' (op.cit., p.847). He does not give any evidence to suggest why it is theoretically appropriate to use learning theory to interpret the phenomenon of addiction. Heather also objects to Gorman's use of Kuhn, stating that for the latter, 'a paradigm change is precisely constituted by social and political conflict among scientists'. It would perhaps be more accurate to say that this was considered only one of the aspects of paradigm change, but it is interesting that Heather considers it a sufficient condition.

Robertson also contributes to the debate by reiterating that 'The disease model has singularly failed to generate useful hypotheses leading to effective treatment and management of drink problems because of failure to generate equally specific hypotheses.' (to those of the learning paradigm). This statement is an appropriate criticism, though it would be more accurate to say that the disease model has not produced testable hypotheses. The inability to produce experimentally testable hypotheses within a positivist framework does not of course preclude the ability to form hypotheses and gather data within structured theoretical frameworks.

The knowledge derived from qualitative data collected by AA members allows interpretations of the individual change process. It does not however allow general predictive conclusions and this is a serious disadvantage as the hypotheses can not then be tested. The behavioural sciences can derive predictive knowledge from quantitative data and formulate testable hypotheses. However it is very difficult to construct abstract theory from specific testable hypotheses, which can later be generalised to encompass many different phenomena (or applied to situations that differ from the conditions under which they were initially tested). Much of the research underlying the learning and social learning paradigms involved testing hypotheses that were not specifically concerned with problem drinking. It might therefore be considered less than appropriate to apply this 'wider body of knowledge' directly to a variety of phenomena which are outside its usual territory.

Behavioural science, has therefore been criticized for attempting to be scientific in a field not its own. The appropriateness of behavioural interpretations and research methodologies have been questioned. These criticisms have not been levelled by proponents of Alcoholics Anonymous, nor by academic researchers but largely by medical and psychiatric practitioners. It is suggested that the practice of medicine is not perhaps so entrenched in scientific methodology as research in this field.

For example, the discussion above is concluded with a letter from Edwards, one of the foremost psychiatrists in the field. He argues that there was no obvious old paradigm to displace in the alcohol field and that no new one has emerged. He argues forcibly that alcohol studies should remain an area where no one discipline dominates, but where 'great varieties of hypothesis, conjectures, models and theories' can operate. This final remark aptly illustrates the general attitude of many eclectic practitioners in the field (and also their clients), who do not seem unduly concerned with the inherent theoretical contradictions involved in using more than one approach.

Opposition to the theories of behavioural psychologists illustrates that the 'scientific' data obtained by controlled studies of human behaviour is not necessarily acceptable to the medical community of clinicians. It is possible that, while scientific data are useful to researchers, in the area of clinical practice itself the quantitative data of the positivist social sciences is less useful than the qualitative data derived from individual case studies. As much clinical knowledge is built on the accumulated information of casework experience, many clinicians may come to view both diagnosis and treatment as professional crafts, dependent on qualitative data concerning process and interpretation, rather than scientific procedures.

This difference between the preferred knowledge base of researchers and practitioners is probably best illustrated by a recent phenomenon in the addictions field, that of 'motivational interviewing' and the related idea of 'stages of change'. Methods of interviewing and counselling in the field were developed in the late eighties utilizing notions of individual change processes, apparently in the absence of any coherent theory or testable hypotheses.

The popularity of these methods among practitioners spread rapidly in the early part of the 1990's. These ideas were popularised and now form a base for specialist and non-specialist training in Britain (See Aquarius, 'Managing Drink') and counselling techniques themselves (Robinson, Rollnick and MacEwan, 1991).

Many academics were unable to explain the popularity of this unproven method. However its relevance to practitioners can be easily understood in terms of the importance of individual differences and individual change processes to clinicians. Data concerning individual change process cannot be gained using positivist methods, therefore scientifically orientated research can do little to provide the practitioner with guidance for work with individual clients. The motivational interviewing method offered a means of integrating notions of long term individual change with more general theories of aetiology and treatment.

The notion of the importance of individual change processes was publicised by Prochaska 'Systems of Psychotherapy: A Transtheoretical Perspective' (1979). He then worked with DiClemente to develop the idea of Transtheoretical Therapy. (Prochaska and DiClemente, 1982.) and in 1983 in they produced their much quoted paper 'Stages and Processes of self-change of smoking: Toward an integrated model of change.'

This work was paralleled by W.R. Miller's development of the concept of motivational interviewing. Both concepts were based on ideas about change processes and stages of change. Miller's work was published in *Behavioural Psychotherapy* in 1983 and again (with Sovereign and Krege) in 1987.

The ideas of change process and motivational interviewing have been subject to criticism on the grounds that they have no underpinning theory and that they are not testable (See *British Journal of Addiction* letters and articles 1992/93). Academics from the psychological and medical fields have expressed surprise at the widespread popularity of the approach amongst practitioners. It is therefore interesting to examine the enthusiasm for clinical methods not accessible to positivist based research.

Individual change process and subjective interpretation are the subject area of the phenomenological methodologies, using qualitative methods. It is not possible to measure either process or interpretation in positivist terms. Both the medical and behavioural disciplines are based on explanatory theories developed from experimental research designs. It is difficult for these disciplines to integrate notions of qualitative data for interpretative theory, as Nick Heather illustrates in a rather ambivalent introduction to an edited collection of papers (Robinson et al., 1991). He states that the idea of change processes is of 'limited explanatory value but its descriptive value is high' and that it is 'an elegant heuristic device', rather than a model or theory.

It can perhaps be suggested that the limitations of positivist research are more apparent to practitioners than academics and in order to study areas of interest to practitioners it may be necessary to utilize methods derived from phenomenology rather than positivism. This issue is of particular importance in this study, as the focus is on the need to study individual subjective interpretations of the therapeutic change process.

This gap between a medical or therapeutic approach and the notion of an experimentally proven reality is perhaps best illustrated by Griffith Edwards' argument that the established methods of individual case study have been neglected in this field, 'To introduce into scientific debate the unvalidated retrospection of one selected drinker might be viewed as unusual or even out of order. It could on the contrary be argued that the scientist should be willing to return again and again to exactly such material.' (1990, p.448.)

This decline of the importance of the 'clinical reality' can perhaps be correlated with a similar reduction in the importance of case study data for research purposes. As data collection became more 'scientific', individual change processes and client interpretation became less important as they could not be measured or researched in a 'scientific' way.

Edwards continues, 'One might speculate on the possible impact of changes in the relationship between the world of clinical authority and the high ground of scientific authority.' (ibid., p.451). So as Edwards laments the absence of clinical data, the phenomenologist perhaps voices the same complaint in different language about research data. However, although the complaint may be the same, (that most of the research in the field in undertaken within the narrow confines of the medical and behavioural sciences), these two disciplines have little else in common. Though both approaches are interested in understanding individuals as separate entities, there are important differences between the old clinical case study methods of doctors and psychiatrists and those of the phenomenologists. The phenomenological issues are discussed more fully in Chapter Four, but it is necessary to stress that medicine is firmly grounded in research terms within a positivist, not a phenomenological reality.

The notion of accurate diagnosis in medicine and mental health is extremely significant in predicting outcome for particular treatments. The data needed for predictive purposes are dependent on definition of causal relationships. This kind of information cannot be derived from qualitative data, but is derived from single case design experiments. (That is attempts to control variables in order to compare one individual at different time periods.) Although it is not possible to generalize widely from this type of study, attention can be focused on individual differences, which are often excluded from experimental research.

A criticism which both clinicians and phenomenologists level at positivist research in the field is the lack of information about individual differences. This has resulted in a dearth of outcome studies indicating overall success of particular approaches, but giving no indication of which approach might work best for which client.

It is not necessary to look far for an interpretation of this situation. It is possible that sociological and public health measures, together with behavioural approaches to addiction have undermined the importance of individual differences in assessment and treatment. This is particularly true of the Public Health or Health Promotion approach to the problems of alcohol, drugs and HIV. Where prevention, early intervention and harm reduction become the aims of educational programmes, the aetiology of addiction is of little interest. 'Understanding' the problem becomes unimportant, as it becomes necessary only to 'do something about it'. Statistical survey research demonstrates whether or not 'something has been done about it'. Survey research offers statistical analysis of correlations between variables in a rough duplication of the experimental method. But rather than identifying and isolating important variables in order to develop explanatory theories, researchers simply concentrate on the incidence of misuse in the population as a whole.

However it is clear that these differences in research methodology lead to each discipline focusing on different aspects of the phenomenon to the virtual exclusion of others.It should also be mentioned that though researchers may focus on what is methodologically and theoretically fashionable, many contemporary practitioners in the field of addictions would profess to work in an 'eclectic' way, using methods derived from various theories.

It is possible to use cognitive and behavioural methods irrespective of the theoretical interpretation of the problem. Within the field of addiction, as in the field of psychotherapy generally, the actual methods used by different types of therapist are often similar, though the interpretations may be diverse. For example, the practice of the Minnesota Method could be seen as involving a large cognitive/behavioural element. To some extent, any therapeutic technique can be seen to involve cognitive and behavioural elements in terms of restructuring cognitions and reinforcing behaviours. Likewise, any 'behavioural' technique can also be seen to incorporate other therapeutic elements, resulting from a therapeutic relationship with a 'powerful, helping' figure. An analysis of similarities and differences between the Minnesota approach and other therapies later in the book attempts to isolate different aspects of the therapeutic process, and to clarify the alternative interpretations.

It is probable that eclectic psychotherapy is at least as effective as any one specialist type (See Chapter Seven). However, the fact that clinicians can combine methods does not mean that it is possible to combine theories under one umbrella paradigm, as has been attempted in the research field. The proposed 'biopsychosocial' solution to the theoretical controversy will be examined later. It should be mentioned here, however, that the problems highlighted in the study of dependence and addiction seem to reflect the age old controversies between biological, psychological and social approaches. It seems unlikely then that these basically conflicting paradigms and their attendant research methodologies can be at last reconciled and united in the field of addictions, simply by labelling an eclectic approach as 'biopsychosocial'.

Different theories of addiction can be seen to be inadequate in some respects. They do not offer an overarching or comprehensive interpretation or explanation of this 'multi-faceted' phenomenon. Yet both the disease and the behavioural approaches offer effective methods for dealing with alcohol related problems for some people. The conflict between disciplines has been analyzed in terms of conflicting methodologies, the positivist approach emerging as the clear winner at present. Consequently most of the research in the field is seen as undertaken within the confines of the medical and behavioural sciences. The established research methods therefore ignore the data relevant to process and interpretation and consequently also the methodology and expertise of Alcoholics Anonymous. As might be expected, AA members themselves consider positivist data irrelevant and that the theories obscure the importance of individual differences and stages in the recovery process. It is perhaps more surprising that medical/psychological clinicians find the quantitative data of the positivist social sciences less useful than the qualitative data derived from individual case-studies.

Edwards (1977) is perhaps one of the most respected critics of the disease model, arguing against the notion of total loss of control and the unitary concept itself, yet he points out 'in the very recent past the received wisdom was exactly the opposite of what we accept today.' (Edwards, 1989) He reminds us that in the 19th and early 20th centuries withdrawal symptoms were recognised as a clinical reality and continues 'At some point in the first half of the 20th Century, clinical awareness of withdrawal phenomena faded.... an inspection of a few contemporary texts certainly suggests that over the decades the dependence potential of alcohol was generally downplayed.' (ibid., 1989, p.449).

Edwards attempts to examine the reasons why the questions of the physiology of alcoholism (neuroadaption, tolerance and withdrawal) are considered 'redundant' today. He laments the absence of 'The full history of the way in which medicine and science have regarded alcohol withdrawal symptoms.' He describes the rise of medical or 'disease' theories in America in the 1950's, quoting the work of Victor and Adams (1953) describing the time course and clinical spectrum of alcohol withdrawal and the WHO report of 1955, comparing alcohol withdrawal symptoms to those of opiate withdrawal and suggesting a common syndrome.

Edwards considers that things changed after the war when the newer theories 'of the founding fathers of post-war alcoholism' stressed that 'tolerance and withdrawal were matters only very peripheral to the view of alcoholism which they were at that time developing.'(ibid., p.450). The work of Jellinek (see below) was in direct contrast to this, defining particular types of 'alcoholism' as diseases, and consequently withdrawal symptoms and tolerance as among the most significant factors in the study of alcohol.

Edwards sums up, 'How is the ebb and flow to be explained? Without making harsh judgements from the privileged position of hindsight, how is the ability of experts to forget or deny what was known earlier to many shrewd practitioners to be explained?' He adds that, 'One might speculate on the possible impact of changes in the relationship between the world of clinical authority and the high ground of scientific authority.' (ibid., p.451), but draws no general conclusions, except strongly to emphasise the importance of 'Clinical experience', even though it 'is a notoriously unreliable arbiter on complicated issues'.

The above critique of contemporary approaches to addiction gives some idea of the criticisms of the psychological approach, but also gives an idea of the level of exposure and acceptance of this approach. Criticism has been largely directed at the main areas of contemporary consensus, namely psychological interpretation and positivist research methodology. This is not due to any inbuilt bias, but a desire to balance the usefulness of positivist behavioural studies with alternative methods and research methodologies.

The AA and Minnesota approaches

There is a general belief among many lay people (and some professionals) that Alcoholics Anonymous is a very successful organization in combating alcoholism. However there is very little research available to substantiate these beliefs. The work of the AA General Service Board Survey of members in the United States and Canada concludes that the service is effective (Robinson, 1979). However, the work of an outsider, Bebbington (1976), indicates that no such conclusion can be drawn. A recent survey of Alcoholics Anonymous in Great Britain was carried out by the General Service Board of Alcoholics Anonymous (1986). Prior to this a survey was carried out in 1981 also by the General Service Board (1982). These reports gives a favourable impression, stating that in 1986 there were 2,176 groups in Britain. (3,904 members, fifty percent of all groups, returned questionnaires)

The survey work is interesting and indicates that large numbers of people have derived benefit from the help offered. Unfortunately there is little information concerning those people who do not succeed either in remaining abstinent or in continuing to attend groups.

The survey research also gives little indication of the theory and methods employed in the helping process, nor any indication of which people can be considered potential clients. That is, exactly who is an 'Alcoholic' and who is likely to benefit is unclear.

The use of the Minnesota model is widespread in treatment services in both Britain and America. Although studies carried out would seem to indicate that a third to half of clients appear to benefit from this approach, there is little research carried out independently.

As with the monitoring of Alcoholics Anonymous, most of the evaluative studies are produced by adherents or clinicians working with this model. However the Minnesota Method does lend itself to more structured outcome studies. Spizer and Barnett (1980) have produced work for the Hazelden Foundation (The source of most Minnesota literature); and Rossi, Stach and Bradley (1963) have conducted a study of the effectiveness of the methods. These studies suggest 45 per cent success or 'effectiveness', but as Cook (1988b), points out, their work has a number of methodological flaws. Similarly, Laundergan (1982) carried out a follow-up study of discharges over a two-year period. However, the sample of clients who responded to questionnaires was not necessarily representative of the population leaving treatment and, as with other similar studies, the sample of clients who drop out of treatment (especially at an early stage) was not considered in any detail. These two methodological flaws are not uncommon in the evaluative research. The implications of the flaws for this research are discussed in some detail in Cook 'The Minnesota Model in the Management of Drug and Alcohol Dependency'(1988b) and Gilmore 'Hazelden Primary Residential Treatment Programme'(n.d.).

Laundergan's work, in spite of its weaknesses, provides some interesting data, such as the results of a residential Minnesota Programme in America shown below.

Table 2.1
Outcome at one year after treatment for patients discharged from Hazelden between June 1, 1973 and December 31, 1975

Patients	N	Abstinent	Improved	Not improved
Responding	1,899	50%	17.6%	32.4%
Completing treatment	1,598	50.9%	18.3%	30.8%
All discharges	3,638	37.8%	9.2%	53.1%

Quoted in Cook (1988a)

Although this type of outcome research is useful, information is seldom available concerning the seriousness of the problems prior to treatment. Although screening instruments are being developed at present (eg. the SADQ used in the study and the World Health Organisation instrument AUDIT), much early research did not use standardized measures of problem. The disease models are based on the premise that only a certain proportion of the population are prone to the disease and these people can be identified for treatment before any serious alcohol problems or dependency is manifested. This has serious implications for assessment and treatment of alcoholism dividing disease model adherents and those who do not accept the notion of disease in terms of the type of criteria they use to assess the problem. LeFevre (Minnesota school) estimates that only ten percent of the population are vulnerable to alcoholism and suggests that it is possible to tackle the problem before it fully manifests itself, 'Alcoholics who still had everything began to recognise their alcoholism. ... they were joined by young people who were scarcely more than potential alcoholics.' (LeFevre). This suggests that some of the differences between academics and professionals can be traced back to differences in measurement and assessment respectively, of the phenomenon of 'alcoholism'. So differences in theoretical conception can lead to researchers measuring different variables and clinicians treating symptoms. There are clear implications for comparison studies.

Critical studies of the disease theory and AA

Despite difficulties in problem definition, interesting empirical data can be derived from information about consumption alone. A major criticism of the disease model and AA is derived from population studies. While it should be remembered that the behavioural models suffer from a lack of epidemiological data, it is possible to argue that studies of general population alcohol consumption distributions indicate that these are normal (unimodal) distributions. (See for example, De Lint, 1969). There is therefore clearly not a small minority of the population with severe problems, as the disease model would suggest, but a fairly even distribution of dependency across the general population. This statistical information is not, however, relevant to individual drinking careers, as Edwards (1989) points out:- 'Static data cannot reveal whether there is a small sub-population at the upper end of the seemingly smooth unimodal curve, characterised by "through-time" (dynamic) likelihood of continuing to drink very heavily.' (p.151) It is likely that drinkers fluctuate during their drinking careers. (Clark,1976.)

However, there is much data to substantiate the claim that controlled drinking is possible. Critics would argue that this shows that the disease concept is untenable and the AA treatment aim of abstinence unnecessary. Studies by Davies (1962) and Litman (1977) indicate that clinically diagnosed alcoholics may either return to normal drinking or show great malleability of drinking behaviour in response to experimental manipulation of cues or rewards. Although there has been more empirical evidence recently to substantiate these views, (Orford, 1985, Babor, Ritson and Hodgson, 1986, Heather and Robinson, 1986, Sanchez-Craig, 1986, Donovan and Marlatt, 1988 and Edwards, 1986b and 1988.), the difficulties of defining the problem of addiction or dependency itself remain.

The evidence from population studies and controlled drinking studies undermines to a large extent previously held views concerning a disease concept of alcoholism that underlies AA. These data are open to an AA interpretation, for example population studies could be seen as reflecting fluctuations in the disease as 'alcoholics' pass through stages of 'recovery' and 'relapse': similarly, the controlled drinking studies could be regarded as reflecting a wider definition of dependency than alcoholism. However, there is no doubt that these data seriously undermine conceptions of alcoholism underlying AA. They do not, however, explain why the AA treatment programme is so popular or so successful with some people.

The aetiology of spiritual disease does not fit well with the evidence of drinking behaviours or population distributions, however the therapeutic technique is useful for some people with drinking problems. If the AA interpretation of the problem and its treatment is inaccurate, this begs the question, what is happening at AA and during Minnesota treatment and why does is the programme effective with some people ?

There is little doubt now that cognitive behavioural methods can be used to change drinking behaviour irrespective of the cause, but the professional world perhaps find it more difficult to accept that this may also be the case for the AA programme.

It is therefore important to separate out research and theories based on population studies and the phenomenon of alcohol dependency itself, and focus instead on the treatment methods available. It then necessary to determine which therapies are useful for whom.

There are several problems inherent in contemporary outcome research. Firstly the relevance of the concept of outcome itself has been questioned. As Edwards states, it is difficult to determine the appropriateness of outcome measures generally for evaluation of therapeutic processes. Evidence suggests that a person's drinking fluctuates a good deal over the course of their lifetime and to record this process at any one point may be misleading. (Edwards, 1991, 1992).

If outcome is accepted as a reliable measure of future drinking, there are difficulties involved in determining which measures of outcome are appropriate. Data from alcohol treatment studies are often flawed and difficult to compare due to less than standardised procedures (Lindstrom, 1992). However studies reflect the findings of general psychotherapeutic studies, in that few differences can be identified across therapies.

Although retrospective studies have been conducted to compare treatment programmes, prospective studies involving initial random allocation of subjects to services have only recently been undertaken, the most notable being the 'MATCH' study in America and a similar project in Australia. It is unlikely that random allocation of clients to services will illustrate how effective any one model will be for appropriate clients, until the interaction between individual differences and treatment process is examined. (See Chapter Eight.)

There has therefore been a change in focus in the alcohol field as in the psychotherapeutic profession, from working out which method is best, to attempting to determine which treatment is best for which client.

For this type of research to progress it becomes necessary to have a clear understanding of each model. Largely because the research methods and means of communication of AA are so different, the adherents of the disease model in Britain do not have a great deal of access to the professional journals. Consequently detailed knowledge of AA methods is lacking.

In contrast to the psychological and medical literature much of the Anonymous Fellowship literature does not identify an author and is produced in pamphlet form for members and clients. AA is concerned to convince or convert members rather than to justify and substantiate the theory and methods for a professional population. Not only do the established professions tend to ignore AA methodology and expertise, but AA members themselves consider behavioural and medical theories misplaced and disruptive and professional skills less than necessary, if at all appropriate, to the problem with which they are dealing. It is therefore necessary to rely to some extent on recorded conversations and unpublished or anonymous documents, when presenting the view point of the disease model advocates. For this reason although a brief review of research and criticism is presented below, the following chapter examines AA in more detail using qualitative and descriptive accounts of members themselves.

It will become clear that the disease model used by the Anonymous Fellowship and the Centre in the study has by no means received either the exposure or acceptance in the field in Britain as have psychological theories. It is will therefore be necessary to examine a more thorough critique of this particular approach in this study.

To some extent the disease model of addiction has indirectly received support from this research, in that the increasing emphasis in the field on the importance of process and the possible significance of individual differences reflect age old beliefs of the AA Fellowship and the disease model.

The historical context of theory development has been discussed earlier, illustrating the melding of spiritual and medical models to produce the notion of 'spiritual disease' central to AA. The idea of alcoholism as a disease without spiritual elements was also more common in the USA when this conception of addiction received formal respectability through the work of Jellinek, popular in the 1950s and 1960s. AA advocates were reassured to find that much of Jellinek's work fitted with the AA concept of addiction. His work was therefore assimilated by both AA and Minnesota. For example Max Glatt (1972) developed material based on Jellinek's work that could be used within AA treatment programmes. Jellinek is therefore often understood as providing the evidence for AA. This is not the case, as although Jellinek categorized some forms of alcohol problems as diseases, he stressed that there were many different kinds of alcohol problem which did not fit into these categories. However Jellinek's notion of the 'Gamma' form of alcoholism became most influential in the field, together with the idea that alcoholism was a unitary disease. These concepts reinforced and maintained AA, but the success of AA itself also helped; it is the mutually reinforcing elements of Jellinek's work and AA that are of interest as it is these that kept the disease model alive.

To some extent the disease theory of alcoholism was maintained because the AA methods were seen to be effective for some people; if the therapy worked, people assumed the theory was 'right'. This process was of course reversed for academics; when the theory was shown to be wrong, they assumed that the AA methods did not work.

As the notion of alcohol dependence as a unitary disease is increasingly questioned by both the psychiatric profession and the behavioural psychologists, Jellinek's theory and AA therapy have become less influential and are seldom referenced in contemporary British journals. As Lindstrom (1992) points out, 'Jellinek's working hypothesis had a salutary effect on alcohol research. Today many researchers regard it as a principal obstacle to the advancement of knowledge and the emergence of interdisciplinary approaches to alcoholism.'(p.54)

This is unfortunate as Jellinek had identified important aspects of alcohol dependency and treatment which are have been largely ignored in Britain. He focused on the sequential aetiology of the disease and the importance of individual differences. He stressed the 'need to establish criteria for the suitability of any given method to a given patient, stating that the 'criteria so far established are superficial.' (Jellinek, 1941 quoted in Lindstrom, 1992, p. 3).

In the same way the therapeutic methods of AA have been overlooked, particularly the emphasis on initial client attitudes and beliefs and the stages of recovery. However, in the past few years there has been revived interest in both the process of treatment and recovery (Prochaska and DiClemente, 1983, 1986. Miller, 1986) and the importance of individual differences in treatment (See Chapter Eight). As a consequence some of Jellinek's earlier work has been revived, for example his ideas about different individual types may receive a higher profile again, but so little is known of the AA recovery process that no connection has yet been made between this older work and the new ' Stages of Change ' model of Miller and Prochaska and DiClemente.

Although Jellinek's model of a progressive disease is often criticized, his work is useful in underlining the limitations of a behavioural analysis which ignores physiological aspects of the phenomenon. It is often forgotten that Jellinek (1960) made the first attempt to construct a theory integrating biological, psychological and social aspects of alcoholism. (Genetic vulnerability, physiological addiction, personality characteristics and cultural factors). However these aspects of Jellinek's work are less relevant to Alcoholics Anonymous and therefore will not be discussed further. For an exposition of this author's work see Jellinek, (1946, 1957, 1960).

Jellinek has then been much criticized in the past few decades. This is reflected in the criticism of both AA and Minnesota. Perhaps it is not surprising that an integral part of the development of psychological theories of dependency has been a concentrated attack on the 'disease' model of Alcoholics Anonymous. Nick Heather and Ian Robertson are two of the main proponents of this attack, (1981 and 1986). They see the disease theory as a serious threat to the development of a psychological 'controlled drinking' approach. 'Most influential disease formulations demand abstinence due to the central feature of irreversibility in the theories. The feature has great practical significance for society's response, in that it undermines a "controlled drinking" approach.' (ibid., 1981). It is interesting that Heather and Robinson suggest that the disease theory is problematic because it is disruptive rather than because it is inherently unsound.

Unfortunately the Anonymous Fellowship have not contributed much to the debates in academic journals. However, in response to the initial criticism by Heather and Robertson, it is not difficult to frame a reply from them. Many individuals have commented that they consider that their opponents' theory and methods are undermining their own attempt to control addiction, by colluding with clients in their denial and therefore actively encouraging the development of the disease. (See Chapters Five and Six).

One of the most vocal critics of the spiritual disease model in the past few years is an American where, in contrast to Britain, the general consensus is that the disease model is the correct way to conceptualise and treat alcoholism. As a consequence the critic, H. Fingarette, and the publication

Heavy Drinking, The Myth of Alcoholism as a Disease, (1988), evoked an angry and emotional reaction from the American public. This is hardly surprising, as Fingarette introduces the book by stating that, 'Almost everything that the American public believes to be the scientific truth about alcoholics is false.' (p.1). He continues, explaining that scientific 'facts' concerning alcoholism are often treated as heresy, 'More than once when I have lectured about the scientific facts about alcohol abuse, I've been told by listeners "Though these things may be true, you should not spread the word because it will shake peoples' faith in a useful lie", but hiding our heads in the sand or repeating folkloric formulas certainly is not the best we can do, as individuals or as a society, to respond to the personal, medical, social, and economic problems of alcohol abuse.' (p.28).

Before continuing it should be pointed out that Fingarette's faith in science and 'scientific facts' is probably partly due to his own background as a lawyer unfamiliar with academic notions of knowledge. It is by no means shared by any of the different factions in the academic and professional disciplines. Sociological and philosophical theories of knowledge have established only that theories can be disproved rather than transmuted into proven 'facts'(Kuhn 1962); and that several of these theories can be used concurrently though the basic premises of each may be in contradiction.

Fingarette's work is however of interest as it illustrates not only the widely held belief in the disease model in contemporary America but also the way in which opposition to the model is seen in terms of scientific knowledge invalidating more subjective or interpretive kinds. Fingarette argues that positivist knowledge derived from scientific experiments is the only proper study of man. He criticizes the use of concepts such as 'loss of control' and 'craving', (used in the disease interpretation of addiction) as inappropriate as they are not measurable in any scientific manner.

The use of these terms is also widespread in Britain and attempts have been made to define and describe what clients understand and describe as loss of control and craving. It does however seem to be difficult to do this in positivist or behavioural terms (Tiffany and Drobes, 1991). Fingarette, although accurate in his criticism of the lack of clarity in the use of these terms, does not offer alternatives. If these terms are discarded it would be difficult for the clinician or the client to interpret and communicate; this giving perhaps an indication of why clinicians may be more dependent than academics on phenomenological data and interpretive theories.

Although Fingarette has not developed a sophisticated critique of the disease model he has however illustrated the lack of consensus and strength of feeling in the field of addiction. He quotes from a monograph published by the National Institute on Drug Misuse (1980), 'A selection of specially interesting theories (sic.) - forty three of them.' He continues 'The temptation to doubt that the theories could all be wrong must be balanced by the thought that, however plausible they seem, at least most of them must be wrong. After all, how many true explanations can there be?' (p.50). Although this level of argument has no academic credibility and would be dismissed by the very 'scientists' that Fingarette himself appeals to, it serves as an illustration of how the old fashioned notion of science is often raised in opposition, not only to the disease theory, but also to the idea that more than one treatment can be useful in the same field.

While Fingarette has achieved a certain notoriety in contemporary America, his views were put more succinctly by an earlier American critic of Alcoholics Anonymous, recorded in the *American Evening Post,* 1965 (quoted in Kurtz, pp. 143/144). 'AA has become a dogmatic cult whose chapters too often turn sobriety into slavery to AA. Because of its narrow outlook, Alcoholics Anonymous prevents thousands from ever being cured. Moreover AA has retarded scientific research into one of America's serious health problems.'; (Cain, 1961, see also Cain, 1964). This remark, together with Fingarette's commentary perhaps best illustrate the response of those who do not want to mix their 'pure scientific facts' with any other 'less scientific' kind of knowledge, whether it be phenomenological or spiritual.

There is no doubt that both Fingarette and others are right to be concerned about the limitations of the AA model. Much of this chapter has been critical of the territorial constraints of scientific methodologies and cognitive behavioural interpretations. The last word has therefore been given to critics of AA in order to emphasize that both parties are guilty of the same crime. This book is largely concerned with Britain, where the consensus favours the cognitive behavioural approach to the detriment of AA, but the converse is clearly true for America where cognitive behavioural theories have not been developed in research or treatment due to the dominance of AA and Minnesota.

It can be seen that opposition to AA is often based on misconceptions of science and psychotherapy. Rather than a theory being seen as a useful addition to a range of psychotherapeutic models, it is seen as a block to the search for the absolute scientific 'truth'. Similarly criticism of the behavioural approach in America may be founded on misunderstanding of the interpretative nature of theory and its various uses. Perhaps it is necessary to educate the public about both the advantages and the limitations of scientific endeavour.

Although Alcoholics Anonymous has received little exposure in Britain, either good or bad, criticisms are directed largely at its lack of 'scientific proof'. The basic proposition of this study is that not only are the theories and treatment methods of AA different to statutory service provision, but that the research methodologies of AA and psychologists/ psychiatrists are inherently different. This is not seen as an advantage or disadvantage, but an indication that both the usefulness of theory and the usefulness of the methodology itself require further examination.

It is suggested that the proponents of both AA and cognitive behavioural psychology are self limiting, as each ignores aspects of alcohol treatment which could be effective, so depriving the field of wider research and treatment options. This chapter has emphasized the need to look further than cognitive behavioural theories and to use a greater range of methodologies than those of positivist science. However, it is not suggesting that a disease model and a phenomenological methodology will be a better option, simply that they will increase the range of alternatives for both research and treatment.

3 Alcoholics Anonymous and the Minnesota Method

Alcoholics Anonymous

Alcoholics Anonymous is one of five self help groups within the 'Anonymous Fellowship' based on a model of spiritual disease. The other four groups are: Alanon (for families of alcoholics); Alateen (for the teenage children of alcoholics); Narcotics Anonymous (for drug addicts); and Families Anonymous (for the families of drug addicts). Alcoholics Anonymous is, however, by far the largest and has a longer history (founded in 1935); the other Anonymous Fellowships developing more recently as offshoots from the original Fellowship.

The AA approach is in direct conflict with conventional medical, psychological and sociological concepts of alcoholism in Britain and shares instead the concepts of early 20th Century models of spiritual disease. But despite its opposition to British establishment views, the Anonymous Fellowship has established a widespread network of self help groups and residential rehabilitation centres in Britain today.

The views of many British statutory specialists in addiction differ to various degrees but the majority share one thing in common, they feel strongly that the disease model of addiction developed at the turn of the Century is 'wrong'. Contemporary professional consensus in Britain, in common with the public health campaigners at the end of the 19th Century, argues against any moral or disease model of addiction.

In contrast, in America the 'spiritual disease' model and the Minnesota Method derived from it, provide the dominant theory and method. Although the approach is most prominent in the Northern states of America and in the alcohol rather than drugs field, it is clear that professional respectability is conferred on the model there, whereas the opposite is the case in Britain. (Sanchez-Craig, 1990, Fingarette, 1989).

As discussed earlier, the theory underlying AA and the Minnesota Method are often poorly understood by outsiders who have not actually gone through the process of 'working the programme'. However the publications of those who have been through the programme are often uncritical.

Therefore it is necessary to give a straightforward description of the philosophy and methods of AA and Minnesota before examining the importance of process and interpretation.

Research methodology and understanding AA

The folklore of AA will be described in this section. Knowledge and understanding within AA itself are derived from individual case histories. Much of AA literature consists of life stories of particular individuals, reflecting the therapeutic process itself which involves individuals relating their own life stories to each other.

As a research method, this descriptive form of case study serves an illustrative purpose, examining subjective interpretations and individual change processes. For AA members themselves this type of case study gives them information about others' experiences and interpretations. In effect AA itself utilizes case studies and ethnography as part of its underlying methodology. This type of data is therefore readily available to those attempting to understand AA in terms of both its theoretical methodology and therapeutic practice.

So subjective interpretation and the stages of change are important for researcher and AA member alike, though the former will retain distance from the data, whereas the members themselves will learn experientially in the tradition of dynamic psychotherapy.The methodological issues underlying this study are discussed in the following chapter, but it is important to highlight the relevance of qualitative data and subjective interpretation at this stage.

Alcoholics Anonymous: philosophy and method

The disease or more specifically, the 'spiritual disease' model is encapsulated in the philosophy and methods of the Alcoholics Anonymous and Narcotics Anonymous groups in Britain and America, and has been integrated into what is now called the 'Minnesota Method' of therapy.

The basic ideas underlying the disease model have been discussed in the previous chapter (Jellinek, 1946a,b, 1957, 1960). However, although the AA model of spiritual disease and the disease model of Jellinek have much in common, the disease model did not incorporate the spiritual and moral components of AA. Although Jellinek accepted the usefulness of the AA model, he did not wholeheartedly endorse it. He rather saw it as a temporary stage in developing a comprehensive approach to addiction. However much of his work was utilized by those in AA to give the approach professional credibility. Although AA may have utilized the work of Jellinek for this purpose, it is probable that it is not Jellinek, but AA itself, that is responsible for the maintenance of the disease model of addiction throughout the 20th Century.

Chapter One has given some indication of how the idea of addiction as a spiritual disease developed from notions of a material soul in conjunction with medical notions of addiction.

The Chapter also shows how it became established within the context of the general professional and cultural changes at the turn of the century. The following section will examine the historical development of Alcoholics Anonymous and the 'Anonymous Fellowship' from its beginnings in America in the 1930s.

A plain description of the AA programme in the words of its followers

The following descriptions are based largely on accounts of AA given by members themselves, including the AA textbook *Alcoholics Anonymous* and the accompanying *Little Red Book,* together with examples gathered by Kurtz (*'Not God': A History of Alcoholics Anonymous*) and Denzin (1987 a,b,c).

Individual stories as case studies

The individual life stories which make up much of the AA literature give the reader a partial experience of the first stage of the programme itself. It is in this way that new members are often recruited, by the simple procedure of an established member relating his or her own story and explaining to the new recruit or 'pigeon', how this could apply to him/her.

The story of Rowland H

The earliest example of an individual story or case study, cited by members of AA is that of 'Rowland, H.' a patient of Carl Jung. The story teller often relates how Jung had failed to treat Rowland's alcoholism and had emphasized the importance of spiritual components of therapeutic change. He had advised Rowland to seek 'A spiritual or religious experience - in short a genuine conversion.' Rowland H. followed this advice and joined an evangelical movement, the Oxford Group. This sect emphasized the importance of self-survey, confession, restitution and 'the giving of oneself in service to others' (E. Kurtz). While attending this group Rowland H.

had a conversion experience and was cured of his alcoholism.

This case history is an integral part of the folk lore of AA and can be seen to illustrate the perceived importance of spiritual conversion. This story and the following one are also part of a longer narrative recounting the development of the AA philosophy, illustrating how particular ideas were developed and integrated in the formation of the AA programme.

Bill's story

Probably the most famous and most quoted story in the annals of AA is that of its founder, Bill Wilson. His own case history will be described in some detail as it again illustrates not only the 'process of recovery' for a particular individual, but also demonstrates how the basic theory underlying AA was developed. The story of Bill has been passed from person to person largely by word of mouth. The following account is therefore unlikely to accord with all versions, but is taken from Kurtz's comprehensive description and from interviews with AA members themselves.

It should be remembered that although this story is about the development of AA itself, events are interpreted in terms of the finished AA philosophy. In common with all AA members' stories it is a re-writing of history using Alcoholics Anonymous theory to interpret events.

The story starts here; Bill was an alcoholic. His problem was his inability to accept this fact. It is his friends who first notice his problem as he is blind to it himself. His old friends, Ebby and Shep C. had themselves become religious and had as a consequence given up alcohol. They had trouble convincing Bill of the advantages of this change as Bill saw religion as anti intellectual. Bill valued his intelligence above his sobriety and at first he was not prepared to sacrifice it. He writes that his two friends were 'now asking me to give up the one attribute of which I was most proud - my inquiring rational mind. And they wanted me to give this up for illusion.' As a consequence of not surrendering his intellectual faculties at this stage Bill continued to drink excessively and ended in hospital.

While he was in hospital Bill read William James's *Varieties of Religious Experience* (1958). It had a tremendous influence on him and before leaving hospital he had his first religious experience.

After this Bill began to see more clearly. He accepted that not only was Jung right, in that a religious experience was a necessary part of the cure, but that James's emphasis on the importance of the prior condition of hopelessness and despair was also significant.

Many of the ideas Bill developed at this stage came from discussions with his doctor. Dr. Silkworth thought of alcoholism as 'a compulsion, a pathological craving, a disease. An obsession of the mind that condemns one to drink, and an allergy of the body that condemns one to die.' However, as Kurtz points out, he later changed his views, considering 'recovery as possible only on a moral basis' and stating that 'unless (the alcoholic) can experience an entire psychic change there is very little hope of his recovery.'

Bill's ideas developed along similar lines to those of Dr. Silkworth and the notions both of allergy and moral recovery were established. Bill then added a further condition to recovery, developed again from his own experience. He believed that he needed to work with other alcoholics in order to maintain his own recovery so he started to try to help others. Initially he failed and then as time passed he himself came close to relapse. He became convinced that he 'needed another alcoholic'.

He managed, luckily, to find one and immediately told his story to this man. He then said 'I needed you, probably a lot more than you'll ever need me. So, thanks for hearing me out. I know now that I'm not going to take a drink'.

The story ends at various points depending on the story teller, but it usually includes the following discoveries:- the need for various stages in the recovery process; the need to 'hit rock bottom' in terms of despair; to experience a spiritual conversion; to develop a belief in the moral and physical aspects of the disease; and finally to help others to recover.

The concepts of helplessness and despair, spiritual conversion, moral development and helping others that Bill integrated into the early AA philosophy are all clearly derived from a religious base. The history of Alcoholics Anonymous emphasizes the influence of these basic Christian principles.

The history of the programme

Following 'Bill's' personal progression through the stages of change and the 'discovery' of the foundational beliefs, the AA programme developed slowly over the next 10-15 years. Initially it closely resembled the Oxford Group, a religious group based on early Christian principles, in that small group discussions took place in informal settings and the process of individual change was emphasized, members working at changing their lives through a sequence of stages. The Oxford group stages consisted of the five C's - 'Confidence, Confession, Conviction, Conversion and Continuance'. The early procedures of AA were based to some extent on these principles:-

(1) Give to God
(2) Listen to God's directions
(3) Check guidance

(4) Restitution
(5) Sharing: a) 'sharing for witness' (narration of how one's life had changed)
b) 'sharing for confession' (to soothe guilt).

Eventually, these small social groups developed into formal 'meetings' to which new clients could be brought after they had 'made surrender'. These meetings are referred to by Kurtz as a 'crash-course socialization'. (p.56).

By 1937 the AA programme had began to take shape, and new members were recruited. Recruitment involved both personal story telling and reinterpretation of new members' circumstances. New members would be taught that they had a spiritual disease, were at 'rock bottom' and that they should surrender themselves to God and AA. As the groups became established the basic beliefs were developed into clear cut stages of change. These stages became established in the textbooks *Alcoholics Anonymous*, the *Little Red Book* and in many leaflets produced by the Minnesota Press and AA. The stages became a framework for all AA groups, residential treatment facilities and the local Centre examined in this study. Although both Minnesota programmes and this Centre modified the methods of imparting the AA knowledge or philosophy, the basic beliefs remain the same across all programmes. It is these beliefs that will be outlined below with reference to the main AA textbooks and to staff accounts from the Centre. Slight alterations in methods used in the Centre are discussed in more detail in Chapter Five, but the basic stages or steps to recovery utilised in 'working the programme' at the Centre are outlined below.

The centre study

Although the Centre examined in this study followed the theory and therapeutic methods of AA, it was not a self help service, but a day centre staffed by salaried workers and supported by central government and local health authority funding to provide a service for people with alcohol problems in a particular area.

AA itself is a voluntary self help organization and believes that all members should attend purely on a voluntary basis. Nobody is involved in a professional capacity, and the degree of involvement of each member is entirely up to them. AA does not work within a structured environment and offers no external discipline or restraint. AA members who feel that they need structure and professional support do however attend agencies such as the Centre, and various residential rehabilitation centres (for example, Broadway Lodge and Weston Counselling Services in S.W. England).

The Centre is concerned only with the first five steps of the Alcoholics

Anonymous twelve step programme; these stages are worked through under the supervision of Centre staff. The Centre differed from AA self help groups in that staff were more directive than AA members, giving clients work to do on the first five steps and teaching concepts they may not understand. The following seven steps are then completed with local AA self help groups, all twelve steps being considered necessary to recovery. This is similar to structured residential treatment centres in both Britain and America, many simply working on the first few steps, in order that clients are then ready to attend AA self help groups to complete the programme.

Success in treatment is thought to be related to the great emphasis placed on the need for continuing maintenance therapy through ongoing involvement with Alcoholics Anonymous over average periods of five or six years.'Attendance at such groups helps to maintain healthy thought processes in the patient and reinforces the need for continuing positive changes, thereby safeguarding against relapse.' (Minnesota Press Pamphlet)

Working the programme: the twelve steps

The textbooks and AA leaflets used in this section outline the basic stages of the Alcoholics Anonymous programme and give personal accounts in the words of AA members themselves. These books and pamphlets were available to all clients at the Centre. Many of the texts in AA and Minnesota literature are anonymous accounts of the steps and are presented as if from a group of AA members, in the first person plural. This style illustrates the involvement and experience of the writers and has not been changed here.

Beginning the treatment process

Step One

Step One is probably the most significant part of the programme. The essence of the Step is that clients should believe or accept that they are an alcoholic or an addict and that they are powerless over their lives as a result. (i.e. Admit that their lives are unmanageable). If clients do not accept this interpretation of their experience the treatment programme cannot proceed. This stage is often referred to as 'breaking denial'(Centre staff comment). This first step is perhaps the most significant to this study, as the beliefs of clients in the initiation stages of treatment were of particular relevance to later attitudes and behaviour. This stage is therefore examined in some detail.

Step One refers to 'the foundation of recovery' and involves members coming to an understanding of their own powerlessness. The authors state, 'We admitted we were powerless over alcohol and that our lives had become unmanageable.' The pamphlet examines the experience of AA members when they first encountered the programme and the 'new knowledge'. 'Reluctance to examine our powerlessness is as much a symptom of our illness as liver damage, withdrawal, or digestive disorder. Social pressures centred around the myth that "willpower is all that is needed to control a drinking or drug problem" can result in unwillingness to study our powerlessness.'

This emphasis on acceptance of personal powerlessness can be seen to be an integral part of the notion of alcoholism as a disease and an essential starting point for the programme. 'As we develop a thorough understanding of alcoholism... we will not be ashamed to admit that we are powerless over it, just as we would be powerless over any other disease. We will also learn that we will not be able to adapt our lives to the disease of alcoholism unless we have a thorough, ongoing program of recovery in the same way that a diabetic or heart patient has an ongoing program to keep the disease in check.'

However the notion of disease and powerlessness is also linked to the notion of responsibility for one's own recovery. This may appear to be paradoxical, but is explained within the AA philosophy in the following way; 'Personal responsibility for alcoholism occurs when we have recognized it in ourself, or others have pointed out the symptoms to us, and we realize we are afflicted with a disease. It then becomes our responsibility to start a recovery programme.'

Step One then integrates the concept of unmanageability with the notion of powerlessness. 'Personal unmanageability relates to our attitudes and beliefs....In many cases, personal unmanageability was present many years before chemical addiction.' 'The A.A. philosophy is that putting the cork in the bottle is not enough. We need to rejuvenate our personalities. We have to learn about ourselves on an intimate level. We have to discover what the A.A. programme calls our character defects and shortcomings in order to accept ourselves as human beings with strong and weak points just like everyone else.'

The concepts of powerlessness and unmanageability are linked to the idea of an 'alcoholic personality' which can only be controlled through adherence to the programme and abstinence. 'There are some character weaknesses that chemically dependent people do seem to have in common. One is self-centredness. This defect has to be present in each of us for our disease to prosper. Selfishness seems to need a direct assault to break our denial system and rebuild trust in and concern for other people. Another area of common personal unmanageability is the basic immaturity that seems to be prevalent among chemically dependent people. Immaturity may not be obvious. A person may be able to function very well when sober, but the least amount of agitation or disruption of the normal pattern will cause extreme reaction. Overreacting is definitely immature. Some other examples are temper tantrums, not sharing feelings and emotions honestly with others, insisting on having one's own way and the like. Such behaviour patterns enlarge and gradually take over a large part of one's personality.'

These principles of Alcoholics Anonymous are evoked early on in the Centre's programme. Clients are asked to consider personal examples of their own powerlessness and unmanageability, to write these down and discuss them both with their Centre Counsellor and in their therapeutic group.

Step Two. Hope

This step involves recognizing and 'coming to hope' that one has the need to and ability to change, with the help of the programme and more importantly with the help of a 'higher power' or 'power outside of oneself'. This step was a necessary follow up to acceptance of powerlessness, as without hope and faith in outside help, little progress could have been made. In effect the first step in isolation could be worse than useless.

Many clients at the Centre found difficulty accepting the notion of a higher power (especially if they had been atheist or had non Christian religious beliefs). However some solved this problem by defining their higher power as being the Anonymous Fellowship itself, or their therapeutic groups, that is, without recourse to ideas of a spiritual God.

Step Three. Commitment to change

This step involves not only making a commitment to change, but also 'handing yourself over to others in the programmes, that is, learning to trust others.' This stage involves an effort on the part of the client to stop 'controlling or manipulating others,' that is, relinquishing control over both him/her self and over others. The idea of 'getting out of the driving seat' is also an important part of this process. This aspect of the programme was emphasised by the Centre Director. His statement that the process involves 'sacrificing your individuality to the group, and receiving back their interest in you', sums up this stage accurately.

Step Four. The moral inventory

This stage involves the client writing a list of his/her previous character or personality defects prior to treatment. This list is referred to as a 'searching moral inventory'.

Step Five. Confession

This stage involves sharing this 'moral inventory' with, or telling, someone else. This is often referred to as the 'confessional' step. The benefits felt by clients are often described as very similar to religious practices.

The final steps (six to twelve) do not form part of the treatment programme at the Centre. They are part of the continued experience of all those who complete the programme successfully. The twelve steps can be split into two stages, the first five steps concerned mainly with changing or converting the client; the last seven steps concerned with maintaining this change or conversion. The programme of treatment is not therefore complete without the second stage, (or AA equivalent of relapse prevention).

Step Six involves emphasizing the willingness to change and to have the higher power remove defects.

Step Seven involves putting the initial commitments into action.

Step Eight involves becoming willing to make amends to people one has harmed.

Step Nine involves actually making amends, as far as this is practicable.

Step Ten involves learning to take a personal moral inventory on a regular basis, that is, continually monitoring and evaluating what happens in one's life, admitting when one is wrong and changing if necessary.

Step Eleven involves building and improving on faith, and improving one's relationship with one's higher power.

Step Twelve. The final step is considered of extreme importance (see Director's comments and 'Bill's story'), as it involves helping others, consistently reminding oneself of how bad one was, and reminding oneself of the principles of the programme by teaching them to other alcoholics or addicts. 'Twelfth Stepping' is thought to give members 'a purpose, an identity and self-respect' and is seen as an integral part of recovery and sobriety.

It can be seen from this description of the structure of the programme that a range of therapeutic and 'spiritual' processes are involved. It appears to be important that a client fully understands and accepts each stage in turn before progressing to the following stage in the sequence. Problems are likely to occur if a client does not fully participate in any one part.

The role of the counsellors at the Centre was to ensure that clients had assimilated the ideas of AA at each stage, each counsellor 'guiding' the client through the first five steps in a way that was less likely to occur at Anonymous meetings. The client was asked to read the relevant literature and write down his/her understanding of the ideas and discuss the ideas with the counsellor. In this way the counsellor could assess whether the client has firstly understood and secondly accepted (believes) the new ways of looking at themselves. The Director of the Centre emphasized that these two processes which he defined as 'intellectual understanding' and 'faith', were distinct and that each in isolation was a necessary but not sufficient condition of change.

The Centre groups and Alcoholics Anonymous groups in effect reinforced a new set of beliefs and interpretations. A new client or AA member would often be advised to stay away from old friends or acquaintances if they drink or use drugs and to develop instead a new social life around AA meetings. Many successful clients would continue to socialize mainly with other AA or NA members, their social environment as a whole acting as a reinforcer of the new beliefs. The programme at the Centre was seen by staff as likely to be effective only when the client attended regular AA meetings and kept in close contact with their AA sponsor; clients would therefore usually be asked to leave if they did not attend AA meetings.

Finally staff also advised that a client's spouse or family should attend the relevant Anonymous Fellowship groups (Alanon, Families Anonymous and Alateen), where the 'programme of recovery' is very similar. Though an addictive substance is not involved, the family will work through the same steps and so acquire the same beliefs and attitudes.

Basic beliefs

It can be seen from the description of the programme that the basic premise underlying AA is that the 'alcoholic' is not normal, but that he/she suffers from an illness of the whole person. The client him/her self is seen as an alcoholic, rather than a person who has an alcoholic disease. The alcoholic is seen as having three characteristics; a physical allergy to alcohol, an 'alcoholic personality' (described as immature and self-centred) and a spiritual sickness. The distinguishing feature of the AA disease model is the idea that the disease of alcoholism is the primary cause of all secondary problems or 'symptoms'.

The alcoholic disease model can be applied to various kinds of individual 'disfunction' or excessive behaviour, from drugs to sex and love. The model of addiction can be applied to families who live with addicts. The recommendations made to an individual client; i.e. to attend regular meetings of the Anonymous Fellowship, to read regularly the approved literature of that Fellowship and to work the twelve steps for recovery suggested by the Fellowship, are therefore recommended to all family members. In this way a client involved in the treatment programme can in effect be surrounded by both family and social groups that concur with the basic beliefs of the programme. This tends to happen with 'successful' clients, who socialize more and more with AA or NA members, rely a good deal on their AA/NA sponsor and try to get their families involved in similar groups. It is important to emphasize that although the important treatment element seems to be the process of individual change (of cognitions, behaviour, emotional response) it takes place within a social context which reinforces and maintains this change as well as playing an active part in its initiation.

A spiritual programme?

Alcoholics Anonymous members would describe AA as bridging 'medicine' and 'religion'. This belief which probably grew out of late 19th Century Quaker notions of the 'material soul' has been discussed previously. The idea of an incurable disease with spiritual ramifications fitted well with the concept of the hopelessness of the condition of alcoholism. This was then followed logically by the notion that 'deflation' arose from perception of this hopelessness and so if one had reached 'rock bottom' there must therefore be something else 'higher' to aim for. Here lies the essence of the spiritual content of the programme and the concept of a conversion from alcoholism to a total life-style termed 'sobriety'. If drink (a malevolent power) has proved itself to be stronger than the individual, it is not such a leap of faith to believe in a benevolent power stronger than the individual.

Bill Wilson, the founder of AA, had suggested that alcoholism itself has a spiritual component and he found this idea reflected in the work of Jung and also of Aldous Huxley. For example Huxley described drink as 'the poor man's spiritualism', and 'Jung portrays the drinker as one who is seeking a spiritual release through alcohol'. (quoted from letters of Bill Wilson). AA members themselves consistently note that successful affiliation with AA depends upon the capacity of the individual to experience 'a conversion with its attendant emotional components'.

However not all AA members see the programme as inherently spiritual. Kurtz concludes from his study that the basis of AA is 'not God', but the acceptance by the member that he/she is an alcoholic, 'essentially limited, but able to find a healing wholeness in the acceptance of this limitation.'(p.4)

However he also points out that 'sobriety' is seen as the AA equivalent of the 'classic religious salvation or 'justification of faith.' (p.183). In the same vein, R. Jones (1965) in a paper entitled 'Sectarian Characteristics of Alcoholics Anonymous' states that 88 per cent of AA members interviewed in research admitted to some kind of 'conversion'. Other authors have described AA in religious terms, for example: 'A socio-religious group' (Ritchie, 1948); 'The emerging church of the twenty-first century' (Mowrer, 1961); and finally Gellman (1964) described AA as 'a formal organization of a group of worshippers who share a common and defined set of beliefs and rituals.'

Contemporary opinions differ as to the significance of the spiritual aspects of AA. There is however no doubt that the basis of AA in the early phases had much in common with Christianity and the founders of AA felt the importance of the spiritual element in the conversion process.

There are clearly problems in attempting to integrate ideas of spirituality into the dominant paradigms of the natural sciences, psychiatry and psychology. These difficulties are highlighted both in the previous chapter concerning contemporary treatment controversies and in the following chapter on methodology. Many professionals and laymen alike do not accept the underlying spirituality of AA and object to the anti-professionalism and anti-intellectualism involved in the approach.

Minnesota: treatment philosophy and method

The Centre treatment programme is based largely on AA, and the Minnesota model of therapy is seen as an extension of the AA philosophy and method. This section will briefly outline the Minnesota approach and illustrate how it links with AA.

LeFevre is a prominent representative of the Minnesota Model in America and Britain and is highly regarded by adherents of this approach. His book *How to Combat Alcoholism and Addictions; The Promis Handbook on Alcoholism, Addictions and Recovery* (ND), is utilised to provide the basis for the following examination, together with information from a booklet concerning the practice of the Minnesota method, *The Minnesota Experience* (Anderson, 1981).

Anderson states that the fundamental consensus between those involved in the development of the Minnesota programme was that 'alcoholism is a complex, multi-phasic, usually progressive, chronic illness - a primary pathological process.'

Lefevre sums up the essentials of the five steps used in the Minnesota Model and his interpretation of the essential steps illustrates the fit with the steps of Alcoholics Anonymous.

Firstly he identifies the essence of AA in Step One. 'The essential process of Step One is surrender: the recognition that one is beaten, that one's own perceptions of reality are inappropriate and that one's life has become unmanageable.' Step Two is seen as taking away the 'false self-reliance' and leading the client to 'come to believe that a power greater than ourselves could restore us to sanity.' The Minnesota model does however allow flexibility with regard to the spiritual aspects of AA. 'To expect a sudden conversion to spiritual belief, is to expect too much and it is fortunately completely unnecessary. The group itself is commonly adopted as the "Higher Power".'

Step Three involves a logical progression from Steps One and Two, to make 'a decision to turn our will and our lives over to God as we understood him' and Step Four involves 'a searching and fearless moral inventory of ourselves'. Step Five involves telling someone else these wrongs.

These five steps are obviously closely related to those of AA. Minnesota Treatment Centres (in common with the local Centre) will direct the client through these first five stages, the client then leaves the treatment project and works through the final eight steps in Alcoholics Anonymous self-help groups, under the guidance of a sponsor.

It can be seen that the basic assumptions of the Minnesota model outlined by LeFevre are very similar to those of AA. A disease of the spirit leads to a disorder of mood, which in turn leads to excessive use of chemical substances. This usually causes inappropriate behaviour and problems and therefore further disorder of mood. LeFevre concludes that 'The process of recovery involves the gradual reversal of all the processes of the disease. As in the AA Fellowship, alcoholism is seen as a primary illness and this concept of addiction is considered relevant to all substance misuse, gambling, dependent relationships and some forms of behaviour. The common criteria used to identify an 'addictive disease' are defined as: Any behaviour that is used inappropriately and compulsively to suppress uncomfortable emotions to change a disordered mood or to which someone repeatedly returns despite negative consequences can be defined as a form of addictive disease. (p.43)

There are no data given to indicate the extent of the problem but LeFevre estimates that 'Chemical dependency appears to affect approximately ten per cent of the population, though there are cultural variations.' Addictive disease is assumed to 'originate as a disease of the human spirit', and 'this pre-disposition may be genetically determined'. LeFevre defines the disease in a slightly convoluted way, but basically conforms to the beliefs of AA itself, stating that this disease of the spirit 'leads to a disorder of mood' and 'affects intellectual processes.' These people may then discover specific substances or behaviours which trigger the underlying addictive potential so that they come to be used inappropriately and compulsively. (pp.45-7)

Having discussed the similarities between the Minnesota Method and Alcoholics Anonymous, it should be noted that there are differences, the most obvious being that the Minnesota Method has led to the formation of therapeutic communities, whereas AA has not.

This difference can perhaps be best explained in terms of different responses to a common problem. The disadvantage that both the Minnesota Method and the AA philosophy share is the difficulty of providing continuing social support and reinforcement of treatment ideology in the outside world, where belief systems may diverge radically from those of AA. This problem is compounded in Britain by the divergence of AA philosophy from conventional psychiatric and psychological opinion.

The adherents of the Minnesota Method decided to tackle this problem differently to AA. AA continued to provide a wide network of free self help groups that required no professional involvement or statutory support. These support networks included provision of daily meetings and a system of sponsorship which gave any one member access to another on a 24 hour basis. The group meetings often provided the starting point for other social activities among AA members themselves, so a supportive social environment could be constructed independently of non-AA influences.

Supporters of the Minnesota Method saw the answer in terms of closed therapeutic communities; 'the challenge was to develop control over the total treatment environment in which alcoholics lived'. The rationale was that 'if the alcoholic had to learn to live with and cope with a chronic condition that would never go away' what was needed was 'a separate community for the chemically dependent patient.' 'What emerged (from the development of therapeutic communities) was the concept of a completely structured and disciplined environment utilizing a number of meaningful patient activities intended to produce positive behavioural changes.' It was felt preferable to keep the programme short (60 days) and therefore necessary that 'it must be intensive to produce rapid change'. (Anderson, 1981)

Apologists for the Minnesota Model and the AA philosophy believe that intensive involvement is necessary for people to work through the programme successfully. For example, AA members are often advised to attend at least two or three meetings a week, and sometimes to attend 'sixty meetings in sixty days'. (See Centre data).

To sum up, the ideology and treatment process of the Minnesota Method and Alcoholics Anonymous are easily integrated but these concepts can be translated into practice in different ways. Although the Centre fully embraced the philosophy and ideology of both AA and Minnesota it did not attempt to reproduce the self help format of the former nor the residential community concept of the latter. Instead it attempted to combine the advantages of both AA and Minnesota in a day centre with a structured programme of regular weekly day-long sessions.

The accounts of the AA and Minnesota programmes in this chapter have deliberately been given in the words of the adherents themselves, as to rely only on outsiders' interpretations and outcome data would be likely to produce a distorted picture of any ideology or process. These insider accounts have been placed within an historical and academic context. It is now necessary to place this type of data within the methodological context of the research study.

Part Two
A STUDY OF CLIENT THEORIES OF ALCOHOL PROBLEMS

4 Research design and the case study: Methodological issues

The previous chapters of this book provide a critique of popular and professional beliefs about 'addiction', analyzing the methodology and professional paradigms utilised to interpret this phenomenon. This critique allows for the categorization and contrast of beliefs of clients and therapists and the formation of a research hypothesis examining the influence of subjective beliefs about 'addiction' among all the participants in a particular treatment centre.

Contemporary methods derived from positivist methodologies are seen as limited, as the influence of possible variables such as individual beliefs cannot be examined within this scientific framework. However, although phenomenological interpretation is useful for understanding, qualitative methods derived from this methodology are not appropriate for assessing outcome. The aim of the study is therefore to illustrate that qualitative data are necessary though not sufficient for a full understanding of the interaction of individual differences and treatment process.

The second part of this book explores the conclusions derived from the review of theories and methodologies with a case study of a particular treatment centre. The study explores why different therapies can be effective and why contradictory theories can exist side by side in the field of addiction. In order to understand how conflicting theories can coexist it is necessary to examine the difference between the kind of methodology and knowledge informing each. The previous chapters indicate that the AA approach is based on different methodological assumptions to that of other models in this field. This review led to a consideration of methodological questions about the relevance of subjective interpretation involved in the empirical research. This present work was initially designed to examine the theory and treatment process of Alcoholics Anonymous as it took place in a Treatment Centre. It became apparent early on that these methodological research issues were reflected in the AA theory and practice itself. The positivist methodologies of medical and behavioural research could be seen to be inherently different to those of the adherents of the Treatment Centre methods and Alcoholics Anonymous. Therefore it should come as no surprise that their observations and conclusions are different.

The AA approach emphasized the central importance of the AA ideology or theory and the belief or faith of clients. The literature is based on the use of case studies (or life stories) as theoretical building blocks and as therapeutic tools. So AA can be seen to be utilizing the equivalent of academic phenomenological methods in the development of both its theory and practice. As the subjective interpretations of clients were so important to the Centre staff and AA members it seemed inadequate to exclude them from an evaluation of their service. It therefore seemed appropriate to use phenomenological methods in order to assess the subjective interpretation and also in order to examine AA in its own terms, that is using the methodology on which, in effect, this model itself is based.

If these factors were to be studied, qualitative data would be needed for analyzing the main research questions. However, if these data were to be understood as influential variables in the treatment process, they would need to be examined within the context of positivist analysis. This led to more general questions about the importance of process and interpretation in researching addiction and treatment generally, as potentially influential variables seemed only accessible through phenomenological data. Finally a specific research hypothesis was formulated concerning the importance of individual subjective interpretation in matching clients to treatment models.

The aims of the following study are, then, simply to apply phenomenological methodology to individual therapeutic change processes within a structured comparison study. That is, to utilize both qualitative and quantitative data in an attempt to understand influential variables in the treatment process. Therefore although the case study offered a comparison of different groups, this was supplemented by the use of qualitative methods and research methodology not normally associated with research in psychology or medicine, but those of anthropology, sociology and perhaps also old fashioned clinical psychiatry.

These methodologies offer the means to study individual differences in interpretation and the therapeutic process itself.

This work therefore attempts to redress the positivist balance somewhat, suggesting not only that AA should perhaps be taken seriously, but also that the wider implications of phenomenology should be taken into account by psychological and medical researchers. However, the comparable outcome measures of a positivist approach were not discarded, as it was clear that to obtain some measure of the relevance or influence of any variable, structured comparisons would be necessary.

If the phenomenological assumption of the significance of subjective interpretation is given importance, the role of individual clients' beliefs can then be seen to be significant in the treatment process. It is this proposition that came to be the focus of the research study.

Much of the research in the field is undertaken within the confines of the medical and psychological (behavioural) sciences. These essentially positivist approaches in effect presuppose that 'addiction' can be defined and isolated, all peripheral variables controlled and experimental comparisons made. This approach is seen as both necessary and sufficient for understanding and responding to 'addiction'. This study is not concerned with whether the experimental approach is necessary, simply whether it is sufficient; as the methods derived from this approach tend to ignore individual differences, particularly subjective interpretations and the therapeutic change process. Methodological constraints are can also be compounded by the limitations of particular theoretical perspectives. For example, previous attempts by 'outsiders' to explain and understand the theory underlying the AA disease model have often been made within the context of psychological (behavioural) theory (Heather and Robinson, 1981, 1986; Fingarette, 1988). This theoretical framework is limited by its basic (questionable) premise that 'addiction' can be adequately understood as a learned behaviour (Gorman, 1989).

Positivist studies comparing outcome statistics do not help clarify what actually happens in AA and do little to explain why an approach at odds with both the methodology and beliefs of contemporary professional consensus should survive and flourish alongside its scientifically credible opponents. Such approaches based on a positivist methodology assume an objectively measurable reality which is difficult to reconcile with the various differing subjective interpretations. The data gained from empirical evaluations are also limited in that they do not convey information concerning the individual change process within therapeutic change programmes.

Positivist research tends to ignore individual differences in an attempt to compare and contrast different treatment interventions. This can lead to outcome evaluations where successful interventions with some individuals are effectively cancelled out by unsuccessful interventions with others.

The deficiencies of the phenomenological approach will not be discussed in detail, as the intention is simply that both methodologies be considered, not that positivist approaches be discarded. Although the methods derived from the phenomenological approach do not confer scientific credibility they serve an interpretive and illustrative purpose, examining subjective interpretations and individual change processes.

The AA programme differs from cognitive/behavioural or medical approaches in that the emphasis in the AA programme itself is on the subjective beliefs of the individuals concerned and the process of individual change. If the folklore of AA is described, (Denzin, 1987a, 1987b, 1987c.) it becomes clear that knowledge and understanding within AA itself are derived from individual case histories. This also reflects the therapeutic process itself which involves individuals relating their own life stories to each other.

AA is therefore utilizing case studies and ethnography as part of its underlying methodology and as such has more in common with the methodology underlying qualitative social science such as the ethnographic methods of anthropology or the (now, old fashioned) individual case studies of psychiatry; rather than the controlled outcome studies and the statistical analysis of quantitative social science methodology.

In effect then, this study will be partially using the same methodology as AA itself, in terms of both its theoretical foundations and therapeutic practice. While psychology and medical science determine the research methodology of the addictions it is hardly surprising that the focus should be on controlled outcome studies. This type of research method gives no understanding of the role of either process or interpretation in treatment, both so significant within the philosophy of AA.

It should be emphasized that research methods in the medical and psychological fields are not the equivalent of clinical methods. Although quantitative methods are essential for social researchers to attain scientific status, they are less essential or useful to clinicians. Clinicians themselves may be more dependent on qualitative data derived from individual case studies than academics. For example, concepts such as 'loss of control' and 'craving', are not accessible to scientific experiment as they owe much to subjective interpretation. Yet if discarded, it would be difficult for the clinician or the client to interpret and communicate, that is to 'recognize' or make sense of certain phenomena or experiences.

Diagnosis and treatment are often based as much on individual clinical casework experience as research findings. So many clinicians may view both diagnosis and treatment as professional crafts, rather than scientific procedures. Psychological therapies are often based on phenomenological philosophies, for example psychodynamic models, and cognitive psychology is based on notions of the significance of subjective interpretation. There is little academic research in this field based on phenomenological methodology.

It can be seen therefore that two separate bodies of knowledge exist, based on different methodologies. These different types of knowledge have resulted in the formation of different theories of addiction or alcohol dependence. The therapeutic programmes derived from these theories are radically different and as might be expected neither can be 'proved' to be superior to the other. The relative assessment of 'goodness of fit' and usefulness of these theories varies depending on the theoretical orientation and job of the professional concerned. The arguments proffered by both camps are discussed later; suffice to say here that nether side can see the relevance or credibility of the other's knowledge base. The theory underlying the approach and the methods used in AA and the Minnesota Method are often poorly understood by outsiders who have not actually gone through the process of 'working the programme'. These studies have often been cursory and limited to measures of outcome and behavioural descriptions of therapeutic process. The studies by insiders have likewise often been badly designed replicas of 'scientific' outcome studies, surveys or simplistic assertions of a particular creed.

Not only do the established professions tend to ignore AA methodology and expertise, but AA members themselves consider behavioural and medical theories misplaced and disruptive. Consequently professional skills are seen as inappropriate to the problem with which they themselves are dealing.

The study

This study initially derived from an early small scale evaluation of an alcohol treatment centre in Britain (referred to in the text as the Centre). This early work lasted two and a half years, from March 1986 to October 1988. Parts of the data proved difficult to understand and interpret within the usual methodological research contexts. It is the resulting questions and dilemmas that form the main focus of the case study described here.

The aims of the original study were to evaluate the specific approach embodied in the Centre, examining not only its general effectiveness, but also the theory underlying its practice. One of the main objectives of the study was to determine which individuals the programme was useful for, and which did not appear to benefit, exploring the possible variables influencing different outcomes, in an attempt to discover how and why particular individuals 'succeeded' in treatment while others 'failed'. This was to make possible a consideration of options for future development in the field.

It became clear that the scientific or positivist approach to measuring outcome was not sufficient. The research involved the study of complex interactions of varying beliefs and understandings about the processes of acquiring, maintaining and recovering from addiction. The degree of 'fit' between the different perspectives held by service providers and service users appeared to be an important determinant of 'success', and 'success' itself was best understood as a social construct from someone's particular point of view.

The present study is therefore concerned with the possible influence of individual differences on treatment process and consequent outcome. The specific focus is the differing beliefs and ideas about addiction among all participants in the treatment process. A case study of forty clients in one centre is recorded and placed in the context of an analysis of popular and professional beliefs about addiction.

The empirical case study is eclectic, a combination of quantitative and qualitative methods was used to achieve 'methodological triangulation' (Brewer and Collins, 1981; Denzin, 1983). This approach is based on the expectation that no single method or measure will be adequate, but that if multiple methods are used, the resulting intersection of measures will provide a more useful interpretation of the phenomenon as a whole.

However, it is clear that the qualitative data are most useful for analyzing the main research questions. This then gave rise to more general questions about the two methodological perspectives discussed above, as the central problem seemed only accessible through phenomenological means. Therefore the study became a platform for a much wider consideration of general theoretical issues in this field.

A research question was formulated based on the premise that if phenomenological assumptions about the significance of subjective interpretation are given importance, the role of an individual client's beliefs can be seen to be significant in the treatment process. The question therefore concerned the relevance of subjective interpretations in the treatment process itself. Qualitative data were collated, but this was followed by data analysis within a positivist framework in order to illustrate the relevance of qualitative data for psychological and medical research in the addictions.

Quantitative measures used throughout the evaluative study included basic demographic details of clients, Severity of Alcohol Dependence Questionnaire scores (Stockwell et al., 1983) and routine documentation of individuals' attendance at the Centre. These data allowed later comparison and analysis of different client groups in terms of initial dependency scores, attendance and recorded progress.

Qualitative methods were drawn from the repertoire of the social researcher, in order to give both client and therapist accounts of problems and treatment process. In this way a client's subjective understanding of the problem could be related to the therapist's understanding of the problem and how it was dealt with in terms of the treatment programme. Qualitative data were obtained that allowed an understanding of the subjects' views in terms of their own concepts and beliefs. As Lofland (1971) states, 'In order to capture the participants "in their own terms" one must learn their analytic ordering of the world, their categories for rendering explicable and coherent the flux of raw reality...The qualitative analyst seeks to provide an explicit rendering of the structure, order and patterns found among a set of participants.' (p.7).

Consequently, these qualitative data assumed considerable importance. The analysis of staff records and staff interviews could be related to data collected from client interviews at various stages throughout treatment, to allow comparison of different viewpoints on the treatment process. Ethnographic data collected from participant and non participant observation could be categorized in order to describe the interaction of individuals with different beliefs and attitudes. The results could then be set in the context of statistical data regarding client characteristics and progress.

These qualitative methods were also extremely useful in the early stages of the research as, in the words of Spencer and Dale (1979), they gave 'many opportunities for developing and refining concepts rather than relying on the assumption that we know the relevant properties and categories in advance.' (p.697).

The methods used for collecting qualitative data ranged from structured and semi-structured interviews to informal observation. Structured and semi structured interviews were used to record ethnographic accounts of individual beliefs and social processes, to provide descriptions of clients and staff, their views, initial problems and difficulties in interacting with each other and negotiating the process of treatment at the Centre. This work was supplemented by participant observation in informal settings, non participant observation in meetings and counselling sessions and what Spradely (1980) calls 'passive observation' (p.59), (That is, where the observer does not participate or interact with subjects to a significant degree during involvement with therapeutic groups).

Research programme

Initially the researcher was involved as much as possible in the general day to day work of the Centre, spending time chatting to staff and clients, sitting in on counselling sessions and attending therapeutic groups. This general participant and non participant observation was followed by structured interviews with both staff and clients. The content and form of the interviews were developed partly by following up those topics identified through passive observation, found to be important in understanding the significance of particular social meanings in interactions. This work was supplemented with a comprehensive study of the AA literature which the Centre staff used extensively in their work with clients. The object of this aspect of the research was largely to understand different subjective interpretations of what was happening.

The present study concentrates on the findings which emerged from detailed studies of the progress of all clients who attended the Centre during a particular three month period in 1986. There were forty of these, and the information on which the case study is based includes both data collected as outlined above throughout the study and additional interviews with clients and staff before, during and after treatment, concentrating on how they understood and experienced the process of treatment. There are unfortunately methodological limitations which unavoidably arise from the fact that this work was developed as part of a 'broad brush' evaluative study rather than a project initially designed to study client and therapist beliefs about treatment. It should therefore be regarded as a first step only in research in this area and as suggestive rather than conclusive.

Interviews were conducted by the researcher at three points during each client's progression through treatment: firstly at the client's first appointment at the Centre, prior to assessment by agency staff; secondly between four and eight weeks into the programme and lastly close to the end of the programme. These structured interviews were supplemented by participant and non-participant observation in both formal and informal settings with staff and clients. The qualitative data used for the dialogue extracts were selected specifically in order to illustrate the degree of compatibility or incompatibility between the views of clients and staff. That is, all comments illustrative of client and staff views were recorded. Those offering the most 'apt illustrations' (Gluckman, 1961) of each subject's general views regarding his/her 'addiction' are reported. In this way a client's understanding of his/her problem and the treatment programme can be related to the therapist's beliefs.

It should be emphasized that the aim of the study of this group of clients was to examine the process of responding to and working through the programme rather than assessing long term outcomes. However, it was necessary to define what was meant by success and failure, and the qualitative approach tends to modify our notions of how 'success' and 'failure' can be measured. Instead of the objective (if transient) states they often appear to be in conventional outcome studies, they can be viewed as personal judgements made from particular points of view. The staff of the Centre considered its aims, and therefore also criteria for success, in terms of abstinence. An improvement in drinking behaviour only, or control over drinking and lifestyle would be seen as failure by adherents of the programme. It would have been difficult to use definitions involving criteria such as controlled drinking, in an environment where clients left the programme if they could not remain abstinent. It was felt that this difficulty in definition could be best overcome by defining 'success' in the way that staff did, as achieving and maintaining abstinence. This was judged to have occurred when client and staff member both reported successful abstinence at the end of treatment or, in the case of early leavers, at a time when treatment would normally have ceased. The reliability of the judgement is increased by the fact that most clients and staff were in continuing regular contact through a self help organization as well as through the Centre. Only clients for whom we had reasonably reliable outcome information are included in the forty case studies.

Considerations regarding practical constraints apply largely irrespective of the theoretical perspectives adopted in the research. However, the methods used clearly need to fit with the theoretical perspectives, in the light of the aims of the research. The aims were to do a small scale intensive study, which would not generate very large amounts of quantitative data, but would give insight into the process of treatment (ie. change and maintenance of change). The qualitative data collected give an indication of the degree of compatibility between views of clients and the beliefs of staff, together with the Alcoholics Anonymous philosophy. In this way, the aim was to provide an understanding of individual processes within the context of social interaction at the Centre.

5 A treatment centre examined

This chapter will begin with a descriptive account of the development of the Centre, followed by quantitative material relevant to the effectiveness of the programme and finally 'insider accounts' of the Centre and its functioning. The main focus of the chapter is concerned with individual staff accounts of their working philosophy and methods. Having given accounts of differing sets of beliefs, it will then be possible in the following chapter to categorize and contrast the beliefs of clients and therapists in the actual treatment process.

The Centre examined was one of the few such centres in Britain which was neither residential nor privately funded, receiving funding from the local Health Authority and central government. Clients attended for individual psychotherapy and group therapy for one or two days a week. Length of stay varied depending on the time taken to complete the programme, but generally lasted from three to six months, with a smaller group staying up to a year. The average length of stay was five months.

Development

The following section will include a brief description of the development of the Centre, but will focus largely on the two and a half years of the research work, from 1986 to 1989.

In 1979 the Welsh Office and local Health Authority agreed to fund the project. The Centre was initially established as an alcohol service and until that date this part of the country had no such statutory service. However it is significant that the Centre's Director had previously been active in setting up self help Alcoholics Anonymous groups in this area. Many individuals took an interest in the developing service, Local Social Services, Health Authority, Council for Voluntary Services, Probation Services, psychiatry and the Police were all represented on a Management Committee for the new alcohol service. However, the practical consequences of limited funding resulted only in a small rather insecure service in the early years.

This consisted of one full time worker (the Director) and one part time secretary. In 1984, temporary finance was gained under a community programme, providing funding for one more full time and two part time counsellors. In 1985, further funding was obtained from central government, resulting in a grant to continue financing the staff team. The Health Authority itself continued to fund one worker and one part time secretary. With the exception of the secretary and a part time counsellor (a retired psychologist), all staff had been through the AA programme and considered themselves recovering alcoholics. It is significant that the psychologist had recently returned from America and had consequently worked with AA and the Minnesota Method in his professional capacity. These personnel were trained by the Director and were working effectively by January 1985.

The service provided

Any client contacting the Centre regarding their own drinking was usually seen within one or two weeks. Referrals were accepted from any source, but it important to note that, as can be seen from the statistics, many are self referrals or referrals from friends and family. Appointments were made to see one of the counsellors at the Centre for an initial assessment interview, to discuss the seriousness of the problem and the kind of service available. The counselling styles of staff varied slightly, but the client or relative was generally encouraged to talk openly about their dependency problem and any other issues related to it at the first interview. Staff members then carried out an assessment based on the AA model: this procedure utilized criteria based on the identification of symptoms of the disease. Although social and psychological problems are an integral part of this assessment they are seen as secondary manifestations of the alcoholic's disease. This initial stage of problem definition, although obviously of significance in determining who was dealt with and why, also played an integral part in the early stages of treatment itself, staff seeing the assessment as a chance to 'break denial'.

The counsellor would then suggest a possible course of action, which in most cases involved regular weekly attendance at a therapeutic group and a weekly individual counselling session lasting about an hour. It was usually recommended that clients stay at the Centre for a complete day, if possible, once a week, (a therapeutic group in the morning and further group activities, discussion or individual work on the programme in the afternoon). This however, though considered necessary, was not thought sufficient; all clients were strongly recommended to attend Alcoholics Anonymous meetings on a regular basis, often one or two a week, sometimes more. As can be seen from data in the following chapter, clients could be dismissed from the programme at the Centre if they did not attend outside AA groups.

Clients were seldom turned away by staff at the assessment stage, though they often left of their own accord or were discouraged from attending if they did not co-operate fully in the early stages of the programme (see following chapter). If the counsellor felt that an in patient detoxification was necessary, the patient would be referred to the local Psychiatric Hospital prior to commencement of the Centre programme. The Centre staff would also offer support to G.P.s prescribing out patient detoxification to patients, if they considered it appropriate.

Staff workload and weekly activities

The staff members worked almost exclusively doing counselling and therapy, only the Director taking on all liaison and training tasks. The staff themselves were happy with this arrangement, feeling that this work was both physically and emotionally demanding and that they did not have the time or the motivation to take on other tasks.

The time table below gives an indication of the workload of staff during the year 1986. There are one full time (male) and two part time counsellors (one female, one male). There were also two female graduates of the programme, who worked on a voluntary basis, helping as cotherapists with group work.

Table 5.1
Timetable Sept. 1986

	A.M.	P.M.
Mon. Individual Counselling sessions:-	4	4
Tues. Individual Counselling sessions:-	2	4
	Women's Group	
Wed. Individual Counselling sessions:-	0	4
	Two Groups	Group activities
Thurs. Individual Counselling sessions:-	2	2
	One group	Group activities
Fri. Assessment and Counselling new clients.	4	4

NOTE:
Counselling sessions were limited to four clients a day (i.e. two per half day); 30 counselling sessions per week, (22 regular clients and space for eight new clients).

The timetable of staff activities indicates that much staff time was taken up with group therapy, group work activities and individual counselling sessions. However, this gives only an indication of the formally structured programme. Support and help were also offered to clients on an informal basis to supplement formal appointments. The main office often functioned as an informal 'drop-in' centre for aftercare support and extra help for those still in treatment. The secretary took a large part of the responsibility for this aspect of the work. She had learnt the AA model from the staff as she started work, and unquestioningly utilized this approach in her work with clients. Many clients felt that the friendly informal support consistently available in the main office was an integral part of their recovery programme. Staff not working with clients would spend any free time in the office, and an atmosphere of friendly interest and genuine concern encouraged clients who did drop in to stay to discuss problems and support each other.

Finally it would be incomplete to conclude a section concerning staff and workload without including the contribution of volunteers. It was difficult to estimate the quantity or quality of their work, but the majority of clients attending the Centre were helped and supported by members of the Anonymous fellowships, both in the Centre itself and outside within the self help networks. Many clients had a personal sponsor from these external self help groups and it was not unusual for members of the Anonymous fellowships and ex clients to help out at the Centre itself. A quotation from the Director's report at the 1986 Annual General Meeting gives some indication of the extent of this help:-

'Needless to say a lot of our success is due to A.A., Alanon and a few behind the scenes workers who are always willing to befriend, do a hospital visit, take people to their first meeting etc. The helpers would be too numerous too mention.'

Training, education and liaison

Although the Centre had the primary function of counselling and therapy, the Director was also responsible for education and training sessions, both to the general public and various groups of interested professionals.

The following table gives an indication of the amount of time spent on these activities for the nine month period March 1986 -November 1986.

Table 5.2
Education, talks and lectures

Schools and Youth organisations	4
Probation (training courses)	2
Commerce and Industry	3
Technical colleges, university	5
Hospitals: nurses, doctors	7

This structured educative work was supplemented by discussion both over the telephone and at the Centre itself, with most professionals, particularly with General Practitioners, Psychiatrists, Probation Officers and Social Workers.

To give an indication of the extent of the liaison with professionals and support/contact with clients, a breakdown of incoming telephone calls over a nine month period is tabled below:

Table 5.3
Incoming phone calls, 1986

1986	M	A	M	J	J	A	S	O	N
Professionals	65	72	61	52	65	65	67	67	61
Clients	100	106	100	106	104	67	89	99	107
Administration	9	10	10	15	3	18	20	25	28

Despite educative functions, the Centre was primarily responsible for providing a therapeutic treatment service. Because of this there was little research focus on the Director's training courses for professionals, or in educative programmes for lay people. In retrospect this had unforeseen consequences as there were indications that the philosophy espoused by the Director was more acceptable in some areas than others (see Table 5.9 for referral sources). The researcher attended training courses given to probation and it was clear that many probation staff were antagonistic to the AA approach which conflicted with the beliefs underlying the alcohol education groups which they themselves provided.

This conflict in ideologies and methods was reflected in the Centre's relationship with the local specialist drugs agency. This project utilized the 'harm minimisation' approach to drug misuse and was opposed to the abstinence model of Alcoholics Anonymous and its sister group Narcotics Anonymous. The two centres did not manage to develop good working relations during the research period. The disagreements between the Centre and other agencies were based on the controversies about theory and methods discussed in earlier chapters. Statutory agencies tended to work with a 'controlled drinking' approach based on Social Learning theory.

The Centre also had difficulty working with psychiatrists. Alcohol problems in Britain remain the professional remit of psychiatry, and the views of local psychiatrists reflected those of the Royal College of Psychiatrists discussed earlier. During the study there was conflict between the Centre and psychiatric consultants regarding the Centre's antipathy to any form of prescribing. This resulted in an agreement during the research period, between local psychiatrists and the Centre staff, that both would not deal with a patient concurrently, though consecutive working was tolerated, each party referring on for detoxification or after care respectively.

However, despite differences between the Centre and some professionals, it is significant that many general practitioners and others did utilize the Centre (see Table 5.9). Most of these practitioners were in agreement with the AA model as this approach to alcohol and drug misuse was fairly widespread in this part of the country at the time of the research. (See Keene et al., 1991, 1993a.) It was also true that some professionals referring clients were not aware of the philosophy and practice of the Centre. The attitudes of GP's became apparent when an alternative alcohol service (A consultant led Community Drug and Alcohol Team) was later set up in the area and GPs did not initially utilize its facilities but continued to refer to the Centre.

The major advantage of the AA philosophy was that the Centre was able to use the widespread and comprehensive network of (cost free) self help groups in the county. The Anonymous fellowships offer support and aftercare and in a small minority of instances clients did not use the Centre after their assessment interview but attended AA or NA instead. The Centre was also able to refer clients to residential establishments working with the AA and Minnesota Method, in the knowledge that they would be using exactly the same approach. For example, over a period of 18 months, twenty nine clients were referred to the following centres:-

Broadway Lodge - 12;
Western Counselling Services - 3;
Farm Place - 1;
Rhoserchan Project - 13.

Information and monitoring: quantitative data

This section gives an outline of the numbers and characteristics of the clients attending the Centre for the year 1987, together with retrospective statistics for the years 1985 to 1987. Comparisons are made between 1985 and 1987, in order to illustrate changes in the Centre during the research period. Particular interest is taken in those variables that may be seen to correlate with 'successful' outcome or completion of treatment. These data are included to provide a context for the case study of a group of forty clients (including all clients attending the Centre within a three month period during 1987).

Methods and research instruments

1) Initial contact sheet.

2) Staff assessment questionnaire.

3) Structured client interview, including informal discussion with every client on first arrival and follow up interviews during and after treatment programme.

4) The Severity of Alcohol Dependence Questionnaire. (S.A.D.Q.).

Information collected on a regular basis included basic demographic data, 'addiction' histories, home and social circumstances, an assessment of severity of dependence (S.A.D.Q.) and more detailed material concerning personal history, client's own attitudes and opinions of their problem and the service available. (Interviews were conducted with all clients prior to, during and after treatment).

The statistics examined in this section indicate the numbers of people who use the Centre, the extent of its use and the type of client attending. These descriptive statistics give an idea of the numbers who benefited from treatment and which variables seemed highly correlated with success.

Population of clients first attending the Centre during 1987

Total number of clients, including family = 156

Number of family members seen independently = 21

Total group of problematic alcohol users = 135

Each of the tables giving data for 1987 is followed by a brief comparison with retrospective statistics for the year 1985. This additional retrospective information is given in order to illustrate the kind of changes that characterize the Centre's development during the research period, rather than simply giving a snapshot of one year.

Table 5.4
Number of clients making contact: by month

Month	Clients	Family/Relatives	Total
January	8	1	9
February	12	3	15
March	14	2	16
April	11	2	13
May	7	0	7
June	9	3	12
July	17	1	18
Aug	13	0	13
Sept	8	2	10
Oct	16	1	17
Nov	14	5	19
Dec	6	1	7
Total	135	21	156

135 clients initially made contact with the Centre in 1987 as compared with 190 in 1985. The average number of contacts per month in 1987 was 11, and in 1985 was 16.

Table 5.5
Age of clients

Age of Clients	Number of clients	Percentage clients
Under 20 years	7	5%
20-30 years	31	23%
30-40 years	43	32%
40-50 years	37	27%
50-60 years	12	9%
Over 60 years	5	4%
TOTAL	135	100%

In 1985, 28% of clients were under 30 years and 13% of clients were over 50 years: these figures remained the same in 1986.
It is interesting that the age of the client groups has remained fairly stable over this period, except for a slight increase in young people. In 1985 2% of clients were under 20 years and in 1987 this figure was 5%.

Table 5.6
Sex of clients

	Clients	Family	Total
Male	79 (58.5%)	5 (24%)	84 (54%)
Female	56 (41.5%)	16 (76%)	72 (46%)
Total	135	21	156

1987: Male = 54% Female = 46%. 1985: Male = 60% Female = 40%
It can be seen that there has been a slight increase in the number of women attending the Centre. It should be noted however that only 7% of the 1985 sample were family members, whereas this increased to 13% in 1987. (In 1985 all family members were women: in 1987 only 76% of family members were women).

Table 5.7
Marital status

Single	41	30%
Common law marriage	4	3%
Married	51	38%
Separated	5	4%
Divorced or widowed	34	25%
TOTAL	135	100%

Table 5.8
Dependent children

	Clients	Percentage
One child	21	(26%)
Two children	35	(44%)
Three or more children	24	(30%)

Total number of clients with dependants (N = 80).
No data for 1985.

Table 5.9
Referral source

	Clients 1987	percentage 1987	percentage 1985
Self referral	24	18%	24%
Family/Relative	27	20%	19%
NA/AA group	18	13%	5%
G.P.	17	13%	13%
Psychiatric hosp.	13	10%	2%
Social Worker	7	5%	3%
Probation Officer	11	8%	19%
Solicitor	11	8%	7%
Employer	2	1%	2%
Other	5	4%	6%
TOTAL	135	100%	100%

It can be seen from this comparison that an increased number of clients were referred by professionals in 1987, notably from the local psychiatric hospital. Also more were referred from AA, whereas less were referred from probation. There were therefore less clients attending the Centre as a condition of probation. This latter change may have been partly due to disagreements between the Centre and probation as to the writing of reports for the courts - but was probably also due to the organisation of Alcohol Education groups within the probation service itself. As mentioned previously, relationships between the Centre and the local psychiatric hospital, varied over the years, but in 1987 they were fairly good following an agreement that patients would not be attached to the Centre while they remained patients of psychiatrists at the hospital, but consultants continued to refer patients for aftercare support and surprisingly an AA group flourished at the Hospital.

Retrospective statistics 1984-86

The following tables give statistics from a period of three years prior to the case study to allow larger groups of data for analysis. These data give an indication of the correlation between length of treatment and 'success' (as defined by staff in terms of abstinence). These statistics refer to 210 clients making contact and attending the Centre in the 18 month period from October 1984 - March 1986 up to the time of the case study.

The associations of variables were tested for significant correlation, using the chi square test.

Table 5.10
Association between number of weeks attending the Centre and success

No. of weeks	Success	Failure	Total
1	0	68	68
2-4	3	65	68
5-7	3	14	17
8-10	2	9	11
11-13	1	7	8
14	4	1	5
15+	22	11	33
TOTAL	35	175	210

2 x 2 Chi square on group data. (attendance up to 13 weeks: attendance 14 weeks or more).

Chi square = 89.48 $p < 0.01$ ie. Significant at 0.01

There is a significant correlation between number of weeks attendance at the Centre and success.

Table 5.11
Association between referral source and success

Referral source	Success	Failure	Total
Self/Friend/G.P.	28	127	155
Prob/S.W/Courts	7	48	55
TOTAL	35	175	210

Chi square = 0.832 (1 df.) i.e. Not Significant at 0.05.

It should be noted that 17% self referrals proved successful whereas only 13% of statutory referrals were successful.

In a group where the majority are 'failures', that is where both distributions (self referrals and statutory referrals) are skewed towards failure, then very large samples are needed if there is to be any chance of finding a significant difference between the proportions that fail.

Table 5.12
Associations between regular attendance at AA or NA meetings and success

	Success	Failure	Total
AA/NA Attendance	32	54	86
No AA/NA Attendance	3	121	124
TOTAL	35	175	210

NB. regular attendance = once a week or more at the time of interview.

Chi square = 44.25 (1 df.) i.e. significant at 0.01

These retrospective statistics indicate only association of variables and not causal direction. Although these data give an indication of the interaction between success and attendance at the Centre and self help AA groups, it is unlikely that a simple Chi square, two by two test is adequate to represent the complex process involved in determining 'success' or 'failure'.

These data taken as a whole give a description of the numbers and characteristics of the clients who have attended the Centre. The statistics also indicate which variables may interact with 'success' in terms of continued abstinence.

Background and beliefs of individual Centre staff

In order to give a clearer picture of the aims and beliefs underlying work at the Centre, it is necessary to examine qualitative data providing an account of the subjective interpretations of staff themselves. The staff accounts examined here are particularly important for the case study in the following chapter where interactions between staff and clients are examined. The data recorded below thus give each individual staff member's account or interpretation of their working philosophy and methods. These data are derived from structured and unstructured interviews with staff members. In order to place these data within context they are preceded by an account of the background and experience of each staff member.

All staff had experience of the Alcoholics Anonymous philosophy and method, and all had received training in the Minnesota Method. The level of commitment to this particular method will be evident from the staff interviews. The staff had, with the exception of the part time psychologist, all been through an AA or Minnesota programme themselves and continued to attend AA. They accepted the basic tenets of AA and the Minnesota approach, regarding addiction as a primary disease characterized not only by an inability to control the use of alcohol, but also by a delusional state of mind in which the sufferer is unable to recognise his dependence. This is in accord with the fundamental consensus between those involved in AA and the development of the Minnesota treatment programme that 'alcoholism is a complex, multi-phasic, usually progressive, chronic illness - a primary pathological process.' (Lefevre, ND.) Staff also believed that therapeutic input in the form of group work and individual counselling provided the necessary help and support for clients to work through a programme of recovery. It should be noted that (as can be seen from the interview notes), there were disagreements between the staff on particular aspects of working. These variations however indicated only slight differences in interpretation of the basic premises. The consensus of opinion was that the Centre worked with the AA philosophy and the Minnesota Method.

The staff saw the Centre as working in conjunction with Alcoholics

Anonymous and utilizing both the philosophy and the support network provided by this organization to help provide a more intensive, accessible (24 hours) service to clients.

As all staff took for granted the basic premises of AA and saw the Minnesota Method as integrating and structuring this model, much of the ideology of AA and Minnesota was reflected in the staff interviews; this was often repeated word for word from pamphlets used by staff in work with clients. (See Chapter Three for excerpts from various leaflets available at the Centre.) Where staff simply reiterate the material in Chapter Three, this has been omitted from the interview data; instead information is included where staff express themselves in their own words.

The Director

The Director left school to join the army in 1944. On leaving the army in 1948 he worked for Customs and Excise from 1948-1979. During that time he worked for seven years as 'Dangerous Drugs Trainer' for South Wales and the Borders, and took an interest in counselling techniques at the time. He took an interest in alcoholism in 1967, when he became a founder member of Alcoholics Anonymous, having stopped drinking himself and being as he says 'in the early stages of his own recovery'. At the time he arranged a series of training sessions concerning alcohol use and counselling skills. By 1973 the Director was a trustee of Alcoholics Anonymous and a member of the General Service Board. He retained this post until 1979. The Director's interests included membership of the following groups: in 1967 he became a member of the first AA group in his home town and in 1969 a member of the first intergroup AA in South Wales; 1969/70 he was a founder member of the National Association of Alcohol and Drug Abuse Counsellors (NAADAC) and in 1983 a founder member of the Federation of Welsh Councils on Alcoholism.

The Director himself was largely responsible for early campaigning to create and fund the Centre, for establishing the initial base and programme and for maintaining and developing its work. At the time of the research he did little 'face to face' work with the clients but devoted a large part of his time to administration, liaison, education and training; the supervision and training of staff being an essential aspect of this workload.

The Director had a clear conception of the aims and practice of the Centre, he was a strong advocate of the AA disease model of alcoholism and believed that his staff should have themselves 'worked the programme' before 'they would be able to help other alcoholics'. He felt that he could not explain the therapeutic process intellectually, but said that working as a counsellor/therapist he would guide people through an experience. He stated that it would be difficult for a counsellor to do this guiding if she/he had not been through the process themselves. He therefore stressed the need for a core of people with personal practice at going through the experience through which they would be taking clients. He stated that 'this experience is structured by the twelve steps or stages of AA.'

The Director stated that he believed there to be three fundamental aspects of the programme. These were: 'Self worth; a need for belief in a power outside the self (the second step); and helping others (twelfth step)'. This latter aspect he considered very important and stressed that the helper would be working in a specific way (the way that had worked for him). He emphasized that there were particular ways of helping that were as rewarding for the helper as for the receiver. For the helper because it reminded him of where he had been and how bad it had been and how he could be again, together with the intrinsic rewards to be had from seeing someone else improve.' Help from experience is in itself a learning process.'

The Director then summed up the aspects of the Centre's work which he felt were not replicated by the Alcoholics Anonymous Fellowships. Firstly, 'The Centre gives clients work to do on the first four steps and insists on clients working the initial four steps. That is, the Centre "forces clients to look at themselves". The Centre introduces clients to AA concepts they may not understand and teaches them to understand.' and finally the Centre 'will ensure that clients are allocated an experienced guide for the fifth step'. The Director stressed that he felt that AA was not directive enough and that there was a need for some sort of overview of the fourth and fifth steps; that is, that the client should be directed through them.

The Director saw the general aim of AA and the Centre itself as enabling people to live happy, free and rewarding lives without the use of mood altering drugs. He defined the aims of group work and counselling in the following way. 'The therapeutic process involves encouraging people to take emotional risks within a group environment which is based on gradually developed feelings of trust, honesty and integrity. Within the security of the group, through the method of experiential learning, clients learn how to handle emotions appropriately.' He stressed that reoccurring themes in the sessions included emotions, needs and wants and constructive means of dealing with them. 'The commonest problems that arise are those concerned with interpersonal relationships and conflicts; depression; denial and manipulative strategies or games.'

He considered that the problem of dependency on alcohol or drugs was that one became dependent on them to the exclusion of everything else. 'This is a bad or destructive dependency in that it is one on something that no longer rewards you.' It becomes so dominant that you give up on the dependencies that were more rewarding. 'The solution therefore is partly to become dependent on something else, outside yourself.'

The Director described the therapeutic process of the programme as 'dynamic and constantly changing'. He saw the programme as different for each individual, because each person's background and experience were different. He did not see himself as making the process happen but as an important part of that process. The basic underlying action lay with the client, and this consisted of 'sacrificing your individuality to the group and receiving back their interest in you'.

Counsellor One

Counsellor One was employed as a miner for the first ten years of his working life, followed by a period of work for British Rail. He himself had problems with his use of alcohol and drugs until he was thirty one years old. He entered treatment at Broadway Lodge in 1978. Since that time he has became very involved with Alcoholics Anonymous. He has now been attending AA for eight years and continues to do so on a regular basis.

He is a full-time senior counsellor at the Centre. He works as a co therapist in two groups a week, helping with the activities and assignments that follow a group session. He also sees clients on a weekly basis for individual counselling. He considers it necessary to see clients twice a week (one group and one individual appointment) and together with the other staff emphasizes the importance of this. He also carries out assessment interviews and occasionally visits clients at home.

Counsellor One stressed that the work at the Centre was based firmly on AA and the Minnesota Model; he also emphasized the importance of an intensive programme. He stated that he felt there was a need for a residential treatment centre (similar to Western Counselling Services) or a day care or aftercare service. He also said that the clients at the Centre are now encouraged to stay there for at least one complete day a week, this being a recent development arising from staff feeling that more client contact with the Centre would be beneficial.

He stated that most clients are expected to attend a therapeutic group. He is prepared to see a client on a purely individual basis, only if she/he is in full time employment (the groups are held during the day). It is made clear for all clients (especially those who do not attend a Centre group), that they are expected to attend the local AA or NA groups on a regular basis and that this is considered an integral part of each person's recovery programme. He also stated that he sees the relatives or family of about twenty five per cent of his clients and will occasionally offer support to the family of an alcoholic independently of seeing the alcoholic him/herself. He stated that the Alcoholics Anonymous philosophy was used in the Centre, the programme at the Centre being the same as that used in the first four steps of the AA programme.

Counsellor one stated that by the time a client has progressed to the fourth step of the AA programme, it is felt that he/she has developed far enough to cope without support from the Centre groups. It is usual for the client to have developed firm links with AA groups by this stage, and to have been allocated an AA sponsor who acts in a supportive, advisory capacity to the client/member. Although AA is clearly an integral part of the support network for Centre clients, the Centre itself does offer aftercare support, and will see clients monthly for about six months after termination of the Centre programme. Many clients, having completed treatment, will return to the Centre on a casual basis just to keep in touch for several years. Finally he stressed that Alanon (the AA sister organisation for families of alcoholics), Alateen (for children of alcoholics) and Narcotics Anonymous, were all recommended to clients, and that the Centre worked in coordination with these voluntary organizations for mutual benefit.

Counsellor Two

Counsellor Two had worked at various jobs before becoming employed at the Centre, where she initially served as a part time secretary/administrator. After training and supervision from the Director, she became employed as a part time counsellor and group therapist. She is herself a 'recovering alcoholic' and attends AA meetings regularly. As a part time counsellor, her duties largely involved assessment, individual counselling and group therapy.

Counsellor Two defined the aims of her work as 'enabling patients to face reality; to cope with stress without chemicals. To help patients become happy, useful members of society.' She saw her role as that of supporting clients and, when necessary, to deal with 'denial'. She stated that 'themes' that came up in her work were concerned with the problems of everyday living, for example, the need to work at relationships, to talk honestly about problems, overcome pride, accept the reality of a situation and then do something about it.

She saw the main problems as being concerned with attaining people's trust and honesty. She spoke of the problems caused by clients who 'attended for a short time only and fought against authority, thereby unsettling groups initially.' She stressed the importance of working with friends and relatives of clients, saying that the Centre would try to treat a couple or family as a whole. Finally counsellor Two described alcohol problems as caused by the disease of alcoholism, stating that she believed entirely in the methods of AA as these had worked for her.

Counsellor Three

Counsellor Three spent much of his early life in the army, moving to America after the Second World War, where he studied clinical psychology. He took early retirement and moved back to Swansea, where he has worked for the Centre for the last two years. His work involves mainly one to one counselling. He also writes reports for the courts and assessment interviews.

Although this counsellor was the only staff member who had not worked the programme himself, he explained his own belief in AA and Minnesota by stating that in America, AA and Minnesota were 'far more generally accepted by professionals than in Britain'. He had worked as a psychologist in an American prison, specifically with addicts and alcoholics, and during that time he became familiar with the Minnesota Model of treatment and the AA philosophy. He stated that he believes that the aims of the project are 'both attainable and realistic.' He said that AA had evolved the philosophy of the twelve recovery steps, but that the Centre provided more than an extension of Alcoholics Anonymous. He cited as examples; first, counselling (following that set forth in the Minnesota Model and requiring clear-cut commitments from clients) and second, follow-up support and aftercare.

Counsellor Three talked of the importance of the Centre links with AA, stating that the Minnesota Model integrates the AA approach as part of the overall treatment package. He also spoke of the ability of Centre staff (themselves AA members) to monitor progress through AA group attendance. He highlighted particular aspects of the Minnesota Model, which he considered of importance and relevant to the work of the Centre: Firstly, 'That initial motivation for treatment is unrelated to outcome'; he stressed the importance however of establishing rapport in initial interviews and defined his own approach as 'talk quietly and carry a big stick in your pocket'. Secondly, 'That the concept of alcoholism is changing to one of sickness or "individual pathology", and the community needs education to understand that all forms of chemical dependency should be seen as illnesses.'

He identified an important aspect of treatment as the process of identifying 'Games', and 'Roles' played in social games. Once identified, these 'games' were interpreted as 'defense mechanisms' and as such, were bad or wrong. 'Games are played by frightened neurotics who cannot relate properly to reality.' 'Part of the therapist's task is therefore to convince the client of the validity of the prescribed forms of interaction (reality) and of the invalidity of the client's previous roles and forms of interaction.' He stated that staff often have problems with 'intellectuals', because they 'will not keep things simple'. He emphasized the necessity to 'surrender' or 'have faith' and 'accept what is said' saying that this may have been more problematic for some clients than others.

The Secretary

The Secretary was involved in all aspects of the work at the Centre, often dealing with difficult telephone calls and supporting clients in an informal capacity in the Centre.
She had no links with AA when she first arrived. She says that she is comfortable with the philosophy now, but that it took time to understand it and adapt. She spoke of the support and understanding of the team members for each other and felt that staff members offered each other much help and that this led to a good working team. She saw this supportive, caring atmosphere as partially 'growing from the aims and beliefs of AA', that is, that 'if people believed the basic principles, this would enhance the quality of human interaction.'

Summary

It can be seen that the philosophy of AA was accurately reflected in the opinions of the Director and these beliefs were shared by staff and 'successful' clients. The methods of the Centre involved more structure than those of voluntary AA groups themselves but the ideas of AA were implemented in both individual and group counselling at the Centre. It was generally believed that 'the process involves taking away one destructive addiction and replacing it with a constructive dependency on AA groups, the personal AA sponsor and counsellors at the Centre.' That is 'social processes' were used to enable clients to learn to cope with basic needs and to build up constructive dependencies. The basic concepts underlying this process were that the addict/ alcoholic 'has a disease, but is also responsible for his/her own cure'. This notion of responsibility for one's own 'recovery' did not seem paradoxical to staff who defined self responsibility in terms of seeking help from AA and following the programme.

It was thought essential that new clients believe not only that they have a disease, but also that they are helpless to deal with it on their own and must turn to a 'power stronger than themselves'. These premises were seen as the necessary precursors to 'surrender' and the consequent handing 'themselves over' to the AA programme. Implicit within these concepts was the necessity of accepting the staff knowledge and AA at face value, without questioning it. Questioning or arguing with staff was construed in terms of 'rationalization' and 'denial' and seen as a symptom of the underlying disease. This chapter has given a general description of the Centre and an account of the beliefs of staff members. The following chapter examines the interaction between these beliefs and those of clients themselves, during the process of treatment.

6 Treatment process and interpretation: A study of forty clients

In this study it was hoped to learn as much about treatment processes as outcomes, and a combination of quantitative and qualitative methods was used in an attempt to achieve 'methodological triangulation'. Quantitative measures were analyzed in the last chapter. This deals with the qualitative data. These data were gathered using methods drawn from the repertoire of the social researcher rather than the psychologist, in order to develop an ethnographic understanding of beliefs and social processes at the Centre. The methods used were described in Chapter Four. They allow an understanding of subjects' views in terms of their own concepts and beliefs (Lofland, 1971), and are particularly useful in exploratory research. The results should be regarded as a first step only in research in this area and as suggestive rather than conclusive; however, they seem of sufficient interest to stimulate future work on the relationship between client and therapist beliefs and outcome.

Detailed case notes were kept of 40 clients who first attended the Centre during a three month period in 1987. The aim is to describe how both clients and staff understood and experienced the process of treatment.

The following information was collected for each client:-

(1) Initial questionnaire and interview on arrival at the Centre.
(2) Initial staff questionnaires and interview data.
(3) In treatment interview.
(4) Ongoing staff records and attendance.
(5) Post treatment questionnaire and interview.
(6) Information on continued post treatment attendance at Alcoholics Anonymous, and post treatment drinking behaviour.
(7) Severity of Alcohol Dependence (SADQ) Questionnaire.

Interviews were conducted by the author at three points during each client's progression through treatment: firstly at the client's first appointment at the Centre, prior to assessment by agency staff; secondly between four and eight weeks into the programme and lastly close to the end of the programme. The qualitative data used for the dialogue extracts were selected specifically in order to illustrate the degree of compatibility or incompatibility between the views of clients and staff. That is, all comments illustrative of client and staff views were recorded. Those offering the most 'apt illustrations' of each subject's general views regarding his/her 'addiction' are reported in this chapter. In this way a client's understanding of his/her problem and the treatment programme can be related to the therapist's beliefs.

It should be emphasized that the aim of the study of this group of clients was to examine the process of responding to and working through the programme rather than assessing long term outcomes. However, it was necessary to define what was meant by success and failure, and the qualitative approach tends to modify our notions of how these can be measured. Instead of the objective (if transient) states they often appear to be in conventional outcome studies, they can be viewed as personal judgements made from particular points of view. The staff of the Centre considered its aims, and therefore also criteria for success, in terms of abstinence. An improvement in drinking behaviour only, or control over drinking and lifestyle would be seen as failure by adherents of the programme. It would have been difficult to use definitions involving criteria such as controlled drinking in an environment where clients left the programme if they could not remain abstinent. It was felt that this difficulty in definition could best be overcome by defining 'success' in the way that staff did, as achieving and maintaining abstinence. This was judged to have occurred when client and staff member both reported successful abstinence at the end of treatment or, in the case of early leavers, at a time when treatment would normally have ceased. The reliability of the judgement is increased by the fact that most clients and staff were in continuing regular contact through a self help organization as well as through the Centre. Only clients for whom we had reasonably reliable outcome information are included in the forty case studies.

When the data from the case studies were examined it seemed after inspection that two dimensions were likely to be fruitful for analytical purposes. They were length of time spent in treatment and success/failure, which provided a simple two by two matrix which could then be applied to the material. Although other dimensions may have been relevant, it was decided initially to use these two to structure further work. These four categories of clients could then be examined in detail, material being used from particular client case studies to illustrate general characteristics of each sub group.

The table below illustrates the two dimensions studied: length of time spent in treatment and success/failure.

Table 6.1
Four outcome subgroups

	A	B
	Unsuccessful Stayers	**Successful Stayers**
1	Those who stayed in treatment more than four weeks but did not succeed in achieving abstinence.	Those who stayed in treatment more than four weeks and succeeded in achieving abstinence.
	(n = 5)	(n = 5)
	Unsuccessful Leavers	**Successful Leavers**
2	Those who did not stay in treatment more than four weeks and did not succeed in achieving abstinence.	Those who did not stay in treatment more than four weeks but did succeed in achieving abstinence.
	(n = 15)	(n = 5)

Four subgroups studied

It is difficult to identify particular characteristics which distinguish clients in one sub group from those in another. There were no significant differences between sub groups in terms of age or gender. The seriousness of the drinking problem, measured with the Severity of Alcohol Dependence Questionnaire (S.A.D.Q.) is not correlated either with continued attendance at the Centre, with success in treatment or with staff opinions as to severity of problems. The clients who accept the programme are not necessarily those with the most serious addiction in terms of the SADQ and the programme seems to be of equal benefit to those who are addicted and to those who are not. However, careful examination of the attitudes and behaviour of clients **and** of the staff in response to clients before, during and after the treatment process, gives some indication of why particular clients fail and others succeed.

Clients have completed 'before' treatment, 'during' treatment and 'post' treatment interviews and questionnaires with the researcher. Information from these interviews (client view) is collated with information collected from staff records and interviews in order to develop a full picture of the experience of clients and opinions of staff during the period of treatment for each client.

In the following section each sub group will be examined in detail, material being used from particular client case studies to illustrate general characteristics of each sub group.

Information concerning each client will include past history, attitudes and opinions towards their own addiction and towards the programme (these attitudes may change during the course of treatment), and comments and opinions of staff regarding the client and his/her progress and problems.

The comments of staff are set alongside those of clients to illustrate different points of view. Client comments are placed in the left hand column and staff comments in the right. The researcher's comments are included after each set of quotations. The comments in each column are in chronological order, the first taken from the pre treatment interviews and following blocks are taken from interviews during treatment and at the final contact session. The clients in this section will be referred to by number.

Subgroup A1: the unsuccessful stayers

This group consists of those clients who stayed in treatment for more than four weeks (average 19 counselling sessions and 19 groups) but who failed to achieve or maintain abstinence. These clients attempted to overcome initial difficulties with the programme but were unable to do so. Some detail from each client is given here as the difficulties illustrate the problems that occur with many clients. Differences between the client viewpoint and that of the Centre staff may be resolved during the course of treatment (the clients may change their beliefs), however the clients in this sub group were not able to do this, nor to work constructively within the constraints of the therapeutic programme, despite their efforts to do so.

Client 1.

Attended ten individual sessions and groups.
SADQ score = 47
Referred by Probation Officer
Male

Client comments

Pre treatment
I drink to forget things, it affects my relationships badly and causes too much trouble to other people. I've had bad experiences in my life and drink to insulate myself against this.

During treatment
You can be helped by talking to people with the same problems. I have to change my lifestyle. I see my drinking as an illness. But I want to get back to what I was, a normal person.

Staff comments

I have informed client that he is an alcoholic and told him to attend AA four times a week together with his Centre attendance. He has been prescribed a reducing dose of Heminevrin by his GP.

He has committed himself to attend AA and get a sponsor, also to complete Step One and buy the 'Big Book'. He is having severe physical withdrawals. He is not attending AA, however he did complete his work on the first Step, he understood his problem. I have given him a six week therapeutic discharge and told him only to return if he attends AA during this time. He did not return

Client 2.

Attended eight individual sessions.
SADQ score = 11.
Referred by GP.
Male.

Client comments	Staff comments
Pre treatment My drinking is symptomatic not causative. I suffer depressive illness and was prescribed anti-depressants for two years. I was drinking to cover depression. However I am receptive to these ideas. My Psychiatrist is not against controlled drinking.	There are strong indications that he is a chronic alcoholic. I have recommended that he attend AA five times a week and continue Heminevrin detoxification prescribed by GP.
During treatment I see it as a sickness now, not a weakness or immorality, perhaps it has some form of associated mental illness. I don't know if I am covering the symptoms of depression. I had a depressive illness, but I don't know if alcohol was the cause or symptom of this. Because I don't know I'm getting desperate. I'm confused between what my GP and Psychiatrist and counsellor at the Centre are telling me.	He is an arrogant man, full of anger and resentment, he wants to know all the answers as to why he is this way. He needs to do more work on Step One. I told him to buy the 'Big Book', read two chapters ready to discuss with me. He is still rationalizing and is deep into denial and projection. He seems to have an excuse for everything. I have told him that he is a very ill person and needs the facilities of the Centre to get well. Client never really got onto the programme, he continued to take pills prescribed by GP and remained under a Psychiatrist. I eventually asked him to take six weeks off from the Centre to give our programme serious consideration. He did not return.

Client 3.

Attended twenty six individual sessions and groups.
SADQ score = 30.
Self-referral after detoxification
Female.

Client comments	Staff comments
Pre treatment It can't be half measures I suppose, but I cannot discount the possibility that I may start drinking socially in six months or so. When I'm working I don't need to drink - it becomes secondary if I have other interests. Booze is a ubstitute for my lost world.	Client is willing to do anything that is suggested. Her true self will emerge when she is detoxified from Heminevrin. Client would not go to residential rehabilitation as suggested.
During treatment I see my own addiction as a very strong weakness, a form of illness. I find AA less useful than the Centre (also AA meetings tend to be taken over by unconstructive members). I disagree with the expectation that I should not go to pubs and I do not accept that I will have to cut off from my old friends completely. But I will have to change my lifestyle and way of thinking. Since I have stopped drinking, my old personality is coming out again.	Client is not attending AA and keeps having odd drinks. She is erratic, over-intellectualizing and denies everything. However she got over her initial attitude to AA eventually. She has had several slips, each time is told to keep going to AA and to get in touch with her sponsor. There has been a lot of procrastinating and she will not do her assignments when required. She keeps intellectualizing, she is not keeping it simple. She seem incapable of keeping it simple. Her priorities are wrong. She will not stick to the programme.

Client 4

Attended forty one individual sessions and groups.
SADQ score = 33.
Self-referral after previously failed inpatient detoxification.
Male.

Client comments.	Staff comments.
Pre treatment I feel it is a moral issue, a man should be able to control his appetites. I will have to change my lifestyle and attitudes.	At first he seemed a little confused. he got angry with the Centre for telling him to cut out the wrong pills (he needs certain pills for fits).
During treatment I expect problems with Step Two as it involves a 'higher power'.	He has put a lot of effort into Step One which has been painful to him, but now he understands it. He wanted to detoxify his own way, but he did not complete it. He has been told to give a firm commitment regarding detoxification or the Centre will no longer be involved. He did Step Two by defining his 'higher power' as 'fellowship', and finished Step Three. He has a lot of understanding, perception and insight.
Since slip, I feel more in tune with the programme than when I first started.	Then he had a slip (drink), he felt very bad, I talked to him and his wife. His wife has agreed to go to Alanon herself. He is now attending a lot of AA meetings. He will need to do Steps One and Two again since slip. He has also changed his AA sponsor. He is working well and has completed Steps One, Two and Three again, also sorted out several domestic problems with the help of the Centre. He has done Steps Four and Five and agreed on the importance of continuing to attend AA on a regular basis.

However he then relapsed.

I found the programme useful. I appreciated the unique value of having to 'share' with others your predicament. I think regular visits to AA are essential to continued sobriety. I find AA supportive. I have changed and am more honest with myself. AA meetings give each day a planned and committed structure.

He intellectualised and never really accepted that he was an alcoholic. The trouble with intellectuals is that they will not accept the definition. It's too simple for them. They are so convinced that they are right that they won't see that there is another way to look at things.

Client 5.

Attended twelve individual appointments and groups.
SADQ score = 27.
Self referral
Male.

Client comments

Pre treatment
My behaviour has gradually become childish, petulant and inexplicable. Because of the intellectual and emotional damage done by my drinking I cannot manage situations which in previous years I would have dealt with good grace.

I also started to mix with my intellectual and social inferiors, and began to be shocked, appalled and quite frightened by my behaviour.

I started drinking gradually but in

Staff comments

He intellectualizes and is cocky, arrogant, a smart arse.

later stages although it affected my work, I was never confronted by senior colleagues.

During treatment

All aspects of alcohol unmanageability shown on the Jellinek chart were either blatantly evident or just below the surface.

Often intellectualizes, almost everything is intellectualized. He was cocky and superior, taking the counsellor role in groups.

Procrastination, irresponsibility and general fear of confrontation were typical of my behaviour in the past. The Centre and AA are unlocking doors to the better parts of my nature.

I am beginning to see my 'history' in perspective. Since I can compare it to the experience of others. I am learning to live life as an integrated adult personality for the first time.

The staff have shown me examples of my behaviour to which I've been quite blind to with the perverted thinking of an alcoholic.

He has found the Centre very useful, counselling has made him see things differently.

Initially I had a reluctance to accept what I was being told, I got resentful of the counsellor (I believe this was transference). I got very angry.

Initially he did not realize alcoholism was an illness in itself. He thought he was drinking to cover depression. Now he feels that drinking causes the depression.

Although it is a 'cruel to be kind' policy here, I genuinely believe the staff care about the people who come here. The groups have an accumulated wisdom which is more than the sum of its parts. You need group support to change

He was arrogant and angry and often rationalised things such as his use of pills. He changed as he worked the programme, became less arrogant and apologised for his bad behaviour.

attitudes and maintain attitude change. Therefore I will need to continue attending AA after completing treatment at the Centre.

However he soon reverted to his old self and had more arguments with staff. After four months he left without finishing the programme. He didn't attend AA.

Summary of group A1 the unsuccessful stayers

All the clients in this group made some form of progress before relapsing or leaving the programme. It is interesting to note, however, that the clients in the successful group occasionally came up against similar problems but overcame them and went on to complete treatment. All five clients were articulate, educated and middle class, and held or had held in the past professional posts involving some responsibility. All had some knowledge of the various theories of addiction to the extent that they were aware of differing viewpoints to that of the Centre, and were therefore perhaps less likely to accept unquestioningly the basic beliefs of the staff. Staff references to 'arrogance', 'rationalizing', and 'intellectualizing' for clients in this group are common. It is seen as a common deficiency of these clients that they are unable to see things simply and to accept simple ideas and facts. A tendency to intellectualize is seen as a handicap to progress.

Subgroup B1 the successful stayers

This group consists of those clients who stayed in treatment for fairly long periods (average 14 individual sessions and 14 groups) and who succeeded in achieving and maintaining abstinence. Clients in this group either believed initially that they had an addictive disease (i.e. accepted the initial diagnosis and prognosis), or came to believe this as they worked through the treatment programme. It is interesting to note that the great majority of clients who stayed in treatment more than four weeks did eventually accept the beliefs of the staff, i.e. that their problems were symptomatic of their addiction, rather than the equally plausible converse. It is clearly difficult to determine whether this was actually true for these 'successful' clients, or simply that the programme was effective if the clients believed in it. NB. Two clients in this group did not agree to be interviewed in depth, qualitative data is therefore not included.

Client 1

Attended seven individual and group sessions.
SADQ score = 39.
Self referral.
Female.

Client comments	Staff comments
During treatment. The Psychiatrists I saw did not consider me an alcoholic. However I agree with the Centre completely. I understand that I had an illness which I am trying to recover from. I see it as a soul sickness. I have to change myself and my attitudes. People who go to AA are spiritually bankrupt, it is a spiritual programme.	Client has written a long, painful life story, demonstrating a good deal of suffering, but she is over controlling and most of her resentments are groundless. She worked the programme successfully and is a regular attender at AA.

Client 2.

Attended thirty one individual and group sessions.
SADQ score = 30.
Self referral (serious medical condition).
Male

Client comments	Staff comments
Pre treatment I consider it a weakness, to see it as a sickness is an easy way out. I know no way except self discipline and self respect.	
During treatment I will need to change my	It is difficult working with this

personality and how I derive my self respect. I am being persuaded that it is a sickness. I would like to believe this.

It may be necessary for me to see it as a sickness or a disease over which I have no control and therefore no responsibility before I can get well.

client, he finds it hard to trust. He has done Steps One and Two.
He has relapsed, he still wants to do it his way. I told him he must become sober or leave.

He is trying, has completed assignments. But is blaming and rationalizing. I told him to go to more AA meetings and talk more to his sponsor.

He has a medical condition which is a strong motivator in keeping him sober.
He succeeded in working the programme and now attends AA regularly.

Client 3.

Attended twenty three individual and group sessions.
SADQ score = 25.
Self referral
Male.

Client comments

Pre treatment
I did not recognize it as an illness until recently. I feel it is necessary for me to admit my powerlessness. My drinking is totally out of control. I have to trust that they know what there are talking about.

During treatment
I think I'm in a state of chronic alcoholism and so I don't have any

Staff comments

He realises he is an alcoholic. he is working well and is doing option but to go through the programme. I need to change my mental attitudes.

everything he is asked.

There are some problems with the religious content of the programme but he has adapted to the whole programme very well.

Since being on the programme I have actually watched my thought processes change. It follows a particular pattern, eacn time I come off my thought processes change in the same way.

Successfully completed programme, though had one slip.

Now a regular attender at AA.

Client 4.

Attended fourteen individual and group sessions.
SADQ score = 31.
'Referred' by friends from AA.
Male.

Client comments

Pre treatment
I see it as a sickness I will have for the rest of my life. I think there is a spark of alcoholism in all of us, I fanned mine until it became uncontrollable.

Staff comments

A good start in that he had already been attending AA for some time.

During treatment
Once you change your attitudes, everything else falls into place. It was only when I finally accepted that I was totally powerless over alcohol and believed in a higher power than myself, that I found an inner peace and a great new way of life, a life of sanity, sobriety and happiness.

Initially there were some difficulties; he kept slipping and could not accept in every sense that he was powerless over alcohol. However, he began to attend AA more regularly and got himself a sponsor (who he sees twice a week).

I could not do it without the Centre and AA, as the Centre is only open nine till five and I need continual support.

He had a mental block with Step Two, but did a lot of sharing about his resistance to doing the Steps, and is now committed to using the concept of a higher power.

I then had a period of residential rehabilitation, I could probably have done it without this, but it would have taken longer. think AA and the Centre are magic.

He is now sober and continues attending AA regularly four times a week.

Client 5.

Attended eight individual and group sessions.
SADQ score 17.
Self referral
Female.

Client comments

Pre treatment
I am worried about my health and mentality, my memory is going. I am slowly driving myself mad. I want to stop but I can't do it on my own.

During treatment
I am now going to seven AA meetings a week and attending the Centre. I get a very strong feeling of fellowship.

I am beginning to accept what they say, but I find the 'God bit' a bit difficult to accept. I thought I would be able to go back to social drinking, now I realize that I

Staff comments

Spent only a short time at the Centre, then a lot of regular attendance at AA after being introduced by the Centre.

She will probably reduce meetings to two a week in the future on the advice of her sponsor, in order to achieve greater balance in her life, so that she can do more living.

can't. I didn't realize how dependent I was. I had a different idea of alcoholism when I first came. I thought I was a depressive person and that drink would get me out of this state. The staff told me that drink causes the depression. I believe this now as life is getting better without it.

I though at first the Centre and AA people were phoney, but now I think they are genuine; they give so much time to me that I don't want to let them down. So I make an effort, I feel obliged to return their caring.

Client 6.

Attended eighteen individual sessions and groups.
SADQ score = 18.
Self referral
Female

Client comments

Pre treatment
AA makes you realize that you are not alone.

During treatment
I agree absolutely with the ideas. Although I also think it was partly due to a deprived childhood (I was brought up in care), but my brothers and sisters don't drink.

I think abstinence is the only way.

Staff comments

Client was very shy and reticent initially.

She is playing games with her detoxification. I made it clear that if she doesn't do it our way, she can go, and I told her to make more use of her AA sponsor.

She initially struggled with the work because she couldn't

understand. I needed to simplify the ideas for her as she had trouble with the book work. She had many problems with her family which we discussed, but I told her not to put her family before her sobriety, talked about priorities.
She attended Centre for nine months and continues to remain sober attend AA.

Client 7.

Attended seven individual sessions and groups.
Referred by GP who also prescribed tranquillisors.
SADQ Not known.
Female.

Client comments

During treatment
I'll have to start believing what other people tell me. My Psychiatrist tells me I should not come here as I'd be mixing with the wrong people. I believe it is a weakness and I don't have the will power to stop.

Staff comments

Peer pressure is a problem, her Psychiatrist also does not want her to stop drinking.

After three months she was referred to a residential rehabilitation unit. She did well and is now abstinent and attending AA.

Client 8.

Client comments

Pre treatment
I don't see it as a serious problem.

Staff comments

His wife attends Alanon He doesn't really want help badly

I've never craved a drink and I don't want to be a 'born again Christian'.

enough. He is minimizing.

During treatment

I'm doing it for my wife's sake. But I think she's over reacting.

Either he is in denial or he is not an alcoholic. He stopped drinking and occasionally attends AA.

Client 9.

Attended eight individual and group sessions.
SADQ score = 10.
Referred by his wife.
Male.

Client comments

Staff comments.

During treatment

How can you disagree with something if you know it is going to help you in the end ? But I still don't think I have any special reaction, it's an addiction not a sickness. I think a lot of it is greed. I haven't said I'm an alcoholic yet.
I want my business to succeed, that is more important to me than drink. I have to get my priorities right, drink used to be first, now work is.

At the start he was into denial, he wanted to control his drinking. He did Step One then relapsed. He did Step One again and this time succeeded. He is now abstinent and attends AA twice a week.

He is a workaholic.

Client 10.

Attended twenty two individual and group sessions.
Self referral
Female.

Client comments

Staff comments

Pre treatment

I needed to talk and feel a lot about a personal loss.

Client's difficulties mainly with physical withdrawals.

During treatment

My Psychiatrist is not in agreement with the Centre.

She had not deteriorated morally like the others and therefore had no need to do Steps Four and Five, the moral inventory and confession.

Client 11.

Attended thirty four individual and group sessions.
SADQ score = 32
referred by relatives.
Female.

Client comments

Pre treatment

I'm a binge drinker, my main problem is with the police and courts. I can't go on because of the way they treat you in police cells.

During treatment

I have found the Centre and counselling very helpful. I think support groups are very important, but with counsellors present. It is a very strict programme but very caring.
If I stopped drinking I'd change automatically. I believe I will not be able to drink at all. When you think you are cured, it gets dangerous because you think you can handle it.

Staff comments

Initially very frightened about detoxification. We talked about avoidance games she is playing.

After detoxification she was confused, doesn't know what is happening to her. I explained that this is normal. She has done a good Step Two, but her over-reaction to situations bothers me, games! Her thinking is disorientated. I told her to get out of the driving seat and stop controlling.
I found out today she has been lying about abstinence. I asked her to let me know if she wants to

leave. She says she will drink if she has to go (manipulation).

She is confused about Step Three, I got her to ring her sponsor every day this week and meet her for coffee. She is getting to like herself better, she has changed completely since coming to the Centre, including her clothes and her language. We turned her into a lady.

Client 12.

Attended twenty eight individual and group sessions.
SADQ score = 12.
Referred by Social Worker.
Male

Client comments	Staff comments
Pre treatment I initially tried to substitute pills for alcohol, the result was that I became cross addicted. I didn't think I was an alcoholic before I came here. I thought I just had very bad anxiety and panic attacks and that drink was covering these problems.	Client was shocked to find out how bad his drinking really was, but he could understand after talking about it. He realizes now he has had a serious drink problem for some time. He also said that this is the first time in his life that he has talked in depth about himself.
During treatment I found attending groups very difficult and meaningless at first. Now I find I can communicate with people better. I was not aware of my character defects until I joined the group. I think these defects made it more	He says that this is the best he has felt for a long time. His wife will come to Centre and go to Alanon. Talked of his fears of what his daughter will think if he is labelled as an alcoholic. He now sees this

difficult for me to give up.

as guilt.

I find AA very good medicine and I am a very calm person after attending Centre groups and AA.

I asked him to agree to go to three AA meetings a week. He has completed Step One and I feel he has come to terms with his powerlessness and unmanageability.

Having been a very sick person when first attending the Centre, I will always be very grateful to them for showing me the road to recovery.

I talked about AA and the necessity to get to two meetings a week. Also he is to feed back to me what he has got out of his reading of the 'Big Book' and the 'Little Red Book'. He does need help to clarify what he is reading. I talked with the whole family about the unmanageability of their lives. All have agreed to go to their respective meetings.

Good quality work for Step Three and getting ready to do Four and Five with the support of his sponsor.
Has done Step Four (personality defects) and Step Five. Successful outcome, now sober and regularly attending AA.

Client 13.

Attended thirty one individual and group sessions.
Self referral after detoxification.
Female.

Client comments

Staff comments

Pre treatment
I can't think straight, I'm having suicidal thoughts.

Client is desperate, will do anything. I wanted to be sure

I've had psychiatric help and group psychotherapy, which did me some good, but was only concentrating on problems.
I think if you are an addict you need to be told what to do.

During treatment
I don't disagree with anything. I think you need to leave yourself open for people to criticize you or you will not change or get better.

I like AA and the Centre because they offer intensive treatment. I am a born addict , I do anything to extremes, I will need to change my lifestyle and mental obsession.

I will have to change my attitudes (ie. that I know it all and that nobody else does, and that I'm better than them). I have to change my personality to be more assertive and adult about things.
The Centre and AA have been extremely useful to me. I would never have managed to give up my addiction without the help of the Centre group. Being able to be open and honest and having feedback on the others experiences has meant a lot. People like myself make me feel at ease and give me constructive and helpful advice.

(Data from two clients withheld.)

client would go to any lengths, including her marriage. I feel she is.

Client has done Steps One and Two and life story. She is worried that her feelings for people seem to be changing. Each week she seems to grow. She is considering leaving her husband. We did Step Three.

She is having trouble with Step Three and projecting like mad, complaining about others. I told her she'll 'have to accept what she cannot change', I emphasized the programme on this.

Client is screwed up about the Centre group and the personalities in it and she wants to deal with her feelings in the group instead of taking them away with her. She made commitment to attend AA.

She has decide to be chairman of AA group, it will help her grow.

Summary of subgroup B1 the successful stayers

Clients in this group tended to define their problems - whether psychological or social - in terms of personal pathology, that is as symptomatic of a disease, and therefore dealt with them by changing themselves (beliefs, behaviours etc), using the programme. They then defined their success in terms of their initial diagnosis. To an outsider this process may seem to involve self fulfilling prophecies. However, from the client's point of view, once they had accepted the basic beliefs which made sense of their personal situation and followed the prescribed directives, their lives would improve. In academic terms, these clients have been provided with a theoretical model which to some extent 'fits' their personal experience and which suggests ways to change this experience.

Subgroup A2 the unsuccessful leavers

This group consists of those clients who attended the Centre for between one and four sessions and who failed to work the treatment programme or achieve abstinence. It should be noted that of the 20 clients who attended the Centre less than four times, 15 failed to achieve abstinence. It can be seen that many of this group were not self referrals. However, the general statistical data would indicate that this is not a significant variable in treatment success.

The categories of 'pre treatment' and 'during treatment' are not used where clients have only been interviewed once, prior to treatment.

Client 1.

Attended two individual and group sessions.
SADQ score = 4
Referred by GP.
Female.

Client comments	Staff comments
It is difficult to accept what I am told. I can't imagine myself as an addict, I turn to alcohol under stress. It is up to me, but it is useful to have someone to listen and give advice.	Only attended twice, then left of her own accord.

Client 2.

Attended two sessions.
SADQ score = 30.
Self referral
Male

Client comments	Staff comments
I started drinking after a relative died. Alcohol has a particular effect on me, but not on other people. I think it is immoral, a weakness and a sickness. You start drinking to solve a problem and in the end you don't know why you're drinking.	He decided to work the programme but did not return.

Client 3.

Attended three sessions
Using alcohol, Cannabis and mushrooms.
Referred by probation.
Male.

Client comments.

I'm not addicted to anything, it is not a problem to me. My probation officer thinks it is a problem. I disagree that I won't be able to drink. I only use mushrooms a few months of the year and Cannabis is not addictive.

Staff comments

Little motivation.

Client 4.

Attended one session
SADQ score 31
Referred by probation
Male.

Client comments

I don't see myself as sick, I just drink too much. I enjoy drinking and the lifestyle, it is something to do. I like going to the pub. I think I'll be able to control it.

Staff comments

I recommended he get medical help, see a Psychiatrist. He has underlying problems. His dependency on alcohol only aggravates his anti-social feelings.

Client 5.

Attended two sessions.
SADQ score = 18.
Male.

Client comments

I think I should not drink at all - but I don't really believe it, not yet. I have difficulties with the quasi religious base.

Staff comments

He was anxious and willing to try Step One. His mother paid for him to go to a residential rehabilitation centre. His mother was referred to Alanon.

Client 6.

Attended two group and individual sessions.
SADQ score = 3.
Referred by probation.
Female.

Client comments

Drinking is not my problem. Circumstances and people are my problems.

Staff comments

Client came to interviews and groups slightly drunk, therefore difficult for staff to communicate. Client is strongly into denial that alcohol is the main cause of her problems. Unless she comes to terms with this we cannot help her. she is all the time trying to rationalize - she is finding it hard to surrender, but I think she can make it.

Client 7.

Attended two individual and group sessions.
SADQ score 18.
Previous inpatient detoxification.
Referred by probation
Male.

Client comments

These people can see you teetering on the brink and fish you out, it can't be a bad thing. The people at AA seem a little obsessive,

Staff comments

Possible underlying psychiatric problems.

everybody seems messed up. I've got no time for God or higher power.

Client 8.

Attended three individual and group sessions.
SADQ score = 30.
Referred by probation.
Male.

Client comments

I don't think anyone else can do much to help.

They could be guides, but when it comes down to basics, its up to me.

Staff comments

Client came for a couple of weeks but continued to drink. Although I have not done a diagnostic interview, I believe he is a chronic alcoholic.
He made a commitment to attend AA five times a week. He did not go. He was told that if he was not prepared to keep his word that there was little the Centre could do for him. I told him not to come back to the Centre until he had attended AA. He did not return.

Client 9.

Attended one session.
SADQ score = 18.
Referred by social worker.
Female.

Client comments

It has affected me physically but not mentally. It is a weakness or personality deficit rather than an illness. I blame myself totally. I thought I had the will power but

Staff comments

Difficult woman. She behaved in a superior way.

didn't use it, then suddenly realized my will power was non-existent. My dependency seems very extreme, like a total insanity; 'the devil himself, with all his disguises pulled away.'

They tell me it is a sickness, but I find it difficult to believe. I'm not going to let go of my own responsibility for myself. The battle is still mine, even with their help. But I need help.

Client 10.

Attended two individual and group sessions.
SADQ score not known.
Referred by probation.
Male.

Client comments

I'm just bored and I have nothing to do.

I don't believe what I'm told here is necessarily best for me.

Maybe I can be helped, it depends on how they go about it.

Staff comments

In my opinion this client is very immature and of low intelligence. We are not prepared to help until he comes to the full realization that we can only help him if he acts in a more responsible way towards his recovery.

Client 11.

Attended one session.
SADQ score = 44.
Referred by Psychiatrist
Male.

Client comments

Drink has taken over my life, I am obsessed with it.

I also see my drinking as self-medicating depression and anxiety. I have found a way to smooth the edges of life and make it easier.

I think I will have to change my attitudes and become less gregarious. But I haven't formulated an opinion about what I think about all this yet.

Staff comments

Did not return, but attend AA several times.

Client 12.

Attended one session.
SADQ score = 34.
Referred by solicitor for report.
Male.

Client comments

Drink causes more trouble than it is worth. I tried AA last year but just got fed up and started drinking again. If I was employed I wouldn't drink.

I'll change my lifestyle but I am not going to change my character. Sometimes I feel that they are trying to run your life for you, telling you what you should and should not do.

Staff comments.

Tried several AA meetings, but only came here once. Did not return after court case.

Client 13.

Attended two sessions.
SADQ score = 9.
'Referred' by AA members.
Male.

Client comments

I drink because it's social, to avoid loneliness. I want to stop because its too expensive. I draw the line at a pound a pint. Also it's upsetting my family.

I didn't know the Centre was different to AA. I didn't think my drinking was a problem before. I see it as a sickness now, a sickness that needs repairs. I have come to believe that it is in-built, something to do with my make-up.

He has attended AA several times. In my opinion he is a chronic alcoholic. We discussed his alcoholism and difficult home situation. He is a very angry man.

Client 14.

Attended one session.
SADQ score = 11.
Referred by probation.
Male.

Client comments

I am not abnormal, it is only a problem because I get into trouble. My friends are all the same. I do not see myself as an alcoholic.

If I gave up I would enjoy things less, but I could cut down with my girlfriend's support.

Staff comments

He left after one appointment.

Client 15.

Attend one session.
SADQ score = 26.
Referred by Psychiatrist after inpatient detoxification.
Male.

Client comments	Staff comments
I get very depressed and disorientated, and also I have hallucinations. I am not sure if these are causes or effects of my drinking. I tried AA years ago, but talking about drink made me feel like a drink. What the staff here think makes sense and I want to be cured - but I can't imagine what my lifestyle would be like.	Left after one appointment.

Summary of subgroup A2 the unsuccessful leavers

This group is interesting as it consists of those clients who did not accept the philosophy and beliefs of the Centre and/or felt that the Centre was not catering to their needs. They are people who saw their problems and therefore their needs and goals and methods of attaining them in different ways from the Centre staff. Members of this group tended to view the beliefs and methods of the Centre as dogmatic and inflexible, and often felt that their own opinions were undermined or ignored. They also believed that while the staff's beliefs may have been right regarding some people, the theory was not necessarily accurate in all cases.

The clients in this sub group who refused to accept the Centre Staff's beliefs usually saw themselves as having problems, but reversed the causal direction attributed by staff, seeing the drinking as a solution to these problems. They therefore wanted help with the problems and perhaps help to learn to control their drinking behaviour ('controlled drinking' approach), but did not tend to diagnose themselves as sick.The two most popular ideas amongst this group were that their use of alcohol was a behavioural disorder that they needed to learn to control or that alcohol was a medicine or solution for problems of personality or life generally.

Subgroup B2 the successful leavers

This group consists of those clients who attended the Centre less than five times, but who succeeded in remaining abstinent without attending the Centre programme. All continued to attend AA self help groups and viewed themselves as succeeding because of the support of AA. It is interesting that three of the group were actually referred by AA for extra help; though they did not take advantage of the programme, they stayed within AA. Follow up information was more easily available for this group as all continued to attend AA. Again, the categories of 'pre treatment' and 'during treatment' are not used when the subject was only interviewed once prior to treatment.

Client 1.

Attended three individual and group sessions.
SADQ score = 25.
Self referral.
Male.

Client comments

I have ruined relationships and lost jobs due to my drinking. I can't control it any more. I believe a weakness led me to getting the disease.

It seems impossible to work in the way the Centre and AA say, but it does work, the proof is around.

Staff comments

He came for counselling, then had a bad slip and left the Centre. But he continued regular attendance at AA and succeeded in maintaining abstinence through AA.

Client 2.

Attended three group and individual sessions.
SADQ score = 11.

'Referred' by AA members.
Female.

Client comments

I had been going to AA for four months, some AA members dragged me to the Centre. I think there is too much strong undermining criticism here- when someone might be in need of help or support.

You don't need sympathy but you need support.

Client came to the Centre a few times then disappeared.

When she was ready she could do it at AA. She is now a regular AA attender and is doing very well.

Client 3.

Attended three sessions.
SADQ score = 24.
'Referred' by AA members.
Male.

Client comments

I am a born alcoholic. I had been attending AA on and off for a while. I didn't think I could work the AA programme without support. other AA members suggested I go to the Centre to 'get the Steps right.' so I came for structure and guidance.

Staff comments

Client did not complete treatment at the Centre, but was successful through AA, where he is sober and a regular attender.

Client 4.

Attended two sessions.
SADQ score = 29.
Referred by Psychiatrist.
Male.

Client comments

I think I have worse nerves than most people, but it is a circular thing, I also get nervous because of my drinking.

I also drink because there is nothing else to do. If I stop I will have to do something to occupy me, I will have to keep busy.

I will have to stop drinking completely - there is no use trying to control it.

Staff comments

Client came to Centre for a short while then went to a residential rehabilitation for a 'top up'.

He now goes to AA on a regular basis and is doing well.

Client 5.

Attended two individual and group sessions.
SADQ score = 49.
'Referred' by AA members.
Female.

Client comments

I had been attending AA before the Centre. I had found AA very useful, two women were especially supportive. I had been drinking very heavily, initially it gave me peace, but in the end I began to neglect myself and become a recluse. I couldn't cope and I wanted to die. Since going to meetings I found out that I am not so bad; that it is not such a terrible thing for a woman to drink so much.

Staff comments

She succeeded through AA and is still attending AA on a regular basis.

Summary of group B2 the successful leavers

It is relevant that three of the group were actually referred by AA for extra help; though they did not take advantage of the programme, they stayed within AA. The Centre staff and AA members do not see themselves as distinct, in that Centre clients must attend AA in order to stay on the treatment programme at the Centre. AA is seen by the Centre not only as a place to continue the last eight steps of the treatment programme but also as a supportive aftercare service. Good links are consistently maintained between many AA members/sponsors and the Centre staff allowing for useful communication and co-ordination of help and support.

Discussion

The aim of this analysis was not to assess two (often conflicting) points of view and to determine which is accurate, but to illustrate how discrepancies in beliefs between therapist and client might affect outcome. The staff diagnosed the great majority of clients who attended the Centre as being 'alcoholic' or as having an addictive disease. The prognosis therefore was that unless they worked the programme there was no hope for them. All problems associated with alcohol use tended to be defined in terms of signs symptomatic of the disease and one of the most important concepts of the disease model is 'denial'. In the words of a Minnesota advocate, LeFevre: 'Alcoholism is a disease that tells you that you do not have it.'

The clients who refused to accept the Centre staff's beliefs usually saw themselves as having problems, but reversed the causal direction, seeing the drinking as a solution to these problems. They therefore wanted help with the problems and perhaps help to learn to control their drinking behaviour, but did not tend to diagnose themselves as sick. It can be seen that clients themselves were initially unlikely to define their own verbal response in terms of 'denial', but those who successfully complete treatment will redefine their responses in these terms later in the programme. The two most popular ideas amongst this group of 'unbelievers' were that their use of alcohol or drugs was a behavioural disorder that they needed to learn to control, and that it was a medicine or solution for problems of personality or life generally. Most clients who drop out of treatment do so in the very early stages. If clients are not prepared to accept the Centre's basic assumptions concerning themselves and their lifestyle, they will be unlikely to continue and will not be encouraged to continue by staff at the Centre, who felt that they could not work with people who were 'stuck in the denial stage'. If a client is able to accept a theory, even one with limited scientific support, such as the 'spiritual disease' model, then it is likely to work as well for him or her as other more 'scientific' ideas.

This chapter has not focused on external measures of the problem in each subgroup, however a baseline measure of the initial problem is necessary to check that levels of dependence did not vary greatly between groups. Before concluding this chapter the Severity of Dependence scores for each subgroup are reported below. These are then compared with scores for other agencies to give a rough idea of the seriousness of dependency problems dealt with at the Centre generally.

Table 6.2
SADQ questionnaire scores associated with length of attendance and success in each subgroup

Group 1B (Successful stayed in treatment)	Group 1A (Successful did not stay)	Group 2B (Unsuccessful stayed in treatment)	Group 2A (Unsuccessful) did not stay)
6	25	47	4
10	11*	11*	30
39*	24	30	31
30	29	33	18*
18	49*	27	30
31	23		18*
17			44
18*			34
32*			9*
12*			11
25			26*
36			
totals			
274	138	148	272
means			
22.8	27.6	29.6	22.6

The overall mean for the above table is 24.4.

SADQ scores:

Non-Dependent > mild dependence = 0-14
Moderate dependence = 15-29
Severe dependence = 30+

It should be noted that five scores were unavailable and eleven (*) of this set of 35 clients were using prescribed drugs in conjunction with alcohol. This use may have affected their SADQ score (little research has examined the scoring of cross addicted patients regarding severity of addiction, though many of the variables on the SADQ apply to people addicted to all depressant drugs).

The differences regarding the mean SADQ scores for each group are illustrated below:-

Table 6.3
Mean SADQ scores

	A	B
1	27.6	22.6
2	22.8	29.6

It can be seen that there was little difference in severity of alcohol dependence between the subgroups (subsets).

The reliability of the SADQ questionnaire has been relatively well tested in recent years. (See Stockwell et. al., 1983.) The questionnaire was administered to all but five subjects from the 'indepth' set (these five were considered dependent purely on drugs and not alcohol). It should be noted that there may be inaccuracies concerning those clients using both alcohol and drugs as symptoms of alcohol dependence may be complicated or accentuated by symptoms of dependence on other drugs.

The results of diagnostic interviews carried out by Centre Staff were also compared with the results of SADQ's. Although there was some correlation between those considered very serious alcoholics ('chronic phase') and the higher SADQ scorers, there was little general correlation. Centre Staff often accorded a level of seriousness to the problem not reflected in the SADQ results.

However, the seriousness of the problem (in terms of SADQ scores) seems to have no direct correlation to either the length of stay in treatment or successful outcome. The Centre Staff seem to deal equally well with seriously dependent clients and clients who may not be physically dependent but have a range of problems related to their alcohol and drug use (disabilities rather than dependencies). However, the less dependent clients are perhaps less suited to this programme and/or less in need of the facilities and staff time.

It should also be noted that the SADQ scores as a whole are lower than average for treatment services studied elsewhere. The following table gives the means and standard deviations of SADQ scores taken as norms for an Alcoholism Treatment Unit and a Detoxification Unit (see Stockwell et.al., op.cit.).

Table 6.4
SADQ scores taken as norms for treatment units

Source	
Alcoholism treatment Service	33.6 (S.d. = 16.1)
Detoxification Unit	33.8 (S.d = 1.3.7)

Although these data are presented here it should be noted statistical analysis of the subsets is limited as the subset size is too small for this type of analysis to yield any useful or accurate information. However, of the total set of forty, thirteen were female and twenty seven male. It can be seen that females responded slightly more successfully to the treatment programme than males.
The 'successful' females (nine) constituted 69% of the total subset of females. The 'successful' males (eleven) constituted 41% of the total subset of males.

Conclusions

The data analyzed in this chapter illustrate which clients gain most from the therapeutic process of AA. These were not necessarily those with the most severe problems, but rather those who were able to participate fully in the sequential treatment process because they were able to believe the theory and so utilize it as part of the process of recovery.

It appears that the Centre does well with those clients whose beliefs about their own condition are close to, or at least not incompatible with, the convictions of staff and the ideology of AA, or can be brought into close agreement during the treatment process. If clients do not keep to the basic tenets of the Anonymous Fellowship and progress through the treatment or 'work the programme' in the prescribed manner, then the outcome was unlikely to be successful.

The correlation between beliefs and benefits is however, difficult to determine. An essential aspect of the therapeutic programme at the Centre involves restructuring thinking and if this takes place the client will, by staff definition, be benefiting. If it does not, the client may be seen, by staff, as failing and is likely to be rejected from the programme. It therefore follows that most interviews conducted during treatment and at its completion involved client definitions of experience that coincided with those of AA and staff at the Centre. After treatment, consumer views are taken as a valid measure of whether consumers think that, from their present point of view, things are better. However, successful completion of treatment can also be seen to indicate that clients have crossed the boundaries of two 'incommensurable paradigms' (Kuhn, 1962). In terms of cognitive psychology the client in an untreated state will try to resolve dissonance in the direction of maintaining the untreated paradigm. After successful treatment she/he will try to resolve it in the direction of maintaining the new paradigm and a new social group will help him to do this. However, the initial proposition that lifestyle has improved, can to some extent, can be substantiated with reference to drinking behaviour or abstinence.

It can be seen from these data that the phenomenology of addiction is diverse. The term 'addiction' means different things to different people and therefore it is, to some extent, different things to different people. If it is accepted that people interpret and experience the phenomenon differently, it should not come as a surprise that no one theory will 'fit', or adequately interpret, the different groups or clusters of behaviours and experiences variously described as 'addiction'.

There appear to be no clear objective criteria for determining or predicting with any accuracy which clients will benefit from the treatment Centre which was the focus of this study. Although Edwards (1989, 1990) has suggested that the seriousness of addiction and the disabilities caused by it may offer possible predictions of outcome, depending on the type of treatment response, the significant differences in this work seem to be whether the clients see themselves, or will come to see themselves, as disabled because of their alcohol use, and whether they believe or will come to believe that they have an addictive disease.

The central question underlying this study is not 'Is it true that addiction is a disease?' or 'What is the cause of addiction?' but 'Can people be helped if they believe it is a disease?' or, 'Is it useful to believe the disease theory is true ?' The answer is that it is useful for some people, but not for others. For some clients the theory does not make sense of their experience, i.e. is not coherent. For others it is impossible to believe or have faith in the theory, though they can understand it. However, for a certain group of people the theory both makes sense intellectually and inspires their faith. These clients will in all probability be 'cured' in the sense that they can learn to live without drugs or alcohol and substitute a new social life, spiritual beliefs, emotional contacts and moral behaviour for the old way of life.

In the light of this situation, it is suggested that the clinical usefulness of a theory is of particular relevance and that this aspect of any theoretical model should be examined. Theories could be considered in terms of their therapeutic usefulness as instruments or methods, as a means to an end rather than an end in themselves. Some theories are obviously more useful in some circumstances than others. Rather than attempting to develop a comprehensive theory of addiction, it may be more useful to ensure that present theories are fully documented and understood. This would lead to a better understanding of their impact as theories - in - use, and contribute to a more pragmatic approach to theorising about addiction which would be closer and more relevant to the complex and confusing world in which addicts and their helpers must live.

The significance of this becomes greater when the Centre is considered as part of a system aiming at a comprehensive service. All potential clients do not see themselves as the Centre would see them, and a comprehensive service would need to cultivate a 'fit' with a wider range of conditions and subjectively defined needs. An apparent paradox arises, in that the most effective treatment will often be provided by those with the greatest faith in the particular model they are using, while the most effective referral service, and the 'matching' of clients to services likely to suit them, may depend on a more agnostic, provisional or sceptical approach to the claims of competing models, and particularly to each model's claim to exclusive validity.

7 Psychotherapy and the therapeutic process within AA

The academic and professional literature review in Chapter Two gave an account of the behavioural and medical theories of alcohol dependency and highlighted the inability of AA to provide a testable theory and method. When compared with medical and behavioural approaches, the theory of addiction underlying AA appears inadequate and invalid; that is the internal logic is tautologous and the external validity is questionable.

However, although criticisms of AA may explain the failings, these critiques do not address the successes. Both AA and Minnesota can be successful, yet the reasons why remain a mystery to outsiders because of the limitations of research frameworks. Treatment in the alcohol field can be interpreted and explained in different ways. This chapter examines literature from outside this field in order to understand why AA can be successful despite its theoretical limitations.

The relevant literature includes studies of group and individual change processes; not theories of psychotherapy, but theories of change process in general. This new perspective allows an examination of the AA treatment process itself in order to shed light on how and why this can be effective. Within this framework, the AA theory can be viewed as an ideology or a therapeutic tool and assessed in terms of its therapeutic usefulness rather than its academic utility. The focus will therefore been on therapeutic change as a whole, not on theories of addiction.

Therapeutic processes can be defined or made sense of using different theoretical models, for example; behavioural psychology allows the definition and measurement of behavioural change; cognitive psychology examines cognitive change and small group psychology attempts to describe change in terms of group processes. Unfortunately, as discussed earlier, the methodologies underlying scientific method do not extend to the measurement of subjective interpretation or processes of change. Therefore they do not take into account either the influence of ideology or the importance of individual processes. This short chapter reviews some of the work of authors attempting to integrate these factors into their understanding of therapeutic and religious change.

There are more than two hundred distinct psychotherapeutic theories (Ivey et al., 1987), yet most have elements in common and these 'essences' of psychotherapy can also be identified in individual change during 'conversion' experiences. It is useful to consider what the Centre programme has in common with other 'human change programmes' in order to understand its therapeutic usefulness. The processes identified earlier by clients and staff of the Centre are often described in therapeutic terms or in terms of conversion and it may become apparent that there could be similarities between the Centre programme, psychotherapy generally and religious or political 'conversions'.

The theory or beliefs underlying the Minnesota and AA treatment approaches have been discussed previously. The theory itself is not easily testable in a positivist or scientific sense, many of its premises appear tautologous and predicted outcomes seem rather like self fulfilling prophecies. However, the question of whether AA can be tested and compared with other programmes is perhaps less significant than the question of whether the therapeutic change processes in AA can be understood in the same way as those of any other therapeutic programme.

The AA programme is useful for a large number of people, having an accuracy of 'fit' with their personal experiences, making sense of their circumstances and prescribing a series of actions to help. Many theories of individual and social functioning can be seen as little more than particular interpretations which are useful to certain people in certain situations. This is particularly true of theories underlying much psychotherapeutic technique, where clinical experience has led to interpretation, rather than process acting as the precursor to clinical methods.

This chapter is therefore not concerned with how the Centre programme differs to other approaches to alcohol problems, but with what it has in common to other programmes of individual change. To do this it is necessary to examine psychotherapeutic processes as a whole, and to describe what the Minnesota programme and the AA philosophy have in common with all therapeutic treatments both individual and group. Attempts have been made to construct a general theory of psychotherapeutic intervention and similarities have been identified between cultures and civilizations in terms of other helping or 'persuading' procedures (political and religious programmes).

The function of persuasion in bringing about change is often ignored in psychological literature whereas conventional psychological theory is often ignored by members of self help programmes. Successful clients and staff at the Centre believed, in common with AA members, that behavioural and cognitive processes were incidental, signs or symptoms of far more significant change factors in the programme. The participants themselves believed that the knowledge and wisdom (ideology) were the main effective characteristics of the programme. Therefore before considering 'psychological' interpretations of the programme it is intended to examine the connections between ideology and therapeutic change. The work of Antze helps clarify issues here, examining the importance of the beliefs and ideologies of programme participants.

Theories of psychotherapeutic change: the importance of ideology

Antze examines the characteristics of self help groups generally in his paper 'Role of Ideologies in Peer Psychotherapy Groups' (1979). He criticizes much of the general literature concerning peer group psychotherapy on the grounds that it has one serious drawback: 'It neglects the very feature of these groups that their members take most seriously. Each self help group claims a certain wisdom concerning the problems it treats. Each has a specialized system of teachings that members venerate as the secret of recovery. These are often codified in a book or recited in capsule form at the start of each meeting.' Antze calls these teachings 'ideologies' and includes not only the group's explicit beliefs but also its rituals, rules of behaviour, slogans, and even favourite expressions. He goes on to state 'as far as members themselves are concerned a group's teachings are its very essence.' (op.cit., p.273).

Antze accepts the social psychological interpretation of peer therapy groups as 'arrangements for mutual support' (ibid., p.274). He agrees that the key characteristics of these groups - specialization, use of mutual confessions and quasi religious style - (see also Bales, 1944 and Clinard, 1949), can be understood as serving a supportive purpose. However he suggests that because researchers and social psychologists have 'neglected ideology, that they have missed another, equally crucial function of these groups - a persuasive function.' (ibid., p.274). He goes on to state that 'No understanding of how these groups help their members can be complete without examining this persuasive process.' (p.274).

There is no doubt that Antze's sentiments were reflected in the Centre, this 'persuasive process' was an essential aspect of the AA and Centre philosophy and an integral part of the everyday 'therapeutic process'. Its importance is perhaps best highlighted by the emphasis placed on 'twelfth stepping'; the practice of helping newcomers and maintaining one's own recovery by telling one's own story in terms of the AA philosophy.

However, the importance of ideology is generally neglected in psychotherapeutic literature, each school assuming the 'truth' or theoretical validity of their own approach. In an attempt to overcome this difficulty this section will combine psychotherapeutic concepts with anthropological concepts. Theories and therapies will be redefined as myths and rituals in order to allow an analysis of their social function in therapeutic groups. Myth is used in the anthropological sense of a picture of the nature and the meaning of the universe and man. The sociological meaning of the term is broader including a whole world picture held by a social group and the value system anchored in that view. (Gould and Kolb, 1964). The word is used in this context to indicate not only the questionable 'absolute truth' of the ideologies but also their function. The anthropological functionalist interpretation of the purpose of myth is that 'Myth fulfils in primitive culture an indispensable function; it expresses, enhances and codifies belief; it safeguards and enforces morality; it vouches for the efficiency of ritual and contains the practical rules for guidance of man.' (Malinowski, 1948).

The **content** of the 'myths' of AA will be discussed and, in the light of the particular significance of the ideology of AA to the Centre programme it is necessary to examine the **functions** of myth and ritual in psychotherapy generally. (NB. the term ritual denotes symbolic actions which are not necessarily purposive;) The terms myth and ritual would be unlikely to be accepted by any particular school or group of adherents, but enable an analysis of function independent of theoretical issues. That is, in order to be able to look at similarities between the **function and utility** of different theories, rather than analyze the theoretical content, it is necessary to define this content as serving the function of myth, independently of its internal consistency and external validity.

Therapeutic myths and rituals have several functions: these are outlined by Frank (1981). Firstly they can be used to strengthen the therapeutic relationship. A shared belief system is essential to the maintenance of groups, and creates a powerful bond between therapist and client. A large part of the therapeutic benefit at the Centre could be seen to be derived from the confidence the client develops in his therapist, the groups and later on, his sponsor. The ability to inspire and maintain the client's expectation of help is possible largely through the beliefs implicit in the Centre's 'programme'. In this sense the myth and ritual of the Centre are powerful morale builders in themselves. Frank emphasizes the function of ritual in providing new learning experiences. Behavioural psychology would endorse the notion that the more experiential, as opposed to purely cognitive, learning takes place, the more chance of change. Exposure to new experiences in the Centre groups gives clients the opportunity to 'try out' or practice different ways of behaving.

Frank emphasizes that cognitive and behavioural change are necessary but not sufficient for change, the element of emotional arousal is considered extremely important, making the client more 'suggestible', that is more sensitive to other influences. Arousal intense enough to be disorganizing further increases the dependence on the therapist and may facilitate the achievement of a better personality integration, by breaking up old patterns of thinking and behaviour. It is also interesting to note that eliciting intense emotions characterizes healing rituals in many non industrialised societies. (This is particularly well illustrated in the writings of Levi-Strauss, 1968). The myth also serves to enhance the client's sense of mastery or self efficacy by introducing a conceptual scheme that labels and explains symptoms and supplies the rationale for the treatment programme. These interpretations need not be correct, merely plausible.

The general training of therapists gives some insight into the common features of therapies. Frank remarks that even if all therapeutic techniques did prove to be fully interchangeable, it would still be necessary to master one or more approach. (This would be confusing the *content* of therapeutic conceptualizations and procedures with their *function*). Most skilled therapists need to master at least one therapeutic rationale and ritual. The therapist needs this almost as much as the client to maintain his sense of competence, especially in the face of failures. Therefore he needs techniques that are irrefutable and are supported by the like minded group to which the therapist belongs. (Festinger, 1957.) The therapist's choice of procedure/theory seems less important than his ability to believe in his particular myths and rituals and so appear convincing to his clients.

Antze agrees with Frank about the importance of ideology, though differs in that he distinguishes between psychotherapy and peer therapy, stating that myth is far more central to peer therapy groups than to other forms of psychotherapy. 'Peer therapy organizations are like religious sects, and unlike most other forms of therapy, they are fixed communities of belief.'(p.274). He states that studies of religious conversion show that this peer association is a very powerful force (see also, Berger and Luckman (1967) and William James (1958)). This process has also been likened to brain washing, for example in China in the Korean War, Sargant (1957). These authors would also be likely to concur with Berger and Luckman when they state that the most 'important aspect of a conversion is not the actual conversion but the ability to keep on taking it seriously; to retain a sense of its plausibility'.(see Antze, p.275).

Antze is therefore emphasizing the significance of the 'sharing of experience' in order both to convert and maintain conversion. 'Stories that members tell become an object lesson, an illustration of certain ideas. In this sense, the sharing of experience runs well beyond confession or catharsis and operates as a subtle form of indoctrination.' (p.275). He cites Festinger's (1964) work regarding social influence, which indicates that the persuasive effect is likely to be strongest for the person telling the story, since that person is actively recasting his or her experience in the light of the group's ideas. It is of interest that this technique is used in brain washing or Chinese thought reform and also in psychoanalysis (Lifton,

1961, Sargant, 1957).

Antze continues his analysis of the structural characteristics of 'persuasive' groups by suggesting that all those who join a particular group tend to be alike in certain ways and goes on to say 'In many groups, the uniformity of members is also enhanced by a natural sorting process that tends to exclude persons who feel out of place.'(p.276.) This seems particularly relevant to AA and the Centre. Clearly uniformity makes mutual identification easier; it also ensures cohesion which is important in strength of influence (Bednar and Lawlis, 1971). Significantly Antze also cites Festinger as confirming that the strongest influences are those whom the subject sees as like himself but more successful. (ibid., p.277)

Having identified the structural characteristics of 'persuasive groups', Antze then proceeds to identify five ideological tenets specific to AA itself (pp. 280-281) :-

1) The nature of alcoholism.
2) 'Hitting bottom.'
3) The Higher Power.
4) The moral inventory.
5) 'Twelfth-stepping.'

He then illustrates how these tenets provide a 'cognitive antidote' to the cognitive and emotional experiences of 'alcoholism' (p.281). At this stage Antze draws on the work of Frank, particularly focusing on the supposition that every effective therapy achieves its ends by changing the client's 'assumptive world' (i.e. cognitive change). The work of Frank will be examined later in this chapter in some detail, with the aim of identifying commonalities between psychotherapies and placing the AA philosophy and the Minnesota Method within the context of psychotherapy generally. Antze substantiates Frank's view of the therapeutic process as involving modification of 'values, expectations, and images' (cognitive change) by citing empirical support in a major study of encounter groups (Lieberman, Yalom and Miles, 1973). He describes the 'cognitizing' process as being similar to what he calls the 'persuasive process'. Lieberman et al. also use such concepts as 'frameworks for how to change' and 'the translation of behaviour and feelings into ideas'in their research.

Antze then expands his particular notion of a 'cognitive antidote' that particular groups use in order to understand and attempt to reverse the basic features of the specific condition shared by everyone who joins. He talks specifically of four aspects of AA and alcoholics themselves that enable this 'antidote' effect:-

1) The four 'structural characteristics'.
2) The five ideological tenets of AA.
3) The three 'experiences of self characteristic of an Alcoholic'.
4) The notion of cognitive antidotes to these 'experiences of self'.

Antze's work on the 'persuasive function' of psychotherapeutic groups is not necessarily exclusive to therapy; religious and political changes can be produced and maintained by the same mechanisms. However, it is clear that cognitive change and persuasiveness are an integral part of the AA programme. The next section will indicate how Antze categorizes the cognitive elements of the programme and suggests how its essential points could be construed as 'antidotes' to the problems faced by an alcoholic.

Antze reduces the AA philosophy to five essential points. (ibid., pp. 279-287). First, he outlines the 'nature of alcoholism' and describes the rather paradoxical juxtapositioning of the disease concept with the moralistic language of AA. He states that the contradictory stance adopted, of stating that an alcoholic is constitutionally different from other people, yet that this is rooted in a moral failing, would suggest 'that neither is quite what it means'. (p.280). It should be noted that AA members themselves would dispute this. To them the idea that one has a constitutional weakness does not conflict with the idea that one has a moral responsibility to control it.

Second, Antze describes the concept of 'Rock bottom' and again points out the irony or inconsistency in the belief that 'the alcoholic is ready for change only when persuaded that all efforts at self-control are hopeless.' (p.280). Third, he describes the concept of the 'Higher Power' in terms of a guide or protector who will help the AA member to remove his moral shortcomings. He then enumerates the 'Moral Inventory' and twelfth-stepping' as the fourth and fifth essentials of the programme.

Antze then describes certain 'traits' common to compulsive drinkers in Anglo-American countries. Evidence for these traits is demonstrated by Jones (1965) and McCord and McCord (1960). Antze considers the possibility that such 'traits' may be personality traits but states that 'it seems at least likely that they are learned in the course of the addiction process' (p. 282). He lists these traits as :-
'Great ambition, perfectionism, impulsiveness,narcissism, low frustration-tolerance, unreliability, grandiosity, defiance, extreme defensiveness and proneness to bouts of remorse accompanied by resolutions to do better.' (p.282).

Antze believes that all these traits can be shown to stem from a common root. He suggests that the alcoholic differs from the 'normal' person in 'one key respect: he exaggerates his own authorship in the events of his life; sober or drunk, he tends to perceive his world as fashioned mainly by his own acts.' (p. 282). He states that the result of these beliefs is 'a growing isolation of self from world; an isolation that is ultimately very painful' (p.283). He then attempts to describe this 'condition' of the alcoholic in terms of three distinct 'experiences of self' and demonstrates how the ideology of AA can be understood as providing an antidote to this 'way of being' or these 'experiences of self'. These three experiences of self are described as 'the omnipotent self', 'the embattled self', and 'the accountable self' (pp.282-284).

This idea of characterizing individual experiences of self particular to 'alcoholism' is referred to by Cook (1988 b.), who states that there are 'three experiences of self, characteristic of alcoholism.'

Antze then discusses the therapeutic benefits of the AA ideology in terms of the 'experiences of self' of the alcoholic. He states, 'to absorb the AA message is to see oneself much less the author of events in life, the active fighter and doer, and much more as a person with the wisdom to accept limitations and wait for things to come.' He goes on to say that these changes 'provide the member both with a sound defense against alcohol and with a greater reduction in his need for it.' (p.284).

The therapeutic or psychological benefit to be gained from 'letting go' or asking less of oneself and putting trust in forces beyond one's own control can therefore be seen as an antidote to the alcoholic's experiences of self. Antze describes each of the five essential essences of AA in terms of its psychological benefit for a person with the particular 'traits' identified as those of an alcoholic.

Finally it should be mentioned that the therapeutic programme of AA has also been found to be useful for people who are not alcoholic, e.g. families of alcoholics. The study of the Centre would indicate that people who are not physically addicted to alcohol would also seem to benefit from the therapeutic programme. Although Antze assumes that the personality 'traits' that he describes are peculiar to the alcoholic, it is possible that they are also the experience of many isolated or unhappy people who may derive the same comfort and benefit from the AA ideology and support that 'alcoholics' do. This would seem to be the case for some of the clients attending the Centre.

I have included a fairly detailed summary of Antze's theory that change induction can be best understood in terms of value transformation/alterations of belief systems, partly because this seems a plausible account or analysis of the processes involved in research into the Centre itself, and partly because this account is very similar to descriptions of the process by participants, staff and clients. This is not to suggest that ideology is of paramount importance but simply that theories ignoring the persuasive function of programmes are inadequate to explain the whole process.

Theories of psychotherapeutic change: common processes and 'essences' of psychotherapy

To understand the relation of the Minnesota model and AA to psychotherapy, it is necessary to examine psychotherapy generally and then compare general processes that can be identified in psychotherapeutic groups with those identified as operating in the Centre. The therapeutic change processes at the Centre not only have much in common with general therapeutic techniques but also with political and religious conversions. An understanding of how and why these conversions or changes take place and the kinds of people and problems that they benefit, should throw light, not only on the therapeutic process at the Centre, but also on the kind of people likely to benefit and why.

It can be seen from the previous discussion that Antze and Frank have stressed the importance of factors not usually identified in the psychotherapeutic literature or in the alcohol field. Psychotherapeutic techniques are usually explained in theoretical terms that specify the basis for the development of the problem and the way in which the treatment operates to produce change. Theory specification is seen as the precursor of practice, not an integral part of it. Technique specification (clarification of method) is seen as necessary simply to ensure that techniques can be replicated.

This sequence is effective where techniques are, for example, based on deterministic theory and involve directive and concrete procedures, e.g. behaviour therapy techniques. But it is less useful with those treatments which are based on a phenomenological approach and identify individual and interpersonal processes rather than particular procedures as the significant therapeutic factors. Examples are the 'client-centred' therapy of Carl Rogers and the Gestalt therapy of Fritz Perls. In these cases it is more relevant to examine and specify processes, the way processes develop and the therapist's role in their emergence in treatment. As Alan Kazdin (1977) has warned, without improved attempts to specify processes, many treatments are likely to be ignored for research purposes.

The problem of interpreting and assessing the effectiveness of psychotherapeutic techniques has been much debated since Freud first formulated theories of psychological dynamics. Much of the confusion lies in difficulties in defining psychotherapy itself. Strupp (1973 and 1976) attempts to clarify this problem by identifying the basic features which psychotherapies have in common. He sums up his conclusions by stating that psychotherapy is concerned with personality and behaviour change. 'The patient who seeks help ... desires change - he or she wants to feel or act differently - and the psychotherapist agrees to assist the patient in achieving this goal.' He attributes the confusion surrounding the definition of psychotherapy to a tendency to regard it as 'analogous to medical treatment', whereas he sees psychotherapy as having 'only a superficial resemblance to this model'. He develops this argument by examining the history of psychotherapy, stating that it 'bears a much closer relationship to the teacher-student model. As early as 1905, Freud characterized psychoanalytic therapy as a form of "re-education" or "after-education"... Psychotherapy is a learning process, the role of the therapist is analogous to that of a teacher or mentor.' (Strupp, 1976 passim.)

Strupp emphasizes that no single definition of psychotherapy or behaviour therapy has received universal acceptance and adds that any single definition is unlikely to be given it. He argues that personal definitions are dependent on the therapist's theoretical orientation and other factors; 'psychotherapy is seen by some as a psychosocial treatment, by others as a form of education, and by still others as a means of promoting personality growth and self-actualization.' The same can clearly be said about the AA twelve step programme, which is described in many different ways.

Outcome research in the field of psychotherapy has reinforced the notion of common processes across different theoretical types. It has been difficult to conduct outcome research and is often flawed. However, the following summary by Frank (1981) clarifies the basic conclusions. First, patients who receive any form of psychotherapy can be seen do somewhat better than controls and second, most patients who show initial improvement maintain it. This would suggest that therapy accelerates improvement. Frank states that most of determinants of success lie, first, in the relationship between therapist and patient: second, in cognitive therapy restructuring cognitions is particularly effective with depressed patients: third, that the features shared by all therapies account for an appreciable amount of the improvement observed in most psychiatric patients who respond.

Frank has no confidence in the possibility of validating any one particular theory or technique. 'No form of therapy has ever been initiated without a claim that it had unique therapeutic advantages. And no form of therapy has ever been abandoned because of its failure to live up to these claims....To my knowledge, no therapeutic school has ever disbanded because it concluded that another's doctrine and method was superior.' (Frank, passim.) He states instead that all therapies share certain 'healing components.' It is worth considering these 'essences of psychotherapy' in some detail, as the therapeutic process at the Centre can be better understood within the context of the psychotherapeutic process generally. Although Alcoholics Anonymous and the Minnesota Method are seen by many in this country as rather obscure phenomena to which they are denied access, on closer examination it becomes apparent that, though the ideology differs from more conventional forms of psychotherapy, the therapeutic process differs very little.

Before reviewing the content of psychotherapeutic techniques, it will be useful to consider what the task of psychotherapy is. That is, what is 'wrong' with clients who request this kind of help ? It is apparent from the descriptions, statistics and SADQ scores of clients attending the Centre that many were not actually physically addicted to alcohol. They used it to help them deal with unpleasant feelings or circumstances, often becoming dependent in the process. It is therefore relevant to consider why the form of psychotherapy used at the Centre with the features that Frank describes should be beneficial both to those clients who are addicted to drink and to those who are not.

Frank has attempted to define what the clients of psychotherapists have in common and in doing so has formulated what he has called the 'Demoralization Hypothesis' (see Frank, 1974, pp. 314-5, 327 and 339-40). This hypothesis is based on conclusions of outcome research, that is, that patients, whatever their symptoms, must share a type of distress that responds to the components common to all schools of psychotherapy. Frank proposes that patients seek psychotherapy not for symptoms alone but for symptoms together with demoralization. He characterizes this demoralisation in terms of; subjective incompetence, loss of self esteem, alienation, hopelessness and helplessness and loss of control. (See also Brown and Harris, 1978.)

Demoralization leads to lack of certain skills or confusion of goals, so patients become persistently unable to master situations (subjective incompetence plus distress). The descriptions of demoralization that Frank offers (pp.270, 236, 314-6, and 278-8) seem particularly apt for describing the condition of clients who are addicted to or have problems with drink. This is perhaps partly due to its physiological effects and also to the consequences of the lifestyles adopted by those who are dependent on it. However, it should be noted that the concept of utilizing basic psychotherapeutic techniques to help those who show evidence of the symptoms and distress that Frank describes would seem particularly appropriate for the client group studied in this research. Frank then sees demoralization as a core problem and therapeutic components as a means of directly or indirectly combating it.

Therapy at its most basic is seen to consist of the application of special techniques to combat maladaptive patterns and encourage more appropriate ones. Frank often refers to a basic underlying premise of cognitive psychology, attributing this to all psychotherapies, that humans react to their interpretation of events, the difficulties arising when these interpretations do not correspond to events as they are in reality. All psychotherapies, therefore, can be seen as trying to alter patients' views of themselves, their relations with others, and their system of values.

Frank identifies the following elements of psychotherapy:-

1) An emotionally charged, confiding relationship with a helping person, often with the participation of a group. This relationship involves a non judgemental empathetic response from the helping person.
2) Confession, in the context of a supportive helping person or group.
3) Forgiveness or some form of absolution from the helping person or group.
4) Positive and negative reinforcements.
5) Modelling of the helping person or group.
7) Creation and maintenance of a particular set of values.
8) Creation and maintaining of particular myths, theories or beliefs. A rationale, conceptual scheme or myth that provides a plausible explanation for the patient's symptoms and prescribes a ritual or procedure for resolving them.
9) Creation and maintaining of particular rituals.
These rituals should require active participation of both patient and therapist and is believed by both to be a means of resolving distress etc.

Some of the properties of therapeutic groups at the Centre were clearly intrinsic to most small therapeutic groups, as can be seen from chapters Five and Six. For example, the emotionally charged therapy and support visible in Centre groups have much in common with other therapies. Other factors which coincide closely are the confession and the resulting acceptance within the group, modelling of the group and the maintenance of the group beliefs through ritual.

The aspects of therapeutic functioning listed above are not of course limited to psychotherapeutic groups. Religious and political groups may be said to contain many of these properties. While it is clear that AA and the Centre have much in common with psychotherapies generally, it is also apparent that they have moral and spiritual components not present in many forms of therapy.That is, although AA has much in common with psychotherapy, it differs in significant ways, highlighting the importance of values and sharing moral and spiritual similarities with religious and political movements. The importance of moral and spiritual values is often covert or absent from psychotherapy generally. However, it is very visible in religious and political groups and particularly in change processes or conversions. The next section will therefore examine the influence of these aspects within group processes as a whole and examine the similarities between AA and non-therapeutic groups.

Theories of group change processes: values, morals and spirituality

The place of values in psychotherapy

The social context of psychotherapy itself is often downplayed: if social values underlie a therapeutic approach they are often implicit or taken for granted in both therapy and research. However, studies of therapy cannot be complete without an understanding of the therapeutic aims within the context of social life as a whole. Strupp (1973, 1976), for example, sees psychotherapy and the problem of treatment outcome as extremely complex and not conducive to simple answers; 'it touches on many facets of human life, and conceptions of mental health and illness cannot be considered apart from problems of philosophy, ethics, religious and public policy. Inescapably we deal with human existence, the person's place in the world, and ultimately we must confront questions of value.' (1976) He sums up the moral dilemma of social conformity and individualism that lies at the base of most therapy, as follows; 'In the end, someone must make a judgement that a person's compliance with requests from others is a virtue or an indicator of pathological submissiveness.' Either we accept a patient's judgement that he or she feels better or we redefine it as in some way pathological, deluded or simply inappropriate, a 'reaction formation', or 'denial'. These decisions can only be made by reference to the values society assigns to feelings, attitudes and actions, that is decisions and outcome assessments are made with reference to a socially defined, not an absolute, reality.

Values are clearly inherent in conceptions of mental health and illness as well as in diagnosis and clinical judgements based on these models. Strupp points out that 'One of the great stumbling blocks in psychotherapy research and practice has been a failure to realize the importance of values.' This conclusion has also been given substance by the work of Garfield (1971) and Bergin (1978), who have done much work together and separately in this area. They have demonstrated that outcome assessments by patients, peers, independent clinicians and therapists correlate only moderately. They stress that raters in their research bring different perspectives to bear and that the relative lack of correlation found in their analysis can be explained largely in terms of the different perspectives of those involved.

It is therefore necessary to discuss the various definitions or interpretations of psychotherapeutic processes of change within the context of social psychological and sociological paradigms. That is, to look more closely what Strupp calls the problems of 'philosophy, ethics, religious and public policy' or the 'values' inherent in describing and evaluating psychotherapy.

These issues are developed by Frank (1974) and are summed up in his paper 'Therapeutic Components Shared by all Psychotherapies' (1981).

Frank states that the conceptual schemes which structure all psychotherapeutic procedures reflect not only a particular society's conceptualizations of illness and health but also its values.

The AA programme incorporates the 'basic ingredients' of most psychotherapeutic treatment programmes, but in contrast to many psychotherapies, clearly defines the values involved. It places its therapeutic techniques well within the context of a particular social reality, defining this social context as **real** and the beliefs and values as **real**, (though the'reality' of the AA programme does not necessarily correspond to the wider social paradigms). Certain forms of social interaction and certain self images are defined as good, real, etc., that is morally and spiritually right, while others are dismissed as games/roles and therefore morally invalid.

It has been argued here that Frank's 'essences of psychotherapy' are involved in all individual psychotherapeutic change processes, but that the values inherent in the cultural or social context influences the aims and structure of the therapy itself.This is particularly clear in the group processes underlying AA because overt values are seen as an integral part of the change process.

Overt moral and spiritual values are also a large part of 'non-therapeutic' group changes processes, such as religious and political conversions. Further understanding of these aspects of AA can be gained from a closer examination of these groups.

Religious and political conversions

This section looks at similarities between therapy and religious and political conversion. Therapeutic change has much in common with religious conversion, and political conversion or 'thought reform' has similar aims and methods to both religious and therapeutic conversions. As AA combines the characteristics of religious and therapeutic change, it might be expected that it would provide an ideal case to illustrate the commonalities between the two. It is also likely that similarities between AA conversions and political conversions would be very pronounced.

The positive side effects of religious and political conversions seem much the same as those of effective psychotherapy in terms of therapeutic value, relief of distress and symptoms, both emotional and behavioural, and particularly similar to effects of group therapy. If therapy is seen as attempting to bring about enduring modifications in the patient's assumptive world that will enable him to function more effectively (i.e. to facilitate 'development' or 'maturation' of the patient's personality, to help him become less 'conflicted' or better 'integrated' - to help him, in some sense, become a better person); it has much in common with faith healing, religious revival, political conversion,'thought reform' and brain washing. The processes involved in conversion may however be different to those involved in the maintenance of the conversion. A significant feature or 'problem' of religious or political conversions is that they do not often last very long. This can also be said of the changes brought about by intensive psychotherapy. The way AA **maintains** conversions is one of the most interesting aspects of the programme and perhaps has more in common with religious and political programmes than with therapies.

As discussed earlier, successful psychotherapy often includes changes in patients' values and the development of a more optimistic view of life. In this sense its results resemble those of a religious conversion. This may be characterized as a change in the person's attitudes towards God or the universe, with the knock on effect of changes in his attitudes towards himself and the people significant to him. It is important to note that 88% of a large sample of AA members reported a (spiritual) 'conversion' of some kind. (See Robinson, 1979.)

Conversions can be the undramatic reawakening and reaffirmation of previously held beliefs, the end result of a slow maturational process (such as might occur in long term psychoanalysis), or the result of an abrupt shift in assumptive systems, e.g. in encounter groups. The most dramatic are sudden conversions characterized by drastic and far reaching psychic upheavals, usually accompanied by strong emotion and sometimes leading to permanent changes in attitude and behaviour.

In common with psychotherapeutic change, a sudden religious conversion is typically preceded by a period of severe demoralization (see Frank, pp.314-5.) It is significant that Alcoholics Anonymous and the Minnesota Model require clients to have reached 'rock bottom' before they can effectively embark on the therapeutic programme (see chapters Three and Five). Frank suggests that this demoralization prior to an effective religious conversion is sometimes so intense that the person becomes confused, often to the degree that he attributes these experiences to the outside world. 'A sense of isolation and estrangement from others characterizes the pre-conversion state, the candidate is tormented by guilt and self-doubt. Effects include despair, hatred, resentment, helpless anger etc. In such a state he longs to submit himself to an all powerful, benevolent figure who can give him absolution and restore order to his world.'(p.80).

Frank describes the resulting change in the religious convert's perception of himself in relation to the deity as involving certain changes in his picture of himself and of others, and changes in his patterns of social participation. It increases the clients self worth though paradoxically also increasing feelings of humility. (p.81). This description closely parallels that of clients at Step Two of the Minnesota programme, involving the necessity 'to hand ourselves over to a higher power'.

Frank (1974) in an attempt to understand the mechanics of religious conversions examined the work of a famous religious revivalist, John Wesley. It should be remembered that the early AA members based the initial principles of AA on those of the early Protestant teaching in England and America: the groups were also similar in form, if not content, to the Oxford Group. That AA reflects Wesley's teachings is not therefore coincidental, the founders of AA perhaps preempting Frank in his search for understanding.

Wesley recognized the importance of a like minded group in sustaining the assumptive world of its members. The importance of continuing group reinforcement in sustaining new attitudes is implicitly or explicitly recognized in and many different schools of psychotherapy including psychoanalysis programmes for alcoholics and drug addicts. (See Deissler (1970) and Janov (1970). The importance of this aspect is also paramount in the Minnesota and AA models. Wesley placed great stress on continuing class meetings to consolidate and strengthen the new world view. He divided his converts into groups of not more than twelve who met weekly. Problems relating to their conversion and their future mode of life were discussed in agreed secrecy. (See Frank, pp.82-3) These observations regarding Wesley are also formulated by Sargant (1957), and bear remarkable resemblance to early AA groups. The leader of these groups kept close watch for evidence of backsliding and members who 'grew cold and gave way to the sins which easily beset them' (Sargant p. 83) were expelled from classes and Methodist society. Once again there are clear similarities with the Minnesota and AA methods adopted by the Centre. Clients were asked to leave or take a six weeks break from the Centre if they were seen as sliding back into old habits and old ways of thinking. It is significant that the majority of clients asked to take a six week break did not return. There is little knowledge concerning social and personal factors that might heighten susceptibility to conversions. Personal attributes related to general susceptibility to influence seem to predispose people to conversion experiences. For example, hysterics, people with low self esteem and those with undue fear of social disapproval seem to be good candidates. Feelings of anger, guilt and isolation are characteristic of the pre-conversion state. Many converts have a religious upbringing, so that for them conversion is more a resurgence of dormant attitudes than a shift to totally new attitudes or beliefs. However, clients can shift to entirely new ones, especially if in a state of high indignation at meetings. As Sargant states, 'The best way to avoid possession, conversion, and all similar conditions is to avoid getting emotionally involved in the proceedings.'(p. 99 and 108.)

Religion tends to flourish under conditions of personal or social misery and frustration, especially the emotionally charged conversion experiences. In more affluent societies less religion or less dramatically emotional religions are the norm. Frank suggests that religion can be seen as a means to obtain release of frustrated emotions and from monotony and satisfying of basic psychological needs. Confusion, guilt, frustration seem to heighten the attractiveness of emotional conversions and religion and enhance their effectiveness. This suggests that these feelings may increase a person's susceptibility to emotionally charged methods of influence that offer detailed guides to behaviour, based on an inclusive, infallible assumptive world, which also strongly arouses hope. The similarities between the potential convert and a person experiencing the psychological and social consequences of addiction seem clear.

There are similarities between political and religious conversions and therapeutic change processes. Frank focuses on the importance of preaching or proselytizing in all three, stressing that this is structured by a systematic and comprehensive world view, which purports to govern every aspect of thinking and behaviour of its disciples. (Frank, pp. 85-105). These factors together with emotional arousal and group pressure are present in all three types of conversion.

Frank emphasizes the similarities between psychotherapy and 'thought reform' by stating that 'All psychotherapy tries to modify certain assumptive systems of its patients, along lines which the therapist believes will help them function better, and that this process inevitably creates distress.' (p.87) He also refers to the ways in which these processes differ.

Differences between 'therapy' and 'thought reform'

Therapy	Thought Reform
1) Treatment	Method of indoctrination
2) Help persons in distress	Creates distress to facilitate the indoctrination process.
3) Therapists usually adhere to the same world view as their patients. (Success may depend on this).	Different world views.(opposed).
4) Mild overt pressures	Extreme pressures.

It can be seen that the AA methods more closely resemble thought reform than therapy in some respects. However a psychotherapist can also waver from Frank's criteria, deliberately causing emotional distress in order to facilitate change. A client may also be ignorant of the therapist's model or world view, necessitating a form of indoctrination, if the patient's values are to change. Group pressure within therapeutic groups can be extreme and psychiatric patients subjected to 'firm discipline' may well perceive therapy as coercion, though their therapists do not. This they would have in common with politically motivated 'helpers': Chinese communists saw thought reform as a 'morally uplifting, harmonizing and scientifically therapeutic experience.' (Lifton, 1961).

Thought reform differs from religious conversion and has similarities with therapy in that it involves a detailed, open ended review of past history in a setting of a prolonged, intense relationship between a distressed person and a person whom he perceives as having some control over his welfare. In the case of civilian prisoners and intellectuals in the Chinese 'Revolutionary College' this 'confession' was a detailed life history. 'Wrong thoughts as well as wrong deeds, were a crime - confession included actions and also attitudes, motives etc. All this had to be expressed in such a way to demonstrate complete adherence to doctrine.' (Frank, p.96). In the Russian form 'the method of interrogation ... consisted of making it the arrested man's primary task to build up the whole case against himself ... [He] ... not only had to invent his own "legend" but ... to do his utmost to make it plausible in every detail.' (Beck and Godin, 1951, quoted in Frank p.99). Unfortunately, there appears to be no literature concerning possible varieties of British or American thought reform, though Americans were 're-acclimatised' on their return from Chinese revolutionary colleges, so the examples must be understood largely in terms of Western perspectives on the techniques of foreigners.

This phenomenon of 'confession' is perhaps the most significant factor shared by thought reform, and certain religions and therapies and is the most similar to the conversion process at the Centre. It can be seen from Chapter Three and especially the client accounts in Chapter Six that the process of writing a 'life-story' in the Centre was considered an essential part of the early stages of the treatment process. The difficulties the clients found in constructing a 'life history' and listing their faults or sins, with little guidance at this stage as to what these faults were, seems similar to the experience of political prisoners undergoing thought reform.

The focus on a confession is also an integral part of many religious programmes and the Centre programme, in its later stages, bears more resemblance to Roman Catholicism than thought reform. For example, in Step Four making an inventory of their 'sins' and in Step Five confessing to another person. The preparation of a confession was used in thought reform in order to undermine an individual's own assumptive world and as a way of gauging a prisoner's progress. It also serves this purpose, as a sign of therapeutic progress, for the staff at the Centre (Step Four), and perhaps also indicates progress in religious terms.

The compulsory regime underlying Chinese thought reform differed from religions, therapy and AA in many respects but the process can be construed as similar. Confession was produced partly by group pressures, the most severe being 'tou-cheng' or accusation process. In this, each group member had to criticize himself before the others, going into all his supposed misdeeds and his motives, while they pressured him to confess more. These are also recognisable patterns in AA groups, and play a significant part in the group process at the Centre.

When prisoners of thought reform came 'voluntarily to think of their past life in the conceptual framework of the Chinese - then conversion (was) underway.' In this way the interrogator emphasized the guilt and inner conflicts of prisoners, (the free association technique in psychoanalysis has similar effect), and then demonstrated that their own ideology could not protect them. The prisoner's state of confusion increases his susceptibility to influence; the prisoner may find himself so disorientated that he will take any restructuring which gives some cognitive clarity or resolves his guilt.

Frank emphasizes that two particular aspects of thought reform are very relevant to psychotherapy; participation and repetition. Here again it must be emphasized that the voluntary participation in psychotherapy and AA differs to compulsory thought reform, thought reform forcing the person to participate actively in bringing about his own change of attitude. Thought reform depended on the active participation in groups and criticism of 'fellow students'. It was believed that if a man could be made to participate he would come to believe what he and the group were saying. Once again, certain aspects of these processes are reflected in AA and Minnesota methods. The importance of participation was consistently stressed in the group therapy sessions, to the extent that my role as researcher was changed by mutual consent, from participant observer to passive observer. Repetition also played a large part in the routine of the Centre, as in the revolutionary colleges, most of the techniques used were made more effective by being used in a repetitive way until the prisoner could no long sustain his resistance.

Finally, completion of the confession to the interrogator's satisfaction meant the end of the torment and the reintegration of the prisoner's world view along lines that would enable him to become a valued member of the group. It was therefore often accompanied by a feeling of relief and even joy, analogous to that following a religious conversion. This phenomenon is graphically described by clients of the Centre and also by the staff who had gone through the programme themselves.

It is interesting to note that a political interrogator could see himself as a therapist, in the sense that he is trying to help a prisoner become a better, more effective person by helping him to see the error of his ways and accept his penance: after which he is ready to become a fully fledged member of (the new) society. Also, like the therapist, he may have considerable emotional investment in the prisoner's progress. (However, it should be stressed that a prisoner of thought reform has no rights or civil liberties and may well be subjected to physical coercion and torture.) Confession and conversion of people tends to reinforce the helper's world view and self-image/esteem. It also helps justify the helper's behaviour and the suffering he inflicts on others. So both client/therapist; prisoner/ interrogator may collaborate in erecting a shared belief system, each confirming the other in particular beliefs. (Frank has suggested the term 'helper' to encompass the three categories of therapist, interrogator, and preacher).

To sum up, Chinese Communist thought reform relied on four basic factors; psychological pressures, manipulation of group forces, genuine conversion and the potential convert had no freedom or rights - i.e. was an involuntary convert.

The processes involved included extreme emotional arousal, total control of the environment and interrogation. An attempt was made to produce an intense, disorganizing emotional state, to cut off from other social supports of their previous world view and immerse them in a social milieu that consistently represents the new one. The focus of the attempt to persuade or influence is interrogation and confession. This is brought together with enforcement of behavioural conformity which tends to bring about changes in belief system to harmonize with it. (This proposition is similar to the theory of 'Cognitive Dissonance.' Festinger, 1964).

Similarities with descriptions of beliefs and process of AA and the Minnesota method are clear. However it should be noted that it is usually the initial addiction itself which will cause a client discomfort, disorientation and isolation, rather than the intervention of the Centre staff or AA members. In the case of some clients who had come to the Centre at the instigation of family or probation officers, it was less clear that they attended voluntarily or that their addiction caused discomfort to them rather than their family or society at large. This point is significant in ethical terms, as many clients found parts of the treatment programme distressing and unpleasant. Yet the voluntary status of the client was not considered a necessary condition of treatment by staff, who considered that it was equally effective if compulsory, if not more so.

Finally,it is worth considering the nature of failure in all three areas (political, religious and therapeutic helpers). The phenomenon of failure can be described in terms of the client/ convert's ability to resist the processes of change. The following list of features of resistance incorporates Frank's proposed significant elements of this resistance;

1) Anger at being bullied.

2) Personal qualities and attitudes that enabled the person to maintain a sense of personal identity and group solidarity.

3) The ability to detach emotionally from the proceedings. A prisoner's conviction of the correctness of his own world view and the more firmly it was anchored in his group identification influenced how difficult his conversion would be.

4) An important source of resistance was the ability to construct a theory of what was going on, ie. the client/convert's ability to produce a theory of his own that was different to that of the therapist/converters). This ability to make sense of the proceedings would give the person a sense of being able to predict what would happen next and so help counteract the fear of the unknown and sense of helplessness.

5) Intellectualization can serve as a means of avoiding emotional involvement.

These findings concerning 'resistance' are reflected in the comments made by clients and staff during the treatment programme. (See Chapter Six.)

Although thought reform succeeded well in producing false confessions, its ability to produce sustained attitudinal change seemed to be very small unless the new attitude was constantly reinforced by the group the prisoner joined after his release. Frank states that 'Many Americans who were "partly shaken" returned to their former value system after being re-immersed in American culture. No long-lasting changes were achieved unless sustained by subsequent group support.' (ibid., p.102). Conversions apparently fail to produce permanent attitudinal changes. 'Changes such as those produced by extreme environmental pressures tend to snap back once circumstances change and these are removed.'(ibid.)

If, as seems to be the case, there are similarities between conversion processes whether therapeutic, political or religious, these findings obviously raise some doubts about the ability of particular types of psychotherapy and 'conversion' programmes to produce fundamental personality change. Frank states that these 'changes may be analogous to false confessions.' 'The person has not changed fundamentally, but rather has learned to couch his problems and to report improvement in the therapist's terms.' (p.102). He concludes that 'long-term, gradual pressure would be more effective in producing personality change than a crash programme' (pp.102-3).

This is Frank's conclusion following an exhaustive survey of conversion processes and techniques. It is possible however that the 'crash programme' and the 'long-term gradual pressure' are not mutually exclusive, but that the processes of change/conversion and maintenance of change/conversion could be part of the same process. Alternatively, they could be seen to constitute separate and entirely different processes.

The staff of the Centre and adherents of AA continually stress the necessity of continued involvement of Centre clients in AA groups and AA support networks. This involves their continued participation in groups which reinforce the same ideological tenets as those of the Centre. The informal 'after-care programme' also involves the clients progressing through a further seven steps, and usually means that participants will tend to socialize with other AA members to a large extent for some time after their initial 'conversion', sometimes to the exclusion of a 'normal' social life. (The overall average length of attendance at AA is estimated at six years, see Alcoholics Anonymous General Service Board survey 1981.)

These final seven steps, which are not part of the Centre programme, involve repetitions of the initial processes, but also include helping, supporting and 'converting' new members. In this way older members actively 'preach' the ideology of AA and continually repeat not only the basic tenets but also their version of their own 'life-story' and reaffirmation of their 'faith'. This aspect of the AA programme is extremely significant in examining the maintenance of the therapeutic changes achieved at the Centre in conjunction with AA groups. The final seven steps give an indication of the processes involved in maintaining the initial 'conversion', rather than in achieving the initial change. Unfortunately, there is not space to discuss the implications of this second stage to the AA programme for psychotherapy generally, but it may be useful to examine the notion of two separate processes when considering what Frank calls the 'essences of psychotherapy'. This division of treatment into two stages is discussed in the following chapter.

Conclusion

This chapter has been concerned with an analysis of AA therapy, rather than its theory, and has examined this therapy within an alternative context to that of contemporary alcohol research. In the alcohol field today, it is assumed that the proper study of alcohol treatment is within the context of behavioural psychology and medical science. This has led to a neglect of sociological concepts and both individual and social processes. If the AA programme is interpreted in terms of small group processes within the frameworks of Antze and Frank an alternative interpretation of its effectiveness becomes apparent. If theory can function as myth or ideology then the beneficial aspects of theory as a therapeutic tool need to be examined more closely.

The data analyzed in the previous chapter illustrate which clients gain most from the therapeutic process of AA. These were not necessarily those with the most severe problems, but rather those who were able to participate fully in the sequential treatment process because they were able to believe the underlying rationale and utilize it as part of the process of recovery. The ability of a client to engage with the therapist and participate in a group process may be dependent on more than the scientific credibility of the theory and method.

If this is so, the boundaries between treatment and persuasion will become blurred. It is suggested here that AA provides one of the most apposite examples of this concept.

As Frank points out, the English language lacks a common word for patient, client, penitent, unbeliever, prisoner, and for therapist, doctor, healer, evangelist, interrogator. Although these roles differ in the way the needs and rights of 'patients' are defined, the basic psychological processes undergone between two people or within groups seem remarkably similar. Frank calls the roles 'sufferer' and 'persuader'(pp.103-4) and attempts to summarize the core elements of these roles. He describes the sufferer's position, emphasizing that the sufferer's distress has a large emotional component, 'produced by environmental or bodily stresses, internal conflicts and confusion, and a sense of estrangement or isolation from his usual sources of group support.' He concludes 'He is demoralized, despairing and hungry for supportive human contacts.' (p.103) From the point of view of the sufferer, the persuader represents a comprehensive and pervasive world view, which incorporates powerful forces (political, spiritual, humanitarian). The world view is often seen as infallible, the persuader's powers as benevolent, the sufferer comes to believe that he can obtain favour if he shows the right attitude and self-submission. In this way suffering ceases, there is a resolution of conflicts, an absolution of guilt, and finally a warm acceptance or reacceptance by the group.

The means by which changes in the 'sufferer' are brought about include a particular type of relationship and some sort of systematic activity or ritual. The essence of this is that the persuader invests great effort to change the sufferer's state of mind, emotional state and attitudes, in ways he regards as beneficial. This is similar to the accounts given both by the Centre staff and by AA 'sponsors' of their own roles.

This effort to change the 'sufferer' often 'involves a means of emotional arousal, often to the point of exhaustion, leading to an altered state of consciousness that increases susceptibility to outside influences.' Frank notes that 'This may be unpleasant - but occurs in the context of potential support from persuader and group.' (p.104). This experience has been vividly described by clients at the Centre. Frank defines this activity as requiring the active participation of the sufferer, persuader and group and he describes it as highly repetitive. 'The sufferer may be required to view his past life in more or less detail, with emphasis on occasions when he may have fallen short of the behaviour required by his world view, thus mobilizing guilt.' (p.104.) This process is also described by both staff and clients themselves, together with the highlighting of cognitive contradictions (as in the rational emotive therapy of Ellis, 1962). The resulting feelings of confusion and guilt can then only be relieved by the confession and penance which are necessary for modification of attitudes.

Frank gives an indication of the possibility of 'post conversion' processes, though not defining them as such; he states that after conversion, 'the sufferer is able to function effectively again as a significant member of a group which by its acceptance, helps to consolidate the changes he has undergone.'(p.104.) This factor, though not examined in detail by Frank, was extremely important in the maintenance of change in clients of the Centre and AA members. Clients became integrated and accepted within social groups, both at the Centre and in the outside world, and were likely to lose this social acceptance and return to what were previously often isolated existences, if they transgressed in word or deed for any period of time. It is of significance here that surveys of reported emotional distress and presence or absence of social networks concluded that the presence of supportive social networks is correlated with lower levels of distress. It has also been reported that people who join a religious cult report a sharp decline in anxiety, depression and general emotional problems and attribute this decline primarily to emotional support from all the group members.

The similarities between religious, political and therapeutic conversions and the Minnesota or AA therapeutic process are interesting. The implications; clinical, ethical and academic, justify a far more detailed examination than can be included here. However, it is hoped that this chapter and the previous one, will have given a clearer picture of what actually happens during the therapeutic process at AA and a useful interpretive framework for examining it.

8 The development of clinically useful theories

'If men define situations as real, they are real in their consequences.' (W.I. Thomas 1958).

This chapter discusses the results of this study in the context of contemporary literature and considers the possibilities of applying the theoretical idea developed in the course of the research.

Firstly it is argued that there is at present a range of helpful treatment models incorporating both clinically useful as well as academically proven theories. Although it can be demonstrated that dependency can be analyzed in behavioural terms this does not rule out alternative interpretations. It is important to ensure that present theories and methods are fully documented and understood in order to provide an accessible and understandable range of treatment options.

Secondly it is argued that there may be a range of individual differences which are important in determining treatment outcome. These differences should be explored further and clearly identified if clients are to be effectively matched to different treatments. That is, it is necessary to develop an understanding of which individual differences are significant in each treatment approach.

Finally it is suggested that it will be necessary to provide an administrative system to enable the delivery of a range of services effectively; that is, an unbiased eclectic structure for the assessment and allocation of clients to these treatment models.

1. The identification and clarification of a range of clinically useful theories

Attempts to construct universally applicable definitions of 'addiction' have been unsuccessful. This is hardly surprising since any definition or description which attempts to incorporate the physiological, biochemical, psychological, legal, moral and religious nature of the phenomenon, together with its aetiology, prognosis and its effects on the wider society are likely to be either too general or abstract to offer predictive hypotheses or too narrow or specific to allow for generalization. Yet definitions are necessary for helping agencies to be able to match cases to a classification which implies certain therapeutic or helping procedures. The following section discusses possible practical solutions.

Recent attempts to combine different aspects have resulted in a 'biopsychosocial' model, (Orford, 1985, Galizio and Maisto, 1985). However this generalized approach is limited in its clinical usefulness and difficult to test. Any model that attempts to combine different disciplines must also combine different methodologies and as a consequence is difficult to measure within the context of behavioural science alone. (Schwartz, 1982.)

Attempts to combine models for practical purposes are perhaps best illustrated by the development of screening instruments for clinical and epidemiological purposes. It is perhaps in these areas that most difficulty is encountered. The most common screening instruments until very recently were the MAST and CAGE questionnaires (Mische and Venneri, 1987) both developed in America and based on notions of alcoholism and addiction to the exclusion of other types of alcohol related harm. Recent criticisms of these questionnaires reflect differences in beliefs about addiction as a concept. For example, the latest British attempt to design a screening instrument is based on very different criteria, identifying significant psychological and social aspects rather than physiological or disease criteria (Duncan et al., 1994).

The development of an international instrument led to a less rigid formulation of dependency. The 'Dependence Syndrome' developed by Edwards (1977) was incorporated into the international WHO screening instrument (AUDIT), but as only part of a larger instrument including alcohol related social damage and health.

The difficulties inherent in designing a standard screening instrument where there is little agreement on the nature of the phenomenon to be screened are best summed up by Wanburg and Horn (1983) who developed their own screening instrument (Alcohol Use Inventory). They commented on the difficulties and concluded, 'We refer to our descriptions as multidimensional, multiple pattern, or multiple condition accounts of such problems.' They cite Pattison (1982) 'The general consensus now at hand is that there are multiple types of alcoholics and drinking problems, requiring a spectrum of therapies appropriate to the type of problem....a major hindrance to the development of selective treatment of alcoholism has been a unitary concept of alcoholism.'

The difficulties of defining criteria for selection in screening instruments are reflected in everyday treatment practice. A basic practical problem arising from the theoretical controversy is that communication and coordination between professionals and between professionals and clients, is difficult. The client's view of his or her own experience may differ from that of the practitioner. The practitioner initially contacted may have a view which differs from that of the professional to whom s/he refers on. For example, the word 'alcoholic' can mean different things to different people and likewise the implications of alcoholism may be variously construed. In this way what could have been a healthy academic controversy produces a chronically unhealthy clinical environment.

The problems arising from this confusion are often highlighted in the literature. The report by a Special Committee of the Royal College of Psychiatrists *Alcohol and Alcoholism* (1979) discusses the difficulties of reconciling notions of 'illness' and 'self responsibility'. A 'common starting point for any constructive changes in behaviour has to be the individual's personal admission and realization that he has a drinking problem; this is equally true whether he is going to remedy the matter by his own efforts, or with professional help, or AA.' The passage continues, 'Certainly the person who has contracted the 'dependence syndrome' may well find it impossible to deal with their situation without special help: (but) with society's present lack of information on the nature of dependence, that person may not even have a clear idea of what he has to deal with, until he can obtain some informed advice.' (p.118).

Griffith Edwards emphasizes this point when he states that it 'seems probable that terms such as "alcoholism" and "alcoholic" are now so lacking in precision as only to be passports to confusion.' (1977). It is clear that if successful communication between referring agents and between different members of any treatment team can greatly increase the efficiency with which the needs of patients will be met (Robinson, 1976), then unsuccessful communication leads to inefficient service provision.

The confusion between professionals is if anything surpassed in the relationship between professionals and clients. It is here that disagreement is perhaps greatest and it is this disagreement that is of particular interest in this book. It is therefore relevant to highlight the discrepancy between academic/ professional and lay views about alcohol problems. Although much of the specialist literature in Britain is now based on taken for granted notions of behavioural dependency and controlled drinking treatments, these notions are far from those of the general public. Much of the general population view alcohol problems in terms of 'alcoholism' though there is some uncertainty as to the exact meaning of the term. This is apparent throughout the media and is also reflected in the few research projects based on consumer opinions. However, work in this area is severely limited at present though of intrinsic interest if considering service provision.

Cartwright et al., (1975), whose work involved designing a community response to problems of alcohol abuse, gathered data on ordinary people's concepts of abnormal drinking. They state that there is widespread token acceptance of 'alcoholism as a disease', although little depth of understanding as to what is meant by this phrase. This is borne out in an unpublished Welsh Office survey of people with alcohol problems in South Wales (Keene, 1992). A common complaint among clients was that service providers were not themselves familiar with the disease or AA model and often did not refer to AA groups or Minnesota residential units and/or did not offer AA based therapies themselves. The major criticism of service provision was that workers were not properly trained in different models.

Perhaps because there was disagreement as to the nature of alcohol problems amongst their sample, Cartwright and her colleagues concluded that 'There is no functionally useful concept of alcoholism latent within our society which can be used when a patient and clinician meet.' It would be equally valid to acknowledge that there is more than one concept of 'alcoholism' latent within our society which can be used when patient and clinician meet.

Although it appears as if both the disease model and the behavioural model can be practically useful, little consideration, in British literature, has been given to understanding the disease model and how and why it is effective for certain clients. It is clear from critiques of the model in the literature that there is little understanding of the theoretical framework or therapeutic process of AA amongst those who are not involved (See Chapter Three). In contrast, the evidence to confirm the usefulness/ effectiveness of behavioural interventions has been consistently examined in much of the research over the past 10-15 years.

It is suggested that greater understanding of both are necessary, since evidence to show that one theoretical model is effective does not of itself prove that an alternative theoretical model is ineffective. Much of the literature purporting to be neutral in its examination of different models is biased towards one perspective. 'Overviews' are often marred by lack of understanding or the inherent belief that if one's own model works, then alternative models must be flawed.

The dogma of AA enthusiasts is often commented on, many refusing to countenance any explanation of alcohol problems except that of the disease model. Recent 'reviews' by cognitive/ behavioural apologists take a similar stance. For example, although some behavioural psychologists tolerate the incongruence of etiological theory and treatment in their own work (Marlatt, 1988), they are quick to criticize it elsewhere. 'Traditional views of alcoholism, defined as an inherited biochemical disease, is thought to be best treated by self-help spiritual fellowship, AA. Strange bedfellows! A disease of the body is 'treated' by surrender to a higher power.' (Marlatt, 1985, p.475). This criticism is common to many AA opponents and reflects general lack of information and understanding. The aetiology underlying AA and the Minnesota Model defines alcoholism as a 'spiritual disease' and then 'treated' as such. However, this lack of understanding of AA serves to illustrate a common problem in developing a range of service provision.

Maisto and Conners (1988) follow Marlatt in suggesting that cognitive behavioural psychology offers a superior theory and method. Rather than attempting to examine the philosophy and practice of an alternative theory, they assume that 'A look across the board at AA' is sufficient and that it 'suggests that for strong adherents of this model, alcohol consumption is the most important question about a person's behaviour, with little competition from other behaviours for that position.' (p.426) This is a revealing criticism as it implicitly assumes that 'behaviours' are the most important, if not the only, variables. AA adherents would suggest that information about lifestyle, including spiritual and moral issues, is equally important, and that the behavioural variables are not inherently significant but only indicative of underlying problems.

In a similarly reductionist manner, Maisto and Conners see success in AA only in terms of abstinence. 'In the behavioural approach, the measurement of drinking is required for outcome assessment, but measures of other areas of functioning are also seen as part of good outcome evaluation. This follows from the view that an understanding of the causes and effective treatments of alcohol abuse requires looking at alcohol use in the context of the individual's internal and external environment.' (p.427). Advocates of AA would themselves be more likely to see outcome as an ongoing process involving changes in a person's social and personal life, if not radical changes in personality brought about by conversion and maintained by changes in behaviour determined by a newly developed concept of social responsibility. They would also perhaps dismiss behavioural outcome studies as merely describing behaviour that could well be masking underlying problems.

Ironically, Maisto and Conners themselves highlight the problem inherent in attempts to analyze any work in this field: 'It would be an advance if all outcome researchers in the addictions clearly presented their theoretical beliefs about the behaviours they are treating before presenting data. It would make their data far more interpretable for all.'

There is self evidently a need for clearer understanding of AA and Minnesota as many criticisms by outsiders are based on ignorance or misunderstanding. Likewise with cognitive/behavioural approaches, the move towards a 'biopsychosocial' approach has broadened the psychologists base further than many clinicians or AA advocates would realize.

Previous attempts to explain and understand the disease model and Minnesota Method have often been made in a cursory manner, and more significantly are made within the context of behavioural psychology. It has been suggested that this theoretical framework may be limited by its methodology and that qualitative work concerning process and interpretation would give greater understanding. An initial attempt has been made in the previous chapter to examine the **processes** involved in therapeutic treatment.

In summary, it is often argued that the problems inherent in the field of service provision are caused by the lack of one generalized theory of addiction and exacerbated by conflict between professionals with differing beliefs as to both theory and practice. There seems little likelihood of consensus developing. However, it may be that the breadth and variety of service provision would suffer in some respects if this 'ideal' were to be achieved. It therefore seems sensible to attempt to adapt intellectual models to the practical purposes for which they are most useful.

At present many areas offer a spectrum of services to a wide range of clients with differing problems and needs. It is suggested that the kind of solution needed does not involve intellectual consensus regarding one particular approach, but one that allows assessment of clients' levels of problems and needs, without depending on a paradigm which is incapable of assessing them in more than one way.

This solution of matching for treatment purposes brings with it a range of problems, not least the need to develop a system of classification of each model. In this book it is also suggested that subjective interpretation of the problem influences treatment process and outcome. If this is so, the problem of matching the client's perceptions of the causes and treatment of his problem to those of the therapist is clearly dependent on a categorization of models which includes basic underlying beliefs and taken for granted 'understandings'.

In an attempt to develop a useful classification system, Maisto and Connors have utilized a model developed by Brickman et al., (1982), to place the disease and behavioural models within the same structural framework. In their general model, Brickman et al. constructed a four category classification of theoretical models of 'helping'. The significant criteria used to distinguish models are whether the client is considered to have responsibility for the development of his/her problem and/or responsibility for its solution. Brickman argues that the 'moral' model ascribes responsibility to clients on both counts; that the 'compensatory' model ascribes responsibility only for the solution; the 'enlightenment' model ascribes responsibility only for the development of the problem, and the 'medical' model ascribes no responsibility to the client at all. This classification could be contentious in itself, particularly in Brickman's categorization of the medical model. However it is interesting to test out the usefulness of this structure.

Maisto and Conners suggest that AA provides an example of the medical model and that the behavioural/ Social Learning approach can be classified as 'compensatory'. Marlatt in a subsequent paper (Donovan and Marlatt, 1988), quotes Brickman himself as placing AA into the 'enlightenment' category, - 'Clients bring a problem such as drug addiction, for which they feel responsible and yet without resources to cure.' To confuse this issue still further, it would seem from the data collected in the course of my research that members of AA and the Anonymous Fellowships believe that they are responsible for their recovery, though not responsible for their illness. The adherents of the disease model would therefore see it in the same category as the behavioural model.

The problem with this type of classification is that it assumes clearly defined underlying philosophical premises. The model of man underlying the disease model of AA is developed from the ideas of morality, spirituality and pathology of the late 19th Century. The model of man implicit within Social Learning theory is less easily described and the moral issues of responsibility and choice are to a large extent ignored within what is often construed as a 'science' of behaviour.

The difficulties inherent within categorization of models are reflected in the critiques of models themselves. Observers often have a greater understanding and affiliation for one perspective or model and this limits the overall vision. To some extent this situation may be improved by greater understanding of not only the models themselves but also of the methodologies that can be used to obtain information and understanding about each approach.

2. The identification and clarification of clinically significant individual differences

One of the important questions at issue appears to be whether or not all clients demonstrating a particular type of behaviour should be treated in the same way. This is of particular importance as this study proposes that different theories and practices will be more or less effective depending on individual variables other than behaviour, such as the clients' own model of addiction or understanding of their problem.

This section examines the research evidence concerning individual differences as a whole. It considers the implications of not measuring those that are potentially relevant before examining the possibilities of 'matching' individual clients to different treatments. The implications of ignoring individual differences in research are highlighted by Glaser (1980) who states that 'In addition to being generally ineffective, uniform approaches to complex problems may compound therapeutic pessimism by disguising or obscuring significant interactions between sub groups and the treatment provided.' This point is of particular importance, as much of the more recent research in psychological, sociological and particularly public health studies is limited to surveys of fairly large populations or to comparisons between groups of subjects. As Edwards (1977) points out, '...when two or more interventions are compared with each other the most common result is a tie.' Glaser reiterates this conclusion: 'Uniform approaches to complex problems rarely produce satisfactory results in more than a small number of cases.'(p.80). He concedes that this type of result may be due to 'unrecognised but common effective factors in all interventions', but stresses that it is more likely that the 'assumed homogeneity of the target population is illusory.' It seems clear that if a heterogeneous group is treated as if it were homogeneous, 'those variables which are critical for successful client-treatment interactions for both forms of intervention will tend to be uniformly distributed in the differing conditions of the experiment, and the results in each condition will be the same for the same reason.' (op. cit.)

Marlatt also points out that comparative studies matching clients to different treatments have not been common but that some have been carried out in the past few years. He discusses the problems of ignoring interactions between client variables and type of treatment. He suggests that 'these variables may interact in such a way as to obscure any main effects due to treatment type.' and discusses a comparative treatment outcome study (Marlatt, 1986, Miller and Hester, 1986). He illustrates the point with the following analogy; if treatment 'B' has a better outcome with low educational level clients, and treatment 'A' has a better outcome with high level of education clients, then 'If all educational levels were averaged, no main effect would appear, leading to the erroneous conclusion that the treatments were equivalent. In fact, however, there is an underlying significant interaction between educational level and treatment type; for certain clients there is a substantial difference in effectiveness between treatments "A" and "B".' (p.474).

Evidence in the seventies and eighties has resulted in growing agreement that individual differences complicate the outcome of studies on addiction and dependence. For example Skinner et al., (1974) state that 'Most studies consider alcoholics as a unitary group, thereby tacitly assuming within group homogeneity. If a group average personality profile does not adequately represent most patients classified as alcoholics, then analyses using a group profile could wash out meaningful individual variances... Certainly, the most important finding in this study is that there are many distinct types of personality and psychopathology..this may prove useful during hospital intake for classifying and then channelling patients into optimal treatment programmes.' Similar conclusions were reached by Pattison et al., (1977). 'The population of persons with alcohol problems is multivariate. Correspondingly, treatment services should be diverse, emphasising the development of a variety of services, with determination of which treatments delivered in which contexts, are most effective for which persons and which type of problems.'

Research in the early eighties has added extra weight to these arguments, several authors stressing the influence of individual differences in treatment process and outcome (Caddy and Block, 1985, McCrady and Sher, 1983). However discussion of client matching has remained largely abstract and the practical implications for treatment allocation remain vague.

Glaser (op.cit.), considered the implications for treatment and the possibilities of matching clients to different services, stating 'The question is not whether similarities and differences between individuals exist - they do, but which is prepotent in determining the outcome of treatment?' (p.178) Glaser makes the point that 'In most circumstances at the present time, the similarities between individuals are assumed to be prepotent, and hence all individuals presenting are dealt with in the same way...which is perhaps why the matching hypothesis in most fields remains a hypothesis.' He continues, 'Yet in certain circumstances, such as with respect to alcohol problems, controlled experimentation has suggested that the results of uniform experimentation applied across the board are no better than those achieved with minimal interventions.' (The Edwards and Orford, 1977 study illustrates this point well.) These conclusions lead both general therapists and specialists in addiction towards what Glaser refers to as a 'growing consensus' in accord with the belief 'that the differences between groups of people are of the greatest importance in terms of outcome of various kinds of interventions, and hence that these intervention should not be uniform.'

It is open to debate whether or not this 'growing consensus' has led to any changes in basic theory or practice in the field, as it is now thirteen years since Edwards produced his initial results and thirty years since Jellinek first commented on the significance of individual differences. There is still very little work, either in terms of theories or development of methods, to suggest that these initial ideas have been taken seriously: 'the similarities between individuals are (still) prepotent.'

Matching is often discussed within the context of a 'biopsychosocial' model (Miller and Hester, 1986a, Moos and Finney, 1981). Schwartz (1982) considered the potential implications in terms of improved assessment and better treatment matches. Yet despite an academic interest in matching and increased evidence for the effect of individual differences on treatment outcome, there has been little concrete guidance for clinicians. (Miller and Hester, 1986b). So although people are starting to take Glaser's early work more seriously, we still seem no closer to identifying the significant differences in terms of treatment outcome.

It is suggested that one of the reasons that matching has not become a reality is that research in the area is methodologically limited and as a consequence individual variables and process have not been fully examined. The practical difficulties of research are perhaps best illustrated by examining one of the largest and most comprehensive projects to date, the American study, 'Project MATCH'. This large multi-centre trial compares client characteristics and treatment outcome across three distinct models; Minnesota, Motivational Interviewing and Relapse Prevention. Rather than focus on testing the matching hypothesis itself, the study compares different methods. It follows the tradition of medical and epidemiological research using a randomised controlled multicentre trial to allow for demonstration of a statistically significant effect.

The MATCH study used approximately 1,600 subjects within eight centres. The problems with this type of largely positivist study are dealt with to some extent by incorporating qualitative methods and data. For example, the MATCH study integrates qualitative methods as independent process measures of treatment, distinctiveness and specificity. This has been necessary as different treatment methods are often not clearly specified, resulting in a need for treatment manuals and some form of quality control process measure.

These problems in the general field have resulted in an increasing focus on process measures in treatment, in order to examine the links between treatment components and outcome and the inclusion of qualitative methods.

A more significant problem generally encountered in comparison studies is the wide range of conflicting standardized outcome measures, and the continuing controversy as to which are most appropriate. This is of course due to the different theoretical understandings underlying different treatment methods; definitions of the problem are different and the definitions of success are different. These issues are often not addressed in outcome studies. MATCH attempts to overcome this problem simply by using a large number of measures. There is little indication of how these different measures might be analyzed. This issue is indicative of a much larger difficulty with this type of research, the lack of theory in the field. It is this that makes it difficult to design general hypotheses or specific variants of matching hypothesis.

An alternative to the straightforward comparisons of different methods undertaken by the MATCH study would be to focus on the matching hypothesis. Although retrospective searches for matching contingencies are possible, it is clearly preferable to test specific hypotheses. However, the lack of theoretical structure limits the ability to design these hypotheses in the first instance.

In addition, the perennial difficulty of biased baseline assumptions is clearly apparent in the MATCH study. It is based on the premise that abstinence can be the only realistic aim for any treatment. 'Since abstinence from alcohol is the ultimate aim of all three therapeutic interventions, the primary statistical analyses will test treatment matching hypotheses in relation to two key measures of alcohol consumption, percentage days drinking and percentage days heavy drinking in three months.' (Project MATCH protocol 1991). This underlying assumption reflects the American emphasis on abstinence and would not be the case in Britain where controlled drinking is often the treatment goal.

MATCH has then attempted to overcome the difficulties listed above by working with large samples, clearly defined and closely monitored treatment protocols and a variety of standardized outcome measures. However, problems inherent in the study remain, not least the inability of the research design to measure the influence of client beliefs or client choice in outcome. The work is likely to produce extremely useful data, but excludes variables such as client interpretation and process.

The possibilities for developing work on these elusive variables are perhaps most apparent in the psychotherapeutic literature; particularly comparisons of attributes of clients with those of therapists and with treatment goals, and attempts to correlate the problems of clients with specific capabilities of treatments. Glaser lists some of the research undertaken in each of these areas, including work on therapeutic techniques generally, as work specifically concerned with addiction itself is scarce. Some of the categorizations and comparisons of variables which he suggests are included here.

Firstly, work which considers the personalities and moral values of clients and therapists. Such studies which attempt to compare attributes of clients with those of the therapists are rare. For example Mclachen (1972) pointed out that the advantages of group therapy were related to the match of patient to therapist in conceptual terms. As Glaser points out, this type of work would emphasize the importance of the specificity of the therapist, rather than that of the therapy. (Though it may be difficult to distinguish clearly between the two.)

Secondly, work which attempts to compare the attributes of clients with treatment goals. Again, it is often difficult to distinguish between treatments and goals, and this type of approach is likely to emphasize the specificity of the goal and underemphasize the specificity of the therapy. Thirdly, work which considers the problems of clients compared with the specific capabilities of the treatments. Glaser comments that this seems to him to be the most practicable of the approaches. He notes that some therapies are targeted upon clients with specific problems (eg. Family Therapy), but that other therapies are not so targeted as they are presumed to be useful to clients. With regard to alcohol problems he quotes Rathod (1976), 'Group therapy seems to stand supreme in modes of treatment, even though it has never been proved or disproved that it is necessarily the best type of treatment to offer alcoholic patients.' Glaser notes more significantly that 'the particular type of problem addressed by group psychotherapy has not been clearly specified.' (p.182)

He concludes that 'Irrespective of the type of match under study, it is clear that matching experiments require the specification of clients, therapists, interventions and goals, at least along some dimensions that are considered crucial to outcome.' (p.182). He reiterates the call of Jellinek and Bowman thirty four years earlier 'The only possibility (of improving treatment for alcoholism) is to bring greater order into psychotherapeutic procedures. By this we mean that a definite effort has to be made to establish criteria for the suitability of any given method to a given patient.'

It can be seen that academics and clinicians alike see the need for developing matching in practice, but are prevented from doing so, either by dreams of an overarching theory or an overarching methodology. If individual differences cannot be measured in research we will not be in a position to determine how relevant they may be. Perhaps we are not able to provide the right answers simply because the right questions have not been asked, nor the relevant means for answering them utilized.

3. The significance of treatment process in matching

It has been suggested that qualitative data are not available to inform us about individual differences and subjective interpretation, because qualitative methods have not been used. The same can also be said for treatment process. We know very little about it simply because process research cannot be undertaken within the confines of behavioural science or medicine. If we wish to find out about treatment process we must use qualitative methods.

As our knowledge is very limited, much of this section is supposition. However, if it were possible to distinguish and define each stage of a treatment process as a separate entity, it may be possible not only to match one overarching theory to each individual client but also to use different models at different stages of the process of change or recovery. The implications of this could be that a theory of aetiology could be matched to the client in the first instance,(eg. a social/cultural theory); that a different theory of 'treatment' could be utilized (eg. an abstinence theory); and finally that a post treatment theory of relapse prevention be employed to enable the client to return to controlled use.

As Marlatt (op.cit.) explains, there are 'Various conflicting positions put forth to explain the etiology of addiction, along with corresponding recommendations for treatment.' He goes on to state that 'A one-to-one correspondence between models of aetiology and the effectiveness of various treatment modalities may not exist in the area of addiction treatment....there is no consensus of opinion or convergence of evidence concerning the underlying cause of addiction.' He states in true Behavioural tradition, that 'treatment' itself can be effective even when the causative factors are unknown or considered irrelevant to treatment outcome. That is, there is much disparity in the field generally between models of etiology and treatment. This can also be seen to be true for psychotherapy generally, where a non directive, reflective type of therapy based on what is loosely called a 'humanistic' or 'holistic' theory, can be seen as utilizing behavioural techniques of reinforcement and modelling; and where behavioural and cognitive theories can lead to therapies which involve the 'unconditional positive regard', warmth and empathy considered central to the more holistic theories (eg. Gestalt). Therefore it is not perhaps surprising to find that 'behavioural' and 'cognitive' techniques are used by therapists who believe firmly in the disease model.

A distinction can also be drawn not only between aetiology and treatment but also between initial change and maintenance of change. This is significant in the processes involved in treatment at the Centre. Marlatt himself is particularly concerned with prevention of relapse. Working in America where the disease concept of alcoholism has widespread professional acceptance, he has utilized these arguments to adapt a behavioural theory of relapse prevention to fit with the disease model of treatment. This came about largely because he was facing a good deal of pressure to work within a disease model and to illustrate the cost effectiveness of his approach within this context. (Personal communication, Psychology of Addictions Conference, Cardiff, 1988).

Whatever the practicalities determining the focus of Marlatt's work it does seem possible to distinguish the process of relapse itself from that of initial change or 'stopping' use. Relapse prevention techniques can be used both to reinforce abstinence or controlled drinking strategies.

It seems clear that within the field at the present time there are theories of the aetiology of addiction, treatment and relapse prevention. It cannot be taken for granted that practitioners use corresponding theories for each stage. It may be that they can select several different theories for each client, describing the development of the problem in terms of a particular theoretical perspective, and then, perhaps independently of this initial understanding of the aetiology of the problem, choose a particular theoretical understanding of a treatment process to structure their practical response.

It is no doubt true that academics would require some degree of 'fit' between a theory of aetiology and a theory of treatment. This is not however necessarily true for either practitioners or clients in the field. It seems possible for clients to work both with therapists who take a cognitive/behavioural approach and those who work with the disease model:

it is also possible for 'eclectic' practitioners to use both. The cognitive dissonance which would be generated in many academics is also problematic for many practitioners and clients but for a certain proportion of individuals these discrepancies are not of any importance, if they are recognised at all.

In summary, it may be useful to conceive of three layers of theory: first that of the aetiology or development of the phenomenon; second that of initial change or treatment/cure; and third that of maintenance of change or relapse prevention. These considerations have some relevance in considering the possibilities of matching clients to different treatments. It is argued here that the client's own model or understanding of his or her problem will be a significant factor in determining response and treatment outcome. If this were true it would become relevant to be able to distinguish the clients' understanding of the causes of their problem from their understanding of its cure and of the maintenance of this cure.

In practice, perhaps the two significant stages in treatment are those of initial change and maintenance of change. If a distinction is to be drawn between these two stages, identification and understanding of each will depend on knowledge of the treatment process itself. As discussed in the methodology chapter, any understanding of different stages calls for process research and theory of process. In this field this type of theory has been conspicuously absent. However, in the clinical environment the need for an understanding of process has led to the widespread acceptance of a simple process model, despite its lack of theoretical base or research evidence.

The 'stages of change' model developed by Prochaska and DiClemente (1983) offers a structure with which to identify particular stages of change, independently of the therapeutic input. These are defined as pre contemplation, contemplation, decision making, maintenance of change and relapse. This model offers not only a method of assessing client motivation for change, but also perhaps for determining which type of theoretical model is most appropriate at which stage. (Theory of etiology or maintenance of change). Although this type of approach would allow for different theories and methods to be used at different stages of the treatment process, it does not unfortunately overcome the problem of identifying which diagnostic criteria are most useful in determining which theory to use at each stage.

This model is now widely used in both Britain and Australia, though not (as might be expected) in America, where the AA disease model already provides a ready made process interpretation, through the twelve steps. 'Since 1983 the Stages of Change model has become rapidly influential in the UK and several well known treatment services are now based on it. Moreover it is hardly possible to read an article on interventions for alcohol problems by a British author...without finding the model referred to.' (Heather, 1991) Heather explains the British and Australian enthusiasm in terms of an 'openness to new ideas in the alcohol field' which he finds 'paradoxically' absent in the USA.

It is interesting to examine in some detail the response of a representative of the behavioural school to a process model, as it is indicative of the problems involved in integrating the two approaches. Firstly this model, in common with all process models including the disease approach, suffers from a lack of 'scientific' evidence and a scientifically testable theory. It is, as Heather himself points out, essentially descriptive, not explanatory. This has led to cautious acceptance in the academic journals where few articles researching the model have been published (though it is, as Heather states, often referred to). The subject is limited to counselling and practice books and training packs.

Heather explains this phenomenon by relegating the model to the status of an heuristic device. 'It is as a simple, but elegant heuristic device to assist thinking about a range of possible interventions and how they can be matched to important characteristics of the problem drinker, that the model has proved most helpful.' He continues 'It is apparent that the model has a kind of face validity for many workers in the alcohol field and this presumably means that it is a meaningful enough representation of the manner in which change actually occurs in the real world.'

More practically, Heather criticizes the model in clinical terms as being too simplistic 'Simply locating someone in one of the stages may not be enough to decide what type of intervention might be appropriate...This clearly implies the need for further refinement of the model by research.' Unfortunately he does not clarify which kind of research methodology nor how different methodologies could be combined to make this research feasible.

Although this model has only been received cautiously in the professional and academic world, it does indicate a clear need in clinical practice not yet provided for by either. Academic scepticism is based on the fact that it is not possible to test a process model within the confines of behavioural medicine. It is perhaps for this reason that the largest research project of this decade 'Project MATCH', collects no qualitative data regarding either treatment process nor subjective interpretation.

Heather criticizes the USA for not taking the change model seriously as a consequence of adherence to one model; however it should be remembered that both the British and Americans suffer research limitation due to adherence to one approach. Neither can examine the relevance of process or subjective interpretation to treatment. Even though the USA maintains a model which cannot be adequately scientifically tested, no academic attempt has yet been made to analyze the model in other terms using qualitative methods. Each country either elevates or denigrates the disease model with no attempt to examine or understand it fully.

As discussed earlier, 'Project MATCH' is an American outcome study attempting to compare Minnesota, Motivational Interviewing and Relapse Prevention, yet each is seen within the context of abstinence. The work is likely to produce extremely useful data, but is limited because it is based within a tacit acceptance of abstinence as treatment goal and ignores variables such as client beliefs about their alcohol problems and excludes much potential process data. It is possible that all models may be useful to different individuals at different stages, but this research is unlikely to allow exploration of this possibility. If theories of matching need to be based within a process model, a clearer understanding of the process of development and treatment will become a priority.

4. Matching different clinically useful theories to different individuals

a) Theoretical issues

The theoretical problems of developing an overall theory of addiction or dependency have been discussed in detail in the book so far. There are also both theoretical and practical problems of developing Glaser's notion of matching. In order to understand the basic problem of matching client to theory, it is necessary to examine the difficulties inherent in clearly identifying comprehensive theories which can be matched to clients. The research in this book suggests that there is a relationship between what the client and therapist believe and outcome. This relationship is not evidence for the truth or falsehood of particular beliefs but of the practical utility of beliefs in particular social contexts of addiction and cure. Up until now, studies of matching clients to particular treatments have attempted to group together patients who fall in the same diagnostic category as perceived through a 'scientific' model of the diagnostic process.

The approach to matching which has not been explored, and which this research tends to support, would be based more on grouping together patients whose beliefs about their situation were both similar and within the (broad) range of those belief sets known to be potentially useful in helping people to control addiction. This research illustrates that the particular treatment studied is likely to be effective only if the client believes in the basic tenets of the programme and goes through the treatment process in the prescribed manner. The significant factor is not that theory should be scientifically correct but that it should be capable of playing a role in interpreting and managing the condition.

Sociological studies have illustrated that imposed diagnosis excludes the patient from having any influence on the definition of his own problem. Diagnosis which purports to be a scientific act could equally well be construed as a social act of assigning people to categories and exercising over them the power of classification. The section on theories has shown that different theoretical interpretations can be made of the same condition. The section regarding the common elements of psychotherapy has illustrated that many different therapies can be used for the same purpose. These models or interpretations are not however limitless, neither therapists nor clients can believe what they like as relativist models would suggest. A theory chosen from a range of interpretive frameworks can structure experience in a variety of ways but will not be useful and therefore will not be used, if it does not fit to some extent with other frameworks.

There must therefore be some 'fit', though not necessarily a direct correspondence in the positivist sense. Communication depends on mutual comprehensibility and shared pragmatic utility. This is not simply a process of matching corresponding beliefs, but of matching 'beliefs that are likely to be useful'. Many different beliefs may be utilised if faith in their usefulness is shared and the experience of applying them confirms, for the believer, their utility.

b) Practical and administrative issues

It is hoped that this book demonstrates the need for clear understanding and categorization of a range of models and clear identification and assessment of a range of relevant individual differences. But, however useful these instruments will be for research, in clinical terms they cannot be implemented seen independently of a practical system of administration. It has also been suggested in this study that within the context of treatment matching, clients' beliefs will be of significance in determining whether or not they respond to a particular treatment ideology. This is not necessarily to propose that clients themselves should choose which model and which methods they want. The above suggestions raise a series of issues concerning whether the clients' beliefs should be taken at face value as the objective assessments of rational beings or treated 'as if' they were artifacts or ideologies; together with considerations concerning whether the therapists' beliefs should be seen as professional expertise in assessment and diagnosis or also be treated 'as if' they too were ideologies. If both client and therapist beliefs are treated 'as if' they were useful ideologies there would be a necessity for an outside 'assessor', not functioning within any of these ideologies, to play a large part in assessing suitability of both clients and therapists for each other. If any treatment process can only be understood by reference to one of several incommensurable paradigms, it becomes necessary to be able to 'match' clients and therapists working within the same paradigms. There are clearly problems in defining the role and necessary credentials of an effective assessor but these are beyond the scope of this book.

There is however clearly a need for some form of an **independent** assessor to match the beliefs and methods of a range of services to the beliefs and problems of a range of clients. In this way cost effective services can be developed which are appropriate to the needs and likely response of the clients. The task of assessing attitudes and needs of clients will clearly be difficult, as it would involve both initial assessment and continued monitoring, together with an ability to equip or reinforce prospective clients with those beliefs about their condition which best 'fit'.

If the matching hypothesis were to become a clinical reality, the main priorities would be understanding and clarification of alternative models and research into individual differences to allow an understanding of criteria for selection and the design of an assessment instrument. However even if this were possible, there would be both bureaucratic and professional constraints. In administrative terms there would clearly be extra costs in administering extensive assessments, but more prohibitive perhaps would be the costs of providing a range of services rather than one.

In professional terms there may be difficulties in achieving assent between existing agencies and professionals to the idea of an external assessor taking over a clinical role. In practical terms there would also be difficulties in finding a competent, yet neutral, assessor, as the difficulties of any one individual making 'objective' assessments independent of particular theories are clearly problematic in themselves. However, there are advantages to a system of effective matching. From the evidence available it seems as if the idea of matching or 'fitting' particular theories and methods to particular clients may prove practically and administratively useful. Marlatt (1988), in an article considering the possibilities of matching, has noted two possible advantages of matching clients to treatments. First, this 'may enhance motivation for treatment and/or compliance and adherence to the treatment programme, regardless of the eventual outcome', and second, that matching may 'enhance treatment efficiency or cost-effectiveness, criteria that have important economic implications for health care delivery.' (p.475)

There are also practical advantages of using both approaches in Britain today. The Centre clients and other Minnesota 'successes' seem to have had more in depth and consistent support than most professionals could ever afford to give, either in the form of residential rehabilitation, or AA attendance on a frequent and regular basis (two to three times a week or more for an average four to five years). AA support is free, in the form of a countrywide network of self help groups. To take full advantage of these self help groups professionals need to work with similar concepts in their own therapy groups. It would therefore seem that the rationale of providing a service working on the same model, to enable a link in to AA, has a good deal of sense. On the other hand, the 'controlled drinking' approach may be more accessible to generic professionals such as health care workers and social workers, as a social learning approach to drug and alcohol abuse and treatment often forms part of their basic training. Although these workers may have difficulties in integrating the disease model approach with their own working practices, it should also be noted that in terms of input and results, the disease model often requires more intensive input than a behavioural or social learning approach. (see Brown and Lewinson, 1984; Goldfried and Bergin, 1978; Mash and Terdal, 1976.)

It is likely therefore that there are advantages to both models, although it is not yet possible to identify reasonable criteria for matching. It is important to note, however, that if a client is not suitable for any one approach this does not necessarily increase the probability that s/he is more suitable for the other. It is also not necessarily the case that clients who have been physically addicted to alcohol for a long time are any more likely to believe that they have a primary addictive disease, though it may well be the case that they will find it more difficult to control their drinking.

The disadvantages to using either model are of course the constraints that each places on alternative options. The basic premise of AA rules out possible alternatives which theoretically may be equally viable and perhaps with a greater 'fit' for some individual experience. If these basic beliefs are accepted, alcohol problems cannot be seen as a disorder of behaviour, so excluding methods which involve teaching individuals to control and modify their own behaviour. The same is true for the behavioural approach. If clients except the initial premise that they can control their own behaviour, they can not then admit powerlessness and hand themselves over to a higher power.

However, it is likely that for each particular therapeutic programme to work effectively, clients must believe one interpretation. For cognitive/behavioural programmes clients may need to believe that they have the capacity to control their drinking behaviour. For AA clients involvement entails belief in their individual powerlessness in the face of a disease. If clients at AA continue to believe that their problems are the cause of their alcohol use and that they do not have a primary disease but have merely developed (controllable) drinking behaviours or physical addiction, they are unlikely to benefit from the service offered by AA and at the Centre. This is not to say that either of these theoretical interpretations is more accurate, useful or 'true', but that the addictive disease model will be of no use unless it is construed by the client as accurate and 'true'. There is no doubt that the treatment programme carried out at the Centre in this study is useful and beneficial to those clients who believe its basic premises and work through the programme. It not only results in these people abstaining from alcohol but also results in changes (self-reported improvements) in the lifestyles of clients, their families and perhaps also those people whom these clients themselves will go on to help through AA or NA. However, as can be seen from the statistics in this study (and others) approximately only a third of those who arrive at the Centre actually work through the therapeutic programme successfully.

If there is only one alternative for people in any geographical area (as in this study), or if the system of allocation remains fairly arbitrary as it is at present, it is possible that there may be serious disadvantages for some clients if allocated to particular 'badly matched' models. For example the disease model may reinforce failure, as a 'slip' becomes defined as a 'relapse' rather than a 'lapse to be used as a learning experience'. Similarly, behavioural/cognitive models' may fail to take into account the seriousness of a lapse for someone with an advanced physiological addiction or to someone with a strong belief in the disease model.

It is proposed that, rather than attempt to structure one comprehensive theory of addiction, it may be more useful to ensure that present theories are fully documented and understood. The theoretical components that both inform and partly constitute current experiences of treatment should be maintained and developed, taking into account not only the internal consistency and external validity of each separate approach but also its usefulness as a therapeutic tool. It is suggested that theories and ideologies can be a useful part or tool in the process of therapeutic change and that theories need not be coherent to be efficacious.

Information concerning process and outcome would allow greater awareness of the clinical advantages of different models. Researchers may then be in a better position to clarify and classify models and so study the relevance of individual differences to each.

The work in this study has explored the relevance of one individual variable and led to the tentative conclusion that there is some correlation between the beliefs and theories of client and therapist on the one hand and successful outcome on the other. The central question underlying this study is not 'Is it true that addiction is a disease?' or 'What is the cause of addiction?' but 'Can people be helped if they believe it is a disease?' or, 'Is it useful to believe the disease theory is true?' The answer is that it is useful for some people, but not for others. For some clients the theory does not make sense of their experience, i.e. is not coherent. For others it is impossible to believe or have faith in the theory, though they can understand it. However, for a certain group of people the theory both makes sense intellectually and inspires their faith. These clients will in all probability be helped, in the sense that they can learn to live without alcohol and substitute a new social life, spiritual beliefs, emotional contacts, and moral behaviour for the old way of life.

At present we have little information about the range of models or the significance of individual differences. However it is suggested that if, as its opponents suggest, the AA disease model is flawed, it is necessary to provide explanations as to why it can be effective for some people. Researchers may be better employed exploring why and for whom models do work rather than explaining why they should not.

Postscript

The recent domination of scientific methodology and the behavioural model has been placed in its historical and clinical context in this book. Attempts to fit the phenomena of interpersonal change and maintenance of change into a general theory of diagnosis and treatment of addiction could be seen not only as unproductive, but as counterproductive to the development of therapeutically useful approaches in this field.

It has been proposed in Chapter Eight that theories of aetiology (explanatory or causative theories), theories of treatment change processes (practice theories) and theories of maintenance of change (small group processes and/or 'lifestyle' theories), could be separately identified and used independently and interchangeably. It is suggested that the need for diagnosis or explanation in terms of aetiology may be unrelated to the clinical or therapeutic response; that 'practice' theories can be used independently of causal explanations.

It should be emphasized that the proposed pre treatment process of 'matching' clients to particular therapeutic interventions could not be usefully described or interpreted in terms of diagnosis. It is also suggested that the concept of 'treatment' itself is not necessarily an accurate description of the interactive processes involved in individual change and maintenance of change in this field.

These rather abstract theoretical issues cannot be adequately dealt with here. Although it is suggested that a broader approach to understanding and managing addiction would be useful, it cannot said with any confidence that the constraints of the medical paradigm in this field necessarily outweigh the benefits. If the field of alcohol abuse dispenses entirely with the concepts of diagnosis and treatment it is not at all certain whether there would be an adequate theoretical structure for the identification, assessment and allocation of clients to replace them, but hopefully the need to examine this area further has been demonstrated.

Bibliography

Alcoholics Anonymous (1981), *Survey of AA in Great Britain,* General Service Board of Alcoholics Anonymous Ltd.

Anderson, D. (1981), *The Minnesota Experience*, Hazelden Foundation, Minnesota.

Anonymous (1976), *Acoholics Anonymous,* Third edition of the 'Big Book' (The basic text of AA), Watson and Witney.

Anonymous (1970), *The Little Red Book,* Hazelden Foundation, Minnesota.

Antze, P. (1979), 'The Role of Ideologies in Peer Psychotherapy Groups' in Lieberman et al. (eds) *Self Help Groups for Coping with Crisis,* Jossey Bass, San Francisco.

Babor, T. F., Ritson, E., Hodgson R. (1986), 'Alcohol related problems in the primary health care setting: A review of early intervention strategies', *British Journal of Addiction,* vol. 81, pp. 23 - 46.

Bales, R.F. (1944),'The therapeutic role of Alcoholics Anonymous as seen by a sociologist', *Quarterly Journal of Studies on Alcohol*, vol.5, pp. 267-278.

Bandura, A. (1977), *Social learning Theory,* Englewood Cliffs.

Bateson, G. (1973), *Steps to an Ecology of Mind,* Paladin.

Bean, M. (1975), 'Alcoholics Anonymous', *Psychiatric Annals,* vol. 5, no. 20.

Bebbington (1976), 'The efficiency of AA; the elusiveness of hard data',

British Journal of Psychiatry, vol. 128, p. 527.

Beck, A. T. (1976), *Cognitive Therapy and the Emotional Disorders,* International Universities Press, Inc.

Beck, F. and Godin, W. (1951), *Russian Purge and the Extraction of Confessions,* Viking Press, New York.

Becker, H. (1974), 'Labelling Theory reconsidered' in Rock P. and McIntosh (eds.) *Deviance and Social Control,* Tavistock, London.

Becker, H. (1964), *The Other Side,* Free Press, New York.

Bednarr, R.L. and Lawlis, G.F. (1971),'Empirical research in Group Psychotherapy' in Bergin A.E. and Garfield S.L. (eds.) *Handbook of Psychotherapy and Behaviour Change,* Wiley, York.

Berger and Luckman, (1967), *The Social Construction of Reality,* Anchor, Garden City, New York.

Bergin, A. and Garfield, S. (eds.) (1978), *Psychotherapy and Behaviour Change,* Wiley, New York.

Bolles, R.C (1979), *Learning Theory,* Holt, Rinehart and Winston, New York.

Berridge, V. and Edwards, G. (1981), *Opium and the People,* Allen Lane, London.

Brewer, M. B. and Collins, B. (eds.) (1981), *Scientific Inquiry and The Social Sciences,* Jossey Bass.

Brickman et al. (1982), 'Models of Helping and Coping', *American Psychologist,* vol. 37, pp. 384-6.

Bromet et al. (1977), 'Post-treatment functioning of alcoholic patients; its relation to programme participation', *Journal of Consulting and Clinical Psychology,* vol.45, pp. 829-42.

Brown, G.W. and Harris, T. (1978), *Social Origins of Depression: A Study of Psychiatric Disorder in Women,* Tavistock Publications, London.

Brown, R. and Lewinson, P. (1984), 'A psycho-educational approach to the treatment of depression: comparison of group, individual and minimal contact procedures', *Journal of Consulting and Cinical Psychology*.

Caddy, G.R. and Block, T. (1985),' Individual Differences in Response to Treatment' in Galizio M. and Maisto S.A. (Eds). *Determinants of Substance Abuse: Biological, Social and Environmental Factors,* Plenum Press, New York.

Cain, A.H. (1961), *Seven Sinners,* Harcourt, Brace and World, New York (This is a novelization of his unpublished dissertation).

Cain, A.H. (1964), *The Cured Alcoholic,* John Day, New York.

Cartwright A. et al. (1975), *Designing a Comprehensive Community Response to Problems of Alcohol Abuse,* unpublished report by the Maudsley Alcoholism Pilot Project to DHSS.

Catania, C. and Harnad S. (eds.), (1988), *The Selection of Behaviour,* Cambridge University Press.

Central Policy Review Staff. (1979), *Alcohol Policies: Volume 1,* ('Think Tank'), unpublished report.

Chick et al. (1985), 'Counselling problem drinkers in medical wards: a controlled study', *British Medical Journal,* vol. 290, pp. 965-7.

Clark, E. (1958), 'The Psychology of Religious Awakening', MacMillan 1929. Quoted in Argyle M. *Religious Behaviour*, Routledge and Kegan Paul, London.

Clark, W.B. (1976), 'Loss of control, heavy drinking and drinking problems in a longitudinal study', *Journal of Studies in Alcohol,* vol. 37, pp. 1256-90.

Clinnard, M. (1949) 'The group appproach to social reintegration', *American Sociological Review,* vol. 14, pp. 257- 262.

Cohen, S. (1973), *Folk Devils and Moral Panics,* Paladin, London.

Cook, C. (1988a), 'The Minnesota model in the management of drug and alcohol dependency: (part 1) 'philosophy and programme', *British Journal of Addiction,* vol. 83, p. 625.

Cook, C. (1988b), 'The Minnesota model in the management of drug and alcohol dependency: (part 2)' guidance and conclusions', *British Journal of Addiction,* vol. 83, p. 735.

Courtwright, D. (1982), *Dark Paradise: Opiate Addiction in America Before 1940,* Harvard University Press, Cambridge, Mass.

Davies, J. (1962), 'Normal drinking in recovered alcoholics', *Quarterly Journal of Studies on Alcohol,* vol. 23, pp. 94-104.

Deissler, K.J. (1970), 'Synanon, concepts and methods', *Drug Dependence,* vol. 5, pp. 28-35.

De Lint, (1969),'The status of alcoholism as a disease: a brief comment', *British Journal of Addiction,* vol. 66, pp. 108-9.

Denzin, N.K. (1987a), *The Alcoholic Self,* Sage.

Denzin, N.K. (1987b), *The Recovering Alcoholic*, Sage.

Denzin, N.K. (1987c), *Treating Alcoholism. An Alcoholics Anonymous Approach,* Sage.

Ditton, J. (1979), *Contrology; Beyond the New Criminology,* MacMillan Press, London.

Donovan, D.M. and Marlatt, G.A. (1988), *Assessment of Addictive Behaviours,* Guilford Press, New York.

Edwards, G. and Grant, M. (eds.) (1976), *Alcoholism: New Knowledge and Responses*, Croom Helm, London.

Edwards, G. and Grant, M. (eds.), (1977) *Alcoholism*, Oxford University Press.

Edwards, G., Gross, M., Keller, M., Moser, J., Room, R. (1977), *Alcohol Related Disabilities,* WHO. offset publication no.32. Geneva: WHO.

Edwards, G. and Grant, M. (eds) (1980), *Alcoholism Treatment in*

Transition, Baltimore University Press.

Edwards, G. and Orford, J. (1977), 'Alcoholism: a controlled trial of treatment and advice', *Journal of Studies on Alcohol,* vol. 38, pp. 1004-1031.

Edwards, G. (1985), 'Paradigm shift or change in ownership' in *Drug and Alcohol Dependence,* vol. 15, pp. 19-34.

Edwards, G. (1986a), 'The Alcohol Dependence Syndrome' *British Journal of Addiction,* vol. 81, pp. 171.

Edwards, G. (1986b), 'Normal drinking in a recovered alcohol addict' *British Journal of Addiction,* vol.81,p. 127.

Edwards, G. (1987), *The Treatment of Drinking Problems: A Guide for the Helping Professions,* Blackwell Publications.

Edwards, G. et al. (1988), 'Long Term Outcome for Patients with Drinking Problems: the Search For Predictors', *British Journal of Addiction,* vol. 83, pp. 917-927.

Edwards, G. (1989), 'As The Years Go Rolling By: Drinking Problems in The Time Dimension', *British Journal of Psychiatry,* vol.154, pp. 18-26.

Edwards, G. (1990), 'Withdrawal Symptoms and Alcohol Dependence: Fruitful Mysteries', *British Journal of Addiction,* vol.85, p. 447.

Ellis, A. (1962), *Reason and Emotion in Psychotherapy*, Lyle Stuart, New York.

Ellis, A. (1987), The evolution of Rationale-Emotive therapy (RET) and Cognitive-Behaviour therapy (CBT). In Zeig. J. *The Evolution of Psychotherapy,* Brunner/Mazel, New York.

Festinger, L. (1957), *A Theory of Cognitive Dissonance,* Row, Peter and Company, Evanston, Illinois.

Festinger, L. (1964), *Conflict, Decision and Dissonance,* Tavistock.

Fingarette, H. (1988), *Heavy Drinking: The Myth of Alcoholism as a Disease*, University of California Press, Berkeley.

Frank, J. (1959), 'The dynamics of the therapeutic relationship; determinants and effects of the therapists influence', *Psychiatry,* vol.6, pp. 17-39.

Frank, J. (1974), *Persuasion and Healing: A Comparitive Study of Psychotherapy,* Johns Hopkins University Press.

Frank, J. (1981), 'Therapeutic components shared by all psychotherapies', *Psychological Association: Master Lecture Series,* vol.1.

Friend, J.K. (1981), *Alcohol Related Problems: A Study of Inter-Organizational Relations.* Tavistock Institute of Human Relations.

Garfield, S. (1971),'Research on Client Variables in Psychotherapy' in Bergin A. and Garfield S.(eds.),*Handbook of Psychotherapy and Behaviour Change,* J. Wiley and Sons, New York.

Galizio, M. and Maisto, S.A. (1985), Towards a biopsychosocial theory of substance abuse, in Galizio, M. and Maisto, S.A. (eds.), *Determinants of Substance Abuse: Biological, Psychological and Environmental,* (pp. 425-429) Plenum, New York.

Garfield, S. and Bergin, A. (eds.) (1978), *Psychotherapy and Behaviour Change,* Wiley, New York,.

Gellman, I. (1964), *The Sober Alcoholic: An Organisation Analysis of Alcoholics Anonymous,* College and University Press, New Haven, Conn.

General Service Board of Alcoholics Anonymous, Great Britain (1986), *Survey of Alcoholics Anonymous in Great Britain.* York.

General Service Board of Alcoholics Anonymous in Great Britain (1982), *Highlights of the 1981 Survey of AA in Great Britain.* London.

Gilmore, K. (n.d.) *Hazelden Primary Residential Treatment Programme,* Hazelden, Centre City, Minnesota.

Glaser, F. (1980), 'Anybody got a match? : treatment research and the matching hypothesis.' in Edwards, G. and Grant, M. (eds.), *Alcoholism Treatment in Transition,* Baltimore University Press.

Glaser, F. and Skinner, H. (1981), 'Matching in the Real World: A

Practical approach.' in Gottheil et al., Matching Patient Needs and Treatment Methods in *Alcoholism and Drug Abuse,* Springfield Ill.

Glass, I.E. (1986), 'Alcohol and Alcohol Problems: A Review of Research in England, Wales and N. Ireland', *British Journal of Addiction,* vol. 81, pp. 197-215.

Glatt, M. (1972), *The Alcoholic and the Help He Needs,* Priory Press, London.

Gluckman, M. (1961), 'Ethnographic Data in British Social Anthropology', *Sociological Review,* vol.9, no.1, pp. 5-18.

Goldman, M.S., Brown, S.A., and Christiansen, B.A. (1987), Expectancy Theory: Thinking about drinking. In Blane, T. H. and Leonard, K.E. (eds.), *Psychological Theories of Drinking and Alcoholism,* Guilford Press. New York.

Gould, J. and Kolb, W.L. (eds.), (1964), *A Dictionary of the Social Sciences,* Tavistock.

Gorman, D.M. (1989), 'Is the new problem drinking concept of Heather and Robertson more useful in advancing our scientific knowledge than the old disease concept ?', *British Journal of Addiction,* vol. 84, pp. 843-5. NB. Various letters submitted in reply to this article:- Heather, N., Robertson, I., Gorman, D.M., and Edwards G. (1989) in *British Journal of Addiction*, vol. 84, pp. 843-5.)

Gottheil, E., McLellan, A., Drule, K. (1981), *Matching Patient Needs and Treatment Methods in Alcoholism and Drug Abuse,* Springfield Ill.

Gusfield, J. (1981), *The Culture of Public Problems: Drinking, Driving and the Symbolic Order,* University of Chicago Press.

Hacking, I. 'How should we do a history of statistics', *Ideology and Consciousness,* no. 81984.

Harding, G. (1988), *Opiate Addiction, Morality and Medicine,* MacMillan.

Harrison, B. (1971), *Drink and the Victorians. The Temperance Question in England 1815-1872*, Faber and Faber Ltd.

Harrison, P. and Tether, N. (1988), *Alcohol Policy and the British Government Bureaucracy; Data Note 13.* in the 'Data Note' series edited by Robinson D. ESRC Addiction Research Centre, University of Hull.

Health Advisory Committe for Wales (1987), *Dealing with Alcohol Problems in Wales,* Welsh Office Publication (HEAC(WJ)1987).

Health Education Advisory Committee (1986), *Dealing with Alcohol Problems in Wales,* Welsh Office Publication, (HEAC(WJ)1986).

Heather, N. and Robertson, I. (1981), *Controlled Drinking* Menthus.

Heather, N. and Robertson, I. (1986), *Problem Drinking, The New Approach*, Penguin Books.

Heather, N. (1991), Foreword in Davidson R., Rollnick S. and MacEwan I. *Counselling Problem Drinkers,* Routledge.

Hester, R. and Miller, W.R. (eds.) (1989), *Handbook of Alcoholism Treatment Approaches: Effective Approaches,* Pergamon, Oxford.

Hodgson, R. (1976), 'Modification of Compulsive Behaviour' in Eysenck H. (ed.) *Case Histories in Drinking Behaviour*.

Hodgson, R. J. and Stockwell, T.R. (1977), 'Does Alcohol Reduce Tension' in Edwards, G. and Grant, M. (eds.) *Alcoholism*, Oxford University Press.

Hodgson, R. J. (1980), 'The Alcohol Dependence Syndrome, a step in the wrong direction', *British Journal of Addiction,* vol.75, pp. 255-263.

Jaff, A. (1990), *A Guided Tour of Developing Ideology,* unpublished paper.

James, W. (1958), *Varieties of Religious Experience*, New American Library, New York.

Janov, A. (1970), *The Primal Scream-Primal Therapy: The Cure for Neurosis*, G.P. Putnam and Sons, New York.

Jaspers, K. (1968), 'The Phenomenological approach in psychopathology' reprinted in *British Journal of Psychiatry,* Jellinek, E.M. (1946), 'Phases in the drinking history of alcoholics', *Quarterly Journal of Studies on*

Alcohol, vol. 7, pp. 1-88.

Jellinek, E.M. (1957),'Phases of alcohol addiction', *Quarterly Journal of Studies on Alcohol,* vol. 13, p. 673.

Jellinek, E.M. (1960), *The Disease Concept of Alcoholism*, Hill House Press, New Haven.

Jellinek, E.M. and Bowman (1946), 'Alcohol addiction and its treatment' in *Quarterly Journal of Studies on Alcohol,* vol 2. pp. 98-176.

Jones, M.C. (1965), 'Personality correlates and antecedents of drinking patterns in adult males', *Journal of Consulting and Clinical Psychology,* vol.32, pp. 2-12.

Jones, R. (1984), *Ideological Groups,* Gower.

Jones, R. (1965), 'Sectarian characteristics of Alcoholics Anonymous', *Sociology,* vol. 4, p. 181.

Kazdin, A.E. (1977),'Assessing the clinical or applied importance of behaviour change through social validation', *Behaviour Modification,* vol. 1, pp. 427-451.

Kelly, G.A. (1955), *The Psychology of Personal Constructs,* Norton, New York.

Keene, J. (1992), *Alcohol Services in Wales: A Consumer Survey* Unpublished Report to Welsh Office.

Keene, J. and Raynor, P. (1993), 'Addiction as soul sickness: the influence of client and therapist beliefs.' *Addiction Research,* vol. 1, no. 1.

Keene,J. , Stimson, G., Jones J. and Parry-Langdon N. (1993), 'Evaluation of syringe exchange for HIV prevention among injecting drug users in rural and urban areas of Wales.' *Addiction, vol. 88, pp. 1063- 1070.*

Kerr, K.A. (1985), *Organised For Prohibition*, Yale University Press.

Kerr, K.A. (1894), *Inebriety or Narcomania: Its Etiology, Pathology, Treatment and Jurisprudence,* 3rd ed., H.K.Leis, London.

Kuhn,, T. (1962), *The Structure of Scientific Revolutions,* University of Chicago Press.

Kurtz, E. (nd.), *Not God: A History of Alcoholics Anonymous.*

Laundergan, M.A., Borman, L.D., Antze, P. (eds.) (1979), *Self Help Groups for Coping with Crisis,* Jossey Bass, San Francisco.

Laundergan, M.A. (1982), *Easy does it! Alcoholism Treatment Outcomes, Hazelden and the Minnesota Model,* Hazelden, Centre City, Minnesota.

LeFevre, R. (nd.), *The Promis Handbook on Alcoholism, Addictions and Recovery,* Hazelden, Centre City, Minnesota.

Lemert, E. (1967), *Human Deviance, Social Problems and Social Control*, Prentice Hall, New Jersey.

Levi-Strauss C. (1968), *Structural Anthropology,* Allen Lane, Penguin Press.

Lieberman, M.A., Yalom, I.D., Miles, M.B. (1973), *Encounter Groups: First Facts,* Basic Books, New York.

Lifton, R. (1961), *Thought Reform and the Psychology of Totalism: A Study of Brain Washing in China*, Norton, New York.

Lindersmith, A.R. (1965), *The Addict and the Law*, Vintage Books, New York.

Lindstrom, L. (1992), *Managing Alcoholism. Matching Treatments to Clients,* Oxford University Press.

Litman. (1977), *Once An Alcoholic, Always An Alcoholic: Controlled Drinking As The Goal of Treatment* Addiction Research Unit Paper.

Lofland, J. (1971), *Analysing Social Settings; A Guide to Qualitative Observation and Analysis,* Belmont, California.

Luborsky, L. (1970), 'New directions in research on neurotic and psychosomatic symptoms', *American Scientist,* vol. 58, pp. 661- 68.

Magaro, P.A., Gripp, R. and McDowell D.J. (1978), *The Mental Health*

Industry: A Culteral Phenomenon, Wiley, New York.

Mahoney, M. (1978), 'Psychotherapy and Human Change Processes' in Garfield S. and Bergin A. (eds.) *Psychotherapy and Behaviour Change,* Wiley, New York.

Mahoney, M. (ed.) (1977) *Psychotherapy Process: Current Issues and Future Directions,* Plenum, New York.

Maisto, S. and Connors, G. (1988), 'Assessment of Treatment Outcomes', in Donovan and Marlatt (eds.) *Assessment of Addictive Behaviours,* Guilford Press, New York.

Malinowski, B. (1948), 'Myth in Primitive Psychology' *in Magic, Science and Religion and other Essays,* The Free Press.

Marlatt, G.A., Demming B., and Reid, J. (1973), 'Loss of control drinking in alcoholics: an experimental analouge.', *Journal of Abnormal Psychology,* vol.812, pp. 233-241.

Marlatt, G.A. (1978), Craving for Alcohol, Loss of Control and Relapse: a Cognitive - Behavioural Analysis, in Nathen P., Marlatt, G.A., and Loberg, T., (eds.), *Alcoholism: New Directions in Behavioural Research and Treatment*, Plenum Press, New York.

Marlatt, G.A. (1986), *Personal communication* and paper given at Psychology and Addiction conference. Cardiff.

Marlatt, G.A. and Gordon, J. (1985), 'Relapse Prevention' in *Alcoholic Relapse Prevention and Intervention: Models and Methods,* Guilford Press, New York.

Marlatt, G.A. (1988), 'Matching Clients to Treatment: Treatment Models and Stages of Change' in Donovan, D.M. and Marlatt G.A., *Assessment of Addictive Behaviours*, Guilford Press, New York.

Mash, E.J. and Terdal, L.G. (eds.) (1976), *Behaviour Therapy Assessment: Diagnosis, Design and Evaluation,* Springer, New York.

McCord, W. and McCord, J. (1960), *Origins of Alcoholism*, Stanford University Press, California.

McCrady, B.S and Sher, K.J. (1983), Alcoholism Treatment Approaches: Patient Variables, Treatment Variables, in Tabakoff, B., Sutker P.B., and Randall C.L. (Eds.) *Medical and Social Aspects of Alcohol Abuse,* Plenum Press, New York.

McLachen, J. (1972), 'Benefit from Group Therapy as a Function of Patient-Therapist Match on a Conceptual Level' in Scofield, W. *Psychotherapy: The Purchase of Friendship*, Prentice Hall, New Jersey.

Miller, W.R. (1983), 'Motivational interviewing with problem drinkers', *Behavioural Psychotherapy,* vol. 11, pp. 147-72.

Miller, W.R. and Hester, R.K. (1986a), 'Matching Problem Drinkers with Optimal Treatments' in Miller, W.R. and Heather, N. (eds.) *Treating Addictive Behaviours: Processes of Change*, Plenum, New York.

Miller, W.R. and Hester, B.K. (1986b), 'The Effectiveness of Alcoholism Treatment: What Research Reveals' in Miller W.R and Heather N. (Eds.), *Treating Addictive Behaviours; Processes of Change*, Plenum, New York.

Miller, W.R., Sovereign, R.G. and Krege, B. (1987), 'Motivational interviewing with problem drinkers II: the drinkers check-up as a preventive intervention.', *Behavioural Psychotherapy,* vol. 16, pp. 251-68.

Mische, H. and Venneri, R. (1987), 'The reliability and validity of the MAST, Mortimer-Filkeins Questionnaire and CAGE in DWI assessment', *Journal of Studies on Alcohol,* vol.48, pp. 492-501.

Moos, R.H. and Finney, J.W. (1981),'The expanding scope of alcoholism treatment evaluation', *American Psychologist,* vol. 38, pp. 1036-1044.

Mowrer, O.H. (1961), *The Crisis in Psychiatry and Religion,* Van Nostrand, Princetown.

Ogbourne, C. and Rush, B.R. (1990), 'Specialised addictions assessment/ referral services in Ontario: a review of their characteristics and roles in addiction treatment systems', *British Journal of Addiction,* vol. 85, no.2, pp. 197-204.

Orford, J., Oppenheimer, E. and Edwards, G. (1979), 'Abstinence or control: the outcome for excessive drinkers two years after consultation', *Behaviour, Research and Therapy,* vol. 14, pp. 409-418.

Orford, J. (1977), 'Alcoholism and What Psychology Offers' in Edwards and Grant (eds.) *Alcoholism,* Oxford University Press.

Orford, J. (1985), *Excessive Appetites: A Psychological View of the Addictions*, Wiley and Sons.

Parker, H., Baker, K. and Newcombe, R. (1988), *Living With Heroin,* Open University Press.

Parliamentary Group of the Standing Committee on Communications, (together with the British Psychological Society), (1987), *Psychological Aspects of Alcohol,* HMSO.

Parssinen (1983), *Secret Passions, Secret Remedies,* Manchester University Press.

Pattison, E.M. et al. (1977), *Merging Concepts of Alcohol Dependence*, Springer Publishing Company, New York.

Popper, K. (1986), *Logic of Scientific Discovery,* Harper and Row, New York. (First edition, Hutchinson, London 1968.)

Prochaska, J.O. (1979), *Systems of Psychotherapy: A Transtheoretical Perspective*, Dorsey Press, Homewood, Ill.

Prochaska, J.O. and Diclemente, C.C. (1982), 'Transtheoretical therapy, towards a more integrative model of change.', *Psychotherapy Theory, Research and Practice*, vol.19, no.3, pp. 276-88.

Prochaska, J.O. and Diclemente, C.C. (1983), 'Stages and processes of self change of smoking: towards a more integrative model of change', *Journal of Consulting and Clinical Psychology* vol. 51, pp. 390-5.

Prochaska, J.O. (1986), Towards a Comprehensive Model Of Change, in Miller, W.R. and Heather, N.(eds.), *Treating Addictive Behaviours: Processes of Change,* Plenum Press, New York.

Raistrick, D. (1985), 'Some Advantages and Disadvantages of combined Alcohol and Drug Misuse Services' in *New Directions in the Study of Alcohol,* Group Booklet no.10, NDSAG, Leicestershire Alcohol Advisory Service.

Raistrick, D., Bradshaw J., Tober G., Weiner J., Allison J. and Healey C. (1994) 'Development of the Leeds Alcohol Questionnaire', *Addiction,* vol. 89, no. 4.

Rathod, N. (1976), 'Making Treatment Better' in Edwards, G. and Grant, M.(eds.), *Alcoholism: New Knowledge and Responses*, Croom Helm, London.

Richie, O. (1948), 'A socio-historical survey of Alcoholics Anonymous', *Quarterly Journal of Studies of Alcohol,* vol. 9, no. 19.

Robinson, D. (1979), *Talking Out of Alcoholism: The Self Help Process of A.A.* Croom Helm, London.

Robinson, D. (1987), *Data Note series no. 13,* Addiction Research Centre, University of Hull.

Robinson, D., Rollnick, S. and MacEwan, I. (1991), *Counselling Problem Drinkers,* Routledge, Tavistock.

Robinson, I. and Heather, N. (1986), *Lets Drink to Your Health: A Self Help Guide to Sensible Drinking,* British Psychological Society.

Rogers, C. (1965), *Client-Centred Therapy: Its Current Practice, Implications and Theory*, Constable, London.

Room, R. (1972), *Quarterly Journal of Studies on Alcohol,* vol. 33, pp. 1049-59.

Rossi, J., Stach, A. and Bradley, N. (1963), 'Effects of treatment of male alcoholics in a mental hospital', *Quarterly Journal of Studies on Alcohol,* vol. 24, pp. 91-8.

Royal College of General Practitioners. (1986), *Alcohol. A Balanced View*, Tavistock, London.

Royal College of Psychiatrists (1979), *Alcohol and Alcoholism,* Tavistock, London.

Royal College of Psychiatrists (1986), *Alcohol Our Favorite Drug* Tavistock, London.

Sanchez-Craig, M. (1986), 'Is it useful to think of alcohol dependence as a continuum', *British Journal of Addiction,* vol. 81, pp. 188-190.

Sanchez-Craig, M. (1986), 'Disadvantages of imposing the goal of abstinence on problem drinkers; an empirical study.', *British Journal of Addiction,* vol. 81, pp. 502-512.

Sanchez-Craig, M. (1990), 'Brief didactic treatment for alcohol and drug related problems: an approach based on client choice', *British Journal of Addiction,* vol.85, pp. 169-177.

Sargant, W. (1957), *Battle for the Mind*, Science House, New York.

Schacter and Singer (1978), 'Cognitive, Social and Psychological Determinants of Emotional State', *Psychological Review,* vol. 69, p. 379.

Schein, E.H. (1956), 'The Chinese Indoctrination Program for Prisoners of War', *Psychiatry,* vol. 12, pp. 58-71.

Scott, N. (1987), 'The Fingarette Fallacies', *Alcoholism and Addiction,* vol. 8, no. 6, pp. 17-19.

Schwartz, G.E. (1982), 'Testing the biopsychosocial model: the ultimate challenge facing behavioural medicine', *Journal of Clinical Psychology,* vol. 50, pp. 1040-1053.

Shaw, S. et al. (1978), *Responding to Drinking Problems.* Croom Helm.

Skinner, H.A. et al. (1974), 'Alcoholic personality types: identification and correlates.', *Journal of Abnormal Psychology,* vol. 83, pp. 658-66.

Smart, G. et al. (1989), 'Decreases in alcohol problems and increases Alcoholics Anonymous membership', *British Journal of Addiction,* vol. 84, pp. 507-513.

Spencer, L. and Dale, A. (1979), 'Integration and regulation in organisations; a contextual approach.', *Sociological Review,* vol. 27, pp. 679-702.

Spicer, J. and Barnett, P. (1980), *Hospital Based Chemical Dependency Treatment. A Model for Outcome Evaluation,* Hazelden, Centre City, Minnesota.

Spradely, J.P. (1980), *Participant Observation,* Holt, Rhinehart and Winston, New York.

Stimson, G. (1987), 'British drug policies in the 1980s.', *British Journal of Addiction,* vol. 82, pp. 82-5.

Stockwell, T., Murphy, D. and Hodgson, R. (1983), 'The Severity of Alcohol Dependence Questionnaire: its use, reliability and validity', *British Journal of Addiction,* vol. 78, pp. 145-155.

Strupp, H. (1976), 'The Nature of Therapeutic Influence.', in Burton A. (ed.) *What Makes Behaviour Change Possible ?,* Bruner Mazel.

Strupp, H. (1955), 'Psychotherapeutic technique, professional affiliation and experience level.', *Journal of Consulting Psychology,* vol. 19, pp. 97-102.

Tether, P. and Robertson, D. (1986), *Preventing Alcohol Problems. A Guide to Local Action,* Tavistock, London.

Tiebout, H. (1944), 'Therapeutic mechanisms of Alcoholics Anonymous', *American Journal of Psychiatry,* p. 468.

Tiffany, S.J. and Drobes, D.J. (1991), 'The development and initial validation of a questionnaire on smoking urges', *British Journal of Addiction,* vol. 86, pp. 1467-1476.

Tiffany, S.J., Singleton, E., Haertzen,C.A. and Henningfield, J.E. (1994), The Development of a Cocaine Craving Questionnaire. (Ms in preparation.)

Wanburg, K.W and Horn, J.L. (1983) 'Assessment of alcohol use with multidimensional concepts and measures, *American Psychologist*. pp. 1055-1069.

Watson, G.B. (1940), *Alcohol and the Nation,* Nicholson and Watson.

Wilkins, L.T. (1967), *Social Policy, Action and Research: Studies in Social Deviance,* Tavistock Publications.

Williams, G.P. and Brake, G.T. (1980), *Drink in Great Britain 1900-1979,* Edsall, London.